W [illegible] 1958 he left a detailed and almost continuous diary that he had kept for nearly forty years. In 1918 he had arrived in Europe, a young American from Chicago, just twenty-one years old. With his charm, ability and ambition he made a rapid rise in English society. He married Lady Honor Guinness, became an M.P., and, in the crucial years 1938–41, served at the Foreign Office as Parliamentary Private Secretary to Mr R. A. (now Lord) Butler. He was M.P. for Southend-on-Sea from 1935 to 1950 and subsequently M.P. for Southend-on-Sea (West) until his death. From the late twenties he was a leading personality in London society. His friendships were many and varied; King Edward VIII, the Duke and Duchess of Kent, Lady Cunard, Terence Rattigan, the Duff Coopers and the Wavells, among many others, attended his famous salon in Belgrave Square. His publications include *Joan Kennedy*, 1929; *Paradise City*, 1930; *The Ludwigs of Bavaria*, 1933.

Robert Rhodes James, a former fellow of All Souls College, Oxford, has served as an Assistant Clerk and a Senior Clerk in the House of Commons. He is Director of the new Institute for the Study of International Organization at Sussex University. His other publications are: *Lord Randolph Churchill*; *Rosebery*; *An Introduction to the House of Commons*; *Gallipoli*; and *Memoirs of a Conservative*: *The Papers of J. C. C. Davidson*. He was a contributor to *Churchill: Four Faces and the Man* (published by Allen Lane The Penguin Press), and has edited a study of the Czechoslovak crisis of 1968.

CHIPS

The Diaries of Sir Henry Channon

Edited by Robert Rhodes James

Penguin Books

Penguin Books Ltd, Harmondsworth, Middlesex, England
Penguin Books Australia Ltd, Ringwood, Victoria, Australia

First published by Weidenfeld & Nicolson 1967
Published in Penguin Books 1970

Made and printed in Great Britain by
Cox & Wyman Ltd, London,
Reading and Fakenham
Set in Intertype Plantin

Contents

Introduction

'ALTHOUGH I am not Clerk to the Council like Mr Greville nor Secretary to the Admiralty like Mr Pepys, nor yet 'duc et pair' as was M. de St Simon, I have, nevertheless, had interesting opportunities of intimacy with interesting people and have often been at the centre of things.' Henry Channon wrote these words in his diary on 12 September 1924, on the occasion when he resolved 'to collect various notes from my several diaries and assemble them into a consecutive whole'. He was then twenty-seven, and although his claim was perhaps somewhat exaggerated at that time, subsequent events gave the assertion justification. It is true that although he was a Member of Parliament for more than twenty years, he never rose to any political office higher than that of Parliamentary Private Secretary to the Parliamentary Under-Secretary of State at the Foreign Office. Nevertheless, he was close enough to important events and important people to give his later Diaries, covering the years 1934–52, considerable social and political interest.

There is no doubt that he intended that the Diaries should one day be made available for inspection. 'I sometimes wonder', he wrote in November 1936, 'why I keep a diary at all. Is it to relieve my feelings? Console my old age? Or to dazzle my descendants?' By 1951 he was writing of the Diaries that 'I feel that some day they may see the light of day and perhaps shock or divert posterity a little.' The fact that he took good care of the Diaries and deposited them in the British Museum – and even so, in 1940, buried some at this Essex home in case of bombing or invasion – demonstrates the importance that this personal record came to have for him.

He originally left instructions that his diaries should be deposited in the British Museum and not examined, edited, or published until fifty years after his death. However, in the last year of his life, when faced with the inactivity of a semi-invalid, it was suggested to him that he should start editing the diaries himself. He received this suggestion with enthusiasm and was about to set to work when he died. Under the circumstances, and also due to the fact that the British Museum authorities cannot accept documents to which they are not allowed access, his son, Mr Paul Channon, MP, decided that it would be possible to publish an edited version ten years after his father's death. The task of selection and editing was entrusted to me.

Henry Channon was born in Chicago on 7 March 1897, the only child of a Chicago businessman, Henry Channon II, and Vesta Westover Channon. His paternal family roots were English. His great-grandfather was born in Ottery St Mary, Devonshire, and his grandfather – Henry Channon I – had been born in Bridgwater, Somerset, in 1834. Henry Channon I left home to go to sea at the age of fifteen, and eventually settled in Chicago, where he founded a ships' chandler's business – the H. Channon Co – and acquired a fleet of sailing vessels for the Great Lakes shipping. Both businesses prospered greatly, and their success was the foundation of the fortune of his son and grandson.

Henry Channon II was born in Chicago on 9 November 1868, and he married Vesta Westover in London on 1 August 1892. The couple returned to Chicago, where their son was born five years later. The marriage was not successful, and, after a long period of separation, there was eventually a divorce.

It is always perilous to judge parents by the estimates of their children, and is perhaps particularly so in this case. The comments of his son on Henry Channon II are of interest in that they demonstrate the gulf between them. Of his father the son wrote that he was 'a dull, charmless, uneducated, unexciting, unhappy, untidy little man . . . A cypher, really. But I always quite liked him, and he doted on me' (9 November 1950).

Mrs Channon was, by all accounts, a woman of charm and intelligence, but – and particularly as she became older – eccentric, nervous, and difficult. Her son regarded her with affection, but often with dismay. He was probably right in considering that in character and appearance he most resembled his maternal grandmother, Sarah Miller Westover, always known as Libby. She had, as her grandson had, brilliant brown eyes and a love of parties and gaiety that made her family call her Sortie. Her forbears were MacLarens, and the grandson was justified in ascribing the main features of his personality to this very strong strain. It can hardly have been from the hard-working and practical Channons that he acquired an attitude to life that once prompted him to write (7 May 1925):

> One of those London days when one's blood surges within one and one is madly, desperately happy, when one is tempted to spend a quarter's income on flowers, and something puckish impels one to a thousand capers. Oh, this London!

And it is also difficult to imagine either Henry Channon I or II approving of the remark (27 September 1935) that 'It is very difficult to spend less than £200 a morning when one goes out shopping.'

'Grandmother Libby' often features in her grandson's Diaries, and one reference to her may be inserted at this point, written on the anniversary of her birthday (7 April 1937):

> She was married in 1868 in Brooklyn where she was born, and died in March 1911. I loved her as a child more than anyone else, though it is from her that I inherit all my most unattractive traits – love of display, grandeur, money for its spending sake, and social position.

The Channons, although astonished by their son, watched his progress with increasing pleasure and pride. After a reconcilation between father and son in 1925, relations were good, but never really close (see the entry for 6 February 1937).

Henry Channon III was always called 'Chips' by his European friends. No one has been able to explain exactly how he acquired the sobriquet. One suggestion was that he introduced potato chips as cocktail party fare to London. Another version – considerably more plausible – was that he once shared a bachelor house with a friend known as 'Fish'. It has also been suggested that it originated as a bad pun on his family business in Chicago. Whatever the origin, the name was acquired in Europe, and there are some hints that it was acquired even before he went to England at the end of 1918. But although he was always called

Henry by his American relations, it was as 'Chips' that he was universally known in Europe.

Not very much is known about his childhood, although it is known that he attended the Francis W. Parker School in Chicago, and that he went to a school in Paris for three months in 1907, when he was ten. He was also in Paris at least once again for a short period before the outbreak of war in 1914. His mother was an enthusiastic member of the Alliance Française, and it is quite possible that she took her son to France on more than these two known occasions. Certainly, by the time that he went to Paris with the American Red Cross towards the end of 1917 he had acquired a considerable knowledge of French literature and society.

Chips's dislike of America is one of the most striking themes of his extant Diaries, which begin in 1918, and cover the years 1918, 1923–8, and 1934–52. It is impossible to give the causes of this antipathy with any real precision. Perhaps the unhappiness of his parents' marriage and the atmosphere of Chicago – described well in his book *Paradise City* (1930) – played their part. The spending of money always interested Chips far more than its acquisition. But the principal reason seems to have been an intense feeling for European culture and civilization, and the warm attraction of glamour and tradition to someone whose outlook on life was a highly romantic one. 'The more I know of American civilization,' he wrote, as a very young man, 'the more I despise it. It is a menace to the peace and future of the world. If it triumphs, the old civilizations, which love beauty and peace and the arts and rank and privilege will pass from the picture. And all we will have left will be Fords and cinemas. Ugh!'

It was for England that Chips entertained the deepest feelings of love and admiration – 'Oh, land of freedom, where women are all sirens and men are all gods. What a joy to be with you again!' (6 March 1925) – and although it could be argued that the England he loved was very much that of London Society and large country houses, of rank, privilege, and wealth, his feeling for the country of his adoption went far deeper than this. As he once wrote, 'I have put my whole life's work into my anglicization, in ignoring my early life' (31 May 1927).

It is to be hoped that the extant Diaries for 1918 and 1923–8 will, one day, be published, for they give an excellent portrait of a particular segment of French and English life, and have, in the full, an admirable 'period piece' flavour. Because of their length they have had to be omitted from this volume, but a brief summary of their contents must be given.

As has been related, Chips went to France in October 1917 with the American Red Cross, and he subsequently became an Honorary Attaché to the US Embassy in Paris. In spite of the hazards of bombing and shelling, most vividly described ('The red buildings with great sheets of flame against the black un-illuminated city had a terrible lugubrious beauty,' he wrote of the rue de Rivoli on one occasion), this was an ecstatically happy period:

> What would I not do to have NOW last for ever – to be for ever 20 in Paris in the springtime, what could be more divine? It is dreadful my life – dreadful yet wonderful to skim the cream off life, gliding along on oceans of delight when the world is mourning and is suffering. In the world drenched in misery, is one drop of happiness a sin? (16 May 1918)

And again, on 21 June:

> How wonderful it is to be young, to have the world at the tip of one's fingers – oh, the mad, mad waltz of youth – the lights are on, the stage is set, the music is playing, I am exuberant. How long will it last? Morality, I am sure, is an 'invention des laids', it is their revenge.

But, even at this early age, the interest of the Diaries lies very much in the contrasts between Chips's manifest enjoyment of life and society on the one hand and his seriousness and compassion on the other. He was fascinated by the famous Abbé Mugnier (1853–1944), who was always welcomed by the aristocracy and the faubourg, but who lived in poverty as an almoner to the Missionary Sisters of St Joseph of Cluny in the rue Méchain. Chips noted the contrast in Mugnier's life – 'his flat is hideous, an odd collection of old books, dreadful furniture and modern religious images; but there is always a queue of princesses waiting to see him' (15 May 1918) – but was deeply impressed by the character of the man. 'At the end of two hours my hereditary [Protestant] resistance was broken down and I became a Roman

Catholic in heart at least and realize I will continue to be so all my life' (11 April 1918).

Marcel Proust and Jean Cocteau also took an interest in him. He greatly admired Proust, and wrote of Cocteau (23 February 1918) that 'like some satyr of old – his wit is dazzling and his manner electrifying. . . . He told me that my eyes were set by Cartier, which nettled me.' At a dinner shortly after the Armistice he sat between Proust and Cocteau, and described the occasion:

Their manners, usually so bad, were excellent tonight, and they seemed to compete as to which could be the more engaging. I felt stupid between the two wittiest men in Europe, drenched in a Niagara of epigrams. Jean is a stylist and his conversation is full of fire and rapier thrusts. He is like some faun that is indulged too long. He is haggard at 26, and his figure and smile have something mythological, something of the centaur, in them.

Proust is quieter, longer-winded and more meticulous. His blood-shot eyes shine feverishly, as he pours out ceaseless spite and venom about the great. His foibles are Ruskin, genealogy and heraldry. He knows the arms and quarterings of every duke in Europe. His black hair was tidily arranged, but his linen was grubby, and the rich studs and links had been clumsily put in by dirty fingers.

Proust has always been kind to me, and I don't like to libel him in the pages of my diary, so I will boil down to the minimum all the rumours about him: that he loathes daylight and is called at tea-time, the world knows. Does the world know that he tips with thousand franc notes, and that he has prolonged evening gossips with the Figaro coiffeur at the Ritz? With questionable taste, I asked him if it was true at dinner, and he nodded.

When I first met him long ago, he was particularly agreeable to me. A few days later, when walking with Maurice d'Astier, we met him. Maurice bowed, but I hadn't noticed him until too late, never thinking he would even remember me. The next day he wrote Maurice the letter of a madman, asking in twenty-seven pages of superb prose, for an explanation why I had cut him. Long drawn out pompous suppositions in a super-Henry James manner, as to why a young man should dare to be rude to him. (16 November 1918)

The contrasts in Chips's life at this time may be glimpsed from the next entry, for 19 November:

I went to a cocotte's ball which I enjoyed wildly. I had always found them so dull and difficult to talk to, until someone advised me to pinch them instead of making conversation! I tried this new manner tonight with great success.

Although Chips relished the faubourg life and the Ritz – 'the centre of all that the pre-war epoch has left' – he was censorious of the faubourg attitude to the war:

It takes more than an offensive and an invasion to stir their lethargy, and they have ignored the war as far as possible. They have lost their sons, but most have tried to be embusqués, and their women, with a few outstanding exceptions, have done nothing but wear black. (2 June 1918)

It is not difficult to draw a portrait of the young Chips from these Diaries. The Abbé Mugnier described him as 'an extremist, a sensationist, an individualist, an original, and half a mystic', and the description, although somewhat involved, has comprehension. Although gay in the evenings, he worked hard during the day. Although he loved revelry, he was contemptuous of the idle. He moved easily and happily from frivolous to serious company. As always, his friends could do no wrong, and of the Duchesse de Brissac, who had befriended him, he wrote that 'she has a sweetness and gentle touch on life that is not of this world'. He disliked Gide – 'a dreadful, unkempt, poet-looking person' – and was delighted by Mrs Elinor Glyn, the romantic novelist. Her philosophy, she told Chips, was 'To live! To love! And to write! And to read the Bible!' 'I must learn to do all these things,' Chips wrote; 'so far only the first has interested me'. Mrs Glyn also urged Chips 'to embark on a career of love', and startled the upright Lady Congreve during a discussion on reincarnation by suggesting that 'she may have been a painted courtesan in Pharaoh's days'.

When he left the Red Cross to take up his duties at the Embassy, Chips wrote:

I have spent the happiest year of my life in its service, the year in which I found myself and took on what will probably be my permanent mould. (8 October 1918)

At the end of 1918 Chips was summoned home by his parents. On his way back he stayed a few days in London, and was enraptured. The 1918 Diary ends:

I am in love with London already, and feel that it is pregnant with my destiny.

There then occurs a four year gap in the Diaries. It is not known whether Chips kept a diary during these years; if he did, it has either been mislaid or was subsequently destroyed. (I will forbear to mention the name of a now eminent Oxford contemporary of Chips who, when told of this melancholy gap, muttered fervently, 'Thank God!'). During these years Chips was an undergraduate at Christ Church, Oxford, where he was very happy. After leaving Oxford he shared a house in London with two friends made at Oxford, Viscount Gage and Prince Paul of Serbia.

It is at once evident that Chips had definitely 'arrived'. The Diaries are filled with accounts of London dinners, luncheons and balls, or long country-house weekend parties. He is a close friend of Lord and Lady Curzon, and stays often with them. The future Duchess of York, Lady Elizabeth Bowes-Lyon (now HM the Queen Mother), the Prince of Wales (now HRH The Duke of Windsor) and the future Duchess of Kent (Princess Marina) and friends.

If Chips had been merely social – and there were many then and later who regarded him as such – there would be little real interest in his Diaries. What saves him is his eye and ear for interesting detail and the facility and skill with which he described people and occasions. Thus, he was fascinated by a room at Kedleston which Lord Curzon kept as an exact replica of his Eton room. Chips was also intrigued by a number of photograph albums kept by the then Foreign Secretary. Most were of Eton contemporaries, with their names, details, and dates of death meticulously recorded. Another consisted of photographs of beautiful women, each with a single date but no other comment, 'and only their collector knows what secrets bind their faces to him' (7 October 1923). When Curzon died in March 1925, Chips recorded that 'he told me once that the secret of life was ASSUMPTION. Few people will challenge what appears to be a fait accompli' (23 March 1925). Perhaps it also explained Curzon's eventual failure. But Chips liked Curzon, who had explained to him with great gusto his grandiose plans for Kedleston and

Bodiam. Chips was one of the small party that attended Curzon's funeral at Kedleston on 26 March 1925.

I shall never forget the simple service and the great beauty of the bereft widow, the absence of ostentation, and, also, the absence of friends. Where were the royalties he had served? Where were the statesmen he had made and terrified? Where were the oriental potentates he had cowed; where were the companions of his Oxford days? No one. Only the Duke of Devonshire, who had come over from Chatsworth, and our little group from London.

Chips's comments on contemporaries are always interesting, and are sometimes disconcertingly acute. Many are too acute for publication at present. Of Sir Philip Sassoon's astonishing house at Lympne he wrote that it was

a triumph of beautiful bad taste and Babylonian luxury, with terraces and flowery gardens, and jade green pools and swimming baths and rooms done up in silver and blue and orange. A strange hydro for this strangest of sinister men.

And there is an excellent portrait of Asquith at The Wharf in 1924, his long political career almost over:

Mr Asquith, benign, beautiful and patriarchal, presided at the end of the long table and talked, in his clear bell-like Jacobean English, with a wealth of metaphor. Mrs Asquith, distraite, smoked and read the papers during luncheon, and occasionally said something startling like, apropos of spiritualism, 'I always knew the living talked rot, but it is nothing to the nonsense the dead talk.' She also said she could not help being sorry for ghosts – 'Their appearances are so against them.' (3 March 1924)

Some of the portraits are less kind. He regarded Hugh Walpole as 'noisy, common and uninteresting, and quite devoid of the rarities – the voluptés almost – that make an English gentleman, such as Thomas-made boots and Eton-made inflections' (20 October 1923). He liked Harold Nicolson, but considered that he had 'a subtle mind but an unsubtle character. He is really affectionate, domestic and simple, but his brain has an exotic bent, and he is ever striving for the unusual' (27 August 1924). The famous hostess Lady Cunard is already a great favourite.

At a luncheon in January 1924 in Paris there was a discussion about Tiberius, who was a hero of Lady Cunard's, in which Lord and Lady Crewe and Winston Churchill were also involved. Lady Cunard, Chips recorded,

> lays all the blame on Tacitus, and says he was the creature of Germanicus and dismisses him as a gross libeller and a pamphleteer; she ended triumphantly by saying, 'As for Capri! It was only the Chequers of the time.'

During this period Chips was maintained first by an allowance from his father, which seems to have been modest but sufficient. In 1924 his father gave him a settlement of $90,000, providing him with an income of some £800 a year; in May 1927 he inherited an additional $85,000 from the estate of his grandfather, and, as he triumphantly wrote, 'belong definitely to the order of those that HAVE – and through no effort of my own, which is such a joy' (3 May 1927). He was accordingly spared the necessity of having to work for a living, and the thought of doing so does not seem to have occurred to him. In January 1924 he accompanied Lord Buckmaster, the former Lord Chancellor, to the League of Nations as an Assistant British delegate, and enjoyed it greatly, even though Geneva was a sad disappointment:

> A most unattractive city – so clean, so damnably prosperous, so smug, so Protestant, so oppressingly Calvinistic. I like my 'abroad' to be Catholic and sensual. I long for yells and smells, cathedrals and great market places, old streets and antiquaries. . . . The Swiss are so unimaginative, practical and charmless that they might almost be Americans. (18 January 1924)

In the General Strike of 1926 Chips was a Special Constable ('Terror grips my heart at the prospect of the unpleasant baton charges') and sold newspapers. But during this time he was working on his first novel, *Joan Kennedy,* published in 1929. [*Paradise City,* a series of sketches of Chicago life, was published in 1930, and a well-informed history of the Ludwigs of Bavaria was published in 1933. Each of these books, and particularly *The Ludwigs of Bavaria,* has lasted well.]

A feature of Chips's character as glimpsed through his Diaries is his frequent bouts of depression, in marked contrast with the outward gaiety and even vicarious splendour of his life, as at Ayr races, where

> the members of the Caledonian Club appear in pink coats and top hats, while Lord Bute has a private tent and Lord Lonsdale's party arrive in yellow phaetons with outriders. (21 September 1923)

But there were periods when he craved solitude, and when he relapsed into melancholy:

> I fear I am the saddest of mortals, a rake grown old before his time. How empty is success and fame, how maddening defeat, how fleeting good health, how rare high spirits, how impossible true friendship, how disappointing companionship, how vacant solitude, how dull drunkenness, how prosy sobriety, how stale literature, how fatiguing sexual intercourse, how surfeiting wealth, how debasing poverty, and how impossible life and how futile philosophy. (19 October 1925)

The extant Diaries end at the close of 1928 and resume at the beginning of 1934. In this period he had published three books and had married, in 1933, Lady Honor Guinness, the eldest daughter of the second Earl of Iveagh. The young Channons lived in a style that was, even then, becoming unusual in London. Their second London house, 5 Belgrave Square, became famous, and Harold Nicolson, a frequent guest, has described it thus:

> Oh my God how rich and powerful Lord Channon has become! There is his house in Belgrave Square next door to Prince George, Duke of Kent, and Duchess of ditto and little Prince Edward. The house is all Regency upstairs with very carefully draped curtains and Madame Récamier sofas and wall-paintings. Then the dining-room is entered through an orange lobby and discloses itself suddenly as a copy of the blue room of the Amalienburg near Munich – baroque and rococo and what-ho and oh-no-no and all that. Very fine indeed.[1]

Chips's marriage had also brought him into the House of Commons. Lord Iveagh had been Conservative MP for Southend-on-Sea from 1918 to 1927, when he succeeded to the title on the death of his father. Lady Iveagh succeeded him as Member until 1935, when Chips was selected to succeed her.

1. Nigel Nicolson (Ed.): *Harold Nicolson, Diaries and Letters 1930–39*, p. 244.

Chips himself was succeeded by his son, Paul, as Member for the revised constituency on his death in 1958 – a remarkable example of family service to one constituency, running without a break from the end of the Great War to the present day.

The published Diaries commence at the beginning of 1934, shortly after Chips's marriage and before his entry into the House of Commons. It is best that the Diaries speak for themselves, without further comment from their editor. But for those who did not know Chips at all, some further details may be desirable.

In appearance, he was of middle height, and perhaps rather too carefully dressed for English taste. He often claimed, whether seriously or not, to have Red Indian blood, and there was certainly something about his sharply cut features and brilliant brown eyes to give plausibility to this claim, which is, however, denied by his American relatives.

His friendships were extensive, and extraordinarily varied, and the guests at 5 Belgrave Square tended to be a bewildering but carefully blended mixture of politicians, diplomats, royalties, soldiers, publishers, authors, courtiers and – particularly in later years – actors, actresses and theatrical producers. He was always alert to the possibility of making new friendships, and, to those he loved he was both kind and sensitive. As Lady Diana Cooper has written of him, 'never was there a surer or more enlivening friend. . . . He installed the mighty in his gilded chairs and exalted the humble. He made the old and tired, the young and strong, shine beneath his thousand lighted candles. Without stint he gave of his riches and of his compassion.'

As a politician, he was an exceptionally silent Member in the Chamber, but the Lobby and the Smoking Room and those long, fascinating panelled corridors were his true domain. To those who dismissed him as a dilettante it often came as a real surprise to discover the deep knowledge he had of his constituency and the great trouble he went to on his constituents' behalf. He loved the House of Commons, 'this smelly, tawny, male paradise' as he once called it. For once *The Times* obituarist did not exaggerate when he wrote that 'however silent he might have been during debates, there have been few men in the Commons so universally popular as Channon. He was regarded with real affection by political friend and foe alike.' This feeling was not, of course, total; it never is in the House of Commons. But there was justice in this obituary tribute. The House of Commons, by some strange intuitive process, knows those Members who love the place and are proud to be there, and invariably responds.

I hardly knew him at all, and what I did know about him I rather disapproved of. I knew that he was prominent in London Society. I also knew of his pre-war political attitudes. But it was curious how, of all those Members whom I knew slightly when I was an officer of the House of Commons, Chips made the strongest impression. I remember him most vividly in the Members' Lobby during the magical half-hour between 2.30 p.m. (when the House meets) and 3 p.m. For it is then that the Lobby is astir, with Members coming in to collect their papers and chat to friends (and foes) before entering the Chamber. It is the best time to seize a Member, to pick up gossip and impart it, to study groups in furtive conclaves, and generally to absorb atmosphere. I had the impression that Chips – head slightly cocked, hands in trouser-pockets, sharp eyes missing nothing – was more at home in this fascinating maelstrom than anyone else. I was not surprised to find him writing in his Diary:

> I held my little court in the Members' Lobby. I love the racket and would not be out of it for the world. (24 April 1940)

Of course, it would be wrong to pretend that his political career had any great importance. Chips's excitement at reaching the lowest rung on the official ladder, Parliamentary Private Secretary, in 1938 shows that he had hopes of greater things, but that he did not rise any higher does not seem to have caused him much distress. In office or out of it, he was always an observer, and it is as such that the value of his account lies. If it is difficult not to feel that he wasted his talents, such stern judgement is neither helpful nor reasonable. As Lady Diana Cooper has written of him, 'Life he saw as a Disraelian fairy story.' And Chips was probably right when he wrote that 'reformers are always finally neglected, while the memoirs of the frivolous will always eagerly be read' (7 July 1936).

He was the best of friends, and his friendships meant much to him. That with Prince Paul of Yugoslavia reveals their strength and duration, particularly when Prince Paul was being vilified during the war; that with Wavell reveals their surprising width. Although he loved intrigue, he rarely intrigued for himself. And he had the priceless quality of laughing at himself. 'Fashionable crêtins all,' he dismissed a house party in 1924, then adding '– but am I not one too?' Or – 'I adored my fat, beautiful grandmother, who was such a liar, and so charming and vain and silly and amorous – like me' (7 April 1926). Or, again – 'The Crown Prince Umberto is charm itself, but has no great intelligence. He reminds me of myself.' And, although it is severe, it is difficult to improve upon this self-portrait, written by Chips on 19 July 1935:

> Sometimes I think I have an unusual character – able but trivial; I have flair, intuition, great good taste but only second rate ambition: I am far too susceptible to flattery; I hate and am uninterested in all the things most men like such as sport, business, statistics, debates, speeches, war and the weather; but I am rivetted by lust, furniture, glamour and society and jewels. I am an excellent organizer and have a will of iron; I can only be appealed to through my vanity. Occasionally I must have solitude: my soul craves for it. All thought is done in solitude; only then am I partly happy.

Chips was in poor health for the last four or five years of his life, although he kept the fact well hidden, and his relatively early death on 7 October 1958, in London, at the age of sixty-one came as a considerable shock to his friends. He had been knighted in the previous year, and the only child of a Chicago businessman, who had spent forty years in Britain and was a naturalized Englishman, died Sir Henry Channon. He was buried at Kelvedon, his lovely Essex home for over twenty years.

The formidable length of the Channon Diaries – over thirty volumes, which must total some three million words – has meant that only a very truncated version could be published. But, in selecting those passages that should be retained for this version, other considerations must be taken into account. 'What is more dull than a discreet diary?' Chips once wrote; 'one might as well have a discreet soul.' On 31 December 1937, he wrote:

> As I re-read my Diary, I am frequently horrified by the scandalous

tone it has; one might think we lived in a world of cads; this is far from true, but the weakness of one's friends are more amusing to chronicle than their dignified conduct, which one takes for granted. But perhaps the age is casual and a little under-bred, or modernised by contact with 'levelling' America; but I don't think it dissolute.

It will be clear enough from these extracts that the Diaries contain much material that must be forbidden fruit for present generations. But, although they do contain many sharp comments on individuals, and describe episodes which are best undisclosed for the present, the adjective 'scandalous' requires qualification. There are very few passages that really justify such a description.

This does not mean that it is necessary to amend the Diaries so piously that all the flavour and interest of the originals has been lost. I have endeavoured to retain that which is of real interest without causing distress to living persons or the direct descendants of people who figure conspicuously in the Diaries. In this I have had to use my own judgement on each occasion as it arose.

In preparing the Diaries for publication I have been conscious of the necessity for retaining the balance between the political and social parts of Chips's life, in order to present a fair facsimile of the balance of the original. It has been a very difficult balance to keep.

It is not clear whether the 1918 and 1923–4 Diaries are originals. Indeed, it would appear from an entry for 12 September 1924 that they were, in his own words, 'mostly copied from older, incomplete, records. In writing some from memory I am aided by Engagement books and half a ton of forgotten letters and faded invitations that help one to recapture the atmosphere of "lost Aprils and lost Mays".' This extract also seems to indicate that there were records for 1919–22 that have since been destroyed or lost. On 13 January 1944, he wrote that he had deposited in the British Museum all the Diaries 'that I did not destroy, though gone are all the Proust letters which in my youth and folly I burnt'.

But it does seem that the Diaries at least from the beginning of 1934 were in the main written up shortly after the events they described, and became almost a daily occupation. Diaries of this length and detail are always somewhat self-conscious literary productions, and the versions of events given by all diarists should be approached with caution. Even if the diarist is not attempting to give a deliberately false version, a talented writer can easily over-dramatize, and the accounts can be written for effect rather than as a strict factual record. This word of warning is necessary, but, with this qualification, the Channon Diaries can be enjoyed as one man's view of the world in which he lived, and which has now vanished. The fact that the reader may disagree with many of his judgements, and historians take issue with his version of particular episodes, does not seriously undermine the significance of the Diaries. They must be approached with the same caution that historians approach those of Greville, with which the Channon Diaries have much in common.

I have always been irritated by Editors of papers intruding too much upon the narrative they are presenting. I have tried to keep all comments and footnotes to a minimum. My occasional interpolations are marked with square brackets in the narrative; my brief introductory comments to each chapter are italicized. I have standardized the headings to each day's entry – which varied in the original – and have corrected obvious misprints.

I am most grateful to Mr Paul Channon for having entrusted these very personal Diaries to me, and I am also indebted to Mr Peter Coats for having arranged the preparation of a complete typescript; as Chips's handwriting was often difficult to read, this eased my task considerably. I am also grateful to Mr Coats for much assistance and advice. We are both obliged to Mr William Burry of Chicago, for many years a close friend and legal adviser of the Channon family, and to two American cousins of Chips, Mrs Henry Cave of Mansfield, Ohio, and Mrs Charles P. Sturges of Chicago, for information about Chips's family and childhood.

Robert Rhodes James

CHAPTER ONE

Politics: 1934–5

There is a gap of five years in the Diaries after the 1928 volume. It is not clear whether these are among the destroyed papers, or are mislaid, or that Chips neglected the Diary in these years. When they begin again, at the beginning of 1934, Chips has married. He married Lady Honor Guinness, daughter of Lord and Lady Iveagh on 14 July 1933, Lord Birkenhead being his best man. The Channons lived at 21 St James's Place, for the first two years of their marriage, and it is from this address that Chips resumes the Diary on 12 February 1934. His ambitions to enter the House of Commons have now matured, and a highly appropriate constituency was available – that of Southend, a seat traditionally held by the Guinness family, and whose MP had been Lady Iveagh, Chips's mother-in-law, since 1927: she had followed her husband, who had represented the constitutency from 1918 to 1927.

1934

12 February *Moir House, 21 St James's Place*

Diana Cooper rang me with the dawn and in her fog-horn voice announced that the King of the Belgians had been killed 'Rock-climbing', which it appears was his favourite sport. All Belgium will be plunged in gloom and I can imagine how the Belgians will revel in the crêpe and veils, and mourning generally. Mourning is the only fun that the Belgian aristocracy – that awful 'Salon Bleu' – ever gets. I wonder whether the heir – the youthful Duc de Brabant – will be able to keep in the saddle, for the whole world, Belgium included, seems in a ferment, though no one takes much notice. Serious rioting all last week in Paris; civil war in Austria and now strikes in New York, yet all is calm and halcyon in St James's Place, and last night we had a dinner party; came: the [Duff] Coopers, Emerald [Cunard], wittier and more exquisite than ever, Ivor Churchill, chetif and complaining, and Cole Porter. We used the new gold plate I bought in New York and it was much admired: it belonged to Mrs Rockefeller McCormick, and I used to see it in her house and also at the Art Institute. She died, poor eccentric, last year. The service was originally made as a wedding present from Napoleon to his sister, the seductive Pauline Borghese. It bears the Borghese arms with the French Imperial Crown, and very grand it looks.

20 February
Am I wise to embrace a Parliamentary career – can I face the continued strain? James Willoughby[1] told me today that he nearly gave up his parliamentary campaign in November, as he just could not stand the ordeal of speaking: when he confessed this to his agent, the man replied, 'Don't let not speaking well dishearten you: I have known candidates who could not even read.'

21 February
Honor and I drove to Southend. Oh, Southend, what part will you play in my future? The two of us sat in silence all the way, each trying to compose a speech. We smiled and mumbled at each other from time to time, irritated when the other interrupted. At first sight, Southend seemed charming with the grey sea coast, the mud and the sea and the little rococo band-stand. In the evening, Honor and I drove in state with Lord and Lady Iveagh to the Conservative Ball, where we were met by the Committee, and I tried to be very charming to everyone, especially the women. We shook hands, received 300–400 people. . . . Later we were led by the Mayor and Mayoress to a dais. Lady Iveagh made a good speech – Lord Iveagh was very funny and reduced the audience to hysterics of laughter. Honor spoke extremely well, and was both amusing and dignified. Then my turn came. I found I was not in the least nervous and I spoke, for me, rather well. The evening passed off pleasantly. How many of all these people, those Southend people, will play a role in my life? Will they help me or hate me? What I dread most in political life is boredom, the interminable conversations with brains that are

1. Conservative MP for Stamford and Rutland, 1933–50; succeeded his father to Earldom of Ancaster, 1951.

slower, though perhaps, more sensible than my own. Next morning, while Honor dressed, I walked along the sea coast and wondered at the strangeness of life. What a strange road I have trod – from Chicago to Southend – via Paris, London and God knows where else.

Later, we returned to London, and I now hear that we were a definite success. I may be asked to stand for Parliament very soon.

25 February

This evening, we had the second of our London festivals, a riotous outrageous success. Most of the afternoon, a grey London Sunday, I spent in fussing and telephoning. Eric Duncannon and Seymour Berry chucked at 7 o'clock and so I rang up Douglas Fairbanks, Jr. who immediately accepted. Dinner was staggering, champagne flowed and the food was excellent. We began with blinis served with Swedish schnapps, to wash down the caviare. Then soup, followed by salmon, then an elaborate chicken. Then a sweet and savoury. The candlelight was reflected in my gold plate and the conversation was incessant. Honor got on well with Edward Stanley, who was less deaf than usual. . . . Eventually Cole Porter was sufficiently intoxicated to play the piano. He played for hours, all the latest American airs. I got to bed at 4.30 absolutely exhausted . . . but I suppose what we take from our nights we add to our days.

27 February

Anne Wood brought her father, Lord Halifax,[2] to lunch; his charm is proverbial. He was born with one hand, and he looks like a dashing Cecil, if one can imagine that priest-like race ever looking dashing. We made instant friends, and my success with him was reported to me later by my parents-in-law who dined with us, before going to Noel Coward's play, 'Conversation Piece'.

7 March

My 35th birthday. Actually I have lied so much about my age

2. 1st Earl of Halifax (1881–1959). Viceroy of India (with title of Lord Irwin), 1928–31. Chips's uncle by marriage.

that I forget how old I really am. I think I look 28, and know I feel 19.

20 April *21 St James's Place, S.W.1*

After endless false starts, I have decided definitely to begin my diary again, and only hope I shall have the patience to continue. But as I am dictating it, it may be less scandalous and spontaneous than before.[3]

1 May

In the evening Freddie Birkenhead and Norah Lindsay arrived to stay with me. . . . Freddie more charming than any human being I have ever met. After dinner we sat until midnight listening entranced to this dark Hermes as he poured forth a torrent of wit. He has just completed a herculean task having finished the second volume of the Life of his father – 50,000 words in three weeks. The manuscript lies here in my study.

2 May *21 St James's Place*

We lunched chez Lady Colefax (her house is called 'Lions Corner House') a rather silly jabbering sort of lunch.

3 May

Southend is peaceful and quiet – like a Bonington, with ships with red funnels in the Estuary. I walked along the promenade by myself for an hour and wondered, as I passed all those hundreds of people whether they would all know me in the future. There are 140,000 of them, and at the moment very few know me by sight.

In the evening I walked along, this time to the end of the Pier and absorbed a little of the atmosphere of the town in which I hope to play a great rôle one day.

4 May

At 8.30 the Large Selection Committee met in the Conservative Hall. There were about 100 present. They all stood up when I went in, and when I began to speak they shouted for quite five minutes and would not let me go on. At the end of my little

3. See pp. 52–3.

speech they broke into 'For he's a jolly good fellow', and sang lustily – women waved flags and handkerchiefs, and when I came in again to parade round, I really thought I was going to be kissed. Everyone jumped up and shook me by both hands, and practically hugged me. I was then told that I had been selected unanimously as Conservative Candidate for the Borough of Southend.

Back to London, and found Honor and Freddie both out, and the house gloomy and deserted. Slight anti-climax.

8 May *21 St James's Place*

Paul of Serbia and Princess Olga and Princess Marina lunched with us here. They are surely the two most beautiful Princesses, if not women, in the world. Princess Marina is very much thinner, and I hope one day she will make a suitable marriage with the House of Windsor.

9 May

We lunched in, with the Brownlows who are staying with us, and Harold Nicolson. Harold's book about Lord Curzon comes out today[4] and has been well reviewed. Harold was in an anecdotal mood, and we talked until about 3 o'clock. He is obsessed by Lord Curzon, and all his thoughts run to him . . .

In the evening we dined with the Bismarcks – their first dinner party in a new house in Stanhope Street. Lady Milbanke, Lady Warrender, and others. I talked with the German Ambassador for about half-an-hour over the port, and we discussed Bavaria. He has read my book [*The Ludwigs of Bavaria*] several times. Paul of Serbia told me this afternoon that when he went into Prince Rupprecht's bedroom in his Munich Palace, he found my book next to his bed. The Prince said that he had read and enjoyed my book, and was pleased about the things I had said about him and his family.

12 May *Breccles*

Drove to Breccles, and arrived exhausted. Here I found Maurice Baring, Diana and Conrad Russell playing brilliant 'Soul' paper

4. *Curzon: The Last Phase.*

games, which I loathe, so I went to bed at once, and read *Oliver Twist*.

17 May *Southend*

We drove here yesterday and I spent the morning nursing my constituency; in the afternoon, we drove up in state to St Clements Ward Committee Room. We both spoke, I first. I was a little nervous until after the first few sentences, and then I got used to the sea of faces and rather enjoyed myself. There was just a tiny pause when I forgot what I was going to say next, and suddenly heard my watch ticking. Honor spoke better than I. I thought she would never sit down. I watched the clock – 17 minutes without a pause. We were then professionally charming to lots of people, and drove away.

16 December

A new lease of life for my long neglected diary. I really must try to keep it regularly as once I did – though I am still recovering from the efforts of my slight abdominal operation, and am easily tired – I who once disdained sleep and despised fatigue. . . . So we are taking it easy, though today we lunched with Emerald: Emerald says that she is bored with Christianity, and all its festivals, Christmas especially, which she says is 'only for servants'. But she graciously accepted a green Sèvres cup – circa 1755 – which we bought her. She collects Sèvres, and it suits her. Emerald twitted the Italian Ambassador Grandi[5] unmercifully and accused him of having led Mussolini's March on Rome. Perhaps he did? He is young, bearded, gay and Latin, with a charm which is just a trifle too great to be entirely unselfconscious . . .

Also at lunch were Count Mensdorff, the Austrian Ambassador here in Edwardian days, who is deaf and has such a deep, deep horror of the untitled. Also Evelyn Waugh, alias Mr Wu. I never know . . . is he good, trying to be wicked? Or just wicked trying to be nice? He looks like a ventriloquist's doll, with his shiny nose; I feel his ideals are measured by publishers' royalties. He

5. Count Dino Grandi, formerly (1929–32) Italian Minister of Foreign Affairs, was Italian Ambassador in London, 1932–9.

told me today that he thought that anyone could write a novel given six weeks, pen, paper and no telephone or wife.

Afterwards I walked to Westminster Cathedral to pray that I too should write another book, and to pray for a son. For a year or so I have not missed my writing, but of late there is something stirring – is it a new work being conceived? Or has my feeble talent died? Did it always need necessity's spur?

I am having a rest from Southend, where I have been for weeks on and off. I don't like speaking – yet I can, tolerably, if briefly, when forced to do so: I have made many friends there already; nice, homely 'bodies'; will they elect me? I have tried to be conscientious and painstaking and, I think to a certain degree, I have been effective.

18 December

The Yugo-Slav Cabinet has fallen, and trouble looms once more in the Balkans: I hope my Paul will be strong enough to hold power; what a strange slant in my life – that the person I have loved most and the longest, should be Regent of that remote Kingdom. He is the only human being with whom I am completely, wholly natural; such is my devotion to him there is no treachery too dark, no deed too second-rate, that I would not confess to him; and I now really like Princess Olga too. She and I are old friends, but until now I have thought her standoffish, and a wee bit Royal . . . Emerald, with more than her usual hyperbole, described him to someone recently, in my hearing, as having 'the wit of Voltaire . . . the sad beauty of Apollo, and, Chips tells me, . . . the heart of Jesus'.

19 December

This morning I Christmas-shopped with Diana [Cooper]. What an amazing character she is, with her energy, her beauty and her calm wit; her broadmindedness is staggering and she is still startlingly beautiful, with her wide, rather vacant, staring eyes; no detail of life is too much trouble for her; her interest in everything is acute, operative, and her taste exquisite and flawless. We bought dozens of presents; most from Lady Colefax's chic shop. Sibyl is as slim, able and vivacious as ever; she reminds me of Obsidian or Onyx – shiny and metallic.

1935

4 January *Elveden*

We are having our second shooting party, including, among others, the Milbankes, Eric Dudley and Venetia Montagu. David Margesson is also here, and is a charmer, but a somewhat bromidic one: without brilliance, he reflects the mentality of the 'man in the street'. As Chief Whip, he has undoubtedly as much power as anyone in the land: for there is always a 'little man behind the scenes': and the Chief Whip is he.

8 January

I drove to Southend to address the Primrose League, of which I am the Ruling Councillor. . . . There was a fog on my return, and I arrived back at Elveden late, cold and hungry. Our guests were all still up but all the fifty servants had gone to bed, and I could get nothing to eat. In spite of that, of all the Iveagh houses I like Elveden best. I love its calm, its luxurious Edwardian atmosphere. For a fortnight now I have slept in the Kings' bed, which both Edward VII, and George V have used. And this morning, in the wee sma' hours, I had a humiliating accident – I somehow smashed the royal Chamber pot. It seems to be a habit of mine, and one much to be discouraged. At Mentmore once, staying with the Roseberys, I broke Napoleon's pot in similar circumstances, a very grand affair covered with 'N's and Bees.

11 January *Belton House, Grantham*

We drove here in the cold to find our hosts the Brownlows, Coopers, Weymouths and Piers Leghs, who are frankly bores: he is in waiting to the Prince of Wales. The house, which was built by Christopher Wren, is almost overfull of treasures, Grinling Gibbons carving, etc.

After dinner we went to the Belvoir Ball, given by the Rutlands for their daughters, Ursula and Isabel, both dazzlers. Ursula is already out and is chic and sleek and onyx-y, and the younger Isabel is a dream of romantic loveliness, with her green eyes, sophisticated clothes and baby smile. She is not yet 17. The ball was a glorious Disraelian festival, and the Castle illuminations could be seen for miles. Little coloured lights lined the winding avenue: most of the men were in pink coats, which matched their shining pink huntin' faces. The women were magnificent, and Honor wore her tiara, and John Rutland looked as dix-huitième as only he can look, with his romantic looks and long gold chain on his shirtfront. But I thought that old Violet Duchess looked the best, tired, eighty and in white: she was a romantic, rather triste figure in the castle where she reigned so long, and which she made so famous. She was surrounded by all her descendants – there must have been 30 of them, including several little boys in black suits, Charles Granby and the younger Rutland children, all scampering about.

15 January

Tonight we dined with the [Duff] Coopers at 90 Gower Street: their tiny house, simply run, seems palatial, and there is even an enfilade. The Regency decoration of white and gold makes a highly effective background for Diana's beauty. She has lost none of her radiance and looks and moves like Helen of Troy.

17 January

Emerald Cunard swept in to tea and stayed two hours. I had never seen her so brilliant. She now gives off an ambiente that completely lights up her pretty wrinkled, Watteau face. She had had a dinner party last night (to which we were bidden and refused) for Diana Cooper.

At 11.30 the front door bell had rung and there was the Prince of Wales accompanied by Mr and Mrs Simpson. It was an imprévu visit: the Prince was as charming as only he can be sometimes, and now is so rarely. Later he took them all to the Embassy Club for supper. Diana and the Prince talked politics for 2 hours. Emerald said 'The little Prince talked like a Prophet and drank Vichy water' and she said to him: 'You are not David, Sir, but Daniel'. She is in an excellent mood.

18 January *London*

We lunched with Cecil Beaton – he is a quaint creature, gay, insinuating with great flair and cunning, but sunny and kind. He has made a position for himself in the world by his personality. I remember when he first appeared: I was staying at Longleat, in about 1926, I think, and we went to Wilton to a Ball: suddenly there was a slight commotion – young Cecil Beaton had been thrown into the pond and appeared in Van Dyck's Double Cube drawing-room – dripping. Now his erstwhile tormentors are his staunchest supporters. Rex Whistler,[6] chetif, goat, or perhaps faun-like was also at lunch . . .

We dined in: somehow Honor and I, although not whoopee-minded ourselves, seem to have a quality that attracts others. Tonight came, more or less self-invited, Emerald Cunard, Brendan Bracken,[7] red-haired, gormless, lying, and yet an old tea cosy; Ivor Churchill, an Objet de Vitrine, and the newly engaged couple, Michael Duff and Joan Marjoribanks. We went to a cinema. 'Tom' Mosley[8] was next to us with Baba Metcalfe, 'Ba-Ba Black-shirt' as she is maliciously called. Tom was charming and gentle and affectionate as he always is, except on the platform where he becomes the demagogue. Ivor Churchill is a sad specimen, a typical victim of the System. At Oxford he was considered the cleverest of us all: he had brains, romantic looks, £12,000 a year; he was a Duke's son with every advantage – he would go far. But what has he done or accomplished? Nothing, except be bored and miserable. Of our Oxford set, Anthony Eden has made the most progress, Lord Privy Seal at 35. Then Paul, Regent of Yugoslavia – but he had that thrust upon him. Bob Boothby has become well-known but he was only on the fringe of our Oxford Group. Who else? Perhaps me – 3 books, a certain position?

21 January

People are amused, on the whole, by Randolph Churchill's decision to stand as an Independent Candidate at Wavertree. The Rothermere press . . . is naturally giving Randolph much publicity and backing.

6. Artist and designer, killed on active service, 1944.

7. Conservative MP for North Paddington; a close associate of Winston Churchill.

8. Sir Oswald Mosley (b. 1896). Conservative MP for Harrow 1918–22; Independent MP for Harrow, 1922–4, and Labour 1924–31. Expelled from Labour Party March 1931, and formed the New Party.

23 January

Lunched with Emerald to meet Mrs Simpson. . . . She is a nice, quiet, well-bred mouse of a woman with large startled eyes and a huge mole. I think she is surprised and rather conscience-stricken by her present position and the limelight which consequently falls upon her. Emerald dominated the conversation with her brilliance, her mots and epigrams, some mild, some penetrating, darted like flashes from a crystal girandole. She had that morning . . . rung up Kingsley Wood the Postmaster-General himself, about her telephone being out-of-order.

24 January *Southend*

The Churchill campaign at Wavertree is a boomerang; everyone is wild with Randolph, for he may easily put the Socialist in by splitting the Conservative vote; I think he has finally cooked his goose, and I hope so. I have never known so much social and public indignation.

I canvassed here; I like canvassing; one gets peeps into other people's lives, close-ups which may be useful should ever I return to novel-writing.

26 January *Himley*

It is bitterly cold. We came here by train; the house is large, gay, and modernised, with a swimming bath, but the bedrooms are cold. The party consists of: Sheila Milbanke, calm, lovely, gentle, restful and perfect; Brendan Bracken; . . . Freda Dudley Ward, tiny, squeaky and wise and chic; Pempie Ward her daughter. . . . Our host, poor Dudley is lovable and yet so moody and irritable; people say that accidents only happen to others but look at him, his mother drowned, his little boy run over and killed on the Embankment, and his charming wife killed in an aeroplane disaster . . . in 1930. I remember the evening – a gloom fell on London – but to return to Himley. Emerald Cunard is actually staying in the house, she has hardly paid a real country house visit within human memory.

27 January *Himley*

A lazy morning in the bitter, bitter cold. I went for a walk with

Hore-Belisha,[9] the much advertised Minister of Transport. He is an oily man, half a Jew, an opportunist, with the Semitic flare for publicity. Belisha Beacons, unheard of a few weeks ago, are now world famous.

29 January *London*

Norah Lindsay lunched, bubbling with enthusiasm for the beauty of Philip Sassoon's Austrian rococo rooms he has recently put in his house in Park Lane. Philip and I mistrust each other; we know too much about each other, and I can peer into his Oriental mind with all its vanities. . . . But I admit he is one of the most exciting, tantalizing personalities of the age.

We dined with Lady Colefax, garrulous, gracious, and absurd as ever; Sir Arthur deaf, and unfortunately the very reverse of dumb. Later we went to a small 'conversazione' at Audrey Parr's. Only she can assemble 100 people, give them cheese and punch and get away with it. I felt Honor and I were suddenly unpopular: I have noticed it before of late – is it jealousy? Why is it one tires of people; has said all one wants to say to them long ago? I am becoming stale; hardly anyone amuses me, and even their presence is wearisome. Perhaps my manner shows.

31 January *London*

Leslie Hore-Belisha dined, and we liked him; he adored his evening, and we took him to the scintillating revue at the Gate Theatre. There was one number about him; and he squirmed with embarrassed pleasure as the audience, which had recognised him, hooted with laughter. He is the most advertised man in England today.

Randolph still continues his losing fight at Wavertree. Basil Dufferin spoke against him, his old friend, and compared him to a 'drummer boy'.

3 February *Sandwich*

The cobwebs are cleared, indigestion is subsiding, nerves are nicely patted into place all through the joy of being alone. I am

9. National Liberal MP for Devonport since 1932; Financial Secretary to the Treasury 1932–4, Minister of Transport 1935–7, Secretary of State for War 1937–40.

only really happy alone. Solitude is necessary to me, and solitude combined with sea is the greatest value and luxury in the world.

Peace – slept 14 hours. The roar of the sea slashing the rocks – is there any more soothing sound?

5 February

Georgia and Sacheverell Sitwell lunched – Sachie garrulous, quaint and charming with his rustic clothes and mediaeval appearance . . .

I talked for a long time this afternoon with Harold Nicolson who was having his hair cut. He sails tomorrow in the 'Berengaria' for New York and Mexico where he is going to write the life of Dwight Morrow. He looks young, Harold. He wants to stand for Parliament and asked me to find him a seat. Tomorrow is the big day of Wavertree election. Randolph Churchill's tide is running out.

6 February *London*

Towards evening there was great excitement in smart London; people looked at their watches and wondered how young Randolph was doing at Wavertree. People began to think that he might perhaps 'not do too badly' – a safe prediction, and useful either way.

We dined at Emerald's. As we walked in we saw three girls shimmering like goddesses – Isabel and Ursula Manners, daughters of Kakoo Rutland and Liz Paget, their Anglesey cousin. I have never seen such a beautiful trio. Then my eye caught old Winston Churchill – he was bowed with anxiety over Randolph . . . and his hand shook. He was especially cordial to Honor and me and hinted that whatever the result, we need have no fear that Randolph would ever interfere at Southend . . . then in walked Lord Stanley . . . Edward. They do not and did not speak. Only last night in Wavertree they had been on opposing platforms – now they were only a few feet apart with only me between them, but there was really all India too, all that dark, vast Continent. Conversation was only of Wavertree, and was embarrassing because of Winston's presence and very obvious anxiety. He offered to bet anyone that Randolph would be either

1st or 2nd. Buffles Milbanke took the bet. I bet Ursula Manners £5 that Randolph would *not* be 1st or 2nd, too. Gradually people's voices rose. ... Emerald had included Mr Simpson in her curious crew of insincere worldlings, ... the husband of the Prince of Wales' lady – and a goodlooking Barber's Block, knowing no one, and painfully embarrassed.

At 11.30 we went on to the Westminsters' Ball in Davies Street. Loelia Westminster in white and diamonds, received us. The party had no stimmung, perhaps because it was held in the offices of the Grosvenor Estate in Davies Street, and the rooms looked improvised, which indeed they were. People wandered about awaiting the Wavertree result: no one, I think wanted young Randolph to win or even do well. (Winston had gone to the H. of C. and had said to Honor 'I'll come on to the ball only if he wins'). I introduced Honor ... to Bendor,[10] who was courteous and charming, with only a suggestion of his usual halitosis. About midnight someone came in and announced 'Randolph has got 10,000 votes'. The National Candidate, official Conservative, polled 13,000 odd whereas the Socialist was RETURNED with 15,611. Randolph was third with 10,575 and the Liberal lagging far behind. It is monstrous, and it quite spoilt my evening. I was so enraged that I dragged poor Honor home.

7 February *London*

We went to a supper party at Syrie Maugham's[11] in her smiling, shimmering, all-white house. We were sitting in front of the fire, Margaret Birkenhead, Honor, Lady Colefax, 'Teenie' Cazalet[12] and I, when in walked Randolph. There was no ovation, not even a slight sensation. I got up without speaking to him, and walked away, and his dramatic entrance was a fiasco. London is seething with indignation about Wavertree.

15 February *Oakleigh, Southend*

And so to Southend: a gale lashed the sea-front. I spent the afternoon alone with my papers. Given a few hours of complete calm

10. The Duke of Westminster.
11. Wife of Somerset Maugham.
12. Victor Cazalet, Conservative MP for Chippenham since 1924.

and I can accomplish all. In the evening I addressed the people of Westborough Ward with an ease and fluency which surprised me. There is no doubt I am improving, and I seldom now suffer from nerves. Serenity is descending on my spirit, my energies are less, for my ambition is for the moment satisfied. Now I only want a son.

20 February

Honor in bed with a cold. I lunched with Freddie Birkenhead at Boulestin's, and we happened to refer to Somerset Maugham's novel *Cakes and Ale* in which Hugh Walpole takes a critic out to lunch and feeds him over-well. Suddenly we looked up, and there was Hugh Walpole almost opposite with a critic, and a magnum of Napoleon brandy. He is an awful old hypocrite.

21 February

In the evening I went to Lady Astor's ball: though the house was literally lined with lilac, there was little – if anything – to drink. The Duchess of York was in pink and very charming to me. She danced with Anthony Eden who is really becoming very handsome and important, and with Gage,[13] and Duff Cooper.

The War killed or ruined millions; it must have made a few people, a few young men, like Anthony Eden, who would not be where he is except that there are so few; it certainly made me, or was my vitality, my personality so strong that it would have emerged anyhow?

The belle of the ball was Isabel Manners; they are angels, those Manners girls. But I was cross, in a bad mood, and felt I was charmless.

28 February *London*

At 4 o'clock two Southend ladies came to tea, and we took them to one of Mrs Baldwin's 'At homes' at 11 Downing Street. It was crowded with bores but we were able to introduce them to Lady Astor[14] who was breezy and funny. She is almost a great woman, but I cannot like her. She is warm-hearted, a whirlwind

13. 6th Viscount Gage. A contemporary of Chips at Oxford, they had subsequently shared a house in London.

14. Conservative MP for Plymouth since 1919.

and a wit . . . but an unconscious snob and a hypocrite. Her Christian Science wraps her in a veil of sham and she believes, as they all do, only what she wants to . . . we then took our ladies on to the H. of C., and as we walked in the corridors I wondered how much I should grow to love them.

2 March *London*

Honor ill. I lunched with Emerald and was next to Sir Austen Chamberlain; he talked too much and his frosty eyes stared. I asked him what in life had given him his greatest aesthetic thrills; he named these in this order:

His view of the sunlit Parthenon
His first view of the Velasquez in the Prado
The Rubens in the Cathedral at Antwerp

Then a conversation followed about the present lack of great men. Austen said that great men were like high mountains; one had to be away from them to appreciate them.

7 March

My birthday: I awoke charged with vitality. I am thin, weighing 12 lb. less than in the Autumn. I am well, I am happy, rich and flourishing and very much to be envied, with a lovely sympathetic wife . . . a dog I love . . . and perhaps, soon, a son.

We had a luncheon party. Came : Mrs Keppel, seventy now, still magnificent and charming, this mistress of Kings; her husband, the amorous old George; the Iveaghs (my father-in-law had not met 'Mrs G. K.' as he calls her, for 35 years – how curious), Lady Ribblesdale, chic and complaining about her children who, she declares, treat her so cruelly. The French Ambassador, M. Corbin, an intelligent upper-middle-class Frenchman who goes down well in London, though he lacks the panache of Hoesch the German, and of Grandi, the Italian.

10 March *London*

I returned to London – no letter from my mother, and I am worried about her. She did send me a birthday cable – 2 days late, of course. I think she is mentally ill. I wish her well – wish her anything in fact, except that she should come here. I don't think I could get through a London visit. She is so queer, so eccentric, and her appearance is so frightening. She has never been altogether normal.

16 March

Today's big news is that Germany has decided to re-arm, and has ordered conscription. This means the end of the Treaty of Versailles. I think France, as usual, is to blame. I think I am personally safe – war won't come for some years and perhaps I shall then be too old and feeble. In any case, my feet are too flat. Now people are prattling of war again – every few years we have these scares.

17 March

I shall never stay in London for peace again – the telephone rang the whole morning, Diana, Alice,[15] Sheila, Emerald – all the beauties of London. It was quite like my bachelor days again.

Lady Londonderry told me of a strange anonymous letter she had recently received: it was dated AD 2035 and described the visit of a mother and daughter to 'Ulster House' (Londonderry House) by that time, apparently, a museum. The child, pointing to a portrait of 'The Duchess of Ulster' (i.e. Circe Londonderry) asks 'Who is that pretty lady?' 'Don't look at it – she was an evil woman who tempted the Labour Prime Minister, Ramsay MacDonald, and turned him into a Tory. She ruined England and was very wicked.' Circe L. is enchanted with the ingenuity of the malice and is preserving the letter; but when she showed it to the Prime Minister, he was very annoyed. He has little sense of humour . . . Ramsay MacDonald. Personally, I have always disliked and distrusted him . . .

18 March *London*

Golfed in the morning at Trent[16] with Diana Cooper, who plays badly but amusingly – who else has ever lent a Greek Goddess his niblick or putted with Helen of Troy? Trent is a dream house, perfect, luxurious, distinguished with the exotic taste to be

15. Mrs Von Hofmannsthal.
16. The Hertfordshire residence of Sir Philip Sassoon.

expected in any Sassoon Schloss. But the servants are casual, indeed almost rude; but this, too, often happens in a rich Jew's establishment.

I lunched with the Coopers en ménage, and we discussed politics and the effect of Hitler's dramatic repudiation of the Versailles Treaty, and his militaristic attitude generally. Duff thinks it is as well as we know where we are. Duff thinks that Ramsay MacDonald will resign in the early summer soon after the Jubilee celebrations, and he predicts that Beaverbrook will join the Cabinet and that Empire Free Trade will be adopted by the Government. This will bring the Beaverbrook press definitely onto the side of the Government – a very good thing at Election time. It is possible that Lloyd-George will be invited to join the Cabinet, too. Am I interested in all this – I do not really know. Sometimes I wish I was not in politics; I am not naturally suited to them but could make myself, but it takes an effort.

22 March *London, 1.30 a.m.*

A day by myself by the sea, at Southend, which I am really getting fond of. I fear Murray Gladstone, the garrulous Liberal, in the Election, more than Miss Keynes, the blue-stocking Socialist.

23 March

We decided today to buy 5 Belgrave Square. It is not too grand and is dirt cheap compared with all the other houses we have seen. It has a distinguished air and we will make it gay and comfortable. We hope to be living there by 1 September. I think it is just possible. It will be fun arranging it . . .

27 March

In the evening to Londonderry House where we found half political and social London at the Londonderrys' old-fashioned, distinguished 'do'. We supped with Mrs Keppel, Lady Oxford and poor Sir John Lavery, nearly eighty and recently a widower. Circe L. took in Corbin, the French Ambassador. Bridge, sepulchral conversation, though some spiky chat about the Duchess of Atholl who is called 'The Begum of Blair' in the

H. of C. Honor bored and lovely and splendid: I enjoyed myself; for me L. House parties always have glamour.

29 March

So we are going to live for ever at No. 5 Belgrave Square. I spent much of the day there today, buying bibelots, etc. from the collection of Mr Victor Hanbury, the dotty bankrupt present owner . . .

1 April

All Fools' day, and I lunched with Victor Cazalet, my dear devoted old chum. I always find that he exudes a kind of middle-class atmosphere. It was a luncheon party for Emerald who was three-quarters of an hour late, but desperately amusing once she had arrived. How good her digestion, how efficient her liver, how active her bowels, must be to make possible such a torrent of wit.

5 April *Southend*

A full, exhausting day. We had a luncheon party here, and the plot was to do a 'politesse' to Mrs Simpson. She is a jolly, plain, intelligent, quiet, unpretentious and unprepossessing little woman, but as I wrote to Paul of Yugoslavia today, she has already the air of a personage who walks into a room as though she almost expected to be curtsied to. At least, she wouldn't be too surprised. She has complete power over the Prince of Wales, who is trying to launch her socially . . .

I drove to Southend to attend a businessmen's banquet of about 90 men, all bigwigs, and I was sorry for Murray Gladstone, my political Liberal opponent, who arrived late, shy and badly dressed. I had never seen him before, and put myself out to be charming to him, and I think I succeeded, so I have thus established the note. He is only twenty-four, and I don't think he will prove troublesome at the Election. Afterwards, I went on to a Billiard Tournament and four Conservative Clubs, and presented the prizes and made yet another speech.

6 April

This Southend visit has been the most valuable of all my

expeditions, and I came in contact with many new people. I now definitely know that I do not mind speaking.

I rushed back to London arriving at 11 p.m., changed, and went with Honor to the Stanley's party, given by Portia and Edward for their father, Lord Derby, who was seventy yesterday. All Lancashire, where he is virtually king, was en fete and 80,000 people each subscribed 1/- to give him a birthday present. To-night it was London's turn. Lord Derby[17] was fat, smiling and amiable, though his enemies refer to him as 'genial Judas'. Lady Derby, grey, dignified and magnificent. The party became riotous and the fine fleur of England let itself go.

8 April

Honor has taken to reading George Moore, and when I found her with one of my old books in her hand, I thought of the days when I knew that old charlatan well. For he was a bit cheap, though the greatest singer, perhaps, of English, that ever lived. His work to me is always more like music than prose, and indeed when once I asked him if he was rewriting Ulick and Soracha, he replied: 'My dear young man, I have re-orchestrated it.'

He was pink, querulous, wounding and witty, and lived in a dream world of his own. His house in Ebury Street, where he worked for so long, was run by two excellent maid-servants, who adored and petted and protected him. The walls were hung with French pictures, usually modern. He could be very rude, particularly to other or younger writers. He pretended never to have read anything and indeed this was partly true, but he could be courtly to ladies when they were beautiful, or sufficiently important.

He was fond of society but thought it tied him and took up too much of his time. He was mean financially, never saw his relations, and was unapproachable. He had blue eyes, pink face, white moustache and white hair, and looked like a walrus; and was as pleased as a child with attentions from the Prince of Wales, when he was over eighty. I was once present at a peculiar scene when Lady Cunard was living at 5 Carlton House Terrace, some years ago. Her daughter, Nancy, became involved in the first of her many public scrapes, and I was sitting in the morning-room

17. The 17th Earl of Derby.

with her mother talking about it, when George Moore was announced. Emerald leapt up, saying: 'There's little George Moore' as she always called him. They discussed Nancy and he made some tactless remark, which I do not recall, whereupon Emerald lost all control and in a frenzy of rage struck him with a paper cutter that lay on a Buhl table. She shook him, chased him and rained a volley of abuse on his bald, shining head. He was apologetic, cringing, and ran round the room to avoid further blows. At last he retreated, but it was odd to be present at this little scene between the greatest writer in Europe and the most sophisticated woman in London, and one wonders what their relations were that they could have been so intimate as to exchange blows. George Moore was licentious in mind and collected photographs of his woman adorers, and told racy little anecdotes with the idea of appearing to be more of a rake than he was. I think he was really an old monk, living in the wrong century, and it pleased him to play the rake. I told him once that my favourite book was *Abelard and Heloise*, and that I thought it much the most beautiful of all his works, and I was pleased when he said he thought so too. He adored Emerald for 25 years; certainly she was his greatest, and perhaps, only friend, and his manner with her was always that of the courting suitor.

18 April *Ritz Hotel, Paris*

Crossing from Dover the boat was crowded with fashionables on holiday, going away for Easter. I sat with Lady Astor, who was chic, ondulée and gay. She accused me of introducing Honor to dreadful people like 'that Cunard woman', and asked me how it was that I, born of respectable American parents, could have such 'low tastes'. She is a queer combination of warm-heartedness, originality and rudeness. I find her antipatica.

21 April *Easter (Villa Ombrellino, Florence)*

A pleasant party in this super-luxurious villa full of treasures. Mrs Keppel at 70 is grey and magnificent, and young in spirit, but she cannot resist lying and inventing, and saying anything that comes into her Roman head. It is a habit she contracted long ago when, to amuse the blasé King Edward, she used to tell him all the news of the day spiced with her own humour. She is like a worldly Roman matron, but minus the cruelty. I fear I am at home only with worldlings.

4 May

The Jubilee excitement and atmosphere is increasing. We lunched with Emerald, with a lot of boring antiques. . . . Somerset Maugham was also there with his shrewd brain, and Chinese face. Though he is a brilliant writer he is not, of course, a gentleman. . . . There was a trace of subservience in Maugham's manner to the supercilious Stonor[18] and a touch of contempt in Sir Harry's condescension to Somerset Maugham.

6 May – Jubilee Day

I couldn't sleep for excitement and got up at 7.15. I dressed, woke Honor, and we walked through Green Park to St James's Palace to the Ponsonbys' house where a group of friends had collected to watch the procession. The usual people fainting in the heat (Royal weather) . . . guards lining the street, bunting and after a long wait the first procession, and the Speaker (Honor's cousin, Fitzroy) passed at a walking pace in a gorgeous coach. Then came the Prime Ministers of the Dominions, led by Ramsay MacDonald, seated with his daughter, Ishbel. He looked grim and she dowdy. No applause. Then the Lord Chancellor, wig and all; then the minor Royalties – a few cheers. Then masses of troops, magnificent and virile, resplendent in grand uniforms, with the sun glistening on their helmets. Then thunderous applause for the royal carriages. The Yorks in a large landau with the two tiny pink children. The Duchess of York was charming and gracious, the baby princesses much interested in the proceedings, and waving. The next landau carried the Kents, that dazzling pair; Princess Marina wore an enormous platter hat, chic but slightly unsuitable. She was much cheered. . . . So it passed. Finally the Prince of Wales smiling his dentist smile and waving to his friends, but he still has his old spell for the crowd. The Norway aunt who was with him looked comic, and then more troops, and suddenly, the coach with Their Majesties. All eyes were on the Queen in her white and silvery splendour.

18. Hon. Sir Harry Stonor.

Never has she looked so serene, so regally majestic, even so attractive. She completely eclipsed the King. Suddenly she has become the best-dressed woman in the world.

In the evening, we saw the bonfire in the Park, and crawled home in the car cutting a way in the vast crowds. Oxford Street, especially Selfridges with their great figure of Britannia, was magnificent. In Dover Street we abandoned the car, and walked down St James's Street, it was like Ascot on Gold Cup Day. One met everyone. We saw Loelia Westminster and Colin Davidson ... Then Lord Beaverbrook, who was charming. A tipsy voice called out 'Chips' and it was Hartington sitting on a stand. Honor and I walked to Buckingham Palace, which was floodlit, and joined in the chorus of calls and cheers for the King. All night the crowds in Piccadilly kept us awake, with their shouts and singing. Quelle journée.

9 May

We dined with Lord Beaverbrook at Stornoway House – a typical Max evening. He was loquacious, knowledgeable and gallant, as he received us in the dimly lit drawing room. At dinner he held forth on John Knox, displaying his knowledge of 18th-century politics, his erudition and broad-minded outlook, in the most Rabelaisian language.

14 May *London*

There is tremendous excitement about Mrs Simpson, who has now banned — and all her group from York House. It is war to the knife between the past and the present. Officially I am on —'s side but secretly delighted, for she was always an appallingly selfish, silly influence. Mrs Simpson has enormously improved the Prince. In fact I find the duel over the Prince of Wales between Mrs Simpson, supported by Diana Cooper and, strangely enough, Emerald, and the — camp is most diverting. In fact, the romance surpasses all else in interest. He is obviously madly infatuated, and she, a jolly, unprepossessing American, witty, a mimic, an excellent cook, has completely subjugated him. Never has he been so in love. She is madly anxious to storm society, while she still is his favourite, so that when he leaves her (as he leaves everyone in time) she will be secure.

Empire Day

We had cocktails at Mrs Simpson's little flat in Bryanston Court; there I found Emerald, David Margesson, the Prince of Wales and one or two others. The Prince was charm itself. He is boisterous, wrinkled and gay, and he made a great point of being amiable to Honor. His voice is more American than ever. (It doesn't matter, since all the Royal Family except the Duke of Kent have German voices.) He wore a short, black coat and soft collar, checked socks and a tie. . . . He shook and passed the cocktails, very much the 'jeune homme de la maison'. London Society is now divided between the old gang, who support —, whom the Prince now ignores, and Emerald Cunard, who is rallying to the new regime.

25 May *Belton House, Grantham*

Much T. E. Lawrence talk whom I knew slightly and always thought a bore and a bounder and a prig. He was intoxicated with his own youth, and loathed any milieu which he couldn't dominate. Certainly he had none of a gentleman's instincts, strutting about Peace Conferences in Arab dress. Storrs thinks he was unhinged by his manhandling by the Turks which he described in 'The Seven Pillars of Wisdom'; a glorious book. Whatever else he was, Lawrence was a gifted and distinguished writer. John Buchan lent me his annotated copy of the 'Seven Pillars' some years ago, and I read it all night and was called, finishing it, the next morning.

28 May

During the entracte of Götterdämmerung, I had a talk and a drink, with Dr Axel Munthe, who had read and liked my Ludwig book. He is an old man now and has only recently recovered his lost eyesight. One eye now sees perfectly. A famous Zurich oculist performed the operation. Munthe told me many things, how he had had two audiences with my mad Ludwig II (for already in the eighties he was a nerve specialist). He also knew the Empress Elizabeth well, and she had, he said, the saddest eyes he ever saw. She wanted to buy San Michele, his Capri house, now so famous. His book about the house, translated, he said, into 27 languages, including Hebrew, had ruined his life, for it had made his home impossible for him: it had made him rich and famous, but cheap.

29 May

Sometimes when I think of my poor mother, lonely, abandoned, half-mad, I have fits of remorse – am I a young Nero, heartless and selfish? But what else can I do? She has never been able to keep a friend or be with anyone for long, she is so eccentric . . .

We dined, cum Coopers, at the House of Commons in the Harcourt Room where Mr Baldwin, known as 'Dormouse' was the centre of all eyes since he must reconstruct the Cabinet next week. Duff hopes for preferment, and all the young men were sucking up to him. It is a race between Sir Samuel Hoare and Anthony Eden for the Foreign Office.

31 May

We went to the Opera (the Barber of Seville, with Lily Pons) and were joined in Emerald's box by the Prince of Wales and the Ménage Simpson. I was interested to see what an extraordinary hold Mrs Simpson has over the Prince. In the interval she told him to hurry away as he would be late in joining the Queen at the LCC Ball – and she made him take a cigar from out of his breast pocket. 'It doesn't look very pretty', she said. He went, but was back in half an hour.

3 June *London*

We watched the Trooping the Colour. That supreme ceremony, with the seventy-year-old King reviewing his troops; the sun on the helmets, the pretty pink Princesses peeping from the Horse Guards window.

7 June

The new Cabinet was announced late tonight. Ramsay MacDonald has resigned, and the King has called upon 'the Dormouse'[19] to form a Government.

8 June *Aldwick, Bognor*

We are staying with the Duff Coopers in their delightful modern

19. Mr Baldwin had been Lord President of the Council since 1931. MacDonald now took this post.

white house overlooking the sea. It is cleverly arranged by Diana whose touch is really faultless. Duff is in a good mood but somewhat chagrined about the new Cabinet which does not include him. There are not many changes, and the balance between the 3 parties remains. Sir Sam Hoare is promoted to the Foreign Office, thus disappointing Anthony Eden, and the surprise is the retention of Londonderry, who, relieved of his portfolio as Air Minister, is made Privy Seal, in theory a step-up; in practice a sop. I believe Circe Londonderry, the only political hostess left, bullied Ramsay MacDonald into stipulating that Londonderry should not be dropped altogether. Honor's pacifist Uncle Edward Halifax is now Secretary of State for War, a position which he has accepted reluctantly. I am glad Ramsay has gone: I have always disliked his shifty face, and his inability to give a direct answer. What a career, a life-long Socialist, then for 4 years a Conservative Prime Minister, and now the defender of Londonderry House. An incredible volte-face. He ends up distrusted by Conservatives and hated by Socialists.

Whitsuntide *Bognor*

Much gossip about the Prince of Wales' alleged Nazi leanings; he is alleged to have been influenced by Emerald (who is rather éprise with Herr Ribbentrop) through Mrs Simpson. The Coopers are furious, being fanatically pro-French and anti-German. He has just made an extraordinary speech to the British Legion advocating friendship with Germany; it is only a gesture, but a gesture that may be taken seriously in Germany and elsewhere. If only the Chancelleries of Europe knew that his speech was the result of Emerald Cunard's intrigues, themselves inspired by Herr Ribbentrop's dimple!

13 June

We dined with the Fitzgeralds for the Court Ball; Honor very resplendent in her sapphire parure, diamond tiara, and many other jewels. She looked radiant, Rubenesque and gorgeous. When we arrived at the Palace at 9.50, the ballroom was already overcrowded, the Ball may have been a respectable function but it was dam' dull. At first one saw no one one knew but gradually, like feeling in the dark, I saw familiar faces. We danced or rather pushed our way round the floor. The Duchess of Kent winked and gave us both dazzling smiles; like Honor she was dressed in dark blue to hide her pregnant figure. The Queen glittered and heaved under her jewels. I saw her send for the Begum Aga Khan and motion her into the King's throne. Maureen Dufferin sailed past on the arm of a black potentate. Emerald Cunard nearly fainted in the heat, and 'the Coalbox', dripping with Kitty Winn's diamonds, chattered and chirped to everyone. But it was not a fashionable function, though, of course, a magnificent sight to the uninitiated. As we left, we met Beaverbrook on the staircase and I said 'Oh! Prince Metternich himself' – he pinched me and passed on. The Prince of Wales seemed in a very bad temper but looked about twelve. Alfred Potocki, Lord of Lançut, told me it was a delight to see the rage of the French in Paris when they heard of his recent speech extending a friendly hand to Germany.

16 June *London*

All day long I spent alone with Bundi, who is an undemonstrative dog but always charming, until six o'clock when I went to see Emerald. She was in bed looking very seductive as she reclined in blue and lace. I sat on her bed for two hours, and we gossiped. She leaves on Tuesday to do hostess for the Prince of Wales at Fort Belvedere for his Ascot party, which, of course, includes the Simpsons – but Emerald is wobbling a little bit about Mrs Simpson because Portia Stanley so attacked her about her. In the midst of our talk Ribbentrop rang up, the arch-Hitler spy of Europe. Emerald flattered him for a few minutes and then asked him to join her at the Opera tomorrow. She then suddenly said: 'Corbin, the French Ambassador, says that you are perfectly charming.' I could hear the German's voice drop with surprise and when, a minute later, I asked Emerald whether Corbin had ever said such a thing, she laughingly admitted that she'd invented it, on the spur of the moment.

17 June *London*

We spent the afternoon working at 5 Belgrave Square. Monsieur Boudin from Jansen's in Paris has come over, and we hope he is to do our new dining-room built like the Amalienburg. It will be a symphony in blue and silver . . . cascades of aquamarine. Will it be London's loveliest room or is my flame dead?

18 June

At lunch Oliver Stanley told Honor that Lord Halifax had recently heard the word 'Pansy', and had to send for one of his Secretaries to ask the meaning of the word.

Emerald was provocative, outrageous and more mischievous than usual. She has made friends with the Baldwins and declares that Mrs B is the dictator of England. There is something in it.

20 June

The world of fashion is away at Ascot so there is peace or, at least, a truce in Royal circles. The Princes and Princesses have now all met Mrs Simpson. Ruffled feelings are being soothed.

28 June *Longleat*

Surfeited, Honor and I left in the morning for Longleat, sleeping and picnicking on the way in a field. We found the splendid domain lying in the full heat of a June day – with its amber-stone, gardens, dogs and almost overpowering beauty.

4 July

At Stornoway House, Lord Beaverbrook received us 'aux bras ouverts' – he likes Honor, and is interested in me and my career. He was particularly gracious tonight, small, wizened, and smiling, with a quaint way of speech which makes him endearing. He can be an excellent host.

I am tired of being 'tiddly' by night and 'gaga' by day: the season has lasted long enough.

6 July

There is something classical in Mussolini's seaplane flying to Rome being struck by lightning. It would seem as if the Gods themselves were jealous of this dynamic man. Only once have I met him. It was in 1926. Gage and I were motoring through Europe and turned up at Perugia. The whole town was en fête with garlands and bands and photographers and we were told that Il Duce was arriving the next morning. At 4 a.m. next day the streets were crowded with singing, black-shirted boys and George and I leant out of our window watching them. I got tickets for a lecture Mussolini was going to give at the University, and we duly arrived and found ourselves in a small room along with 40–50 other people, the cream of Perugian society. Suddenly the door opened . . . a little man, Napoleonic in stature, in a black coat, raised his right hand in a Fascist salute and advanced down the room as the audience stood up. He mounted the rostrum and spoke for an hour, very fast in flowing Italian, about Hannibal and the Punic Wars. My Italian was never very good, nevertheless I understood almost every word he said. He held the audience spell-bound, and made cold chills run down my spine. It gave me more of a thrill than my interview with the Pope.

When it was over we were led up, because we were English, and introduced to him and I shook his warm big hand.

This is my only personal contact with Mussolini. Now all our Roman friends meet him often, as during the past few years he has deigned to go out into Society . . .

We spent seven hours today with Monsieur Boudin from Paris. He is considered the greatest decorator in the world. He brought the plans for our dining-room: I think it is going to be stupendous. There is to be a small ante-room opening into a gallery – orange and silver like the Amalienburg; then another door, and then I hope, stupefaction – a high banqueting hall, all blue and silver. Constructing it will take six months, and Boudin is going to Munich for inspiration.

19 *July*

Sometimes I think I have an unusual character – able but trivial; I have flair, intuition, great good taste but only second rate ambition: I am far too susceptible to flattery; I hate and am uninterested in all the things most men like such as sport, business, statistics, debates, speeches, war and the weather; but I am rivetted by lust, furniture, glamour and society and jewels. I am an excellent organiser and have a will of iron; I can only be appealed to through my vanity. Occasionally I must have solitude: my soul craves for it. All thought is done in solitude; only then am I partly happy.

20 July *London*

A full but unexpectedly enjoyable day. At 3.30 I left in my grey Rolls to pick up Miss Regina Evans at 31 Buckingham Gate. ... Regina Evans is one of the forces of the Conservative Party, and has held every Office. She is an able, even a brilliant speaker, and can handle the roughest crowd. I was slightly alarmed by her; but she immediately became loquacious and charming and we chatted for two whole hours as the car raced on our expedition to Essex. We arrived, enfin, at Stansted Hall, Halstead, the home of the Butlers. He is MP for Saffron Walden, and Under-Secretary for India[20]: she is a daughter of Sam Courtauld who was also there. Millionaire picture-collecting Sam.

Our host and hostess were nervous and affairés; and no wonder as there were 10,000 people roaming in the gardens and Park, and the Baldwins were receiving in the Hall: he looked nervous. We then proceeded to a covered-in platform. I sat between Mrs O. Lewis, the pretty wife of the Member for Colchester, and Mrs Butler herself. Immediately in front of us was Mrs Baldwin and next to her the Prime Minister. It began to drizzle and 2,000 umbrellas went up looking like a sea of black mushrooms – but the rain passed as the Prime Minister began to speak. He was slow, steady, uneloquent but convincing, with his agricultural arguments calculated to appeal to the audience. But there was little, almost no applause. He sat down, and pressing his notes into Geoffrey Fry's hands whispered 'Never let me see them again.' He looked relieved, and I heard Mrs Baldwin murmur '39 minutes' as she handed him his gold watch. She then pulled his coat and told him to get into his mackintosh which he smilingly did. We then proceeded back to the house and the Baldwins gruffly gracious, cracked jokes with us all. Dinner was very welcome.

26 July *Pyrford*

I feel caddish, even treacherous sometimes keeping this diary from the eyes of my wife – yet it is our only secret. She knows I keep it, but if she were to read it, and I knew she were, it would lose much spontaneity, and cease to be a record of my private

20. This was apparently the first occasion that Chips met R. A. Butler.

thoughts. Once or twice in the past I have dictated a few harmless paragraphs to a Secretary – and they have never been the same, becoming impersonal and discreet immediately. And what is more dull than a discreet diary? One might just as well have a discreet soul.

28 July *Pyrford*

Monsieur Boudin of Jansen came to us this morning with his final drawings and estimates for our dining-room which is to imitate and, I hope, rival the Amalienburg. It will shimmer in blue and silver, and have an ochre and silver gallery leading to it. It will shock, and perhaps stagger London. And will cost us over £6,000 . . .

— came to lunch and was her usual calm, divine self. She is, however, hipped about the Prince of Wales and Mrs Simpson, and talks of little else. She is deeply hurt, not only by his sudden neglect of her, but more by his disloyalty to the — gang. Secretly I am on his side. The — milieu, while amusing and witty, is small – small and suffocating, with their high-pitched voices and pettiness and criticism and anti-everything. It is destructive. Mrs Simpson, who wants to get on, is a much bigger better woman than all of them put together.

30 July

I am bored by this Italian-Abyssinian dispute, and really I fail to see why we should interfere. Though, of course, the League of Nations will stand or fall by it. But I am a little uneasy that the destinies of countless millions should be in the exquisite hands of Anthony Eden, for whom I have affection, even admiration – but not blind respect. Why should England fight Italy over Abyssinia, when most of our far flung Empire has been won by conquest?

13 August

I motored to Bailiff's Court, the Moynes' 'seat' near Littlehampton. It is fantastic; they have created almost a community in the Norman-Gothic style; the house, chapel, guest-house, and dependent buildings, even the garden are medieval. There is a stillness that reminds one of the Emilian plains near Ravenna.... Nevertheless, the general effect is depressing for the rooms are small, badly-lit, and there is no comfort, although every guest-room is decorated to resemble the cell of a rather 'pansy' monk.

18 August *Bognor*

A pretty comedy this morning. Honor found a stray, frightened dog that had come into our garden. It was pathetic and half-starved; after much coaxing and chasing it was caught. Luckily the name of the owner was still distinguishable on its worn collar, and we rang up the Bognor police – no result. We then searched the London telephone directory and discovered a likely number; and rang it. A male voice said 'his people' were staying at East Wittering; a ramshackle middle-class ville d'eau near Chichester. And to East Wittering Honor and I, plus the lost dog, now asleep after a good meal, went in the grey Rolls. The rich car caused a slight sensation amongst the sea-shanties. At last we discovered the owner.... He was a lean little man of fifty and he cried when he saw his dog – burst into tears as he hugged the animal to his bosom. He led us to his house – a sort of converted railway carriage where he was spending a brief holiday. He pressed cider and biscuits upon us, whilst his family gathered round, all too shy to speak, and too overjoyed at the return of their pet to be more than just polite to us. We left, touched by the joy of the little household...

All day I have felt that perhaps I am in a trance: it is not me but someone else sitting by this silent sea.... Some sunburnt Samurai, revelling in Lady Murasaki's long novel. What an epoch! I should like to have been Japanese in the 10th century. No riches, no complications, only scented notes and endless acrostics and the flapping of cranes as they passed over one's palace, to break the monotony of endless, inevitable adulteries.

21 August *Bognor*

War?[21] War? I wonder. The conversations between Anthony Eden and Monsieur Laval in Paris have broken down. Tomorrow the Cabinet meets to take the fateful decision.

21. Over Italian ambitions in Abyssinia.

22 August *Bognor*

If only a European war can be postponed until I am too old to go . . . I know that I should be utterly worse than useless as an Officer in the trenches . . . and yet, such is my love of England I should probably enlist.

23 August *Bognor*

England has asked the League for sanctions, which she knows will never be given, and we have saved our face with no greater loss than the good-will of the Italian people, which we will, no doubt, regain one day.

9 September

Today we spent with Rex Whistler whom I have persuaded to paint a fresco for our drawing-room. He is chetif, mild and has faultless taste, even genius. Cecil Beaton also lunched looking très 1830. He was wearing a stock and large pin. He is so insinuating, so clever, so gentle and '*fin*' in the French sense . . .

Sam Hoare has made a great impression by a terrific Geneva speech in which he backs up the League of Nations, and pledges Britain's word to uphold the Covenant, provided the rest of the world does likewise. We now await France's answer.

13 September

France is hedging: but has come out for the Covenant. Is it war? All now depends on the Megalomaniac Mussolini. But how can he hope to fight all Europe unless Hitler decides to back him up?

I fear I am really superstitious, and Honor confirms this – she has caught me crossing myself in Catholic churches and whenever we pass a funeral or a piebald horse.

14 September

The newspapers announce Mussolini's firm and emphatic refusal to listen to the League of Nations; he still does not believe that England will apply sanctions. The war alarums increase. My poor mother, with her distorted brain, was right. She always said that if I became a naturalised Britisher, I should be obliged to fight; but there is still hope; we may only send an Expeditionary force abroad, and have a mild Colonial War. Personally, I know, that I could never be a soldier; I should be hopeless.

15 September *London*

The shadow of war darkens everything, and overnight, Hitler has become the arbiter of Europe. Will he remain aloof, turn a helping hand to us, or to Italy? Are we, in the name of the League, not forcing Mussolini into Hitler's arms?

21 September *London*

Mussolini has turned down the League's offer for a peaceful settlement; general opinion is that this is final and grave; I, on the contrary, think it is the beginning of the end, and that the bargaining will now start . . .

24 September

I rushed to Southend. All afternoon and evening I was on tiptoes, hoping and expecting a message to say that 'it had begun'. For my son is due today. I have always felt he would come on Saturday, and have even inscribed MFNE –Meus filius natus est – in my diary for that day.

26 September

No baby yet.

Lord Beaverbrook has sent masses of yellow chrysanthemums to Honor with a card inscribed 'From the Crabbed Old Man of Stornoway . . .'

I am tired of the Abyssinia crisis – though a crisis a day keeps the war away.

27 September

It is very difficult to spend less than £200 a morning when one goes out shopping.

3 October

War. The Italians have bombed Adowa, killing 1,700, including nurses, women and children. Their first victim being a Red Cross

Hospital. All day news has drifted in, much of it, no doubt, false and exaggerated. Where shall we be in a fortnight's time? Winston Churchill has made a stirring speech at Bournemouth demanding increases in our defences.

4 October

The war in Africa and our own baby suspense are getting a little on my nerves . . .

The Abyssinian war goes on; the Italians advance and have invaded Ethiopian territory.

7 October

Diana Cooper rang early; she had been to the Fort last evening to dine with the Prince of Wales, who was, she said, 'pretty and engaging'. Mrs Simpson was glittering, and dripped in new jewels and clothes.

I went to Claridges to have tea with the Nicholas' of Greece who are here for the Royal confinement. The Duchess of Kent was there in a brown dress and much bejewelled, and rather large, but not so large as Honor. Her curls were faultlessly done at the back. She was sweetness itself, but she has not become in the least English. We had many pregnancy jokes, and she asked tenderly for Honor, and said it would be 'so amusing' if her baby was born first, or on the same day as ours.[22] This unlikely coincidence now seems possible. Hers is due on 16 October, and ours was on 24 September. I adore this family, and loved them when they were down on their luck; now their star is rising, especially since the Kent wedding (these damned, inefficient and all too numerous servants never fill my ink-stand). At one point the Grand-Duchess sent her daughter into the next room to fetch her spectacles and the Duchess went meekly. She has been well brought-up in an old-fashioned, affectionate way.

I feel quite confident that my son will be born before morning.

22 November *21 St James's Place*

Too much has happened: I am weary unto death, yet calm – and

22. The Duchess of Kent's baby (the present Duke of Kent) was born on 9 October, on the same day as Chips's son Paul.

thin for me, only 11 st 5 lb. A father and now an MP,[23] all in a few weeks . . .

At 5 the Duchess of Kent came in, in green with a red feather like Robin Hood. She was gay with her wondrous smile and glow, and adored baby Paul, and held him up affectionately. He had been vaccinated and was a little cross, but sweet. The Duke of Kent followed, blue-eyed, . . . insinuating, and – to me – though not to Honor – altogether irresistible. After they left, Laura Corrigan[24] arrived from Paris and she hugged the baby tightly to her thin childless bosom.

Brendan Bracken has sent Paul a baroque carved walnut cradle, magnificent but highly unsuitable; it must have been made for some Venetian Grandee's baby in the Settecento.

Duff is Secretary for War at the age of forty-five and everyone is enchanted. The secret has been well kept. Diana denied it up to the last minute. Emerald telegraphed him 'Hail Mighty Mars'.

I am so happy for Diana; she will be happy and gleeful. But personally and privately I am not altogether happy in my own mind about Duff's appointment. His is too bellicose a nature for the job. He belongs to or rather leads, the extreme pro-French Group in the House of Commons . . .

26 November

After luncheon at Emeralds to meet the Kents, I drove at breakneck speed to the House of Commons, and hurried into 'The House' – no clerk, no policeman asked me my name. The Chamber was crowded, and I stood up in the gangway. Everyone was nice to me, but I, ever over-intuitive, felt less so than usual; there was a touch of the old boy and the new frightened freshman. Only I wasn't in the least frightened, only bored, a bit amused and desperately self-possessed.

27 November

I motored to Southend, where I noticed a change, not a very

23. For Southend. The General Election had been held early in November. The Conservatives won 385 seats, with 32 National Liberal and 8 National Labour allies, making a Government total of 425; the Opposition consisted of 180, of whom 154 were Labour.

24. Mrs James Corrigan.

subtle one, in people's manner towards me. I was 'Sir-ed' at every sentence; people who weeks ago were bombarding me with advice, were now obsequious. I was treated very much as 'the Member'. I opened a fete for Holy Trinity Church in Southchurch, signed over 900 letters and returned to London to a peaceful evening.

I now only like dining quietly with Honor in her bedroom. We eat well, drink Guinness, talk to Bundi until 10 p.m., when we adjourn to the nursery to watch Paul being fed. I love holding the little bundle in my arms, tight and close.

28 November

I went to the House of Commons and joined the queue to take my oath, and in a few moments found myself swearing and signing and then shaking hands with the Speaker, who is Honor's cousin. He looks so ordinary in morning clothes; but today, aloof and bewigged, he seemed terrific. I wrote my first note on House of Commons paper to Paul reigning in Yugoslavia, and then left. I have time enough . . . months, perhaps years to be spent in 'The House'.

29 November

A full day, furniture, fixtures and fatigues: I am *determined* to move into Belgrave Square in January whilst the House of Commons is not sitting.

Honor is full of energy and glowing health; her accouchement has done wonders for her looks and well-being. She is an angel of goodness, gentleness and grace: I love her more every day. Our baby boy now smiles and weighs nearly 11 lb and Honor is content to sit holding him for hours on end while he gurgles. And for me it is an extraordinarily satisfying emotion to meet a white pram in the Park which contains one's own son.

30 November

Little John Julius Cooper came to tea wearing a kilt. He sang, showed-off, played the piano, did tricks and was altogether enchanting. I wonder whether Paul will be like him?

5 December

I do not really think the House of Commons 'My Cup of Tea',

I am too much of an individualist, and also, too self-centred and set in my ways. Enough if I remain a mute, just adequate back-bencher, but frankly most of the problems that so excite 'the Hon. Members' leave me quite cold and indifferent.

6 December

There is considerable indignation caused by the Monarch's cavalier treatment of Lady Sysonby. For 30 years Fritz Ponsonby[25] was the King's closest friend, his most devoted counsellor, Keeper of the Privy Purse, and general adviser. He was witty, devoted, discreet, and sincere. He died literally *penniless*. His widow, whom he adored, has now been given only 3 months to turn out of St James's Palace, where she has lived all her married life...

... I am shocked by the whole story – I am always shocked by meanness.

I think the Court is dead and out-of-date. Emerald told us how she had lunched today with Alec Hardinge[26] who, though quite young, has already taken on the Court 'colour'. He very much criticised the Prince of Wales and his entourage. It is high time such dreary narrow-minded fogies were sacked, as, indeed, they will be, in the next reign.

9 December

In the House of Commons I was struck by David Margesson's changed attitude; for years he has been my firm friend; but now he seems aloof and pre-occupied. Is he being the big boy ...? Perhaps it is the House of Commons manner.

I roamed about the House of Commons and I have learned the geography; that is something.

We dined with Victor Cazalet in a private room at the House of Commons. ... We talked until 10.30 and then I went into the Chamber, where J. H. Thomas was ragging the Labour Opposition, and a sorry sight it was to watch them wincing under the gruelling. J. H. knows them so well, speaks their language,

25. Sir Frederick Ponsonby, subsequently Lord Sysonby.

26. Lord Hardinge of Penhurst, Equerry and Assistant Private Secretary to King George V, 1920–36; Private Secretary to King Edward VIII, 1936, and to King George VI, 1937–43.

and is aware of their tricks and he went for them. The Socialist Opposition seem appalling; uneducated, narrow and unattractive, and the Independent Labour Party, headed by Maxton, are a quartette of loquacious jokers – a super-night at the House.

10 December

Most of the day at the House of Commons. Today for the first time I really liked it; boredom passed and a glow of pleasure filtered through me. But I wish I sometimes *understood* what I was voting for, and what against.

12 December

House of Commons all day and it seems interminable. Am I to sit and smoke and drink myself to death in the smoking-room, thus making myself better-known and, perhaps liked? Or shall I burrow in the library for the next five years and re-become what I once was, well educated and well-read? Most of today I spent reading Lamartine.

But I am forgetting the trial. At 10 a.m. Alfred Beit fetched me and we drove to the Royal Gallery in the House of Lords to attend the much-discussed trial of young Lord de Clifford.[27] The Hall resembled a Venetian canvas, gilt and red. There were places assigned for the Peeresses, others for Ambassadors, for strangers, for Members of the House, for witnesses, etc. At 11 o'clock the Lord Chancellor, red-robed, bewigged, entered and was followed by the Peers; about 105 of them in glorious robes and cocked hats. But I noticed that the more venerable peers, including Desborough, Scarborough, Londonderry, etc., were not in their robes, whereas others such as Donegal, Faringdon, etc., were resplendent in red. Some documents were read, old fashioned Norman documents sounding like Froissart. Then young de Clifford was brought in . . . tall, good-looking and sufficiently distinguished; he was wearing morning clothes. He was charged and pleaded 'not guilty' in an audible voice. The trial then proceeded; it was like Iolanthe. The policemen who were witnesses wore new uniforms; and they were followed by 2 pretty girls who testified. As one gave her name and address I saw one old Peer raise his robes, fish out a pencil and, no doubt,

27. On a charge of manslaughter.

note down her address. I went to the trial thoroughly believing in de Clifford's guilt, as did many others, considering him a déclassé night-club Peer, and a semi-drunkard. Within a quarter of an hour, so clear and concise is British justice, everyone was convinced of his innocence.

When the verdict was announced, it was a unanimous one – a complete acquittal. There was no case against de Clifford, scarcely a shred of evidence, and he is a teetotaller. It has now been divulged that the man who was killed had four motoring offences against him, some for driving when intoxicated. These were not mentioned at the trial.

It was a glorious sight, and perhaps one that will never be seen again.[28]

16 December

I met Aldous Huxley slinking out of a bank, as if he was afraid to be seen emerging from a capitalist institution, from where he had doubtless withdrawn large sums.

17 December

A political crisis has burst on the country: who would have thought a few weeks ago when we were on the hustings, that this would happen? Sam Hoare, ill and disillusioned, realist and unimaginative . . . crossed over to Paris late on Sunday. He conferred that evening with Laval, the tottering Prime Minister of France and again on Sunday, and between them they drew up proposals which were to be a basis for negotiations for peace between the League of Nations . . . Italy and Abysinnia. Italy was to have been given large tracts of land, etc. . . . Hoare communicated these proposals to Mr Baldwin in London, and yesterday there was a Cabinet Meeting at which they were discussed. Unfortunately there has been a leak, and today the Press of the World knows the truth. The country, or rather a noisy section of it, pro-sanctions and loud in the praises of the League is now campaigning. The terrible truth is that many sensible people like Duff Cooper are taken in. . . . But this afternoon I attended a thrilling meeting of the Foreign Relations Committee presided

28. It never was. This was the last trial of a Peer by his fellow-Peers.

over by Austen Chamberlain[29] and almost everyone spoke against the peace proposals, and in favour of a League policy. Chamberlain, aged, cadaverous, correct and polite, refused to say what line he would take on Monday at the full-dress debate on Foreign relations . . .

Home at 1.30, ill and flu-ish. I am sick to death at all this talk about Hoare's peace proposals. He wants to keep England out of war and he wants to prevent a European conflagration; I should have thought two estimable, patriotic ambitions.

19 December

What a day. Sir Samuel Hoare has resigned. Honor and I went to the House of Commons for the great debate. I was clever enough to wangle her a ticket for the Members' Gallery and there I deposited her. Questions were galloped through and no one listened; the House was packed. Sir Sam Hoare sat in a corner of the 3rd bench, a place usually accorded to fallen Cabinet Ministers. He looked thin and ill, and had a plaster across his nose, which he broke in Switzerland a few days ago.

There was considerable tension; many people, I amongst them, felt that the Government has behaved with almost incredible stupidity. It wobbled. First it displeased the Left-Wing by its seeming acceptance of the Hoare-Laval proposals, and then suddenly it made a volte-face, and dropped Hoare and the Proposals, thus enraging the Right-Wing. The Socialist Opposition have put down a Motion of Censure.

At last Sam Hoare got up, and in a flash he had won the sympathy of the House by his lucidity, his concise narrative, his sincerity and patriotism. He told the whole story of his negotiations and added that not a country, save our own, has moved a soldier, a ship, an aeroplane – was this collective action? He was a Cato defending himself; for 40 minutes he held the House breathless, and at last sat down, but not before he had wished his successor better luck, and burst into tears. I have never been so moved by a speech. It may have been only a Mea Culpa; but to me it was more – it was the voice of a large section of sensible

29. Sir Austen Chamberlain (1863–1937). Former Chancellor of the Exchequer and Foreign Secretary. Half-brother to Neville Chamberlain.

England; perhaps the swan-song of a certain Conservative spirit. . . . He may be down today, disowned and disgraced, but he will rise again, I am sure, and soon, to high office. . . . But his health is weak and his nerves seem shattered. The house vibrated with emotion as he spoke; and had it been possible to put a vote I am sure he would have won. But he was followed by the Prime Minister, who was embarrassed and spoke lamely, though he was honest enough to admit his mistake in accepting the proposals. In no other country could the Prime Minister stand up in the Chamber and calmly say 'I made a mistake, and I am sorry'. But Mr Baldwin can do this better than anyone. The House took him at his word. There were a few 'back-benchers', murmuring inaudible complaints including myself. If I had been in the House longer, I should have struck a note of *reality*, and expressed the opinion of everyone one meets – for God's sake, Mr Baldwin, make peace. Instead he has allowed himself to be bullied by the Left-Wing Conservatives and by Liberals. Attlee, the Socialist Leader, followed. He looks like a black snail and is equally ineffective: he challenged the Government, in a long, unconvincing speech; indeed, given his case, almost anyone could have made a better job of it. The House emptied . . . Austen Chamberlain rose, gaunt, deaf, and was mildly conciliatory and then made a sudden assault on Attlee which made the little man seem to shrink. Harold Nicolson made a good 'maiden' – the Liberals talked a lot of nonsense. The vote was put: and the Government won with a majority of 232. Cheers, and then an Amendment which we again won, and then home. The Government is saved.

20 December

Who will be the new Foreign Secretary? Betting seems to be on Austen Chamberlain as a temporary appointment. But he is too old and does not want it,[30] though he would be an excellent stop-gap for a few months, until the Government regains its prestige.

I walked to the House and arrived at 11 punctually. There were only about twelve or so supporters of the Government present, all were either exhausted by yesterday's proceedings, or had left for the holidays. I noticed that the Socialists were in force, and

30. This is incorrect; Chamberlain did want the Foreign Office.

chuckling. One of them moved that 'this House re-assemble on 23 January' – and I saw we could not defeat this Amendment. But the Whips quickly twigged, and we were given orders to keep the debate going at all costs. Several Members got up and talked drivel in order to prevent a 'snap' division. Meanwhile the Whips telephoned frantically to White's, Buck's, Government Offices, etc., and by the time Mr Speaker ordered the Lobbies cleared, it looked as if we might just win after all. The division bell rang, and we poured into the Lobbies. We won, but only by 30 votes.

23 December

Anthony Eden has been appointed Foreign Secretary by Mr Baldwin. His appointment is a victory for 'The Left', for the pro-Leaguers. He has had a meteoric rise, young Anthony. I knew him well at Oxford, where he was mild, aesthetic, handsome, cultivated and interested in the East – now at thirty-eight he is Foreign Secretary. There is hardly a parallel in our history. I wish him luck; I like him; but I have never had an exaggerated opinion of his brilliance, though his appearance is magnificent.

CHAPTER TWO

The Year of the Abdication: 1936

The abdication of King Edward VIII has been the subject of many accounts, of varying interest and objectivity. Chips's account is of particular interest in that although he was not an admirer of the King he liked Mrs Simpson, and was extremely sympathetic to her in the tragic predicament in which she and the King found themselves. As a result of his close friendship with the Duke of Kent and certain members of the Government, Chips's information on the course of the drama was extremely good and detailed – too detailed in fact for complete publication at this stage.

After the crisis Chips wrote two portraits of the King and Mrs Simpson, parts of which can be conveniently inserted at this point, as an introduction to his narrative of the Abdication Crisis:

KING EDWARD VIII

I first met him in 1920 and I have known him fairly well ever since, but there have been long intervals when I never saw him, or when I did he barely recognised me. At other times he was exceedingly friendly towards me, and in Chicago greeted me as a very old friend when we happened to be there at the same time.

It was — who first 'modernised' and Americanised him, making him over-democratic, casual and a little common. Hers is the true blame for this drama.

The late King and Queen Mary too are not without blame. For the 26 years of their reign they practically saw no one except their old Courtiers, and they made no social background whatever for any of their children. Naturally, their children had to find outlet and their fun elsewhere, and the two most high-spirited ones, the late King and the fascinating Duke of Kent, drank deeply from life . . .

He takes up things with violence – golf, hunting, flying, drink and latterly gardening; since Wallis's influence, Society. He has the easy gift of smiling, and popular he always was and always will be. He is fanatically loyal whilst his friendships last. For two years he has played the bagpipes, sometimes all night, and drank next to nothing and then only whisky with plain water, claret or Vichy water, because Wallis drinks these things. His amazing energy makes him indulge frantically in exercise, or stay up all night . . .

MRS SIMPSON (THE DUCHESS OF WINDSOR)

Wallis Simpson I first met at Emerald Cunard's in 1935, and Emerald begged us to invite her to dinner sometime. Instead we asked her to luncheon at 21 St James's Place. . . . Three days after our luncheon party she invited us for a cocktail at Bryanston Court where she was living in a dreadful, banal flat. The Prince of Wales arrived, and I saw a signal pass between him and Wallis, and he went at once to Honor and talked to her for an hour . . .

Our acquaintance drifted into genuine friendship, and I grew to admire and like her. . . . She is a woman of charm, sense, balance and great wit, with dignity and taste. She has always been an excellent influence on the King, who has loved her openly and honestly. I really consider that she would have been an excellent Queen. She is never embarrassed, ill at ease, and could in her engaging drawl charm anyone. . . . Her reserve and discretion are famous, and proved by the fact that no one knew of her impending divorce, also by the fact that she never confided in anyone her hopes of becoming Queen. I think that the idea grew, gradually. She was encouraged by the King to believe that he could marry her, and indeed there was nothing legal to prevent him doing so. Perhaps at first the idea was a joke, which blossomed into a plan. . . . Not until too late did she realise the gravity of the position and then even she could do nothing with the King.

Now she is 'de-throned', almost an outcast, and her social ambitions – always very great – have crashed. But she will recover everything except the Throne. . . . I hope she will be happy. She has always shown me friendship, understanding, and even affection, and I have known her do a hundred kindnesses and never a mean act. There is nothing sordid or vulgar in her make-up, but she is modern certainly. She has a terrific personality and her presence grew as her importance increased: we are far from being done with her yet.... She would prefer to be grand, dignified and respectable, but if thwarted she will make the best of whatever position life gives her.

Chips's feelings in this crisis were complicated by his friendship with the Duke and Duchess of Kent and his warm feelings for the Duke and Duchess of York (subsequently King George VI and Queen Elizabeth). As was perhaps not surprising, he had little in common with the Duke of York, whom he described as 'good, dull, dutiful and good-natured', and his friendship with the Duchess had been intermittent since her marriage. He regarded her with warm affection as 'well-bred, kind, gentle and slack ... always charming, always gay, pleasant and smiling ... mildly flirtatious in a very proper romantic old-fashioned Valentine sort of way.... She makes every man feel chivalrous and gallant towards her'. Thus, throughout the Abdication Crisis, as the result of his friendship with, and admiration for, Mrs Simpson, Chips found himself in a difficult position. He subsequently tended to deride the post-Edward VIII Court, and he never forgave the Royal Family for its icy treatment of the Duke and Duchess of Windsor; his dislike of Sir Alexander (later Lord) Hardinge became intense, and, indeed, he retained for the rest of his life an aversion to the members of the Court who had opposed Edward VIII. This was all the more remarkable because, as is plain enough from the diaries, he had little real liking for the unfortunate King.

This narrative is therefore of real interest in that it is written by someone who was closely involved in the crisis, was exceptionally well informed about its course, and who supported the King because he admired Mrs Simpson. The latter has never really received proper recognition for the honourable part she played throughout the unhappy affair. In Chips's account we have, for the first time, a contemporary day-by-day account which entirely takes her side and seeks to give justice to her actions.

The account is very long and very detailed. For this reason alone, severe pruning was necessary. But it also contains much highly confidential and private material. Although it is over thirty years since the events which are described, many of the principal participants are still alive, and it has been necessary to delete much. But this narrative is of such interest that I have excised material with very great reluctance and care, and have retained enough to maintain the flavour and information contained in the full account, so that nothing of real importance has been omitted.

In order to retain a complete narrative I have put the account of the Channons' 1936 visit to Germany as an Appendix to this Chapter, and have reduced the volume of entries relating to matters other than the Abdication Crisis to an absolute minimum. For this was the main crisis in Chips's life in this year, and for him – as for so many others – 1936 was indeed The Year of the Abdication.

The narrative opens with the death of King George V.

1936

18 January *London, 21 St James's Place*

The year has, indeed, begun in gloom. The King ill, and Kipling dead[1] – Kipling was a great man, a writer whom I personally could never read nor appreciate, nevertheless he was certainly an Empire figure. I once met him in the 20's; I was staying at Fairlawne with the Cazalets, and towards tea-time a middle-aged couple and daughter arrived. Hugh Walpole and Lady Russell of 'Elizabeth and Her German Garden'[2] were also there, I think. I did not take in the newcomers' names, and I thought they looked far too dowdy and middle class for me. But over the port I found myself next to the little man, and was immediately struck by the long hairs protruding from his ears. Somehow the conversation got onto bullfights, and he recounted in vivid language one he had witnessed. A few moments later I discovered he was Kipling.

1. Rudyard Kipling died on 18 January.
2. Elizabeth Mary, Countess Russell.

Kipling has little or no message for the youth of this country, the present youth that is; certainly none for our class by whom he was respected, but not liked; though I believe that in America he is still a best-seller.

As for the King, I have been gloomy about him all day, for three days ago I dreamt that he died. It seems that the Prince of Wales has gone to Sandringham, where the Duke of York has been for nearly a week, and I have it from an unimpeachable authority that he rang up Mrs Simpson last night after the Queen had gone to bed, and he told her that the King's cold was worse than he had thought. The Princess Royal and the Kents are also at Sandringham. This afternoon there was a crowd outside Buckingham Palace, just as there used to be in 1928. Honor and I leapt out of the car, and a policeman informed us that a new bulletin would shortly be issued. We paced the pavement for ten minutes as the anxious crowd thickened. . . . The new bulletin was not encouraging – 'increased cardiac of the heart'. We came home, and I rang up Diana Cooper, and Emerald Cunard rang me; both had talked to Mrs Simpson whom the poor Prince loves so desperately. They were gloomy. My heart goes out to the Prince of Wales tonight, as he will mind so terribly being King. His loneliness, his seclusion, his isolation will be almost more than his highly-strung and unimaginative nature can bear. Never has a man been so in love. . . . How will they re-arrange their lives, these people? I stood near George V at the last Garden Party, and for minutes saw his light blue eyes, tobacco-stained beard, and heard his famous guttural laugh.

20 January

About 7 o'clock we heard that the King's strength was diminishing . . . and we sat in consternation. At 9.35 came the fatal news over the wireless, 'The life of the King is moving slowly to its close'.

21 January

The King is dead – Long live the King. The eyes of the world are on the Prince of Wales, the new King Edward VIII. This morning everyone is in mourning, and the park is full of black crows. I went to the House of Commons at 6, which had been summoned by gun-fire – and unofficially, by radio. About 400 MPs out of 615 turned up, then the Speaker came in, and took his oath to Edward VIII, and we followed; the Prime Minister first . . . it took hours and I sat in the smoking room with A. P. Herbert and Duff Cooper waiting my turn. We talked of Royalty. Today is the anniversary of Lenin's death; tomorrow that of Louis XVI and Queen Victoria. . . . Duff had just come on from St James's Palace where he attended the Privy Council to announce the accession of the King, and there they witnessed the King's Oath. 60 or 70 patriarchs, and grandees, in levée dress or uniform, presided over by Ramsay MacDonald as Lord President of the Council. They make an impressive picture, it seems, not unfunny and reminiscent of charades in a country-house; then they processed into yet another Long Gallery where they were received by the Princes . . . a few moments later the new King was sent for, and he entered . . . solemn, grave, sad and dignified in Admiral's uniform. Everyone was most impressed by his seeming youth and by his dignity. Much bowing, and he in turn swore his Oath. When he left some of the Councillors were overcome by their emotions . . . all this from Duff.

22 January

This morning I walked to the foot of St James's Street to witness the Proclamation, and found a crowd already gathered before St James's Palace. Soon the carriages of the Herald's Office arrived; very grand, very gold and scarlet and heraldic were the various Heraldic Kings, Norroy, Garter, Clarenceux, etc. In the first carriage sat Bernard Norfolk, Earl-Marshal of England. The trumpeters blew a bugle, and proclaimed the accession of King Edward VIII. It was a fleeting brilliant ceremony which I shall surely never see again. Afterwards I saw a large black car (the King's) drive away, with the blinds pulled half down. The crowd bowed, thinking that it contained the Duchess of Kent, but I saw Mrs Simpson . . .

We are all rivetted by the position of Mrs S—. No man has ever been so in love as the present King; but can she be another Mrs Fitzherbert? If he drops her she will fall – fall – into the nothingness from whence she came, but I hope he will not, for she is a good, kindly woman, who has had an excellent influence on the young Monarch.

23 January

Baldwin spoke for 20 minutes about the late King. It is the sort of thing he does very well, and every word perfectly chosen, and perfectly balanced. He had had a trying day as he was pall-bearer in the morning at the funeral of his first cousin Rudyard Kipling. Mr Baldwin's speech was 'The Question was —' that messages of condolence be sent to the King, and to Queen Mary. He was followed by Major Attlee for the Socialists. We on our side thought he would jar, and do badly, but on the contrary he was excellent ... he, too, held the House. At 3.40 the Speaker left the Chair, preceded by the Serjeant-at-Arms and Mace, etc., and we followed in pairs. Harold Nicolson said 'Let's stick together', and we did. In solemn silent state we progressed into Westminster Hall, lining the East side. Harold and I were at the end of the queue, as befitted 'new boys' and thus were nearly on the steps and found ourselves next to the Royal Family[3]; I could have touched the Queen of Spain, fat and smelling slightly of scent, and old Princess Beatrice. Opposite us, were the Peers led by the Lord Chancellor, who, unlike the Speaker, always seems a joke character. In the middle of the Great Hall stood the catafalque draped in purple.

We waited for 10 minutes ... and I was rather embarrassed as my heavy fur-lined coat has a sable collar, a discordant note among all the black. I had been tempted to come into the Hall without one, but that would certainly have meant pneumonia. I was sorry for the aged Princess next to me, shivering in her veil.... After a little some younger women, heavily draped, came in, and were escorted to the steps. I recognized the Royal Duchesses. Princess Marina, as ever, managed to look infinitely more elegant than the others; she wore violets under her veil and her stockings, if not flesh-coloured, were of black so thin that they seemed so.

The great door opened ... the coffin was carried in and placed

3. For Sir Harold Nicolson's account, see Nigel Nicolson: *Harold Nicolson, Diaries and Letters 1930–39*, pp. 240–41.

on the catafalque. It was followed by King Edward, boyish, sad and tired, and the Queen, erect and more magnificent than ever. Behind them were the Royal brothers. There was a short Service . . . and all eyes looked first at the coffin, on which lay the Imperial Crown and a wreath from the Queen, and then we turned towards the boyish young King, so young and seemingly frail. Actually he is forty-two, but one can never believe it. After a few moments, the Queen and young King turned, and followed by the Royal Family, they left. The two Houses of Parliament then proceeded in pairs round the catafalque now guarded by four immobile officers and by Gentlemen-at-Arms . . . there was an atmosphere of hushed stillness, of something strangely sacred and awe-inspiring.

This King business is so emotional, it upsets and weakens me, and I am left with the feeling that nothing matters . . . almost an eve-of-war reaction. As we left, we were told that on the way to Westminster Hall, the top bit of the Imperial Crown had fallen out during the procession, and had been picked up by a Serjeant-Major.

Saturday, 25 January

London is once again taking on a highly emotional atmosphere – it is like the Royal Wedding and the Jubilee all over again. The foreign potentates are soon due, and the capital is filling up with foreigners come to pay homage to the dead King. The centre of the universe seems to be Westminster where thousands upon thousands of reverend people pass. Some of them stand for hours, sometimes five hours, in the long queue . . .

After luncheon, I took Emerald, Diana and young Howland[4] to Westminster Hall. As an MP I can walk through the Private Members' entrance, and take any friends. We saw the great catafalque, the purple-draped coffin, bearing the Queen's simple wreath (changed daily), the orb, sceptre and Imperial Crown. The crowds passed in silent, reverent procession on either side, but it is the men on guard whom impress one most. Four officers, frozen into silence, stand motionless for 20 minutes on end, and are then relieved: it is a great strain for they must look down

4. The present Duke of Bedford.

all the time, and see nothing but shuffling feet, at least so Cranley and Charles Wood, Honor's cousins, say, who have both done it.

Monday, 27 January

I took a large party, Maurice Baring, Victor Rothschild, etc., to Westminster Hall. Just as we arrived, the Queen arrived too, and I saw her well. She was erect, composed, magnificent as she stood near the bier. Her dignity and fortitude have caught the heart of the whole nation . . .

There is much gossip and speculation about the new court. What an upheaval. Will the King keep his own entourage or take on his father's? And will he (I doubt it) continue the same old round of Sandringham, Ascot, Cowes and Balmoral?

Tuesday, 28 January

The dreadful day dawned early for us as I was awakened at seven by my old Belton, with the words: 'Dr and Mrs Walker from Southend are here'. I had rung them up the night before, offering them my parliamentary tickets for the funeral procession. Honor and I had been invited by Loelia Westminster to go to St James's Palace to her mother's house. I dressed hurriedly – it was grey, almost black without, but already, as on Jubilee Day, the Green Park was full of hurrying sombrely clad people. I called to Honor and went down. The Walkers and I had a melancholy breakfast and they left on foot . . .

Presently, the Iveaghs came in from the hotel opposite where they are staying, in unaccountable and acute discomfort, and Honor and I set out at 8.50, and I wondered if we should ever arrive? However we slipped into St James's Palace easily. Half the house had been commandeered for Mrs Simpson and her party. I didn't see her. Apparently she did not go to Windsor, having refused, with dignity I consider, the offered invitation. From the windows of St James's we watched the crowds battling with the police. Honor secured a front place while Eric Duncannon and I went out on the roof. It was a long wait in the cold, but at last the procession came, with detachments of many different regiments, and all the three Services represented. As it passed, unendingly, a silence fell on the vast crowds, who still struggled, noiselessly, to get a better view. A feeling of awe came over us as we knew that the gun carriage was approaching and at last, drawn by Marines at an easy pace, it did. The monarch of the world lay in that small coffin, draped with the Union Jack, and immediately behind walked his son. As he passed, the new King looked up, no doubt seeking Mrs Simpson at the window, and he caught my eye. I bowed, as if to the gun carriage. He has a curious way of darting a look at one in an intense, ardent and rather alarming way. Behind him were his brothers and the Princes, and the Kings, and amongst them Paul next to the Prince of Piedmont. Paul looked well, but shuffled in his long coat and ugly uniform. Fritzi of Prussia looked very handsome in a white uniform, and the King of Rumania, as ever, looked ridiculous. There were also the Kings of Norway, Denmark, Belgium, Bulgaria and a score of other Royalties. Slowly the gun carriage went up St. James's Street, watched by ten thousand wet eyes. Then the Queen's coach came, magnificent with its red trappings. The Queen sat at the window, all in black, with her sister-in-law, the Queen of Norway. She looked incredibly magnificent and composed and held a handkerchief. The carriage was driven very close to the kerb, so that people on the left side of the street could easily see her. The procession took well over an hour to pass.

Silent and sad, I joined Honor, and followed by the Thursbys, Georgia Sitwell and Sheila Milbanke, we returned to 21 St James's Place.

The shops are shut, life is at a standsill. Only the banks are open; apparently it would have needed an Act of Parliament to shut them.

Friday, 31 January

This morning we said goodbye to No. 21 St James's Place, where we have lived for two years, where we have loved and been happy, and where our little boy was born, where we have both been ill, where we have entertained and developed and become, perhaps, too fastidious. The great move, our belongings, bibelots, servants, luxuries and loveliness have all been transported to 5 Belgrave Square.

Saturday, 1 February *5 Belgrave Square*

Though our new house will one day be a dream of beauty, at the moment it is still unfinished and smells strongly of paint. I slept for the first time in my new white, modern Biedermeyer room, which the eccentric old Bowring Hanbury lived in for so long, and where the great philanthropist, Lord Shaftesbury, died.

Sunday, 2 February

We are concerned that some of our friends should be trying to poison the Kents against Mrs Simpson and hence the King, and are attempting to drive a wedge between the Royal brothers.

Tuesday, 4 February

Routine again. I wish I felt more at home in the House of Commons. I like the glamour, the kudos, the Oxford atmosphere, but I do not want to speak, yet I know that I must lose my maidenhead soon. But it will be an ordeal, and perhaps I won't speak well?

12 February

Honor and I went to tea with the Brownlows.[5] There we found assembled the 'new Court', Mrs Simpson very charming and gay and vivacious. She said she had not worn black stockings since she gave up the Can-Can, a remark typical of her breezy humour, quick and American, but not profound. We discussed everything except the King. She drinks whisky and soda instead of cocktails.

Saturday, 15 February *5 Belgrave Square*

Sir Arthur Colefax died today; he was a good man, talented, high-idealed, kind but boring beyond belief. Berners once said of him that he 'had been offered £30,000 per annum to bore the channel tunnel'. His wife, the curious, many-sided Sibyl, will miss him, for she was, strangely enough, genuinely devoted to her loyal, proud, adoring, deaf husband.

5. Lord Brownlow was Personal Lord-in-Waiting to the King.

Monday, 24 February

The day was devoted, in the House of Commons, to a discussion of Foreign Relations. Anthony Eden, looking immaculately distinguished, spoke well: the attacks fell flat: and I personally had great sympathy with Amery's 'die-hard' repudiations of the League of Nations and of the policy of Sanctions, which I have always deplored. He is speaking now, as I sit in the balcony and write. People in this country are coming around to the folly of our pro-Geneva, anti-Mussolini policy. It took the expense of it to do that: English idealism, especially when false, falls like a punctured balloon when the question of expense crops up. The £7 million spent on our fleet in the Mediterranean has brought home to many people our extravagant misguided folly. Today, for the first time, although we always said it must soon happen, regrets were expressed that Sir Samuel Hoare's proposals were not put into operation. In time he may become a hero ...

These late nights in the foetid atmosphere of the House of Commons nearly kill me, though Mr Baldwin was quite amiable to me in the lobby today, while Lady Astor rushed about like a decapitated hen, making naive remarks.

Thursday, 27 February

At a Foreign Affairs Committee Harold Nicolson gave a brilliant address on 'Anglo-German relations'. It was shrewd, but alarming and we almost heard the tramp-tramp of the troops. Harold predicted that trouble would come from the German source in 1939 or 1940; perhaps I shall be too old. Certainly I feel too infirm at the moment to join any army, and my feet are too flat.

4 May

Since last I kept you my neglected, imperfect, haphazard diary much seems to have happened. I have twice spoken in the House of Commons, been to America, dined with Kings, recovered and lost again my high spirits.

No one now enjoys the House of Commons more than I. I am truly bitten by it. The first week I was shy but flattered, then I had a fortnight of doubt, and of boredom, but ever since I have loved every minute of it. I like the male society. It reminds me of Oxford or perhaps of the private school to which I never went.

5 May

This evening in the House of Commons there were many divisions on the Civil List, twenty-two voted against the Duke of York's rise, while only three were against providing for the King's unborn children. The Civil List was really passed with amazing smoothness, the majority of Socialists tumbling over one another in order to laud the Royal Family: one might think that they had invented them themselves. This extreme royalism has increased very much since the rise of the dictatorships in Europe. Of course the ILP, charming fellows all, protested at the vast expenditure, and declared that 'this one family' had spent eleven million pounds during the last reign. I wonder if that is true?

10 May *London*

Emerald came to lunch and regaled us with stories of the royal racket. It appears that the King is Mrs Simpson's absolute slave, and will go nowhere where she is not invited, and she, clever woman, with her high pitched voice, chic clothes, moles and sense of humour is behaving well. She encourages the King to meet people of importance and to be polite; above all she makes him happy. The Empire ought to be grateful.

14 May

The Budget leakage continues to absorb everyone's thoughts, and poor old Jim Thomas,[6] risen from nothing, will now return to it; what a rise and fall. I have watched him in the House lately, and he looks sad and answers questions haltingly: his resignation is now imminent. It seems that young Jim Thomas junior stood for Parliament at the last election for the Leek Division, an unfortunate coincidence. Four different people told me that joke today.

15 May

At nine o'clock punctually Honor and I arrived at Emerald's. I wore a black waistcoat and my white tie, as is correct during Court mourning, and Honor was in black satin and diamonds. ... At 9.15 the King entered, smiling, gay and happy, wearing a

6. J. H. Thomas, the Colonial Secretary 1935–6. (See p. 85.)

black waistcoat and magnificent diamond links in a square design. He had a bandage on the index finger of his right hand. 'What is that, Sir', asked Harry Rosebery.[7] 'I cut myself gardening', HM smiled. 'Usually one gardens with one's left hand', Winston laughed. After a little parley we went into dinner.

Dinner was gay and animated, but no gossip, as the King disapproves of it. Winston greeted me with the words 'Why do you avoid me in the House of Commons?' A brilliant beginning, flattering and unanswerable. He told us of the day when he was already a Junior Minister and Baldwin only a whip. He is consumed with contempt, jealousy, indeed hatred, for Baldwin, whom he always denigrates. The King was reasonable and talked well about traditions and ceremonies which he intends to keep up so long as they do not interfere with ordinary life, as he thinks they serve a valuable purpose. The ladies all curtseyed when they left the dining room, and Winston then led the conversation ... We talked for a little, the King drinking Vichy water and eventually he poured about three drops of brandy into a large glass and played with it and then drank it. At last he rose; there was a pause in the Morning room whilst he talked to Wallis Simpson and later when the King wanted some more Vichy water and couldn't find the bottle opener, Wallis said 'Ask Ernest for his'. 'Ernest' apparently wears one on his key chain, so the Royal bottle was finally opened. At 1.30 the party broke up, the King leaving a trail of regret behind him, he was so charming. He seemed pathetic driving away alone.

20 May

A luncheon party here at which the star was 'Shakes' Morrison,[8] a man of tremendous charm, a North country accent, a brain of very varied and great power, and wide vision. Thick sensuous lips, wild white hair and clear laughing eyes make up his startling appearance. He is young, alert, eager, kindly, polite, and amused, always amused.

'Shakes' is a typically House of Commons man, always there, always anxious to take part in any debate. He is thoroughly

7. The 6th Earl of Rosebery.
8. Conservative MP for Cirencester and Tewkesbury.

English. . . . 'Shakes' will surely be PM after the next Socialist government, if ever we have one. Meanwhile the Baldwin mantle must certainly fall on Neville Chamberlain, who has earned it, if he wants it: I think it may be soon, as Mr Baldwin looks disgruntled and tired, and is getting deafer; David Margesson now has to repeat 'questions' to him and the PM frowns as he listens. Like all deaf people he is a little annoyed when he has happened to hear, and the remark is nevertheless repeated to him.

26 May

In the House of Commons people are a bit on edge and it is time for a recess. The last few parliamentary days are always stale and bad-tempered, nevertheless the Baldwinites, the good boys, including myself, are happy. The naughty boys, an insubordinate and ambitious group consisting of Winterton (a finicky goat), old muddle-headed Austen Chamberlain, who abuses his position as doyen of the House, Winston Churchill, Sir Henry Page-Croft and their satellites are very disgruntled. They spent last week at Shillinglee, the guests of Winterton and no doubt concocted dark schemes to torpedo the government. They are now known as 'The House Party'.[9]

28 May

Today, the 'naughty boys' delivered an attack on the Government but were easily worsted. Inskip made an impressive speech, his second this week and silenced his critics. Winston is angling to be made Minister of Munitions, but Baldwin hates him so much that I doubt if he will succeed. I am loving the House of Commons, yet I wonder shall I ever make my mark? Harold Balfour says that I shall be in the Government in ten years time. I wonder if, when re-shuffles are discussed in five or ten years time, people will be saying 'will Chips get a job?'

29 May

The last day of Parliament. Honor and I lunched with Laura at Crewe House (which she has taken for the season) to meet Herr Von Ribbentrop und Frau. Frau Von Ribbentrop is

9. It was this episode that provoked Baldwin's remark about it being 'the time of year when midges come out of dirty ditches'.

distinguished in the Berlin manner, that is she has intelligent eyes appalling khaki coloured clothes and an un-powdered, un-painted face. How can the Germans be so silly about things that don't matter, or is it because their women are so unattractive that the race is largely homosexual? He, Ribbentrop, looks like the captain of someone's yacht, square, breezy, and with a sea-going look. Actually he was once a wine merchant. He is not quite without charm, but shakes hands in an over-hearty way, and his accent is Long Island without a trace of Teutonic flavour. Afterwards the Ribbentrops, Laura and co. left with Lord Londonderry for Mount Stewart for the Whitsun holiday. The Ribbentrops are intimate with the Londonderrys, and he is known as the Londonderry Herr.

30 May

We were rung up by Lord Beaverbrook and asked to dine at Cherkley and we started late and then, of course, lost the way. My nerves were on edge, but after endless wrong turnings, we eventually arrived, breathless and angry. They had waited dinner for half an hour. Beaverbrook was charm and courtesy itself, as he always is, and was attentive to Honor. The house, or rather overgrown villa, is hideous but lies magnificently in an old park with fine yews and trees. Dinner was indifferent but conversation sprightly. Present were, darling Jean Norton cool and chic and ultra charming, Mike Wardell[10] and his new wife. Brendan Bracken, rather silent. After dinner we had to sit through a film in Max's private cinema recently hung with silver silk. Honor has asked the Beaver to dine on 11 June to meet the King. He pretended that he did not want to come, il se faisait prier, but I think he will in spite of his asthma and low spirits.

4 June

After the opera (Bohème) and supper at the Durhams, Pat Jersey, Princess Bismarck, Honor and I and Herr Ribbentrop looking like a jolly commercial traveller, went to a night club. I certainly never expected to go on the Bummel with Ribbentrop, but we laughed a lot, and he has now invited us to stay as Hitler's

10. Editor of the *Evening Standard*.

guests for the Olympic Games in August. Honor accepted gleefully.

5 June

Sam Hoare is now back at the Admiralty as First Lord, in the place of Bobby, otherwise Lord Monsell, who resigned. It is a long sad tale. Six months ago Hoare was ignominiously turned out, and had it not been my first week in Parliament I should have risen in his defence. The Government simply bowed to public opinion and chucked him overboard. Events have now proved him a hundred times right, but he was discredited, humiliated and let down. Ever since his great 'mea culpa' speech there has been a movement to bring him back to the Cabinet. At first he was discouraged, disillusioned and stayed in Switzerland to mend his ailing health (and broken nose). Of late he has been 'desperately well and dumbly ambitious' as Billy Ormsby-Gore[11] said to me of him. Now he is back, and the newspapers predict his appointment will mean a revulsion of policy and that the Government will become less anti-Italian, pro-realist, less Genevaist, less visionary. I fear they exaggerate, but still his presence will serve as a brake against Eden, Cooper and Co. who I should like to see out of the Cabinet altogether, as I so distrust their policy . . .

We dined with the Kents to meet Grace Moore, the Prima Donna who has fantastic orange hair, and a wide bosom hung with emeralds . . .

After dinner Grace Moore offered to sing, and we put out our cigarettes. When this was done, and the room was aired, she started. Now the drawing room at Number Three is large, but not enormous, and we were not quite prepared for what happened. She went to the piano, and began with a bit from 'Butterfly' and the first few notes shook the chandeliers, nearly blowing us from our chairs. She has a voice of tremendous volume, but to my mind no very great beauty. We literally vibrated until she adapted her notes to the size of the room. We stayed late and that arch social barometer Philip Sassoon invited us to Lympne for the Bank Holiday. . . . Our social stock seems to be rising.

11. Subsequently Lord Harlech.

9 June

Honor came to the House of Commons to dine, and I collected Alan Lennox-Boyd[12] the charming, big sized, big hearted member for mid Bedford, and others.

11 June

'When royalty comes in, friendship flies out of the window' Sheila Milbanke said on the telephone and how right she is: tonight's dinner has cost me Laura's friendship, at least for the moment. She is still in a rage. I rang her up, repeated my invitation for her to come in after dinner and she rudely refused, but I thought right up until the end of the evening that she would arrive. Beaverbrook to our sorrow, and Ernest Simpson, to our relief, both chucked dinner. We arranged the house until it was a bower of flowers: then there was a long pause, as we were both dressed at 8.30, Honor looking lovely and a little nervous, I quite calm. We both drank a brandy and soda and waited for the guests to arrive. The King had rung up and said it was to be white ties. The first to arrive were Leslie Hore-Belisha and Barbie Wallace,[13] and then quickly the others followed. The men still in white ties and black waistcoats, the women in black dresses. The Kents were punctual at 9.05 and as we were introducing people to them, though they knew them all except Harold Balfour[14] (my new House of Commons friend, and the member for Thanet), the King drove up. I went to meet him, and he did the circle charmingly, calling everybody by their Christian names except Harold to whom he said 'I don't think we have ever met before' very politely. He kissed Princess Marina who curtsied. Dinner was announced, doors were flung open, and we suddenly realized Lady Cunard had not appeared, but we processed into dinner and there was a pause as everyone's breath was quite taken away by the beauty of the dining room. There was an awkward gap next to the King where Emerald should have sat and several

12. Afterwards Chips's brother-in-law. Conservative MP for Mid-Bedfordshire since 1931.

13. Mrs Euan Wallace, afterwards Mrs Herbert Agar.

14. Conservative MP for Isle of Thanet, 1929–45; Parliamentary Under-Secretary for Air, 1938–44; Minister Resident in West Africa, 1944–5. 1st Baron Balfour of Inchrye, 1945.

moments of anxiety on my part until she arrived, apologetically. . . . Dinner proceeded well, and Philip Sassoon, who has not yet been given the job of Commissioner of Works, which he longs for, asked Emerald to say a word for him to the King, which she did. Dinner was perfect, we began with Blinis and caviar then Sole Muscat followed by Boeuf Provençal. It was served so speedily that we had finished before eleven, and then the ladies left, curtseying as they got up. I then moved over to the King and we talked à trois, he, Duff and I, about the Amalienburg dining room which he was in ecstasies over. He and Honor had got on very well together at dinner, and she liked him and happened to show him her 'Map' cigarette case[15] which I made for her, and the King produced his saying 'I must confess mine is a copy of yours'. They were almost identical. The room was full of glamour and candlelight, everybody was gay and a little elated. I drank a little and became somewhat befogged but no more. After dinner we went up to the drawing room and library, and scattered. It was only 11.15 and the pianists were not ordered until 12 o'clock. Honor looked in despair, but groups were soon formed, the King with Emerald and Wallis and others, while I found myself with Princess Marina in the drawing room. The moment I could, I stole away to hurry up the musicians. The pause, the gêne, if any, only lasted five minutes when conversation became general. It was twice interrupted, once when Lady Colefax arrived and again when the Hofmannsthals came, but no sign of Laura. Every moment I hoped that she would turn up. At last the two musicians from the Ritz appeared and they began to play Austrian music and eventually jazz. The King asked Mrs Simpson to dance, but she politely refused . . .

At last at 1.45 the King rose and I showed him to his car. The others soon followed and by 2.10 a.m. the party had broken up. I was sad when it was over, it was the very peak, the summit, I suppose. The King of England dining with me! But I wish I too had only drunk Vichy water; I should have enjoyed myself more, and remembered more.

The dinner party took up so much of my energies today that I have not chronicled today's drama in the House of Commons. I reached the Chamber at 3 p.m. and found it expectant and

15. Engraved with a map showing their honeymoon trip.

nervous. At 3.30 J. H. Thomas entered, sad and aged, but sunburnt still.

He sat immediately below the gangway on an aisle seat. Very soon took place one of the most poignant scenes the House has ever witnessed, when the Speaker quietly said 'Mr Thomas' and the poor man rose. He read a written statement which was simple and rather heartrending.[16] He accepted the findings of the tribunal, but declared that he had never consciously betrayed a budget or any other secret. He was leaving the ''Ouse' after twenty-seven years in its midst. He had now only his wife who still trusted him and loved him. He hoped no other member would ever be in a situation as cruel, as terrible as the one he today found himself in. Then he sat down for only a second, and there was a loud murmur of pity and suppressed admiration through the House. There was scarcely a dry eye. Mr Baldwin sat with his head in his hands, as he often does, Winston Churchill wiped away his tears. Thomas then rose again and slowly made his way out, not forgetting to turn and bow, for the last time, to the Speaker. His young PPS also strangely enough called Jim Thomas[17] followed him, and patted him affectionately on the back, as did 'Teenie' Cazalet; and he left, a broken, ruined unhappy man who had known triumph, success, high position all built on his personality, and now crashed. Afterwards Baldwin made a few remarks, and he is so good at that sort of thing. He buried poor Thomas, for ever barring him from public life, but admitting how much he must have suffered.

I told the King at dinner of 'J.H.'s' speech, and he told me that J.H. had said to him pathetically 'my only consolation is that the old King did not live to know of my disgrace'. They were great friends. HM further said that he would contribute anonymously to any fund organised to help. Obviously there will be one.

12 June

I woke feeling terribly ill and old and world-weary, the result of

16. Thomas had been found guilty by a Tribunal set up by Parliament of passing on Budget secrets to Sir Alfred Butt, MP.

17. J. P. L. Thomas, Conservative MP for Hereford since 1931. (Subsequently First Lord of the Admiralty, 1951–6; Lord Cilcennin 1955.)

too much champagne. Everyone rang up to say how successful our party had been. 'A wow', as Diana put it. Philip Sassoon, Barbie Wallace and others wrote.

Wallis Simpson said that the King had much enjoyed his dinner with us. Laura Corrigan was freezingly polite, and is still deeply hurt over last night's party, but really one invites the King's friends to meet him, not one's own. Harold Balfour was the exception.

Oh, social rows! There is nothing so trivial and yet nothing so wounding and discouraging.

15 June

There is now another political crisis. The Government is indeed unlucky. A few nights ago Neville Chamberlain, in an impromptu speech at a semi-public dinner declared that the continuance of Sanctions was 'mid-summer madness'. I should have thought that any sane man would agree, but his indiscretion has caused a tempest. It is of course an indication that all is not well within the Cabinet. Now all the cranks, lunatics, Socialists in the country are trying to stampede the Government into maintaining Sanctions against Italy.

18 June

A full dress debate on Foreign Affairs. It was a remarkably poor performance. Anthony Eden, lame and halting, had to announce that the Government had decided to drop Sanctions. He was vigorously attacked by the opposition, principally by Lloyd George, who gave a remarkable performance of virility, vitality and unscrupulousness. For forty minutes the aged wizard harangued the Government making them, each one of them, uncomfortable in turn. The House roared with laughter as it always enjoys a little fun at the expense of the great. Mr Baldwin tried to answer but was ineffectual and boring. He is ageing and seems worn out and one wonders whether he has lost his grip. Will his strength survive, or will it tide him over next year?

20 June *Sutton Courtenay*

We came here to this floral, lovely paradise, world-worn and nerve-shattered. But a few hours here, and we were both once more ourselves. The smell of the roses, the lapping of the water, the colours and above all Norah's tremendous charm and personality work wonders. At night I lay awake thinking of all the hours I have passed here and with whom, in this very emotional, very sensuous house; happy years with Paul, wild expeditions for dinner and bathing with poor Ivo Grenfell and with Gerry Wellesley: now Honor and I are happily here. We had dinner in the courtyard, and Norah played the piano. There was scent, sensuousness, simplicity, serenity, and finally sleep.

What a house Sutton Courtenay is. For two generations it has moulded the youth of England, it has seen them go forth into battle and into the world; all must have carried away memories of bathing in its Thames backwater, of reading poetry in the rose garden, of cutting trees and gardening, of listening to, and loving, Norah Lindsay.[18]

23 June *London*

The Foreign Affairs debate lasted all day, and it was a very crowded House, in which I longed to speak, and yet was relieved when I was told that I could not. Sir John Simon made the speech of the day, and he held the House fascinated for over an hour. Baldwin summed up in his best manner, and scored a bulls-eye when he related how he had said to his honourable friend next to him (David Margesson) six months ago that his greatest difficulty would be how to keep the Opposition out of war. The debate fizzled out, and I think even the Socialists realized how futile had been their Sanctions mania.

24 June

We lunched with Victor Cazalet, who had already, since sanctions are to be lifted, invited the Grandis. He is the most successful Italian Ambassador of the age, gay, bland, flirtatious in the extreme. He gets around everyone, and has skilfully kept his personal and social position here during the long months when we were so hostile to Italy. Now, after all the shouting and clamour against his country has died down, he is delighted to hear what he describes as 'the noise of a sudden silence'.

18. Mrs Henry Lindsay was a well-known hostess and passionate gardener.

This evening at the Holland House Ball we found the whole noblesse of England assembled, enough to kill any festival stone dead.

2 July *London*

We dined with the Marlboroughs, who I am becoming very fond of. . . . Later, we went on to Emerald's, who had a dinner for the King, and we sat with Grandi, the Italian Ambassador, his great eyes twinkling over his moustache, Wallis Simpson, demure, thin, simply dressed, but with a new parure of rubies, Portia Stanley, Philip Sassoon and others. Soon Ruth Draper arrived, and began one of her famous imitations. She was finished and clever, but too much drawn out, and finally became almost unendurable: at first the King laughed, then he suddenly became fidgety and left at 1.15. Laura Corrigan was in the seventh heaven of bliss, though I gather the King never spoke to her. There can be no doubt Royalty casts a strange atmosphere. It makes many people self-conscious and either wish to thrust themselves forward, or else become too self-effacing; both forms of behaviour are equally tiresome.

6 July

What a bore week-ends are, forty-eight hours social crucifixion. Ours this summer have been curious. 13 June, the Dufferins, in a hideous villa, with cocktails, gramophones, pekes and bridge. 20 June, Sutton Courtenay, roses, the river, and the youth of England splashing in the Thames, and Norah, the sublime Norah. Russian ballet food in the courtyard, Chopin, colour, gardening, a riot, but a healthy riot of the senses, and a deep thirst for life. 27 June, Villa Trianon, Versailles, super sophistication. Toile-de-Jouy, French princesses, Sèvres, gardens lit by Wendel, flowers, one feels, by Cartier. 4 July, Tredegar; glorious house, but the feel and even smell of decay, of aristrocracy in extremis, the sinister and the trivial, crucifixes and crocodiles.

7 July

Vansittart[19] lunched with us, and said that never had the inter-

19. Sir Robert (later Lord) Vansittart, Permanent Under-Secretary of State for Foreign Affairs since 1930.

national situation been so dangerous. There is no point, according to him, of trying to be friends with Germany and at the same time insulting her, à la Duff Cooper, and that she will never be content until she regains her lost colonies. If we ever want lasting peace we must restore them to her; the House of Commons would never agree to such a step, I fear.

The Simpson scandal is growing, and she, poor Wallis, looks unhappy. The world is closing in around her, the flatterers, the sycophants, and the malice. It is a curious social juxtaposition that casts me in the role of Defender of the King. But I do, and very strongly in society, not for loyalty so much as for admiration and affection for Wallis, and in indignation against those who attack her.

Jimmy Maxton[20] is sitting opposite me as I write; in what different paths our lives lie, and yet I wonder, shall I not be known when he is forgotten? Reformers are always finally neglected, while the memoirs of the frivolous will always be eagerly read.

8 July

George Gage lunched, and was enthralling about his visit to Germany last year, when he was received by Ribbentrop, Hitler, and escorted everywhere by Storm Troopers. Honor and I can now hardly wait to go. Harold Nicolson and Lady Colefax disapprove of our journey, and so, I felt, though they have not said so, do the truculent Coopers.

It was a long day today at the House of Commons, six divisions. The subject was malnutrition, a vote of censure on the Government, and the Socialists as usual mishandled their case. Kingsley Wood[21] and Walter Elliot[22] were our brilliant defenders. Harold Macmillan, the unprepossessing, bookish, eccentric member for Stockton-on-Tees (and incidentally the Duke of Devonshire's son-in-law), having voted against the Government on the Foreign Office vote of censure, has now repudiated the Government Whip, and has received a frigid note from Mr Baldwin.

20. James Maxton, the fiery and independent Labour MP.
21. Minister of Health.
22. Minister of Agriculture.

9 July

In the House of Commons I chatted with Ramsay MacDonald, and observed his determined chin, his good health, live intelligence and shifty eye. He still wears two gold wedding rings on his left hand, on his third and on his fourth finger; and he is so pleased, so relieved, and still betrays it after five years, at being on the gentleman's side, where of course he is more at home. He loathes the Socialists, whom he led so long, and certainly they have treated him ungratefully.

11 July *Blenheim*

It is a long time since I have been to Blenheim, where we are spending the weekend, and where I spent much of my youth under the old régime. This is Honor's first visit to this colossal and very beautiful house, and my first since the present people succeeded. Mary Marlborough has improved the house and has enhanced the atmosphere. It is now gay and healthy, and the long corridors echo with childish laughter and screams, and huge dogs sprawl about. In the evenings, the fantastic terraces and gardens are floodlit (I think that all gardens should be floodlit now, it is a wonderful invention and the effect is fantastic, rich and beautiful). On Sunday I was next to Mary Marlborough at luncheon, and got to like her quite enormously. She is an efficient Duchess, handsome, gay, and serious-minded, very English, very balanced, very conventional and brings up her children in a rather snappy, almost Spartan simple way: and they seem to adore her.

15 July

I must soon make up my mind whether I really want to carve out a career for myself in the House of Commons, but is it really worth the sacrifices? I should like about five or ten years here, and then a peerage. I shall steel my mind towards that goal, and perhaps I shall reach it.

16 July

I went with Diana [Cooper] to Hyde Park for the Presentation of the Colours by the King, and we drove there in a War Office car, and were soon shown to our seats, the very best ones, as befitted the wife of the Secretary for War. Next to us sat the new

Court: Emerald in a sable coat (Emerald up at 10.30!), Wallis Simpson, the Fitzgeralds, and others. In the adjoining stand, the Royal Pavilion, I saw the Queen, the two little princesses, etc. The great parade ground was lined with troops and in the middle was a raised platform: soon the King arrived, looking very young and charming and dignified, and he made a short simple strong plea for peace as he presented the Colours to his Guards. The ceremony lasted about an hour, and it was London at its very best, London well dressed, London in high summer, the grey sky, the green of the trees, and then the sun coming out at the right royal moment, the bayonets glistening, and the horses ... the Waterloo-ness of it all. Afterwards, I went back to Belgrave Square for luncheon, and on my way to the House of Commons I read on a placard: 'The King shot at'. It seems that an unbalanced man called Mahon pulled a revolver from his pocket, and had been about to shoot the King, when someone knocked it out of his hand and it fell at the feet of the King's horse.... No one knows yet.[23] It was on his return ride to Buckingham Palace. It is very unfortunate that this should take place in England, where, until now, Royalty has always moved about freely and with safety.

17 July

A very Royal day. This morning I received a message that the Queen[24] would come to Belgrave Square at 3.25 to call on us. Honor and I had a hasty consultation, and decided to ask only Lady Iveagh. We spent some time arranging, 'tidging' the house with flowers, etc. Punctually at 3.25 the green royal car drove up, though there had been policemen hovering about for an hour before.... I was on the pavement, and Honor three yards back on the red carpet on the front steps. We came into the morning room, where we had five minutes conversation, and the Queen kissed my mother-in-law. We then began a minute detailed examination of the house, the Queen at once revealing her very great knowledge and flair for pictures, furniture, and bibelots. I found her absolutely delightful, indeed I have never

23. In fact the revolver (unloaded) was thrown onto the road.
24. Queen Mary.

liked anyone so much so quickly. She was dressed in black, of course, and carried a black sunshade, but there were no weeds, no crepe, and she referred several times to the late King as 'my husband'. There was not a piece of furniture, not a rug or chair, which she failed to notice and comment on. She was in ecstasies over the small black anteroom, and did not hide her delight when we came to the Amalienburg. I have never known such praise. She felt the walls in her black gloved fingers and she patted the stove, then examined the Dresden pieces. We were there quite twenty minutes, and then again the anteroom fascinated her. She sat on the uncomfortable little oyster seat, and was generally so gay and so pleasant that soon I was twitting her gaily, and I really found her rather like Lady Scarbrough.[25] We then walked up to the Library, the drawing room, even to our bedroom, and climbed to the nursery, and the Queen picked up Paul and played with him. He clutched the royal nose, to her amusement, and tried to tug at her earrings. She stayed in the nursery for some time, and seemed delighted with my beloved baby boy, who always plays up on these occasions. We then took the lift, Her Majesty and I alone, and shot down, and I showed her into the cloakroom and 'loos' which we have arranged so gaily. 'Ah', she laughed. 'What a place to keep the family,' and she pointed to the Third and Fourth Georges on the walls. I had forgotten them. We then returned to the morning room and although she had sent word not to have tea we had provided lemonade, cakes, etc. . . . At last, at five o-clock the Queen rose and the visit, alas, came to an end. It was a *riotous* success, and one felt it.

An hour later, after a cigarette and a rather strong drink, we drove to Wallis Simpson's. She was alone, but the King soon came in, and we were just the four for an hour. The King laughingly said: 'I know, Chips, why you are dressed like that. I've just seen the Queen.' We invited him to Austria to stay with us and he accepted, which has thrown us into a flurry. He could not have been more friendly, and talked of yesterday's incident, saying that when he saw a black object lying at his horse's feet yesterday he thought 'It is a bomb. Will it go off?' And he had said something of the sort to his brother, of York, immediately

25. See p. 486.

behind him. Then he talked mild politics, and I told him that I thought we should live to see his country ruled by Shakespeare Morrison, and occasionally by Herbert Morrison the Labour Leader. A succession of Morrisons. The King doesn't like Herbert Morrison, though he once did. He thinks that the man will rule, never lead, but admitted that there was no one else. . . . Home to bed at 1 a.m. utterly exhausted, and I dreamed of lions and unicorns.

18 July *Bognor*

We motored to Bognor where we found the [Duff] Coopers, our hosts, in most charming mood. Also here, are Conrad Russell, . . . Venetia[26] and Hilaire Belloc. At dinner, preceded by much drink, Belloc sang Provençal lyrics and recited Ronsard and du Bellay, and Jacobite songs and early English ballads. A rivetting evening which almost became a bore as we sat clustered about the great man who looked for all the world like a French-Canadian priest, and applauded while he chanted. It was quite a unique experience – but not to be repeated.

20 July

At the Kemsleys' ball at Chandos House, a grandiose, high season affair with 'all London' present, a curious scene took place whilst I was at the House of Commons. Honor sat with Wallis Simpson who was in a rage, as she had just received a letter from an MP signed by a well-known name, which she was clever enough not to reveal, in which he warned Mrs Simpson against Lady Astor and her campaign. Wallis asked Honor for her advice, and soon Honor had spilt the beans about Nancy A's various attacks on me in regard to Wallis at the House of Commons. I fear that there may be a proper scandal and 'bust up' as Wallis will, and in fact, already has, told the King.

24 July

We had a dinner party, Osbert Sitwell, fat and gay and sardonic, Sachie Sitwell, lean, insinuating, clever and flushed; Georgia Sitwell, dark, flirtatious with much joie de vivre. Sir Archie

26. Mrs Edwin Montagu.

Clark-Kerr, fascinating, able and now Ambassador to Baghdad, his Chilean wife, the diminutive chirping Tita, and one or two others.

27 July

I hurried to the House of Commons for the Foreign Affairs debate, during which old Austen Chamberlain, the doyen of the House of Commons donkeys, made a really stupid speech in which he attacked Germany with unreasoning violence. He is ossified, tedious, and hopelessly out of date.

The situation in Spain, where civil war has been waging, is very serious. The army of the Right elements, revolted by the appalling Left government, have tried by a coup de main to seize power. For a few days, we had hoped that they would win, though tonight it seems as if the Red Government, alas, will triumph.

At Supper at Emerald's, Mrs Simpson was literally smothered in rubies, and looking very well, as she has been on a fish diet for four days. Like me, she is worn out, but looks handsome, as I do too.

1 August

We left with Norah Lindsay for Lympne to stay with Philip Sassoon, whom, as we arrived, we met in the road. He waved us a welcome and went on. 'Very Jewish of him', Norah remarked. We were received at his fantastic villa by armies of obsequious white-coated servants who seemed willing enough, but second rate. I whispered this to Duff Cooper, who was busy with a jigsaw puzzle, 'Yes, one sees who has the upper hand here,' he laughed. The house is large and luxurious and frankly ugly. Honor said that it was like a Spanish brothel. The drawing room is a mixture of fashionable whites, distressed white, off white, cream, and even the famous frescoes have been whitewashed.... There was the usual German argument after dinner with Philip and Duff attacking the Nazis with the violence born of personal prejudice. I said never a word. After dinner ... a young R.A.F. pilot whispered to me 'Is Duff Cooper off his rocker, or what?' Indeed he seems obsessed at times.

2 August *Lympne*

Lovely weather and the scent of magnolias overpowering. Honor and I have the so-called Alhambra suite looking onto a sort of courtyard, attractive but uncomfortable. The whole affair is second rate, even the lavish lapis dining room, and especially the white coated footmen who will wait on one at tea, always a bad sign.

In the evening more flying boys to dine, whilst all day their planes roar about us.

3 August

At dinner, the Coopers and Aberconways having left, we were a small party enlarged by the presence of young Max Aitken[27] and his co-pilot. Someone referred to the Olympic Games, where we ought to be now, and the opening ceremonies which are supposed to have been stupendous. Max Aitken then proceeded to describe the scene. He had flown over with his father, and had only just returned. Teenie [Cazalet] tactlessly flew at him (he hates the whole Beaverbrook crew) and a dreadful discussion ensued during which everyone lost their temper.

1 November

We drove down to Coppins to call on the Kents. . . . They have modernised and re-decorated it with skill and success. The result is charming, and the rooms now glow with luxe and gaiety. It is entirely Prince George who has transformed it, and he now thinks of little else. We had a massive tea, and then the besotted father carried in the pièce de résistance, the curly-haired, very red, howling Prince Edward.[28] He had fine blue eyes, golden curls and looks like all four Georges rolled into one. Princess Marina, Honor and I sat on the floor playing with him. He is smaller, crosser, than our baby, but possibly prettier.

2 November

Tomorrow I shall have closer information about the royal situation. Of course all the world is saying that the King intends to

27. Son of Lord Beaverbrook.
28. The future Duke of Kent.

marry Wallis, now that her divorce is over. Personally, I suspect that this is true, and that we shall live to see a great dénouement, for the King is naturally uxorious, a trait he inherits from his domestic father. . . . He thinks only of Wallis.

3 November

Some days are fuller, more dramatic than others. Today was one: we rose early to attend the Opening of Parliament, though the day was wet and the procession was cancelled. However I took my seat in the North Gallery of the Lords and watched the fantastic scene of red splendour below, watched the peeresses, a dowdy lot I thought, file in in evening dress and jewels and the peers in their robes. My father-in-law looked like a Doge of Venice, or some Longhi Podesta. The Duchesses' bench was full, with several unknown ones, though Eileen Sutherland looked splendid. The gallery for Ministers' wives held an oddly assorted collection, with Mrs Baldwin next to Diana Cooper who looked pale and ethereal. At last, the King entered, looking exactly as he did in 1911, at the investiture at Caernarvon. Not a day older, a young, happy Prince Charming, or so he seemed. He walked with dignity and calm and took his place on the throne (I watched Ribbentrop's face, he was in the ambassadors' box). Lord Halifax then advanced and, on bended knee, handed the oath of the succession to the King, who read it, and kissed the Bible, swearing that he was a faithful Protestant. Lord Halifax then presented the Address, which the King calmly read, in an English voice, but he said prog-ress and rowts instead of roots, as I do. He was not nervous, not fidgety, but serenely dignified, watching his long train being put in place with some amusement. Then he rose, as we did, and followed and preceded by Poursuivants, Heralds, etc., he left and we returned to the Commons. The whole scene was like a six no-trumper at bridge.

Later, I heard the Address moved and seconded. The mover was Miss Florence Horsbrugh,[29] Member for Dundee, an extremely likeable and able woman. She used simple, but magnificent prose, and scored a great success; she was wearing a dark-

29. Conservative MP for Dundee, 1931–45; and Moss Side, 1950–59. Minister of Education, 1951–4; Baroness Horsbrugh, 1959.

brown, flowing dress and fawn gloves. She was followed by Harold Nicolson, from whom so much was expected. He was in diplomatic uniform, and somehow looked ridiculous, and I remembered him in the same uniform at a Court Ball in 1924. He rose, and immediately 'lost' and annoyed the House. Indeed, his speech was one of the saddest I have ever heard, so well meant and so well phrased, but meaningless to the point of absurdity. He began with a tribute to Ramsay MacDonald, which irritated both sides of the House, then he stumbled, and at one moment I feared that he was breaking down. I felt sick for him. . . . He sat down, at long last, in complete silence.[30]

This evening, we had a brilliant dinner of fifteen. I was between Portia Stanley and Wallis Simpson, who was gay and amusing. We discussed her divorce, which she says was at Ernest's instigation, and at no wish of hers. . . . Wallis talked of the King, and told us that he had wanted to dine with us tonight and asked why we had not invited him, etc.?

Later, rumours began to drift in of the overwhelming Roosevelt victory in the United States. I never thought he would do so well, but it seems that it is a landslide.

5 November

A plot came off, instigated by me, tonight. Last summer, I thought it would be wise if the King and Lord Beaverbrook were to meet, and I tried to bring it about, but failed, but I put the idea into Wallis Simpson's clever and retentive brain. Dining here the other night, she told Perry Brownlow that she thought a meeting would be a good idea. It took a day or two to arrange, but tonight the dinner took place at 4 Seamore Street, chez the Brownlows. It consisted of the King, Wallis Simpson, the Brownlows and Honor. The men wore dinner jackets, and the King affected the fashionable American double collar. Dinner was immediately successful, but Honor thought, and Perry corroborated, that Beaverbrook was at first a bit touchy, though obsequious. Royalty always affects people differently. However, conversation soon flowed and Max ended by being charming. I arrived, as invited, at 11.15, but as the men were still at dinner,

30. This unhappy speech is described by Sir Harold Nicolson on pp. 277–8 of *Diaries and Letters*.

I went up to the drawing room for fear of breaking the flow of conversation. Soon they came up and the King looked well, bronzed, freckled and fair, and in a very good temper. I went up to the nursery and carried Edward Cust, aged seven months, down to the drawing room, much to the King's amusement, who said, 'Chips is mad about babies'. I put him in the King's arms, who said 'He is my grandchild, I mean godchild'. Afterwards we played a game, introduced by the King. He gave us each ten matches and we sat huddled in a circle on the floor, and an empty bottle was sent for and the idea was to pile matches on the top, in turn, without letting the pile collapse. It seems silly and it was, but it was most innocent and enjoyable. I won. The King's attention to Wallis was very touching. He worships her, and she seems tactful and just right with him, always prefacing her gentle rebukes with 'Oh, sir ...' She confessed to Honor that she always kicks him under the table hard when to stop and gently when to go on. Sometimes she is too far away and then it is difficult.

I like the King very much. He is so manly, so honest and far shrewder than people pretend. I discussed Anthony Eden with him, and I said in his defence, that he was an idealist. 'Heaven spare us from idealists, they cause all the trouble', the King laughed, and Beaverbrook agreed. I am worn out. Honor has so changed now that she wants to go to every lighted candle and a peaceful evening is never, never mine, though I enjoyed tonight.

7 November

Jean Norton, Honor and I had a long discussion as to the King's matrimonial plans. He certainly wants to marry Wallis, but she is probably too canny to allow it, yet what a temptation it must be for a Baltimore girl: one could not blame her if she did. If he married her, both Honor and Jean argued, he would have to abdicate immediately, for if he did not, we would have unrest, a Socialist agitation and a 'Yorkist' party. There would be empty streets when they processed, and general unpopularity. I maintained that marriage would regularise the situation, that there would be an outcry, of course, but that the throne, although blown up, would certainly survive. I don't think Wallis would be content to be the consort of an ex-King. The situation would be untenable, for the smart world would soon be bored with them, and gravitate around the new Court. Already the press here is beginning to register digs and slight disapproval, and it is quite true that the monarchy has lost caste enormously since last January. All the world knows is that the King is the slave of an American, who has had two husbands and two divorces. It does not know how charming, how wise and sympathetic she is, nor what an edifying influence. It seems the whole press angle has been clumsily handled. The King is at his worst with Fleet Street, off-hand, angry and ungracious; he never treats them in the right way, or realizes that his popularity largely depends on them . . .

Last night was a calamity. We went to the opera as the guests of Emerald in the Royal box, to hear Richard Strauss conduct 'Ariadne auf Naxos'. As we arrived, we were handed a note, 'Lady Cunard wants you to go to the Duke of Bedford's box'. We tried to do so, but it was nearly full and so, we returned to Emerald's. When Emerald arrived, accompanied by Wallis Simpson, she was in a rage because there was so little room, so I led Mrs. Simpson (in a simple black dress with a green bodice and dripping with emeralds – her collection of jewels is the talk of London) and Diana Cooper, back to the Bedford box. Emerald was furious that the semi-queen was not with her. We joined up again in the interval and Emerald presented the Cromers to Wallis. The Cromers, suave aristocrats, were obsequious, and Honor remarked that they did everything except curtsey. Poor Wallis, the cynosure of all eyes, she can do no right. All her tact, sweetness and charm – are they enough?

Later, Honor and I spoke to the Ribbentrops. My feeling is that they will not be a social success in London, though at first I prophesied great things for them; but, for all their ambition, they have not the well-bred ease which Londoners demand, and Frau von Ribbentrop really dresses too dowdily. She will be the liability, though he has not started off well, either.

Sunday, 8 November

A full week is over. The Socialists suffered severe rebuffs at the municipal elections all over England. President Roosevelt was re-elected with a fantastic majority; and, with an idea of taming the Press, I was instrumental in bringing the King and Lord Beaverbrook together. Parliament opened, and now Madrid has fallen. The Communist Government has left the capital and it is occupied by the Insurgents.

We dined with Venetia Montagu in her little house in Onslow Gardens. There were the usual lot . . . the cleverest, wordiest, quickest people in London, but I found them, for the first time, boring, and worse, out of date. They do not know that it is all about now, I fear, and they are all too pro-semite. 'Crinks' Johnstone,[31] capitalistic and a gourmet, began dinner by saying, 'Here's death to Ribbentrop'. Diana Cooper turned on him, but Duff Cooper laughingly said, 'I only hope he dies in pain'. Then the usual long, anti-German tirade began.

10 November

I walked to the House of Commons, as we had been warned not to bring cars. The lobbies were full of hunger marchers come to protest against the new unemployment regulations, the so-called Means Test.

During questions, someone asked, innocuously, about the coming coronation. McGovern[32] jumped up and shouted, 'Why bother, in view of the gambling at Lloyd's that there will not be one?' There were roars of 'Shame! Shame!' and he called out, 'Yes . . . Mrs Simpson'. This was the first time her name has been used in the House of Commons, although the smoking room and lobbies have long buzzed with it. I was shocked, but the truth is that the monarchy has lost ground in a frightening manner. Prince Charming charms his people no more . . .

Later, I went out into the lobby and found it full to suffocation with marchers, who were being incited by Communists. Many of them wore red shirts and ties. At the door was a queue singing the Red Flag. It really seemed as if trouble must break out. But it didn't, and about 8.30 I took the last look at these unfortunate people who have been goaded and misguided by their leaders into walking from Lancashire and South Wales. David Balniel and I went out into the cooler evening air and were

31. Harcourt Johnstone, Liberal MP for Middlesbrough.
32. Labour MP for Shettleston (Glasgow).

amused to see strings of taxis depositing the walkers at St Stephen's. On my way home, I passed the Abbey, which looked beautiful and calm, and flood-lit because it is Armistice eve. Many people, mostly women, were planting little crosses tied to poppies on the lawn surrounding the Abbey, and in the cool light they looked, holy, sad and peaceful. As I watched the silent scene, the grey, middle-aged women, thinking of their lost sons, I thought of my warm, gold and pink boy waiting for me at home.

Armistice Day, 11 November

I dined at the House of Commons, and what was to have been a quiet snack developed into an acrimonious argument over the eternal problem – will the King marry Mrs Simpson? MPs are like a lot of old concierges on this matter, and can think and talk of little else. But the situation is extremely serious, and the country is indignant; it does seem foolish that the monarchy, the oldest institution in the world after the papacy, should crash, as it may, over dear Wallis. Yet why should we forsake our Sovereign? He has been foolish, indeed almost brazen. The Mediterranean cruise was a Press disaster, the visit to Balmoral was a calamity, after the King chucked opening the Aberdeen Infirmary and then openly appeared at Ballater railway station on the same day, to welcome Wallis to the Highlands. Aberdeen will never forgive him. The Simpson divorce has caused all this talk, and the American newspapers have had a Roman holiday. The headline in one, referring to the Ipswich divorce, ran, 'King's Moll Reno'd in Wolsey's Home Town'. A pleasanter tale is of Wallis taking a taxi on her now famous journey to Scotland. 'King's Cross', she is reported to have said. 'I'm sorry, lady,' answered the driver.

12 November

We had a large cocktail party to meet the Prince Regent and Princess Olga, who are staying next door with the Kents. He, my beloved Paul, was as charming and gentle as ever, while she was shy and distinguished. Half London came. . . . The house was a dream of lit-up beauty and everyone was intoxicated by the Amalienburg dining room . . .

I rushed back to the House of Commons directly I could, and

found it packed. Winston Churchill had just delivered a smashing attack on the Government defence programme, or rather, the Government's neglect of our defences during the years 1933–4. Baldwin rose, as I came in, and made a long, too long, honest, too honest, speech which, while the truth and rivetting, will damage him politically. He said, by inference, that he had not dared, especially after the Fulham by-election, to rearm, as the country was not then in a mood for it.[33] He is right. Later, with his huge victory, which amounted to a mandate, he proceeded to do so.

Dinner was a repetition, only more exaggerated, of last night's wild talk . . . absurd, unfair abuse of Mrs Simpson. Everyone was unanimous in agreeing the King must marry soon, almost anybody except Wallis.

Friday, 13 November

I feel a foreboding of impending doom. What can it be – that the throne will totter, or perhaps cease to be, that I shall be ill, or perhaps my baby Paul? In any case, I am gloomy, though perhaps it is only surfeit combined with constipation. I am too rich, and I dine with kings . . . but I am bored, even sometimes lonely. But my child fills me with such tenderness that I can hardly bear to be away from him . . .

I must take a pull, write a book, become a miser, or perhaps, most important, speak in the House of Commons. I am a good attender and popular, I think, but I cannot just take that small hurdle of speaking constantly. I must. What a Parliament! We saw the death of the late King, the accession of the new. Shall we see yet a third . . . or none? We are faced with an impasse. The country, or much of it, would not accept Queen Wallis, with two live husbands scattered about . . .

I dined with Emerald Cunard, a dixhuitième atmosphere, with the hostess aged, wrinkled, vivacious and glittering in the candlelight. I was between Mollie Buccleuch and Eileen Sutherland, and afterwards escorted them in my car to the Yugoslav legation, where there was a charity concert. Places were reserved for us,

33. This is the speech which has become known as 'the appalling frankness' speech, in which Baldwin, in a long extempore passage, spoke of the strong pacifist sentiment in 1933.

and soon the Royal party arrived, Paul dark and distinguished, Princess Paul angular and handsome under her vast tiara, the Infanta Beatrix and the Duke of Kent. The programme proceeded in intense stuffiness and afterwards Madame Grouitch became quite maddening; while leading the royalties down to supper, she suddenly spied Mrs Simpson, and seizing her, dragged her, in spite of her protests, before the photographers, and then pushed her into the Royal supper room. It is this sort of behaviour which causes Wallis such trouble and she, poor woman, was indignant.

14 November *Sutton*

I spent the whole day, a long, rich, companionable one, with Paul. I told him of the appalling impression that the King was making, and that the House of Commons openly talked of abdication, etc. He was horrified. We discussed all the eligible princesses in Europe, and tried to agree on one whose charms we could urge on the King, but we could find none: perhaps he had better marry Wallis and be done with it, and brave the storm.

17 November

A pompus, manqué dinner at Emerald's. . . . Honor looked lovely in cyclamen and wore her rubies. Walter Buccleuch acted as host, and Emerald, looking like Pavlova in white, slipped a crumpled note into my hand for me to read. It was, she said, an anonymous missive she had received. It began, 'You old bitch, trying to make up to Mrs Simpson, in order to curry favour with the King'. Emerald was frightened, and yet rather flattered. It was in an educated handwriting.

At dinner I sat between Diana Cooper, looking wan and thin, and Bridget Parsons, and I had heart-to-hearters with both. Diana told me that Duff is tired of politics, and is thinking of retiring from them and devoting his life to literature, for which he is better suited. An admirable decision, which I hope he will soon take . . . Diana confided to me that she thought Neville Chamberlain was obstructing him: I have heard that he dislikes and disapproves of him.

After dinner, I sat on a sofa with the Pauls and Mrs Simpson, who looked very well tonight, like a Vermeer, in a Dutch way.

The conversation got on to tiaras, and Princess Olga said that hers gave her a headache. Wallis Simpson laughingly added, 'Well, anyway, a tiara is one of the things I shall never have . . .' There was an embarrassed pause. Diana is convinced that Wallis and the King will marry in secret, immediately after the Coronation. I half hope so, half believe it is fated.

18 November

I sat, sleepy, cold and disgruntled and yet strangely excited, all night in the House of Commons waiting for a division, which only came at 6 a.m. How I scatter my forces! I should have been better employed supping with all the royals, as in society I am a power, and here at the House of Commons I am a nonentity. At 7 a.m. I went home in my new Rolls and Bundi was so effusive in his welcome that I was touched. I worship that dog, and he, at least, loves me . . .

Our dinner party for the King tomorrow will be complicated. Is it our high water mark socially? HM has just rung up to ask that decorations should be worn.

We were invited to eleven dinner parties tonight. The Iveaghs, while amused by our royal activities, are nevertheless impressed. Their gangster son-in-law from Chicago has put their daughter into the most exclusive set in Europe!

Thursday, 19 November

Everybody says that our party tonight was unbelievably beautiful and brilliant – but to go back: all morning I rushed about getting a film, as the King, most kindly, had put his apparatus at our disposal.

It came from Buckingham Palace, and was put up in the drawing-room. It was enormous and enclosed in a steel cage, and was formerly the possession of the late King.

I thought that our dining room looked a cascade of beauty, for the table seemed literally to swim with Dresden. Then at 8 o'clock, I read that Don Alonso, second son of the Infanta Beatrice of Spain, had been killed in an aeroplane accident while fighting with the Insurgent forces in Spain. Bang goes our royal evening, I thought, and how ridiculous and manqué we shall appear. Then Princess Olga rang up Honor, and I was certain she was chucking, but no. . . . She only said she would be late as she was rushing to Claridges to console the Infanta. At 8.30 the guests gradually arrived. . . . At 9.20 I went to the front door to await the Kents and Yugoslavs, who were late. Two minutes later the King's car drew up, and he got out breezily, followed by Perry Brownlow, his Lord-in-Waiting. At once I saw he was in a gay mood – no doubt a reaction from his depressing Welsh tour, two dreadfully sad days in the distressed areas. I led him in and he spoke to everyone, and I then went back to the door to meet the Kents. Paul of Yugoslavia followed, and for a moment, I hesitated. Should we go into dinner, or wait for Princess Olga? We decided to go in. Dinner was announced and Princess Marina, in a trailing black velvet tea gown which half hid her pregnancy, led the way. The king said: 'Who is that man? Is he on your list?' It was Pierre de Monaco, whom I had asked at 8 o'clock, so he had not been on the King's list which I had sent him, and which he was clutching in his hand. But nothing could mar his excellent temper and we marched into dinner, the ladies leading. The King will never precede the ladies, and dislikes being asked to do so. There was an awkward pause at first as Princess Olga had not yet arrived, and soup was served before she finally appeared, in a vast tiara and wearing two ropes of diamonds. She greeted Honor, and curtsied to the King and then dinner proceeded, and well. I had the two sisters on either side, and talked to both throughout the dinner until they both turned and I was left alone. Honor got on famously with the King who ate a lot, drank claret and laughed much. . . . Tiaras nodded, diamonds sparkled, the service was excellent, conversation flowed, and I thought of Sachie Sitwell's description of a supper party at Louveciennes chez Madame Dubarry. Would ours be as ill-fated? The ladies rose, each one curtseying to the King as they left the dining room. The King called to me 'Sit on my left, Chips. Come next to me, Paul'. We thus had a three-handed conversation – two reigning sovereigns and Chips. The King was jolly, gay and full of cracks. He returned only tonight from the distressed areas, and must have felt as elated as I do after two or three days in my constituency. We talked for nearly an hour, and he criticised the National Government 'for playing too much to the Opposition' as he put it. Then we went up to the drawing room which I had converted at endless trouble into a cinema. The King, however, said 'It's too late for a long film now'. So I cancelled it and only the topical budget, showing the King at Portsmouth, etc., were shown followed by a short Mickey Mouse. Then conversation ensued, and Paul went up to Wallis Simpson and begged her to ask the King to telephone his sympathy to the bereaved Infanta. 'Couldn't I do it in the morning?' the King asked, gaily. 'No, now, to please me, sir', Wallis said. I interrupted, 'I'll get the number, sir', and the King followed into my little study, and I rang the Grosvenor Hotel. As he was talking I dialled the wrong number, but finally, I got on and asked for the Infanta. Then the King took the receiver and I left him. On my return the room seemed to sway with jewels, and at 12.30 the King, who had talked with Emerald, Princess Olga and Portia and others, rose, and I escorted him downstairs to the front door, where he thanked me warmly. . . . Our party then went on for some time, everyone agreeing, I think and hope, that it had been sensationally successful. They all left at about 1.30, exalted and impressed, and exhausted, I crept up to bed. The atmosphere had been terrific; so many royalties, so many jewels: the King told Honor that he approved of spendour.

Friday, 20 November

I woke early with a headache, caused by reaction, not by drink. Then the telephone began, and nearly everyone congratulated us on a brilliant evening. Emerald said she had never known an evening go so well – certainly never a royal one.

I sometimes wonder why I keep a diary at all. Is it to relieve my feelings? Console my old age? Or to dazzle my descendants?

22 November

Two days later: London is suddenly seething with rumours; sinister, unlikely rumours. This morning Emerald rang me up to say that a 'Cabinet Minister' (there are, I think, 18) had confided in her the news of the impending crisis. Would I go and see her . . . I did, with Honor, and she told me this amazing tale. On Friday evening, the night before last, Leslie Hore-Belisha dined with her and as the hours passed he became rather tipsy and confidential so Emerald plied him with more drink and encouraged him to talk. He told her that Mr Baldwin had spoken separately to all the Cabinet, telling them that he had seen the King, and had with all respect 'protested at his association' with Wallis, and declared that unless the King promised never to marry her, his Government would resign. He gave the King three weeks in which to make up his mind. The King is alleged to have been defiant. He intends, so Belisha believes, to speed up the Simpson divorce, and in about three weeks time to marry her in the Chapel at Windsor. Immediately afterwards he will broadcast to the nation that he has devoted his life and his energies to the welfare of the Commonwealth, and that it is his intention to continue to do so, and that he, in marrying the woman of his choice, has only claimed the privilege allowed even to the very humblest of his subjects. A bombshell; Leslie thinks that the Conservatives will resign, and that the premiership will be hawked about to anyone who will take it, and that Winston Churchill will summon a party meeting, create a new party and rule the country! All this in three weeks time. I tried to dampen Emerald's excitement by telling her that Leslie Belisha is an imaginative Jew, that his mentality is a Hollywood one, but she believes it . . . and so, in a way do I. The King is insane about Wallis, insane. He, too, is going the dictator way, and is pro-German, against Russia and against too much slip-shod democracy. I shouldn't be surprised if he aimed at making himself a mild dictator, a difficult task enough for an English King. There are corroborating tales. Someone at Cartiers foolishly told Bertie Abdy that they are re-setting magnificent, indeed fabulous jewels for Wallis, and for what purpose if she is not to be Queen? And the Duke of Kent's mysterious remark to Kitty Brownlow here at dinner that 'in a month or six weeks time something terrific will happen. I wish I could tell you now'. Everything I fear points to the truth of Leslie's tale.

Emerald, wrongly informed over this at least, thinks that Beaverbrook is returning from the US to attack the King, as most newspapers will certainly do. In fact, Beaverbrook is rushing across the Atlantic in order to help him, for Jean Norton confided to Honor another story. Beaverbrook apparently sailed ten days ago for America en route for Arizona in the hope of curing his asthma, and was bombarded all the way over with cables and appeals from the King to return urgently. The crossing in the 'Bremen' was bad and Beaverbrook, tired and ill, cabled back that he would return in a few days time, after a short rest in New York. The King cabled through his solicitors that it was urgent, and that there was not a moment to be lost and Beaverbrook sailed seven or eight hours after his arrival in the same ship.[34]

I can think of nothing else but the changes and terrors ahead, the Conservative party divided, the country divided, mental civil war going on, and schism in the Royal Family.

I personally think, though Honor disagrees, that there will be an upheaval, that the Throne will sway a little, but that it will survive and that the King will get away with it. We are working up to something terrific. What is history unfolding?

23 November

We had a dinner party here this evening for the Ribbentrops and to say goodbye to the dear Bismarcks who leave us on Thursday for ever, after eight years of London fun and friendship. I am sad, as I like them both. Annemari with her gay Swedish face and flirtatious little manner suggesting a Valentine, her gaiety and laugh, and Nordic prettiness and sweetness, and Otto with his blunt Prussian ways, his directness and bullying, and underneath his great good nature. They have had much success here. At dinner I was between Frau von Ribbentrop and Annemari, and we had a long talk. Frau von Rib said 'I know that in five years I shall be liked in London, but I am going to have a lonely five years until that happens'. She dresses very badly, with high fronted evening gowns . . .

All through dinner, though it was not discussed, I could not get the King situation out of my mind, and I remember now that a few days ago I saw Wallis Simpson lunching alone with Esmond Harmsworth at Claridges, and this morning the 'Daily Mail' publishes a leader of praise for the King, so fulsome and exaggerated as to be almost dangerous.

34. See Lord Beaverbrook's account in *The Abdication of King Edward VIII* (1966), pp. 36–8.

24 November

There is little fresh King news today except that 'The Times', already a bit left wing, attacks the 'Daily Mail' for its eulogy of the Monarch.

I am convinced now that the marriage will take place, although Kitty Brownlow has been invited by Wallis to go away on a trip for a few weeks in the winter.

25 November

The possibility of a royal marriage is still the talk of London. Two remarks are worth chronicling: The Duke of Kent asked Kitty Brownlow last night what she thought of 'this marriage'. Kitty tried to nance out, but he insisted. 'After all they are my relations.' Then he made an astonishing rejoinder: 'I am very discreet'. 'As discreet as a Chubb safe when you've given away all the keys', Kitty retorted. The other is graver. The King said to Perry Brownlow: 'I think — ought to marry Lord —. She is in an invidious position. Men have no right to compromise women, and put them in doubtful positions.' Was this a hint of his own intentions?

26 November

Beaverbrook arrived back from USA today, and there's been no word about it in the Press. He was met at the station by the King's messenger who took him at once to Fort Belvedere. The King could hardly control his impatience to see him. No one knows this story, and when I found it out I thought, will Wallis be at dinner tonight at the Stanleys' where we are to dine? When we arrived at 43 Belgrave Square for dinner, there she was, and I sat next to her. She was wearing new jewels – the King must give her new ones every day. She was charming, sweet and gay, and we had a semi-confidential talk about dictators, communism and how much we both disliked Americans. She has never liked them, and has always felt herself alien to them. 'They have no air', she said, and she likes air. I asked her if the Americans ran after her now, and she smiled a little. She made one confession – that she had not dared be funny for three years. We talked of houses, and I suggested that she should move to Belgravia and she didn't reply. It is these occasional lapses which are mysterious. Why not say 'I'll look about' or something casual instead of leaving one with the feeling that she won't want a house in May, as she'll be living in Buckingham Palace. I personally think that he'll marry her, and soon.

27 November

Princess Olga rang up the House of Commons asking me and Honor to go to a play with her and the Regent tonight, but I had to say that we were already dining with the King and Mrs Simpson. When the House rose and I walked home, I found a message to say that Mrs Simpson was indisposed, and was obliged to postpone her dinner. It came at 4.30. What's happening? It appears that Beaverbrook dines with the King tonight . . .

28 November

The Battle for the Throne has begun. On Wednesday evening (I know all that follows to be true, though not six people in the Kingdom are so informed), Mr Baldwin spent one hour and forty minutes at Buckingham Palace with the King and gave him his ultimatum that the Government would resign, and that the press could no longer be restrained from attacking the King, if he did not abandon all idea of marrying Mrs Simpson. Mr Baldwin had hoped, and thought to frighten the Monarch, but found him obstinate, in love and rather more than a little mad; he refused point blank, and asked for time to consult his friends. 'Who are they?' Mr Baldwin demanded. The audience was not acrimonious, but polite, sad and even affectionate, I am told. 'Lord Beaverbrook', the King retorted. The Prime Minister gasped and departed. On Thursday Beaverbrook arrived back from America, and spent the evening with the King. Yesterday the Cabinet again met at an emergency meeting and the PM told them of the King's determination. The King saw Beaverbrook yesterday and last night Beaverbrook went to see Wallis and thus our dinner party 'chez elle' was postponed. Now no-one knows what will happen; the atmosphere vibrates, and the storm may break at any moment. The Bishop of Oxford (dear old Tommy Strong – who was Dean when I was an undergraduate in 1919) told Thomas Beecham that the Archbishop of Canterbury will refuse, not only to marry the King, but even to consecrate him at the coming Coronation. Everything looks like being sacrificed 'for a plain gold band, not quarter of an inch thick' for it is the marriage state that the people object to, not the immoral one of a liaison. There is no doubt that Wallis' dinner party was postponed, and only at 4.30 yesterday afternoon, because of the situation.

29 November

Honor had a charming note from Wallis to say that she had a sort of break-down yesterday, and must be kept quite quiet and away from visitors and the telephone for a week: and what a week! What will emerge triumphant – passion or the Empire? I am strongly opposed to the Conservative party or the National Government taking the line that Wallis is not good enough for the Throne, as such an attitude reflects snobbishly on us, and only the Socialists would gain from such an attitude, which of course they will in any case. This marriage must help them, and therein lies its danger. The Royal entourage must indeed be in a stew and turmoil today.

30 November

The month is closing and the love crisis of the King is now acute, but not yet public, for there is hardly a ripple in the House of Commons, only occasional malicious and jocular gossip about Mrs Simpson.

Late last night, or, rather early this morning, I talked with Jean Norton, who is very much in the know, about abdication, for that is what the King now threatens. The Government will not resign, nor will Mr Attlee accept office on behalf of the Socialists. He has intimated this, and the King has been told that he must behave himself. He rages and storms and says 'these damned politicians have made Wallis ill'. Apparently he has no sense of reality, and whenever Beaverbrook, whom he looks on as a supporter, gives him adverse advice, the King not only refuses to believe it, or take it, but actually only says next morning to his advisers and solicitors: 'Lord Beaverbrook was in a bad temper last night'. Beaverbrook, while enjoying his role of Mr Fixit, and the power he now holds in his horny hands, is now nearly distraught, and has told the King honestly that it isn't the support of the penny press that His Majesty most needs, but that of the more respectable Conservative dailies, such as the 'Telegraph' and 'The Times', and they are both in governessy, middle-class hands. There is no hope for the King, none, and it looks almost certainly as if the Yorks will succeed. . . . Honor and I will be out of the royal racket having backed the wrong horse, but I don't much mind. . . . Of course it is still possible that the King may decide to be crowned, and later on marry Wallis morganatically, and get away with it that way.

This evening, on my way to the House of Commons, I found the dark sky was ablaze with light, and it looked like a Venetian sunset. It was the Crystal Palace which was burning. It was one of the largest fires ever known in London and for hours the glass melted; now there is only one tower left – a reminder of the Victorian Age. Osbert Sitwell has been agitating for some time in a facetious spirit to get the Crystal Palace moved back into Hyde Park where it once stood, and Sir Edwin Lutyens is said to have suggested putting it in a glass case.

1 December

Honor came to dine with me in the House of Commons. She is bored, idle, and doesn't sleep or take exercise or do anything, but in spite of that is looking extremely well. She tells me that last night the male dinner party at Stornoway House consisted of Beaverbrook, Esmond Harmsworth, Perry Brownlow and Monckton,[35] the King's Solicitor. They were all in agreement that the marriage cannot be allowed to take place, and that the only avenue of approach to the demented lovesick sovereign was Wallis Simpson herself. And they bullied Perry Brownlow into promising to see Wallis today, and warn her confidentially that the country will not accept the marriage, and that she must go away for a few weeks, and allow the talk to simmer down, and to put all thoughts of marriage out of the King's mind. Perry reluctantly but very patriotically agreed, but this morning he discovered that Wallis is at Fort Belvedere and ill – so ill, with a form of nervous exhaustion, that the King refuses to leave her. . . . I don't personally see how the tension can be kept up, for things are boiling over. Perhaps we can anticipate an abdication

35. Mr Walter (later Lord) Monckton.

shortly. Things are moving in favour of the Yorks, and from a realistic point of view I must confess that this seems the best solution.

2 December

The storm has burst. Yesterday a provincial bishop, the Rt Rev Blunt – as usual aptly named – unknown outside his own diocese in Bradford, made a startling speech in which he referred to the coming Coronation and the King's 'unawareness'. This morning the 'Yorkshire Post', 'Birmingham Post' and other provincial dailies quote the bishop's utterances and some run leaders in which the King is criticised. The fat is now properly in the fire. Tomorrow, the world will know all. The Cabinet met from 10 until 1 p.m. discussing what must be a constitutional crisis, and at 6 o'clock the King received Mr Baldwin. Meanwhile, I went around to Kitty's for a drink where the Kents were expected, but they sent a message refusing to come. We dined with the Brownlows, the others at Quaglino's, and I returned to the House of Commons, and lured Shakes Morrison, and a whip, J. C. Llewellyn, to the Smoking Room where we talked long and late after the House rose. I put my cards on the table, and told them that I knew all, and they had to admit the crisis. I appealed to Shakes Morrison, after all a coming man, to intervene and save the King from the coming disaster, but he was adamant. 'He must go', he repeated, and explained that when a responsible Civil Servant is proved unworthy of his office he is removed, and Members of Parliament, too, were not allowed by custom to marry when the alliance was unwise or scandalous. I saw he was firm, as his beautiful, negroid mouth twitched and his dark eyes flashed with rage. 'The King', he said, although I knew this rather better than he did, 'has behaved like a petulant lunatic, and there is nothing to be done except save him from himself. He must go – in fact he has nearly gone already'. It was he, Morrison insisted, who had sent for Baldwin and told him of his intention to abdicate and marry Wallis. I did not say that I knew as a fact that the King had also summoned Duff Cooper for an audience ten days or more ago and told him, too, that he was going to abdicate, and how should he do it in the most dignified manner: or that Duff had said wildly, 'If only you'd wait a year, perhaps we could make her Queen', and that the King had nearly shot out of his chair with surprise and delight.[36] From that moment on, he had made up his mind to keep Wallis and the throne. . . . The Royal Family, it seems, have long been prepared for the marriage. I was sad, and disillusioned with Shakes. If only he could do something, he could make himself the man of the moment and of the Empire, but he was too North-country, too adamant, and too middle-class. Honor says that Beaverbrook and Rothermere will support the King to the end, and thus cause division in the country. This afternoon, I saw Baldwin, smiling and puffing at his pipe in the Smoking Room, being amiable to unknown members; and only a little later, he was hectoring the King for an hour and fifty minutes. Later, I am told, peaceful relations were restored, and the King was tearful and Mr Baldwin sad, impressive and firm. The sleeping country yet knows nothing.

3 December
The Country and the Empire now know that their Monarch, their young King-Emperor, their adored Apollo, is in love with an American twice divorced, whom they believe to be an adventuress.[37] The whole world recoils from the shock; but very few know that she is a woman of infinite charm, gentleness, courage and loyalty, whose influence upon the King, until now, has been highly salutary. 'The Times' has a strong leading article, every other newspaper follows suit, though both the Beaverbrook and the Rothermere press is favourable. There is talk of abdication; of the King sticking to his guns, and marrying her; of a morganatic compromise. Beaverbrook says that he fears the King will abdicate this afternoon, and that his abdication is written out, and it only remains to be signed.

I went shopping with the Regent, and when I returned Honor met me. 'It's all over', she said. I seized her, and we rushed next

36. This appears to be a somewhat exaggerated version of the meeting. Duff Cooper's own account is given on p. 201 of his autobiography, *Old Men Forget*, in which he relates how he suggested postponement, and the King 'refused to consider the suggestion'.

37. It was on the morning of 3 December that the national Press abandoned its self-imposed reticence on the subject of the King and Mrs Simpson.

door, where we saw the Duke of Kent, who was upset. We threw all discretion, all reverence overboard, and I advised him to go at once to the Queen, to take his brothers with him, to call a family council, and in a body to implore the King to change his mind, so as to gain time . . .

Our interview with the Kents made us late for our Admiralty lunch with Sir Samuel and Lady Maude Hoare. Luncheon was endless, the food bad, and everyone distrait. Afterwards Sam Hoare (who is now openly mentioned as Prime Minister, if Baldwin fails) showed us over the Admiralty, showed us the famous Fish furniture, the Admiralty table cut so that William IV could sit at it, the pictures, the Dresden figure of Augustus the Strong, and all the while Princess Olga was pinching me, and whispering, and I begged her, 'Go to the Queen. Quick, take Princess Marina'. At last the strain broke. Sam Hoare conducted the Royalties to the side door, and we were away. I went to the House of Commons and found it astir as it had probably never been before. When Questions were over Mr Attlee rose, and asked the Prime Minister if he had a statement to make. Baldwin rose amidst cheers and said that there was as yet no constitutional crisis, and that it was inexpedient to say more. Winston Churchill then got up, his voice breaking, and with tears in his eyes, said he hoped nothing irrevocable would be done before reflection, or words to that effect, and the din of cheering was impressive.

Baldwin answered non-committally, but the sentiment of the House of Commons is pro-Government and pro-Baldwin; it feels that the King had no right to plunge us in this crisis and that the Dominions would not stand Wallis as Queen, even if England did.

There was a dramatic moment when Black Rod summoned the House to the Lords, and everyone rushed to the Bar thinking it was the Abdication, but it was merely routine, to give the Royal Assent to the Bill passed on Monday about vessels carrying munitions to Spain. One wondered, was it the last time we should be so summoned, the last time we should hear the Clerk intone 'Le Roi le veult'? Perry Brownlow, who has left officially for Plas Newydd to shoot, has in reality escorted Wallis Simpson to France in all secrecy, crossing by the Newhaven boat tonight.

She was advised to leave as 'she was in danger'; last evening her windows in Cumberland Terrace were broken.

At midnight, just as I was leaving for a Costume Ball at the Austrian Legation – I was in lederhosen, bare legs and Austrian dress – the Duke of Kent rang me up to come next door, which I did. I found Paul, Princess Olga, Princess Marina; the Queen of Spain had just left. I told them the news; that the King was still fighting, that the Abdication had been delayed for a day or two, perhaps even over the weekend. The others went to bed and Prince George followed me home, where we found Honor and Jean, and we talked and deplored until 4 a.m. The Duke of Kent unburdened his heart; said he loved the King more than anyone, how the King ignored him, how he had not even seen him since the Balmoral visit until the evening in our house at our now historic dinner on 19 November. The King had rung him on the telephone before dinner that evening, to say he was going to marry Wallis, and the Duke of Kent had not known whether to congratulate him or not; hence his nervousness and irritability. And he had only rung him because he knew he would meet him at our dinner. The King, it seems, had however dined with his mother about a week before the 19th, and afterwards sent the Duchess of Gloucester from the room, and then told the Queen and Princess Mary of his matrimonial intention. The Queen, it seems ... twice warned Mr Baldwin, once in February and again in July, that she feared for the future, and hinted that the King was bewitched and intended marriage. But she was shy, nervous and ineffectual. All her life she has been reserved with her eldest son, and the habit of a lifetime was too strong for her to break it. Mr Baldwin, as the lady was not divorced, tried to let matters slide, but he did twice try to broach the matter to the Monarch, who remarked icily that it was not a discussable question ...

At 4.15 we all separated and went to bed, but Belgrave Square was an unusual sight in the December dawn, the Duke and I with our dogs, I sleepy and in despair, walking, whilst gay revellers in Tyrolese dress were shouting and yodelling as they emerged from the Austrian Legation.

The King ... is driving straight to the precipice; if he defies the Government and persists with his marriage plan the Cabinet will resign, and there is no alternative Government as the Socialists have refused office under the present circumstances. Only a possibility of Winston Churchill . . .

Wallis Simpson, a chauffeur, a detective and Perry Brownlow are at this moment speeding across France, and Beaverbrook is plotting at Stornoway House trying to keep up the King's courage, the courage of a broken man at bay.

4 December

There is no real news, at least no decision. I went to the House of Commons and again Attlee questioned Baldwin, who replied that while aware of the public anxiety he had nothing to add to his statement of yesterday. But at 2.30 I heard that a statement would be made shortly, and I was able to get hold of Honor who arrived in time, with Jean Norton. The news spread . . . the Chamber filled up with the result that a minor Bill regulating offices which the Socialists hoped to pass, was overwhelmingly defeated by the Conservatives who rarely attend on Friday. By 2.30 there were cries of 'Divide! Divide!' but the Government put up someone to keep the debate going for a quarter of an hour until Baldwin arrived; as he did, an awful stillness fell on the House, and the Cabinet, looking like a picture by Franz Hals, a lot of grim Elders of the Kirk, squirmed uneasily. Then he rose, and in a stentorian voice, unsmiling and ungracious, I thought, announced flatly that there was no middle course, that a morganatic marriage was not to be considered, that none of the Dominions would agree and, even if they did, the present Government was not prepared to introduce such legislation. He was greeted with cheers, but they were more for the man who has been through an appalling few days, than for the pronouncement, which slams the door to any possible compromise.

This evening Baldwin drove again to Fort Belvedere to see the King.

London is now properly divided and the King's faction grows; people process the streets singing 'God Save the King', and assemble outside Buckingham Palace, they parade all night. After the first shock the country is now reacting, and demands that their King be left in peace.

We had people to dine, all Cavaliers, except Duff Cooper who is revolted by the King's selfish stupidity. The King cannot understand that Wallis is still legally the wife of Ernest Simpson, and that the Courts are not disposed to hasten up the decree. Apparently the King talks of her as a free woman already, which is both untrue and in bad taste.

I rang Beaverbrook late for news and he said 'Our cock would be all right if only he would fight, but at the moment he will not even crow'. 'Cocks crow better in the morning,' I suggested. 'Not this one,' he laughed.

So the appalling drama goes on.

5 December
If only I had power – My God, I'd do something! Anything! Nothing matters now, no details, they are forgotten. We can only combine to try to save the Sovereign. All day there were telephone messages and plots. I went in to see the Kents, and found Princess Marina looking ill and sad. He is at the Fort, with the King, whom he adores. The Yorks are staggered and behaving well; he intends to call himself George VI instead of Albert which people think too Germanic: but there is still a chance, Edward VIII still reigns, and may do so over the weekend. It seems he is cheerful on the telephone, at least when he spoke to Kitty Brownlow. Yet how terrible that he should have no real friend in the world to turn to, except Beaverbrook.

6 December
The crucial day. I woke late with a heaviness of heart, feeling all was over unless something very drastic was done – the God from the Machine. I thought over the situation, rang Hore-Belisha and we talked for 40 minutes. I then put in a trunk call to Cannes to speak, if possible, to Wallis or failing her to Perry Brownlow. Nervously I drank my tea and soon the telephone tinkled; it was Perry, surprised to hear my voice, and annoyed that he had been traced. I told him that his whereabouts were an open secret, and tomorrow would be in every newspaper. I then pleaded with him to induce Wallis to do 'something', and tried to make him understand the gravity of the situation. He was, he said, doing everything, and that Wallis was in fact very reasonable, and ready to renounce the King, would do any-

thing, in fact, to keep him on the throne, but thought that an independent statement issued by her would only mean that the King would fly to her in his plane, an undignified exit for the Emperor of India and King of England. Perry said he would go on trying. Apparently the King is now prepared to wait six months or even two years if Baldwin will give him time. I then called Belisha back, and said that Perry still hoped to get some statement out of Wallis. Leslie thought this was a cheerful sign, and then suggested that Perry ring him so that he, Leslie Hore-Belisha, could go and see Mr Baldwin before the Cabinet meets: he wanted the credit. Today the atmosphere seems better, and I rang Kitty Brownlow and said that I had been speaking to her husband, and soon she and Belisha were in communication, and again rang up France. The lines to Cannes are tapped (and I think ours are, too) and it is increasingly difficult to reach the Villa as Wallis spends several hours a day talking to the King.

In the evening we had a dinner party and half expected everyone to come late as the Cabinet was sitting. The Oliver Stanleys had a rival festival of 11 people, all Roundheads and violently anti-King, particularly Maureen Stanley. Our dinner assembled punctually and Esmond Harmsworth was the first to arrive, soon followed by the Cabinet boys, Duff, Belisha, and David Margesson. Dinner progressed with little embarrassment, although both Duff and David were extremely cold to Esmond Harmsworth who has so strongly supported the King on the morganatic compromise. Honor begged David that someone should 'get at' Mrs Simpson direct, and he promised to tell Baldwin tonight. Everyone admitted that no decision had yet been reached. ... At the end of dinner, Duff, David Margesson and Belisha moved to the end of the table and held a private conclave for two hours, from 10.15 until after midnight, discussing the problem and hoping for a way out, as we all talked or played bridge upstairs.

I slipped away for five minutes and telephoned to Coppins and spoke to Paul. He had been having tea with the Yorks at Royal Lodge, and says that they know nothing. The Duke of York is miserable, does not want the throne, and is imploring his brother to stay.

I have felt all day today that the tide is turning against the

Government, and is more pro-King. Indeed that a definite reaction has set in. Will it last? I fear not, as the King is so badly advised, he seems destined to rush to his fate and no human agency, nor divine, can save him unless the country rises in his defence, which it will not. Oh why did Baldwin slam the door against a morganatic marriage so firmly and irrevocably? What about Queen Mary's uncle the Duke of Cambridge who married an actress, and lived happily ever after, and the Duke of Sussex?[38] He delivered a blow to the Monarchy on Friday almost as great as the King's.

We must keep our King, until now the most popular man the Empire has ever known; but I wonder whether his selfishness and stupidity over this muddle do not really make him unfit to govern?

7 December

The world is now divided into Cavaliers and Roundheads. Belisha is a secret Cavalier, and there are many in the Cabinet: Duff Cooper is one, Sam Hoare is another, and the newspapers this morning are tamer; other news is beginning to creep back on to the front page.

People are weary of the crisis, and public opinion is hardening on both sides. What meanwhile is in the Monarch's mind?

I walked to the House of Commons where I found much excitement and a full House and one could hardly bear to listen to questions and answers, as every one watched the clock and every brain thought only of one thing. Only the supplementary question 'Where is the Spanish Government now?' aroused any interest, when Maxton shouted 'Where is our own?' The Prime Minister had a rousing reception, and Attlee was called by the Speaker, and he asked Baldwin whether he had anything to add to Friday's statement. The PM then rose and made a frank statement that really meant nothing except that no decision had yet been reached and that the Monarch was still making up his mind. The PM does not want to hurry him, yet at the same time he realizes the dangers of a too prolonged delay. He sat down amongst cheers, although there was a quiet corner of non-

38. Queen Victoria's uncle, who married a commoner, whom Queen Victoria created Duchess of Inverness.

cheerers where I sat. I was numb. Winston Churchill then rose, misjudged his cue, and was booed. 'Drop it', 'Twister' were taunts hurled at him. He tried to stand his ground, but lost the House, and I fear did the King's cause harm. We then, after dividing perfunctorily on the 11 o'clock rule, emptied into the Lobbies. I had a feeling at first that all was over, that the King was about to abdicate. Walking by the Lords I bumped into Bob Boothby and buttonholed him, and he then let me into his confidence. Last night at Chartwell, he, and Archie Sinclair, leader of the Liberals, and Winston Churchill drew up a paper which they hoped to get the King to sign to the effect 'As long as I am King I will never contract a marriage against the wishes of my Ministers'.

They think such a document would give him a way out for in the future, as he could still abdicate or, as might easily happen, future Ministers might allow the marriage. The problem was of course, how to get the King to sign it? The draft paper was sent around to Buckingham Palace addressed to Godfrey Thomas whom Bob knows intimately. An hour passed and when I again met Bob Boothby in the Lobby he had had a message to go at once to Wyndhams Club to meet Walter Monckton, the King's solicitor, who happens to be an old driend of Bob's too. Why should Monckton send for him if there was not some hope of the King climbing down? I see light, a ray of hope ahead.

Beaverbrook and Co are hopeful that the King will stay, but he is losing ground, and in a day or two it will be too late for him to remain. No such tragedy of human folly has ever been enacted; things move so quickly that one cannot even chronicle them.

This evening when I got home, Honor gave me the astonishing news that Wallis had signed her renunciation at Cannes and that it would be published in tomorrow's press.[39] I rang up Beaverbrook at Cherkley and he confirmed the rumour. By this time, it

39. The statement read: 'Mrs Simpson throughout the last few weeks has invariably wished to avoid any action or proposal which would hurt or damage the King or the Throne. Today her attitude is unchanged, and she is willing if such action would solve the problem, to withdraw forthwith from a situation that has been rendered unhappy and untenable.'

was nearly midnight, but we went to the Savoy to Freddy Birkenhead's birthday supper party which proved a disastrous function, as opinion was so bitterly divided; I personally lost my temper with any Roundhead I could see, and hurled abuse at them in my Royalist fury.

I then went out and bought the 'Daily Mail' which had just come out with the signed statement 'Mrs Simpson renounces the King'. Either the crisis has passed or at least is much better, the change is electric. Meanwhile the King still reigns.

8 December

The press receives Wallis's statement with mixed comments. Rothermere and Beaverbrook hail it with great jubilation, and the 'Express' announced 'End of Crisis' but 'The Times' and 'The Telegraph' barely disguise their disappointment for they are both determined to get the King to abdicate. Perry Brownlow, apparently summoned thirty journalists to a meeting yesterday afternoon at the Hotel Majestic, Cannes and made a dignified statement on Wallis's behalf, but now everyone asks, rather ungraciously, why didn't she make it months ago? and the newspapers, reflecting the temper of the people, are showing signs of irritation with the King. Even I, who had my great Royalist outburst last night, am beginning to think that he had better go. He has kept the whole Empire in suspense too long . . .

I walked to the House of Commons where the excitement has somewhat abated, and there is a feeling of hope. The Stock Exchange certainly reacted favourably this morning, but the early spurt was not maintained. Baldwin did not appear and Sir John Simon, answering for him, said that there would be no statement today. Later we read the tape that Mr Baldwin had left for Fort Belvedere to see the King, and that the Dukes of Kent and York were with their brother too. Their conference there must have begun at about 4.30. Bob Boothby, informed by Walter Monckton, who has sprung into such unexpected and highly powerful limelight, tells me that he believes the King will give in, or already has: now there are rumours of an aeroplane, specially chartered by three mysterious men which has flown to Cannes.

I came in at 8.30 and found that the poor Duchess of Kent

had been ringing me, as the Duke of Kent is still at the Fort. I went next door to see her and Princess Olga; they were dining alone, in despair and with heavy colds. They knew nothing.

Later. The news has now got out that the three men who flew so secretly to Cannes were Mr Goddard who is Wallis Simpson's solicitor, his clerk and a doctor, Dr Kirkwood who is a well known gynaecologist.[40] This is foolish and most unfortunate and typical of the mistakes made by Monarchs who have lost their heads and are doomed to perish.

We arrived, very late, to dine with Emerald Cunard at 7 Grosvenor Square, for the party which was to have been in the King's honour; he himself had chosen the date. Could he have foreseen this tragedy then? We found a brilliant company ... Londonderrys, Marlboroughs, Coopers, Fitzgeralds, Ribbentrops, Eric Dudley, old Mensdorff[41] and others; there was nervousness and subdued whispering, and the Ribbentrops were even later than we were and I stood for a time with Mary Marlborough who asked me, in her frank breezy way, did I not think that all the while Wallis had been playing a double game? She herself has not yet made up her mind, but she added that it enraged her when people attacked Emerald for entertaining her, as Emerald was only one of many. 'We had her to stay at Blenheim; I liked her,' was Mary's summing up.

Afterwards I returned to the House of Commons to vote and found that antagonism to Mrs Simpson, the double-divorced foreigner, had grown. When I went back to Emerald's the music was starting and I found Honor and the Coopers hovering on the threshold trying to leave as Duff cannot be in the room with music of any kind. At that moment the butler said I was wanted urgently on the telephone by a lady. I went, kept my head, and recognised the Duchess of Kent's voice. She asked us to go and see her, and Honor and I stole away to 3 Belgrave Square, and had a long talk with the two sisters who were alone except for Mrs

40. Dr Kirkwood was a House Surgeon at St George's Hospital; he was in general practice with an interest in female disorders, and had a connection with Queen Charlotte's Hospital. Hence the origin of the story that he was a gynaecologist. In fact he went on the trip as Mr Goddard's personal physician.

41. Austrian Ambassador in London before 1914.

Campbell.[42] For two days now the Duke of Kent has been with his brother at the Fort, never leaving him for a second and trying by every means in his power to persuade him to stay. The King told him that over two years ago while he knew that he was an excellent Prince of Wales and liked his job, he nevertheless felt that he could never 'stick' being King as he puts it, he was afraid of being a bad one. He could never tolerate the restrictions, the etiquette, the loneliness; so perhaps if this issue had not arisen something else would have. The country thinks that we shall hear the decision tomorrow but I understand that it will not be until Thursday, the 10th, that the abdication will be announced ...

Bed at three, nervously racked.

9 December

A day of doubt, torment and indecision. The King's delay, his silence, is losing him thousands of supporters. People are saying that he has no right to let us down like this, and the Cavaliers, yesterday in the ascendant, are now losing ground. Towards six in the evening we knew definitely that the abdication was signed. Honor went to Kitty Brownlow's at midnight and the Buists came in, hysterical and weeping. They had a plan, a mad one, of rushing to the Fort in a last final attempt, and they rang up Osbourne, the King's valet, and he said that the King refused to see them, or even speak on the telephone. Then they went to the Kents where they stayed very late talking and arguing. The Duke of Kent, who had only just returned after two days at the Fort, said that there was nothing to be done, that the King's mind was made up and no-one on this earth could stop him. Meanwhile Kitty got through to Cannes, and talked to Perry who is half mad with grief and anxiety. He said that Wallis and the King spend several hours a day telephoning to each other, whilst the anxious world waits. Wallis had cajoled, threatened, implored, done everything to make the King stay, to stay at all costs, but even to her, the woman who he loves so madly, he is adamant.

The Duke of Kent said that he was in good spirits, even cheerful, and this corroborates an account given by Tommy Dugdale,

42. Mrs James Campbell, born Princess Galitzine, a life-long friend of Princess Marina's.

that dinner last night at the Fort was almost a festive occasion. It was the only dinner table, probably, in the Empire where 'Topic A' was not under discussion. Present were the King, his brothers of York and Kent, Monckton, Mr Baldwin and Tommy Dugdale himself.

I still feel that the refusal to countenance a morganatic marriage was a calamity.

10 December

The dreadful day dawned coldly, and my limbs were numb and chilled. The telephone began early, and I talked to the Duchess of Kent who told me that all was over. The Duke of Kent returned to the Fort very early. I drove to the House of Commons and noticed that the Royal Standard was still flying.

At 2 p.m. Honor and I left for Parliament as I had secured her a ticket for the fateful day. The House was full, for there has not been an Abdication since 1399, 537 years ago.[43] I thought everyone subdued but surprisingly unmoved, and Lady Astor actually seemed to enjoy herself, jumping about in her frivolous way. Baldwin was greeted with cheers, and sat down on the front bench gravely. At last he went to the bar, bowed twice 'A message from the King' and he presented a paper to the Speaker who proceeded to read it out. At the words 'renounce the Throne' his voice broke, and there were stifled sobs in the House. It was a short document, more moving by implication than by phrase, to the effect that the King could no longer remain on the Throne. The Speaker was tearful, but very few others were though Geoffrey Lloyd was in tears, and so I thought, was David Margesson. . . . Then Baldwin rose, and in half an hour told us the tale of his meetings with the King and their protracted discussions. He was a little muddled, there were many notes scattered on the Despatch Box, but a few points, spoken simply, emerged, as Mr Baldwin paid His Majesty tribute after tribute. That the King throughout had behaved in a constitutional and upright manner, and that the Cabinet was dead against morganatic marriage, which was only suggested by the King on 1 December, long after the original marriage scheme had been

43. Of Richard II.

broached. Mr Baldwin admits that he had little time to consider this second proposal, (and to my mind he committed a crime in not allowing it). He said the Cabinet would not agree, nor would the Dominions, but surely he could have persuaded them. Winston Churchill sat doubled up throughout the speech. One other fact came out and of this I was always sure, that at no time did the King really hesitate, it was always a choice between marriage and abdication. At last Mr Baldwin sat down, and the Speaker adjourned the House until 6 p.m. I found Honor, put her in the car, and am now writing these lines. It is 5.42 and the House empty, the Chamber has witnessed yet again a scene that will always live in history. As I walked to my locker and fetched this diary, Lady Astor sang out to me 'People who have been licking Mrs Simpson's boots ought to be shot'. I was too tired to retort and pretended I did not hear.

It is not known when the King will leave, nor how, but probably he will go tomorrow; what a heart-rending farewell.

11 December

'The King is gone, Long Live the King.' We woke in the reign of Edward VIII and went to bed in that of George VI. Honor and I were at the House of Commons by eleven o'clock, and as she stood for a time in the queue waiting to go to the Strangers Gallery, I talked with Mikey and David Lyon who were waiting to hear their sister made Queen of England. They were simple, charming and bored as ever. When the Bill came it was passed into Law with the minimum of time. Lord Halifax who moved it, and Lord Onslow who was on the Woolsack, are both Honor's uncles, and I realized how vested and what a closed corporation the aristocracy of England still is. Then the Royal Commission was sent for, and the Lords Onslow, Denman and one other, filed out of the Chamber, and returned in full robes and wigs. Black Rod was sent to summon the Speaker, who, followed by his Commons, appeared at the bar. The Clerk read the Royal Commission. The three Lords bowed, and doffed their hats. The Bill was read. The King was still King Edward. The Clerk bowed 'Le Roi le veult' and Edward, the beautiful boy King with his gaiety and honesty, his American accent and nervous twitching, his flair and glamour, was part of history. It was 1.52.

We went sadly home, and in the street we heard a woman selling newspapers saying 'The Church held a pistol to his head'. In the evening we dined at the Stanleys' cheerless, characterless house, and at ten o'clock turned on the wireless to hear 'His Royal Highess, Prince Edward' speak his farewell words in his unmistakable slightly Long Island voice. It was a manly, sincere farewell, saying that he could not carry on the responsibilities of Kingship without the support of the woman he loved. There was a stillness in the Stanleys' room. I wept, and I murmured a prayer for he who had once been King Edward VIII.

Then we played bridge.

12 December *Arundel Castle*

We came here this morning, in a new reign, the third in 1936, year of the three Kings. The ex-King left Portsmouth at 1.45 this morning, having boarded a destroyer, and left the country which he has ruled for only 10 months . . .

Honor and I drove down through the fog and found a large party of frumps. The great castle is cold, and Honor shivered as we walked through the big Hall and were led to 'His Grace's study' where we found a fire, and Bernard[44] shaking cocktails. He is charming, shy and very 'John Bull' in his outlook. At dinner I was next to the Duchess, Bernard's mother, who, with all her dowdiness, is a worldly old girl, like most Roman Catholics, and she said in no uncertain terms that she was against the abdication. She regretted Mrs Simpson, but thought that a morganatic marriage should have been permitted.

We have the best rooms but oh! how cold they are, and there is a gale blowing like at sea. Where is poor Edward, ex of England and of India? I thought of him this afternoon as I passed through the crowds waiting to see the proclamation ceremony outside St James's Palace. Only last January I saw the carriages, gorgeous and gold and red, with the Heralds drawn up in Friary Court, and Wallis at the window with the King.

14 December *London*

People are beginning to rat. They 'never really liked Mrs Simpson', always disapproved of the King and thought him

44. The Duke of Norfolk.

obstinate and insane; already. I wrote to Wallis at Cannes, sympathising with her, and suggesting that the Duke of Windsor should buy Wasserleonburg.[45] I also wrote to him personally on Friday to Fort Belvedere, as did Honor. The rats, oh the rats. The Coopers are in a difficult position for they have week-ended for a year with the King, and accompanied him on the 'Nahlin' on that ill-fated cruise which jeopardised the Throne.

Of course the most conspicuous rat of all is the Archbishop of Canterbury, Old Cosmo Cantuar, who, in a monstrous broad-cast last night, poured scorn on the late King, and branded his social circle as people whose ways of life were alien to all that is best in the instincts and tradition of the English people. This is a terrible indictment and an unfair one. The King's circle, since Wallis, at least, has consisted of Ambassadors, Cabinet Ministers, the Coopers, the Edens, the Brownlows and many more whose personal reputations are quite unsullied.

16 December

I felt shy and self-conscious in the House of Commons as if the episcopal attack had been directed at me alone, and I heard that garrulous gossip Malcolm Bullock, with an expertise of felinity, remark (for me to overhear) 'I don't know whom the Archbishop meant, as the late King had no friends'. It is terribly true; only Fruity Metcalfe with his checks and his brogue. No other man friend did the King ever have.

17 December

Much talk of the rats. Osbert Sitwell has written a poem, not a very good one, called 'Rat Week' in which he lampoons many deserving people. It is cruel, funny and apposite in spirit, if not in the letter.

We had people to dinner, and Raimund Von Hofmannsthal suggested that, as a gesture, we should tear down our Amalien-burg dining room so that it might be remembered as an exquisite salle-de-parade for the elegant reign just ended. I see the point, a folly built for a King's pleasure, but I have no intention of doing it . . .

45. A castle in Austria.

Just before dinner the Brownlows looked in, Perry having just returned from Vienna where he left the Duke of Windsor. His role in the drama has been far from easy. Having been summoned early on, and ordered by Edward VIII to escort Wallis secretly to Cannes and to look after her, suddenly he became the centre of the world's interest, and perhaps for some days the whole fate of the Monarchy hung on him. It was an anxious time. He had first to ward off, and then placate and finally interview the Press, and control and try to influence Wallis; he was rarely off the telephone to the King at Fort Belvedere. He is firm about one thing: he repeats and insists that Wallis did everything possible to prevent the King's abdication, and he showed me a letter written in his handwriting and dictated by Wallis, in which he authorises her solicitors to withdraw the divorce proceedings at Ipswich. This letter is signed by Perry, her solicitor Goddard and herself and is a valuable historical document. Perhaps it was too late, but her wishes were not acted upon. Perry is going to show it to Mr Baldwin who has summoned him to Chequers tomorrow for an interview. Perry is wild with justified rage against the Archbishop of Canterbury, and I myself wrote a dignified snorter to His Grace today. I hope the old gentleman has asphyxia.

19 December

It was Perry Brownlow (he told me at luncheon today) who arranged for the Rothschilds to invite the Duke of Windsor to Enzesfeld, not their idea. Perry says that the King is quite pathetic and highly nervous. He sleeps in a room at Enzesfeld entirely devoid of anything personal except several large photographs of Wallis. No bibelots, nothing personal at all except a little yellow pillow on his bed that once was hers. The ex-Monarch of the world has no possessions, nothing. Everything belonged to the palaces which are entailed 'on the King'. All he has is twenty-six suits of clothes and a Cairn terrier, but apparently the new King has behaved well and the brothers have spoken several times on the telephone. On one occasion the Duke of Windsor complained bitterly of the Archbishop's broadcast. The Duke of Kent has also been in constant telephonic communication with Enzesfeld. Perry says that the Duke knows exactly who has and who has not been loyal to him, and he is desperately sorry for him, and does not know which of his moods is more tragic, when he is angry, and delighted to have cut the painter thinking only of his marriage with Wallis, or when he is gayer and chatters of old days and of his intention of keeping his Colonelcies, etc., in various regiments. He seems to have made no plans for the future other than for his reunion with Wallis.

Perry's interview with Baldwin passed off well and he told him the whole story of his trip. Baldwin was interested and sympathetic. Perry has now demanded an interview with the Archbishop of Canterbury who was gracious in his reply, and set Monday for the audience.

20 December
The Archbishop of Canterbury's indiscretion has not been forgotten. In today's 'Referee' H. G. Wells writes a most bitter and scathing attack on him and advises horse whipping for the sanctimonious Prelate. It is not the first time he has been in trouble. Last year when the old King lay dying at Sandringham, the Archbishop of Canterbury was most officious, and later gave

21 December
Perry Brownlow was rivetting at lunch. He gave us a detailed account of his interview this morning with the Archbishop of Canterbury who was unctuous, adamant, tearful and angry. Perry very civilly demanded an apology as his actions in being loyal to his King can scarcely be described as vicious, etc. The Archbishop, his tiny eyes screwed up, refused any recantation. 'The innocent must suffer with the guilty', he remarked in true Christian spirit. He was unable to see that he had done the Brownlows incalculable harm, and in fact the aged Prelate showed himself to be quite unrelenting. When Perry asked him who he meant by 'The King's Circle' the Archbishop was at a loss for a reply. In fact he did not know. The interview was hardly satisfactory though Perry was delighted to talk to him as no one else has dared to do for many a long year, the Archbishop admitted that he had had 'a most disgusting' post. He showed slight signs of panic.

Walter Monckton's description of the last family farewell is poignant. It took place at Royal Lodge, Windsor, and there the ex-King said goodbye to his family. His mother, Queen Mary, ever magnificent, was mute and immovable and very royal, and had thoughtfully left off her mourning black for the evening so as not to cast more gloom. The brothers were sad and showed their emotion. . . . At last he left, and bowing over his brother's hand, the brother whom he had made King, he said, 'God bless you, Sir. I hope you will be happier than your predecessor', and disappeared into the night, leaving the Royal Family speechless.

22 December

Today there has been a development, and I think an important one. Perry Brownlow was to have gone into Waiting yesterday, and he received his usual card of warning which he acknowledged. Yesterday he was told that he need not really appear at Buckingham Palace in the afternoon as the King had only the Archbishop of Canterbury to receive, and it was to be informal and at 145 Piccadilly. Perry was disappointed, as he had rather looked forward to the fun of showing in the Archbishop, whom a few hours before he had almost insulted.

Then this morning he read (as I did) in the Court Circular that 'Lord Dufferin and Ava had succeeded as Lord-in-Waiting'. Immediately Perry rang up Buckingham Palace, and was told that his name could never appear in the Court Circular again. He demanded to speak to Lord Cromer who told him that 'his resignation had been accepted' though he had never resigned. 'Am I to be turned away', he asked, 'like a dishonest servant with no notice, no warning, no thanks, when all I did was to obey my Master, the late King?' 'Yes', was Lord Cromer's anwer. This trivial act of shortsightedness may create an anti-Court faction. They have simply sacked Perry from his job as Lord-in-Waiting to the King, for the offence of having been loyal to the last one, and for having acted on orders in escorting Mrs Simpson to Cannes. All Courtiers are always kept on for six months, and this is a deliberate slap in the face and a serious one. I feel this means there is to be a 'Black List' and the Court will try to damage everyone who was a friend of the late King. . . . A foolish small-minded policy, as it will only create enemies to the new régime and make their difficult roles still more so. Are we all on the 'Black List'? Are the Sutherlands, the Marlboroughs, the Stanleys? I cannot believe that it is Queen Elizabeth's doing. She is not so foolish. It is those old courtiers, Wigram and Co. and above all Alex Hardinge, ever both the late King's and Perry's relentless foe.

Later. There have been further developments, as both Lord Cromer and Lord Wigram have rung up Perry and admitted that the present King had not dismissed him, thus admitting that it had been done as a result of a Court plot engineered behind the King's back. If they attempt to form a Court Clique, taking decisions without even consulting the King, it will lead to trouble. I am very sorry for the Brownlows.

23 December

The Archbishop of Canterbury must be losing his enfeebled mind. He has given a press lunch and is about to launch a 'Back to God Campaign' and has roused other Bishops to support him. A more efficient way of making the Church of England ridiculous I don't know. He has mis-read the feeling in the country, for whatever people may have thought about the King/Simpson situation, no-one wanted religious recrimination afterwards and the Church of England has certainly not gained adherents by its un-Christian attitude. Indeed it has lost much support, and has now become ridiculous.

The Royal Family left yesterday for Sandringham amidst much publicity. The press is trying to work up popularity for the new régime, and perhaps in time it will succeed. After all George V and Queen Mary were actually unpopular when they began their long reign, and they lived to see themselves adored.

Everyone agrees that 'finis' should now be written to the tragedy of Punchinello and Columbine.

APPENDIX TO CHAPTER TWO

The Channons' Visit to Germany August–September 1936

The narrative for 1936 has not been interrupted by Chips's account of the visit he and his wife paid to Germany, Austria and Yugoslavia in August and September. It was of considerable importance on Chips's attitude towards the Nazi régime, and should be included for this reason alone. But it also gives a vivid picture of the régime and of its principal members.

As Chips did indeed fall under what Harold Nicolson has called 'the champagnelike influence of Ribbentrop and the youthful influences of the Brunswicks, the Wittelbacks and the House of Hesse Cassel,'[1] it is important that this fact should not be omitted in any dispassionate editing of his diaries. If modern readers may be surprised that anyone could be so completely misled about the true nature of the Nazi régime, it can only be said that it was indeed surprising, but that many other British politicians were equally misled.

4 August

Sad goodbyes this morning to Paul and to 'Bundi'. I love that boy almost to distraction and his gay alert face fascinates me, and my woolly dog, that warm bundle of canine charm. To-morrow, Berlin!

5 August *Berlin*

We took off from Gatwick for Berlin at 9.30. In the early afternoon we landed at Templehof, much enlarged since I landed there with George Gage nine years ago, where we were met by Baron von Geyr, who is to be our personal ADC, and driven in a Government car to the Eden Hotel, where we were given a magnificent suite of rooms: Berlin crowded with foreigners, and the streets be-flagged. Honor and I went for a walk down the

1. Harold Nicolson, op. cit., p. 273.

Unter den Linden, an avenue of banners blowing in the breeze, and everywhere we heard the radio booming 'Achtung', and then giving the latest Olympic results. About six, we went to the Bristol for a cocktail, where we found the whole English contingent very excited. . . . We dined with the Bismarcks, a party of over fifty in the Eden roof garden, and Otto, ever gauche, put German women on his left and right. It was a brilliant, cosmopolitan dinner of Viennese, German and English. . . . Bed about 4, and we came for a rest!

6 August

Breakfast at 12.30 and no lunch. Our ADC, in a grand car with a Storm Trooper at the wheel, called for us soon after and we whizzed off to the Olympic Stadium, which is really a collection of stadiums. First we watched indifferent polo, then we walked to the largest stadium of all, and watched hurdling and running, which bored us, though the great bowl, which seats 100,000 and is always full, is terrific. After an hour or so of watching this, the crowd suddenly bellowed 'Heil!' and there was a sudden movement and a surging forward; a large rotund figure, dressed in a white uniform, appeared. Goering. He waved a greeting and sat down in the front of the official box. The crowds roared again, and the amplifiers called out, 'We want our Herman'. Goering rose and bowed again and the games proceeded. Whenever there was a win, the entire stadium stood up and, with right arm uplifted, sang the National Anthem, as best they could, of the victorious country. German wins were frequent, and then, not only Deutschland über Alles was bellowed, but also the Horst Wessel song, the Nazi anthem, which I thought had rather a good lilt. Thus an hour or so passed, and then, suddenly the audience was electrified. Hitler was coming and he looked exactly like his caricature – brown uniform, Charlie Chaplin moustache, square, stocky figure, and a determined but not grim look. . . . I was more excited than when I met Mussolini in 1926 in Perugia, and more stimulated, I am sorry to say, than when I was blessed by the Pope in 1920.

We left about six with our rather gloomy ADC, Baron von Geyr, and returned to the hotel to prepare for the evening gala. At eight o'clock, piloted once more by a Storm Trooper in a khaki shirt, we arrived at the Opera House for the State Banquet. We were in evening dress and Honor in full regalia, with her rubies, but minus tiara. A hundred or more footmen in dix-huitième pink liveries and carrying torches in glass holders, lined the entrance. A reception took place in the foyer, and here Frau Goering, a tall, handsome, and seemingly almost naked woman, was the principal figure and moved about amongst an obsequious crowd of Royalties and ambassadors. Berlin has not known anything like this since the war, and one was conscious of the effort the Germans were making to show the world the grandeur, the permanency and respectability of the new régime. At last, dinner was announced, and we went into the Opera House itself, where a floor had been laid. Dinner was then served, hitchlessly, on two thousand people. Honor and I, Pat Jersey[2] and an aged German General shared a small table in a conspicuous position. The food was good, and the wines flowed. During dinner, a corps de ballet entertained us. The auditorium glistened with flashing jewels and orders. To the right of what in ordinary times would have been the stage, sat Goebbels and his wife, with the Crown Prince of Italy. On the left were the Goerings, with the Crown Prince of Sweden and the King of Bulgaria, who looked very like Mr Attlee. After the performance, Prince Philip of Hesse came down to our table, and said that Goering would like to meet us. . . . He was flirtatious, gay and insinuating, and exchanged German banter with Honor, and presented her with a bell, a model of the Olympic bell. . . .

At last we left, tired and impressed. The new régime, particularly Goering, are masters of the art of party giving. Tonight, in a way, must have been a little like the fêtes given by the Directoire of the French Revolution, with the upstarts, tipsy with power and flattered by the proximity and ovations of the ex-grand, whom once they wished to destroy.

7 August

Although we have only been here for 48 hours, we are already conscious of an atmosphere of intrigue; we are told that Ribbentrop is a waning star; that Goering and Goebbels hate each other;

2. The Countess of Jersey.

that Hess, the deputy leader of the party, is Hitler's favourite. There is talk, too, of a Hohenzollern, or perhaps Brunswick, restoration.

The games were boring today, and it was hot and dusty, so we returned early to Berlin, stopping to have tea with the Duke of Saxe-Coburg-Gotha,[3] a grandson of Queen Victoria, who is a fervent Nazi. He speaks English perfectly, was at Eton, and is, indeed, English. He was Duke of Albany, until he forfeited the title during the war, when he chose to remain German.

A different evening. We dined with a collection of young Berliners, plus Pat Jersey, at a small restaurant, and then went on the Bummel, flitting from Restaurant to café, all through the night. I was bored, but Honor was very amused and sat up till 6 a.m. She has great success with young Germans. I was interested to see the general gaiety of Berlin; the ugly city pulsates with life, and, it would seem, with money and prosperity.

The English pour in, and are jealous of one another's activities and privileges. That we are perhaps the most favoured is due to George von Wüssow, our German buddy. He is a strange man, Baltic by origin, not a member of the Nazi party, and yet beyond doubt Ribbentrop's most trusted agent. He has Berlin in his grasp, yet is un-German. He is gay and light in hand, but there is some mystery about him.

8 August

Harold Balfour and I walked about Berlin and passed Hitler's house in the Wilhemstrasse. No-one is allowed to walk immediately in front of it, and sentries motion one to cross to the other side of the street; there is always a crowd waiting in the hopes of seeing the Fuehrer. The guards, picked SS men, wear black breeches, unlike the Storm Troopers, who wear brown.

We lunched with Ribbentrop, in his Dalheim villa. It is small, but has a large dining room, attractively furnished with Biedermeier, and has a tennis court and a swimming bath. Ribbentrop seems genial, but gives the impression of being steel under all that suaveté. . . . She is tougher, browner, more German and looks more intelligent, and also controls the purse strings, being born

3. Brother of Princess Alice, Countess of Athlone.

Henkel. The lunch party was large and cosmopolitan, Potockis, Kemsleys, and Lady Chamberlain, looking sour and disapproving. She is on board the Kemsleys' yacht, as is also Sir Austen, but he refuses to put foot on German soil. . . . Luncheon was unendurably long and it was 3.30 before we escaped.

Dinner, again, was in a completely different milieu . . . with the Horstmanns in their house, 14 Tiergartenstrasse, over-full of glorious objets d'art, Meissen and bibelots. In my wife's honour, Freddie Horstmann had had the Bruhl swans put on the table, which was decked with water lilies . . . very beautiful. I was next to Countess Wilczek, who is half Spanish and the wife of the German Ambassador in Paris.

At the British Embassy reception, the Ambassadress, Lady Phipps's place was taken by her sister, Lady Vansittart. The Vansittarts are notoriously pro-French, and I hope their Berlin visit will go some way to neutralise their prejudice; I think it has. 'Van', talking to me at the Opera House banquet, admitted to being impressed by the Nazi régime, and the way it had transformed Berlin and rejuvenated the country. The Embassy reception was boring, crowded and inelegant.

10 August

Yesterday Fritzy[4] rang up to say that his mother, the Crown Princess, expected us to luncheon today, and we wondered what to wear for this royal engagement.

I thought that grey flannels would be appropriate for lunch in the country anywhere, but, on the whole, we decided black might be more correct and so black it was, with Harold Balfour and I in our House of Commons uniforms, and Honor beautifully dressed in semi-grand 'dayers'. Cecilienhof, which the Imperial family thinks looks very English, is a dreadful Lutyens sort of house, ugly and bogus Tudor, built just before the war. That it overlooks a lake is its only consolation. Fritzy met us and led us to the water's edge, where we found Princess Cécile, his second sister, an intelligent, half cross-eyed girl of eighteen, bathing with young Lord Jellicoe. The house inside is very royal with plush, palms, bareness, and faded, signed photographs of

4. Prince Friedrich of Prussia, the Kaiser's grandson. He subsequently married Lady Brigid Guinness.

dead monarchs. Fritzy showed us his mother's bath-cum-dressing room, which she has fitted up as a yacht, to remind her of Kiel, and we were laughing a little, when the door opened and the Crown Princess walked in, large, smiling and gracious. 'Thank you so much for all your kindness to my child', she said to the curtseying Honor. She looked very, very royal, with gold, jingling bracelets, large single pearl earrings, simple clothes and a Fabergé brooch. We filed in to luncheon in a large dining room and Honor was between the two princes, I on the right of the Crown Princess. She is indeed very much a Mecklenburg, that is, dark and rather Russian (she is a double first cousin of my adored Princess Nicholas, whose mother, the Grand Duchess Vladimir, was a Mecklenburg). All the Mecklenburgs have a frivolous outlook and are dark, charming and well-bred. Princess Marina, for instance. They all have a habit of talking in a slightly guttural voice, and their catch phrases are 'poor thing', 'do you find' and 'it makes me the impression'.

11 August

On our way back, driving up Unter den Linden, which was patrolled by khaki shirted storm troopers, our chauffeur said excitedly, 'Der Führer kommt'. Instantly, four black cars, filled with black uniformed protective police, rushed passed at terrific speed.

The Ribbentrop party. The Dalheim villa had been transformed into a scene of revelry. On arrival, we were received by ADC's and led up to the Ribbentrops, who were busy thanking people for their congratulations on his appointment as Ambassador to London. No-one quite knows why he has been selected. Is it because his power is waning? Have the machinations of his jealous colleagues led to this dignified banishment? Is it because London is considered so important a post that their best man had to be sent, or is it simply because there is no-one else? But, back to the party. We were presented with a catalogue of the guests, a thick pamphlet with our names inscribed, showing us where we sat at dinner, which was for six hundred people and served in an enormous marquee. . . . Honor was next to the Duke of Saxe-Coburg-Gotha and I was next to Lady Camrose.

After dinner, as the marquee was being noiselessly cleared,

we listened to some very good singing . . . perfection, and not too long. About midnight, the older people began to drift away, whilst the others returned to the marquee, where there was a band, dancing, a cocktail bar and much drink. Goering, his merry eyes twinkling, shook us both by the hand: he really is a most disarming man. Frau von Ribbentrop was simply dressed, unlike the other Nazi ladies. There were many English MPs present, and I talked, rather drunkenly, with Kenneth Lindsay.[5] . . . He is of some importance, being Civil Lord of the Admiralty. . . . We stayed at the party until three, and I enjoyed myself quite wildly. The lovely evening, the fantastic collection of notabilities, the strangeness of the situation, the excellence of the Ambassador's (or more correctly Frau von Ribbentrop's) champagne, all went somewhat to my head.

12 August *Berlin*

I cannot put the French Directoire and the Consulate from my mind, and am always seeing a parallel, no doubt a faulty one, between Nazi leaders and society and those French days of the 1790's. Will the parallel become more complete? Shall we live to see an Emperor too? I should not be surprised, but it will never be Hitler. He might, however, accept the Cromwellian title of Life Protector. It is known that he is not altogether deaf to the ambitions and rights of the deposed Hohenzollerns. . . .

This afternoon, Honor and I went for a long drive along the Hitlerstrasse, the magnificent new road which will one day lead from the Baltic to the Adriatic. We drove out to a fantastic water lift, a gigantic bit of engineering. It lifts three boats, full of people, 96 feet from the river to the canal. It is frightening, the solitary steel skeletons which lift a bit of the river. We watched the barges and pleasure steamers hoisted in the air and discharged with ease and rapidity into the canal 108 feet above . . .

A crowd watched us assemble at the Bristol. Were they pleased or sulky, looking at well-dressed 'elegants' going into dinner? Did they think it a return of the old régime? Berlin is still very crowded, and everyone goes to the Olympic Games all day: we pretend to, and don't, as they are very boring, except when Hitler arrives.

5. Independent National MP for Kilmarnock Burghs, 1933–45.

13 August

The Goering Party

I don't know how to describe this dazzling crowded function. We drove to the Ministerium in the centre of Berlin, and found its great gardens lit up and 700 or 800 guests gaping at the display and the splendour. Goering, wreathed in smiles and orders and decorations, received us gaily, his wife at his side. When he spied Honor he was especially genial; a table was reserved for us, with the Brunswick clan, Ernest August, in a green uniform, and the daughter Princess Frederika,[6] typically royal of another age with a marabou boa, and the Hamilton boys. Towards the end of dinner a corps de ballet danced in the moonlight: it was the loveliest coup-d'œil imaginable, and there were murmurs of delighted surprise from all the guests who agreed that Goering had indeed eclipsed Ribbentrop, which indeed we had been told had been his ambition. The end of the garden was in darkness, and suddenly, with no warning, it was flood-lit and a procession of white horses, donkeys and peasants appeared from nowhere, and we were led into an especially built Luna Park. It was fantastic, roundabouts, cafés with beer and champagne, peasants dancing and 'schuhplattling', vast women carrying pretzels and beer, a ship, a beerhouse, crowds of gay, laughing people, animals, a mixture of Luna Park and White Horse Inn, Old Heidelberg and the Trianon . . . Reinhardt could not have done it better. The music roared, the astonished guest wandered about. 'There has never been anything like this since the days of Louis Quatorze,' someone remarked, 'Not since Nero', I retorted, but actually it was more like the Fêtes of Claudius, but with the cruelty left out. . . . Goebbels, it appears, as well as Ribbentrop was in despair with jealousy. We wandered back into the gardens where we found dance floors had been laid and bands playing. Frau Goering asked if we would like to see the house, and eagerly we followed her indoors into the vast Ministerium where the Goerings live in theatrical magnificence. The rooms are all large and nearly empty, unimpressive except for their size; alone Goering's private study is interesting with his writing table and its collection of telephones and many outsize photographs. Every-

6. Afterwards Queen of Greece, and mother of King Constantine.

thing on the table is like Goering himself, too large, ostentatious and yet rather disarming. . . . Two large portraits also hang in this room, those of his wives, and there are flowers before his first wife's picture, as at a shrine. He adored her, and has built a fantastic tomb on his country estate. There is something un-Christian about Goering, a strong pagan streak, a touch of the arena, though perhaps, like many who are libidinous-minded like myself, he actually does very little. People say that he can be very hard and ruthless, as are all Nazis when occasion demands, but outwardly he seems all vanity and childish love of display.

15 August
I spent the morning with Philip of Hesse and we talked of how most of the royalties of Europe have a cockney accent acquired from English Nannies. At one moment English Nannies played a great rôle, and indeed directed the politics of Europe – and what a hash they made of it.

This evening was the Goebbels party, the last of the fantastic entertainments, and in a way the most impressive, though it lacked the elegance and chic of Ribbentrop's and the extravagance of Goering's. There were 2,000 people invited, and we drove out in a queue of cars, all excellently controlled by the police. Bridge and pontoons had been thrown across the water to an island, a former imperial possession. The arrangements were colossal and we were greeted by girls in theatrical uniforms (a vulgar touch) and the whole fête was, while larger, much less elegant than Goering's. At neither did the men dress, as the invitations read 'Sommerfest'. We were received by the slightly sinister Goebbels and his milder wife. Honor and I walked about for a little until we spied a table, and had dinner; at the end of which cannons roared and fireworks began on a scale which would have impressed the Romans, had they known about fireworks – perhaps they did. For half an hour the German Himmel blazed with coloured light, and the noise was deafening. When at last the fireworks were over, the skies were still light for some time before darkness dared to defy Goebbels and steal back again . . .

Berlin of all the cities I have ever known, next perhaps to New York in boom days, has the most stimmung and the least beauty.

16 August

Honor and I accompanied by Von Geyr went to the Stadium for the end of the Olympic Games and the crowds were enormous but really amazingly well-controlled. A long yet exciting afternoon followed. There was International Jumping and for hours we watched the competitors, saw the humiliation of England, in a field where she surely ought to excel, and witnessed the German and other countries' victories. For hours we watched the hurdle jumping; it was very exciting, even breathless, and it lasted until after dusk. As each horseman rode into the arena, he smartly saluted Hitler, who always lifted his hand in return. We saw him all the time in the distance and he seemed amiable and enjoying himself. At long last there were more processions, the orchestra played, Hitler rose, the great torch faded out, and the crowd, 140,000 strong, sang 'Deutschland über Alles', with arms uplifted. There was a shout, a speech or two, night fell and the Olympic Games, the great German display of power and bid for recognition, were over.

17 August

We tried to leave Berlin today, but every plane, every train, was full, and the roads are solid queues of departing motor cars.

10 September

[*Schloss St Martin, Im Innkreis, where the Channons had been staying.*]

Two telegrams from the King today that he cannot come here;[7] it seems that he is having daily treatment from the famous aurist Neuman for his increasing deafness. He is very deaf in one ear, and I cannot remember which one it is, but I think the left. Geordie Sutherland and Edward Stanley suffer from the same complaint. I am both disappointed and relieved that the Royal visit has not come off.

14 September

San Sebastian fell to the Insurgents yesterday, and it now definitely seems that the Red Government forces are losing

7. This was the result of a casual invitation earlier in the summer which had been provisionally accepted.

ground. But the tales of their fiendish cruelties are unbelievable . . . and yet, for a race brought up on bull-fighting, a race that invented the Inquisition, nothing can be too bad.

20 September

Harold Nicolson arrived, dear, sentimental, hard-working, gentle Harold, who is always a victim of his loyalties. He refused to go through Germany because of Nazi rule.[8] Lalli Horstmann[9] and Colin Davidson[10] came yesterday, so I am worn out with anti-Nazi discussions.

8. For Sir Harold's account of this visit, see *Diaries and Letters*, 272–3.

9. Wife of Frederick Horstmann, the German diplomatist. A determined opponent of the Nazis.

10. Lieutenant-Colonel C. K. Davidson, killed in action in 1943.

CHAPTER THREE

Politics and Preferment
January 1937–August 1938

Politics was increasingly fascinating Chips, and the House of Commons, which he had so disliked at first, quickly became to him what he called 'this smelly, tawny, male paradise'. His political views at this time might be best described as vehemently conventional. He had supported the Hoare-Laval Pact over Abyssinia, believed that the German and Italian dictators should be left alone, and was a supporter of Franco. Harold Nicolson records a conversation with him in September 1936, in which he said that 'we should let gallant little Germany glut her fill of the reds in the East and keep decadent France quiet while she does so. Otherwise we shall have not only reds in the West but bombs in London, Kelvedon and Southend . . .'[1]

In holding these views, Chips represented a substantial body of opinion in the Conservative Party and in London Society, against which a handful of Conservatives, dominated by Winston Churchill, and a few officials, notably Sir Robert Vansittart, struggled in vain. As the international scene became gradually more ominous and dangerous, these internal strains in the Conservative Party became more serious and acute. There was a two-year gap between the remilitarization of the Rhineland in March 1936 and Hitler's seizure of Austria in March 1938; during this period the Spanish Civil War flared up terribly, and led to the undisguised participation of Germany, Italy and Russia; the British policy of complete non-involvement was generally supported in the Conservative Party, but for a variety of reasons. Chips, like so many other Conservatives, ardently wanted a Franco victory.

Chips had identified himself so enthusiastically with the official attitudes of the Conservative Party that it was natural that he

1. Nicolson, op. cit., p. 273.

should be given an appointment of some kind, and thus he secured the post of Parliamentary Private Secretary to the Under-Secretary of State for Foreign Affairs (R. A. Butler) in March 1938 in the reshuffle of appointments caused by the resignations of Anthony Eden (Foreign Secretary) and Lord Cranborne (Under-Secretary) earlier that month in protest against the Prime Minister's attitude towards Mussolini. They were replaced by Lord Halifax and Butler.

Chips's account of his eagerness to secure this very minor political appointment has a certain engaging naïveté, and his undisguised joy when he achieved his ambition is both amusing and understandable. His actual influence on public affairs was small and he became an ardent – even fanatical – admirer of the Prime Minister and the foreign policy that the Chamberlain Government pursued. The interest of his account lies in the fact that, from this point, Chips becomes far better informed about contemporary events, and he gives a vivid and illuminating portrait of the prejudices and attitudes that lay behind the policy of Appeasement.

1937

23 January

After dinner with the Kents I went on to Venetia Montagu's and found Winston Churchill playing Bezique with Diana, while Duff played Rummy with Brendan Bracken and Venetia: How I loathe those games of chance. They were all very tense, dynamic. . . . I am beginning to dislike this milieu, though I stayed till 3 a.m. and drove the Coopers home.

26 January

In the House of Commons today old Ramsay Macdonald was quite inarticulate and inadequate at Question Time. He never smiles except when he is talking to an elder son, although he was once very pleasant to me on the day that our last Royal dinner party was described in the Press. Fatuous old snob, he is hated by all parties, and I don't know why the Government keep him on. His name doesn't guarantee us a single vote.

6 February

My son Paul is utterly adorable: he was brought to me in bed while I breakfasted and we had a romp with Bundi. I pray that he will be gentler and kinder to me than ever I was to either of my parents, neither of whom I liked a bit.

Later, I walked with Bundi in St James's Square to call upon my father-in-law, and came upon a levée, the first of the reign. I saw the Royal Procession emerge and I was interested to watch the public reaction to their new Monarch, who looked well and young and remarkably like Edward VIII. He also, I thought, looked lonely and wistful as all the males of this family do on State occasions. He bowed suddenly to the crowd's cheers which, I thought, seemed prompted more by good nature than by any real enthusiasm.

24 February

I lunched with Emerald and sat next to Lady Vansittart who told me much of Van's private mind. He was opposite, looking very gay and young. She told me that he had been much impressed by Berlin and the Nazi Government, and that on his return to London he had warmly advocated the surrender of some of our colonies to Germany, but had encountered tremendous opposition and realised that there was nothing to do. The Government has only two courses before it, to placate Germany, and give her some colonies, or to re-arm.

26 February

I had a large dinner party which started by the Granards proposing themselves, and as usual all day I went through agonies of apprehension lest I should be under-manned. But luckily no-one chucked, and dinner was magnificent. Lady Granard could scarcely walk for jewels and Winston Churchill was all amiability and smiles, his fat body shaking as he laughed. Perhaps my guests were a little too Edward VIII for the Granards? It was, I admit, a thoroughly 'Cavalier' collection. Lord Granard tactlessly attacked the late King and Mrs Simpson to his neighbour, Mrs Churchill, who turned on him and asked crushingly, 'If you feel that way, why did you invite Mrs Simpson to your house and put her on your right?' A long and embarrassed pause followed.

Bridge after dinner, except for Diana who took on Winston at Bezique. He had come up from Kent to attend the Speaker's evening party and was therefore covered with decorations, but he enjoyed himself so much chez moi that he remained until 12.30.

11 March

In the House of Commons this afternoon I saw Mr Baldwin sitting alone in the Chess Room absorbed in 'The Field.' And when, an hour later, I happened to return there, he was still reading it. He often sits alone in the window seat of this room and stares out at the river. He was not at his wife's 'At Home' this afternoon, which I dutifully attended.

14 March

People dined, including Lady Oxford, self-invited as usual. She wore a flowing black dress like a priest and was charmingly cassante, rude, dictatorial and magnificent. She is the cleverest woman I know and is a terrific character. I suppose she must be 75. Her crisp penetrating phrases are rivetting. This evening she played Bridge until 1.30 without a pause, passing judgment on everyone in politics and society the while.

16 March

This afternoon Duff presented his army estimates to the House and spoke for an hour and twenty-one minutes. He never wearied, never bored one and all-in-all it was a faultless performance. Yet I thought it empty, for all his brilliance of diction. His memory is magnificent, and people in this country often mistake feats of memory for intelligence. I personally don't think he will go much further. When he sat down I went up to the Gallery to find Diana who was with Lady Anglesey, Liz Paget and Venetia. Diana looked radiant and relieved and triumphant.

Austen Chamberlain has died suddenly this evening ... no blow for me, as I have always found him humourless and narrow-minded, with none of Neville's shy charm.

There must be rejoicing in Germany tonight that this desiccated patriarch, who played the Roman senator too long, is no more. He used to say that he loved France 'like a woman'.

Nevertheless I was saddened by how the House of Commons reacted to his death, for after all he has been a Member for forty years. People just shrugged their shoulders, saying 'It's not too good a seat'. 'He only held it by about forty in 1929'. Little more.

17 March

A real House of Commons day. We opened, after Questions, with a series of moving tributes to Austen Chamberlain and so eloquent was Mr Baldwin that I wondered whether I had got Austen wrong? But I believe his contemporaries, in their eloquence and loyalty, were stressing the achievements of his long ago youth. It was in his old age that I knew, and disapproved of him. I thought him humourless and rigid though never doubted his honesty and courage. But one incident disgusted me: I approached him one day in the Lobby here and asked his advice as to whether I should continue to be identified with the League of Nations at Southend in view of the fact that they had opposed me at the Election. He impressed upon me with ceremonious courtesy the necessity and urgency, of our continued support of that rickety organisation (the adjective is mine). He was himself on its Executive Committee etc., etc. So firm was he that I should follow his example and I, in my innocence was impressed. Three days later I was astonished to read in the press that he had resigned his office, and had relinquished all association with the League; but all the same, the tributes today moved the House extremely and Mr Baldwin was at his very best. It is the sort of thing that he does magnificently and he reduced many Members to actual tears. His closing sentence 'Austen has at last gone home' made us all think of the attendant's call 'Who goes home?' And Lloyd George, the old rascal, was rivetting with his rich reminiscences: he recalled how he remembered Austen's maiden speech forty-five years ago and how Mr Gladstone had gone up to old Joe Chamberlain and, complimenting him, said his son's speech was one to warm a father's heart. Mr Gladstone once served in the Duke of Wellington's administration! A link with time.

20 March

Tomorrow Honor, who has been away for a month, returns. Hurrah!

22 March

At the House of Commons, nothing much, except that I was startled to see Mr Baldwin and Winston drinking together, and alone in the Smoking Room; this is unheard of, and no one has seen them sitting together for ten years. Is it Baldwin's valedictory policy to be conciliatory to everyone, or is it a genuine reconciliation, or just mere chance? Churchill's stocks will now rise. They were like kittens in a basket, but they were certainly not drinking milk.

8 April

All day I sat in the stuffy Chamber in the hope of speaking, but the Speaker did not call me until 8, and by then, as the dreary hours dragged on, I lost all interest in what I was going to say, as I heard it all being said for me. The subject was 'Widows and Orphans' the Old Age Pensions Bill, a measure which affects Southend and its black-coated workers. At last I rose, and spoke, too hurriedly, to an empty House for 20 minutes. At midnight I went home, and found Honor awake and sweet.

9 April

The Duke of Windsor is to be married on either 30 or 31 May in France. If Honor and I are invited I think, on the whole, we should go. We shall be criticised for either course, for going or for staying away, but historically it will be interesting. Besides, I like and am sorry for both of them.

12 April — *House of Commons*

Oh, the House of Commons and its joys. Everyone was charming to me today and greeted me vigorously. How one's stock rises and falls in this most barometric of all buildings. My speech on Thursday seems to have been well received after all, and Baldwin smiled at me with one half of his face in the division lobby. His smiles are porcine but warm for all that.

13 April — *House of Commons*

At 12.30 a.m. I was walking in the lobby with Harold Balfour, who now never leaves my side, when Sir John Simon[2] came up to us and offered to give us 'breakfast', so we trooped into the dining room, and he ordered a magnum of champagne mixed with stout, what he called a 'Bismarck'. We then breakfasted merrily for an hour.

15 April

Yesterday they discussed Spain again. Why will the Opposition always prefer talking of every country save their own? Winston Churchill made a terrific speech, brilliant, convincing, unanswerable and his 'stock' has soared, and today people are buying 'Churchills', and saying once more that he ought to be in the government, and that it is too bad to keep so brilliant a man out of office; but were he to be given office, what would it mean? An explosion of foolishness after a short time? War with Germany? a seat for Randolph? Of course he gets on better with Neville Chamberlain than ever he did with Baldwin: at least there is no active dislike between the two great men.

The fashionable world, which I have ignored for a fortnight, now congregates, as it did in 1931, at Ciro's, where it has late supper and dances, surely a dullish occupation. Cannot they find something new to do? How I hate pleasure.

17 April

Diana and Duff have returned from Windsor, where they 'dined and slept'. Diana said it was all very different from the atmosphere at the Fort and the late régime. 'That was an operetta, this is an institution' she said.

18 April

A quiet day with my accounts and finances. . . . I find a new, unexpected joy at the age of nearly forty, in accumulating money and watching it grow.

20 April *Budget Day*

My second Budget, both of them Neville Chamberlain's. Of the two his first was decidedly the most popular. This one is too

2. The Home Secretary, former Foreign Secretary (1931–5), etc.

complicated and seems over the heads of the country, which doesn't understand it.

This is how it was introduced. After Questions, Neville came in and was cheered, and he smiled as he sat down next to Baldwin who, half scowling and half frowning as is his habit, 'shoved up' to make room for him. Then Neville rose and in an easy voice, and a quiet ingratiating manner, unrolled his accounts. He was undramatic, unspectacular, even jocular, as he juggled with our hopes and fears. The nation was prepared for the defence deficit and his announcement of another threepence on income tax was received with bored relief that it was not worse ... a little later after playing with us, as if he were an angler and the House of Commons a salmon he revealed his tax on increased profits, a measure which will lead to trouble, litigation and discussion, and probably modification. It was received in bewildered silence, except for a few Opposition cheers. Then he sat down, his sixth and least popular budget (but perhaps his canniest) introduced. The lobbies hummed, and it was not well received.

21 April

All day in Southend, and I half detected unpopularity; am I wrong? Is there a Socialist campaign against me? Are my pro-Franco remarks resented? But it will be a disaster for Conservatism if he is defeated by the forces of Communism and anarchy, which dominate the Madrid Government.

I do too much and yet want to crowd in more – ah, how much more, during the next 10 years. And then peace, perhaps Bradwell,[3] books, diaries and I hope some creative work among the roses.

22 to 23 April

I took Honor to a 'Pay Party' at Eric Dudley's new house – 14 Belgrave Square. ... The House of Commons, when I returned to it, was in an amused uproar and the late sitting began. Hour after hour passed. Aneurin Bevan,[4] the red-nosed publicity seeker, was suspended and the Speaker had to be fetched to do it.

3. A house in Essex – Bradwell-Juxta-Mare, afterwards bought by Tom Driberg, MP, and long coveted by Chips.

4. Labour MP for Ebbw Vale since 1929.

He was evidently asleep as it took 12 minutes for him to appear, bewigged and berobed. Meanwhile, we all sat making friendly conversation – a thing which would have been impossible anywhere else in the world. We all knew that Bevan had only called Sir Dennis Herbert 'abominable' in order to be suspended, and to get the most of the notoriety, which he loves. He was well aware that we saw through his scheme and were indifferent to it.

27 April

I lunched with the Warrenders to meet Count Grandi and the Ambassadress. After lunch, Leslie Hore-Belisha, most tactlessly, told Grandi that he'd been prevented by Anthony Eden from going to Italy at Easter, because of the strained relations. Suddenly Leslie became 'the Jew boy', bungling and self-important, and talked of what he would do when he was Prime Minister, etc. I am fond of him but today I was embarrassed. Grandi remained all smiles, all charm throughout.

28 April

I lunched with Colebox – a pleasant party, with George Gage, Gerry Wellesley, David Cecil[5] and the Guinnesses. . . . They talked of a country house, Kelvedon Hall, near Kelvedon Hatch. I am intrigued about it and shall look at it. Will it prove only one more dream to toy with for a few weeks and then discard, from inertia?

2 May

Honor returned this evening and we discussed Kelvedon. She seems bitten by the idea. Nor is she put off by the story of the strange nuns who have inhabited it. The Superior is a Miss Dalton, who must be half mad. She is a tyrant, given to moods and mental excesses. For a time she had a flock of 17 nuns under her, 'Benedictine oblates' they were called. But the Roman Church has denied all relations with them, although for some years a Roman Catholic Priest was paid £2 a week to go to administer religious instruction to the unhappy females. But the money soon ran out and the Order became impoverished, so they took in mental patients, 'borderline cases' and the like, and lived on the proceeds. But trouble overcame them again. One nun, the

5. Lord David Cecil.

gardener told me, and he knew her well, was so unhappy that she drowned herself in the lake, after threatening many times to do so. And two years ago there was a serious scandal, for one of the patients, a perfectly sane woman, jumped out of the window and was found dead. A few hours before, earlier in the night, she had escaped, in her nightdress (as the nuns had hidden all her clothes) to a nearby farmer's house. He had led her back in tears to the nuns who locked her up. She then killed herself.

One feels these tragedies at Kelvedon, but when I entered the house I was overcome at once by its beauty. It is the interior that is so perfect. Somehow I see myself living there.

3 May

In the early heat, Honor and I motored to Kelvedon and at first she was pro it, wanted it, but as we sat over our picnic lunch her mood changed, and she argued against it. Now I do not quite know what the situation is, or what will happen.

4 May

Lady Iveagh is pro-Kelvedon. I hope Honor will be influenced by her . . .

We were half dreading dining with Sybil Colefax in Lord North Street, though I must say, she has made her little house very charming and cosy. She was dressed like a Winterhalter and told us it was her first dinner party. It proved to be surprisingly agreeable. Present: Winston and Clemmie Churchill (who looks young and well), Harold Nicolson, affectionate, smug and pernickety, Diana and Duff, Barbie Wallace, two Americans, one the head of Morgans, and a Mr Knickerbocker, a redder, wronger, noisier Brendan. He has recently returned from Spain, where for 9 months he reported from Franco's Headquarters. He was dreadful, I thought. He gave us a jaundiced picture of the Spanish War, but he had been falsely imprisoned for 24 hours through a mistake and perhaps the incident prejudiced him. Winston Churchill, gay and plump, gave us a dramatic 10-minutes account of the horrors that are taking place, and how all the original motives of the war have long been obscured in the general ghastliness and barbarity . . .

Winston was charming to me, called me now Channon, now

Chips. My hostess concentrated on me until the arrival of Daisy Fellowes, as exotic as ever, and escorted by Tom Mitford; 'How are your delectable sisters, Tom?' Winston asked. Someone suggested going on to the Londonderry House Reception, but Winston said 'I'm staying here; so that pre-eminently Conservative Party function will lack the lustre of its most brilliant jewel'. He talked, too, of the House of Commons, and said that he was really the leader of the Opposition as the Labour people are so ineffectual, weak and uneducated. And that an uneducated opposition was always powerless. After dinner there ensued a long Windsor argument and — was sickening and unoriginal. He, too, was snubbed successfully by Winston, who remains pro-Windsor to the end.

6 May

Honor, Gerry Wellesley and I went to Kelvedon this morning. We motored about, picnicked in the hot sun as we discussed the house and the whole proposition. Will I now be a country squire?

7 May

At 12.30 I drove to Westminster Hall for the enormous luncheon arranged by the Empire Parliamentary Association in honour of the Dominion Prime Ministers. The old Hall was warmed for the occasion, and there were about 100 tables, and a bustle of activity which seemed curious in the hallowed Hall, which is usually so still. Soon Trumpeters in new liveries blew on silver bugles to announce the arrival of the King. He walked alone, a trifle awkwardly, but not without charm, and we watched the great dignitaries being presented to him. Then luncheon, after Grace was said by that old Humbug of Canterbury, began. A short meal, but the spectacle was brilliant: 700 men in morning clothes, and a few Socialists in flannels.... Then Hailsham stood, proposed His Majesty's Health, and the King rose, the amplifier was put in front of him, and for a few terrible seconds there was dead silence, as he could not (that is his trouble and failing) get the words out. A feeling of uneasiness came over the crowd; but soon the King, controlling himself, read out a short speech of thanks. As he went on he seemed to warm up, and finished in good style, and sat down amidst great applause and relief.

This evening I thought of the grave, grey Speaker of the House of Commons and his dignified address to the assembled Delegates, and the King, faltering, with his halting speech and resigned kindly smile, and everyone pretending that he had done it well.

11 May *Coronation Eve*

London is in its finest clothes and the decorations are gay but not impressive, but the excitement and the crowds increase, and the régime seems overnight popular.

This evening came a message that our offer of £5,000 for Kelvedon has been accepted. So now I am a Squire of Essex and shall probably gravitate more and more towards a country life.

We went to bed at 10 to prepare for tomorrow, the great day.

12 May

At 5.30 the Lord and Lady of Kelvedon woke, thrilled and eager to get to the Abbey, and as I dressed I thought, not only of the approaching ceremony but of Kelvedon: shall I one day take its name? Lord Westover[6] of Kelvedon? Ten years in the Whips' Office might do it, I think. But shall I ever get there? . . .

My baby boy, sleepy but laughing, was brought down to my room to watch his father get into his finery, my velvet Court suit. Honor looked splendid in grey, all her sapphires and diamond tiara. Will Paul remember us, togged in our finery, as we stooped to kiss him?

At exactly 7 o'clock we stepped into the car, and already a crowd had gathered, and they cheered us. Soon we were in a stream of cars all proceeding towards the Abbey: they were wonderful to watch. Some contained friends, the Warrenders, the Marlboroughs, some funny Peers and vast frumpy Peeresses, unknowns, in fact the world and his wife driving off. . . . Everyone was laughing and gay and the thin crowds cheered the few State coaches – I counted only three.

At 7.30 we arrived at the Poet's Corner Door, one hour too soon, so we crossed over to the Commons, and meeting the

6. Chips's mother's maiden name was Westover.

Willoughby d'Eresbys joined them for breakfast. Much chaff as to the possible bladder complications, if we ate or drank too much. Then we returned to the Abbey at 8.30 and found it already filling up. We were conducted by a Gold Staff Officer to seats in the South Transept, where we sat immediately behind the Viscounts and Barons.

The panorama was splendid, and we felt we were sitting in a frame, for the built-up stands suggested Ascot, or perhaps – more romantically – the tournaments of mediaeval days; the chairs were covered with blue velvet; the church atmosphere, I fear, had completely gone; we had an excellent view and we settled down to wait. I looked about me; on all sides were MPs I knew and their be-plumed, be-veiled, be-jewelled wives. Some were resplendent but my Honor stood out. The Peeresses began to take their places, the Duchesses in front, and in front of them the four of their Order who had been chosen to hold the canopy, Mollie Buccleuch, Kakoo Rutland, Mary Roxburghe and Lavinia Norfolk. My mother-in-law, on the Countesses' bench, looked magnificent as her glorious diamond riviere made a circle of blazing light. It sparkled as she moved . . . the North Transept was a vitrine of bosoms and jewels and bobbing tiaras. I recognised many, Eileen Sutherland, Loelia Westminster wearing a heavy necklace of rubies. In the 'theatre', half-way between the two transepts, stood the two thrones, whilst facing the altar was St Edward's chair. There was an excited pause, then a hush as the regalia was carried in and then out again. Then again half an hour to wait, and I went out to prowl, and gossip with friends. The lavatory arrangements were excellent 'Peeresses' – 'Peers' 'Gentlemen', and several of these three orders were smoking cigarettes on the outer built-up balcony. I talked to Vansittart, very dashing in his robes; Winston Churchill, Duff and Diana Cooper and others. Soon the processions began: the foreign Royalties and their suites; our own tuppenny Royalties, i.e. the Carisbrookes, Mountbattens, Carnegies, etc. Then, a pause. And I looked about again, dazzled by the red, the gilt, the gold, the grandeur. After a little the real Royalties arrived, the Princess Royal looking cross, the tiny Princesses excited by their coronets and trains, and the two Royal Duchesses looking staggering. The Duchess of Gloucester looked so lovely that for a moment I thought she was Princess Marina. Another pause, till the gaunt Queen of Norway appeared, followed by Queen Mary, ablaze, regal and over-powering. Then the Queen's procession, and she appeared, dignified but smiling and much more bosomy. Then, so surrounded by dignitaries carrying wands, sceptres, orbs and staffs, as to be overshadowed, George VI himself. He carried himself well. The Peers clustered around him, Lord Zetland, Honor's uncle Halifax, others. And soon the long ceremony began: it seemed endless, and the old Archbishop intoned in his impressive clear voice that was heard so well over the amplifiers. The ceremonies were complicated, but thanks to the books which we found on our seats we could follow the Service with ease. After communion the King resumed St Edward's Chair and we watched him as he undressed and the Canopy carried by 4 Knights of the Garter was held over him. Then he was anointed. Then the homage of the Peers, led by the Archbishop, with all the other Bishops kneeling in a row, looking like a Gentile Bellini. Opposite me, near the throne, sat the 8 representatives of the Free Churches, like crows at a Feast, in their drab 'Elders of the Kirk' black cloth. They looked so glum and disapproving that they reminded me of the present Government as it sat decreeing the Abdication, relentless, perhaps right, but forbidding.... The sun shone through the windows and the King looked boyish suddenly. Then it was the Queen's turn, and followed by her train-bearers, 'Liz' Paget, Ursula Manners and two others, she advanced towards the altar. Once again the Golden Canopy was brought forward, and for a brief moment the four Duchesses held it over her. The second Service was shorter and soon she mounted her throne. And my thoughts travelled back to the old days when I called her 'Elizabeth' and was a little in love with her.

What a happy group we were: – Paul, now Regent of Yugoslavia, Gage and me, The Queen, others, almost all of whom have reached positions of importance and power.... The end of the Service was long, too much of the Archbishop, too little of the Sovereigns; and Honor complained of feeling ill. The heat and airlessness were indeed overpowering. Then at last the procession formed up, and we watched, spellbound, as it uncurled and slowly progressed down the nave. With Hailsham looking, as he invariably does, like a Gilbert and Sullivan Lord Chancellor in his robes and his wig, and Ramsay MacDonald, old hypocrite, who, as Lord President of the Council, had stood almost behind the throne throughout the Service, the Archbishop and others. I wondered what were Queen Mary's thoughts as she swept out? Personally I believe she is a worldly old girl; certainly she and the Court group hate Wallis Simpson to the point of hysteria, and are taking up the wrong attitude: why persecute her now that all is over? Why not let the Duke of Windsor, who has given up so much, be happy? They would be better advised to be civil if it is beyond their courage to be cordial. . . . There was a long wait after the Royalties and processions left, and impatience broke out. Chocolates were munched, and flasks slyly produced; I tried to remember the great moments of the ceremony: I think the shaft of sunlight, catching the King's golden tunic as he sat for the crowning; the kneeling Bishops drawn up like a flight of geese in deploy position; and then the loveliest moment of all, the swirl when the Peeresses put on their coronets: a thousand white gloved arms, sparkling with jewels, lifting their tiny coronets. By now there was much general chaff and when one of the Gold Staff Officers lost his sense of humour, and called 'I say, a Baron has got out before the Viscounts', there was a roar of laughter.

The few Socialists and their wives seemed subdued and impressed by the ancient Service and the grandeur of the feudal capitalistic show. One of them remarked to me, 'Why should we sit behind these Peer Johnnies?' 'It's their show, after all. You are lucky to be here at all' I answered, and he stopped smiling . . .

At home, at 7.45, friends began to arrive, Winston with his wife and youngest daughter Mary; Coopers, Eric Dudley, Jim Wedderburn, others. We listened to Mr Baldwin on the wireless and then to the King, who was adequate, and everyone said 'well done', and the party became riotous. Duff held Brigid Guinness' hand, Winston held forth, champagne flowed, people came in. The party was too hilarious to go out into the wet streets but now and then one heard the hurrahs of the soaked crowds cheering outside Buckingham Palace. At 1.30 our guests left, and Honor with some of them went to a night-club. Then Emerald arrived with Thomas Beecham and the Birkenheads and Basil

Dufferin and we sat up until the dawn, a bit tight, drinking and talking.

I must really try and be a Peer before the next Coronation.

18 May

The Sutherlands' Ball. A dazzling night. Honor looked magnificent with all her sapphires, tiara and a resplendent blue brocade number made to match the Amalienburg and we were hardly dressed and down before that brace of princelings, Ernst August of Hanover, and Fritzy of Prussia, very young, fair and Nordic and dripping with decorations, arrived almost too punctually. Soon after nine we swept into dinner, and the dining room was a gorgeous, glittering sight of jewels shimmering in the candlelight, of Meissen china, of decorations and splendour. Mrs Greville was delighted to be next to the young Prince of Prussia and there was great stimmung and excitement. At 10.45 Honor and I with Ernst August, jumped into our car, and armed with a special white card we drove to the Royal entrance – rather to everyone's annoyance, at Hampden House. The Ball was the best spectacle so far of the summer; we were ushered into an improvised ballroom hung with tapestries, with, at one end, an enormous dais of red baize where all the Royalties of the earth seemed congregated. We had barely arrived when the King and Queen entered with the Sutherlands. All four were gay, smiling and impressive, and I noticed how both the King and Queen have gained greatly in presence and dignity. They went up to the queue of Royalties and greeted them all, kissing many. The Queen was in white, with an ugly spiked tiara, and she showed no sign of her supposed pregnancy, which I am beginning to doubt. The King followed her, showing his teeth. Queen Mary was in icy blue; soon the ball began. Honor and I were dancing near the dais when we caught Queen Mary's eye, and we stopped to curtsey and bow as she held out her hand. Then Honor and I became separated and I danced with Lady Iveagh. Later I danced with Alice Hofmannsthal, and we went up on the dais to talk to Princess Olga who was wearing her mother's ruby parure. We chatted with her for a few minutes, and as we turned we saw the King and Queen coming up to us, and they very smilingly talked to us. Both Alice and I were thrilled, which was unreasonable as we have both known them for years, and at one time intimately. Having talked to the two Queens I decided to enjoy the remainder of the evening. I watched one dark vivacious woman, rather like the Brazilian Ambassadress, with a touch of the Begum Aga Khan, go up to Queen Mary and chat amicably with her but she did not curtsey. I was surprised until I was told she was the Queen of Egypt[7] who has only recently emerged from purdah, but long enough to have become very dashing and elegant. The ballroom was never crowded; it was cool and spacious and when the Royalties processed into supper, forming a formidable crocodile of Crowned Heads there were very few people left . . . Music, champagne. . . . Their Majesties were given a cheer when they drove away but a yet more rousing one was given to Queen Mary by the waiting crowd. I stayed on and on, and in the dawn had breakfast with Eileen Sutherland, the tired but triumphant hostess. The whole evening was an exalted success; both our dinner, and the ball.

19 May

We lunched with Eleanor Smith – unpunctual, untidy, and vivacious; her sister Pam,[8] pregnant, luscious and original; and their mother, Margaret Birkenhead, at the Embassy. They all attacked the Archbishop of Canterbury, deplored the present persecution of the Duke of Windsor, and were as gay and provocative and quick as ever.

20 May *H.M.S. 'Cameronia'*

We left London early this morning and came to Southampton in the Special Train, the guests of the Admiralty, and came on board where we had many cocktails at Government expense. We were asked to sign chits and I persuaded everyone to sign 'Nancy Astor' and 'Victor Cazalet', those two famous teetotallers. The battleships, hundreds of them, lined up as the Victoria and Albert floated between them, were an impressive sight, and the foreign representatives must have realised that England is mighty still. In the evening there were fireworks, but these, after Goebbels' last year in Berlin, were very tame.

7. Nazli, mother of King Farouk.
8. Lady Pamela Berry, now Lady Hartwell.

21 May *Newton Ferrers, Callington, Cornwall*

In lovely weather we motored here from Southampton. On the way we came to a sign-post marked 'Ottery St Mary 2 miles', and I remembered that here was the cradle of the Channons, so we turned down a lane and drove into the small village where Coleridge lived, and where my ancestors came from. My great-grandfather and his wife, a Miss Blackmore, were both born in Ottery St Mary, and emigrated soon after their marriage to Bridgwater in Somerset where my grandfather was born. I wondered whether we should find any family tombstones – and the small grave-yard was full of them; Watkins, Thomases, others, half a dozen Channons! The church is one of the loveliest in England, and I talked to the Verger wondering whether he might even be a cousin! I was thrilled to think that my forebears came from so lovely a spot.

24 May

A fullish day. At 10 o'clock the Regent fetched me at Belgrave Square, and we shopped and gossiped as of old. . . . In the afternoon he gave audiences to Neville Chamberlain, Delbos and others, while I returned to the House of Commons in a gay and happy mood, almost enchanted to get back to this club which I adore, this smelly, tawny, male paradise. I found the House buzzing with reshuffle rumours. The Smoking Room, where the various chances of promotion for the Junior Ministers were being discussed, was more thrilling than the debate on the Civil List in the Chamber, where Winston Churchill made a stirring speech in support of the Monarchy . . .[9]

In the evening there was a stupendous dinner party at Mrs Greville's. The hostess presenting all her 40 guests individually to the fat King of Egypt,[10] who is young and clumsy and continually stepping on his mother, Queen Nazli's train . . . Music played, tiaras nodded, Lady Willingdon dragooned everyone. A really splendid party – one of the most amusing I have ever attended. I was pleased to have had a reconciliation with Edwina and Dickie Mountbatten, who have been cold to me for years.

9. In the debate on the new Civil List.
10. King Farouk.

27 May

I lunched hilariously with the Coopers, and talked about last night. Duff goes soon to the Admiralty, though neither Diana nor he will admit it, while Leslie Hore-Belisha tomorrow becomes War Minister . . .

Tremendous excitement in the lobbies today re the reshuffle, and I have the complete new Cabinet list made out.

28 May *Mereworth Castle*

The great Baldwin reign has drawn to a magnificent and splendid end; this morning at 9.30 he was received by the King who accepted his resignation as Prime Minister, created him an Earl and conferred the Garter on him. Mrs Baldwin, and her homely comic qualities will long be recalled, is made a D.B.E. J. C. Davidson, Baldwin's henchman for many years, is now a Viscount, as is Mr Runciman. So three front benchers will be seen no more. Ramsay MacDonald remains in the House, but has refused any honour hereditary or otherwise.

The sensation of the reshuffle is sending Leslie Belisha to the War Office, which is a staggering appointment and will make or mar his career. Personally, I think he will be successful. His flamboyant personality, his application, his unstinting energy ought to help him and, after all, even if he is a failure, we can cart him, for he is not Conservative, whereas Duff Cooper is. For me the Cooper change is even more startling. Duff, translated to the Admiralty has been both promoted and rebuked. He now commands the Senior Service, has risen in rank, and yet he must be aware that his advancement is due to his failure at the War Office.

A lovely green and blue English evening at Mereworth with champagne under the Palladian portico, well dressed women, ease and well-being, and now a brand new Government.

31 May *Back in London*

A full emotional day. The Conservative meeting took place at noon at Caxton Hall to elect the new leader. Never was there a political meeting so peaceful, so dignified, or so elegant. The MPs, the peers, the prospective candidate and a few others filed in (all the wealth and grandeur of England) and took their places whilst on the platform were gathered the 'Inner Circle' of politics looking like a picture by Franz Hals. Lord Halifax, dignified, ecclesiastic and magnificent, presided. He paid tribute to Mr Baldwin and then called upon Lord Fitzalan to move a resolution which was duly seconded by Sir John Gilmour. Never have praises been so lavished on a man. Then it was moved, with humorous eloquence by Lord Derby to elect Neville Chamberlain as the new leader; Winston Churchill in an able, fiery speech not untouched by bitterness, seconded the resolution, which was overwhelmingly received. The Chamberlains then appeared together, he smiling and in a grey morning coat and she looking twenty years younger in a blue hat which I remember Mrs Simpson wearing. They were led, much touched obviously by the warmth of their reception, by David Margesson on to the platform. Neville spoke movingly and referred to 'the lady at his side' in the best approved George V manner. They had a thunderous welcome and he seemed all the things he is supposed not to be, warm, gentle and even sentimental. He joined in the praises of Baldwin, and the meeting broke up . . .

1 June

This afternoon at the House Winston delivered a philippic, against Mr Chamberlain's N.D.C.,[11] that misguided tax which has failed to please anyone except Gallacher the comic Communist.[12] When the Prime Minister rose to reply, he referred to Winston as his Right Honourable uncle, and conceded that he would withdraw his tax and substitute another. There were cheers and general relief, only Gallacher shouted 'you've thrown me over'. But the House scattered for dinner in a happier mood.

3 June

The Windsor wedding has taken place in a foreign country mid a blaze of publicity and rather cracked trumpets, and the photograps of him and Wallis show an animated ecstatic pair. Reaction here, however, is setting in and people are angrily demanding why

11. National Defence Contribution. It was regarded at the time as one of Churchill's most witty and effective speeches.
12. Communist MP for Fife West, 1935–50.

he should be so snubbed? And the House of Commons is embarrassed and feels guilty . . .

The present King and Queen are popular, very, and increasingly so, but they have no message for the Labour Party who believe them, and rightly I fear, to be but the puppets of a Palace clique. Certainly, they are too hemmed in by the territorial aristocracy, and have all the faults and virtues which Edward VIII lacked in this particular field. Still, it is the aristocracy which still rules England although nobody seems to believe it.

When I got home I found a telegram from the Duke of Windsor saying 'Many thanks for your good wishes. We shall write when we get the present. Edward'. It must have been sent directly after the Service as it arrived at 4 o'clock and is dated Tours.

4 June

Almost every newspaper last night and again this morning has run a leader of good wishes to the Duke of Windsor. 'The Times' however, refrained. It is of course an organ of the Archbishop and he is a power behind it. I think it is disgraceful. The treatment of the Duke of Windsor by the present Government has hurt the institution of royalty far more than ever the Duke of Windsor did himself by his abdication. The Royal Family should be kept sacrosanct, and not turned into puppets.

We lunched with the Ribbentrops, a curious hotch-potch of semi-royalties. . . . We sat about the modern table, drank a great deal, including champagne, and ate ice-cream made of lobster. Ribbentrop has improved in manners and health, and the huge Embassy is impressive by sheer size but is far from beautiful. Luckily they left the frescoes by Watts in the dining room of what was the Marlboroughs' house, untouched. Indeed they have even uncovered bits that were unknown.

6 June

I was having tea with Harold Balfour on the terrace of the House of Commons when Dunglass[13] came up to us and asked us

13. Conservative MP for South Lanark since 1931; Parliamentary Private Secretary to the Prime Minister, 1937–9. Succeeded as 14th Earl of Home, 1951; Foreign Secretary, 1960–63; disclaimed title October 1963; Prime Minister (as Sir Alec Douglas-Home), 1963–4.

if possible to be in the Smoking Room about nine as Neville 'was going to look in' and was 'nervous as any debutante' going to her first party. So the Smoking Room had to be made to look normal and natural for the Prime Minister. I was reminded of the tours that Potemkin arranged for Catherine the Great. It is part of the Prime Minister's business to be pleasant and genial with back-benchers, and occasional attendance in the smoking room is an essential feature of the programme. Baldwin came sometimes, but only rarely, and then he usually read 'The Field' in a lonely corner in the Chess room. Winston Churchill told me once some years ago that he once went into the small lobby w.c. where there are only two pissoirs. To his embarrassment one was already occupied by the Prime Minister. It was too late to retreat as he had been seen and so in he went. Baldwin was silent, but as he did up his trousers he turned to Churchill and remarked 'I am glad that there is still one common platform upon which we can still meet' and walked away. Winston tells the story with a wealth of gesture.

I love the House of Commons so passionately that were I offered a peerage I should be tempted to refuse it – only tempted of course.

8 June

Honor has an axis with the new Neptune, i.e. Duff Cooper and this morning she sent him a handsome present of a pair of library steps with dolphins on the legs. 'A step up for Duff' she wrote.

In the evening, Cecil Beaton came in, in a rollicking mood, and he regaled us with anecdotes of the Windsor wedding. He spent the day before the wedding with Wallis and the Duke helping them to arrange the improvised altar which the unexpected arrival of that hero the Reverend Jardine at Château de Candé necessitated. Cecil repeated that the Duke, although much hurt and wounded by the absence of his relations and former friends, was nevertheless, increasingly besotted with love. He entered into every detail of the arrangements with care and vitality, causing confusion indescribable. Cecil took many photographs of them both in their wedding clothes, which, tempting misfortune, they donned the day before, and left the evening before the ceremony. He showed us some of the pictures he had done, and charming they were. He had been sorry for the couple, attendri towards the Duke, both amused and disgusted by the milieu Bedaux-Rogers. When Cecil left us, he went next door to the Kents to show them the photographs too.

10 June

I have a feeling of temporary unpopularity as if the social arrows were turned against me. Why? Perhaps a few people are jealous. I know I inspire jealousy just as I do loyalty, and after every coup, such as entertaining royalty or buying Kelvedon, I always sense a bit of a backwash. Honor is supremely oblivious and indifferent, and I much admire her patrician hauteur. I am more susceptible.

13 June *West House, Bognor*

Lady Oxford came to call before luncheon and was in a caustic mood.... We sat in the garden and discussed the Government. Lady Oxford, staring at Duff, remarked 'the new Government is pure Lewis Carroll' and continued 'there is not one good appointment, and Mr Belisha at the War Office is sheer "Alice in Wonderland" '.

16 June *House of Commons*

I laughed aloud when I read that Princess Juliana of Holland had herself made a public announcement that she is pregnant. 'People are becoming too intimate these days', I laughingly remarked to the Socialist Pritt[14] who happened to be by me. 'I so disapprove of Royalty and everything connected with it that I am completely uninterested in their trivialities' he retorted, and I was left standing rather stupidly and speechless!

17 June

Sir James Barrie lies a-dying. I have always disliked the little man and thought him boorish and petulant. He allowed himself to be spoilt and made too much of by the Wemyss family. I always thought him hopelessly undistinguished, and his literary gifts were few though he did add Peter Pan and a few other characters to our literature. In early youth I used to stay often

14. D. N. Pritt, K.C., Labour MP for North Hammersmith since 1935.

with the Wemyss family at Stanway, and Barrie was usually there.

22 June

At the Buckingham Garden Party Honor and I successfully avoided all the royalties, and when we saw Queen Mary looking like the Jungfrau, white and sparkling in the sun, bearing down upon us, we bolted.

23 June *Oxford, Christ Church*

In the afternoon I drove to Oxford. The beautiful long drive is shortened now by by-passes and excellent roads. I found Oxford as glamorous and welcoming as ever, like a friendly mushroom, and I went at once to the room assigned to me in Peck Quad, which has been turfed and re-faced and seems much larger. At 7.30, as Tom was striking, we assembled in Tom Quad, a hundred or more dons, M.A.'s, Canons, etc., all in gowns and robes, and the crocodile procession, wended its dignified way up the vaulted staircase and into the big hall. There was good food, fine wine and the many pictures which had recently been re-hung, glowed in the candle light. I chatted with my neighbour who asked me if I recalled old Owen who was senior censor in 1919 when I went up. 'Yes', I said, 'Poor old boy, how long has he been dead, ten or twelve years it must be?' 'He is sitting almost opposite you now' was the retort, and sure enough, there he was, no older and no redder than he was eighteen years ago. He must be nearly ninety now. It is surprising how dampness and port keep one young. Dons live for ever. As a general rule it is considered that it is the old ladies of London, the rival hostesses, who are most malicious about one another but after listening to some of the conversation of the Oxford dons at tonight's dinner I must admit the old ladies in trousers and gowns far surpass the ladies of London in malice at one another's expense, but it is done so exquisitely that it becomes a work of art.

Tonight Roy Harrod[15] looking more than usually 'Ming' had a few quips about Professor Lindemann,[16] who all Oxford loathes.

15. The distinguished economist.

16. Professor of Experimental Philosophy at Oxford since 1919; an intimate friend of, and adviser to, Churchill. Later Lord Cherwell.

After speeches, we rose and I was suddenly alone. I could not face a night of carousal in a don's room, and so fled into the night. For two hours nearly I walked about like a ghost. The quads were flooded with moonlight, and I retraced my steps until I began to think I was myself, or my own ghost, or rather the ghost of my dead youth and remembered dear dead days and thought of poor Ivo Grenfell, his great Herculean frame rotting now in a Taplow grave, then of Paul reigning over millions of people in the Balkans, of George Gage and of others. The four years that I was at Oxford seem to have flashed by me, and I have hardly ever recalled a moment of them until tonight but tonight they came back, flooding my mind and directing my footsteps. I looked for 4 Broad Street, that lovely panelled house, but found it has been demolished. I walked to Micklem now so altered, passed by 12 King Edward Street and thought how dingy it looked. I even remembered the name of my barber who I have not thought of since 1922. At last, worn out, I went back to Peck, and to my room and I wondered how ever I withstood the discomfort of University life for so long. My bed was like a sack yet I soon fell asleep and woke only once when I couldn't quite remember where I was, was I back at Oxford? Had I ever left, were my Honor and my bonny baby boy, Belgrave Square and my myriad millions, all of a dream? Was I really an MP? I was not sure what or where I really was, but soon dozed again in the uncomfortable bed. At 7.30 I was called, hurriedly shaved in cold water and of course had no bath, then donning my gown, attended prayers in Chapel. The beauty of the language and the cool calm cathedral impressed me and I liked sitting in the stalls. Then, after a hearty breakfast with Godfrey Nicholson, MP and Roy Harrod, I went for a walk, and an old gentleman in the street asked me to direct him to Lincoln; so perhaps I do not look so old after all.

Driving back to London I resolved to begin a campaign to reconcile myself to all my enemies: but it will probably take me longer than it did to make them.

25 June, Friday

I rose late, and then came to the House in time to hear the Prime Minister who made an excellent impression. He seemed so calm, and yet so sensible and determined, as he proclaimed our desire to be at peace, and to be friends with everyone, particularly Germany. Anthony Eden wound up, and rose, looking fatigued and fashionable in his pale grey clothes. He spoke well, repeating our determination to remain neutral, etc. But he seemed exhausted. Later in the Lobby I pressed his arm 'You were wonderful' I said, 'Thank you Chips' and he smiled his famous tired smile. He is sometimes very disarming, very endearing, and his sartorial splendour makes every one else look shoddy.

27 June

We spent all day at Kelvedon, every day I like the house better and shall soon love it. But shall I ever quite overcome the slight frisson that I get whenever I enter it. Is it so very haunted? Its atmosphere is almost overpowering.

12 July

At 6 o'clock, six MP's including myself were received by the Prime Minister in his private room at the House of Commons. He breezily motioned us to our seats, and we put our case before him, namely, that our constituencies are growing so fast and that they made so many demands on our time and purses that we would like them split up. We showed the injustice of the present arrangement whereby the Socialists have more members than they ought, since 44 out of 48 of the larger seats in England are held by us. He listened to us gravely and patiently, his onyx eyes sparkling and his small features smiling. Then he spoke for ten minutes repeating our arguments in clearer language. He admitted that we had an unanswerable case, but he doubted the wisdom of tampering with the electorate lest political capital be made by our opponents. He has a way of leaving one in doubt as to his intentions, and I suspect that he will turn down our proposal.

15 July

Exhausted socially and mentally I slept for two hours this afternoon in the Library of the House of Commons! A deep House of Commons sleep. There is no sleep to compare with it – rich, deep, and guilty.

19 July

An all-star performance at the House of Commons. A full dress debate on Foreign Affairs was opened by Anthony Eden, who was forceful but not engaging. Then Winston spoke dramatically, and made a startling announcement that there were twelve-inch Howitzers trained on Gibraltar. The effect was electrifying, and the House was stirred and suddenly less pro-Franco but Winston's authority turned out to be Master Randolph and so the House was merely amused.

I dined at the Carlton Club with Ralph Asheton and Harold Balfour and was impressed by the dignified room, the pictures and the plate. We sat at the MPs' table. I must frequent this club more.

22 July

To the House of Commons, where I found Duff Cooper up, and answering foolish charges brought up by the Opposition on the adjournment. He was angry, and he trounced and pulverised the silly muddled Opposition severely, but I don't know that he did his own reputation any good for he is already thought to be too excitable. Certainly he quite demolished the Socialists . . .

I drove home alone about 11.30 not before I had congratulated Duff on his triumph, and was he pleased! as Americans say.

27 August *Yugoslavia*

The days passed with Paul are always the happiest days of my year . . .

All is not well in Yugoslavia. There seems to be unrest, cabals against the Government, and agitation because of the new Concordat with the Vatican which has given real religious toleration to nearly six million of Paul's subjects. Perhaps the country is bored now, after a too long dictatorship and they may think that Paul is easier, slacker and more enlightened than was the late King Alexander. He is, but I wonder whether he will stay the course or whether the dynasty will one day founder? I saw the little boy King yesterday. He is thin and pale but not devoid of charm, and it is for him that Paul is working, so devotedly, and keeping the throne warm. And the boy when he comes of age in four and a half years time, will he appreciate all that Paul has done for him, or will he reverse his policies? I wonder very much whether the Karageorgevitches are not doomed? Have they not lost all 'erdgeist' feeling? They all talk English amongst themselves, read the Tatler, barely understand Slovenian and Serb, and dream of their next visit to London. I fear that the Yugoslavian one will be the next throne to go bang, perhaps soon after the boy Peter assumes power, though at first there may be a wave of enthusiasm, for certainly King Alexander was more popular assassinated than ever he was alive. Stoyadenovitch, the Prime Minister, is an able, intelligent, manly creature, and on the surface seems devoted to the Regent, but he is a Serb and a Democrat, and of heavier, more male, less civilised calibre than the Royal Family.

7 September *Pfannberg*

In the evening late, David Margesson arrived from London and my cup of happiness was full, with the Chief Whip here. He is so charming and so powerful, and I only hope that he will enjoy himself . . .

12 September *Yugoslavia and Pfannberg*

A fantastic day. I was called at six which is late for this Schloss which is geared to stalking hours, and about 8 we set out. David Margesson, Seymour Berry and I, for Yugoslavia in the pouring rain, a blinding storm in fact. After Graz they began to complain of the distance and grumbled all the way to the frontier, especially when I was a long time over the car papers, although we had 'laissez-passers' from both governments. However, we finally entered Yugoslavia, and at long last we arrived at Schloss Brdo at 1.30 for luncheon. There we found the Regent, Princess Olga, the Kents and the local Prime Minister, M. Stoyadenovitch burly, and intelligent with bushy eyebrows, and I suspect not completely loyal to the Karageorgevitch régime. There was a pause before luncheon while we washed and drank 'Schnapps' and warmed ourselves after the long five-hour drive, and the Regent did a little propaganda with both David and Seymour Berry for Yugoslavia, and I believe and hope opened both their eyes a little to the dangers of Soviet activities. No Englishman will really believe or realise the danger nor will he until we get

Communism at Calais. Luncheon was delicious. The Duchess of Kent was lovely, dark and more glamorous and gentler than ever. Both she and the Duke were brown after their Mediterranean cruise. David and I discussed the H. of C. but never a word did he even hint as to my prospects of being a Whip or otherwise, but I like him enormously.

Over tea and cocktails David Margesson let himself go rather and told us much of the inner political life of the past few years. No-one played so quiet and yet so powerful a role behind the scenes. At one moment, he told us, he was in despair about the fate and future of the National Government. That was in November 1934 when the disastrous by-election at Putney made even the all-powerful Government shudder. David thought there were too many old men in power and particularly he disapproved of Ramsay MacDonald who was becoming increasingly gaga. And when MacDonald once sent for David and asked rather abruptly why the by-election figures were so disappointing David, annoyed, retorted that the country was tired of its leaders, and hinted that they ought to resign. Ramsay bridled and the interview came to a sudden end, and David half wondered whether he would be sacked from his job as Chief Whip. But that afternoon he managed to see both Baldwin and Neville Chamberlain, and he explained to them what had happened. Both Baldwin and Neville were pleased; though their hands were tied, as a similar hint from them, the natural successors to old Ramsay, might have been interpreted as a wish to assume power. However MacDonald soon sent for them and asked their advice, and offered rather reluctantly to resign at Easter. But Easter came, and he put it off until Whitsuntide (it being easier, as everyone agreed, to resign at a time when the House was not sitting). He repeated constantly that he would only hand over when all was peaceful. David and Co. were afraid that some small squall might blow up, which Ramsay would use as a pretext for remaining in office and meanwhile Conservative support for the Government was fast cooling. And sure enough there were soon rumours of a threat to Italo-Abyssinian relations, and at Whitsuntide Ramsay announced that he thought he had better remain in office until the House met in the Autumn. Tremendous pressure had to be brought upon him to resign; he dawdled, snatched at every pretext, hoped that he would be urged to remain, and was not, and at last he signed his letter of resignation, and agreed to go. Still he held it up for forty-eight hours before his decision was allowed to be made public. Then he went, to everyone's relief. The Cabinet was reshuffled on younger more vigorous lines and it was ready both for the Abyssinian crisis and the General Election. Had old Ramsay remained we might have lost the election. He had little appeal and many enemies. Baldwin had much appeal and no enemies whatsoever, then, at least.

I gleaned from long bedroom chats with David Margesson that the Government, backed by the Baldwinites and the Whips' room are pushing Inskip[17] forward for the premiership after Chamberlain, instead of Sam Hoare who would certainly give them more trouble. Inskip's would be a very dull régime and the Socialists would certainly get in again and after making a mess of things would allow the Conservatives once more to ride to victory, this time under the banner of 'Shakes' Morrison who then I hope, would rule us for ever.

Pam and Michael Berry have arrived from Cannes ... gay, dark, vivacious and charming.

7 October *5 Belgrave Square*

This morning before leaving Paris I went for a long solitary walk and soon found myself at No. 7, rue de Mezières where I was once en pension as a schoolboy in 1907 from September to December when at school in the Ecole D'Alsace. The pension had been run by an old lady, the Baronne de Baileul, a relic of the Second Empire, or so she said, and she had an old-maid daughter, Mdlle. de Baileul almost as old as herself. My mother and I stayed there, and I was happy for I was soon the pet of the establishment, and an Englishman of nearly thirty, one Dundas, took a great fancy to me and showed me the sights of Paris – Fontainebleau and Versailles and so on. I remember it well. He was sandy, Scotch, with a little moustache and was devoted to me. I had not given the incident a thought for many years and now suddenly wondered what had happened to him. He was the brother of Lord Melville and I wondered whether he had been

17. Sir Thomas Inskip. A former Solicitor-General and Attorney-General: Minister for Co-ordination of Defence, 1936–9.

killed in the War; certainly he must have forgotten his young friend. I went into No. 7 and said to the rather irritable concierge that years ago I had stayed there with the Baileuls and had she ever heard of them? 'Montez, montez Monsieur au troisième'. Surprised I climbed the shiny stairs and recalled after twenty years the rather sweet smell of bread: I rang the bell. Mdlle. de Baileul, unchanged, gaunt and grey, opened the door to me and I explained my sentimental errand. She invited me in, and it was difficult not to open the conversation with the observation that I thought she had long been dead! She remembered me, or pretended to, and remembered Dundas too but did not know where he was. Her mother died just after the war, worn out by the air raids. The room seemed quite unchanged and I remembered much, only everything seemed somewhat smaller. I stayed for an embarrassed quarter of an hour but I learnt little of the whereabouts of my lost friend.[18] A Proustian dreamlike incident.

26 October

I walked along the crowded streets of Westminster to the Opening of Parliament and took my place in the North Gallery of the House of Lords. Already the Chamber looked like a pack of cards, with the Peers in their warm red robes and the Peeresses glittering. It is always a splendid show; and I thought of last year when I saw King Edward perform the ceremony with his wistful smile and sad doomed manner.

A few moments before 12, the Royalties arrived; Kent looking ill . . . Gloucester heavier and more pompous, both their Duchesses looking lovely. At mid-day the lights were gradually lowered, and the Royal Procession very slowly and with great dignity wended its way in. The King seemed quite at ease and so did the Queen. She has become more matronly, and as she toyed with her jewels, I looked at her and thought of old days when I called her 'Elizabeth' and was even a little in love with her. The King took 10 minutes to read the speech (which he did well) and the Chamber was motionless, with an atmosphere which was almost hallowed. Lord Halifax carried the Sword of State, indeed he held it throughout the ceremony; quite an ordeal for a man with only one hand . . .

18. He become Sir Charles Dundas and Governor of Uganda.

Afterwards I drove to Chelmsford where I attended the Essex Political Rally where Shakes Morrison spoke well in his rich earthy way, and I envied him his ease and fluency. He was followed by 'Rab' Butler, now Parliamentary Secretary to the Ministry of Labour. He is a dull dog all right, but an ambitious one, and he was on safe ground, for he always knows his facts. In fact, I was pleasantly surprised by his thoroughness and knowledge of his subject.

31 October

We decided this morning to give a dinner party and spent all morning telephoning. When I rang up Lady Oxford at 11 a.m. and said 'May I speak to her Ladyship?' 'It's Margot speaking' a high voice retorted. She came, of course, and during dinner was entertaining enough as she described her predecessor 'Mrs Asquith', who was no wife for Henry as 'she lived in Hampstead and had no clothes'. Then she told us how she had once at Mrs Greville's request, taken Mr and Mrs Asquith to Taplow for a long weekend, little thinking that one day she would marry Mr Asquith herself. Joe Chamberlain was there too and she claims wore embroidered slippers and a velvet smoking jacket. True? Margot's reminiscences are usually accurate.

9 November

I shall always remember today, as today I was elected a Director of Guinness and Company, a great honour and a privileged position of power and prestige. Who would ever have thought, five years ago, that I should be on the Board of so rich and grand a company? I must try to be of some service to it.

Ramsay MacDonald has died in the night at sea somewhere en route for South Africa. I feel few will regret him. Yet he had a disarming smile and aristocratic appearance which lent colour to the legend of his birth – an illegitimate Dalhousie! How much happier he was after 1931, when he carted all his old followers and began to breathe freely in the more spacious Conservative air. We treated him with respect, but he inspired no affection and no liking. He could never say yes or no to any ordinary question, never. Evasive, subtle, and eel-like, he trusted no-one. I saw him sometimes in those early months of the first

Labour Government when London society very wisely decided to take him up rather than to ignore him. Defiant at first, he soon took to grandeur and high life and wallowed in it like a man who has been starving all his life. He was much criticised for his pacifism, and his equivocal role during the General Strike.

At the end of Questions, Neville Chamberlain gave a perfect, if slightly perfunctory, tribute to MacDonald although there was no feeling of loss in the House on any side. Nevertheless ex-Prime Ministers do not die every day, and the House adjourned as a mark of respect. Who will be the next to go, Baldwin or L.G.?[19]

At the 1922 Committee dinner at the Savoy, the PM was terrific, first leading the unsuspecting MP's along the paths of speculation, and then pulling them up sharply, with a statement that he was about to make 'a gesture of friendship' to Germany. He even hinted that perhaps the Mandated territories might be returned, or at least that their return might be discussed. He is sending Lord Halifax. . . . The PM had a rapturous reception and was cheered long and loudly when he sat down. I was delighted.

15 November

Vita Nicolson's book about her wild mother, Lady Sackville, is just out.[20] She was an extraordinary woman, whom I knew fairly well when she lived in Ebury Street, and later at Brighton. When I first published a book ('Joan Kennedy') she wrote to me to congratulate me and said that she liked it so much that she was sending me a copy, and did. She died over a year ago, lonely, colourful, passionate and impoverished.

18 November

I was dining with the Kents this evening when suddenly after dinner the King of the Belgians[21] was announced, and I was quite overcome by his appearance and charm. He has an aloof loneliness, a distinction and charm and manner that suggest a king in

19. It was, ironically enough, Chamberlain himself (in November 1940).
20. *Pepita*.
21. King Leopold III.

a fairy tale. He ought really to have arrived in a pumpkin or a golden carriage instead of a banal dark blue royal Daimler. He was wearing khaki uniform and decorations, just having come on from the Foreign Office banquet. We stayed talking for some time, and often I made him half laugh. His English is perfect, his manner shy. He wore a soft shirt and rather common links. . . . We talked mostly of Eton.[22]

31 November

We had a scratch dinner party which included Emerald Cunard and Fritzi of Prussia. The latter looked surprised when Emerald said 'Monseigneur, which do you think the more unfashionable, the Connaughts or the Gloucesters?'

5 December

I had a long conversation with Lord Halifax about Germany and his recent visit. He described Hitler's appearance, his khaki shirt, black breeches and patent leather evening shoes. He told me he liked all the Nazi leaders, even Goebbels, and he was much impressed, interested and amused by the visit. He thinks the régime absolutely fantastic, perhaps even too fantastic to be taken seriously. But he is very glad that he went, and thinks good may come of it. I was rivetted by all he said, and reluctant to let him go.

16 December

Leslie Hore-Belisha and I drove to the House of Commons, through the Horse Guards Parade – I have never done that before, and Leslie showed me his ivory pass, with 'Secretary of State for War' printed on it, with the letters almost worn out. It once belonged to the Duke of Wellington, and Leslie is immensely proud of it. He thinks war will break out during the recess. He always says that, and I reminded him that he had so predicted in the summers of 1936 and 1937. Leslie is getting fatter, he likes the luxuries of life, which have only come to him lately.

22. Harold Nicolson, at his meeting with the King on 22 March 1936, also found himself discussing Eton with him (*Diaries and Letters*, pp. 253–4).

17 December

There is nowhere in the world where sleep is so deep as in the libraries of the House of Commons. This afternoon, waiting for a division I slept soundly for two hours and when I awoke I found Attlee reading beside me. He holds his book with his left hand, his right hand he twiddles, and he rubs his moustache nervously. It is an irritating, nervous trick. He seems still upset by the fiasco of his Spanish visit. After a second nap I woke to find the Duchess of Atholl, so sour, sunken and sallow, peering at me. I glared back.

I really must speak more in the House of Commons. My attendance record is second to none, but I never speak, either from laziness, ignorance or shyness, and I know that it is a mistake and a pity – I must try to make a fresh start . . .

20 December

Today in the House of Commons, Harold Nicolson showed me a letter he had this morning from a man who pretends to be in constant spiritual communication with Lord Curzon. Curiously enough, Lord Curzon was always intrigued by Spiritualism and indignant with Lady Oxford's scathing comments: 'I always knew the living talked rot, but it's nothing to the rot the dead talk' . . .

28 December

The old Duchess of Rutland[23] died on Christmas Day. No one knew her age but I think she was nearer ninety than eighty, though she still was full of youth and vitality. Her energy was astounding and her beauty proverbial. She had a Greek quality of mind and body and was kindness itself yet I suppose devoid of all scruples where her interests or those of her family were concerned. She leaves many devoted descendants who are among the loveliest people on earth.

1938

1 January

I have made the following resolutions for the coming year: (1)

23. The mother of Lady Diana Cooper.

To spend more time in the House of Commons, (2) To bury all my hatchets, (3) To take better care of my health, and (4) To spend a little, but only a little, less money.

The New Year's Honours are dull except for the dismissal of Vansittart, who has been kicked upstairs.[24] The dismissal was done as tactfully as possible, and now poor fascinating, dark Van is out. And what about me? What will the next twelve months bring me? Kelvedon habitable? More money? A step nearer the Whip's Room? A daughter?

5 January

I spent the day at Park Royal going over the vast brewery, revelling in the glory of being a Director of that great organisation . . .

30 January

Great praise of Chamberlain on all sides, and Baldwin has already faded into obscurity. His stock is low indeed, though History may make him out a great man, half Machiavelli, half Milton.

1 February

For luncheon, I walked jauntily to Lady Colefax's attractive little Lord North Street house, where I found the usual mixed bag, including Harold Nicolson (who gets every Parliamentary action just wrong) . . .

Parliament met again, and the members coming in reminded me of schoolboys on the first day of term – except that they all seemed delighted to be back. High spirits, gaiety, reunion back-slapping; some ski casualties were on sticks. But it was not long before a storm blew up, at question time, about the sinking of the British vessel 'Endymion' off the coast of Spain, and Duff Cooper was in serious trouble, as he had omitted to condole with the relations of the victims. The Socialists made a dead set at him. Seymour Cocks, the waggish Labour MP, said to me: 'How can you expect the husband of Diana to be sympathetic over "Endymion"?', a classical allusion which was to the point.

24. Vansittart was appointed to the honorific but powerless post of Chief Diplomatic Adviser.

4 February

Today there is terrific excitement because Hitler has pulled off another political coup; and has assumed supreme control of his Army, sacking Blomberg, the suave, ex-Commander-in-Chief.

7 February

I was suddenly sent for to go to the PM's room; at first I hoped wildly that I was to be offered a Government post: he was calm and smiled gently at me as I entered. What were my impressions of Italy? he asked. I told him frankly what I thought, that Italy wanted to be friends with us and that the only drawback to better relations was Anthony Eden. The PM smiled enigmatically, and Dunglass led me out again. The interview only lasted 4 minutes.

8 February

Prince Nicholas of Greece died this morning after a month's illness. He was only 65. A gentle, dreamy gentleman, he tasted many of the vicissitudes of fortune. At the age of 50 he taught himself to paint. He was bald and brown and wore the eye-glass which is traditional in the Greek branch of the Glücksberg family. When his daughter, Princess Marina, married the Duke of Kent, his paternal pride was a pleasure to see. Prince Nicholas spoke every language, wrote endless letters to his royal relations, and was particularly devoted to the late George V, who was his first cousin. To him, he was in the habit of sending naughty stories and doubtful limericks; for the late King had a racy mind and liked a vulgar joke, so long as the point was obvious.

13 February

The newspapers this morning print the rumour that Anthony has resigned from the Foreign Office, and that there will be a reshuffle. These rumours may have spoilt his big effort at Birmingham last night, where he delivered what was to have been a most important speech, a bid, in fact, for the leadership of the Youth of this country. But my spies tell me that it was a failure, and that Anthony lectured his audience, and even the Cabinet. I fear he is showing signs of 'Mountain Sickness'.

17 February

Today I set out with Diana Cooper to re-join my wife at Sestrières.

In Paris we drove to the Ritz, where we met Harold Balfour, and at 7.55 we left from the Gare de Lyons for Italy. Harold was sharing a wagon-lit with a dark, sinister, Bloomsbury-looking man. I looked at his luggage labels and read 'Dali', and we wondered whether he could be the great surrealist painter. During dinner in the train I approached him, and asked him if he knew Lord Berners, which he did: he then joined us and we had an amusing dinner, rushing across Europe, Diana, Dali, Harold Balfour and I. Dali is Spanish, a native, I think, of Barcelona, but he seemed to be pro-Franco. He told us that the anarchists had burnt his house. Our conversation had a disastrous effect on Diana's night, and she dreamed of women with flies coming out of their nipples and of babies with piano instead of human legs.

19 February *Hotel Duca d' Aosta, Sestrières*

A gorgeous Italian day, azure sky, almost too much snow, and champagne air. Honor is well and in excellent spirits and we all skied, though the snow is so soft that one sinks up to one's waist. Diana is fair and determined. Honor good, Harold middling, Chips hopeless. Tomorrow I return home.

21 February *London*

An incredible day. I woke as the train arrived in Paris, and sent out for newspapers. The wagon-lit conductor, who was Italian, brought them, beaming from ear to ear. They blazed the news: 'Anthony Eden resigned'. I could scarcely contain my excitement as I lapped up every detail. It seems that after a two-day conference, the Cabinet decided to begin immediate negotiations with Italy. Anthony was over-wrought and refused his consent, unless Italy made some preliminary concessions.[25]

25. The break came after a period of mutual mistrust that had existed between Eden and Chamberlain. The actual occasion for Eden's resignation arose when Chamberlain wanted to open negotiations with Mussolini to obtain a general settlement in the Mediterranean, including a *de jure* recognition of his conquest of Abyssinia.

The hours to Boulogne seemed endless, and I was tempted to leave the train and hire an aeroplane. Would there be an election? A reshuffle? At Victoria I rushed to the H. of C. where the excitement was immense, and the lobbies buzzing. Anthony Eden had just finished speaking, as had Bobbety Cranborne,[26] and the general opinion was that their speeches had been eloquent but too bitter. . . . The whole country is in a ferment and no-one knows yet which way the cat will jump. I back Chamberlain, and think today the greatest event since the formation of the National Government. The doctrinaire 'Leftist' policy of the Foreign Office has received a check, and there is jubilation in the House. Excited groups stand about, whispering. Later Harold Nicolson attacked Italy in violent, foolish terms, and thus did the cause of peace as much harm as he could.

The Prime Minister, I have reason to believe, has long been tired by Anthony's pro-French, uncompromising theories, while the Socialists now proclaim Eden as their saviour and leader. Eden, the man whom they have been attacking for years! This evening a group of excited Communists even invaded the Lobby, demanding Anthony's reinstatement. God preserve us from our friends, they did him harm. I thought the excitement in the House was greater than during the Abdication crisis. Sparks flew. At length the Prime Minister rose, and spoke clearly, convincing many.

I congratulated Lord Halifax on his new job – for it is he who must certainly be appointed, and he smiled affectionately at me. Tomorrow is a Vote of Censure.

22 February

The Government has had a triumph: at the end of a long day a majority of 161 against the Censure Vote is a victory indeed. The atmosphere during Questions was excited and no-one listened, as they never do, when a crisis is coming. Greenwood in an almost

---

Eden wanted certain conditions fulfilled first, including withdrawal of Italian troops from Spain and the reduction of Italian forces in Libya.

26. Lord Cranborne, Parliamentary Under-Secretary for Foreign Affairs (the present Marquess of Salisbury) had resigned with Eden.

comic speech attacked the Government. Chamberlain replied. More speeches. At length Winston Churchill rose, and defended Eden, and attacked the Government. It was yet another bid on his part to lead an Independent, perhaps Centre, party. He was followed by Bob Boothby, who was clear, sensible and brief, and sat down amid applause. Then Lloyd George, looking mischievous and hearty, rose, and we knew we were in for fireworks. And we were. At first he was interesting about the Treaty of Versailles, and told the House how there had been arguments at the time for uniting Austria to Germany. He then began a eulogy of Eden, who, to everyone's surprise, was seated with Cranborne and Jim Thomas in the third row behind the Government: people said that it would have been better taste had he followed Sam Hoare's example, and stayed away. Lloyd George ranted on, cheered by the Socialists. Now and then Anthony nodded. Then Lloyd George deliberately accused the Prime Minister of withholding important information, and for a terrible moment the House stormed: the PM went scarlet with anger, but coolly denied the charges. Lloyd George passionately repeated them. The House shouted 'Withdraw', and a duel followed between the old ex-Prime Minister and the present one and Chamberlain's position was not made easier by an interruption from Eden. The battle hung on a telegram from Italy on Sunday which, however, was only delivered by Count Grandi to the Prime Minister on Monday. Suddenly it was clear, even to the prejudiced, that Chamberlain had done nothing wrong and the atmosphere lightened. My heart went out to the PM and I determined to support him always. I feel loyal about him as I never did about old Farmer Baldwin.

Finally, Lloyd George, worsted, angry, discomforted, sat down in comparative silence. I whispered to Ivor Guest, who was next to me, 'That may be an inglorious end to a great career'. 'No fear', he laughed.

24 February

Anthony Eden makes a big speech tomorrow at Leamington. There is some apprehension lest he be too bitter: but I believe not: firstly because he is a gentleman, and secondly because he is too shrewd a statesman to burn his boats irretrievably.

Already there is talk of him coming back, like Sam Hoare, in the autumn.

At a loose end, I went supperless to bed – to read Proust, and rest. And how pleasant.

26 February

The excitement of today was the publication of the two new appointments, Edward Halifax goes to the Foreign Office – and a saner, more intelligent, happier appointment has never been made, and Alan Lennox-Boyd to the Ministry of Labour as Parliamentary Secretary, in the room of 'Rab' Butler who has become Under-Secretary of State for Foreign Affairs. Alan has been living with us here for some time, at 5 Belgrave Square.

Rab Butler is a scholarly dry-stick but an extremely able, cautious, canny man, of great ambition. I must cultivate him.

28 February

I happened to be walking in the 'Aye' Lobby and spied Harold Balfour talking to Rab Butler: I went up to them, by the mercy of God, and congratulated Rab on his recent appointment to the Foreign Office: actually, I said, 'Europe is to be congratulated'. He beamed and as I walked away (so Harold says) he asked about me, and Harold, of course, lauded me to the skies, and then suggested that he made me his PPS. He took to the suggestion, and they discussed it at length. It would be a position of power, great power, for whosoever gets it, since there will be only two MP's in the House of Commons at the Foreign Office. If I got it, I might play a great role.

2 March

Of course, I cannot believe it, I, Chips at the Foreign Office. Will my star lead me there? It cannot happen. But what a romance my life would have been.

Today when I came into the House of Commons, no-one was about, and when I saw Rab Butler he seemed to ignore me. Later, however, Wing Commander James,[27] called to me and told me that he had heard that Rab was considering me. How I

27. Conservative MP for Wellingborough since 1931. Parliamentary Private Secretary to R. A. Butler, 1936–8.

should enjoy the triumph, the power and position; but I would have even less time for Kelvedon and myself, my boy, my Bundi and my books – even my diary might have to be shut.

3 March

David Margesson hinted that the job will be mine, but that I must be careful not to gossip, etc. He is pro-me, and said so to Rab Butler, and will build me up. But he is aware that there may be a small outcry. Perhaps – but I do not care, my whole future depends on it. I feel somehow that I shall get it, though the evening passed, and there was no new development.

I went early to bed, in some apprehension. Am I tempting destiny too much by assuming that this lovely plum will fall into my lap?

4 March

I came to the House, entered the Chamber, and had a temporary 'sinker' when I saw Mr Conant[28] on the PPS's bench. I rushed out to the attendant, and was relieved to be told he was 'Lord Stanley's PPS'. Then I met David Margesson who asked whether I had heard anything, and when I said no, he assumed that Rab was going to consider the matter over the weekend.

Much later, as I was leaving the House, hat in hand, and rather discouraged – politics (even minor ones, I know) bring one these exalted hopes, only to have them dashed – I was caught up by a [Whip's] Runner who told me the 'Chief' wanted to see me, and once again I was ushered into David Margesson's sanctum. He had, he said, spoken to Butler who assured him that his mind was now made up and that he intended to offer me the job, probably on Monday. Almost dancing with delight, but feeling the necessity, already, of discretion, I left the House by Westminster Hall.

There, standing, perhaps waiting, was Rab. Shyly, he said, 'I should like to talk to you for a moment', and we walked off together. Then he spilt the big beans, 'Would I consider being his PPS?' Would I? My heart throbbed, and I felt exhilarated, as I said he was voicing my life's dream. We walked amicably together

28. Mr Roger Conant, Conservative MP for Bewdley.

towards the FO, where he took me to his room, a large one overlooking Downing Street and the Horse Guards Parade. He pointed to what would be my desk, and as we chatted, we suddenly became friends. He would, he promised, send an announcement to the Press. I went home: Honor was out, but I played with my unbelievably beautiful, adorable boy – I, Chips, PPS – how lovely – but to the Foreign Office, is beyond belief exciting. I can hardly wait to take up my duties.

5 March

Chamberlain's stock soars ... I think he is the shrewdest Prime Minister of modern times; and it is a pity he did not drop Anthony months ago. When he first became PM he was recovering from the first set-back of his career, his muddle over the N.D.C. Otherwise, I am told, he would never have taken Anthony on.

6 March

Honor gave me a very magnificent gold cigarette case for my birthday, especially made for me. The lid has been engraved by Professor Lowenthal, who is undoubtedly the Benvenuto Cellini of the age, with a medallion of my child. It looks terrifically Rothschild and rich. But I must no longer think too much of things like that. My frivolous life is over – tomorrow politics, and the dawn of a career. I wonder how I shall get on with Rab Butler?

7 March

Today I celebrated a 'Double', my birthday (which is to be my last for many a year) and my arrival at the Foreign Office. I turned up about eleven, was warmly greeted by Boss Butler, and we got down to work at once, framing the answers to questions, which were then taken over to 10 Downing Street to be OK'd by the Prime Minister. Blandly, smilingly, I took my seat on the PPS's bench directly behind my new chief, and my appearance there made a mild sensation in the House, of pleasure to my friends and rage to my enemies, whom I suppose I must try to conciliate. I hope I behaved with dignity; certainly I was beautifully dressed, though Rab says I must abandon my black Homburg hat – it is too Edenesque – and buy a bowler. Bowlers are back! I made a point of not sitting there all day. What a joy having a room (and one of the best) to myself. There is considerable jealousy about it. Almost all the Cabinet Ministers congratulated me, and Geoffrey Lloyd[29] called me 'Chips' and walked arm-in-arm with me. Letters and telegrams pour in.

Chips at the FO – shades of Lord Curzon, and how pleased he would be.

8 March

The newspapers are full of my appointment. I have not slept, and I am so excited that food gives me indigestion. Several MP's looked darkly at me.

Rab is without prejudices, very alert, extremely able and sensible, in fact the ideal man for his none too easy job. I like him . . .

I am relieved that the FO is not so opposed to Franco as I had feared, and seem well aware of the tricks of Republican Spain. Halifax has sent telegrams to France such as that country has not had since Napoleon! They should make them sit up.

9 March

I am worn, thin, exhausted (but, I believe, handsome): my first day on duty was terrific. I never left the Chamber from 2.45 until 11.30, except for a few moments at dinner time, when I gave a snack to Peter Loxley, the long, delightful, sensible fellow who is Rab's Private Secretary. He was formerly Bobbety Cranborne's and I feared that there might be opposition to us, the new régime. If there was, Peter had the tact to hide it, and it is now dispelled. Dieu merci. But I hope to hoof some of the other FO people out before I am done, though I must feel my way quietly, slowly.

10 March

All morning at the FO reading confidential telegrams, and meeting people.

I went to tea at the German Embassy, where there were many people. I talked to Mr Kennedy the new American Ambassador, whose chief merit seems to be that he has nine children.

29. Conservative MP for Birmingham, Ladywood, since 1931

Lady Desborough came purring up to me with her honeyed and insincere congratulations on my appointment. Of course, to the outside world, it sounds much grander than it really is.

11 March

An unbelievable day, in which two things occurred. Hitler took Vienna and I fell in love with the Prime Minister.

The morning was calm, the PM enchanting. I am in and out of his room constantly now. Early on, there were messages announcing mysterious movements of troops in Bavaria with the usual denials from Berlin. Then there was a grand luncheon party at 10 Downing Street at which, the Chamberlains entertained the Ribbentrops, the Halifaxes, Winston Churchills, etc. By then the news had reached the FO that the Germans had invaded Austria, and from 5 to 7 p.m. reports poured in. I was in Halifax's room at 7.30 when the telephone rang 'The Germans are in Vienna', and five minutes later, 'The skies are black with Nazi planes'. We stood breathless in the Secretary of State's room, wondering what would happen next. All night messages flowed in; by midnight Austria was a German province. Rab Butler was dining with the Speaker, and as he was already late, I drove him there. Later Peter Loxley and I called on him about midnight and told him the latest news; he was still in his Minister's dress and we sat, an unreal trio, in the Butlers' flat in Little College Street, discussing the event. It is certainly a set-back for the Chamberlain Government. Will my adorable Austria become Nazi-fied?

12 March

Honor has gone to Hackwood for the weekend, but because of the crisis, I have stood by, and was in and out of the FO all day. Rab is a curious chap, my charming chief; with the brains and ability of a super clever civil servant, but completely unprejudiced. He seems to have no bias on any subject and looks upon the whole human race as mental! His years of experience with the East are of value to him now. Unfortunately, we do not laugh at quite the same jokes, and I wonder whether we shall really ever be intimates: but I like him, and am out to please him; though we worship at different shrines. There is nothing 'snuff-box' about him; bibelots, Fabergé, royalties, baroque and scandal leave him unresponsive.

Austria has been a severe shock, and already people are saying 'Czechoslovakia will be next'.

15 March

Franco marches on, and will soon split the Red forces in two, when he reaches the sea. The Socialists are terrified.

Peter Loxley took me to tea at the FO.[30] This is a more important function than it sounds; a definite ceremony of the utmost significance which has been often written about and described. It means that one is absolutely in the inner circle of FO affairs.

16 March

I hate society at the moment, and every day cannot wait to take my proud place on the PPS bench. Today the Opposition, as we feared, demanded an adjournment of the House to discuss Spain. They are desperate, as it now seems sure that Franco must win. The thwarted Socialists realise that their sun is setting, and they were like a pack of snarling hounds, attacking John Simon as he wound up. At times he could not be heard at all; yet he scored and won, and made his opponents look uncomfortable and foolish. The Government won by an enormous majority and the Opposition demand for aid for the Spanish Reds was defeated.

17 March

The H. of C. is humming with intrigue today, and the so-called 'Insurgents' are rushing about, very over-excited. They want to bring back Anthony Eden and their Shadow Cabinet is alleged to include Lloyd George, Winston and Eden. Shakes Morrison and Leslie Belisha are said to be concerned in this wild scheme, but I think they are innocent.

18 March

We go from crisis to crisis. Poland has now issued an ultimatum to Lithuania.

There was a terrific rush this morning over Private Notice

30. The daily tea-party referred to later in Chapter VI.

Questions, which had to be ready by 11 o'clock. The ink was still wet on one I was writing when the Prime Minister snatched it brusquely. . . . 'Hurry up, hurry up, he repeated and went off with it. I have never seen him so irritable; but he is very overworked and is 69 today.

20 March

Alan Lennox-Boyd, in a very sensible speech, has declared that it would be ridiculous to promise to defend Czechoslovakia. Perhaps he has put his foot in it? Though it would be utter folly to make new commitments.

21 March

The House of Commons is still full of intrigue. Fearing that Duff Cooper might throw in his weight on the wrong side, I tipped off Diana by telephone that the Insurgents were after the Admiralty: and it happens to be true, as Sir Roger Keyes advised the PM in the course of the Naval estimates to put Winston in charge of the Navy! I am now making enemies fast and furious, and am already feared at the House of Commons.

I spent the whole morning at the Foreign Office where the statement the PM is to make on Thursday was being drafted. It is a highly important one, and the peace of Europe for years may depend upon it. He (no-one knows yet) will not make any promise to Czechoslovakia, but will reaffirm our present commitments. All afternoon in the House, I 'fagged' for the PM – in fact, I never left him; in the middle of it all, someone passed me a note quoting Harry Lauder's famous remark:

'I was vurra thick with the Prime Minister: I dunno who was the thicker of the twa.'

It's true – I am nuts about Chamberlain.

22 March

When I went to bed last night I left Rab Butler closeted here at the House of Commons with Lord Halifax and the Prime Minister in the PM's room; they had sent their secretaries away.

Rab told me this morning that he had stayed until after one. Thursday will be a tremendous day in history and I am up to the neck in it.

The Insurgents

Winston Churchill
Leo Amery
Duncan Sandys
Harold Nicolson
Godfrey Nicholson
Leonard Ropner
Derrick Gunston
Ronnie Cartland
Ronnie Tree
The Duchess of Atholl
Paul Emrys-Evans
Vyvyan Adams
Louis Spears
Bob Boothby
Victor Cazalet
Brendan Bracken
Jack Macnamara

24 March

The big day, so long awaited, is over, and the PM scored a triumph. He laid down his policy to an enthusiastic House, and met little opposition; and, although a 3-line Whip had been issued, there was no vote. The House was packed, and I was delighted that everyone should see me in my new importance, and I thought how typical of this House that a such long-heralded day should finally prove dull! The excitement is so often over before it actually begins.

28 March

I adore my job, and think that I am rather good at it, and I know that Rab Butler is pleased with me. There is no other 'PPS-ship' that I should like, really; though I shouldn't mind being a Whip. And a Whip I shall one day be.

29 March

Franco advances – victory is clearly his. He has been so misunderstood, so misrepresented in this country that to champion him, and I have done, is dangerous from a Constituency point of view.

The Archbishop of Canterbury has made a foolish speech in the Lords in which he defended Hitler's coup in Austria. He will thus lose further support and respect.

4 April

An incident in the House of Commons. Mr Shinwell[31] made him-

31. Labour MP for Seaham; he had defeated Ramsay MacDonald in the 1935 General Election.

self highly objectionable, and unfortunately, Commander Bower, the [Conservative] member for the Cleveland Division of Yorks shouted 'Go back to Poland' – a foolish and provocative jibe, though no ruder than many that the Opposition indulge in every day. Shinwell, shaking with fury, got up, crossed the House, and went up to Bower and smacked him very hard across the face! The crack resounded in the Chamber – there was consternation, but the Speaker, acting from either cowardice or tact, seemed to ignore the incident and when pressed, refused to rebuke Shinwell, who made an apology, as did Bower, who had taken the blow with apparent unconcern. He is a big fellow and could have retaliated effectively. The incident passed; but everyone was shocked. Bower is a pompous ass, self-opinionated, and narrow, who walks like a pregnant turkey. I have always disliked him, and feel justified in so doing since he once remarked in my hearing 'Everyone who even spoke to the Duke of Windsor should be banished – kicked out of the country'. But the incident does not raise Parliamentary prestige, especially now, when it is at a discount throughout the world.

In the evening I took Honor, thin and glittering in her tiara, to Lady Astor's diplomatic reception in honour of the Halifaxes. It was a grand Disraelian 'do' – diamonds, superb wine, and all the 'dips and pols'. The function will be criticised, since there is already talk of a so-called 'Cliveden' set which is alleged to be pro-Hitler, but which, in reality, is only pro-Chamberlain and pro-sense.

The Foreign Office in the morning, House of Commons in the afternoon, and much occupied in arranging Rab's dinner tonight in honour of the Sultan of Oman and Muscat. I did it all, and I invited Gage, Dufferin and others. A most réussi party and we sat down 21. The Sultan brought two Arabs ... much laughter and drink for the occidentals. When it was over we escorted the Sultan to the Chamber, and I introduced Mr Attlee and Gwilym Lloyd George and others to His Highness.

27 April

The question of Freddie Birkenhead's being appointed PPS to Halifax arose, and was referred to me. Such an appointment might be the making of him. Have I his career in my palm?

I drifted reluctantly to Lady Colefax's for a cocktail ...

Lady [Austen] Chamberlain called me to her and we had an enthralling chat. She is outraged with Anthony Eden, whom she has always looked upon as Austen's protégé (as he was).... [Neville] Chamberlain blames Anthony entirely for the muddle we are in. He got out of hand after Austen Chamberlain died, which coincided with the change in régime at No. 10. He could not tolerate the new Prime Minister's supervision after Baldwin's lazy, laissez-faire indifference. Much Lady Chamberlain told me was highly confidential.

3 May

Winston Churchill is even against the Irish Treaty.[32] Is Winston, that fat, brilliant, unbalanced, illogical, orator, more than just that? Or is he perhaps right, banging his head against an uncomprehending country and unsympathetic government? ...

9 May

One triumph for me: I have now contrived, after some slight hesitation, in getting Freddie Birkenhead appointed PPS to Halifax, so we shall now work together in happy harness.

12 May

After lunch I drove away with Leslie Belisha in my car; en route to his house a lorryman recognised him and called out 'Hello Leslie'. He was pleased as Punch. His house, 16 Stafford Place, is a horror, small and though arranged with care, it shows astonishing lack of taste or humour. Wedgwood plaques cover the walls ... old ones, small ones, good ones, bad ones. And his bedroom he has turned into a sort of 'chapelle ardente' to his mother's memory. There are photographs of her taken at all times, and personal relics, as well as a striking portrait, painted of her from memory. She adored him and he worshipped her; she was the passion of his life; he only wants to succeed, he confided in me, to justify her faith in him.

32. This included the renunciation by the British Government of their rights to occupy for naval purposes the ports of Queenstown and Berehaven, and the base in Lough Swilly. Churchill was virtually alone in attacking what he subsequently called 'this improvident example of appeasement'.

After dining at the House of Commons I found myself talking to Lord Nuffield, a pleasant, wrinkled little man, with no 'aitches' and a weak hand-clasp.

This Government has never commanded my respect: I support it because the alternative would be infinitely worse. But our record, especially of late, is none too good. Halifax and Chamberlain are doubtless very great men, who dwarf their colleagues; they are the greatest Englishmen alive, certainly; but aside from them we have a mediocre crew; I fear that England is on the decline, and that we shall dwindle for a generation or so. We are a tired race and our genius seems dead.

13 May

An ominous date. In the morning I met Sam Hoare, and walked with him for a little; he is very worried about the Government and the Air Debate. Next week comes the great re-shuffle. I hope to remain where I am unless I am made a Whip, which would not be until after the Election.

In the evening I had a long talk with my boss, Rab Butler, and we agreed that when a man becomes 'cocu' his political future ends. Something in the man seems to snap, self-confidence goes, and with it motive-power. We cited several examples, and yet recognised that life in the House of Commons encourages infidelity in one's wife.

Herr Henlein[33] is here unofficially and today he lunched with Winston Churchill in his flat: it was a secret meeting, which leaked out. What is Winston up to?

19 May

I lunched at No. 10 Downing Street with Mrs Chamberlain and the PM. In the long drawing room, which they have just done up, there were 6 or 7 other MP's as fellow guests. No-one else, and we lunched in the small dining-room. Mrs C. is good-looking, certainly, and wears her greying hair in majestic fashion over her forehead. She has Celtic charm and smilingly greets her guests. Perhaps she is shy; she has little humour, but a quick mind. She is neither fashionable nor frivolous, nor yet really serious-minded. The PM received us seated, and near him

33. The leader of the Sudeten German Party in Czechoslovakia.

stood his stick. His gout seems very slight – perhaps it is diplomatic. Conversation at luncheon was a touch strained. Mrs C. had set questions for everyone:

> 'Mr Channon, what are you writing now?'
> 'How is Lady Honor?' . . . etc.

and she showed me over the house and I discussed chair covers and curtains with her. She showed me samples . . . her taste, I fear, is elementary.

I dined with the Buccleuchs to meet the Kents. Their dining-room at 2 Grosvenor Place is ducal enough for anyone, with pictures and plate and a magnificent Charles II chandelier – a very different set-up from luncheon, though I did not enjoy it for some reason, though Noel Coward did – very much.

20 May

Decidedly the PM does not like the Japs! And I always notice that he corrects Japanese questions, and makes them terser. Every day he goes over the questions at 12.50. He really is his own Foreign Minister.

22 May

How stimulating it is to wake up in Jesuitical Circles[34] and to breakfast and to share the newspapers (full of alarming rumours) with a bevy of silent-footed priests! And with my adorable Oxford outside, gloriously green, caparisoned in blossom and bathed in loveliness. The bells, the blue warmth, the late morning and even the discomfort brought back Oxford to me and those happy far-off days when my only misery was the dread of ever returning to the transatlantic land which gave me birth, and which I have always loathed as much as I have loved England and the mad English. Now, after just twenty years my infatuation is wearing off – and I am tiring of England, perhaps of the world. But English life remains the only possible existence.

Back at the Foreign Office I found an atmosphere of suppressed excitement. Telegrams had poured in all day, and they were behind with the de-coding. The Germans were moving troops or possibly even mobilising: their rage against the Czechs

34. Chips had spent the weekend at Campion Hall, Oxford.

is boiling over. Meanwhile, in Czechoslovakia elections are taking place. There is rain, and hence quiet in Prague, but in the Sudeten districts excitement and indignation mount over the shooting of two Germans by the Czech frontier guards. The world stands still, and a shiver has passed through every Chancellery. Is it 1914 all over again? The Cabinet was returning when I arrived, and had been in session for several hours. Halifax, whom I saw, seemed aloof and Olympian. He called a meeting of journalists, which I attended. He seated himself at the head of the long table in the Ambassadors' room and briefly addressed them, asking them for their restraint and discretion: he then emphasised the seriousness of the position. As he spoke I stood at the window gazing out over the sunlit Horse Guards Parade and wondered whether the world was going to commit suicide? But it was Halifax who saved it this time. I saw the telegrams he sent to both Germany and France, and the one to Prague. To Germany, he hinted that a war could only please those who looked for the extermination of civilisation, and that England might not be able to keep out. In other words, between the lines, he was warning Germany that if she attacks Czechoslovakia we would go to the immediate assistance of France: this telegram had a sobering effect on Germany, especially on Ribbentrop who has been churlish and violent lately (he had a scene with Nevile Henderson yesterday).

To Prague, Halifax telegraphed urging restraint and advising the Czechs do everything possible to meet the demands of the Sudeten Deutsch, and thus rob the Germans of a pretext for marching in. To France went a firm reminder that he would not FOLLOW her into war: she could fight alone.... Thus might Metternich have played political poker. I pray to God that it will pay off: already the atmosphere is calmer. To both Germany and France we have said 'hold back'. Henderson, remembering Disraeli, has ordered a sleeping carriage to stand by, to take him from Berlin.

23 May

The news at the Foreign Office was better. Halifax's poker-playing seems to be succeeding, and the tension eases.

A Cinderella Evening. Tonight there were two grand balls –

and we were invited to neither: ... But what is sinister is that Lady Astor either forgot us, or deliberately omitted us from her ball tonight in honour of the King and Queen. I thought that such social humiliations were over: that I was too secure, or too indifferent to mind them: but I find I do, which is ill-bred of me.

1 June

Honor has had the most extraordinary letter from Max Beaverbrook, in which he confided that he had recommended Sir Samuel Hoare to have a confidential conversation with her. We were both filled with alarm and curiosity. Why should the Home Secretary want to confer with us? I searched every possible explanation, and to find out, Honor has gone to dinner with Max. I refused, so that she might pump him better.

2 June

Beaverbrook, it appears, is convinced that Chamberlain will die in harness, as Austen, his brother, died suddenly ... at 70. 'The Chamberlains are not a long-lived lot', he says, and he thinks that it is the duty of the Conservative Government to be prepared for such an emergency. Beaverbrook knows that the Baldwin-Whips' Room-Margesson candidate is Inskip: he would prefer Sam Hoare, as I would, who has more personality and drive and charm. Even more convinced than we are that Sam Hoare is the PM's logical successor is Sam Hoare himself, and it appears he asked Max's advice the other day on how he could become the recognised Heir-Apparent. Beaverbrook surprisingly answered : 'Consult Honor Channon; she is the most able politician's wife, and Chips is a brilliant strategist and intriguer. Together they have the facilities – see Honor and talk to her.' Honor is aghast; is she to inherit the mantle of Lady Londonderry and make and unmake Prime Ministers? Sam Hoarse agreed to consult us: already, it appears, he has the Astors' support. Staggered by this news, I pumped Rab, who I felt, too, might be favourable to such a cabal: but he added that personally he would support Halifax, if he was in the running. So should I, of course. But I would prefer Sam Hoare to Inskip.

8 June

At the Opera (Rigoletto – amazingly old fashioned and funny) I had a long talk with the Aga Khan, who told me that he thought there were only three men in Europe who wanted war: Goering, Winston Churchill, and President Benes. We talked of charm, and turning to his French wife, who is beautiful, and chic, asked her who was the most attractive man she had ever met. 'Heetlaire,' she surprisingly retorted. Evidently the dictator turned on his persuasive powers on her, and obviously succeeded completely in demolishing her French prejudices.

14 June

On my way to the House I met the Chamberlains in the Park and duly doffed my bowler (everyone wears bowlers now – since the Eden debâcle black Homburgs are 'out'). I tried to hurry past, but one of the two detectives who always follow the PM caught me up and said: 'The Prime Minister would like to speak to you' – so I had a long talk with them and they were amiability itself. I asked them to come to lunch next week, and they accepted.

15 June

The Foreign Office Banquet – with all the Corps Diplomatique and the Government present in glittering uniforms. The Prime Minister, looking young and smiling, was seated between the Brazilian and French Ambassadors. The dinner was long and excellent, and the wines splendid. No speeches – only toasts. As I arrived, I said to Lord Halifax: 'It's like the Congress of Vienna'. 'You must feel at home then, Chips' he replied. He looked magnificent, and I was amused to see that Duff – to his dismay – was next to the German Ambassador, Dirksen.

19 June

The 'Sunday Express' today published a most extraordinary paragraph to the effect that I am really 41 instead of 39, and hinted that I had faked my age in the reference books. The awful thing is that it is true. Now I feel apprehensive and shy, as one does when one is in disgrace. Honor is being very sweet and loyal about it ... I told her she would be a widow two years earlier.

20 June

I had a drink with Jim Thomas, who told me much of the Eden-Chamberlain controversy.... Jim has kept a diary, dictated daily, he told me, since September, soon after the first major row between Chamberlain and Eden took place. One day Jim intends to publish it, but he dare not do it now. It would, he assured me, 'let in the Socialists for a generation', so dark a villain according to him, is the Prime Minister. I told Jim he was a fool, and that only knaves kept diaries. That from me!

22 June

We dined with the indefatigable Laura Corrigan, a festival of 137 people, all the youth and fashion of London with the Kents enjoying themselves wildly and leading the revels.... There is a new dance called the Palais Glide which smacks of the servant's hall, and, lubricated with champagne, the company pranced about doing this absurd 'pas' till 4 a.m. Leslie Belisha was in the gayest of moods and 'cracked the dawn', as did half the Cabinet. In spite of the general frivolity of the evening, I gleaned some news – i.e. that the King is sound, and is very against Anthony Eden, who, in two years, has caused us more trouble than any Foreign Secretary since Palmerston.

26 June

Our luncheon today for the Prime Minister was a flop. I had miscalculated or at least was extremely unlucky. I invited the guests for 1.15 hoping that the Prime Minister would be punctual, which he usually is. Instead he was delayed by something of which I did not know at the time. At one o'clock, in walked that dreaded creature, the too-early guest, in this case, Bill Astor. For some reason I was feeling ill and detached and could not put into the function that zest which usually characterises a Channon party. Everyone except the Chamberlains was desperately punctual ... then followed a long pause and we waited. As a bad joke Harold Balfour wrote out a message to say that 'Mr and Mrs Chamberlain were very sorry that they are unable to come to luncheon'. Luckily I recognised his handwriting, or I would certainly have had a heart-attack: many cocktails, and soon there was a hum of conversation, and then at 1.30 there came a real message that 'The Prime Minister and Mrs Chamberlain are unavoidably detained and will be late.' The atmosphere became uneasy: Lord Granard looked irritated. At length, Mrs Chamberlain arrived alone, by taxi, wearing little gold bells in her ears which jingled and succeeded in irritating me. I introduced a few people to her and finally we went in – our guest of honour missing – though he did arrive, eventually. Honor was able to make him laugh and he got on well with Mrs Keppel, who was on his other side (Freddie Birkenhead asked her if she was any relation to 'King Edward's friend', whom he thought dead). There was then a hitch about coffee – which I had ordered upstairs – and our guests left coffee-less. Perhaps it did not go too badly – Diana Cooper seemed to enjoy it, and the food was excellent; at least we have entertained the Prime Minister, which is something.

Back to the House, and someone, I can't remember who, whispered to me: 'There is going to be some fun with Sandys at the end of questions, as he is raising privilege'. No-one seemed to be prepared for the storm that followed. Sandys rose, grave, wordy and self-important, and told his tale, of how he had been threatened by Donald Somervell, the Attorney General, with the Official Secrets Acts, and the possibility of a two years sentence! My immediate reaction was that someone, I could scarcely believe it was Belisha, had blundered: but at the same time, what was Sandys doing with State secrets anyhow?[35] The House took a serious view and was instantly on its guard to protect its rights. The whole Socialist opposition was violent. It was very exciting – but as I walked away Rab cautioned me to take no part in the controvery.

35. Mr Sandys, MP for Norwood, had put down a Parliamentary Question about London's anti-aircraft defences that demonstrated detailed knowledge covered by the Official Secrets Act (Sandys was a Second Lieutenant in a West London anti-aircraft battery). The Army Council ordered an enquiry into how Sandys had received such information; Somervell, extremely unwisely, had threatened Sandys with the provision of the Official Secrets Act.

27 June

Sandys makes all the headlines, and has the Press behind him, as it resents the Official Secrets Act: and it has now come out that the Prime Minister was consulted by Belisha and he advised him to send the papers to the Attorney General. The PM was, however, unaware of Sandys' intention to raise the matter with the Speaker until just before our luncheon yesterday, and that is what delayed him.

29 June

There was another flare-up today at Question Time in regard to the suave, freckled Duncan Sandys. The War Office have ordered him to be present tomorrow in full uniform to give evidence at a Court of Inquiry, which is to investigate the leakage of information. Sandys submitted that a prima facie case of breach of privilege had been committed, and he asked for the protection of the House! The Speaker gave it, amidst tremendous confusion, and the PM announced that he would move that a Select Committee be appointed to inquire into the whole matter. There was glee among the Eden-ites.

2 July *Cliveden*

I really wonder why we came here: I hate week-ends, and so often feel desœuvré and bored in other people's houses, and there is nothing so out of date as a 1900 house, which Cliveden is, en plein. But the park is glorious, with its famous views and vistas. Virginia Cowles[36] is staying here, who I call Valencia Cowles, as she is so 'red'. But she is an intelligent girl, who has, in a year's time, made a position for herself in the Press world, and is a really good journalist. But people take her too seriously. She is even feared by the Foreign Office. She adores Vansittart.

8 July

I love my life: I love sauntering through the Park to the FO and meeting the PM on the way: I love the rich flowers and seeing the Horse Guards disappearing under the arch, and I like the atmosphere of despatch boxes, Government messengers, the

36. Now Mrs Aidan Crawley.

whole grey and red Government racket: the hurry and animation of Downing St. How could I have ever lived any other way?

29 July

At the Foreign Office we were in a frenzy of preparations with Questions, when Rab Butler was summoned to Lord Halifax's rooms and remained there a fraction too long, making himself late for the Prime Minister. Miss Watson (the PM's very efficient secretary) telephoned to me frantically so I fetched him from Lord Halifax's room and rushed him to No. 10, where the Prime Minister was pacing the floor saying, 'Where is he? Where is he?' he being Rab. The PM grunted at him surlily but said 'Hello Chips' to me with his usual dazzling smile that so excites one's loyalty. We then rushed to the House of Commons, and arrived on the front bench with only fifty seconds in hand. Questions passed off smoothly.

7 August

My boy is enchanting, so gentle and gay, I hold him in my lap, and see my own dark eyes reflected. That Fate should be kind to him is my deepest wish ... If anything happened to him it would kill me.

All this week there have been war scares.

CHAPTER FOUR

Munich, and the Coming of War
September 1938–September 1939

Chips's position in the Foreign Office, and his close relationship with some senior Ministers, provided him with an interesting inside view of the events of 1938–9. The value of his account lies partly in the fact of his intense partisanship of the Chamberlain Government and of the Prime Minister in particular, and partly because he was involved in – or fully informed of – the numerous intrigues which reflected the serious strains within the Tory Party after Munich.

2 September 1938
I spent the whole day at the Foreign Office. The Czech telegrams are very alarming but I am quite convinced that Hitler is too canny to risk a war, so long as there is a chance of French and Russian participation.

4 September
Tomorrow I leave by car for Geneva to attend the League of Nations Assembly. Me at Geneva! It is almost a Bateman joke, as I have always scoffed and ridiculed that absurd Assembly. But there I go. I hated Geneva when I went with Lord Buckmaster in 1924 – was it 1924? And meanwhile, Kelvedon, that sleeping waterlily of a place, must await my return, as must my white dogs, and my glorious dark-eyed, angelic, glamorous, 'super' son. I love him with every fibre of my body, and he is all mine.

6 September *Luxembourg*
In 'The Times' of today there is a startling leader in which a hint is dropped that the Czech Government would be well advised to consent to, or at least consider, a frontier revision. In other words, cede the Sudeten areas to Germany – the beginning of the end.

8 September *Hotel Carlton Parc, Geneva*

Arrived in Geneva where I found Diana and John Julius Cooper waiting for me at the hotel. Diana (how like her) is already enamoured with Geneva. Perhaps I shall like it more now that I am better acquainted. She had seen no one for days, and so was unusually fascinating and quite seduced the Foreign Office boys. We had a glorious, exciting evening, all rather tipsy. They say that war is inevitable, which seems now the accepted Foreign Office view.

9 September

Rab arrived, looking ridiculously like a Minister, at 7.10 a.m. I met him at the station and rather sleepily escorted him to the hotel. He was a touch aloof, as always when contact has been broken, and his clothes are really tragic. But he has a quiet, strong shyness which is deceiving.

We went to the League building, which is a vast affair, a huge modern, white, dignified, lavish, empty palace, as befits the meeting place of 47 nations. 47 nations in theory, but in reality, the League is now really only an anti-dictator Club. The bars and lobbies of the League's building are full of Russians and Jews who intrigue with and dominate the press, and spend their time spreading rumours of approaching war, but I don't believe them, not with Neville at the helm. He will wriggle out somehow.

We all dined gaily again tonight at the Plat d'Argent, and Rab almost embarrassed us once or twice with his high staccato laugh which, when he is amused, becomes veritably soprano, like a pheasant's call. But he charmed, and was charmed by, Diana.

Tomorrow the League racket begins.

10 September *Geneva*

The first meeting of the Council was held this morning and I saw Litvinoff, the dread intriguer, for the first time. He looked older and more like a Socialist MP than I had expected, and neither so smiling or so evil as Maisky. Every day, after the session, he slips out of the building by a side door, for fear of assassination by White Russians, though on the whole I would have thought that he was safer here than in Russia. Diana, now

Queen of Geneva and John Foster, that dark handsome young intellectual with a touch of the Grenfell charm about him, Fellow of All Souls, prospective candidate, and altogether one of the cleverest young men in England, Roger Makins, gloomy and an Edenite, Peter Loxley and my beloved Peake all dined with me. As we waited upstairs for a table in the restaurant, we did the 'Lambeth Walk' and altogether had a riotous evening. Everyone is indignant with 'The Times' for its article last Tuesday, which they pretend has strengthened Hitler's hand, and the Foreign Office have quickly issued a dementi that 'The Times' in no way reflected the Government's view. I now discover that Lord Halifax dined with Geoffrey Dawson, my informants say, on Monday night, the 5th, and that 'The Times' article was definitely inspired, a ballon d'essai, to see how the public would react, and to prepare them for the Runciman Report.

11 September *Geneva*

Bad news from London. The Czech crisis is looming large. We are trembling on the very brink of war, though neither Rab Butler nor I believe that it will come about. Geneva is full of rumours. The Swiss are alleged to be strengthening their defences, while the Germans are known to have mobilised two million men.

This afternoon Diana let us in for a typical Diana adventure. She had always wanted to see Coppet, with its relics of Madame de Stael, and so telephoned a message to the concierge of the Chateau that the Delegation Britannique would be arriving, and could they please be shown over? She did not realise that the present owners, three granddaughters of Madame de Stael, were in residence. These aged, white-haired garrulous, faubourg ladies received us with some surprise, as in grey flannels and sports shirts and looking most unofficial, we gatecrashed the Chateau. It is much as Madame de Stael left it, and even as her father, Neckar, originally arranged it. I thought how charming some of the things would look at Belgrave Square, the portraits by Ramsey, the books and the wallpaper. Altogether, I thought it had great atmosphere. Thus we spent the last (?) Sunday of peace.

12 September

Today De Valera was elected, thanks to the votes of the British Delegation, President of the Assembly. He is grey and dignified, and looks like an unfashionable dentist. He spoke of Ireland as Ireland and never once use the absurd name 'Eire'.

We spent a long day waiting for Hitler's big speech, which may decide the fate of Europe. One wonders who won the war, now that an Austrian paper-hanger can so terrify the world. Bits of the speech began to come through at dinner time.

13 September

Next day. The news is bad. Hitler has staked his claim, the Czechs will not budge, and the French say they will march if an inch of Czech territory is violated. I don't believe it:

Litvinoff was heard to remark to Monsieur Negrin, the Spanish Premier, who is staying in a hotel, 'Si nous n'avons pas une guerre mondiale, vous êtes foutus.'

14 September

The big Banquet of the British Delegation was held tonight, and I induced Diana, as a Cabinet Minister's wife, to act as hostess, and so she received the guests. De Valera, as President of the Assembly, was invited as Guest of Honour. He has never before attended a British Government official Banquet, and so it was intimated to him privately that if he was going to refuse to drink the Toast to the King's Health it would be more tactful to stay away. He said that he would of course drink it, and did. There were 80 or more at dinner. Towards the end of the Banquet came the news, the great world stirring news, that Neville, on his own initiative, seeing war coming closer and closer, had telegraphed to Hitler that he wanted to see him, and asked him to name an immediate rendezvous. The German Government surprised and flattered, had instantly accepted and so Neville, at the age of 69, for the first time in his life, gets into an aeroplane tomorrow morning and flies to Berchtesgaden! It is one of the finest, most inspiring acts of all history. The company rose to their feet electrified, as all the world must be, and drank his health. History must be ransacked to find a parallel.

Of course a way out will now be found. Neville by his imagination and practical good sense, has saved the world. I am staggered.

15 September

This morning, Neville, accompanied by one or two experts, left London for Berchtesgaden. Of course some Jews and many of the more shady pressmen who hang about Geneva are furious. No war. No revenge on Germany – and they say that Hitler will insult Chamberlain, browbeat him as he bullied Schussnigg. No fear.

This evening I dined with Maurice de Rothschild, a dinner of 17, in his rich house, full of amazing Boldinis and medium Tiepolos. Dinner was indifferent, but the wines staggering. One claret was 69 years old, the same age as Neville, as I pointed out. Everyone was a touch tipsy with Rothschild wine and admiration, even hero-worship for Chamberlain.

16 September

The Chamberlain-Hitler meeting seems to have been a huge success. Neville is returning to London today to lay Hitler's propositions before the Cabinet, though I gather from a private source that Duff, Walter Elliot, Winterton and, of course, that gloomy Oliver Stanley – 'Snow White' as we all call him – are likely to be troublesome.

This morning I stole away from the meeting of the Assembly. (They are almost unsitthroughable) and drove Rab to the far side of the lake where we lunched and talked for two hours. He was charming. He thought aloud; told me his creed, displayed his civil service cunning, his way of handling men, his theory that the man in possession when challenged must eventually inevitably part with something though, as he said, it is better to postpone the challenge as long as possible. That is what these harebrained Edenites do not understand. As we talked, the lake lapped the shores, and I came to the conclusion that there would be no war, no matter what people said. Rab, too, has implicit faith in Halifax and Chamberlain and agreed with me that both were linked together by an understanding. Either would do an even dishonest deed to reach a high goal. The ultimate object was all that counted – Suddenly it was 4 o'clock.

There was glorious weather tonight for Diana's Ball, the Ball that was designed to be the last of peace, and thus to rank with the Duchess of Richmond's famous effort on the eve of Waterloo, but fate and Neville have ruled otherwise. . . . She gave it in the Villa Diodati, a lovely rococo Maison-de-Plaisance overlooking the lake and near an earlier house in which Milton had once lived. It was enchanting with its boiseries and pictures, and had been let for a time to Byron, and later to Balzac who had lived there with both his loves. But tonight, the empty pavilion had been scrubbed, refurnished and lit by candles and filled with flowers. A dozen tables were grouped in the long room, and a buffet supper was served, mostly by me. There was much to drink, provided by Maurice de Rothschild and myself, and nearly 90 people sat down to the 18th century fête, including Carl Burckhart, the High Commissioner of Danzig and a few members of Genevese society. A radio was brought in, and we heard Neville's account of his flight to Berchtesgaden, and heard that he was going back to Germany, perhaps, in a few days time. The company became exhilarated, drank overmuch, danced, became romantic, rowdy, reminiscent, as the candles spluttered. The Genevois were thrilled to see the famous 'Lady Diana'. Rab quoted Lamartine's 'Le Lac' to a very decolletée Swiss miss on Byron's balcony.

17 September

We all awoke to realities, and the war which still looms. Now Henlein, backed by Hitler and his two million men under arms is demanding secession and nothing less than incorporation of the Sudetenland into the Reich will satisfy the Germans. These are Hitler's terms. Will the French reject them? Will Czechoslovakia? There is a Cabinet today.

19 September *Geneva*

I have come to the conclusion that the League has seen its best days. States are resigning every day and it is only Rab's secret persuasion of Poland which has induced her to remain a member. What after all could be more absurd, with the whole world on the precipice of suicide, that the crisis should never once be referred to by the League of Nations? Still, it might serve a useful purpose if it were non-political, and would devote itself to good work about droughts, refugees, etc.

Chips, rejoined by Honor, left Geneva for Yugoslavia via Venice.

22 September — *Grand Hotel, Venice*

I induced the hotel manager to let us listen to his wireless, but the news is no better. I wonder if we are wise to go to Yugoslavia after all? I don't much care. The bottom of life seems to have fallen out.

Neville flew again to Germany today, this time to Godesberg where Hitler is to meet him: he will get a terrific welcome and a Venetian woman in the street said to me today 'Every Italian woman is praying for Chamberlain'.

23 September — *Brdo Palace*

We arrived here this evening and found the perfect, pink palace smiling in the sunlight and the Prince Regent advancing to welcome us. He seemed enchanted to see us, and we are by ourselves, as both the Grand Duchess and Princess Olga have had to rush to Paris to nurse invalids. We are blissfully alone in this glorious place, where above everywhere I am happiest. Of course we discuss the war, listen to the wireless, which is bad and perhaps jammed, and look across at the mountains beyond which lies the Colossus Germany. . . . Paul cannot believe in the war. Messages come in every minute from Belgrade, and his private wireless station takes the news. This evening he gave me his solemn oath that in the event of war he will never do anything – anything to hurt England. At worst, he will be neutral, as he would not dare to come in on our side, as both Germany and Italy would at once squeeze his country to death.

24 September — *Brdo*

The situation seems worse, though there is no real news. Shall we ever get back? And if so, how? Though the Regent has offered us an aeroplane to take us wherever we wish. I rang up Freddie Birkenhead at the FO and he said to come home immediately as the situation could not be worse . . .

I still cannot believe that the worst will happen.

25 September

The PM flew back to London yesterday, convened the Cabinet, and had an audience with the King, who has been fitted, like everyone else in London, with a gasmask. There seems to be some hysteria: here all is calm and great beauty. We have our meals alone, the Regent, Honor and I, and wonder sadly when we will all be together again.

26 September

Parliament is to meet on Wednesday (the day after tomorrow) at 2.45. With luck I shall get there in time.

The King of Bulgaria arrived before dinner, and there was a comedy, as the Regent went to one station to receive him, and he arrived, in Hitler's private train, at the other.

Paul and he had a long talk before dinner, for which King Boris did not change. When we went in, Honor was surprised, and rather offended, that he walked through the door ahead of her – five men and one woman. No other King would do that, and I have met many. Il est très muffle. King Boris sat between us – facing Paul, looking Jewish, though he is really very Coburg and very Orleans in appearance, with the bad traits of both houses. He told us that he had seen Hitler yesterday, and had found him 'sérieux'. He had also seen Mussolini, who, in his opinion, definitely does not want war. He was interested when Honor told him she was Lord Halifax's niece, and became much more deferential. I fear His Bulgarian Majesty is a snob. It was a strange little dinner party – King Boris, Prince Paul, Honor and I and two courtiers – one Yugoslav – one Bulgarian. What has the future in store for us all?

27 September

We left Brdo early and caught the Orient Express, taking a sad leave of my beloved Regent. At the station we were taken for royalty, and there was the usual excess of Yugoslavian bowing and scraping. We spent all day in the train, apprehensive at having no news, and very relieved to cross the Swiss frontier about midnight, and to be out of potential enemy country. It would only be fair to record, however, that the Italians were all charming, all very anti-war and all fulsome about Chamberlain;

but one wonders whether the Duce knows the temper of his people, and how little they want to march.

Rushing across Northern Italy, I thought of my two great friends – Rab and the Regent – so utterly dissimilar. Rab is fundamentally male, endowed with great intelligence and judgement and even some charm: but the lighter graces are certainly not his: he has no superficiality, no social sense. The Regent, on the other hand, is ME, only more so, with every conceivable quality I admire, except physical attraction. Distinguished, affable, entertaining, with sound judgement reinforced by a subtle Slav, almost feminine intuitive sense, which is unerring. One day, Rab will surely pass out of my life – perhaps when he becomes PM, but Paul I hope will be in it for ever.

28 September *Kelvedon*

(The great day in the House of Commons.)

An incredible day which started when I woke in Paris about seven, dressed, and was the first to leave the train at the Gare de Lyon, where I found the French jittery and unpleasant, though I miraculously got a seat on a London plane. At Le Bourget I ran into Barbie Wallace who had just arrived from Geneva. She told me that Rab and Euan Wallace were staying on there until the end of the Council. Barbie, who is an Eden-ite, although intelligent and with a political nose, also said that she had heard that Winston Churchill would be Prime Minister tonight in place of Neville. I replied that anyone who said that could have no knowledge of the House of Commons; to which she said that I did not know the mood of the country, as I had been away. I didn't believe her, but was a bit shaken. Was my world collapsing? I climbed into the plane, after buying all the newspapers, which made harrowing reading ... The Fleet mobilised. Trenches dug in Hyde Park. At Heston there was war atmosphere already, with young airmen lounging about, smoking; we heard the word 'Boche' again, and someone said 'mufti'. It was 1914 all over again.

Home, and I changed and went to the House of Commons, where a crowd was waiting outside to watch the legislators arrive. I made sure of my place on the PPS's bench, and was told as I came in, by Stuart Russell, that all was not quite over, that we were still in communication, at least, with Hitler, although Sir Horace Wilson's flight had been a failure. I was then told by the FO people that the PM had sent SOS messages, in a last attempt to save the world, to both Mussolini and to Hitler this morning. No reply yet had come. . . . The solemn House, unaware of this latest démarche, filled every seat, and everyone was aware of the momentous hour and the gravity of the situation, which was beyond anything perhaps that the House had ever known. The PM at last came in, and was cheered frantically by members in all parts of the House. Everyone appreciates the great efforts he has made. . . . I sat immediately behind him, Lord Halifax and Lord Baldwin were in the front row of the gallery by the clock, immediately over it was the Duke of Kent. . . . The PM rose, and in measured, stately English began the breathless tale of his negotiations with Hitler, with the accounts of his flights to Germany, of Lord Runciman's report, etc. He was calm, deliberate, good-tempered and patient. . . . My eyes stole up to Mrs Fitzroy's gallery and I saw Mrs Chamberlain listening intently. A lovely figure sitting by her made me a gesture of recognition and half-waved; it was the Duchess of Kent. Behind her was a dark, black figure, and I looked again and recognised Queen Mary, who never before, in my recollection has been to the House of Commons; – the Ambassadors' Gallery was full. I was next to that ass, Anthony Crossley, the MP for Stratford, and whenever there was any remark deprecating the Germans he cheered lustily, 'That's the way to treat them' – once when the tide was going with him, he turned scoffingly to me, and said 'Why don't you cheer?' – again he asked 'How are your friends the Huns now?' – I sensed a feeling of unpopularity.

The great speech continued for an hour, and gradually the House settled back prepared for an announcement that must, although perhaps not for several days, lead to War. Hitler has decreed that his mobilisation will begin today at two o'clock . . . magnificently, the PM led up to his peroration – but before he got to it, I suddenly saw the FO officials in the box signalling frantically to me; I could not get to them, as it meant climbing over 20 PPS's, so Dunglass fetched a bit of paper from them which he handed to Sir John Simon, who glanced at it, and I tried to read it over his shoulder, but there was not time, as he suddenly, and excitedly tugged at the PM's coat; Chamberlain turned from the box on which he was leaning, and there was a second's consultation – 'Shall I tell them?' I heard him whisper. 'Yes', Simon, Sam Hoare and David Margesson all nodded, and I think Kingsley Wood did likewise – I am not sure about that, the excitement was so intense – and the conference 'in full divan' was only of a moment's duration. The PM cleared his throat, and resumed his speech, with just a suggestion of a smile. Then he told how he had telegraphed to both Hitler and Mussolini this morning; he had sought Mussolini's eleventh hour help and intervention, and how the Duce had not let him down, but had acted promptly. How foolish the anti-Italians now looked, and Anthony Eden's face – I watched it – twitched, and he seemed discomfited.

The House shifted with relief – there might yet be a respite – the Führer had agreed to postpone negotiations for another 24 hours – and then the PM played his trump ace, and read the message that had been handed to me – 'That is not all. I have something further to say to the House,' and he told how Hitler had invited him to Munich tomorrow morning, that Mussolini had accepted the same invitation, that M. Daladier in all probability would do so too – every heart throbbed and there was born in many, in me, at least, a gratitude, an admiration for the PM which will be eternal. I felt sick with enthusiasm, longed to clutch him – he continued for a word or two and then the House rose and in a scene of riotous delight, cheered, bellowed their approval. We stood on our benches, waved our order papers, shouted – until we were hoarse – a scene of indescribable enthusiasm – Peace must now be saved, and with it the world.

At length some order was restored, and when Mr Attlee rose, I rushed from the Chamber to our room, and put through an urgent telephone call to Rab at Geneva, to be a happy Cassandra. ... I got on almost at once, Peter Loxley answering the telephone, as our Chief was over at the League Building. I told him the news, which he could scarcely believe, and he hung up to rush and tell Rab. Then I ran into Bill Astor who said the House was up, and we watched Queen Mary drive away with the Kents from the Speaker's House. The crowds cheered them. Then I saw Chamberlain's car draw up, and Bill Astor and I rushed up the private staircase he always uses, and met him advancing with Mrs Chamberlain and the faithful Dunglass. He had walked out of the noisy frantic Chamber alone, and a gulf of his own making seemed to open between him and mankind. The Saviour of Peace, got quietly into his car, umbrella and all. He saw Bill Astor and me scampering, and he smiled, as did Mrs Chamberlain, proudly. Bill and I then rushed into the Palace Yard, and cheered ourselves hoarse, and the crowd took it up and gave him a rousing welcome, waving their handkerchiefs and shouting, and his car was soon swallowed up. Exhausted, exhilarated, I went back to the House, hushed now, though the litter on the floor reminded me of a Southend Sunday in September.

I will always remember little Neville today, with his too long hair, greying at the sides, his smile, his amazing spirits and seeming lack of fatigue, as he stood there, alone, fighting the dogs of war single-handed and triumphant – he seemed the reincarnation of St George – so simple and so unspoilt – now in a few hours for the third time he takes a plane to a far country in the service of England. May God speed him, and reward him for his efforts. I don't know what this country has done to deserve him.

29 September *Kelvedon*

A wave of relief has spread over the world. May the indefatigable Neville be successful.

This morning the whole Cabinet, except that absurd dissenting nanny-goat Eddie Winterton, was at Heston (yes, including Duff) to wish the indomitable PM Godspeed. May he be successful.

30 September

I was called at 8 a.m.: by my side lay the newspapers – 'Agreement signed at 12.53 in Munich'. So it is peace, and a Chamberlain, respectable gentleman's peace: the whole world rejoices whilst only a few malcontents jeer.

Alan [Lennox-Boyd] told me that he had met Lord Halifax in the Park and had congratulated him on the great success, the triumph of Chamberlain, and his, Halifax's share. Halifax replied that all the credit was Neville's and that his admiration for him surpassed all bounds; but he added that he foresaw political troubles ahead, both in Parliament and in the country. But I consider Neville the Man of our Age.

1 October
Duff has resigned in what I must say is a very well-written letter, and the PM has immediately accepted his resignation. But we shall hear more of this – personally my reactions are mixed. I am sorry for Diana; they give up £5,000 per annum, a lovely house – and for what? Does Duff think he will make money at literature?

3 October *5 Belgrave Square*
The storm broke over the Government this afternoon, for having preserved peace.

The big debate began: and the crowded House was restless; when the PM took his seat directly in front of us, there was cheering, but not the hysterical enthusiasm of last Wednesday. Duff Cooper rose from the seat traditionally kept for the retiring, or resigning, the third corner seat immediately below the gangway – it was here I heard first Sam Hoare make his famous Mea Culpa over sanctions, and later Anthony Eden. Now it was Duff's turn, my plump, conceited, Duff. He did not impress the House and his arguments were flat, inconclusive, and the House took the speech as a dignified farewell from a man whom they were tired of, for Duff is definitely not a Parliamentarian. His defect is lack of imagination, which makes him a poor writer, although his English is distinguished. Diana was in the Weeping Gallery.

The PM followed Duff's rather contradictory personal explanation carefully, but he was tired and Wednesday's glow had gone. Eden followed, and he was charmless, looked old, and he too now shares the St Helena bench with his old enemy, Duff Cooper. Will they now sink their differences?

The House buzzed with intrigue, but I bet that there would be no serious revolt against the Government, at least not a revolt which would be reflected in the Division Lobbies.

5 October
Winston's contribution today enlivened the House, discomfited the Front Bench, but did not materially weaken the Government's

excellent case. He went on deploring that we had not taken stronger action against the Dictators. . . . Simon made a magnificent speech, quoting Shelley's great lines about Hope. 'To Hope . . . till Hope creates from its own wreck the thing it contemplates . . .'

6 October *Kelvedon*

We met, at 11, and for some anxious hours we listened to the debate. Would the Eden-Cooper conclave actually vote against us and persuade many others to do so? Would the PM do well? At 3.15 he rose and was magnificent, making so moving an appeal, so devoid of resentment or bitterness, that I should have thought he would have led us unanimously behind him into the Division Lobby. The House was with him, and he seemed aware of the strength of his following. Even the St Vitus antics of the Conservative Opposition were powerless to stem the Chamberlain tide, which swelled and swelled as he spoke. At length he sat down and the fateful divisions began, the first was the Socialist Amendment and the figures were:

369 for the Government
150 against

I was almost the first to congratulate the PM and he put out his hand and tapped my arm, beaming with pleasure. There were two red spots on his cheeks, and he looked positively jubilant.

The figures were highly satisfactory, but not so good as those of the French who were almost unanimous (only 73 against and of them 71 were Communists) in their support of Daladier in the Chambre yesterday.

20 October *Kelvedon*

I went to Edward Stanley's magnificent memorial Service.[1] Just before the choir entered, the Chamberlains arrived, and he took his seat in the first stall, and prayed a long time. I watched him

1. Edward Stanley, who was only 44, had died on 16 October; he was described by Chips as 'courteous, almost handsome, gentle, genial, gay, simple and loyal. He enjoyed fun and society, but was quite unmalicious.'

throughout the ceremony; he looked very alive and sad, and when a sunbeam fell on him he seemed, what he is, a saint.

I wonder whether he could be only thinking of Edward, whom he liked, but could not have loved: I suspected his thoughts were further away, at Munich and of the calamity he had averted. Leslie Belisha also in a stall, looked gay and debonair: he is becoming less hideous. All the clergy looked older than the man in whose memory the service was. Leaving, I saw Mr Attlee's eyes were red with weeping: the service, he said simply, had got him down. No wonder: the Last Post followed by Chopin. I never liked him so much before.

30 October *Kelvedon*

Va-et-Vient at Kelvedon. Prince Fritzi of Prussia came here for the day: he is just back from Germany via Doorn where he stayed with his Grandfather the Kaiser, whom he loved. He told us no-one in Germany had wanted war; all Germany had feared it. The Army and the Potsdam group were averse to it and are growing increasingly hostile to the Hitler Régime, to the Régime more than the man. Himmler and Ribbentrop were the dangers. From Kelvedon he went to London to have tea with Queen Mary who dotes on him. He has been working for, and has at last succeeded in once more establishing, good relations between her and her grandfather. The exile of Doorn now writes regularly to Queen Mary and to his old uncle, the Duke of Connaught. They are all in the twilight of their lives, and it is pleasant that between them, at least, there is no more war bitterness. The Kaiser told Fritzi only last week that he is still haunted by the fate which befell the Czar and his family. He had sent the Czar a telegram offering him a free and protected passage through Germany, had he wished to escape by sea. (This was at the moment when the Czar had tried to get to England.) It was Lloyd George who spoilt and stopped everything, and the late King had been weak with him, not understanding the danger. Their responsibility in the matter has ever been a millstone to both Queen Mary and King George, and their failure to help their poor Russian relations in the hour of danger is the one blot on their lives. Of late, Fritzi tells me, Queen Mary has been sorely conscience stricken.

1 November *Belgrave Square*

We are inundated with work and today the Opposition raised 'Munich and what has happened since' on the adjournment. By Opposition, one means nowadays of course, that little group of 'Glamour Boys' who are attempting to torpedo the Prime Minister; he is too lenient with them. Vyvyn Adams, who is much opposed to us, complained to me that he had not been called to speak for nine months. I went to the Speaker and after a little preliminary flattery, suggested that he call Adams. He promised that he would and later did, whereupon Adams attacked us violently! Thus are things done in democratic England.

2 November *London*

The long postponed Debate on the Italian agreement came at last today. The PM, who is becoming increasingly dictatorial (fortunately, he is always right) wants to reward Signor Mussolini for his help at Munich, and the Duce wants the ratification of this agreement, as it will confer recognition on the King of Italy as Emperor of Abyssinia. The Debate was singularly lifeless, dull and foregone, until towards the end of the afternoon, Anthony Eden got up and filled the House. He made a bitter but polite attack on the Government. There was a leftish leer in his eyes, and even his clothes, I thought, lacked their patrician suavity of old.

Later, I found myself completely alone on the 2nd bench, with Ernest Brown the sole occupant of the Front Bench. Suddenly a hand was placed on my shoulder and looking up I saw that it was Anthony himself. We had a long, friendly, unhurried, even affectionate talk. He was charm itself; he had not seen much of me all these years, he had been too busy, did I love the Foreign Office? I was, he had heard it said, a great success there; were we in our Essex house yet? We must meet soon; it was lovely to be able to dine out in peace; he was really enjoying his freedom. He would never again raise his voice about Foreign affairs in the House. We had a surprisingly warm reconciliation and I left him aglow with appeasement. I have always liked him, though I have always thought him 'simple' and still do. Why he should have selected this moment in which to make me an advance, I don't know. Possibly he thought I would intimate to high quarters his determination never to refer again to Foreign affairs. If he thought so, he was, for once in his disastrous career, right; for I rushed to the Prime Minister's room and told him. He smiled, and murmured 'I am glad to hear it'.

The Debate thereafter, was desultory, with nobody much interested; everyone wants friendship with Italy, that is all save a few frenzied enemies of Mussolini and, of course, the Labour Party. Duff voted with the Government tonight. He could hardly do otherwise, as he was a member of the Government when the Italian agreement was negotiated. The figures were good . . . so now the Italian episode is ended. What a triumph for Sam Hoare. He is vindicated at long last. Rab wound up, and very bad he was too.

3 November *Kelvedon*

Lunched alone at the H. of C. and looked quite handsome, though tired. I caught a glimpse in a glass of my slightly overdressed self.

Barbie Wallace is frankly an Eden-ite and told me she had spent the afternoon with all the Glamour Boys buzzing about, talking at Noel Coward's studio where he had a cocktail party for the 'Opposition'. Emerald says he (Noel Coward) is quite out of date. There is a cleavage in London society about Chamberlain; though the ranks may close again when we are faced with an election.

18 November *Kelvedon*

I am dumbfounded by the news of the Bridgwater election, where Vernon Bartlett, standing as an Independent, has had a great victory over the Government candidate. This is the worst blow the Government has had since 1935. Of course, there are extenuating explanations, but these are meagre comfort.

The Central Office machine is cumbersome, inefficient, and wants overhauling, otherwise we shall lose the election; but the election is only poor comfort for the Socialists; they only win seats when they stand down in favour of an Independent.

Honor and I went to dine locally with the 'county' in a ghastly house smelling of gentry – china in cabinets higgledy-piggledy, water-colours in gilt frames on the walls. Horror.

8 November *5 Belgrave Square*

The 4th session of this most fateful, eventful, Parliament started with the Opening of Parliament today. I wonder what it will unfold for us? A war? An election? In the past we have had everything else – scandals, political strife, resignations, an Abdication and a Coronation . . .

The wave of anti-Chamberlain feeling, though at present largely confined to London society, seems to be growing.

15 November *Belgrave Square*

The Pogroms in Germany and the persecutions there have roused much indignation everywhere. I must say Hitler never helps, and always makes Chamberlain's task more difficult.

16 November *London*

I lunched with Loelia Westminster in her lovely, chic, gay house, where I was next to poor Maxine Elliot, now a complete wreck. She looks a hundred, and her figure is catastrophic, but her great eyes are charming still, and she is gay, Edwardian and flirtatious. She was full of Reynaldo Hahn who is performing tonight at 'Winnie' Polignac's. I thought he was dead. I heard him in 1917 in Paris.

In the evening, I thought the Buckingham Palace party very mixed: a third list, I fear; and hardly any of our friends. Queen Mary glittered with five diamond necklaces about her neck. She was in blue with literally mountains of jewels. Pamela Berry whispered to me – 'She has bagged all the best'. She has. Soon she advanced upon us, and beside her, all royalties, except the Kents, look second-rate. She shook hands and joked with Mr Kennedy, the American Ambassador, who was immediately behind us. He presented two of his daughters – entranced they looked – to her. Then the royalties moved into the gallery and Honor, who looked magnificent, began to get tired, and we left. Below we found the Anthony Edens waiting for their car. 'The worst of being sacked, is you can never find your car', Anthony remarked.

17 November *Belgrave Square*

Diana Cooper rang me early to ask all about the BP party to

which they had not been invited. Was it, she wondered, because Duff had resigned, or because she had curtsied to the Duchess of Windsor in Paris?

A long day at the House; I am the Supreme Attender; it was the day when the Glamour Boys hoped to damage us, and Winston Churchill made a terrific attack on the Government, and he begged fifty Conservatives to follow him into the Lobby. Actually only Messrs Macmillan and Bob Boothby went, and the figures, a majority of 196 for the Government, were satisfactory. The PM spoke for 1 hour 1 minute, very well, clearly and amusingly. He refused to create a Ministry of Supply.

21 November *Belgrave Square*

The newspapers splash the arrival of the Regent, my dearly beloved Paul, who comes this evening.

No-one ever accused me of being anti-German, but really I can no longer cope with the present régime which seems to have lost all sense and reason. Are they mad? The Jewish persecutions carried to such a fiendish degree are short-sighted, cruel and unnecessary and now, so newspapers tell us, we shall have persecutions of Roman Catholics too. The secret telegrams do not give a very roseate account of Hitler's present attitude. He is becoming increasingly morose and anti-English generally. He quite likes Chamberlain, but thinks we are an effete, finished race.

Rab told Honor today that I had great gifts, the chief being my writing, which he feared he was preventing me from doing, and was afraid that my pen would become rusty. Honor was pleased; neither knew that almost every day I pen you, Diary, depository of all my secrets.[2]

23 November *Belgrave Square*

I am getting to know Rab. He is shrewd and his mind, while never flashy, is alert and far-sighted. He treats everyone as an oriental, and plays with us all. He sometimes looks, acts and appears as most ingenuous, even naif, but only a fool would be deceived. If he had more outward gifts he might be PM. Yesterday I met his parents. His father is a fat little fellow of sixty, but Lady Butler I thought a grand old girl, rather overdressed, grey

2. See entry for 26 July 1935, p. 52.

and not a day over 58. She is tall, jingles when she walks, worships Rab who – and this is the most charming quality I have observed in him – could not resist showing off to his impressed parents. They sat in our room, 21 D, and after Questions, Rab and I followed by the faithful Peter Loxley, joined them. He gave us all orders, quietly and Napoleonically, interviewed three MP's, and then brusquely dismissed them. Business was dispatched, documents were signed, while his parents sat gasping with pleasure.

The Coopers are feeling the adverse wind. It is so difficult (I find, at least) to be affectionate and, above all, natural with people when one violently disapproves of actions they have taken. Duff himself has referred to the evident relief of everyone at his departure. There, at any rate, he was right.

24 November

I went into Buckingham Palace by the private door, and Paul showed me the so-called 'Belgian suite' in which he and Olga are living. It is hideous, Edwardian, but comfortable, with furniture from Kensington Palace, etc., and wall paper. It is nearly period already and in 20 years such a decor will be the dernier cri. Afterwards, we lunched with the Kents, in their houseful of treasures. I told the Duke that his Australian Governorship would save him £500,000 or more, the money he would certainly have spent in London shops. As far as I knew, I told him, neither Melbourne nor Sydney has a Cartier, or a Rochelle Thomas or a Moss Harris for him to spend thousands in. He laughed.

28 November

I had a cocktail party for the Yugoslavs, and though I feared no-one would turn up, it was a riotous success, only a touch too grand. Emerald arrived an hour early (I could have killed her) and greeted Lady Oxford, who was looking like a death mask, with the words 'Look at little Margot – doesn't she look refreshing?'

6 December

This morning, I rushed to Victoria to take leave of the Regent, who arrived looking smiling and debonair, with Princess Olga, very royal. The waiting-room was full of diplomats, Corbin the Frenchman, and the large staff from the Yugoslav Legation. We were all greeted ceremoniously, and there was just the hint of a twinkle in the Regent's eye. . . . When he got into the train he stood in the doorway of the carriage chatting to us all and, as usual, I had the sinking feeling which I always have when he leaves – for one day, he will go away and never return, the victim of some fanatic's aim.

7 December

Later I had a word with Tommy Dugdale[3] – the government 'spy'. He was Baldwin's PPS and now is being groomed for the future Chief Whip, of that I am convinced. He reports every conversation to the PM or to David, and it is his role to pump people.

Dugdale is surely the mystery-man of the government. He has no opinions; he is not an intriguer; is a good sort and yet is the arch-informer. He listens, listens, offends no-one and reports all. He is square, short, smiling and shrewd, with merry brown eyes, white teeth, black shiny hair, and always a double-breasted pin-stripe suiting. He is married to Nancy Tennant, half-sister of Lady Oxford.

Random Reflections

Over the Munich crisis and its sensible solution, the Astor Dynasty not only had its way, but led the movement. The Rothermere and Beaverbrook Press followed enthusiastically – the powerful Berry clan and Press were however opposed to Munich, critical of Chamberlain and have continued so, although Kemsley, a realist, is giving in; and Camrose, in all justice, has been ill. Nevertheless, over this crisis, the Astors have won, and the Berrys have lost. The Rothermere and Beaverbrook Press have merely joined the winning side. Over the Abdication, the Astors and Berrys vied with each other in traducing Edward VIII and intrigued against him for months: he had, however,

3. Conservative MP for Richmond (Yorkshire) since 1929; he had been Parliamentary Private Secretary to Baldwin, 1935–7; he was a Government Whip, 1937–40.

(and still has at heart) both the Rothermere and Beaverbrook factions. The Astors and Berrys are fundamentally straight-laced, and puritanical; there they converge. But the Astors want peace with Germany, due, I think, to Lothian's influence on Lady Astor.

Over both the Abdication and the Czech crisis, one cannot help being struck by the fact that we had, in each case, the right man for the job. I doubt whether Chamberlain would have been equally successful with the Abdication problem, all through which Baldwin's tact was masterly, wherever one's sympathies lay. Certainly Baldwin as Prime Minister during these recent weeks, would not have behaved in the superhuman way that Chamberlain did. He would not have flown to Berchtesgaden – not he. He wouldn't have known where it was.

14 December *Very early a.m.*

At the Foreign Press Banquet Chamberlain made a very great speech in which he gently castigated the German Press. The German Ambassador and the German Press correspondents stayed away and boycotted the banquet at the last moment, thus creating a bad impression. They are so tactless always; yet we constantly attack Germany, so why should she not attack our statesmen? But the PM's stock rose tonight, perhaps enough to prevent, or at least postpone, an election.

I spoke to David Margesson again and he assures me that following his promise to me he had arranged for Rab to be made a Privy Councillor in the New Year's Honours.

I sat with Leslie Hore-Belisha drinking sweet champagne and drove him home to Stafford Place where he lives. It is snug and luxurious, like the boîte of a well-kept tart! And it is a touch Jewish. But he is a brilliant Minister too, or will be if he doesn't allow himself to become too self-assured.

15 December

I looked in at 11 Downing Street to an 'At Home' given by Lady Simon, a simple hausfrau who is obsessed by slavery and has campaigned against it all her life. 'Hasn't my wife made this house charming' the Chancellor asked us. And the guests were then requested to file out through the study so that they might look at his mother's portrait by Gerald Kelly, a remarkable old lady. She looks like Simon's twin, with a touch of Whistler's mother. Simon worshipped her. He is as mother-mad as Belisha.

19 December *Belgrave Square*

A Parliamentary day, fireworks and fun, but a governmental triumph. All the morning we prepared 50 questions, which is a record for any department, and later took them into the PM's room. We found the little man, as usual, alone (his secretaries are very slack, in my opinion). 'May I give you your Questions, Sir?' 'Yes, come in', he smiled, and we had a few words and I left. The Debate, a vote of Censure moved by the Opposition, began with a diatribe by Dalton. The PM followed and was at his very best – tolerant, easy, smiling but important. He has now learned all the rhetorical tricks and used them all. But it is a very personal government – very one man! He held and thrilled the House. He was followed by Archie Sinclair, who always provides a pleasant interval during which one can go out for a drink or a cup of tea, then by Quintin Hogg, who made his second speech since his recent election.[4] It was good oratorical stuff but the House, whilst recognising its obvious merits, was not altogether pleased that so new and young a member should be so self-assured. He stood behind me and swayed as he spoke, betraying no nervousness whatsoever. Lloyd George, who followed, was frankly funny, and he convulsed the House as he twitted the Prime Minister, but he said little of value. The PM roared with genuine laughter as the arrows hit him.

1939

1 January

Rab has been made a Privy Councillor this morning: it was in the Honours List: I knew, of course, and had David Margesson's

4. For Oxford, where he had defeated the Master of Balliol (A. D. Lindsay) who had stood as an anti-Government candidate with Labour and some dissident Conservative support; Harold Macmillan and Edward Heath (then an undergraduate) had canvassed for Lindsay, as had Randolph Churchill.

promise long ago. Yet I am delighted, for he well deserves it: no-one works so hard.

2 January *A party at Elveden to meet the Prime Minister*

I am quite childish in my fanatical worship of the PM, and was enchanted when my father-in-law asked me to meet him at the front door on his arrival, and escort him to his room, and did so with glee: he and I then talked for twenty dazzling minutes: he is looking forward keenly to his Rome visit[5] and seems quite unperturbed about the future: in fact he was calm, self-assured and very amusing. When we joined the party in the Big Hall, everyone ragged me, and jokingly accused me of having drawn the PM's bath and perhaps rubbed him down?

At dinner, Sam Hoare, who is staying, told Honor a rivetting secret story: he was in Italy in charge of our propaganda during the war, and after the famous defeat of Caporetto when half Italy wanted to get out of the war, had to work hard to keep her in. He was told that there was a powerful Socialist – a fellow called Mussolini – in Milan who owned a newspaper there. He might be able to keep Italy in the clear, at least he would be able to guarantee Milan and the north – if sufficiently bribed. Sam Hoare 'for a very considerable sum indeed' bought the newspaper: Mussolini kept his bargain, and arranged for processions of gangsters and thugs to process the streets in Milan with placards 'Mutilati della guerra'. Already a brilliant showman, Mussolini skilfully embarked on war propaganda, and in so doing, raised the money to form the Fascist party and finance the march on Rome. So English Government funds did much to create the Fascist revolution. This is very secret, and Mussolini, when he meets Sam Hoare now, is inclined to gloss over their former encounter 'Yes – we once met' he says vaguely. Sam Hoare still has in his private possession documents relating to this curious transaction.

3 January

I was up at 8 and down at 9 – the excitement of being under

5. With Lord Halifax, to discuss the proposed Anglo-Italian Treaty with Mussolini.

the same roof as the PM prevented me from sleeping: at 10.30 we went out shooting – a lovely cold Norfolk day, and the flat black country and woods looked sunlit and still. The PM shot well – indeed with amazing accuracy – though Sam Hoare excelled him.

In fact, the whole day was a success, with a bag of 818 without the 'pick-up'. The head keeper – Turner – who is a martinet, and no respecter of persons, as usual rode his pony, and conducted the manoeuvres in a Napoleonic way. He had given the order not to shoot English partridges – and someone slipped up and did; when it was discovered, we placed it surreptitiously with the PM's bag, but he quickly pointed this out, and with much indignation declared that his Home Secretary was under suspicion.

In the evening the PM was in great spirits, and sat up till midnight – midnight, that is by Elveden time.[6] Next day, when he left, he thanked me for all I had done for him, and said that I had been an excellent ADC. I purred.

10 January

I dined with Sir Patrick Hannon, a large dinner of men, and talked to Nevile Henderson, whom, though always distinguished, I found changed; he indeed seems very ill, but he gave us several vivid pictures of his time in Germany, and described how he had once lost his temper last year with Ribbentrop in front of Hitler, and told him that he knew nothing of England, nothing at all. Hitler roared with laughter, and apparently quite enjoyed seeing his jackal attacked. Henderson praised Goebbels, but only slightly, and remains true to Goering whom he definitely likes. Someone asked what would have happened if Chamberlain had not made the Munich Agreement, and Henderson replied that Hitler would have certainly marched into Prague at once, and that, had France stood firm, there would have been general war; though there was always the probability that France might have climbed down. He said, too, that in spite of Hitler's amazing diplomatic success this year his popularity is declining; and the cheers are less; Chamberlain gets the cheers in Germany today.

6. At Elveden, clocks were kept half an hour ahead during the shooting season.

13 January

Lunched alone with Rab (off pork) at Smith Square, and found him very sly and subtle. Reserve, reserve, all the way is his motto.

15 January

Old Brolly[7] got back from Rome – his stature enhanced, his prestige increased. He is winning through and will probably be Premier for years to come. He was well received in London.

23 January

Rab told me that at Geneva Lord Halifax once more raised the question of whether Anthony Eden should be allowed 'back'. He is in favour of his restoration, but the PM is against it.

6 February

As I was standing at the Bar of the House, Anthony Eden came up to me and said angrily: 'I hear, Chips, you say that my American trip was a failure and that I am a disaster'. Surprised, I weakly retorted: 'That's news to me'. 'Well, thank you for your tribute', he announced and walked away. I am sorry, really sorry, to have offended him, but I do consider him a menace, though a diminishing menace.

16 February

Today Lord Halifax addressed the FO Committee, and was brilliant, he cajoled them, led them up the garden path, played with them, impressed them with his charm, sincerity and high ideals. He fascinates and bamboozles everyone. Is he saint turned worldling, or worldling become saint?

27 February

To the House after dinner as there was a threat of an adjournment, and I had to gauge the situation carefully. At 10.15 I concluded that there might be trouble, and I rang the Ritz where Rab was dining, got him to the telephone and warned him. He returned just in time. And I also produced 2 people from the Foreign Office. Promptly at 11.06 Arthur Henderson rose and we

7. Chamberlain.

had our Libyan debate. The Italians, though I hate saying it, are letting us down in the spirit, if not in the letter of the Anglo-Italian agreement by sending reinforcements to Libya. So we were on a bad wicket.

28 February

Franco and the Socialists had their last snarl today. Attlee opened the Debate,[8] which took the form of a Vote of Censure, and he renewed his pusillanimous attack on the Prime Minister, though in so doing he lost the respect of the House, for he said little about the subject. Then, the PM rose, and never have I so admired him, though at first, I feared he would retaliate, as he looked annoyed. Instead, with sublime restraint he coolly remarked that he would resist the temptation to castigate the Leader of the Opposition, and he then proceeded to state the Government's case for the recognition of the Spanish Nationalists as the Legitimate Government of Spain. He was devastatingly clear, and made an iron-clad case which our opponents found difficult, indeed impossible, to answer. Their only reply was rage and abuse. The hours passed and it became increasingly clear that the House was Sick Unto Death of Spain, and that it recognised the necessity, indeed the urgency of establishing friendly relations with Franco, and the sooner the better. When fat, funny Inskip rose to wind up, he had an easy passage.

7 March

I dined in the 1936 Club – which entertained the Prime Minister, who was jolly, enjoying himself and amazingly open and confiding. Members plied him with questions. He smiled, members roared with laughter, as he answered each one with humorous precision. Someone asked him if it was true that Hitler disliked him, and he retorted that he had heard many contradictory reports on this subject, but that his last interview with Hitler was very friendly. He foresees no crisis on the horizon, all seems well; he thinks the Russian danger receding, and the dangers of a German War less every day, as our re-armament expands.

8. On the Government decision to recognize the Franco Government.

9 March

Appeasement cannot last indefinitely. The Boches or the Italians will surely let us down.

14 March

There were rumours at the FO of renewed trouble in Czechoslovakia. We did not at first take them very seriously; but soon learned that the Czech Government had resigned and that Hitler had summoned the President to Berlin. It looks as if he is going to break the Munich Agreement, and throw Chamberlain over.

There were questions in the House about the Czech situation and news came via the tape that German soldiers had invaded Czechoslovakia and that Ruthenia was proclaimed independent. We have another crisis. 'Beware the Ides of March.' It is just a year today since German troops entered and took poor languid, helpless, prostrate Austria. Hitler is never helpful.

15 March

Hitler has entered Prague, apparently, and Czechoslovakia has ceased to exist. No balder, bolder departure from the written bond has ever been committed in history. The manner of it surpassed comprehension and his callous desertion of the Prime Minister is stupefying. I can never forgive him. It is a great day for the Socialists and for the Edenites. The PM must be discouraged and horrified. He acceded to the demand of the Opposition for a debate and the business of the House was altered. Then he rose, and calmly, but I am sure with a broken heart, made a frank statement of the facts as he knew them. The reports were largely unconfirmed and based on press reports; consequently the PM was obliged to be cool and so was accused of being unmoved by events. I thought he looked miserable. His whole policy of appeasement is in ruins. Munich is a torn-up episode. Yet never has he been proved more abundantly right for he gave us six months of peace in which we re-armed, and he was right to try appeasement. I was relieved at how little personal criticism there was of the Apostle of Peace, and Grenfell, who opened for the Opposition, was more impressive than Attlee; he was saner, more manly, more eloquent and he held the attention and regard of the House.

Rab is in a rage with recent events, and Hitler's methods.

The country is stirred to its depths, and rage against Germany is rising. Anthony, by the way, was not hostile to the Government and he took me by the arm at one moment. What a day of shattered hopes.

17 March *Palace Hotel, S-on-S*

I had a big meeting at Southend which opened with the relaying of the PM's speech which lasted 40 minutes. It was strong meat, it was magnificent and held us spellbound. He told in polite but decisive language the whole story of his negotiations with Hitler and his treachery. The PM hinted at a new policy, or rather a return to our old faded friend, Collective Security. The country is solidly behind Chamberlain just now: all criticism of him is temporarily stilled.

18 March *5 Belgrave Square*

On my return to London, I found everyone in a state of excitement. The Cabinet was sitting; the newspapers talked of a German ultimatum to Rumania: I rang various Ministers, and now know the strange truth. Rob Bernays,[9] an excitable, pleasant youth, sensitive and Semitic, left-wing and intensely anti-German, yesterday had tea with Princess Marthe Bibesco, a writer and a famous mondaine and exotic. One can picture the scene, the reclining, luxurious lady in a tea-gown and pearls, surrounded by roses, and the impressed young Under-Secretary, dazzled by the mise-en-scène. She then proceeded to tell him that she knew that King Carol had had an ultimatum from the German Government, saying that they would invade Rumania, etc., etc. How could she get the news to the English Government? She knew no one. . . . Bernays believed her, not realising that the ordinary channels existed for carrying such information, were it true. He rushed to a call-box and frantically poured out the tale to Walter Elliot, who immediately rang up Oliver Stanley at the Foreign Office. Stanley knowing nothing, sent for Tilea, the Rumanian Minister. Tilea was guarded, and thinking that

9. National Liberal MP for Bristol North 1936–45; killed in an air crash, 1945. At this time he was Parliamentary Secretary to the Ministry of Transport.

the FO either knew too much or too little, led them to believe the Bibesco romance: No. 10 was informed, Cabinet Ministers cancelled their week-end plans and this evening there was a Cabinet called to consider the emergency situation which had arisen. Were we to guarantee Rumania her frontiers against German aggression? Meanwhile, late this afternoon a message came from Sir R. Hoare, our Minister at Bucarest, saying nothing was known in Rumania of such an ultimatum. This is the bald truth, but it is midnight now, and this country believes what it has read in the evening newspapers and has gone to bed hating Germany more than ever, and resigned to the inevitableness of war. It has taken me all evening to piece this tale together. Bernays defends himself by saying that it was his duty to warn the Government. Perhaps it was, but he has made us ridiculous in the eyes of Europe, I fear.

Now we have begun to flirt with Russia. We must be in very low water indeed to have to do that.

20 March

Nevile Henderson was recalled yesterday from Berlin, and Herr Dirksen, the German Ambassador, left London. The situation is grave.

Frog Week! i.e. the visit of the President of France and Madame Lebrun, begins tomorrow.

21 March

I watched the procession arrive from the House of Commons. The Lebruns looked well, she was dressed like the Queen, in clinging grey and furs. Much cheering from the crowds. Hitler has guaranteed the success of this visit.

22 March

A Round Robin is being hawked round Europe asking Poland (who was cautious in her reply), Yugoslavia, Rumania and perhaps others, to join in a Non-Aggression Pact. It will enormously enlarge our commitments and give us little advantage, except possibly in the way of prestige and strategic value. The smaller nations are chary, particularly my Paul's régime in remote Belgrade.

Memel was today ceded to Germany by the Lithuanian Government under threats of invasion and aerial bombardment. Memel, not in itself very important, is the camel-breaking straw and the Cabinet is now unanimous that 'something must be done'. And Lord Halifax, at last influenced by the Mandarins in the Forbidden City, i.e. the Foreign Office, is beginning to hate the Devil more than his works, and clever people in the FO, knowing his religious tendencies, have been stressing tales of Church persecution in Germany.

Tonight was the great Grand gala at Covent Garden for the Frogs. I wore my Court dress – and escorted Loelia Westminster to Emerald's where we all dined. Emerald's dinner was a magnificent sight – with ten Faubourg Frogs, the Duc and Duchesse de Mortemart, Prince and Princess Achille Murat, others ... but our London beauties, literally covered with jewels, made a much better show. How shabby French women are, at least aristocratic ones, when compared with our English ones. Covent Garden was breath-taking in its magnficence. There was a vast Royal Box in the centre, designed by Rex Whistler and decorated by Mary Newall. It was light, gay, pretty but a touch tinselly and night-clubbish. I did not approve of it. To the left was the Government box; to the right the Diplomatic one, and we were next but one, with only the Camroses between us. Slowly the whole spectacle opened before us – and we had the greatest fun watching the arrivals. All HMG, Lady Maugham, with a curl on her wrinkled forehead, Simon separated from his wife by a gangway. At last the Prime Minister and Mrs Chamberlain, who looked like a Gunter's cake in pale pink with a pink boa, arrived. Alan [Lennox-Boyd] and I applauded, and the grand well-bred audience took up the cheers, and he had a rousing reception which pleased him and we were rewarded with his now famous smile. They had been at the French Embassy banquet as had the Halifaxes who were the last to come. These functions do not tire Halifax who is fundamentally social, but they are an added strain to the poor PM, who is already very over-worked. Then the Ambassadors filed in, finally the Royal Family arrived with the Lebruns. They quite filled the large box and were given a reception almost as rousing as the Chamberlains. The Queen looked lovely and distinguished. Queen Mary grey and hard. I watched her for a long time. She is ageing. Lebrun sat between the two Queens, his wife between the King and the Duke of Kent. They all looked glamorous, though of course Princess Marina extinguished them all, with her shimmering slimness. Mme. Lebrun behaved with a simply dignity which was warmly commended. Her clothes had been made by Worth and a jeweller in the Rue de la Paix lent her a few ornaments to wear. She looked all right.

Almost everyone in the Opera House was in Court dress or uniform; half the women wore tiaras; it was a brave sight, enough to impress the Frogs. Shall we ever see so grand a gala again? I think so . . .

The performance was adequate, but how much trouble and money it would save had there been no programme at all. At such entertainments people only want to stare at one another.

A grand day. The ancien régime dies hard in England.

23 March

I am glutted with the great. An early start, as I had invited Mrs Gaterhill, a French constituent, to Westminster Hall, and the little woman gurgled with Gallic glee as we drove up to the great doors in my green Rolls. Soon all the great of England filed in, and at the top of the steps sat the Cabinet, the Speaker, the Lord Chancellor and others. At 11 o'clock the bugles blew, and the North doors were opened and the Lebruns entered escorted by Lord Ancaster, as Great Chamberlain of the Palace of Westminster. Mme. Lebrun, who looked self-possessed and amiable, indeed even chic and having considerable chien for an old bourgeoise, smiled and conducted herself with dignity. The President (who, I am assured, calls her 'Pom-Pom'), was immaculately dressed though it is absurd to look as French as he does. 'Vive le Président'. There was much hand-clapping and cheering. I caught his brown eye. Then the Lebruns left for Windsor Castle to lunch with the Monarchs; by having such a success with our Royal Family Lebrun is certain to be re-elected President, for the French say that if he is good enough for Queen Mary, then he is good enough for them.

At luncheon with the Kents, the Duke of Alba asked me whether I knew that Grandi, my dear bearded, adorable Grandi, was to succeeed Ciano at the head of Foreign Affairs in Rome? He, the Ambassador, had heard it from General Franco, and he gave me permission to pass on the information, which I later did.

I was able to tone down the PM's reply to a Question about our 'attitude to recent events' I had seen the flimsy and when I handed it to him, I said 'It's pretty stiff. I suppose it has got to be?' He agreed. But with a pencil he altered a few stinging lines. I encouraged him: though he did not need it. 'I can type', I said. Then he altered it still more, and I rushed back to 21D, and explained the alterations, which were more in tone and manner than in actual fact to Rab, who in my absence had arrived. He agreed – and I hastily typed out two copies of the amended statement which might easily prevent or postpone War rather than precipitate it. It does not actually attack Germany, and now throws the grammar into the subjunctive. Perhaps I have made History – or prevented it, which is often more important.

More French fun in the evening – the FO reception, after a grand dinner at the Bessboroughs'. The India Office, where our party took place, had been skilfully converted into a theatre – Life Guards were drawn up in the passages. FO boys in grand uniforms acted as Ushers. It was a marvellous sight, but not too well done, and certainly not enough people invited, and many of the wrong ones at that, and we soon escaped up to a small room where there were drinks overlooking the court-yard. It was from that window that I had watched the rehearsals this morning. There is a large portrait of Napoleon over the fire-place and Harold Caccia had gone on so long this morning about the Entente and our wonderful Friendship with France – 'Look, there is even a portrait of Napoleon', he said, gloatingly. 'There may be one of Hitler there in a hundred years time', I retorted . . .

To go back – the guests filed in below us, the Government and wives, many of whom had been omitted and were only invited because I had sent a memo to the effect that they must! Alan and I in our resplendent clothes (actually his green Ministerial uniform is rather drab), walked up and down. . . . Suddenly we met Queen Elizabeth and President Lebrun face to face. I did a 'bunk' and half-faded, half-fell into a doorway, with Alan in front of me. The Queen saw me and smiled, with a touch of the twinkle which she keeps for her old friends. The rest of the dinner party followed . . . Anthony, Winston, all the pro-Frog boys. Then the Royal Family. Queen Mary was looking more rested and handsomer than last night. Bonnet was next to her and they chatted animatedly. The room glittered with jewels. The Duchess of Portland looked like a Christmas Tree, as did Circe Londonderry and Mollie Buccleuch and others. The French must have been very impressed by our bejewelled Aristocracy.

At one moment in the midst of the over-long performance there was nearly a disaster; Alan, Jim Wedderburn[10] – in his Archer uniform – and Geoffrey Shakespeare[11] were standing on a sofa next to me, when a little woman seated on the sofa, unaware of her importance as a makeweight, suddenly got up. The sofa toppled over and three senior Ministers were very nearly catapulted into the audience below. They might have gone through the window, fallen on top of Royalties and Frogs below and the evening's entertainment would have ended in disaster. How Hitler would have laughed.

24 March

Chamberlain's note of warning in his statement yesterday has been well received, even in Germany. Thank God I helped to modify it.

26 March

I am not sure that the Polish guarantee is wise. It may stiffen the resistance of the Poles, as we unintentionally stiffened the Czechs last year.

28 March

At the 1922 Committee banquet the PM had a riotous reception and was cheered and cheered so much so that he was much moved and made no attempt to conceal his emotion. He then proceeded to give us (over 100 members) a frank, firm talk; he referred to his betrayal by Hitler, was scathing and yet humorous

10. Later Earl of Dundee.

11. Liberal National MP for Norwich, Parliamentary and Financial Secretary to the Admiralty, 1937–40.

about him – and then touched on conscription. He had decided against it for the moment as he did not wish to divide the nation (It will take another Dictator's coup to bring that in here, as I remarked to Alec Dunglass, and he agreed) . . . I felt warm within as he talked, the way I do when I play with Paul, and I know now that I really love the PM and have great hero-worship for him – I want to embrace him: I trust I shall never be so foolish as to do so.

31 March

Neville made a great and historic statement in the House, and it went extremely well – the unconditional guarantee to Poland. The House cheered.

1 April *Camfield Place, near Hatfield*

Where I am staying with Lord Queenborough, an amiable 'Grand Seigneur' who at the age of 77 entertains la jeunesse politique. His excellent food is served in Edwardian splendour, and the old gentleman is very alert and still keenly interested in politics. He told us many stories at dinner, one of a conversation he had years and years ago with Joe Chamberlain whom he congratulated on the successes of his son Austen. The old man was obviously pleased, but added 'Wait until you see my Neville'. He also told me what Queen Mary had said to him, in reply to a question as to when the Duke of Windsor would return to this country: 'Not until he comes to my funeral'.

Everyone here seems happy about our guarantee of Poland.

3 April

The debate today was a star one. It was opened by Arthur Greenwood who had behaved with dignity and thoughtfulness during the crisis. He is really rather decent at heart. Neville followed and although he pleased the House I was not so enthusiastic about his speech as usual, and I felt that his heart is not really in this new policy which has been forced upon him by Hitler. He was followed by Winston, who for once did not harangue the Government but actually praised it, his speech was not damaging; after the debate, I saw him with Lloyd George, Boothby and Randolph, in a triumphant huddle surrounding Maisky. Maisky, the Ambassador of torture, murder and every crime in the calendar.

4 April

This morning I wandered up into the Private Secretary's room where I found Nevile Henderson, debonair and elegant as ever, sitting on a desk and we had a few words. Hitler, he thinks, is partly mad and completely under the domination of his more violent followers, the companions of his Munich days. They, and Ribbentrop, ever a 'Yes-man', are urging him on to new adventures. Hitler it seems is in a rage against us and our governessy interference. First it was the Communists, then the Jews and now it is the British Empire. He absolutely loathes us and Nevile thought that at any moment he might commit a coup-de-tête. Yet the man, he went on, was not altogether bad. He ought he thought to negotiate an arrangement for the rectification of the Polish corridor and Danzig, which would be quite legitimate and then at the Nuremburg Conference announce to the German people that he had lifted them from being the world's doormat to their present proud position, and that now he was going to retire and live in his mountain fastness. Germany could choose Goering or the Hohenzollerns, or whomsoever they liked. Nevile Henderson doesn't pretend that he thinks Hitler will follow such a course, but more surprising things have happened.

5 April

Colonel Beck's[12] visit is evidently a success, but I cannot trust him. Still we must have allies, and Poland is now our new found friend. The Government are getting the jitters, and are groping for allies anywhere. Rab is annoyed that he has not been more consulted over the Polish Guarantee and thinks that Halifax, who is veering away from the Prime Minister, intends to keep him in the background.

7 April *Good Friday*

This morning early, John Coulson, who is the gargoyle-looking, but charming and intelligent resident clerk at the Foreign Office,

12. The Polish Foreign Minister.

was awakened at 5.30 by a message to say that the Italians are occupying Albania. The report proved to be only too true. King Zog has fled whilst Queen Geraldine (a semi-American née Apponyi) and her two day old baby son have fled to Greece. There is unrest, and international disturbance, and I don't know whether to cable the Iveaghs to return at once from Asolo. The terrible inevitability of war has descended upon us. 'Et tu Benito?' for Mussolini had only recently assured us that he had no territorial claims whatsoever on Albania, and her invasion, or really annexation, is a complete violation of the spirit of the Anglo-Italian Agreement. War seems nearer now that the Dictators are drawing together. Their methods show brutal similarity. We listened in to the radio and were depressed indeed.

8 April *Kelvedon*

The Statesmen are in London and the PM is returning from Scotland. The FO is in a fever of excitement and Parliament may be recalled. The whole country is in a state of jitters.

Pam and Michael Berry have arrived. Much in love, and much depressed by the war situation.

10 April *Kelvedon*

Glorious weather and we lunched out of doors, basked in the sun, and Honor and I actually plunged into the water. Afterwards Paul and I caught frogs together. Kelvedon is a dream of fruit blossom and spring loveliness – war seems really unthinkable.

The Cabinet sat for the first time on a Bank Holiday since the war. I rang up Rab who was quite calm. I gathered from him that Neville will not consider renouncing the Anglo-Italian Agreement; that will cause a Parliamentary storm.

11 April *Kelvedon*

I have long been convinced that the Golden Days of this great Empire are over; this is the decadence, 'the kill', we are degenerate and there are no great men anywhere. The FO is very depressed, Rab alone is not alarmed, but Halifax, who I am beginning to admire less and less, is wobbly. Beware these priests!

13 April

Up to London early for the big debate. Rab walked over to No. 10 with Halifax who remarked 'I suppose you are coming to give the PM moral support'. Halifax is weaned away from Neville now on many points, but Rab, as Alec Dunglass told me, still sees eye to eye with him, and the PM still feels more mentally at home with Rab than with anyone.

The debate was disappointing, and the Prime Minister, though modulated and calm, was not as inspiring as usual. He is unhappy in his new role of the protagonist of diluted collective security. Furthermore to the guarantee of Greece he added, to my surprise, one for Rumania. This was a last moment decision taken after luncheon at the urgent request of the French. It does not really matter, as we should have to come into any war in any case, were Rumania attacked.

15 April *Kelvedon*

Fritzi of Prussia, who is staying here, told me today that Hitler had dined quietly some years ago at Cecilienhof with his parents, and that he had sat on a sofa after dinner, and had solemnly declared that it was his intention of restoring the German Monarchy directly he could. They believed him, and indeed perhaps he meant it, at the time. Perhaps he meant it altogether. Fritzi also told me that he had no intention of fighting for the Nazis, whose régime he thinks not only repugnant but doomed.

20 April

The PM played with the House today. In answer to a question, he confirmed that a Ministry of Supply would be set up, and that the name of the Right Honourable Member who would be appointed to the post of its Minister was – and he paused – the temperature of the House rose. 'Burgin'.[13] The House, expecting, half hoping, half-fearing, that it would be Winston, was amazed.

Conscription has been decided upon.

23 April

I am distressed about an alleged possible rapprochement with Russia. It is surely madness. Already our flirtation with the Bear

13. Leslie Burgin, Minister of Transport.

has ... lost us face in Spain, in Portugal, in Poland and elsewhere.

26 April

In the afternoon I had several long conferences with Alec Dunglass who is a miracle of tact, humour and sound sense. He admires Neville so much that he has even come to look like him. He thinks that there may well be an election should the Socialists overdo their opposition to conscription. When it was announced, Attlee was shaking with rage and there were rude interruptions and shouts of 'Resign', 'Hitler' but the PM was quite unmoved and afterwards I met him, smiling, with colour in his pale cheeks and dark eyes shining. He patted me on the shoulder and said 'That went quite well I thought'. He has the whole country behind him. His amazing physique, his enigmatic personality, his steadiness, have captivated everyone except London Society.

27 April

Blum has telephoned an urgent appeal to Attlee to modify his violently anti-conscription attitude, and his message has had an effect for when I got to the House of Commons the Labour boys were very piano. When the PM gave his calm review of the conscription problem, he was neither barracked nor interrupted. Though Attlee followed, reading a lot of terse rot, the speech of the afternoon was doubtless Winston's, a magnificent effort. Archie Sinclair was singularly bombastically inept, even for him, and throughout his long speech I watched the PM write copious notes on House of Commons writing paper. I wondered what could so interest him in the middle of Archie's diatribe. And afterwards discovered that he was making notes on salmon fishing which he then passed to Anthony Crossley who is writing a book on the subject. What a commentary on Chamberlain, especially as Anthony Crossley has been one of the disloyal band, and nothing has been too bad for him to say against the PM who, now with his infinite patience, finds time to help him with his book. I only hope the Crossleys keep the manuscript.

28 April

At 12.30 a copy of Hitler's speech was delivered to us. He

complains of all the usual injustices, but is conciliatory about England, and the tone of the speech on the whole is moderate.

29 April

Honor is looking lovely indeed just now and this evening she wore her magnificent emeralds which I have given her. I have never seen her look so lovely or be so gay and attractive.

30 April

We are still at peace. I consider that the Press have been unfair in their reception of Hitler's speech, in particular to his friendly references to England. But it is hopeless in England; give a dog a bad name and it can never recover.

1 May

The House was dull today. I had a long conference again with Alec Dunglass, and we agreed that something must be done immediately to make the Poles more reasonable towards the German demands over Danzig, and also to make some overture, however slight, towards Germany. I promised to confer with Rab along these lines and later did so. He immediately asked for an interview with Halifax which later he had.

2 May

I was next to Lady Chamberlain[14] at lunch at Emerald's and we had an hour's talk. She had just come back from Greece via Rome and she gave me much Mussolini news. The Duce is about to become a father. The mother is the petite bourgeoise with whom he has been consorting for two years or more. The husband was sent to Abyssinia and did not get killed, but Mussolini is enchanted with himself. At the same time he is co-habiting with the fair, Nordic, south German girl sent to Rome by the Nazis. Given up to the practices of love he is losing reality and depending more and more on Ciano who has become impossible and is almost certainly in the pay of the Germans. Ciano is an erotic too and the whole Italian Government has now become a sort of brothel, and is losing touch rapidly with the population which by and large is pro-English. All this from Lady Chamberlain who

14. Widow of Sir Austen Chamberlain.

all her life has been pro-Italian and has always used her influence to improve our relations with Italy. She is disappointed with Mussolini, and made no attempt to see him during her 24 hours stay in Rome. Ciano however sent someone from the Palazzo Chigi to call on her. She was interesting too about the Neville Chamberlains. 'Annie' she lightly dismissed as knowing nothing of foreign affairs and told me that the PM gets all his mental stimulus and confidence from his two maiden sisters with whom he corresponds constantly. Neither he nor Mrs Chamberlain care much for their children, and they have always been absorbed in themselves to the exclusion of anyone else. Thus, their sister-in-law.

3 May

Jim Thomas warned me that he will resign the Whip if anything savouring of appeasement begins again, and I foresee a political battle next week, once it is known that Russia is to be snubbed, or rather let down lightly.

I have no doubt that Duff, Anthony, Bobbety Cranborne (who surprisingly enough praised me warmly to Serge[15] on Monday) and above all Winston, see themselves as an alternative Government, so this evening I warned Tommy Dugdale that the 'Glamour Boys' are becoming restive. I had a confidential talk too with Ernest Brown who told me that one member of the Cabinet betrayed its decision to the 'Glamour Boys' as he is secretly one of them at heart. I think I know who it is. I foresee trouble.

As I write these lines a journalist has just rung me up to say that the news has just come that Litvinoff has resigned and has been replaced by Molotov. Will he be shot?

Consternation ensued in the Lobbies, and David Margesson sent for me, as he wanted a line to give the boys. I rang Smith Square but Rab refused to be disturbed, and there was no reply (there rarely is). I then walked over and although I threw pennies at the windows was unable to raise anyone. It was only 11.15. Rab always retires early, that is why he looks so old. The Lobbies were still humming on my return and Jim Thomas rushed up and said 'If you have let Russia slip through our fingers, I will never forgive you'. The ass.

15. Colonel Prince Serge Obolensky, a lifelong friend of Chips.

4 May

Fearing a 'Glamorous movement' I packed the Foreign Affairs Committee with sound Chamberlain chaps and we elected Sir John Wardlaw-Milne, a semi diehard as Chairman in the room of Jock MacEwen[16] recently made a Whip. The new chairman will be fair and will tolerate no nonsense from the Glamour group who are being very tiresome today.

5 May *Kelvedon*

The PM decided to make a statement about Russia this morning, so we all assembled at the FO promptly at 10 o'clock, and later drove to the House of Commons. At 11 the PM rose and in fine fighting fettle he delivered a series of deadly blows at Attlee and others. He was most scathing and clearly revealed both his dislike of the 'Bollos' and of Russia. The Eden-ites had intended to join forces over this issue, i.e. a pact with Russia, but none of them turned up, and I was overheard to say, rather unkindly, that it was because they sit up every night too late at the Four Hundred Club.

Neville was in a rage yesterday and in the morning whilst he was going over questions he delivered himself of an angry tirade against the 'Glamour boys'. More particularly Bobbety Cranborne, who is the most dangerous of the lot. 'Beware' he said 'of rampant idealists. All Cecils are that'.

9 May

I took Rab at luncheon time to the Bath Club where we swam together. He has so little pleasure and complains constantly of the dullness of his life and his uninteresting background. But he has little social sense, no lightness of touch and he is unpunctual. But his charm lends colour to his high intelligence, and his capacity for work is immense; slowly he has become the PM's blue-eyed boy.

10 May

All morning at the FO intriguing and arranging matters, and the hours passed in a confusion of secret telephone calls and

16. Conservative MP for Berwick and Haddington.

conversations. The startling thing about my intrigues is that they always come off.

I am told that the PM is showing signs of strain. That is the danger of the present government, which is almost a one man show. Should Neville collapse or die or resign the whole National Government would cave in, for, excepting Edward Halifax, it is composed of comparative nonentities. I should find myself in the political wilderness, and I could not bear it.

11 May

Lord Perth,[17] somewhat to my surprise, called on me this morning, and we had an hour's conversation. He was rivetting about Italian policy; he said that Italy (like Yugoslavia now too) has decided that it is preferable to have a friendly Germany on the Brenner rather than a hostile one; this was the beginning of the Axis. At Stresa we had not once mentioned Abyssinia, and Simon's silence and Macdonald's aloofness persuaded Mussolini that he was to proceed in Abyssinia. More interesting, probably as it is fresh news, was Perth's impression of the Albanian adventure. He was not shocked by it, as it has long been understood that Italy had a claim over Albania, and had even at one moment been offered it at Versailles. For many years Italy had exercised a sort of semi-suzerainty over Albania and had paid large subsidies for the development of the country to King Zog. On 4 April, a Tuesday, Ciano had sent him an ultimatum which he was convinced King Zog would accept, to the effect that Italy meant business and that he was to become a puppet, like Farouk in Egypt. Zog procrastinated and began to take defensive measures, and on Good Friday, the 7th, the Italians walked in.

Blum is in London. He is the real architect of many of our woes and it is revolting to see the Churchill gang kowtowing to this Jewish agitator who has done such infinite harm.

I saw an unexpected letter at the Foreign Office to the effect that Halifax has arranged for Queen Mary to have copies of all confidential telegrams sent abroad. A box will be despatched to Marlborough House, a quite unorthodox procedure, and possibly a temporary one during the visit of the King and Queen to

17. British Ambassador in Rome, 1933–9. Formerly (1919–32) Secretary-General of the League of Nations.

America. More and more we are being ruled by a small group of thirty or forty people, including myself, for Alec Dunglass and I have woven a net around the PM whom we love and admire and want to protect from interfering, unimportant noodles. Both he and Halifax are oligarchic in mind and method.

15 May

Rab prophesies trouble over Danzig during the next few days. All along he has dreaded the middle of May.

The Russian reply has come, and is a refusal of our terms. We are playing, of course, for time as both Halifax and the PM are reluctant to embrace the Russian bear, and both regret the Polish guarantee. They are determined to prevent an Anglo-Russian alliance – the pet scheme of the leftish clique in the Foreign Office.

16 May

I gather that it has now been decided not to embrace the Russian bear, but to hold out a hand and accept its paw gingerly.[18] No more. The worst of both worlds.

17 May

To hug the bear or not? Every day there is a change, and I am still plotting hard to prevent a Russian alliance unless there are sufficient safeguards. The chances are about even, but I fear we may give in, and thus dangerously imperil our dignity and our future.

19 May *Kelvedon*

A supreme, superb parliamentary day in which I revelled. It was the debate on Foreign Affairs and Russia was of course the clou. The PM looked tired, and seemed a touch rattled, and in fact I rather doubted whether he would make a good speech. The Debate was opened by Lloyd George who spoke for fifty-eight minutes. I was immediately facing him and more than once caught his blue eye. There were flashes of fun and extraordinary vivacity for a man of his age, but his speech moved no-one, and lacked his usual brilliance. The House was patient, but bored.

18. An apt simile for the half-hearted Anglo-Russian negotiations of 1939.

The Gallery of course strained every ear whilst the old wizard poured out his ineffectual, untrue, irrelevant criticisms. I wondered was he at the beginning of his dotage? or merely of the decline of his great powers? He challenged us again and again on Russia, why didn't we come out into the open and embrace her? I looked up at Maisky, the smirking cat, who leant over the railing of the Ambassadorial gallery and sat so sinister and smug (are we to place our honour, our safety in those blood-stained hands?). I carried in messages, papers, telegrams from the Foreign Office. The PM was courteous and smiling, though once or twice he snorted as he does when disgruntled. He loathes Ll. G. Then we had Attlee and his speech was less vehement than usual. Indeed it was, as the PM later described it, a thoughtful speech. He is a bee without a sting, and today there was merely a buzz. But he is much more effective when mild, and even held the House, no easy task for the dull little man. He is really not a bad fellow, and socially he is even pleasant.

Then the PM rose without enthusiasm and I think the House expected an indifferent speech, and so at first it seemed, but after a sly snub for Maisky, whom in veiled language the PM accused of betraying our negotiations to the Press (true!) he warmed to his brief, and went on. After touching on Turkey he proceeded to expand our general theory of present day Foreign Policy, and became magnificent, calm, spacious and added comic relief by several playful shafts at Lloyd George. The PM referred to Russia and the difficulties we encountered with other countries à propos our Russian negotiations. However he did not mention any specifically, and about that there hangs a tale; Winston Churchill had in his pocket, it appears, a letter from the President of Poland saying that he had no objection to our making a Russian alliance. Winston intended to interject and read out the letter thus sabotaging the PM's remarks. He told several people, and I heard it from Jim Thomas, who stupidly taunted me with Winston's triumph-to-be. I was in the Aye Lobby at the time and hurriedly scribbled a pencilled line repeating what I had heard, which I passed to the PM who smilingly acknowledged it. It was lucky I did so as at the end of his speech he was hard pressed by the House, and by Ll. G. in particular, to say 'what countries' he had in mind. But, armed by me, he had been careful not to mention any by name. Old Winston, not three yards away, sat fuming and fumbling with his notes with the Polish letter probably among them. His disappointment was obvious.

Finally Anthony Eden spoke and had nothing new to say. It was a snubbing experience for him since at one moment there were only fourteen members in the Chamber. A few filtered in to hear him, but at no time, although he spoke for half an hour, was the House crowded or even interested. Butler had sensed what was coming, and whispered to me to fetch a Cabinet Minister at once from somewhere, as otherwise it looked discourteous to Anthony, and he feared trouble. I got up and went to the Lobbies, but I took my time about it, as I wanted to draw attention to the poor attendance in the Chamber, and I deliberately waited for five minutes, lit a cigarette, went into the lavatory, etc., and at last went to the dining room, where I found old Walter Elliot finishing off a ripe Camembert, and persuaded him to come and sit on the bench. As he was getting up, the Division bell rang. Progress was being reported! Anthony's humiliation was complete.

24 May

Tonight Rab takes the train from Paris and arrives at 5 a.m. at Geneva. As Lord Halifax is coming back, their trains will cross, like their policies. It appears that during the Halifax reign in India someone asked 'What is the Viceroy thinking?' and the answer was 'Whom did he see last?' I fear that it is very true and I fear the worst about Russia tomorrow.

We have embraced the monster ... at least as they seem to think, but Halifax has been shrewd, and during his prolonged conversation with Maisky in Geneva they have worked out a formula for mutual co-operation against aggression, but based on the Covenant of the League. Thus, really, our new obligation means nothing. A military alliance might have been the signal for an immediate war – 'blown the gaff' but a Geneva alliance is so flimsy, so unrealistic and so impractical that it will only make the Nazis poke fun at us.

Later – The Russian statement in the House was a colourless affair and merely expressed in hopeful terms the belief that an agreement would shortly be reached. The actual terms are not yet agreed upon. The House was enchanted with it. I wonder – I think that the Russians will run out.

25 May

John Simon is taking the Foreign Affairs debate tomorrow raised by the Opposition on the adjournment. It was a struggle to induce him to do so, and he insisted that Rab should 'hold his hand', a monstrous stipulation. Peter Loxley and I had so hoped to get poor Rab off this added and unnecessary chore – but Simon, always bloody-minded, insisted, and was in fact adamant.

26 May

I drove to Croydon to meet the Paris plane which of course was late, though finally Rab descended, already dressed in his House of Commons clothes – short coat and striped trousers. I rushed him to Westminster, but the chauffeur idiotically lost the way and at one point we seemed headed – at sixty miles an hour – for Brighton. There was a moment of panic, and we thought that after all that fuss we would not get to the House in time. Confusion – nerves – we turned, raced back and just got to Westminster in time – but only just. Rab read over the typed answers to his questions which I had prepared for him. Poor fellow, he had got up at six-something in Paris and rushed to Le Bourget to catch an early plane, and was very nervy. Luckily, when we arrived they were still at Prayers, though almost at once our questions were called. Rab answered them perfectly, and no-one was aware of the flurry we had been in. But a morning like that takes years off one's life.

31 May

Disturbing telegrams at the FO – particularly a long report from Percy Loraine on his recent interview with Mussolini. The Duce, it seems, was grim and glum and asked Loraine how we could think that it was still in Italy's interest, in view of Gt. Britain's 'encirclement policy', to adhere to the Anglo-Italian Agreement? He suggested that he was thinking of renouncing it, though he did not say that he would do so. Percy Loraine took a firm line with him, and the meeting, though scarcely cordial, passed off amicably enough. The termination of the Anglo-Italian Agreement would be a smashing blow to poor Neville.

3 June
Philip Sassoon died today – what a loss to the London pageant. No-one infused it with so much colour and personality. Philip was sleek, clever and amiable. Kindly yet fickle, gay yet moody, he entertained with almost Oriental lavishness in his three rather fatiguing palaces (of which Trent is the loveliest) and exerted an enormous influence on a section of London Society. He was always pleasant and witty with me, talking in that clipped sibilant accent which has been so often imitated. 'His teeth rattled like dice in a box' was a favourite remark of his, and, 'it is so quiet at Lympne one can hear the dogs bark in Beauvais' another. He once likened some Lobster Newburg he was eating to a 'purée of white kid gloves'.

Philip was an adequate if uninspired administrator. But more than the air, he loved the Arts, and collected with a flair and a lavishness which was unequalled in London Society. He had a prolonged and hazardous friendship with the Prince of Wales whom he worshipped, though their intermittent quarrels were famous. He was also intimate with the King, Queen and Queen Mary – royalties haunted his house always, and he was loyal to them as he was to no-one else. Politicians he dropped as soon as they fell from power. The Eden reign was the longest but of late he was inclined to drop him too, much to Anthony's amused resentment. Philip was never in the Chamberlain racket and his power waned with Baldwin's retirement, but he never lost his thirst of life. Though Jewish he hated Jews. What he really loved were jewelled elephants and contrasting colours – the bizarre and the beautiful.

8 June
For the Foreign Office Banquet I dressed early in my Lord Fauntleroy velvet number (which I was wearing for the 10th time), drove round to pick up Freddie Birkenhead and we went to the FO together where we were welcomed smilingly by Lord Halifax. The scene was a splendid one – Ambassadors everywhere.

Much good food, served under the glittering chandeliers

which poor Philip Sassoon had brought from our old Embassy in Vienna. Halifax then proposed the traditional two toasts, and the Nepalese Ambassador, in his plumed hat fringed with enormous emeralds, whose religion forbade him to eat with us, came in later to pay his respects. I drove Malcolm MacDonald (flushed and friendly – I like him) back to the House and slipped on a pair of ordinary trousers over my knee-breeches and put on a short coat and black tie to vote. But I forgot my buckled shoes, and was ragged about them.

10 June *Kelvedon*

Laura Corrigan has arrived to stay – a dynamo of energy and conversation. She even talks of royalties when standing on her head, which she does regularly for health reasons. She is a tremendous personality – a great ally and sometimes, alas, a colossal bore, though she was very nice all day today.

15 June *London*

At the 1936 Club dinner Lord Chatfield was the guest of honour and he spoke bluntly and frankly of our defences. He is the Minister of Co-ordination of Defence. Every day – he said – that war is postponed, is of the greatest value to us.

19 June

All day I have been popular, and perhaps powerful. (Does one quality cause the other)? I held almost a court in the H. of C. Lobby – with Ministers affectionate, the PM smiling, PPS's asking me to dine, and Sam Hoare giving me a drink. I am on the crest of the wave.

20 June

There is a great Channon wave on at the moment. We are popular, répandus, indeed run after. We are asked to every lighted candle, to every dinner and everyone is charming to us. Is our success Social? Political? or both?

29 June

The whole outlook is appalling, Hitler is a bandit; we are all mad; and Russia is winking slyly – and waiting.

9 July

The Berry cat, which Seymour hinted about some days ago, is out of the bag, and today the 'Daily Telegraph' produces a full leader of a column and a half demanding the inclusion of Winston Churchill in the Government. It is quite threatening, and the PM is taken aback by it. All day David kept sending for me, and by the afternoon it was clear that a conspiracy had been hatched. The Press Lords are to combine in an attempt to force the Prime Minister into inviting Winston into the Government. The Eden-ites have joined them, hoping to get a Cabinet seat for Anthony too.

In the lobby of the House of Commons I overheard Jim Thomas say to Anthony 'We cannot count on the Evening Standard. They will let us down'. What a clumsy group of plotters they are. But Winston's supporters contend that an invitation to him to join the Cabinet now would be a warning to Hitler that we 'mean business'.

4 July

Jim Thomas is now annoyed by the Churchill plot, to which he originally subscribed, and by the fact that Winston is stealing all Anthony's thunder. There is thus division in Tuscany – I must report all this in the morning.

5 July

The news I picked up from Jim Thomas was warmly welcomed by the Whips; so far it looks as if the plot is a wet squib.

6 July

The plot is finally dying down, but we could never defeat the Berrys combined with the Astors, though on this Churchill issue the Berrys are themselves divided; Camrose being pro-Churchill, but Kemsley anti. The Astors surprisingly enough, take a strong pro-Churchill line. Lady Astor, frightened by anonymous letters and gossip about the so-called 'Cliveden Set', has thrown over her principles and is urging Chamberlain against his better judgment to take the plunge. He won't, David Margesson assures me.

7 July

I awake tired after a late night and went to the Foreign Office. The news abroad is rather better and on the Home Front we have won, at least temporarily.

In the afternoon I drove to Weston to stay with the Sitwells for the Blenheim Ball, which was stupendous. I have seen much, travelled far and am accustomed to splendour, but there has never been anything like tonight. The palace was floodlit, and its grand baroque beauty could be seen for miles. The lakes were floodlit too and, better still, the famous terraces, they were blue and green and Tyroleans walked about singing; and although there were seven hundred people or even more, it was not in the least crowded. It was gay, young, brilliant, in short, perfection. I was loath to leave, but did so at about 4.30 and took one last look at the baroque terraces with the lake below, and the golden statues and the great palace. Shall we ever see the like again? Is such a function not out of date? Yet it was all of the England that is supposed to be dead and is not. There were literally rivers of champagne.

10 July

Little Princess Cecile of Prussia, whom I love, is staying with me at 5 Belgrave Square, and she brought a dark, engaging damsel, a Miss Cynthia Elliot[19] to lunch, and so I quickly collected Master Coats,[20] Tony Loughborough, and young Jack Kennedy[21] to amuse them. We had a hilarious party, and later I took them all to the House of Commons as they wanted to see the PM.

11 July

The war seems a little more remote; perhaps it will never come; it seems less of a reality, perhaps because there is no news . . .

I lunched with Alan and Patsy to meet the Queen of Spain, for whom they collected a pleasant party. Ernest Brown, Yeats-Brown of Bengal Lancer fame (I was disappointed in him, a

19. Afterwards married to Leslie Hore-Belisha.

20. Chips had met Peter Coats earlier that summer at dinner at Lady Cunard's. They were to remain close friends until his death nineteen years later. Peter Coats edited the original MS of the Diaries.

21. The future President of the United States.

thin, crisp, studious creature, and not the beau sabreur I had expected), the Halifaxes, both very gracious, and others.

In the evening at Laura Corrigan's big dinner I found a bevy of young beauties. I was next to the American Ambassadress, Mrs Kennedy, on my left. She is an uninteresting little body, though pleasant and extraordinarily young looking to be the mother of nine. She has an unpleasant voice, and says little of interest. She too keeps a diary, and I always like people who keep diaries; they are not as others, at least not quite.

26 July

I had a tea party for Sir George Sitwell, Sachie's eccentric Renaissance father, who really is a cinquecento character. An old man of over 70, he is capricious, cold, cruel, vindictive and cuttingly witty, yet he adores his grandchildren, though he has been tyrannical to his own children and even allowed that gaunt wife of his, Lady Ida, to go to prison for debt on some trivial charge to do with a cheque. Sachie wanted to show him our famous dining room, so I had it lighted by candles for them. He arrived looking like Barbarossa or Malatesta and today seemed mild, good mannered and cheerful, but I felt his thin lips and tapping fingers could say and do cruel things.

31 July

The great Foreign Office debate opened with Archie Sinclair making a singularly irrelevant vapid speech attacking Neville for an hour. He was followed by that able but unattractive renegade, Hugh Dalton. The PM sat through it with his good humoured dignity. When his turn came he lashed at them both with vigorous skill in what was possibly his most brilliant speech. He seemed to enjoy himself and his quiver was full of arrows which he shot with deadly aim. Both Sinclair and Dalton were hard hit over and over again. The PM walks and talks like a debutante. What a remarkable old man he is. Surely the most miraculous human being alive. He never shows any sign of fatigue, of age, of exhaustion, even of irritation.

1 August

The Regent was reminiscent at luncheon, for our blue rococo

dining room always makes him think of our famous Edward VIII dinner party a few days before the Abdication trouble began.[22] He re-told the story today, of how the then King had sent for his brother, the Duke of Kent, on that famous Thursday, having himself only just come back from his triumphant tour in Wales; he began by saying that he wanted his brothers to know, before they met that evening at 'Chips' Dinner Party' that he was going to marry Wallis. The Duke of Kent gasped 'What will she call herself?' 'Call herself?' the King echoed 'What do you think – Queen of England of course.' 'She is going to be Queen?' 'Yes and Empress of India, the whole bag of tricks.' The King was cock-a-hoop, gay, happy and confident. That was Thursday evening, 19 November, at about 7.30 p.m. The Duke, flabbergasted, rushed home to dress and tell his wife and Princess Olga. Looking back upon it, no wonder Princess Olga was late. Honor and I were sublimely unconscious of the hidden drama lying behind our dinner party. The Duke of Kent had not known whether to congratulate Wallis when he saw her, or not.

2 August

I went to Victoria Station where in the Royal Waiting Room I found a large gathering of top hatted people come to take farewell of the Regent. There were nearly 100 policemen and much confusion. At last Paul and Olga came, and whispered to me 'You have made our visit to London, we love you so much, dear Chips' and I felt rewarded for all the great trouble I had taken. Then the train moved slowly out, and I felt a gulp of misery as I always do when they leave. When I got home, miserable, I found that the Regent's last action in London had been to send my Paul a huge panda; I am so happy that he loves him. It is an added bit of happiness. Sometimes life gives one that.

In the House of Commons there was an astonishing debate on the question of adjourning the House until 3 October. The Opposition tabled an amendment that we should come back on 21 August, the usual political manoeuvre which means little, but this time things did not work out quite like that; it was made an occasion for 'The Glamour Boys' to attack the Prime Minister personally. Churchill, in a funny but sad speech, said

22. See pp. 104–6.

that we must certainly come back early, and gave many reasons including his theme song that the dictators help themselves to a country whilst we are on holiday! Speech after speech followed along those lines, and except for Sir Herbert Williams and Victor Raikes who made commonsense defence of the Government, all were against the PM who grinned and bore it. I left the Chamber for a little, and made a small investigation; Austria was taken on the night of 11/12 March, Friday night, while the House was sitting, but away for the weekend. Prague was raped on 15 March, and all that day, Wednesday, we debated the matter in the House; we talked, but were powerless. Albania was taken by Mussolini on Good Friday, a few hours after the House rose. I made notes of these brief dates and handed them to the PM who put on his glasses, read them, and smiled with approval at me. I had included all the points, either in favour of the House sitting permanently, or adjourning normally (since to go away for only 17 days would be the worst of both worlds). The PM used these notes with devastating effect when he arose for the second time about 7 o'clock. By the very brilliance of his performance, and it was his third in one week, he infuriated the House, as everyone hates the truth about himself. When he sat down there were roars of delight and approval, but also some of rage.

4 August

I drove in the rain to Polesden Lacey where I had not been for 15 years, a long time. The gardens are glorious, the grounds magnificently green and well kept. Everywhere there is the silence, and spaciousness that comes from long established wealth. But the house, whilst Edwardian to a degree and comfortable and full of rare china and expensive treasures, is really a monster. When I arrived I was told, grandly, that Mrs Greville would see me at 7.30, so I went for a walk meanwhile, and got caught in a shower. I returned dripping but was at once shown up to Maggie's little boudoir. I found her changed, older, and thinner. Her hair is quite grey. We gossiped, and she proceeded to be awful about Mrs Vanderbilt whom she hates. There is no one on earth quite so skilfully malicious as old Maggie. She told me that Mrs Vanderbilt had said that she wanted to live in England. 'No Grace, we have enough Queens here already' Maggie had retorted.

She was vituperative about almost everyone, for about 40 minutes and it was a scramble to get dressed.

7 August
Honor comes back tonight and I am thrilled to see her again.

8 August *Kelvedon*
I woke at 6, got up and went for a long walk in the woods with Bundi. There were yokels working, clearing out the debris, and the Essex sun shone through the trees. The noise of chopping and of boughs dragged over the turf was like a Grimm fairy story. Back at 7.30, and I astonished the household by asking for breakfast.

We lazed all day, lay about in the gardens which are looking a dream of vernal lush beauty. But the political atmosphere or rather the international one is worsening, and I am genuinely apprehensive. However, Honor and I intend to spend the rest of the month quietly here, if events in the outside world will let us . . .

22 August *Kelvedon Hall*
A historic day. I feel that a new era, perhaps the last, has opened for England and incidentally for me. It began this quiet, sunlit, morning when I sleepily opened the newspaper and read emblazoned across the ever sensational Express 'German–Russian Pact'. Then I realized that the Russians have double-crossed us, as I always believed they would. They have been coquetting secretly with Germany, even as our negotiations proceeded. They are the foulest people on earth. Now it looks like war, and the immediate partition of Poland. The Russians have decided that the Germans are the best bet, and even as our conversations continue, Ribbentrop is flying to Moscow to conclude their death alliance.

The Cabinet sat all day and it is announced tonight that the House will meet again on Thursday to pass emergency legislation. Perhaps we have a few more days, even weeks, of peace, but a partition of Poland seems inevitable. For if Poland resists we automatically go to war. But I cannot bear to think that our world is crumbling to ruins. I refuse to admit it.

24 August

Early to the House, where I watched the other Members come in and meet one another. They all looked well, many were bronzed. At 2.45 the House met and soon the Prime Minister rose. He spoke in well modulated phrases and was clear and admirable, but with little passion or emotion, and I thought of the Munich crisis last September and all the excitement then. There was little resemblance to that hectic day this afternoon. The House was calm, bored, even irritated, at having its holiday cut short by Hitler. I looked about me. Lloyd George opposite me, and Winston Churchill a little to the right below me, those twin apostles of Russian friendship looked old, and dejected. Winston held his face in his hands and occasionally nodded his head in agreement with the PM. I was directly behind Neville, and admired him immensely as he coolly unfolded the story of Russian perfidy and German aspirations. Everyone secretly or openly, whatever they may say, hopes that the Poles will climb down. But the whole House expect war. Even Rab is pessimistic.

I suppose it is like getting married; the second time it is impossible to work up the same excitement. Certainly tonight London is quiet and almost indifferent to what may happen. There is a frightening calm.

25 August *Kelvedon*

All day at the Foreign Office, wondering whether there would be war. Every few minutes the barometer rose or fell. Halifax is worn out and shows it. The Polish guarantee was his pet scheme and his favourite godchild.

Later Harold Balfour rang me from the Air Ministry to say that news, good news, had come through from Berlin. Hitler had sent Nevile Henderson, who was to return to London tomorrow to report the conversation to Chamberlain. I don't believe in the war, nor does our Italian chef, who today visited his Embassy, and was definitely told that there would be no war as far as the Italians were concerned. That is something. In fact the Italian telegrams to the War Office are very thrilling and it looks as if Ciano and Mussolini will climb down. They are searching for a way out of the Axis. They would like to 'lâcher' Hitler, and we must make it easy for them. The alliance between Germany and Russia is definitely unpopular in Italy.

26 August

I found the Foreign Office in a turmoil, with Sir Nevile Henderson due back from Berlin by air at twelve o'clock. He was late, as the car from Croydon broke down. But he came to the office for a moment before crossing over to No. 10, where he lunched with the Prime Minister en petit comité, with Rab, Halifax and Alec Cadogan. But it appears that Hitler's offer to Henderson was so stiff and our Government's reaction so negative that the door is slamming again. Later Peter Loxley and I walked to the Travellers Club to lunch, and in the park we ran into Leslie Hore-Belisha, walking with Lord Gort.[23] I deserted Peter and joined the War Office. Leslie is pessimistic and is almost looking forward to a war. He thinks we have the Russians cornered. I fear and deplore his attitude. Later, twice, I came across it in David Margesson.

28 August

The Foreign Office have made arrangements to go to Cheltenham, the Ministry of Labour to Leamington Spa, the Air Ministry to Worcester, the King and Queen have taken a country house in the name of the French Ambassador near Worcester. The West Country will come into its own.

And the whole secret story (which we didn't discuss tonight, needless to say) of 'The Walrus', as one of the individuals has come to be known is so extraordinary. A Balt, named Mr D[24] – and a Mr Spencer, of mid-Beds, have it appears been negotiating secretly here, and pretend to come from Germany. According to them Goering is anxious to dethrone Hitler and set himself up as a General Monk, and restore the Hohenzollerns, etc. I doubt the validity of the Walrus's credentials, but he is taken seriously by Halifax, and a secret plane transported the two emissaries here, with special facilities at the airport. The news got out immediately, at least of the arrival, if not the identity of the

23. Chief of the Imperial General Staff, 1937–9.
24. Dahlerus.

men. This foolish, melodramatic story is only known to about ten people.

All night, mostly, at the FO.

29 August *Kelvedon*

I thank God for one more day of peace and beauty here, but will the sun set on peace tomorrow?

30 August

The long answer from the German Government has come today and is thought to be unsatisfactory by most. The Cabinet met to consider it. Meanwhile we are still urging Germany and Poland to negotiate, though the Germans seem determined to have their way, and are as unaccommodating as possible. All day we were on a see-saw Peace – War – Peace. The Italian news however I thought distinctly encouraging and Ciano has now definitely promised that Italy will be neutral and suggested that she was veering round to us. But Leger of the French Foreign Office sent me a telegram warning us not to believe these tales and his gloomy report corroborated Paul of Yugoslavia's impression, who warned me by the telephone not to trust 'The Macaronis'.

Tentative evacuation has been ordered for tomorrow. Peace is in the balance.

1 September

We are on the very verge of war, as Poland was this morning invaded by Germany, who will now carve up the country with the help of the Russians. At home there were more 'goodbyes', and Honor has gone to Kelvedon. There is a blackout, complete and utter darkness, and all day the servants had been frantically hanging black curtains.

2 September

It is really tomorrow, and it is at 1.25 a.m. that, dejected, despondent, despairing I sit down in my bedroom (for the last time?) to chronicle today's events. They are appalling. This morning began with nervous fusses here at home with hysterical and foolish servants. Then I walked to the FO, and talked at length with

Rab, who was strangely cheeerful; but he seemed disappointed when I told him that he is not to be made Minister of Economic Warfare, but to remain on at the FO, when war breaks out. . . . The morning passed in reading telegrams, waiting about; outside all seemed natural, there were possibly fewer cars, but few signs of evacuation in this part of London. At 12.30 Alec Dunglass crossed over from No. 10, and we talked secretly with Rab. Alec still thinks that the brand might be snatched from the burning, some sort of démarche might be made through an intermediary which would induce the Germans to retire from Poland, where the tempo of this half-hearted War increases slightly, though both the offensive and defensive are mild.

I had no lunch, walked with Rab to the House of Commons, and tried on the way, forgetting it was Saturday, to buy him a hat. By 2.30 I was back in my room at the House of Commons, and I rang the Private Secretaries asking where the box was with the Statement which the Chancellor was to make. It had been delayed. At last it arrived, but only two minutes before the Speaker took the chair. Rab and I walked along, and I caught sight of John Simon's bald white head and as we caught him up, he whispered that he had just received an urgent message not to make the statement as important news had come from Italy.

The moment Prayers were over he made a brief announcement to the House that the Prime Minister would make a statement later. I rushed out, found Rab in a deep conference, although a peripatetic one, with Halifax. They walked to the Lords together, and I followed, trying to listen. When we reached the Prince's Chamber, which was full of eager Peers, my father-in-law seized me and delayed me. When I had broken away Rab told me that the Italians had offered to negotiate and to call together a Five Power Conference, etc. . . .

Then we went, followed by Rab to No. 10. The PM apparently considered Ciano's message of sufficient importance to call together an immediate Cabinet at 4.30 at No. 10, and there was a sauve qui peut from the Front Bench, and the House at once sensed that there was something afoot. I remained in our room so as not to be trapped into saying anything indiscreeet. . . . Rab rang me about six, the Cabinet had just risen; it has been, he said, stormy, and Ciano was only going to get a very stiff reply though it would be as reasonable as Chamberlain could make it under the circumstances.

Then there was a long, and most unfortunate wait, which very likely affected the final course of tomorrow's War – for it must be tomorrow now, since we have had our miracle today and did not profit by it; for during the long time which ensued, the nervous House, chafing under delay, and genuinely distressed, some of them, by our guarantee to Poland not having been immediately operative, quenched their thirst in the Smoking Room, and when they returned to hear the PM's statement, many of them were full of 'Dutch Courage'; one noticed their flushed faces.... Meanwhile the Cabinet had risen and retired. The PM was left behind with Halifax to draft his statement, and a clumsy, or rather inartistic, document it was, too. At the same time they had to ring up Paris and convey to them Ciano's offer (at the time I understood this to be so, though now I believe that the French knew of it this morning). In any case the French Cabinet met immediately and began to discuss it. They demanded more time, and it was first suggested that the Germans should be told that unless they evacuated Poland within a week we should declare War jointly with the French (this proposal is supposed to have originated with Bonnet, who is anti-War). There were long telephonic conversations and the time limit was whittled down to 48 hours. The PM arrived at last, and I instantly woke Rab, who had ten minutes sleep, handed him an icy Martini which exhilarated him, and together we walked into the PM's room where we found Alec Dunglass, Rucker[25] and David Margesson. Arthur Greenwood and Archie Sinclair had just been summoned into the inner room and the PM told them of the French evasive delays (they are not so prepared as we are, nor is their evacuation so well advanced). We waited outside, and someone said something funny about Horace Wilson which threw us all into fits of laughter. I suppose it was nerves – the first laugh for weeks, and when Rab gave us his famous cackle, David Margesson and I doubled up, roared until the tears came. ... Suddenly the PM's bell rang, and David was summoned into the presence. By now our spirits were soaring, peace might again

25. A. N. Rucker, Principal Private Secretary to the Prime Minister, 1937–9.

be saved, as by a miracle, by Italian intervention. . . . We followed the PM into the House, which was crowded and grim. The long wait had irritated everyone, and it would have been longer still had I not reminded the Secretaries that Halifax had probably already made his identical Statement in the Lords.

The PM rose, was cheered, but not over-much, and then he read out his statement which I thought ill-conceived. It began by saying that, as yet, no answer had come to our warning to Berlin, and the House, thoroughly prepared to unsheathe the sword, was aghast when it was hinted that peace might yet be saved. Decidedly the PM did not have a very good reception, though Greenwood, who followed him, attempted to soothe the House, whilst maintaining his own dignity. Maxton made an impassioned appeal to the PM to continue his good work, not to be rushed, but he was almost shouted down. All the old Munich rage all over again; the resentment against Chamberlain: All those who want to die abused Caesar. John McGovern leant over to strike Kirby (Labour member for Euston) but the Speaker pretended not to see . . . there were a few other short speeches, after which Chamberlain rose for the second time, and promised a definite answer by noon tomorrow when the House will meet again – for the first time on a Sunday in all its history.

The Cabinet and the Appeasers were discouraged by the reception the insane House of Commons gave to this glimmer of peace, and began to say that the PM was not accurate in reporting to the House the findings of the Cabinet.

All evening at the FO, Butler and I struggled hard. There were countless telephone calls to Paris and we were told that the French, led by Bonnet, would not shorten their ultimatum to Germany which they insisted should be for a whole week! We know we could not hold the House of Commons for so long, but we offered, as a compromise, 48 hours from tomorrow morning – the Frogs, at first, would not agree. And here the War Party, suddenly strengthened by John Simon, who, I suppose, saw his chance of becoming PM, began to argue for a shorter ultimatum still – the Cabinet sat long. Terrific excitement; wild talk of the French ratting altogether, of our fighting them and the whole world . . . Peter Loxley and I crossed over to No. 10 Downing

Street after the Private Secretaries had rung for us to come and join the fun, and it came on to rain – a storm, terrific, ominous – 'When the Rains Came'. I saw Alec Dunglass, 'Are we all mad?' I asked him.

The PM came out of a side room followed by Horace Wilson and Rab. He looked well, almost relieved that the dread decision was taken and the appalling battle on – we were going to give Germany only two hours ultimatum (this was an answer to the French, to make them ashamed). The Cabinet had insisted; the War Party was led by Simon, Oliver Stanley, Walter Elliot and, I believe Shakespeare Morrison; the Overruled Peace Party consisted of the PM and Kingsley Wood. I sat on Rucker's (the most amiable, able Chief Private Secretary) desk, when the door opened into the Cabinet room, and I saw Sam Hoare, alone in a dinner jacket. The various Chiefs of Staff were wandering about in uniform: Corbin, the steely, grey, Frog Ambassador, was soon in conference with the PM. He was told our decision: we had already instructed Nevile Henderson to ask for an interview tomorrow morning at 9 a.m. and to inform the German Government that unless news came by 11 a.m. that the German Government had ordered the withdrawal of their forces from Poland we should be at War.... This message was sent, I think, about midnight or after. The French immediately climbed down, and we understood from Corbin that the French Ambassador in Berlin was to ask for an interview tomorrow at noon, and give the German Government 17 hours, that is until 5 a.m. on Monday morning, to withdraw. The French Government have not sufficiently completed their mobilisation and evacuation and all day they had been pressing us to hold back a few more hours. Brokenhearted, I begged David Margesson to do something; but he was already determined. 'It must be War, Chips, old boy', he said. 'There's no other way out'.

I decided to go home; there were no cars; the rain was blinding – Cabinet Ministers, Chiefs of Staff, all wandered hopelessly about. We left Rab with the PM, who was about to go to bed, for his last night of peace. Wet typists trotted off into the downpour; only people emerging from No. 10 knew the facts.... Peter and I left: I wanted to walk, as it had cleared a little; he would not. It was dark, a precaution against air-raids. We found a taxi.

Peter dropped me. I am home. I shall not sleep; in a few hours we shall be at War, and the PM will have lost his great battle for peace.

3 September

10.57 a.m. The PM is to broadcast at 11.15 and in a few moments a state of war will be declared. The method, while to my mind precipitate and brusque, is undoubtedly popular. Everyone is smiling, the weather is glorious but I feel that our world or all that remains of it, is committing suicide, whilst Stalin laughs and the Kremlin triumphs. If only we can win a quick war, and dislodge the Nazi régime. That would mean a Neville victory, a November election, and triumph. In London the church bells are ringing, people draw more closely together, everyone is kind and considerate, and all are quietly appreciative of what the Government has done. The arrangements have been smooth, swift and skilful. I went up with Victor Perowne to the FO wireless station and listened to the PM. He was dignified and moving, brief and sad. He had barely finished when the sirens announced an air-raid (and later Rab told me that he had been with him in the room at No. 10 whilst the actual broadcast was being done, that the PM had not been warned of the air-raid rehearsal and was visibly shaken when the sirens blew). Though we thought it was a rehearsal we all went to our assigned rooms. Ours is 172 and nearest the garden door, a commodious but comfortless suite. There I found several typists and we were soon joined by Rab and others. The wailing noise continued, and finally the heavy doors were shut. 'It's like the Thetis' I remarked.[26] Soon, however, the all-clear sounded. Afterwards Rab and I, accompanying Lord Halifax, walked to Westminster stared at by a silent crowd.

The House was crowded. There were perhaps half a dozen uniforms. I took my place just behind where the PM sits. He came in looking smiling and well and we all rose and cheered; but the Opposition who yesterday growled at him for not declaring war, today were too churlish to cheer him for having done so. There was a pause, and a feeling of unreality, while the clerks

26. The *Thetis* submarine disaster was still fresh in everyone's minds.

read out their mumbo-jumbo to do with Parliamentary procedure. Then he rose, more cheers – and he spoke feelingly of the collapse of all his hopes. I was wet-eyed, but indignant with the Opposition for their bad manners. Old Josh Wedgwood was disgustingly jubilant. Duff Cooper grinned, Anthony Eden was expressionless, and when Greenwood began speaking, I looked up at the Ambassadors gallery, and there in a distinguished huddle were the Duke of Alba, Joe Kennedy and the Belgian, sitting with the French and Polish Ambassadors, who both looked worn out. A little later Maisky dared to appear, and he beamed his Cheshire-cat smile. No wonder. It is the moment he has long intrigued and hoped for. The other speakers did not hold me, though Winston spoke well.

In the evening I dined with Peter Loxley and Harold Balfour at the Savoy, in semi-darkness. The restaurant was almost empty and the streets completely black. In the night there was another air-raid alarm but I did not awake until called by the butler. Then I joined the servants in the cellar, where I found everyone good-tempered and funny. The Duke of Kent sent me a message asking me to go to his shelter next door, but I was too sleepy, and declined.

CHAPTER FIVE

The Fall of the Chamberlain Government
September 1939–May 1940

The first six months of the Second World War ('the phoney war') were to end with a series of disasters to the Allied cause, starting with the German invasion of Norway and the collapse of France. The Chamberlain Government was brought down after a vote of censure in the House of Commons on 9 May in which its majority of about 240 slumped to 81. Chips's account of these months has a particular interest as it is the first version that has come from the entirely pro-Chamberlain side. His account of the famous debate that destroyed the Government is one of the best pieces of descriptive writing in the whole of the Diaries, and is accordingly given almost verbatim.

Throughout the Diaries dealing with the War, I have excluded the many references to the course of the war except where they have a direct relevance to the diary extracts themselves.

The narrative opens on 4 September 1939.

4 September 1939

I walk to the Foreign Office; all the major new appointments have been announced; Winston is back at the Admiralty and in the War Cabinet of nine. Anthony Eden is at the Dominions Office with access to the War Cabinet, a fact much commented on by the Italian wireless. I talked with Rab about our personal futures; I am in some doubt as to what to do. Remain here? Or break out and take some semi-military occupation – I, with my flat feet, my stomach, my inefficiency and loathing of drill, exercise, discipline and danger? Rab is worried too, and somewhat disappointed at having been refused the new Ministry of Economic Warfare. But really, as both David Margesson and Alec Dunglass told me, he is far more needed at the FO as both the PM and the S. of S. so depend upon him. Indeed he is the PM's 'blue-eyed boy'. He (I have positive information on this point) was considered both for the Ministry of Information and for Economic Warfare, but in each case the PM refused to release him from his present important duties. Rab is pleased but disappointed. Later he will be rewarded.

5 September

I was grateful for an uninterrupted night's sleep, and today I feel like a lion. How enjoyable it would all be if it were not for the war. In fact, I am almost ashamed of my high spirits and rude return to health and energy.

I had tea with the Duchess of Kent, who looked sadly lovely with her amber eyes, and I wondered once whether they were tear stained? We sat in what was once her little private sitting room, but today there were two chairs only and a tea tray. The house had been completely dismantled and there were only a few packing cases and dust sheets about, and few traces of its former gaiety and happiness. All the Duke's expensive toys, his lovely bibelots, his books, his Panninis, his Meissen, all had been removed, mostly to the Pantechnicon. They now have no London home at all. We had a sad conversation about poor Prince Paul struggling and hoping for peace in his mountain fastness of Brdo. . . . It was a sad little talk and I think we both felt a touch like Ruth amid the alien corn, aliens in this incredibly lovely and lovable England. Princess Marina more than me, for I have never known any other life really, except for my youthful Parisian flash.

6 September

Awakened at 6.40 by the siren's sad song. I took to the cellars but shall not do so again. Two dreary hours wasted.

. . . Today I watched Winston whispering to the PM (I was immediately behind them). He is behaving well, but their deep mutual antagonism must sooner or later flare up and make co-operation impossible. Then we shall all be sacked, and there will be a 'glamorous' central Government, reinforced by extreme Left Conservatives and some Socialists who are already saying that while they have refused to serve under Neville that they would agree to under Winston. I see it coming.

7 September

It was a lovely English lush morning, and I walked all the way to the House with Ralph Assheton whose appointment as Parliamentary Secretary to the Ministry of Labour was announced this morning. What a warm-hearted charmer, and so good and honest. He will do well, and I have long urged his claims to office. En route, we met the Neville Chamberlains, followed by two detectives, who gave us dazzling smiles. The Chamberlains, not the detectives.

There is now a Whip's vacancy again, though it may well not be filled as the H. of C. work will be minimised. However, my hopes rose when this afternoon Harris,[1] the eminence grise of the Whips' Room, told me that the Chief Whip was looking everywhere for me. My heart beat fast, then half sank; a Whip at last, and yet not quite when I want to be. Excitedly, I sought out the Chief Whip, but all he wanted was help in getting the Queensberrys out of France, where they have foolishly got themselves stranded. I was at once disappointed and relieved. Yet I feel my present Foreign Office job cannot continue indefinitely.

8 September

I met Nevile Henderson who looked worn, but brown, and as usual, faultlessly dressed. He told me that he and his staff took four days to get back from Berlin, though the German Foreign Office were most polite, and indeed almost cried when they left.

9 September

Emerald is completely discouraged, indeed demoralised by the war, and I heard today at the Foreign Office that the French fear that it will last at least until the spring of 1941; here we are more optimistic, though the news from Poland continues appalling, and, amongst many other places, Lancut, the Potocki's operatic castle, has been taken. It was twice occupied during the Great War. Since then it has stood, like an isolated rock, forgotten by fate and much enjoyed by the privileged few who were asked to

1. Charles (later Sir Charles) Harris, Private Secretary to successive Parliamentary Secretaries to the Treasury, 1919–24, 1924–9, and 1931–61; Private Secretary to Conservative Chief Whip, 1924 and 1929–31.

stay there, though I personally always felt a sense of doom under its roof.

10 September

I went to Kelvedon on Saturday afternoon in lovely weather in the hope of a peaceful perfect Sunday but it was not to be. There were endless decisions to be made; papers to be stored; fuss and confusion; irritated servants; neglected dogs; plate-room and cellar complications. We packed up all our jewelled toys, the Fabergé bibelots and gold watches, etc., and counted the wine, then we welcomed 150 refugees, all nice East End people, but Honor was depressed and worn out, and our Sunday not as happy as I had hoped.

On my way I looked in at Bucks and saw several swaggering officers with highly polished belts stuffing themselves with oysters. . . . All morning I went about carrying an absurd gas-mask in a canvas bag, which I found a bore . . .

13 September

The Windsors arrived back last night, and are staying with the Metcalfes near Ashdown. The journey over was arranged with the utmost secrecy; it is dramatic, the ex-King returning after nearly three years exile, with the woman he loved on his arm, uncertain of their reception . . .

14 September

Diana Cooper rang me this morning for the first time since the war. She is in a terrible state, nervous and apprehensive. . . . Duff, at the moment is out of a job, unhappy and resentful. He knows that Chamberlain will never forgive him. Diana asked me why Duff was not included in the new Government?

This afternoon I saw Duff having a long heart to heart with Winston at the House of Commons. I am told that Winston is already driving the Admiralty to distraction by his interference and energy.

17 September

A glorious September day at Kelvedon where I bathed in the pool, and then in a bath towel rang up the FO to be told the grim news that the Russians had definitely invaded Poland. Now the Nazis and the Bolsheviks have combined to destroy civilisation, and the outlook for the world looks ghastly.

18 September

I drove up to London, and lunched with Emerald where I sat next to old Margot Oxford, crisp, rude but as affectionate as ever. She is very pro-Chamberlain and angry with her step-children who are not. She is against the black-out, deprecates any danger from air-raids, and thinks gas masks unnecessary. I agree up to a point, though I rather enjoy the black-outs. She said one would have disliked Lord Kitchener intensely if one had not happened to like him, whereupon Emerald said she had found him 'alarmingly dull'. Once in desperation she asked him who was his favourite author and after long hesitation he replied 'Stanley Weyman'. We wondered who would be the Kitchener of this war; 'certainly not Hore-Belisha' Margot volunteered. How she dislikes him.

There is now a tendency to say that the Russian intervention in Poland is not so serious as we originally feared. Dalton, who called at the Foreign Office this morning, takes that line.

19 September

What I have always half foreseen, half feared as a nightmare, is now a possibility, that is, an entire alteration in the European system with the power of Russian enormously strengthened. There will be, indeed, some sort of Bolshevik régime over most of our continent; but not quite yet; the USA might save us, but our days of power are over for a long time to come. Meanwhile the war in Poland is drawing to a close, and another few days will see the end. Then activities will be transferred to the Western Front, and *we* shall begin to have a bad time, to put it mildly.

I think that Neville made a mistake in not resigning after Prague; it would have been better for this war to have been declared by the Left, or by the Churchill Centre.

20 September

I think that Kingsley Wood might easily become our next PM and that is now the PM's intention. He purposely put Inskip on the Woolsack in order to clear the way for Kingsley Wood. The PM thinks that Halifax would only be a stop-gap. I am nervous and discouraged; my world has collapsed; I should like to bury myself in Devonshire. I came with a war, perhaps I shall go with one. The fact is, I am just the wrong age for this war. 42. Old enough not to have to do anything, yet occasionally embarrassed and envious of people in uniform. Perhaps unfortunately, I look much younger than I am.

22 September

Honor came up yesterday and I took her, Brigid and Harold Balfour to luncheon at the Ritz which has become fantastically fashionable; all the great, the gay, the Government; we knew 95% of everyone there. But Ritzes always thrive in wartime, as we are all cookless. Also in wartime the herd instinct rises . . .

23 September

I lunched at the Spanish Embassy and talked at great length to Eddie Devonshire who is always kindly, though deaf. But he is obdurate about his son Billy Hartington's engagement to Miss Kennedy; he will not budge; the Kennedy alliance is not to his liking; he has an anti-catholic mania, and has forbidden the match.[2]

24 September

'Musso' has made his long-awaited 'peace' speech at Bologna, and it was temperate, as if he knew in advance that such a démarche would fall on deaf, determined ears. We are resolved to fight this grim war to the end, as it had to come some time. That seems to be the prevailing spirit.

26 September

The PM made his usual dignified statement: unfortunately he was followed by Winston who executed a tour-de-force, a brilliant bit of acting and exposition, in describing in detail the work of the Admiralty. He amused, and impressed the House. . . he must have taken endless trouble with his speech, and it was a

2. Lord Hartington and Miss Kennedy were not married until 1942.

great contrast, which was noticed, to the PM's colourless statement. Already today I noticed signs of the 'glamour boys' beginning to intrigue again. We must watch out.

27 September

The first war budget. At 3.45 Simon rose (he was directly in front of me) and in unctuous tones not unlike the Archbishop of Canterbury, opened his staggering budget. He warned the House of its impending severity yet there was a gasp when he said that Income Tax would be 7/6 in the £. The crowded House was dumbfounded, yet took it good-naturedly enough. Simon went on, and with many a deft blow practically demolished the edifice of capitalism. One felt like an Aunt Sally under his attacks (the poor old Guinness trustee, Mr Bland, could stand it no more, and I saw him leave the gallery) blow after blow; increased surtax; lower allowances; raised duties on wine, cigarettes and sugar; substantially increased death duties. It is all so bad that one can only make the best of it, and re-organise one's life accordingly.

28 September

Very secret. 'The Walrus'[3] is in London. He arrived today by plane and this time his visit is known to Hitler. Halifax and others are seeing him this afternoon. No-one knows of this. What nefarious message does he bring?

29 September

The now fabulously mysterious 'Walrus,' i.e. Mr Lazarus,[4] was interviewed secretly yesterday. He arrived by boat via Holland and so caused no comment. His other trips were all made by air. This morning he walked about the Foreign Office openly ... Also Cadogan had a talk with him and a report of their conversation was given to Lord Halifax, who read it I believe, at the War Cabinet. It is the usual personal plea for peace, and again hints at making Goering head of the German State. Ribbentrop and Molotov had today signed their Treaty for the final partition of Poland and for their future joint action. They now say that all

3. Dahlerus; see also pp. 259–60.
4. i.e. Dahlerus.

responsibility for the future of the war must fall on the Democratic Western Powers. Reactions to the theory are as expected and, the French, always realistic say 'we had better make peace, as we can never restore Poland to its old frontiers, and how indeed should we ever dislodge the Russians from Poland even if we succeeded in ousting the Germans?'

1 October

In the afternoon the House was calm and uninteresting. Rab described a certain official at the much libelled Ministry of Information as being like a nonconformist accountant in a disorderly house which was extending credit. He is enchanting sometimes.

4 October

Hitler made his big but disappointing speech to the Reichstag this afternoon. It was delivered at the Opera House, where Honor and I once attended a sumptuous, almost beyond belief, banquet given by Goering in 1936.

10 October

Russia helps herself to a new country every day and no-one minds. It is only German crimes which raise indignation in the minds of the English.

In the evening I listened to Kingsley Wood's great statement about the air situation. It was a broad, rich speech but badly delivered, and the House slept. He read it as if he was dictating to a typist. I feel that in spite of its definite worth, he was not staking his claim to future premiership. There are already several 'Crown Princes' about.

11 October

This morning Rab was sent for by the Secretary of State and Cadogan, and told them that the statement to be made tomorrow is to be almost, but not quite, a definite refusal of Hitler's terms. Rab has however succeeded in keeping the door slightly ajar.

12 October

An unreal day, and now in the gloaming I sit with my fountain pen in the Chamber and scribble. The front bench is nearly deserted, only Anthony Eden in a flashy grey suit with still some remnants of his fading good looks, Miss Horsbrugh, able and alert, and a brace of dim Whips. . . . Opposite is Stafford Cripps who has just spoken. I have arranged for him to see Halifax tomorrow. Charles Emmett is speaking, or rather dribbling intolerable platitudes. The House is bored and dimly lit. Rab is disgruntled with democracy, and has gone out for a brief respite . . .

The House earlier was crowded and attentive, half hoping for peace, but determined really on war. The PM came in early, calm and icy. I sat immediately behind him. Questions were interminable and he rose at 3.50 and slowly and deliberately made his famous statement which many have read and had a finger in. I have his actual copy and will preserve it. It was messed about by so many people that I feared it would sound stale but it had a facile parliamentary triumph. The House liked it and Neville's stock rose. He was much cheered and I was glad. Even Winston sitting opposite him (there was no room on the Government bench for his baroque bottom) joined in the cheering. I felt however that Neville's heart was not in his speech. Only his personal hatred of Hitler helped him through it.

24 October

I had an hour with Alec Dunglass and we plotted for Rab to go to the India Office as Secretary of State in the Spring; and Alec took kindly to my plea that Nevile Henderson be given a Peerage immediately. Then I tried to wangle the Admiralty for Rab.

2 November

I lunched at the Ritz with Eileen Sutherland, whom I had not seen since the far away Summer, that feverish season when night after night we went to balls and fêtes, each one more splendid and sumptuous than the others; it was a sort of sunset glow before the storm. We sat and drank cocktails, the Dukes of Marlborough (who calls his wife, who is in uniform, the General[5]), Northumberland and Leeds, more like a pekinese than

5. The Duchess was Chief Commandant of the A.T.S. 1938–40.

ever. It was 'The Dukeries' in excelsis. Eileen told me rather sadly that they have shut up Hampden House. I dined there in the summer, her last Dinner Party as it worked out. Londonderry House too, has been shut, and also Holland House,[6] where there will surely never be another Ball – again I was at the 'house cooling'. It is sad that the houses of the great will never again open their hospitable doors. Emerald, too is trying to sell her house. It would indeed be the end of a chapter, were that to go. However, I have had twenty years of splendour, fun and life – the Twilight of the Gods, it was worth it and nothing matters now – I have Gibbonian apprehensions.

4 November

There is no real war. Hitler is indeed shrewd. Is he trying to bore us into peace?

16 November

I lunched with Circe Londonderry and her daughter Mairi at the Dorchester. The only other guest was Harold Macmillan, who for all his intelligence, is lacking in judgment, and is a too facile critic of the Government and the PM.

24 November

The war at sea intensifies and we have had a series of maritime knocks, though none sufficiently serious to be alarming. I trust that Joe Kennedy, the jaunty American Ambassador, is wrong, for he prophesies the end of everything, and goes about saying that England is committing suicide. My reason tells me he is wrong, that everything is on our side, but my intuition warns me that he may have something.

28 November

At the Opening of Parliament the King was in naval uniform, and the Queen wore trailing black velvet, furs and pearls, and I have never seen her so regal and beautiful. She was dressed to perfection. Everyone remarked on it. I have so often watched this ceremony in the days of peace with King George and Queen

6. It was destroyed in the Blitz.

Mary floodlit with splendour; with the Royal Commission, in 1935, because Princess Victoria had died that morning; in 1936 when King Edward VIII opened Parliament looking more curiously boyish than ever in his robes . . . since then the present sovereigns have done it, and there has always been the fear, as there was today, that the King would stammer, in fact, it is always a relief when he finishes his speech. I could not help contrasting this morning's quiet solemnity with all the Nazi fanfare, though there was a Merovingian touch about the King today. The company rose as the King and Queen bowed and slowly left the Chamber, the King holding the Queen's hand. Back in the Commons lobby, several old Members who should have known better, smoked, and were stopped as the House was suspended, not adjourned.

Rab asked me whether Maisky and he could lunch alone at Belgrave Square today for a secret meeting, as did not want to be seen with him in public. The lunch apparently was a success: I never thought that the Russian Ambassador would ever cross my threshold; I checked up on the snuff-boxes on my return but did not notice anything missing. Rab said that His Excellency is an agreeable scoundrel.

7 December

The 'Te Deums' of the unreal League of Nations must be sung next week, and my Rab will be the principal delegate. Should I accompany or stay behind and 'run' the Foreign Office? Which? I am torn with doubt. I don't want to go; but fear it would be occasion manquée not to; but I suggested this morning that Eddie Devonshire be appointed as second delegate under Rab. An Under-Secretary who is a Duke would be perfect. The Cabinet jumped at the suggestion and charged Anthony Eden with a message to Eddie asking him to go.

10 December

An intoxicating day spent with someone I have hardly seen alone since January, i.e. myself. There is no such blissful companionship, no such satisfactory or stimulating friendship. I got up late, wrote many letters, tidied up and telephoned. The war is 100 days old, and a damned bore it is, though no-one seems to talk about it now. It might be somewhere very remote, and I feel that there is a definite danger in such detachment.

13 December

There was a secret session, and Questions proceeded in a normal way. At the end of them I went out for a moment, and ran into the Duke of Kent who was in naval uniform and we chatted. He was amiable enough, and I came back to the Chamber just in time to hear the PM move that 'strangers be ordered to retire' and the galleries were emptied. Peers remained. Quintin Hogg, foolishly and youthfully, rose to protest against the presence of Gallacher, the Communist. It was a mistake, as Gallacher is being carefully watched. Hogg protested with dignity, but he raised the temperature of the House, always an undesirable thing to do. Then the debate began.

14 December

As each session closes, the PM seems to be in even better form and fettle – though I secretly feel he hates the House of Commons: certainly he has a deep contempt for Parliamentary interference and fussiness; and who can blame him?

17 December

The whole world is waiting for news of the 'Graf Spee', which has taken refuge from our fleet in Montevideo. In a few hours time the much vaunted German pocket battleship will have to decide to be interned, to scuttle herself or to fight her way out.

18 December

The scuttling of the 'Graf Spee' off Montevideo is a welcome tonic, and will give a fillip to the Navy and to the world in general. Already our sailors are being referred to as Nelson's grandsons.

The Meet of the hounds took place at Kelvedon for the first time for 40 years – and was a lovely sight. Honor and I dispensed hospitality in the hall where a long table had been set up, laden with cherry brandy and other drinks: the Meet – and the 'Graf Spee', have revived my faith in Old England.

25 December

Essex is wrapt in fog: it is like a winding sheet: but, catarrhal and half suffocated, I came down to breakfast and spoke to Rab who rang me up from Stansted, and we had a good gossip: how he loathes holidays, rest, and country life.

THE RESIGNATION OF HORE-BELISHA

The circumstances in which the flamboyant Secretary of State for War, Leslie Hore-Belisha, was obliged to resign his office in January 1940 have always been surrounded by a certain amount of mystery. One version has been given by R. J. Minney in The Private Papers of Hore-Belisha *(1960); some light is cast by Iain Macleod in his biography of Neville Chamberlain (1961). Chips's account is of considerable interest, for, as will be seen, he describes the intervention of the King into the controversy, with decisive results. There seems no reason to dispute Chips's account, although it is possible that as yet unpublished papers may clear up the mystery. But in view of Chips's close involvement in the episode, and the authority of the information on which his account is based, I have left it largely as it was written.*

1940

2 January

I was sad to leave Kelvedon – though it was intensely cold – but beautiful too: the place is a dream of loveliness now, like a beautiful woman, she flourishes under attention: all our care is at last having an effect.

No sooner had I reached London, than I learned from Rab – who had it from Horace Wilson – that there is a plot to get rid of Leslie Hore-Belisha who, apparently has made the War Office restive by his drastic methods and too great acceleration.

3 January

At the FO we went over the MS of Nevile Henderson's book about the beginning of the War,[7] and decided that it would be

7. *Failure of a Mission.*

disastrous if it was published now, as it lays bare our vacillating policy, our offer of colonies, etc., and it warmly praises both Hitler and Goering: so we have decided to prune it drastically.

The anti-Belisha plot has grown, and is now alarming. The PM is in a dilemma – either Belisha goes or most of the General Staff. Leslie is not aware, so far, of the projected coup-de-main: so I wrote him a private word of warning, and as most of his staff at the War Office are disloyal, I sent it to Miss Sloan, his devoted personal secretary who worships him.

4 January

I am told that David Margesson has now been offered the War Office, and if he accepts poor Leslie is for it. But every effort will be made to find him some other job, as he is personally liked by the Prime Minister, and has been a definite success.

5 January

I hoped last night that the Belisha storm might blow over but this morning Rab saw Horace Wilson get into a taxi and say 'To the Ministry of Information'. Later we were told that the 'changes had all been made' and we do not quite know what they are, but Rab's curiosity is intensely aroused by the impending re-shuffle.

6 January

This a.m. the newspapers blaze 'Belisha resigns'. It is a sensation, and seems to have caught both the Press and the public unaware, and unprepared. I think that it is a calamity, especially as Leslie is to be replaced by Oliver Stanley – a dry stick. Sir John Reith, of whom I disapprove, and whom I dislike, becomes Minister of Information, though possibly he is the man for the job, and Sir Andrew Duncan[8] succeeds Oliver at the Board of Trade, a post Leslie, with dignity refused,[9] and so is now out in the cold.

8. Former Chairman of the Central Electricity Board (1927–35) and the Iron and Steel Federation (1935–40).

9. Chamberlain originally proposed to make him Minister of Information (see Macleod: *Chamberlain*, p. 286).

History will prove Belisha right in his reforms and also that Chamberlain was right in letting him go, since the war must be won – and a divided and dissatisfied War Office would never lead us to victory. Perhaps poor Leslie's methods were too democratic and too startling, but for all that, I feel that he had the youth of the country behind him.

What is the truth of what happened? There has been an anti-Belisha faction in the House, in the War Office and in the Army for some time. His mania for publicity, his courting of public favour, and his democratic methods of re-organising the Army have made him many enemies: every place seeker disappointed in his hopes, everyone refused a commission, and most of the upper-classes who saw their sons serving in the ranks, were against him: but he went blindly and blandly on with his reforms. . . . Then a cabal was formed of people on the General Staff – but they could think of no way to oust him until they hit on the brilliant idea of roping in, of all people, the Duke of Gloucester, as a professional soldier. He took up the cause and told his brother the King. The Crown decided to intervene dramatically, and sent for the PM. . . . The PM, startled by the King's complaint, gave in and that turned the scales. Hitherto, the PM, though aware of the movement, had supported Leslie. On Thursday he sent for him to come to No. 10 – and Leslie, unsuspecting went: they had a long talk during which the PM asked Leslie to accept the Board of Trade. Belisha was staggered, and asked why (evidently he had not believed my too-mildly-worded warning). Then he was told, as gently as the PM could do it, that he must go. Leslie demanded an hour in which to make up his mind, and went for a walk in St James's Park. He could hardly believe what he had been told, and was, of course, quite unaware of the Royal intervention. Later he refused the offer of the Board of Trade and made it plain that he would never serve under Chamberlain in any capacity again, because he no longer trusted him. How could he ever be sure that the PM would not throw him over again? There was some bitterness, but no actual scene, and Belisha agreed not to make a statement, not to attack the Government. Dazed and fallen from power – he left – a very unhappy man.

8 January

London is agog with Belisha tales . . . as it has now leaked out that the King himself insisted on Leslie's resignation. . . . Ever since the Abdication, the Court Minions have been intriguing his downfall . . . all this will do the Monarchy harm, as they should not intrigue or dabble in politics: though I must admit that when the King has done so in the past, he has usually been right: but George VI is not George V, and Alec Hardinge is certainly not Lord Stamfordham.

It seems that Belisha knew nothing until his conversation last Thursday with the PM. Leslie was horrified, as he told Anthony Eden (and others) on the telephone on Saturday evening when Anthony was staying with Teenie Cazalet at Great Swifts. Alone of Leslie's former colleagues Kingsley Wood tried to save him, and urged him at least to consider the offer of the Board of Trade: but, after consulting Beverley Baxter,[10] Leslie decided against it.

Throughout the crisis, David Margesson's stature has increased: he has strengthened his influence over the Prime Minister, he has shown tact with the Palace and has now appointed a great friend to the War Office: En plus – he has succeeded in not offending Belisha personally.

Meanwhile the Prime Minister is put in a difficult position, and is blamed by everyone and it seems that both the Government and the Palace are astonished by the fuss that has been caused – by the publicity and headlines, and are a bit shaken.

*

In defiance of the rules of chronology, it may be more convenient to conclude this account of Hore-Belisha's removal with Chips's account of his resignation speech and the reactions to it.

16 January

The world and particularly Whitehall love a victim – a relic of Roman days and the arena; today the House was crowded for Belisha's 'resignation' speech. Questions were rushed through, and Leslie did not appear until just in time to be called, looking

10. Conservative MP for Wood Green; former Editor of the *Daily Express*.

older and grayer. I was deeply sorry for him. He sat in Winston's old seat, the corner one in the front row below the gangway. When he rose, it was with dignity, and he quietly made his apologies, seeming more broken than bitter. I looked about the crowded House and noticed many Peers, including Boy Munster[11] who is largely responsible for his fall. At the very end of his speech, Leslie became eloquent (a practised effect) about the prosecution of the war . . . and the Ministers in front of me were obviously embarrassed: How far he has fallen; a fortnight ago he was surrounded and flattered by MP's soliciting favours, today he is almost a political outcast. But he will come back to office – unless there is something shady about it that is unknown to me. I recalled other resigning speeches – Sam Hoare's magnificent mea culpa which was Cato-like in its eloquence,[12] and, as it proved, its cold commonsense: then Duff after Munich: I missed Anthony's stinging and reproachful farewell, as Harold Balfour and I were in the train on our way back from Sestrières. Finally, Leslie sat down but there were few cheers. The PM on the other hand, had a warm reception though I did not think him at his best, and he seemed for the first time aged and colourless.

I thought much about poor Leslie's speech – I think he must now know who are the architects of his downfall, and he made two clever digs which could be taken by the uninitiated to be slurs on the PM, but which now seem certainly to have been sad, sly allusions to the Sovereign.

17 January

I met Leslie in the House today and he was affectionate, and seemed to have recovered from his shock; he said he had liked my letter the best of any he had from the House. I admire his jaunty courage, and I now suspect he knows the whole story. Alan dined last night with Max Beaverbrook where there were Sam Hoare and Terence O'Connor, and they openly hinted at the truth, and Max quoted 'There's such divinity doth hedge a king'. To my mind the Monarchy by interfering has cheapened itself – though it has certainly won the round.

*

11. Earl of Munster – Military Assistant to Lord Gort.
12. See pp. 63–4.

10 January

I am appalled by the plan to send an expeditionary force to Sweden,[13] for it is clear that the same brain who conceived the Dardanelles Campaign is responsible for this wild enterprise. Rab is aghast – not only by the folly of the scheme, but by the Secretary of State's curious weakness in allowing it to go so far. For so high principled a man he (i.e. Halifax) can be very two-faced: to him the MEANS never mean anything – it is only the END that counts. Rab and I consulted – decided that Ismay was the man to convince – and Rab accordingly induced him to dine with him tonight, and will try to persuade him.

Alan [Lennox-Boyd] and I dined at the Roumanian Legation – a dinner which began with masses of caviare and vodka, and wonderful wines to follow. Hector Bolitho was in good form, and gradually we all got intoxicated and seldom have I known such a high pitch of gaiety, wit and fun. It was 1.25 a.m. when we left the dining room. But Tilea, our host, did not entirely waste his time wining and dining us. He asked my help in getting our legation in Bucarest raised to an Embassy, and he hinted that we would be well advised to occupy Petsamo immediately. He seemed to know all about our project for 'invading' Sweden.

12 January

The War Cabinet is discussing Sweden today – Ismay is going to back Rab: if they scotch the idea of an invasion, Rab's succinct and excellent memorandum on the subject will have played an important role.

23 January

I dined with Emerald, whose brilliance was fantastic; she has been quite unsurpassable of late, and I really adore her. She is abandoning Grosvenor Square, that house where we all have been made so exquisitely and elegantly happy all our carefree days, and wants to sell some furniture; Alan and Patsy have bought George Moore's spinet. Emerald is seeking refuge in the Ritz, and I wonder if she will ever have the will, energy and luck

13. This is clearly a reference to Churchill's proposed 'Operation Catherine' in the Baltic; see his account in *The Gathering Storm*, pp. 363–4, 420–24.

to re-start her great career in another setting. It was in her house at Grosvenor Square that the great met the gay, that statesmen consorted with society, and writers with the rich – and where, over a year the drama of Edward VIII was enacted. It had a rococo atmosphere – the conversation in the candlelight, the elegance, the bibelots and the books: more, it was a rallying point for most of London society: only those that were too stupid to amuse the hostess, and so were not invited, were disdainful. The Court always frowned on so brilliant a salon: indeed Emerald's only failures were the two Queens and Lady Astor and Lady Derby. Everyone else flocked, if they had the chance. To some it was the most consummate bliss even to cross her threshold. She is as kind as she is witty, and her curious mind, and the lilt of wonder in her voice when she says something calculatedly absurd, are quite unique. We must rally round her now; I love her deeply.

25 January

Lloyd George spoke in the House and ranted for more than 40 minutes, making a political harangue which helped no-one. Most of what he said was inaccurate and rambling, but he can still hold the House with his stagey tricks, and his white mane of hair looked thicker than ever: as he continued to abuse us, I noticed Gwilym Lloyd George, just in front of me, stir uneasily in his seat, a little ashamedly. Papa was going too far.

9 February

I have come to the conclusion that Rab has several faults – minor ones – but faults all the same. He is bad about time – and keeps his visitors talking too long: he is also unpunctual: yet the fact that we are not now at war with Japan is probably due to his efforts alone, and is his greatest achievement, for which he has been working for years.

13 February

In the House I had chats with both Winston Churchill and Lloyd George. Tweedle Dum and Tweedle Dee have rooms on our corridor: indeed we are sandwiched in between them. L. G. seems the more alert and hale of the two, in his too-blue suits, blue tie, and flowing mane of hair: he does not really know me:

Winston, on the other hand, does, and dislikes me intensely, and shows it, though he tries not to: he talks to me as he does to all that are not his fervent followers – i.e. he sidles away from one, and looks down as he talks; he knows that I am a devoted Chamberlain man.

19 February

I set the wheels in motion today to sack Vansittart, who I have decided to have made a Peer.

20 February

In the lobby [of the House] I ran into Lady Astor and puckishly decided to turn my charm on her. Surprised and bewildered, she fell into my trap. She is dynamic, unbalanced, and foolish, and only warm-hearted so long as she can patronise one. But her blue eyes are beautiful still and we chatted almost amicably; she said that my child was the most remarkable little boy that she had ever seen, a short-cut, of course, to my heart.

21 February

This evening, at the House of Commons, I was sitting in the Smoking Room with Jim Wedderburn and Terence O'Connor, when we were joined by Sir John Simon, who was whimsical and discursive, and told us tales of the splendid response that had been made by all sorts of people to his appeal for funds and loans. A few days ago he told us he found a box with his personal letters next to his bed when he was called. He picked it up, and it seemed to rattle, so he rang for his servant and they gingerly carried it to his study, where they placed it in a bucket of water, thinking it must be an IRA bomb. Very cautiously, the Chancellor, still in his dressing-gown, opened the parcel with a pair of scissors. It contained a note, a gold watch and chain, and a few other trinkets which were a poor widow's contribution towards the war. The Iron Chancellor is a shrewd man, who always gives the impression that he wants to ingratiate himself with his companions, and yet always says or does something which prevents him from pleasing. But he is handling the finances of the country in a masterly manner, and may yet save us all from bankruptcy.

22 February

At the Memorial Service for Lord Tweedsmuir the Abbey was crowded with Canadian troops, the Government occupying the stalls and the Prime Minister sitting in his usual seat, the highest stall. I was opposite him and I watched his sad, lean face; he looked like some medieval saint, for his features, when relaxed, have a mystical quality. Next to him was Simon, looking as usual, like a worldly prelate, and then Halifax, who, too, could well have graced the pontifical throne itself. The service was dull, and I was disgusted to see that wicked Archbishop in the procession. His face seemed hard and inhuman, in fact bereft of any of the kindlier virtues. The wonderful Abbey was crowded and I thought of John Tweedsmuir's kindness and how he had helped me over 'Joan Kennedy' and had corrected the MSS, as he must have done for half a hundred other young writers, for he adored youth.

... In the evening Rab came into my room to tell me of the hour he had just spent with Monsieur Maisky. The Soviet Emissary had, it appeared, brought offers of peace: Russia would like an immediate Armistice with Finland, and suggested that England, in the person, if possible, of R. A. Butler, should mediate. A diabolically clever scheme, but Maisky's dove is clearly a vulture, and I hope will be so considered. Rab will report his interview to the Cabinet, and I presume, to the Finns.

29 February

Rab and I went together to the Lobby lunch at the Victoria Hotel; it was in honour of Winston Churchill and he made a most amusing, if somewhat over-personal, speech which lasted 40 minutes. Never once did he mention anything other than himself: nevertheless he was brilliant. He was on the right of the Chairman who had the Prime Minister, jovial and a little flushed, to his left. All seemed peaceful between them, and at the close of his remarks Winston pledged himself loyally to serve the 'Captain' for the duration of the voyage, and Chamberlain bowed his thanks.

6 March

Malcolm MacDonald, who I have always liked, but never

particularly admired ... made a magnificent speech, the speech of his career, in defence of the Regulations. ... I have only once seen such enthusiasm in the House, and that was when the PM announced last year that he was going to Munich: then everyone lost their heads, cheered madly, waved handkerchiefs, and were hysterical. Today the reaction was considerably calmer but MacDonald was cheered far longer than anyone, other than the PM, has ever been in my Parliamentary life. I could not get over it, that little wiry, undistinguished body, pumping forth such eloquence: was it the future leadership for which he was staking his claim? Certainly he was sincere, deeply moved and moving.

Poor Maxine Elliott is dead, aged (officially) 69. She was a great character, an immense bulk of a woman with dark eyes, probably the most amazing eyes one has ever seen. She became a grande dame, via the stage, and collected a huge fortune en route. Pierpoint Morgan, ... Lord Curzon, Edward VII and many others have shared her tempestuous bed. She was lovable, fat, oh so fat, witty and gracious. She always ate too much and I can remember her once consuming pat after pat of butter, without any bread.

7 March

A dreary birthday, with Honor away, I celebrated it by lunching with Margot Oxford at 44 Bedford Square. ... She looked like an antique skeleton in black satin with a bright red coat, and received me in her ground floor library, full of books, photographs and bibelots. She had lunched the day before, in what was once her old dining room at 10 Downing Street, alone with the Chamberlains, and was full of Neville's praises. Also lunching was a German, a Dr Something, a refugee, an iron manufacturer and ex-supporter of Hitler's. He talked at length of the Fuehrer, and said that at times he could be quite normal. Then suddenly 'it', as he called it, a sort of beast or inner monster, would take possession and he would rage and rant and become another creature: then the mood would pass, and gradually he would control himself ... he told us too that he was certainly a homosexual. Papen had looked up Hitler's military record in 1931, and found out that although he had been a brave soldier, Hitler had never risen above the rank of Corporal, and his failure to rise was due to his very pronounced perversion. In later years he reformed; and in the famous 'Purge' he deliberately tried to eliminate all homosexuals from his Nazi Party, which had been (and still is) riddled with it. After the Purge, it appears that sadism became the fashionable Nazi vice.

8 March

I fear we are being defeated all along the diplomatic line.... Harold Nicolson goes about betting that within six months Italy will be ranged against us.

Much to and fro from the Foreign Office, and this afternoon I slipped into Lord Halifax's room; he was alone looking tired and ecclesiastic, and I asked him whether I should go to Belgrade for Easter, and he warmly approved of the project.

At supper at the Savoy Grill with Emerald, Loelia Westminster and Leslie Belisha, Leslie told me how he had behaved at his weekend at Chequers. Mrs Chamberlain said to him at dinner 'Is it true that you never get up until 12.30?' Leslie, nettled, replied: 'Seldom before 3.30 in the afternoon', and Mrs Chamberlain, always gullible, was shocked. However, on Sunday morning he came down at 6.30 and rang the bell, which was answered by a sleepy servant. 'What, no breakfast yet?' he demanded. Leslie waited about, and at 8.15 when the PM appeared, said to him 'Does no-one ever get up in this house?' The PM was amused, and saw through the little plot; this was last summer, before the war. He will go far, Leslie; he is much too ebullient and intelligent to be held down for long. He half attacked Winston for agreeing to return to the Government without insisting, as a sine qua non, that Duff Cooper, too, should be reinstated ...

12 March

I woke with a headache, which was not helped by the appalling news that the Government has promised to send a large Expeditionary Force to Finland to help win the war, if the present peace negotiations broke down. Either way we are in a hopeless jam; if Finland capitulates, the Russians will be released to fight elsewhere; if she fights on we must assist her, and our transports and convoys, some of them at least, will be sunk; the whole expedition will probably end in disaster. Rab is deeply perturbed. Sending troops to Finland, he thinks, may topple the Government, without helping the Finns. Obviously, Halifax has been pushed into this by Winston, who only a few weeks ago was campaigning for an alliance with Russia.

13 March

The Finnish problem solved itself today with the announcement of the tragic capitulation by the Finns to the Russian terms. The epic struggle ended at 11.00 a.m. There can be no worse case of flagrant blackmail in history than this hold-up of the heroic Republic. The Foreign Office was in a frenzy, but secretly relieved, as our Expeditionary Force, ready to sail, would have had a hazardous task and would have been bombed by the Germans en route and possibly encountered opposition in the Scandinavian countries. Sweden has behaved particularly badly, each country hoping that she may be the last to be thrown to the wolves; though Axel of Denmark, who called on us, said we could not reasonably expect the Scandinavian countries to allow the easy passage of British troops, as Germany would be down on them like an immediate ton of bricks. Luckily, Rab's foresight prevented another Munich, which is what we should have been accused of, had we entertained Maisky's proposals: that is certainly not the case this time and our consciences are clear . . .

Rab dined at No. 10 with the Prime Minister, to meet (Sumner) Welles, and I helped to dress him for the occasion at the Office. He is completely devoid of any personal vanity and dresses 'dry' in 10 minutes and, I must add, looks it. He has no time or use for the frivolities of life: but with such a brain he does not need them.

19 March

All my plans for my dash to Belgrade are now made, visas, diplomatic 'laissez passer', tickets, all are in order.

There was a big Finnish debate in the House today. The PM setting a note of challenge, made the speech of his life, and completely demolished the case against him. It was a magnificent effort for a man of 71. The debate continued, and Leslie Hore-Belisha then delivered an over-rehearsed but not particularly offensive oration. Harold Macmillan followed and was irritable and irritating, and Archie Sinclair, who a few months ago was advocating an alliance with Russia, was tonight complaining that we had not invaded her.

I dined at the House with Alan, Patsy, Geoffrey Harrison[14] and [Donald] Maclean[15] of the Foreign Office. Afterwards, I suddenly ran into the PM as he was leaving for home. The supreme lonely old man stopped and smiled, 'Well, Chips, what did you think of the debate? How did it go?' 'You were magnificent, Sir', I answered and he hesitated, smiled again, put his hand on my arm and went away. I felt a wave of sentiment for him, and soon I too left for home. It was a glorious night, and London never looked so beautiful in the clear moonlight . . .

On 22 March Chips went, with Prime Ministerial approval, to Belgrade

22 March *Wagon-Lit*

After delays and queues at Heston and Le Bourget, Paris looked wonderfully gay and cheerful, as I rushed to the Ritz, where Laura Corrigan had put her suite at my disposal. The Lorelei, I call it, and it takes up most of the front of the first floor of the hotel. Laura Corrigan is an amazing woman, and all her great energies are now no longer lavished on entertaining, but on war work: she has organised a great relief fund, known as the Bienvenue-au-Soldat and has sent literally thousands of pounds to a French Regiment which she has adopted. She was very affectionate and pleased to see me and told me that the Nattier of hers that I like so much is safely hidden in a cellar somewhere, and she promised to leave it to me: she is always a woman of her word.[16] She told me that she had invited the Coopers in at 6 o'clock, but as my expedition is a semi-mission, and it is impor-

14. Private Secretary to Parliamentary Under-Secretary of State for Foreign Affairs, 1939–41; subsequently Ambassador to Brazil (1956–8) and to Persia (1958–63); deputy Under-Secretary of State, Foreign Office, 1963; subsequently Ambassador to the Soviet Union.

15. Subsequently defected to Russia with Guy Burgess, 1951.

16. The picture is now in the possession of Paul Channon.

tant that few people know of it, the Coopers above all, who are so anti-Chamberlain, I did not want to see them: so I hid in Laura's dining-room, as they were announced, and I heard Diana say in her booming voice: 'How is Chips? Still praising that awful old Chamberlain?' Laura answered tactfully, and I had dinner in solitary state, unbeknown to the Coopers, who were only a few feet away from me. Finally they left, and Laura drove me to the Gare de Lyons, and I am now embarked on my Balkan adventure.

24 March *Easter Sunday – Beli Dvor, Belgrade*
I arrived at dawn and was driven to this lovely white palace, decorated by Jansen, 7 kilometres from Belgrade, where I found grande luxe, glorious food and silent sullen bowing Serbs, sentries and heel clicking ADCs everywhere.

There are glorious long views over the Sava valley. I changed luxuriously in my very grand suite, and then the Regent, plump and dapper as a partridge, came to me and we embraced warmly . . .

How wonderful it is to overeat again, and to read in bed with the light on: I find splendour very soothing. The Palace is full of treasures, and arranged in excellent taste, with many traces of me. . . . The Regent has reconstructed the old library from Chesterfield House (which I well remember) and it is from there that he rules Yugoslavia. He has fine books, including a set of the first published edition of Goethe, which Hitler gave him but, in spite of that, how he hates the Huns!

Three people in the Palace curtsied to me today thinking that I was a Greek Prince.

25 March
Much talk . . . of the visit to Berlin, where Princess Olga sat next to Hitler for seven evenings running at dinner, and Paul refused a German decoration. Never apparently have the Germans taken more trouble, never has a State visit born less fruit, and Paul described how he had dismissed Stoyadenovitch, the burly MP who had begun to fancy himself as the local Fuehrer: up to now his instinct has been unerring, and he is surely one of the most astute diplomats and statesmen of our time.

26 March

This morning the Regent took me to see King Peter's palace, which shares the same park as Beli Dvor . . . a Californian Hacienda, which might well house a Vanderbilt. It is all a touch theatrical (legacy of the Rumanian family) and the star turns are the subterranean apartments, copied from the Kremlin, a series of hideous vaulted chambers of garish mosaic and painted stone, one of them King Alexander's private theatre.

28 March

German economic penetration in this country is considerable but as a race they are loathed. Sooner or later Yugoslavia will enter the war on our side. Meanwhile the railway sidings are blocked with oil being shipped to Germany, which comes from Bulgaria, Turkey and Russia. Tomorrow, alas, I leave.

29 March

Tonight, I left, and I almost wept as I took leave of my dear host and hostess; it was after dinner and I was rather tipsy. Paul came to the door to see me off, and pressed my hand and watched me drive away. Shall I ever see him again? At least so well and so powerful? Or will the Nazis swoop down upon him and destroy his haven and his people? At 10.20 the train pulled out of Belgrade, and my Balkan adventure ended.

3 April *London*

At the House, Rab whispered to me that the re-shuffle would take place tonight, so I did some rapid ferretting and got all the changes within 20 minutes. Poor 'Shakes' Morrison has had a setback, and an obscure business peer, Lord Woolton, has been made Minister of Food; the return to the Air Ministry of Sam Hoare and the appointment of Woolton are the only sensational changes . . .

I had a friendly conversation with Duff, whom I had not seen since July. He mentioned 'hearing of me' in Paris and I suppressed a smile, remembering how I had eavesdropped throughout his call upon Laura. He told me he made only £1800 out of his tour in America . . .

8 April

The FO was hectic today with Norwegian notes, and fears lest Norway break off her relations with us . . .

9 April

I was rung up by Alan and Honor before 8, both had heard rumours of an invasion of Denmark. I at once rang the FO, who had heard nothing. Then I got on to Reuters and the news was confirmed. It seems that the Germans walked into Denmark at 4.30 this morning. Later we heard the agonising news that Norway too has been invaded . . .

I was later in waiting on the Prime Minister, and he seemed calm, and thanked me affectionately for nothing. But his hands twitched his papers (which I afterwards took from him) as he waited to make his statement. He was calm, courageous and impressed the House, which gave him an ovation. I think that someone has blundered. The FO was in a flurry all day.

10 April

No country has crashed, no throne has tottered today, but there are many disturbing rumours. We have fears for Holland, and there are fears that Sweden will be invaded by Russia and probably the invasion of Salonika by Italy will follow. Everything seems to be crumbling; shall we after all emerge victorious? and will life be worth it?

This afternoon the PM spoke dramatically at the end of questions, and he described the great naval battle of Narvik, a battle which might never have been necessary. Where was our Fleet? and why was the invasion of Norway not prevented?

11 April

I am increasingly disappointed in Halifax: he looks and seems magnificent, but is in reality, weak and too easily swayed, hence the muddle we are in. He has been weak with Winston who arrived today at the end of Questions and took his place on the front bench, greeted only with perfunctory cheers. His long winded dull statement pleased no-one, and he looked tired and ill, and made little attempt to touch the real point; why did we allow Narvik to be captured and where was the fleet, could we not have stopped the Germans, if their invasion had been so long and elaborately planned? Why did we not know about it? Is our Naval Intelligence so weak? He spoke for an hour and his speech was a flop; he was too facetious for the occasion, and a graver manner would have been more appropriate.

All day conflicting news has been coming in of supposed naval battles and victories off the Norwegian coast, but little was substantiated.

12 April

No tragic news today, except that we have not yet had a victory at sea nor have we yet ousted the Germans from Norway: Holland and Belgium may be invaded at any moment, yet such is the vitality and confidence of the country that defeat seems inadmissible to the English mind.

I stayed at the Foreign Office until 8, in order to drive Rab home and at 7.30 I looked out of the window and in the evening light I saw the PM and Mrs Chamberlain, both wearing hats and overcoats, pacing the little garden behind No. 10. Round and round they went; poor Neville, will he be proved wrong about Italy? Will he have to 'eat his hat'?

Mrs Patrick Campbell is dead, aged 75, and her husband Cornwallis-West is engaged to be married for the third time; at 24 he married Lady Randolph Churchill (he liked old ladies, and she young men). Years later he married 'Mrs Pat'. I was present at the party where they met, and I was coming down Ned Lathom's narrow staircase (at his house, 47 Cumberland Place, where he lived in foolish splendour). I was with Lady Randolph, 'Aunt Jenny', as I called her, and at the door we met the newly married couple, Mrs Pat and her husband, face to face. It must have been about 1920. There was a tense moment, and we passed on: no word of greeting was exchanged. Soon afterwards Cornwallis-West, who was known as the Old Wives Tale, left her. I then often saw Mrs Pat, who even in those days was immense, with a deep voice and a heavy manner. She lived in Pont Street in near poverty, in fact she got poorer and poorer.... Finally she went to Hollywood, where I think she had some success, and I never saw her again.

15 April

The news is bad again, and an Italian coup is clearly imminent but somehow I think it will not come just yet: the Duce is an expert sabre rattler.

I joined Emerald at the Gate Theatre to see 'The Jersey Lily', a little play about Mrs Langtry by Basil Bartlett. ... A pleasant trivial little play, interesting because it actually portrays King Edward VII on the stage; the theme is the love affair between Prince Louis of Battenberg and Mrs Langtry (the offspring of this romance is Lady —, who was only told who her father was, when she was 20, by the then Mrs Asquith). I remember Mrs Langtry; she came to Chicago in early 1917, and attended the huge Allied Bazaar and I danced with her several times. She was an old tart of a girl, with, I seem to remember, reddish hair and a flamboyant manner, and was very old then.

16 April

The Norwegian news is so slow, why cannot we take more violent action? The General Staff have let us down, and now I am told that they are all to be replaced: Dill[17] will succeed Ironside (as CIGS), who has proved so slow and ineffectual ...

'The Times' this morning published a ridiculous leader about 'Tired Ministers' which infuriated the Prime Minister, who admits that he is surrounded by 'old men' who get easily fatigued, though they are a lot younger than he is.

17 April

Halifax was most amusing about his interview yesterday with Dr Marie Stopes,[18] who came to the Foreign Office, and said that she had had affairs with over 100 Germans and then with at least 100 Americans, so she knew men better than most women. She was prepared, she told Lord Halifax, to accept Cabinet Office and would he pass on her request to the Prime Minister? ...

The clouds were now darkening ominously for the Chamberlain Government. Uneasiness was developing in the House of

17. General Sir John Dill, Chief of the Imperial General Staff from 27 May 1940 to the end of 1941.

18. The eminent and courageous advocate of contraception.

Commons and the country about the pusillanimous handling of the war. Nerviness was also growing in Ministerial circles, where there were apprehensions of a Churchill intrigue to oust Chamberlain.

Chips's account of these events must be approached with caution. He was not an impartial commentator, and, although he did not blind himself to the failures of the Government, he could not and would not accept the argument that there was a necessity to replace Chamberlain himself.

25 April

The House was crowded and pleasant and I was surrounded by people all day, which always stimulates me. Dunglass pumped me: did I think that Winston should be deflated? . . . Ought he to leave the Admiralty? Evidently these thoughts are in Neville's head. Of course he ought to go, but who could we replace him with? Today I heard that chagrined by his failure at the Admiralty, he has now thrown off his mask, and is plotting against Neville, whom up to now he has served loyally; he wants to run the show himself: all this was inevitable, and I am only surprised it did not come before. Winston, it seems, has had secret conversations and meetings with Archie Sinclair,[19] A. V. Alexander[20] and Mr Attlee and they are drawing up an alternative Government, with the idea of succeeding at the first favourable moment. Eden is on the fringe and is watching and waiting for his chance . . .

The PM looked well, though Lady Halifax said yesterday that whenever she sees him he seems to look smaller, in fact he seems to shrivel before one's eyes. Perhaps that is true, but only physically.

26 April

The plot spreads. Last night Harold Balfour and Kingsley Wood took David Margesson out to dine at the Mirabelle Restaurant and warned him of the 'glamorous' development of which he was already half aware. It was decided to send Kingsley to No. 10

19. Sir Archibald Sinclair (later Lord Thurso), leader of the Liberal Party 1935–45.

20. Labour MP for Sheffield, Hillsborough. Succeeded Churchill as First Lord of the Admiralty.

at ten o'clock to warn the PM and consult with him. He did, and the PM was shaken and indignant. So now we are in for a first class political struggle between the Chamberlain men and the 'glamour' group: we may weather the storm, but there is trouble ahead all of which of course can only cause glee in Germany.

While these intrigues are going on our position in Norway is terrible, desperate, far worse than the public realises – all is à tort et à travers – God help the country . . .

Rab, as we drove round the park, and wondered at its vernal beauty . . . talked of his life, and complained that there was no youth, gaiety or frivolity in it. Rab is so charming, so clever, so balanced: his only weaknesses are his inability to terminate an interview; his unpunctuality and his indecision in trivial, personal matters.

27 April

The news gets more and more depressing. We are about to retire from Norway, or at least the Southern half of it, and there is to be a secret meeting of the Supreme War Council this afternoon. The delay in sending the fleet on that fatal 9 April may well cost us the War.

I came down to Kelvedon this afternoon, which is looking a dream, with swans, blossom, white dogs, and my baby boy, who had tea with me . . .

In the evening we walked about the garden and all was green and luscious with that subtle gauzy haze which one only finds in Essex; but how precarious everything seems just now.

29 April

Rab seems distrait and discouraged today and hinted that the Supreme War Council have definitely, and wrongly, decided to abandon Norway, all except Narvik. What a blow, and perhaps a decisive one, to our prestige.

30 April

In the House, there is more talk of a cabal against poor Neville. 'They' are saying that it is 1915 over again, that Winston should be Prime Minister as he has more vigour and the country behind him.

1 May

Oh! the excitement, the thrills, the atmosphere of ill-concealed nervousness, the self-interest, which comes over the House of Commons when there is a political crisis on, or rumours of a reshuffle. Such it is now. . . . Winston, is being lauded by both the Socialist and Liberal oppositions, and being tempted to lead a revolt against the PM . . . who, outraged and full of fight still, is playing a deep game. To gain time he has given Winston more rope, and made him what amounts to Director of Operations. Tonight Churchill sat joking and drinking in the smoking room, surrounded by A. V. Alexander and Archie Sinclair, the new Shadow Cabinet. A Westminster war added to a German one is really too much.

2 May

The Westminster squall is blowing hard, and it is terrible that the PM and Halifax should have to suffer this additional strain when all their energies are needed to win the war. But I am beginning reluctantly to realise that Neville's days are, after all, numbered.

3 May

David Margesson says we are on the eve of the greatest political crisis since August 1931.

5 May *Sunday*

There is a storm of abuse of the PM in the Sunday Press and I fear he is in for a bad time. Also Dunglass tells me he is very down and depressed. Rothermere has come out against the Government: Kemsley is pro it: the 'Telegraph' and Beaverbrook are mildly critical, but stay their hand. Harold Balfour, who has an excellent political nose, thinks that our game is up. Political life will lose much of its fascination for me if Neville goes, as I shall no longer be in the inner councils of the racket.

7 May

A dreadful day: the political crisis overshadows everything: one cannot eat, sleep or concentrate. The 'glamour boys' are smacking their lips but their full strength is not yet known. I ran into the Prime Minister today in the House, and we chatted for a moment, but it was he who made the conversation, as I was suddenly stilled and made shy by my affection for him. Five minutes later he was speaking, and was given a warm welcome, but he spoke haltingly and did not make a good case: in fact he fumbled his words and seemed tired and embarrassed. No wonder he is exhausted: who would not be? All day and all night he works, while the small fry criticise. I realised at once the House was not with him, and though he warmed up a little towards the middle of his speech, the very crowded House was restive and bored and the Egyptian Ambassador even slept. The PM sat down at last, and the opening attack was a half-hearted affair, almost a failure. But Opposition members were offensive and acrimonious. Attlee followed and then Archie Sinclair, and neither were effective. Then came several long dreary speeches, almost all attacks on the Government. Roger Keyes, an ex-hero, but a man with a grievance, was damning and he had come to the House in the uniform of an Admiral of the Fleet with three rows of medals . . . questionable taste, but it lent him dignity. The atmosphere was intense, and everywhere one heard whispers. What will Winston do? Oliver Stanley wound up for the Government, and it was a shocking performance, luke-warm and ineffectual. I am most uneasy now about tomorrow, as it is rumoured that the Opposition will challenge the Government with a division, and we have scarcely time to collect our troops, as many of them are scattered, or serving abroad.

8 May

The cataclysmic day has drawn to a welcome close and I am worn out, revolted by the ingratitude of my fellow-men, nauseated by the House of Commons, which I really think ought, though I love it, to be abolished.

When I got there the atmosphere of the House was definitely excited and it intensified as the long hours passed. Herbert Morrison opened the debate with vituperation, and announced that the Opposition would challenge the Government into a division. The PM, angry and worn out, intervened to say that the Government accepted the challenge, and he called upon his friends to rally round and support him. Possibly he was tactless, but I do not quite see what other course he could have followed. We then knew that it was to be war. Samuel Hoare, the pet aversion of the Labour Party made a boring contribution in defence of the Government, which did not help. The temperature rose, hearts hardened, tempers sharpened, and I came to the conclusion that there is nothing so revolting as the House of Commons on an ugly night. Little Neville seemed heart-broken and shrivelled (as Lady Halifax said) but remained courteous and patient. I sat behind him, hoping to surround him with an aura of affection. From time to time I looked up into Mrs Fitzroy's gallery[21] and several times I caught the eye of poor Mrs Chamberlain, who has hardly left the House for two days: she is a loyal, good woman. . . . She was in black – black hat – black coat – black gloves – with only a bunch of violets in her coat. She looked infinitely sad as she peered down into the mad arena where the lions were out for her husband's blood.

For hours the issue was in doubt. Duff Cooper made a damaging speech in which he said that he hoped we should get on more actively with the war . . . good advice from someone who has just returned from four months in America . . .

The whispering in the lobbies was unbearable. Ham Kerr[22] offered to bet that 100 Government supporters would vote against the régime; I scoffed. Mrs Tate offered to bet me £5 that over fifty would do so, but refused to take up the challenge, when I agreed. Lady Astor rushed about, intriguing and enjoying the fray and the smell of blood: she has joined hands with the insurgents, probably because she must always be in the limelight, and also because I think she is seriously rattled by the 'Cliveden Set' allegations which were made against her before the war, and now wants to live them down.

At last the atmosphere became so horrible that I decided I must leave for a few minutes – when I came back Alexander was speaking, winding up for the Opposition. The real issue of the Debate – Norway – had long since been forgotten: speakers attacked us on any possible ground, and still the doubt was in

21. Mrs Fitzroy was the wife of the Speaker. She was a relation, by marriage, of Chips.

22. Conservative MP for Oldham, 1931–45, for Cambridge, 1950–65.

everybody's mind, would Winston be loyal? He finally rose, and one saw at once that he was in bellicose mood, alive and enjoying himself, relishing the ironical position in which he found himself: i.e. that of defending his enemies, and a cause in which he did not believe. He made a slashing, vigorous speech, a magnificent piece of oratory. I was in the gallery behind him, with Rab, who was, several times, convulsed with laughter. Winston told the story of the Norwegian campaign, justified it, and trounced the Opposition, demolishing Roger Keyes, etc. How much of the fire was real, how much ersatz, we shall never know, but he amused and dazzled everyone with his virtuosity. He taunted the Opposition and accused Shinwell of skulking: a Labour MP – rather the worse for drink – had never heard the word and thought that he had said skunking. There was laughter, but somehow the tension was increased and poor Healy, the new Deputy Sergeant-at-Arms was quite nervous lest he be called on to eject an unruly Member. It was like bedlam.

I asked Roy Wise how many would vote against the Government – and he said that he would, for one: it was the only way to shock us out of our complacency, he said. I told him that he was playing with dynamite: then Charles Taylor[23] ('Cow and Gate' and looks like a calf) came up to me and said: 'We are trying to get your Government out tonight'. Feeling grew, still we thought we would survive. At last the Speaker called a division, which Winston nearly talked out. I went into the Aye Lobby, which seemed thin for a three line Whip, and we watched the insurgents file out of the Opposition Lobby (Teenie Cazalet could not make up his mind and abstained). 'Quislings', we shouted at them, 'Rats'. 'Yes-men', they replied. I saw all the expected ones, and many more – Hubert [Duggan] among them and my heart snapped against him for ever. Then I voted, as usual everyone wondered how many had dared to vote against us: so many threaten to do so, and funk it at the last moment. Anthony Eden and Jim Thomas in our Lobby looked triumphant, and I saw Winston and his PPS Brendan Bracken there. I went back to the Chamber, and took my seat behind Neville. 'We are all right' I heard someone say, and so it seemed as David Margesson came in and went to the right, the winning

23. Conservative MP for Eastbourne.

side of the table, followed by the other tellers. '281 to 200' he read, and the Speaker repeated the figures.[24] There were shouts of 'Resign – Resign' . . . and that old ape Josh Wedgwood began to wave his arms about and sing 'Rule Britannia'. Harold Macmillan, next to him joined in, but they were howled down. Neville appeared bowled over by the ominous figures, and was the first to rise. He looked grave and thoughtful and sad: as he walked calmly to the door, his supporters rose and cheered him lustily and he disappeared. No crowds tonight to cheer him, as there were before and after Munich – only a solitary little man, who had done his best for England.

What can Neville do now? He can reconstruct his Government: he can resign: but there is no doubt that the Government is seriously jarred and all confidence in it is gone. Hitler will be quick to take advantage of our divided councils.

What changes does that fatal division portend? Neville may survive but not for long: Oh, the cruelty of the pack in pursuit . . . shall I too crash when the Chamberlain edifice crumbles?

I am disgusted by politics and human nature and long to live like Walpole, a semi social – semi literary life in a Strawberry Hill (only not Gothic) of my own. Perhaps one day I will.

9 May

I woke as if from a long nightmare – but the telephone soon brought me back to reality which was worse, first Harold Balfour, who said that the PM would certainly resign after last night's vote – though I think, with a majority of 81, Neville could still make minor changes and remain. Rab was non-committal. I went to the House and found it curiously calm after the roar of last night; the 'Glamour' element tip-toed about, excitedly – but I think disappointed too, as they hoped for a greater number of defections. The PM entered the Chamber calmly, and I had a talk with him behind the Chair, and said that it had been 'terrific' yesterday, and murmured a few banalities which, while nothing in themselves, I hope recorded to him my loyalty and affection. He was geniality itself and did not even look tired. He has

24. 41 MPs who normally supported the Government (33 Conservatives, 4 National Liberals, 2 National Labour, and 2 Independents) voted against it; 65 Conservatives were absent unpaired or abstained.

already conferred with several people about what course to take ... probably the reconstruction of his entire government. But rumours of his retirement are rife. The House was full of rumours and intrigue, plot and counter-plot, and I rushed about talking too much and making myself both conspicuous and a nuisance. Dunglass asked me to find out the attitude of the Labour Party, and whether they would be willing to serve under Neville. I did; I approached the plump Jewish Colonel Nathan.[25] At first he thought something might be arranged, but after several conferences he reported that the position was hopeless, and that even if the Labour leaders would serve under Chamberlain, the back-benchers would never allow it. Sadly I passed this information on.

Rab had an adjournment [debate] and I sat behind him until I was asked to find Herbert Williams and three other powerful Tory MPs who were ushered into the PM's room at 3 o'clock. They agreed to continue their support, but demanded drastic changes in the Government. Everyone agrees – they, I, the Socialists – that Walter Elliot and Sam Hoare must be discarded and perhaps others ... the PM received them courteously.

Earlier, on the motion for the adjournment, Lloyd George, stung into fury by an attack made on him by Beverley Baxter, made a fiery defence of his attitude in a deplorable speech, which will obviously be of immense value to the German propagandists. He practically said that the allies were responsible for the war. Lloyd George is full of fire and beans, and his bronzed skin, white locks and bright blue suits, make him a doughty figure. I stayed in the Chamber till it rose and it behaved as if it had a hang-over; people were ashamed of their behaviour.

I went back to the office, and then went over to No. 10, where a long conversation had been held between Winston, Halifax and Neville each saying to the other two: 'You must be Prime Minister', and each one no doubt wanting it for himself. Various statesmen were sent for – Sam Hoare, Kingsley Wood and others. Sam Hoare was with the PM while I gossiped with Miss Watson and Alec Dunglass. It was decided at last to ask the Labour

25. Liberal MP for North-East Bethnal Green, 1929–35; joined Labour Party 1934. Labour MP for Central Wandsworth, 1937–40. Created 1st Baron Nathan, 1940.

leaders to call at No. 10 and Attlee and Greenwood arrived, and spent three-quarters of an hour with Neville, who tried to persuade them to join the Government, and form a real Coalition. They went away promising to let the PM know their decision tomorrow. I left about 8 o'clock. Neville still reigns, but only just.

10 May

Perhaps the darkest day in English history. I was still asleep, recovering from the emotions of the past days, when my private telephone tinkled, and it was Harold ringing from the Air Ministry to say that Holland and Belgium have been invaded; bombs are falling on Brussels and parachutists on the Hague. Another of Hitler's brilliantly conceived coups, and of course he seized on the psychological moment when England is politically divided, and the ruling caste riddled with dissension and anger. He surely heard of Wednesday's debate and the fatal division yesterday, and at once acted upon them. At the FO all was in confusion, and the Mandarins, some of them, seemed more downhearted that the invasion of the Low Countries has probably saved Chamberlain, than cast down by the invasion itself. It was the popular view this morning that Neville was saved, for after all his policy had been vindicated swiftly and surely within twenty-fours hours. Had he sent an army to Finland, where should we be now? Neville may be saved, though I think that he would be glad to divest himself of his great responsibilities. However, all the morning support for Neville seemed to gain ground, and Roy Wise went to see him and apologised for voting against him; others did likewise.

In the afternoon Princess Olga rang me; she had lunched with the Halifaxes (they didn't invite us, I noticed) at the Dorchester, and had sat between Halifax and Dill, the rising Military star; and she had had a talk with the PM who was calm and charming and showed little effects of the battle that has been waging about him: he did say, however, that Lloyd George's personal attack on him surpassed anything he had ever heard in Parliament.[26]

26. This was the philippic in which Lloyd George, after referring to Chamberlain's appeal for sacrifice, declared that the most notable

Now the drama begins; the Chamberlains returned to No. 10, and some time during the afternoon a message came from the Labour people that they would join a Government, but refused to serve under Chamberlain. Action had to be taken immediately. Neville hesitated for half an hour, and meanwhile Dunglass rang me – could not Rab persuade Halifax to take it on? Rab was doubtful, as he had already this morning and yesterday had such conversations with 'the Pope', who was firm – he would not be Prime Minister. I don't understand why, since a more ambitious man never lived, nor one with, in a way, a higher sense of duty and 'noblesse oblige'. Nevertheless, I persuaded Rab to go along to Halifax's room for one last final try; he found Halifax had slipped out to go to the dentist's without Rab seeing him – and Valentine Lawford, the rather 'Second Empire' secretary, who neglected to tell Halifax that Rab was waiting, may well have played a decisively negative role in history. Rab came back to our room angry and discouraged, and we rang No. 10, but Alec Dunglass said that already the die had been cast. A message was sent to the Palace and an audience arranged for six o'clock – it seemed then that only a miracle could save Chamberlain.

I sat numb with misery, and mused on this fantastic day – and on my lunch with Harold at Belgrave Square and our drive along the Strand with startling placards everywhere: 'Paris Raided' – 'Brussels Bombed' – 'Lille Bombed' – 'Many killed at Lyons' and, finally, 'Bombs in Kent'. We had stopped, bought newspapers and read of the rain of horrors falling everywhere. From 5 until 6.30 or afterwards I was miserable, and rushed from room to room and, incidentally, had tea in the Secretaries' room with the Dutch Foreign Minister, M. van Kleffens, a tall, thin, youngish man with a nose rivalling Cyrano's, and the Dutch Minister of the Colonies, an older man. These 'Flying Dutchmen' had had a day indeed; they were both awakened about 3.30 a.m. by the noise of gun-fire over the Hague, and had quickly dressed. A Cabinet Meeting was called for 4.30 and presided over by Queen Wilhelmina – in tweeds. She was in a towering rage against the Germans and full of fight. A decision was

---

contribution the Prime Minister could render to the nation would be to sacrifice the seals of office.

taken to dispatch some Members of the Government at once to England. So they left the Hague at 8 a.m. in a Dutch sea-plane. Over Scheveningen their plane was hit by German gunfire, and almost crippled. M. Kleffens called to the pilot to continue, and they got as far as Brighton, where they came down in the sea, and after being rescued were promptly arrested as Germans! They then came to crisis-ridden London to plead for help for the Netherlands. All this they told me in broken English, but I think I understood it correctly.

At 6.30 I rang up No. 10, and the loyal Miss Watson told me that the PM would broadcast at 9.00 p.m., and, her voice breaking, hung up the receiver. Shortly afterwards Alec Dunglass and Jock Colville arrived, and told us that the PM had just come back from the Palace, Winston had kissed hands and was now Premier. . . . We were all sad, angry and felt cheated and out-witted. Alec who, more than any other, has been with the Prime Minister these past few weeks, and knows his words and actions by heart, let himself go. I opened a bottle of Champagne and we four loyal adherents of Mr Chamberlain drank 'To the King over the water'.

CHAPTER SIX

With the New Government
May 1940–July 1941

For the following year Chips was still officially connected with the Government, although his lack of enthusiasm for it is evident from the Diaries. He was also troubled by the position of the Regent of Yugoslavia, the beloved Prince Paul. He was a loyal friend; in the case of Prince Paul he was perhaps too loyal a friend, and the latter's apparent betrayal of the Allied cause did Chips much harm politically and personally.

Of particular interest in this period of Chips's life was his visit to Yugoslavia via Egypt and Greece at the end of 1940 and beginning of 1941. The beginning of his subsequent strong friendship with Wavell dates from this journey, fostered by their mutual friend Peter Coats, who was Wavell's ADC.

This section of the Diary is so detailed that selection has been particularly difficult, and much interesting material has had to be deleted to keep the chapter to a reasonable length.

1940

11 May *Kelvedon*

The war news is worse, the invasions of Holland, Luxembourg and Belgium proceed. Will it be our turn next? Meanwhile what will become of Rab, and of me? . . .

At the Foreign Office, we sat about all day restless, irritable and nervous; it seemed impossible to get down to any real work. About one o'clock I heard that a terrific battle had been waging at the Admiralty, where Winston had summoned Neville and Halifax; for it seems that the Labour leaders, goaded by Lord Salisbury, announced that not only would they not serve under Chamberlain, but not with him either. Winston was in a dilemma as he had offered a post to Neville last night which he practically accepted, and announced as much in his broadcast. Now Winston may be forced to choose between Labour and Neville, and may thus be unable to form a Government at all. However, after struggling all day, he was able to effect a last-moment compromise, and the Cabinet changes were announced.

The Press is lukewarm about the new Prime Minister. . . . Norway was Winston's adventure, and poor Neville blamed for it. I wrote him a short, simple, somewhat sentimental letter of sympathy.

13 May *London*

The House today was absurdly dramatic and very Winstonian: first of all we were summoned by a telegram signed by the Speaker, and asked not to mention the meeting. But as both Houses were summoned, over 1300 telegrams must have been sent, and must have been seen by literally thousands of people.

I arrived at 2.15 and found an atmosphere of confusion and embarrassment. No-one knew who had been re-appointed, dropped or changed. It was 'Crazy Week'; I joined a group of bewildered Ministers – Ministers still – who stood in the 'Aye' Lobby. They chattered, amused, apprehensive, uninformed. Ernest Brown was the angriest, and he inveighed against Winston: others did likewise. I was surprised as I thought W. C. would have a triumph, at least today, but he very definitely did not.

After Prayers he went into the Chamber and was greeted with some cheers but when, a moment later, Neville entered with his usual shy retiring little manner, MPs lost their heads; they shouted; they cheered; they waved their Order Papers, and his reception was a regular ovation. The new PM spoke well, even dramatically, in support of the new all-Party Government, but he was not well received. And all the speeches that followed were mediocre. Only references to Neville raised enthusiasm. I met Winston face to face and murmured banal congratulations which he acknowledged very pleasantly, I must admit, and he moved about, enjoying his triumph, talking to everyone. Bob Boothby and Brendan Bracken, his faithful henchmen since many years, are now in for a spell of power and I heard Brendan assure Ernie Brown that he would be given a post – it would be monstrous to leave him out. There was some amusement, too, over the seating quandary. If there was to be no Opposition, who would sit in the Opposition benches? Wedgwood, mad as your hat, attempted to proclaim himself a sort of leader of an official Opposition and sat in Mr Attlee's late place – that little gad-fly looked smaller and more insignificant than ever on the Government Front Bench, dwarfed by Winston. No-one seemed to pay much attention to me – I don't suppose I am sufficiently important to be victimised. I want nothing: only to be left where I am, and feel that Winston will not move Rab, who is 'down' and depressed – today. Poor Sam Hoare is out; but Simon, rather unexpectedly, goes to the Woolsack, kicked upstairs – a dignified end to his political career. He is 67 and a priest at heart, a Jesuit really. In his frequent attempts to conciliate he always further wounds.

I felt so ill that I came home and went to bed. My temperature rose to 103° and I sent for a doctor. I have streptococcal fever and throat – the illness Philip Sassoon died of: but he got up in the middle of it, and went to spend the week-end at Windsor.

14 May

The tales of the bombing of Amsterdam, The Hague, etc., are beyond belief for horror.

Diana Cooper rang up and was gently affectionate and her usual old self; I am forgiven. Naturally she is cock-a-hoop over Duff's appointment to the Ministry of Information.

15 May

Still very ill, and I lie in bed brooding about the grim future.

Harold and Rab have both been sent for by the Prime Minister and asked to continue in their present jobs; both gleefully accepted. Rab tells me that he had a characteristic five minutes with Winston: when he reminded him that they had often sparred in the past, and disagreed on many things, 'Yes', Winston stuttered, 'but you have invited me to your private residence'.

Beaverbrook returns to power and favour; he should never have been cold-shouldered . . .

Duff spoke on the radio, and well. I was impressed; it is the sort of thing he can do.

17 May

The Heads of Government Departments here were sent for tonight, and told that it could not be certain that France's resistance could be counted upon for more than a fortnight. It is expected that Paris will fall shortly. The Nazis are putting every ounce of their power into their offensive and if they fail, which is possible, the war may yet be won for us, as they will have nothing left, and their reserves will have been used up. It is the Gauleiters' last throw, so our experts say, but I am not quite so sure; they are seldom right.

18 May

I am definitely recovering. A lovely day . . . and not far away in France the terrible battle goes on. I hear that Soissons and Rheims are gone.

It is now believed that the war will be over in September – the Germans will either win or be exhausted by this terrific effort which may go on for weeks, weeks of hell and anguish. The new German tanks spitting fire at first caused much alarm, but now our forces are getting used to them. If only the French can hold out.

Brussels has been evacuated.

Lloyd George is jubilant by the turn of political events. . . . It is a little surprising he himself was not offered a decorative post. But stranger people have drawn numbers in this mad lottery. It will be years before a really Conservative Government comes in again.

19 May

I am increasingly haunted by Horace Walpole: can I be his reincarnation? I am extraordinarily like him in many ways; but where is Conway? But who is Mme de Deffand? Old Norah [Lindsay]? Diana Cooper? Or is she yet to be encountered? or more probably she is Emerald with whom I have had a flirtatious friendship for 20 years. She is now in New York; how she must loathe it.

23 May *Kelvedon*

Honor and I have decided to bury my diaries in the churchyard; Mortimer has promised to dig a hole tomorrow evening after the other gardeners have gone home: perhaps some future generation will dig them up.

The news on the radio was grave. Winston announced in the House that Abbeville had fallen and that Boulogne was the scene of a great battle. . . . It is maddening not to be in the House these momentous days . . .

A roar of planes immediately overhead woke me; and I counted 21 fighters rushing towards the coast: they were barely over the tree-tops. The war is at our door.

24 May

This evening we buried two tin boxes three feet below the earth's surface in the little churchyard under a tree near the brick wall – the West wall, which divides the churchyard from Honor's private garden. The larger, lower box contains my diaries, the smaller box my best bibelots, watches, Fabergé objects, etc. Mortimer, who dug the hole, is discreet, and he waited until all the gardeners had gone home; we watched the earth cover them over; may they sleep in peace. Mother Earth must hold many other such secrets in her bosom.

25 May *Kelvedon*

Rab rang up to ask how I was – he remains confident of ultimate triumph.

29 May

The news gets gradually worse. Our troops are behaving magnificently in the face of superhuman odds and are retreating in an orderly manner. The Belgian desertion is a grave blow, and the manner of its delivery incredibly treacherous. . . . France is wobbly; and there is always the danger of a separate peace since she never wanted the war, and was dragged in by us. They expect invasion here next week. . . . I went to the House of Commons, where there was some amusement over Harold Macmillan's so very obvious enjoyment of his new position; he rushed frenziedly about.

I think there is a definite plot afoot to oust Halifax, and all the gentlemen of England, from the Government, and even from the

House of Commons. Sam Hoare warned Rab of this scheme only yesterday, before leaving today to be our Ambassador in Spain.

31 May

The retreat of our troops from France has been little short of a miracle. Up to this morning 151 odd thousands had been rescued. There must be another 100,000 or nearly. As usual the Guards are bearing the brunt of the attack and the casualty lists, once they are made public, will make distressing reading . . .

2 June *London*

The newspapers were sensational and despairing; and the secret telegrams little better. General conflagration in the Balkans; Italy's imminent entry into the war; even Spanish intrigue . . . everything is conspiring against us. The numbers of the rescued from Flanders is now 237 odd thousand and this great retreat magnificently carried out against overwhelming odds, is an heroic feat, and a relief to the whole country which is proud of its troops . . . but nonetheless we are in an appalling position.

The break with Italy will come at any moment now and the elaborate, almost elegant arrangements for the actual declaration of war are bewildering. The Italians are being extraordinarily courteous . . .

I wonder as I gaze out upon the grey and green Horse Guards Parade with the blue sky, the huge silver balloons like bowing elephants, the barbed-wire entanglements and soldiers about, is this really the end of England? Are we witnessing, as for so long I have feared, the decline, the decay and perhaps extinction, of this great island people?

3 June

I met the Halifaxes in the [Buckingham] Palace Yard; he stopped to gossip; they were on their way to call on Queen Wilhelmina. As I walked away I reflected on Halifax's extraordinary character; his high principles, his engaging charm and grand manner – his power to frighten people into fits – me sometimes – his snobbishness – his eel-like qualities and, above all, his sublime treachery which is never deliberate, and, always to him, a necessity dictated by a situation. Means are nothing to him, only ends. He is insinuating, but unlovable.

4 June

The Prime Minister made an important and moving statement. I sat behind him (he was next to Neville who looked tiny and fragile), and he was eloquent, and oratorical, and used magnificent English; several Labour Members cried. He hinted that we might be obliged to fight alone, without France, and that England might well be invaded.[1] How the atmosphere has changed from only a few weeks ago when idiotic MPs were talking academic nonsense about our restoring independence to Warsaw and Prague.

Jock Colville tells me that the Admiralty is fantastic now; people who were at each other's throats a few weeks ago are now intimate and on the best of terms. Winston darts in and out, a mountain of energy and good-nature, the Labour leaders, Brendan Bracken and Prof. Lindemann, sometimes Randolph, Beaverbrook, the Defence Ministers, etc. – the new racket all much in evidence, but no Neville and no Horace Wilson.

6 June

I was on duty as PPS to Winston, Brendan being away. It is fantastic, the turn of the wheel! He was, however, agreeable and easier in his manner – though without, however, the great dignity of Neville. 'Have you two minutes, Chips?' he asked as he arrived. 'Yes', I answered, and he gave me one or two things to do.

8 June *Pyrford*

Every night Night Wardens are on duty in shifts at the Foreign Office. Last night, as they were searching the innumerable rooms and poking every sofa, they eventually reached the Secretary of State's room, the long one overlooking the Park, and someone jabbed the sofa, and was startled by a feminine scream. The surprised warden flashed his torch, and found a couple reclining in 'flagrante delicto'. 'What are you doing?' he asked, somewhat superfluously, as it was quite evident. The culprits were a young typist and a young man in the cypher department. Surely such a thing has never happened in that room before – or perhaps I am wrong?

1. This was the famous 'we shall never surrender' speech.

10 June

The clouds get darker ... the Germans are drawing nearer to Paris, and this afternoon I was told that Mussolini would declare war at 6 p.m. One could hardly believe the rumour as he has threatened for so long.

11 June

War has begun with Italy, but Bastianini actually called today at the Foreign Office! Halifax refused to see him, and he was received by Alec Cadogan who listened to his complaints that Italians were being arrested and maltreated, and then he told the Ambassador in icy terms what he thought of Mussolini.

This afternoon the Emperor Haile Selassie came to Belgrave Square to tea; it was a very secret meeting arranged for him to meet Rab. Philip Noel-Baker was also here. I met the Emperor at the door, and he entered gravely wearing a bowler hat and the famous cape. He has dignity, but he has aged since the night I dined at Boni de Castellane's to meet him in 1925 – or 1926 – I cannot remember. I escorted Haile Selassie into the morning room – how many Kings and Queens have been thus led in – presented Rab and Noel-Baker, and then left them to their own devices.

12 June

I went to see Leslie Belisha this morning and we walked for over an hour in the Park; it was a lovely morning, but the people basking in the sun looked unhappy. No wonder. Possibly in a fortnight's time it will be no longer possible to sit on a bench in St James's Park and watch the ducks ...

Beverley Baxter at lunch said that Beaverbrook is so pleased to be in the Government that he is like the town tart who has finally married the Mayor!

14 June

Paris was occupied by the Germans early this morning, although some advanced troops entered the capital late last night. Thus Hitler's boast that he would have conquered the city before 15 June has come true. Little news has come through, other than that the French have further retreated. The question is, will

France go on fighting? M. Reynaud has asked to be released from his promise not to negotiate a separate peace, and has Marshal Pétain behind him. Winston and Halifax flew yesterday to see Reynaud at Tours to try and dissuade him from giving up, and he said that he would make one more appeal to President Roosevelt for American help; if it were not forthcoming it was probably that the game was up, as the Army could not hold. Halifax and Winston are back, and the situation is very grave indeed; meanwhile all hangs on Washington. What will Roosevelt decide tonight? If he refuses to come in, it would seem that the war must come to an end, and this great Empire will have been defeated and humiliated. Today and tomorrow are probably the most vital days in our history . . .

I had all day at the Office which was extraordinarily calm for such a crisis.

15 June *Pyrford Court*

This morning Valentine Lawford had to go into the Secretary of State's room, and tell him that Lithuania had been occupied by the Soviets. 'That leaves me quite cold', Lord Halifax retorted, immersed in other affairs.

16 June *Pyrford*

The new Government which has been formed in France is a pro-peace one, and a complete surrender is now a matter of hours, if it has not already taken place.

18 June

The Prime Minister made a statement to a crowded House; my usual place was taken, so Rab and I went to the Gallery to listen. I wasn't very impressed, but I suppose that the nation will be.

19 June

The German army advances in France, crushing all before it, and the French Government have announced that they will not accept a dishonourable peace. General de la Gaule [sic] who flew here rather melodramatically with [Edward] Spears is trying to rally the French around him.

Dined with Alice Harding at Hanover Lodge and almost enjoyed myself. Harold Nicolson, Sir Timothy Eden (a tired edition of Anthony, with the same intonation and curious chuckle); Lord and Lady Kinross; Lady Colefax, quite friendly once more, and Vincent Sheehan the writer-journalist, a Chicago journalist who has made good. I drove Harold home, and also Sibyl Colefax. London was astonishingly beautiful in the moonlight. I adore the black-out at this time of year.

20 June

No news yet of the expected peace terms; opinion is divided; one school of thought anticipates that France will be tempted, indeed, lulled by easy terms; another suspects that Hitler will demand complete capitulation. No doubt the Germans consider themselves tricked over the escape of the French Fleet, which has visibly and enormously encouraged people here . . .

I am much encouraged about everything – though I don't know why – and my deep gloom has lifted; but we are living as people did during the French Revolution – every day is a document, every hour history.

Winston wound up with his usual brilliance and out-of-place levity. His command of English is magnificent; but strangely enough, although he makes me laugh, he leaves me unmoved. There is always the quite inescapable suspicion that he loves war, war which broke Neville Chamberlain's better heart!

21 June

I spent an hour in Westminster Cathedral this afternoon, burning candles, listening to a service, and praying for the welfare and safety of my beloved child on his transatlantic trip.[2]

24 June *London*

I was called at 7, dressed and ate nervously; at 8.15 we set out for Euston. Honor and I had the child between us; he was gay and interested. At the station there was a queue of Rolls-Royces and liveried servants and mountains of trunks. It seemed that everyone we knew was there on the very crowded platform. . . . We led our child to his compartment, and clung hungrily to him until the whistle blew and then after a feverish hug and kiss, we

2. Paul Channon was being evacuated to the USA.

left him. I care more for Paul than for all of France, and mind his departure dreadfully. For the first time in my life I felt a surge of remorse for my own appallingly callous treatment of my parents, who perhaps once loved me as I love Paul . . .

As the Cease Fire between France and Germany came into effect at 12.25 this morning, we can now be prepared for the Battle of Britain – or rather on Britain.

25 June

I had hardly got to sleep last night when the sirens sounded, and I went to the cellar where I was soon joined by 4 female servants in various stages of déshabille. The scullery-maid read the financial section of 'The Times'! . . .

The Duchess of Kent, Alice, Brendan Bracken and others lunched. Brendan told us that he had been sitting in the garden at No. 10 last night with the PM when the sirens sounded; but they remained there drinking. From his conversational crumbs I gathered that all is far from well in Churchill's private paradise, and that there are endless squabbles amongst the new Ministers! Brendan attacked Attlee and Greenwood, thus reflecting Winston's mind.

30 June *London*

There seems to be an ominous lull; the German raids have not been intense, although they come every night. . . . I am feeling restless and this morning I thought I looked quite handsome. What a pity it is one is never good-looking when one wants most to be.

3 July

An early telephone call told me the glorious news; my infant is safe, and in Montreal . . . all is well. My relief passed all bounds. . . . Now I care less what happens; my life is over, the rest is residue. I can live on in my dauphin who looks, acts, re-acts, and thinks, just like me.

I walked jubilantly to the Foreign Office and during the luncheon hour shopped, buying 2 dozen pairs of socks to celebrate, and prayed at Westminster Cathedral to St Anthony to thank him. Then I called at No. 10 and had half an hour with

Miss Watson who I heard had been feeling lonely. She is a great character; an expert with Parliamentary Questions, she was brought to No. 10 by Bonar Law, I believe, and has been there ever since, serving all the PMs. She liked Neville much the best after she had got to know him; it is always like that, no-one can resist his quiet charm nor deny his cool judgment. His only enemies are the people who don't know him.

4 July

The newspapers announced the stirring story of our taking-over the French Fleet. I knew that this had been before the Cabinet for some days, and Vansittart, to give him his due, had advocated it; but Alexander, who had been got round by Admiral Darlan, killed the idea originally. But now we have appropriated the ships in Portsmouth, and have also won a great naval victory at Oran! But how ironical that our first victory of the war should have been over our Allies. . . . Later Winston made a very characteristic statement, and it was a theme after his own heart: he recounted the stirring story of the fight, and how we had routed the treacherous French. At the end of his speech the House rose, cheered, waved Order Papers – as I have so often seen them do for Neville. Only it was not little Neville's turn now. Winston suddenly wept.

7 July *Kelvedon*

The Windsors have been appointed to reign in Bermuda, and they will adore it, the petty pomp, the pretty Regency Government House, the beach and the bathing; and all the smart Americans will rush to Nassau to play backgammon with Wallis! It is an excellent appointment, and I suggested it two years ago and have been harping upon it ever since.

10 July

The Third French Republic has ceased to exist and I don't care; it was graft-ridden, ugly, incompetent, Communistic and corrupt, and had long outlived its day. Pétain is to be a sort of Hindenberg, and has divided France into provinces, as she was before the French Revolution, and has appointed local Gauleiters. The old France is dead. The French National Fete day is no more; it is abolished, as is that tiresome motto 'Liberté, Egalité, Fraternité'.

15 July

What can the future hold for us, personally, now? What can one look for? Only to save from the wreckage one's hopes, one's possessions, and some part of one's fortune. What a mess! I have little heart to go on – à quoi bon? All I want is an oval library with doors leading into a rose garden, by the sea.

16 July

Rab and I lunched at the Yugoslav Legation, 3 Upper Grosvenor Street, where there was a little festival to meet the Maiskys. I had arranged this capitulation to the New Order, and found them both far better than I had expected; she is soignée and pleasant and very obviously not a Communist; he is clever, shrewd and humorous. After the ladies left the dining-room we sat about the table drinking. . . . Maisky said that Diplomacy was an art, not a science . . . a little later Maisky and Rab retired into an adjoining room and continued their confidential conversations, while we others joined the ladies. The new order is not so terrible as I feared; one could certainly get on with Bevin and perhaps even with Maisky, too.

18 July

Winston was superb, magnificent, in the House as he answered Questions, and later made the very important statement about the Far East;[3] and he successfully quashed the Leftist Opposition's eagerness for war in the East as well as everywhere else.

19 July

At 6 o'clock, Rab and I turned on the radio to listen to Hitler's speech, but it was so badly relayed that we understood little except that he seemed less ranting and less hysterical than usual. Of course the Foreign Office had made no attempt to take down the speech, and we were later indebted to the Rumanian Minister for accurate information.

3. The Burma Road Agreement with Japan.

20 July

Rab lunched with the Egyptian Ambassador, and although late, he insisted on going by bus. It is a curious trait in so balanced a character, especially as he happens to be the possessor of an ample fortune. Halifax is also mean. Fortunately, I myself have never shown any sign of it, at least I hope not, and I trust my son will not either.

21 July

I call the FO 'Bourbon House' since they have learnt nothing and forgotten nothing: in fact they are still asleep, dreaming in a pre-Hitler, pre-dictator world, foolish, carping, finicky, inefficient and futile; there was an attack on Lord Halifax today by Attlee in 'The Times'. Our reign is slowly ending; I shall regret its close, although I have hardly ever been in complete sympathy with it.

22 July

Dr Benes called at the Foreign Office, and I had a word with him. He has been officially informed that he is recognised as the head of the Czechoslovakian Provisional Government, and he smilingly told me that 22 years ago next month, Lord Balfour had appointed him to exactly the same role. History indeed repeats itself.

23 July

Winston was in roaring spirits today, and gave slashing answers, which he had himself drafted, to foolish Questions, and generally convulsed the House. He is at the very top of his form now and the House is completely with him, as is the country, but he knows very little about foreign affairs. I sat behind him today and he was smiling and friendly, but I am always shy with him, and never get it quite right: I do not know why.

24 July

I lunched with Cecil Beaton in his tiny but super-attractive snuff-box of a house in Pelham Place. I am envious of him and it, and of his curious flair for arranging rooms amusingly.

Lloyd George, whose affection for Winston has noticeably

cooled of late, predicts that after the PM's first great blunder, the country, now admittedly hysterically infatuated with him, will turn against him and only remember his mistakes. I wonder?

28 July *Kelvedon*

A gloriously hot day, and I lay in the sun and got beautifully burnt while planes zoomed on high.

Later in the day I heard that Neville Chamberlain had been taken to hospital for a serious operation; thus fades the last hope of peace. Once again one man's illness may influence the history of the world.

30 July

The big FO debate began with an absurd Alice in Wonderland wrangle about procedure which lasted from 3.45 until 5.30 ... in war time! it was ludicrous in the extreme. [Someone] rose in the middle of it and 'spied strangers' which further delayed matters. At long last the debate began in Secret Session, and Wardlaw Milne opened with a surprisingly bitter attack on our Far East policy and on our closing the Burma Road in particular. Rab replied, and was excellent, really first class, easy, informed, confiding and statesmanlike; he has lost much of his inelegant jerkiness, and I thought it was his most successful Parliamentary performance so far. At about 8, the PM himself rose and we had 40 minutes of magnificent oratory and artistry but he gave away no secrets and, indeed, talked from his heart rather than from his head. He stoutly defended our action in closing the Burma Road.

7 August

I had a talk with Attlee in his room. He is quite agreeable and easy but small and he shook and twitched, and generally seemed very nervous and fidgetty.

8 August

A great air battle over the Channel, and a vast number of German aeroplanes have been brought down over the coast! Our Air Force is sublime. 53 raiders, the newspapers announce, were brought down today.

13 August
Another big day along the Channel, with many planes down; shall we be invaded tomorrow? As I write, I hear the buzzing of planes on high, and think that London will certainly be raided soon. I feel that at long last we are entering upon a decisive phase of the war.

18 August
A new friend of mine, Rodney Wilkinson, has been killed; he flew his Spitfire into a Messerschmitt, and crashed. I shan't forget his engaging charm, his curious shuffle and infectious gaiety. He had strange Egyptian eyes, long limbs and a natural elegance, but seemed fated to die: indeed, he always said so: but destiny, prompted by me, hesitated, since the Duke of Kent offered to take him as an ADC some weeks ago, and Rodney, preferring more active duty, valiantly refused. Later, he was given a Squadron with the greatest of difficulty, as being 30 he was over-age. He was typical of the type which is serving and saving England, and there will be many aching hearts when the news of his death comes out. I wonder why I met him, and why we became such sudden friends?

19 August
Circe Londonderry made me laugh when she repeated Mrs Greville's crack about Mrs Keppel. 'To hear Alice talk about her escape from France, one would think she had swum the Channel, with her maid between her teeth'.

20 August
Winston made a great speech, but somehow I was unimpressed, though he was eloquent and made great play with a peroration on Anglo-American relations. But the House, and the country, loved it. I thought it only another tour de force, not a new word, or fact or hope. Then Archie Sinclair wound up for the Government, and he made the almost incredibly magnificent exploits of our airmen sound dull and trite: his stammer, and his trick of reiterated over-emphasis, are very monotonous.

25 August *still Kelvedon*
The newspapers and the fish were both late in arriving as a bomb

fell on the Epping-Ongar road last night, and there are tales of raids everywhere, particularly in Kent, and two over the London area. I am burying another tin box, containing my diaries for the first year of the war; Mortimer the gardener is again my accomplice.

29 August

I lunched with Alba where I found Dr Dalton, alias Dr Dynamo, who has charm, intelligence, but who can on occasions be more offensive than anyone I have ever heard. Today he was delightful. Also Vansittart, whom I chaffed about his great love, his treacherous mistress, France, and he admitted that they had had a lover's quarrel. 'Vous portez des cornes', I taunted him but he was obviously too downcast and discouraged to take up the challenge; but he was pleasant, and I slyly got back into his good graces. He drove me back to the FO and told me how unhappy he had been all those years with Chamberlain and Halifax opposed to him; but the real culprit, he said, was Horace Wilson whom he hates. Van is charming and I think a bit mad. I do not understand why Neville did not sack him, as he often declared that he wanted to; laziness and inability to cast off disloyal officials was Neville's weakness and ultimately a cause of his downfall.

5 September *London*

In the House, Winston, whom I had met in the passage with Clemmie and two of his daughters, spoke at some length, but he was not at his best, and invoked little enthusiasm; the House has become accustomed to his high-flown rhetoric and thinks that he jokes too much: it is true that he is rarely serious about even sacred things, such as loss of life, and he betrays too easily how he is enjoying power.

9 September

Honor was awakened at 7.30 by her bailiff, who came with the news that a 1,000 lb. bomb had fallen on her farm: we hurried to see the damage, and found a crater only a few yards from the farm buildings, nearly 60 ft. square and over 20 ft. deep. Standing at its edge were two old women who had lost everything; their pathetic wooden shanty nearby was demolished, and a few sad possessions and dead chickens were strewn about. The women refused to leave, and no-one could persuade them.

There is a settembrile feeling in the air – going is the summer, going, indeed, is almost everything.

12 September *London*

I had not long been at the Foreign Office when the siren sounded, and we retreated to the cellar, where Rab sat surrounded by a body of BBC journalists to whom he administered a heartening tonic. He is more optimistic about the war now, as is Harold, who is happier about our air defences and says that the new barrage over London ought to protect it, at least at night. Later Harold and I went to the Dorchester together for dinner, and found half London there. Beaverbrook, smiling, younger and plumper, came up to me very cordially, taking both my hands in his, saying 'Well, Chips, how is Honor?' and we had a talk. The dining room was full of well-known people and friends waiting for the air raid which soon began. Somerset Maugham was nearby, and dozens more. . . . Later, the lobby was crowded and people settled down for the night with rugs, etc. Just before midnight I left, and although warned not to do so, I walked home. It was inky dark and the incessant gun fire was alarming, like the battlefields. The invasion is expected any moment now, probably some time during the weekend.

This island race is extraordinary: everyone I have seen today was in the highest spirits. They are all convinced that an English victory now lies just round the corner, and that our Air Force is actually superior, not only in quality but in numbers, to the Germans. Rab says we are fighting a punic war and that Hitler, the modern Hannibal, will certainly be defeated. Instead of elephants, we have his Dorniers to contend with.

I was distressed to hear that Neville Chamberlain has cancer, and can only live another 14 months or so. The leadership of the party must then become Rab's, if there is a Conservative Party.

13 September *Kelvedon*

I dread being killed or dying before Paul grows up: he must profit by all my mistakes, avoid the pitfalls into which I fell, and emulate my successes and hope for my luck . . .

16 September *London*

I drove back to London via the East End, which is a scene of desolation; house after house has been wrecked, debris falls from the remaining floors, windows are gone, heaps of rubbish lie in the pavements. A large hospital and a synagogue still stand, but they are windowless. Some streets are roped off because of time bombs. The damage is immense, yet the people, mostly Jewish, seemed courageous. I gave many of them lifts.

Everyone still seems cock-a-hoop in the face of almost certain invasion: I am less so, for the German machine is very thorough and very successful; there are ships of all kinds congregated along the French coast, enough, they say, to transport half a million men: luckily a gale is blowing.

17 September

More raids and there were jokes about a probable attack on the House of Commons this afternoon. I went over early, and found everyone expectant: would the raiders come soon after Prayers? Winston, who had been lunching at Buckingham Palace, wandered about without an escort and I chatted to him several times. The sirens blew about ten minutes to three, but the Speaker did not adjourn the House until after 3.30 when the bells rang. Meanwhile, Neville Chamberlain appeared looking fairly well, but lacking his usual colour and animation. He had an ovation as he always does, when he took his place for the first time since his operation: so did Winston when he sat down beside him.

I thought that Neville looked very small: has he shrunk again?

Soon we all trooped down into the cellars, which did not seem very substantial to me: and are really only a shelter from splinters and shells: yesterday one of our AA shells crashed into a window in the Library, and went straight through the floor. As the Prime Minister afterwards said, the Houses of Parliament have become, by their size, their vulnerability, and position, one of the most dangerous spots in London. After a while the all clear blew, and the sitting was resumed. Winston spoke, and soon 'spied strangers' which meant that we had to go into Secret Session. He then elaborated his suggestions for future meetings of Parliament, which, he said, would not yet be announced, and further stressed the imminence of invasion. Afterwards Members went about, chatting vivaciously, each recounting his own adventures: many had had bombs in their houses or in their gardens.

19 September

More raids. I drove to the Foreign Office, Rab had not yet arrived. After nearly 2 hours I began to be anxious about him, and discovered that a time bomb had fallen in Oxford Street, and that all the residents of North Audley Street had been turned out at short notice, though Rab had just managed to get into his clothes before being hurriedly escorted to Claridges' where he spent the remainder of his interrupted night. He arrived at the Foreign Office shaken, unshaved and untidy, and announced that from now on he would stay with me at Belgrave Square. I was delighted and went home, at luncheon time, to order my depleted staff (six instead of fifteen) to make the necessary arrangements. Later Rab moved in, and I lent him clothes and a razor and whatnot. We inspected the bedrooms, and concluded the cellar was safest and he decided to share my cell. He on the bed, and I on an Empire chaise-longue, extremely elegant, but not very comfortable. When we 'retired', Rab put wax in his ears, opened his red box and worked for a bit. After a while I slept, though several times in the night I heard loud reports; Rab snored quietly; what a pleasant human reassuring sound it can be.

23 September

A silly, extraordinary story. On Saturday, after I left the Foreign Office there came a telegram 'very urgent' from Lothian in Washington in which he said that President Roosevelt had learned from a most trustworthy source 'that the invasion was due to start tomorrow, Sunday, at 3 p.m.' A copy of this telegram I myself saw today. The Service Departments were immediately informed, everyone prepared, the whole country alerted. Later it occurred to people here that possibly the President's kindly tip referred to the imminent Japanese occupation of Indo-China, which we have all known about for some time. An inept and comic story; the machinery of Government thrown into confusion by a complete misunderstanding!

General de Gaulle has arrived at Dakar and even now a battle is in progress there; I wonder whether this was a well-advised plan, or just a Winstonian scheme in his earlier, rasher manner?

26 September

The failure, admitted now, of the Dakar expedition, has revealed the PM to be as incautious as ever. It is a deplorable affair, and feeling at the Carlton Club is running high against him.

30 September

The Chief Whip's car was still at the Foreign Office steps at 7 p.m. which usually means a Cabinet crisis. Rab now says that Winston, whilst he had the final say in the matter, was not really in favour of the ill-fated Dakar expedition.

1 October

More raids, and I was rudely awakened by a swaying movement; so was Rab, and we could not at first understand what had happened as there was no unusual noise at the moment. Soon we were told that two bombs had fallen on Belgrave Square, uncomfortably near, and later I walked over to see the damage; the old Austrian Legation, No. 18, had had its façade torn off, and the basement damaged, while the garage at the back was completely wrecked. I thought of other days, of Mensdorff reigning there in Edwardian splendour, before my time, and the Franckenstein parties, little distinguished boring lunches and countless concerts with Dollfuss and Princess Helena Victoria, and latterly costume balls. At one of the last of these a 'Congress of Vienna' Ball, Honor looked superb in an Empire creation, and for the evening they had put masks on the eighteenth century pictures, a charming touch. Autres temps, autres mœurs . . .

People now think that the invasion is either postponed or abandoned.

3 October

Winston is without doubt all-powerful now and, though he talks of resigning directly after the war to make room for younger men, he is at the moment relishing to the full the fruits of power.

I wish I could be made Under-Secretary of Reconstruction,

under Reith: and I think I could do it well. But the Churchill régime will never offer me anything, unless Brendan bestirs himself on my behalf.

7 October *London*

Rab, with his brilliant intelligence, has many ideas of the new England that will emerge after the war: he thinks that our whole system will be drastically modified and perhaps improved: I only hope that it will be he who is the architect of the reconstruction.

Though the post-war new order, I fear, rather bores me, Rab is obsessed by it, and I suppose I shall have to adapt myself to it when the time comes.

I am becoming increasingly attached to Rab and find him fascinating. His perpetual good nature, his shrewdness, his balanced views, and lack of pose and pretence are amazing in one so young: by comparison, the 'glamour boys', now so prominent and powerful, after being fallow for so long, are a makeshift and shoddy lot. Their only merit has been long subservience to Winston. At his almost Papal court, the new Cardinal, Morton,[4] is an Oppenheim character. His rival, Professor Lindemann, the Berlin-born scientist and snob, remains, to his chagrin, no more than Bishop-in-Partibus but yearns for a Biretta. Roy Harrod, a theoretical, oriental-looking don, is the Monsignore of the Churchillian conclave.

10 October

I ran into Winston in the House: I wonder why he always bows and withdraws into himself when he is aware of hostility? When he shakes hands with someone he dislikes, he seems to contract, suddenly to look smaller and his famous charm is overclouded by an angry taurine look.

11 October

After all the disturbed nights and bombs, Rab remarked that I

4. Major (Sir) Desmond Morton, Churchill's personal adviser, 1940–45; previously (1930–39) attached to the Committee of Imperial Defence.

looked dejected and tired, and offered to drive me to Kelvedon, which he kindly did.

As we drove he described going this morning to Buckingham Palace to attend a meeting of the Privy Council; after it, he had a few words with the King, who 'sent me his love'. I never know quite how I am with the present Royal régime, but I do know that they do not impress or thrill me at all: I suppose I know them too well. They do their job well, but 'the divinity that doth hedge a king' is completely lacking.

14 October

Geoffrey Lloyd, Alan and the Butlers dined, and it was a memorable evening ... Sydney Butler's first evening in London since the blitz. Dinner proceeded, and suddenly Lambert, the butler, ushered in what appeared to be a Harlem nigger: it was Harold Balfour, black from head to foot. He had been standing in the smoking room of the Carlton Club with David Margesson and Victor Warrender drinking sherry before going into dinner: suddenly, with a blinding flash, the ceiling had fallen, and the club collapsed on them. A direct hit. Harold swam, as he put it, through the rubble, surprised to be alive, but soon realised that his limbs were all intact; he called out to his companions to see if they were still alive, and fortunately, all answered. Somehow he got to the front door ... to find it jammed. At that moment he saw Lord Hailsham being half led, half carried out by his son, Quintin Hogg. A few other individuals, headed by Harold, put their shoulders to the door, and it crashed into the street, and only just in time as by then a fire had started. Harold remembered that he had left his car, an Air Force one, nearby, and went to it, and found only a battered heap of tin; but the chauffeur, an RAF man, was luckily untouched, as he had gone into the building. Harold came here for a bath, champagne, and succour, and we gave him all three. Seaford House, across the square has also been struck, that huge mansion where I have been to so many balls in old days: I wonder what happened to the famous green malachite staircase? Holland House, too, has gone, and I am really sorry. It seems that it is beyond repair. I have been thinking of that last great ball there in July 1939, with the crush, the Queen, and 'the world' still aglitter.

22 October

At the House of Commons I picked up David Margesson for dinner and later called at No. 10, where I left a note asking Brendan Bracken, as all the Treasury telephones are still down and one can only use the few secret Federal lines; he came and brought David with him in the Prime Minister's armoured car, which looks like a huge painted thermos bottle, and is supposed to be bomb-proof. Brendan drank a whole bottle of hock, David a bottle of Krug '20. A gay, interesting evening. Brendan offered Rab the Presidency of the Board of Education, which I know Rab secretly covets; but I pray that they will leave him at the Foreign Office.

28 October

An historic day. Italy sent Greece an ultimatum at 3 a.m. that she would take over strategic bases at 6 a.m. unless Greece capitulated. General Metaxas refused, and now tonight, the flames have spread to the Balkans, and Italian troops are pouring over the mountain passes into Greece. My poor Prince Paul, what a position he is in. He is holding a cabinet meeting, even now, to decide Yugoslavia's role, and will, I suppose, remain neutral, though Turkey may rush to Greece's aid. I am thinking much of the Regent, my alter ego, who has to decide the destinies of his country and his dynasty: no man is more shrewd. But I can't bear to think of his anxiety, sitting in his library, which was once Lord Chesterfield's, tormented by doubts, scruples, and having to decide the fate of millions.

30 October *Polesden Lacey*

Letters from New York from both Helen Astor and Serge describe a recent tea party at Rhinebeck; a message had come that President Roosevelt was bringing Princess Alice (Athlone) to tea from Hyde Park. Helen told Paul that he must behave himself, and be the host. The little fellow very gravely met the Presidential and Royal party at the door, and bowed deeply. Later he sat on the President's knee, and had a long talk with him about the international situation. As the President left he patted him on the head, and said he was a nice little boy: as he got into the car, Paul shouted 'I hope you beat Mr Wilkie', to which the President remarked to Princess Alice 'He's beginning his political career young'.

1 November

This morning I met David Margesson, by chance, in Downing Street, and followed him into his office; I offered to give up Southend in exchange for a Peerage, as I know Oliver Lyttelton is looking for a safe seat. David was sympathetic, but thought I was too young and had not been long enough in the House to be elevated – 'to be kicked upstairs' – still, if I insisted? I didn't. In any case it was too late, for I believe a seat has been found for Oliver Lyttelton. David made a mental note, and said he would willingly arrange for me to have a peerage later: slightly relieved, I left him; I don't really want to leave the House yet, but the seeds are sown, and in time I shall surely be Lord Chips, which will be fun.

3 November *Kelvedon, or rather Bleak House*

I am beginning to hate this place, and fear the 'Kelvedon Curse' is a real one, though it is supposed only to affect women: nothing has gone right for me, however, since we bought it. Today it is wet, sad and foggy, and I went for a long walk in what might be such beautiful woods and was oppressed by them; the dripping leaves and mud added to the gloom. I like the woods, but love the baroque swimming bath and exquisite pavilion which I created, more. Something tells me that I shall reign here again, one remote day. But shall I want to? I really have no future, a bombed house, probably, in Belgrave Square, the loss of all my possessions, Kelvedon gone, alone[5] . . . my child far away, and perhaps forgetting me. The outlook is bleak and dour indeed. I am wretched tonight, and lonely for the first time in my life, I think . . . painfully lonely. And now I hear that Neville Chamberlain is very ill, and probably will not survive until Christmas: everything seems to come at once.

4 November

Lothian presided over a small meeting of journalists held in the Ambassador's room at the FO and spoke with astonishing frank-

5. Chips and his wife, Honor, had recently separated.

ness for an hour. He is confident of Roosevelt's victory, and was rather scathing about Joe Kennedy, whom he dismissed as an Irish-American, much concerned with the preservation of property, his own in particular, since he has 'nine hostages to the future'.

5 November

I admire the PM's pluck, his courageous energy and magnificent English: his humour too, although often in doubtful taste, is immense. ... This morning one of his secretaries rushed up to me in the House, and asked me if I had seen him? He was apparently due to lunch at the Palace, and it was already 1.15. Luckily I had just seen him 'boozing' in the Smoking Room, and so I volunteered to remind him. I went up to him politely, but unsmilingly, and he got up ungraciously, after grunting at me. He can be very unattractive when he is in a bad temper. Neville, my poor dying Neville, was never like this ...

Harold fetched me, and drove me to the Dorchester, where we dined with the Elvedens, a large party with Peggy Dunne, sweet Nell Stavordale and others. Half London seemed to be there. The Coopers were next to us, entertaining the Walter Elliots. ... Oliver Lyttelton[6] our new President of the Board of Trade, was throwing his weight and wit about. He and his wife were dining with the Lloyd Georges, the Gwilyms ... it was exhilarating, but fatiguing. I gave Bob Boothby a champagne cocktail in the private bar, which now looks, seems and smells like the Ritz bar in Paris, rue Cambon. Our bill must have been immense for we had four magnums of champagne. London lives well: I've never seen more lavishness, more money spent, or more food consumed than tonight, and the dance floor was packed. There must have been a thousand people. Leaving, Harold and I wore our tin hats, and the cloakroom attendant said to me, without a trace of a smile, 'You have a screw loose, Sir, in your hat – if you can wait, I'll send for the engineer'. We left the modern wartime Babylon, and got quickly into Harold's Air Force car. The contrast between the light and gaiety within, and the blackout and the roaring

6. Minister of State in Middle East, 1941–2; Minister of Production 1942–5; President of Board of Trade, 1945. Created Viscount Chandos, 1954.

guns outside was terrific: but I was more than a little drunk.

6 November

As raids are very much increasing in intensity there was a Secret Session today to discuss the House of Commons' future meeting place. Winston came in, 'spied strangers', and then made the Government statement. He told us that we are to meet in future at Church House in Westminster Cloisters, which has been converted by the Office of Works. He was humorous but dictatorial, and hinted at shutting down Parliament altogether if there was opposition to this decision, which on the whole seems a reasonable one. 'We must try the shoe, see where it pinches and perhaps return here later.' 'This procedure will confuse the enemy.' Such was his line. The House took none too kindly to this announcement, and there was chatter of 'funk holes' and 'bad example', etc. However, Winston stuck his ground, and at Church House we shall meet tomorrow, and probably rightly. Members are complaining openly that Winston trades on his position, on his immense following in the country, though his popularity is on the decline: but it is still high. Yet the country does not want a dictator.

President Roosevelt has had an even greater triumph than anyone anticipated. A real landslide, and I have yet to see anyone who is not delighted.

7 November *Pompeii*

I write amidst my ruins – but more, much more about that later. A dreadful day started with the House of Commons meeting for the first time in its new premises which Winston has dubbed 'The Annexe' – a large building, astonishingly well arranged, many Members turned up early to watch the proceedings: it is the first time since the big fire of 1834 that the Commons have met anywhere except at Westminster . . . The Speaker was enthroned under his usual canopy, the Serjeant-at-Arms on a camp chair at the Bar; Members found places as nearly as possible equivalent to where they usually sat at Westminster. The Hall was not too crowded, but the acoustics are indifferent and there was noise and muffled excitement, and ministers tumbling over one another. Winston watched the confusion with amusement. The atmosphere was gay, almost like the Dorchester. Outside in the cloisters, however, I ran into several clerics who seemed indignant that their building should have been taken for such lay purposes as law-making. Proceedings followed their usual course with surprising ease. So strong is tradition among members of Parliament that all the usual forms and customs were observed.

Some chaps dined. . . . Hector Bolitho, Raymond Mortimer and Bill Tufnell and, towards the end of dinner, a terrific barrage began. The House shook, but Hector nevertheless remarked that he had never had such a lovely evening, it was his first night out, really, since the Blitz, and he remarked how soothing it was to sit and dine by candlelight drinking Chateau Yquem, a change from his usual sausages and beer at the Air Ministry. Just after 9 we left the dining room, and as my four guests proceeded, still carrying their brandy glasses, into the morning room there was an immense crash and a flash like lightning.[7] 'That was somewhere near, let's go and see if we can see anything' Bolitho suggested. I protested that there were usually two bombs in quick succession, and that we had better wait a moment. As I spoke I heard the sound of breaking glass and there was a brief pause; no-one was frightened but I heard the voice of Harold, the footman, shouting 'We've been hit'. At this we all rushed into the hall, and were at once half blinded by dust and smoke. A second later, as if we had invoked the devil, out of the darkness sprang an ARP warden, whom I recognised as, of all people, the Archduke Robert.[8] He was followed by a woman and several others armed with pickaxes. They had made their way through the ruined portico to dig us out and they seemed amazed, even a touch disappointed, to find us intact and calm. 'But you've had a direct hit' one of the wardens insisted. 'Are there any dead below?' I said I did not think so, and, surprised by my own calm, I led them into the morning room, gave them drinks, and rang the bell. Lambert appeared, and I asked him if everyone was all right downstairs? He nodded, and I told him to fetch more tumblers and drinks. I nearly said 'The Krug '20', but just didn't. We

7. There is a graphic description of the following incident in Hector Bolitho's book *War in the Strand* (1942).

8. Of Austria.

then stood about, and the wardens put out the electric lights as by now we had no windows, and the shutters had been blown in. I lit a candle and introduced my motley guests, the Archduke with his Hapsburg chin, looking lanker than ever, his female companion, who I discovered to be Mrs Harald Peake, several chauffeurs from the mews, etc. An odd group. Soon we tried to go into the Square, and it was quite a feat to crawl over the fallen masonry and broken columns, etc. The porch had gone, so had the balcony and only a huge heap of rubble and debris remained. Still we were lucky to be alive as the bomb fell within a few feet of where we had been standing. It was all most distressing, but I tried to laugh and make a joke of it to Robert the Archduke, who remained as grave as ever. Tufnell decided to leave for Essex via Claridge's, but when he went to his car, a handsome Alvis, he only found its charred and battered remains, and was in despair. Bolitho went to the telephone; mirabile dictu, it was still connected and functioning, and asked the Air Ministry to send him transport, which they did. At length he left, dropping the others en route. Raymond Mortimer decided to stay the night, as our shelters were intact. He and I, armed with torches, made a tour of the house. Every window on the south side had been blown in, and most of the shutters lay on the floor. The dust and dirt were indescribable. I went to bed in my underground bedroom, took a sleeping draught, and thus endeth a very tiresome difficult day, and a fantastic evening, which began by the Duchess of Kent getting me twice out of the bath to talk on the telephone.

10 November *Kelvedon*

Mr Chamberlain died in the night; and in a way, though I loved him, I am glad: the shafts of malice had hurt him, and probably killed him. Now the reaction, already begun, will have added impetus, and his place in history will be more secure. He had nothing more to live for; all his hopes had gone; this tough race, which is capable of great courage and strength, can also be very cruel; he was against the War, and would have done anything to prevent it. The world has lost its best friend. I shall miss him personally; his wife adored him; Horace Wilson will be broken-hearted.

11 November *London*

I lunched, as did Boss Butler, at the Belgian Embassy, and found myself next to Attlee, whose French is really appalling; but I was pleasantly surprised by the courtesy of the little man. He is a gentleman, or nearly so; no revolutionary he. We discussed poor Mr Chamberlain, whom he once so hated. Today he was kind about him, recalled his sympathetic speech on the Members' Pensions Bill, and lauded his great qualities. But he shied off when I hinted that Neville had saved Christendom, though he did not contradict me. I think that I made a conquest of him; I hope so. He is narrow, nervous, unimposing and well-meaning, and seems more Liberal than actually Socialist: but he could never control the energies of his wilder followers.

12 November *London*

Winston spoke of Neville in measured, stately English, and the general impression was that it was well-done, dignified and sincere: but he looked grumpy enough. . . . The scene seemed so strange in this new, slightly shoddy, 'Annexe'. Attlee followed, and made his tribute on behalf of the Labour Party well, as did Archie Sinclair for the Liberals. About five o'clock, after showing my pass, I walked into King Charles Street and there met 'Steepledick' himself face to face. He was wearing a fur coat with an Astrakhan collar and his curious black hat: he was puffing a huge cigar, and walking quickly, closely followed by a detective. He looked very cross indeed, and half-grunted at me: he knows that we dislike each other. I cannot help but be suspicious of him, and I think he knows it, for he once asked me a year or so ago why it was that I always avoided him in the Smoking Room.

13 November *Albury Park, Guildford*

At the House today there was an atmosphere of suppressed excitement, and Victor Warrender[9] soon whispered the good news to me that half the Italian battle-fleet – 3 out of 6 capital ships and several cruisers – have been sunk or damaged beyond repair. Apparently our fleets caught the Wops napping in the Gulf of

9. Later Lord Bruntisfield.

Taranto, and practically annihilated them, with the loss of only two seaplanes: our own fleet was not engaged. This victory considerably alters the naval balance of power, frees our ships to go elsewhere, and will greatly discourage Italy. I met the PM coming in from behind the Chair ... 'We've got some sugar for the birds this time ...' he said; and even smiled at me. Questions seemed interminable but finally Winston rose and gave the electrified House the wonderful Nelsonian news.

London.

14 November *Neville Chamberlain's Memorial Service*

The Abbey, as the Service had been kept so secret, was far from crowded. There had been some uneasiness lest the Germans would stage a raid and get Winston and the entire Government with one bomb. However, nothing occurred, and there was no alert during the actual service, which was long, dignified and moving. Rab and I were put in the second pew.

There in the Abbey, and it angered me to see them, were all the little men who had torpedoed poor Neville's heroic efforts to preserve peace, and made his life a misery: some seemed to be gloating. Winston, followed by the War Cabinet, however, had the decency to cry as he stood by the coffin, and Mr Speaker and others too seemed deeply stirred. ... The service was long, and the Abbey was cold, that terrible ecclesiastic cold known only to English churches.

Afterwards I heard that after everyone had left the Abbey, poor Horace Wilson, the once all-powerful eminence grise of the Chamberlain régime, was seen alone, his face contracted with grief, praying for his dead friend.

24 November *Coppins*

I came here for the night, and this afternoon tea ended in tragedy as little Edward became bumptious, and knocked over a table, spilling a kettle of hot water over his little pink legs, and he bellowed. The Duke lost his temper, the Duchess was in a flurry, nannies rushed in, but little Alexandra, delightfully unconcerned, turned round, and as if to change the subject said, 'I love soldiers, do you?' ...

We had a lovely evening. I played backgammon with Princess

Marina, whilst the Duke strummed Debussy. He is extremely intelligent, well-informed, but sometimes very nervous and irritable. She, on the other hand, is perfect, and it is touching to see her pride and pleasure in the Greek victories.

26 November *London*

I escorted Halifax to a meeting of the H. of C. Foreign Affairs Committee, and though he looked tired, he was superlatively suave and gracious and even affectionate to me.

27 November *Coppins*

Questions early at the House. We have returned to the 'usual place' and everyone feels relieved and pleased to be home again.

28 November *London*

The House went into Secret Session, and hardly had Anthony Eden got up to give an account of his visit to the Middle East when there was an air raid warning. The news was brought in by a Whip, told to David Margesson, who whispered to the Speaker that planes were immediately overhead. Mr Speaker rose and suspended the sitting, so we all trooped sheepishly into the cellar. Later we resumed our activities and Anthony was adequate and plausible.

I had a dinner party at home for 'Peter' (Sir Charles Portal), Head of the Bomber Command, a man of granite and of ruthlessness. He is young-ish, has a beak of a nose; but one is conscious of his immense personality. He told us of his frequent visits to Chequers, and was as funny and malicious about Winston as he dared be and the other guests, Rab, Harold Balfour and Geoffrey Lloyd my 'little ministers', relished his remarks. Portal said that he looks forward to his fishing, to living in a keeper's cottage in Scotland on £300 a year after the war. Meanwhile he has to put up with the Dorchester.

29 November *London*

Looking lovely, thin and chic, Honor dined with me at the Dorchester, where Charles Peake joined us, and was entertaining with his stories of Winston and Chequers, etc. It seems that

Winston wearing an Air Force cap received the Halifaxes in particularly curious clothes and seemed rather put-out by Halifax's surprise; pointing to his strange garb he said 'Clemmie bought me these rompers!'[10]

30 November
Great news. The Yugoslav minister showed me a cable this morning from his Government to say that the Prince Regent would like me to go to Belgrade. I am very tempted; I might make history, the destination allures me, and the visits en route are dazzling; but what an uprooting, and what a fiendish journey, and perhaps to find myself at Christmas in Takaradi. Still, I shall certainly go if 'les affaires' permit.

To 'tâter le terrain', I asked to see Halifax; Ralph Stevenson waved me to go in, and I did so quietly, I opened the door, saw him standing before the fire, a paper resting on his dummy arm, and he leaning on the chimney-piece: occasionally he puffed at his cigarette-holder and his ecclesiastic face seemed contorted with misery. He frowned, went to his desk, picked up a red pencil and made a few notes; then he picked up another document, returned to the fire, rested it on his withered arm, and it all began again. I coughed slightly but he was too absorbed to see me. I became embarrassed and watched the ticking clock; after 8 minutes I said 'I'm so sorry to interrupt you'. He looked surprised, smiled gravely and said 'Hello Chips, I didn't know you were there'. We had a little chat, and he agreed, indeed, was in favour of my going at once to Yugoslavia. How strange, silent and reserved is this really great man. I am, I know, uneven about him; for I realise his faults, and forgive his frailties.

4 December
Rab addressed a collection of National Liberals on Egypt: he was wily, sly and fascinating, and he scored a brilliant success. Several of them said to me afterwards 'Why look further for a Foreign Secretary or even a Prime Minister?'

5 December
Arrangements for my fantastic journey are advancing. . . . I leave

10. No doubt the famous 'siren suit'.

on Monday, 16 December for Bournemouth, and fly early next day from Poole. I am very excited about it and it will be a welcome change and break.

9 December *London*

Luckily my duties took me to the House of Commons, where a friendly policewoman told me that St Stephen's Cloister had been hit last night. I went into what was the Members' cloakroom and saw a scene of devastation; confusion, wreckage, broken glass everywhere, and the loveliest, oldest part of the vast building a shambles. Suddenly I came upon Winston Churchill wearing a fur-collared coat, and smoking a cigar; he was led by a policeman and followed by Steel, his secretary. 'It's horrible' he remarked to me without removing his cigar; and I saw that he was much moved, for he loves Westminster; I walked with him. 'They would hit the best bit' I said. 'Where Cromwell signed King Charles's death warrant' he grunted. I sensed the historic significance of the scene – Winston surveying the destruction he had long predicted, of a place he loved.

Leslie Hore-Belisha proposed himself to dine, and all day I wondered who I could invite to meet him; a year ago the world would have jumped to dine with the Secretary of State for War. And today, too, at tea at the FO, I mused at the melancholy business of ingratitude. I was in the Secretaries' room at the famous 'Tea-party' when John Simon emerged from Halifax's room. He was jovial, irritating and tactless and no-one treated him with respect, or even marked civility. At last I said – after all, he is Lord Chancellor – 'Can we offer you a cup of tea in this palace where you reigned so long?' And he was mollified, accepted a cup and was amiable. But his smile – 'like the brass knocker on a coffin' – puts me off. A fallen idol.

11 December

Brendan and others dined with me . . .

Brendan told some fascinating stories about Winston. The other day, it appears, the PM heard a noise, rang a bell and hissed to the servant who answered 'What was that noise?' 'I think it was a bomb, Sir.' 'That is a platitude', the Prime Minister retorted. Brendan left at 10.30 in the PM's armoured car.

12 December

Lothian died today; he had been suffering from some slight internal complaint, but being a Christian Scientist he refused to consult a doctor, though he could easily have been saved by a stomach pump or even a purgative.

16 December *Bournemouth*

A fussy day with my preparations for departure . . . parcels, messages, letters and luggage . . . and at the last moment Rab very clearly showed that he did not want me to go; he put up a hundred objections, and I was tempted, for a moment, to chuck the whole expedition: I should be criticised: I should not get back; I should be caught in Spain. It was a risk. He managed to take the gilt off my travelling ginger-bread, and I went into the corridor of the Foreign Office to be alone for five minutes to make the important decision and concluded that I would go (I could probably always turn back, if necessary), and at 4.30 I left, with few misgivings. At the Bournemouth Hotel I found a telegram of bon voyage from Honor, and soon after Alan arrived gaily from Southampton to say goodbye. My last night, possibly for ever, in England. The flight into Egypt has really begun.

Chips, after a lengthy and uncomfortable air journey via Lisbon, the Canary Islands, Lagos ('*a hell of a place; too Kipling to be true*') *and Wadi Halfa, arrived in Cairo on 31 December. The account of this journey, detailed and amusing though it is, has been omitted.*

The narrative continues on 2 January 1941.

1941

2 January *The Embassy, Cairo*

I am luxuriously established, and have already made conquests of the Embassy staff. The Lampsons[11] only returned today, which was bliss, as it gave me time to settle in. I always love staying in people's houses whilst they are away.

11. Sir Miles Lampson was British Ambassador to Egypt and High Commissioner for the Sudan, 1936–46. Created 1st Baron Killearn, 1943.

I lunched alone with the Lampsons. He is a huge, magnificent man of about 60, of enormous physique and easy manners. She is the daughter of Sir Aldo Castellani, the Italian doctor and scientist. Later Peter [Coats] whisked me off to the Wavells' house, where he also lives; a modest villa by Gezira Club which they share with General Wilson.

Lady Wavell, Queenie, is a large, lazy woman with wonderful turquoise eyes, but I was fascinated by him. We had a long conversation and I saw how lovable and gently distinguished he is. He talked first of [T. E.] Lawrence, then of his son whom he wants me to meet. His charm completely engulfed me.

3 January *The Embassy, Cairo*

I am exultant; the Cairene scene is just my affair, easy, elegant, pleasure-loving, trivial, worldly; me, in fact . . .

In the afternoon I went with Freya Stark to an Egyptian cocktail party in a flat overlooking the Nile. Freya, one of my mother-in-law's greatest friends, is here officially to do propaganda. She speaks perfect Arabic and is a sort of Lady Hester Stanhope or Gertrude Bell – in every generation there seems to be one English woman who lives amongst Arabs and knows their language. She is doing excellent work and is popular with everyone. . . . Her eccentric clothes (not unlike Norah Lindsey's) and her habit of attaching any object or bibelot to herself in queer places infuriates Lady Wavell who, whilst she has a good sense of humour, is extremely conventional. Wavell, however, likes Freya . . .

After the Egyptian party I walked to Middle East HQ and was received by Air Marshal [Sir Arthur] Longmore[12] who kept me for an hour explaining our air policy and the difficulties with which he has had to contend. Now things are easier as planes are beginning to come in. I gathered that he does not see eye to eye with Winston, who is always inclined to adventures, while Longmore is against extending his lines of communication. We have been lucky, and it was partly bluff, to have done so well for so long. Now we are winning in the Middle East at last. Already we have captured 500 Italian planes but many of these are antiquated and damaged. I told him of my mission to

12. Air Officer Commanding-in-Chief, Middle East, 1940–1.

Yugoslavia, and he hopes that Yugoslavia will not come into the War until we are prepared to give her arms . . .

I adore Cairo, it is everything I like.

4 January *The Embassy, Cairo*

We went to the races to join the Ambassador and Lady Lampson in their box. 'God Save the King' was played as they arrived. The paddock was crowded, and it reminded me of Newmarket, with Aly Khan leading in his horses and Charles Wood[13] (in Cairo on leave) wandering about with Hughie Northumberland. I found masses of friends and acquaintances.

Later I took Jacqueline[14] to the Mousky with its fascinating shops, although they have very little really that one wants. Back to the Embassy, and we drove in state to the Wavells' mammoth cocktail party of over a hundred people, arranged by Peter, who is their Lord Chamberlain as well as everything else. The joke in Cairo is that at first he looked after General Wavell, but now Wavell looks after him. At the party I had my second glimpse of the great General. He is like his photographs, grey, gracious and smiling, but is alleged to be more silent than Coolidge. He has a queer expression due to having only one eye and sometimes does not seem to focus accurately . . . I soon found him easy, sometimes even a cataract of conversation. After dinner he led me into a corner of the rather bare drawing-room and we talked for over an hour, standing up. He asked me dozens of questions, first about London, then David Margesson whom he has never met, then about other politicians. . . . Then he switched on to books, and I found him charming, one of the most rare, gentle, detached, good people I have ever met. His charm is insidious. I quite understand Peter's passion and devotion for him, which P. told me was only of gradual growth. The Victor of Bardia hardly mentioned his latest victory: typical: all goes according to plan; Wavell does his thinking alone, walking, or on the golf course. His staff is excellent . . . a very cosy evening, with the beam of history on that house, and I alone with Wavell for an hour and a half. He seemed surprised when I told him how famous he was at home, and that a grateful Nation would no doubt present him

13. The present Lord Halifax.

14. Lady Lampson.

with a second Blenheim. 'I hope not' he laughed, and when I said he was a second Nelson (a foolish remark) he retorted, 'Why? because I have only one eye?' We really made friends. Peter, when he drove me back to the Embassy, said that I had had quite an unprecedented success with Wavell, who was not easy, and often bored . . .

7 January

Tomorrow I go on to Greece, and am wretched to be leaving Cairo, though I will be coming back. I would like to be a permanent Pasha.

8 January *The Legation, Athens*

I was called at 5.15, a too frequent occurrence in this aeronautical age, and dressed gloomily, and was driven to Heliopolis. . . . At Tatoi airport there was no car to meet me but a message explained that the Legation – which seems a rather muddled institution – had sent the car to the wrong aerodrome; there are two. I got a lift into Athens, and on the way saw our airmen everywhere. Athens seemed smaller than I thought. The Legation is a pretentious house which formerly belonged to Madame Venizelos. . . . A message came that the King was waiting to see me, so, unchanged, I hurried to the Palace, escorted by Harold Caccia. There we were received by Colonel Levidis, the pompous Chamberlain, whom I had known in London. The King seemed overjoyed to see me; he is thin, lonely and conversational, for he sees few people, but he is quite convinced of victory – if only we would send him more arms, and if only Paul of Yugoslavia would come into the War now. He gave me more tea and showed me over the unattractive Palace which was mostly under dust-sheets. Altogether the King was very nice. I have known him well for twenty years; he is lonely and a mild bore; but kindly, gentle and loyal. He is living officially at the Tatoi Palace at the request of General Metaxas for reasons of security; but he comes up to Athens nearly every day and picnics in the town Palace. He asked me shyly to share his tray; but I refused, pleading the Palairets[15] . . . his uniform, cut like an English one, made him look more English than ever.

15. Sir Maurice and Lady Palairet, the British Ambassador and his wife, were Chips's host and hostess.

9 January *The Legation, Athens*

Got up late and made my arrangements for my appalling journey on to Belgrade tomorrow. I am already against the Balkans and long for Cairo. Then Lilia Ralli, witty, frivolous, sweet, chic as ever, fetched me and we shopped; and we drove up to the Parthenon; it is superb, amber-pink (not beige as Lady Mendl is alleged to have said) and staggering in its quiet splendour. Lilia told me much. The Royal set-up at Athens is complicated; there is the isolated King who sees no-one; there are the Crown Prince and Princess (Frederika), who, madly in love, remain aloof from the world with their babies and their passion. She is a touch unpopular, being German (I met her first dining with General Goering in 1936); there is Princess Andrew who is eccentric to say the least and lives in semi-retirement: there is Prince Andrew, who philanders on the Riviera whilst his son, Prince Philip,[16] is serving in our Navy; there are the Georges who live in France; there is Prince Peter, the Georges' son who has recently married morganatically a woman who is not allowed into Greece at all. ... Life in Athens is simple after the Belshazzars in Cairo and I have not lost my taste for splendour ... but my high spirits continue: is it the thyroid that I am taking or am I drugged with private happiness, and released energy?

I am apprehensive about something the King of Greece hinted to me today that Paul, to whom he talks frequently on the telephone, is having a sort of nervous collapse. The Germans are putting it about that he is mad. I do not believe it. The King and Paul have not actually met since they came for a cocktail in my house in Belgrave Square, three years ago. They are very old friends, but mildly hostile and amusing about each other. Now they talk every night on the telephone and with the line certainly tapped! The King said inter alia that he was aghast at the appointment of Eden to the Foreign Office, but as it was an accomplished fact there was no use making such a song and dance about it, as Paul was doing. He personally very much regretted the departure of Halifax.

10 January *Train in Greece*

Burdened with luggage and three diplomatic bags I only just

16. Prince Philip Mountbatten (now HRH Duke of Edinburgh).

caught the 12.10 train for Belgrade. The Athens station was crowded and I saw many wounded soliders, some limping, others on stretchers. The courier guided me to the one 1st class compartment, and when I got there I found to my dismay that I was next to the German courier plus wife and companion. There was a sudden and frantic move to another compartment which I shared with six Greeks, one of whom spoke a little French. I sat in great discomfort and watched the lovely Greek countryside slip by: we proceeded very slowly. There is only one railway and it crosses many bridges. Why the Italians have not blown it up, I cannot imagine; supplies, reinforcements, in fact the whole Greek effort would have been checked or, at least, seriously delayed, had they done so. At Tatoi I saw the very English faces of some of our grand airmen, and I called out to them. The hours passed; I was cold, uncomfortable, apprehensive for my bags. I occasionally had desultory conversation with my well-meaning but highly smelling companions. The little stations where we passed were crowded with wounded; everything looked bare, except for the olive trees. Somewhere we were greeted with frenzied cheers – Klissura had fallen into Greek hands and the lovely church bells were pealing in triumph. The Greeks in my compartment kissed each other. Joy triumphant. . . . At last I fell asleep, huddled in my fur coat, but clutching my diplomatic bags all the while.

12 January *The Palace of Beli Dvor, Belgrade*

Half dead with fatigue, hunger, thirst and sore bottom I arrived at Belgrade at 6.30. A Courtier met me and I was whisked to the Palace: grave sentries saluted, and the ADC on duty conducted me to my room, the same as I had last Easter. I went at once to bed and rested for an hour while my things were unpacked and breakfast was brought. About nine o'clock there was a knock on my door and the Regent walked in, half-dressed, wearing a dressing-gown. We fell into each other's arms, and hugged each other. He seemed cheerful but said he was distracted with work and complications. I was overjoyed to see him . . .

The Palace is smooth-running, perfect, luxurious, with too much food and drink . . .

After luncheon the Regent and I had a long talk. He is

violently anti-German, cannot abuse them enough, and is well on to their intrigues and double-dealing. He has turned against the whole race; but he is in a difficult position politically and geographically, and cannot enter the War – yet. But he says he is helping Greece as much as he can in little ways. He mistrusts his Croatian advisers who at any moment are prepared to break away from him, and certainly would not follow him into war. He is playing for time; until we are more powerful. Meanwhile he prayed that England would not do anything rash like sending troops to Greece, which would only bring the Germans southwards farther into the Balkans. He dismissed King Boris (of Bulgaria) as a rogue. Carol (of Rumania) as a fool.

At 6 o'clock Ronnie Campbell,[17] the Minister, came to be received in audience and they were closeted in Lord Chesterfield's library for a long time. As I went up to dress the Regent rushed into my room, shaking with rage, and told me that a proposition had come from the Foreign Office that a United Balkan front be proclaimed. Wavell, so Campbell told him, would be in Athens tomorrow. The Regent and Campbell had had rather a heated argument, and it seems the highly strung Paul had eventually shouted 'This stinks of Anthony!' I could not understand his anger though I appreciated his reasoning. He believes, and so does General Metaxas, that such a declaration would be a direct challenge to Germany, and that she would invade Yugoslavia at once – perhaps bomb Belgrade tonight. Paul wants to preserve peace at least until he hands over his country, which he feels he rules only as a trustee, to young Peter next September.

Later in the evening he calmed down; but he complained bitterly of our Foreign Office, and of the mistakes we had made in the past.

13 January *Belgrade*

It is very cold and there is snow everywhere, but the Palace is warm, and the food incredibly luxurious. The cellar comes from Voisin.

15 January *Belgrade, The Palace*

I feel I ought to think about my return arrangements: how I

17. Mr (later Sir) Ronald Campbell, Minister at Belgrade, 1939–41; subsequently Ambassador to Egypt, 1946–50.

dread the long trek, and my arrival back in England. The Regent I find more and more vague: he seems to have somewhat lost his grip on things; though he remains completely loyal and loving. Princess Olga this afternoon showed me their air-raid shelter, a subterranean affair of immense size with bathrooms, its own electricity, kitchens, etc. But all the time there is an ominous atmosphere of feckless politicans, and, in the evening with the lights still blazing, one wonders when the enemy will decide to attack?

16 January *Belgrade, The Palace*

The Regent is so angry over Wavell's visit[18] that he has retired to bed – also he has a cold in his left eye. He is convinced that by our actions we shall draw the Germans south into the Balkans. He is quite unprepared for war.

Beli Dvor is the perfect house: it is too exquisite to be a Palace, for Palaces usually are hideous. Lying about, too, there are many of my presents, a Lamerie gilt coffee pot, always used; snuff boxes; a silver seal box I sent out this Christmas, whilst on the dining table are always four Adam silver candle-sticks which I gave to the Regent in 1935 . . .

Later, a royal car took me to the Legation where I lunched with Ronnie Campbell, the Minister, who asked me a hundred questions about the Regent's intentions next September. In a world crisis, with war threatening, it would be unwise, he insisted, almost impossible, to hand over the reins of power to a boy of 17. I agreed to try and persuade the Regent to 'stay on'. Campbell wanted to know why he had reacted so violently to Wavell's visit to Athens, and I explained his point of view with which, I half suspected, Campbell agreed.

19 January *The Palace, Beli Dvor*

I spent the whole day with the Regent, sad, lonely and affectionate: we were quite on our old basis of firm friendship and trust. . . . The splendour prevails, the over-eating goes on but I have the curious empty vacuum sensation of being on the edge of a volcano which may erupt tonight.

18. To Athens.

20 January *Train between Salonika and Athens*

Last evening the Regent tried to persuade me to stay another week; but it is always a mistake to alter one's plans and perhaps spoil a perfect visit: besides I must get back to England. Many good-byes: for a second I saw tears come into Princess Olga's fine eyes; she is usually so undemonstrative. She came down to the entrance hall with me and I was miserable; what would she and I go through before we meet again? We each have our problems, and are cast in too high positions to be left alone by destiny. ... Then the Regent came running down the stairs and he clasped both my hands in his, and we walked out on to the portico, surrounded by the eternal unsmiling sentries. 'Good-bye, Chips, I fear I may never see you again', he murmured, and I heard him call out as the car moved off 'Good-bye Chips'. Alexander[19] was standing with him, and I drove away from my greatest friends with a heavy heart. At the aerodrome I was met and conducted to a comfortable Lockheed, a luxurious one which is used sometimes by the Prime Minister, but belongs to the King. We took off about 10.30 and I was faintly apprehensive both of the pilot's capabilities and of Greek gun fire ... but we crossed the Greek frontier without incident although there seemed some doubt as to whether the authorities had been warned. About two o'clock we were at Salonika where the heat was intense. The Greeks (I am beginning to dislike all Greeks) refused to allow the plane to proceed without the permission of the Minister concerned, which, in war-time, would take several hours to get – so I decided to go to Athens by train.

The railway station at Salonika seemed as confused as ever; however I got a corner seat, and had no hostile courier to contend with, and so slept peacefully, with my diplomatic bags stowed above me.

21 January *The Legation, Athens*

Bored, bearded and travel-stained, I arrived at Athens where Legation officials awaited me. ... In the evening Lilia Ralli took me to an enjoyable Greek cocktail party. Philip of Greece was there. He is extraordinarily handsome, and I recalled my after-

19. His son, Prince Alexander.

noon's conversation with Princess Nicholas. He is to be our Prince Consort, and that is why he is serving in our Navy. He is charming, but I deplore such a marriage; he and Princess Elizabeth are too inter-related.

22 January *The Legation, Athens*
Lunched at Princess Nicholas' with the King and Crown Prince Paul, who was in Naval uniform, and I thought over be-jewelled, with his several bracelets and rings. His wife, Frederika, has improved, and is pretty but Teutonic. I like her, and see that she has immense character: she will need it for her role may become extremely difficult. We were just the six. I reminded the Crown Princess that the last time we met was at a dinner party in Berlin at General Goering's where I had sat next to her. She looked vague. She is madly in love with her large poop of a husband.

23 January *The Legation, Athens*
A hilarious lunch with the Crown Princess, with wonderful food, in their hideous villa. The Greek family live simply: they are an impoverished lot and have not the riches or the dictatorial powers of the Yugoslavian dynasty. I parted from them with real regret, and Princess Nicholas nearly broke down as I kissed her hand and helped her into her car. Shall I ever see her again? Life is emptying.... My Athenian interlude has ended.

25 January *The Embassy, Cairo*
General Wavell asked me to go and see him; he was shyer this time and more silent and made me so; yet I felt a wave of sympathy between us.... The General advised me to go to Palestine, and then sat down and wrote a letter of introduction to General Neame, the VC, who has the Palestine Command.

26 January *The King David Hotel, Jerusalem*
Before dawn Peter [Coats] and I drove to Heliopolis and were soon embarked in a Lockheed, and, after a quick flight, landed at the Jerusalem Aerodrome which is some eighteen miles from the town. We were met by untidy, officious Jews speaking Bowery English; soon we were driving through Palestine. It

seemed a fascinating country with its vineyards, sunlit orange trees, goats and hills, and the cypresses and towns reminded me of Calabria. It was warm, even balmy and there are precocious blossom trees already in bud. At length the pale pink town of Jerusalem was before us with its dust and donkeys, its dark-eyed women and walls. We drew up to the King David Hotel and at once I fell in love with it: next to the Ritz in Paris, it surely is the world's best hotel. Our rooms looked on to the Garden of Gethsemane and the Mount of Olives. . . . We went for a walk and it was bewildering; noisy Arabs argue, Jews bargain, the Mouskys are a hive of life. We wandered about until the evening copper light fell upon the walls which seemed to glow with history. I was moved.

28 January *Amman, Transjordan*

We left at 8.30 and drove across part of Palestine, crossed the famous Allenby bridge and were soon in Transjordan, which is even more romantic. No Jews, less sophistication and wilder country. . . . Jerash, the ruined city, is splendid in its desolation, and the ruins are immensely impressive. We clambered about amongst the once stately temples, saw the mosaiced floors and frescoes, took photographs and, at length, had an excellent picnic lunch in the Forum. Not a sound, nor a human, broke the warm peaceful silence.

29 January *RAF Mess, Ma'an*

After calling on Mr Glubb,[20] a little quaint person who has succeeded the famous Peake Pasha – we left for Shouneh to lunch with the Emir [Abdullah] of Transjordan who is camping with his followers near the Dead Sea. We were received by an ADC, and the Prime Minister and conducted to the largest tent where His Highness awaited us. He is about 58, a large genial man with a beard, and dressed in a blue robe. A great gentleman with the grand manner. We were placed on chairs, he occupying the centre one, and conversation – and orange juice – flowed for an hour. The Minister of Education [Samer Bey] acted as inter-

20. The famous Glubb Pasha, Chief of the General Staff, Arab Legion, 1939–56.

preter, thus giving us time to think up the next compliment. The Emir is violently pro-British and was rivetted by my accounts of the air-raids, etc. He was delighted when I told him that the Egyptian Embassy (in London) had been bombed. He loathes Egyptians. We made immediate friends, and finally rising, before going off to pray, he removed a cornelian ring from his finger and put it on mine saying, 'Young man, this ring has been in the family of the prophet, wear it; it will bring you luck'. Soon we walked to an adjoining tent, the Emir taking me by the hand, like a bride, the others following. Waiting for us were seven Sheiks who were presented to us. And a sumptuous repast began with the Emir and I seated opposite each other, and served simultaneously. Peter was on his left. Next to me was the local Chieftain, a very grand Arab with a lustful face and painted eyelids, a character straight from Lawrence. . . . Finally we took leave of His Highness all smiles and charm, and drove back to Amman where a curious trolley, a two-seater affair, awaited us. I sat on one seat, the Minister of Education on another; behind us there was an armed guard and a basket of chickens (ugh)[21] – and we were off. The trip took four hours or more, and was cold and dark. We were actually on the Amman-Ma'an railway made so famous by T. E. Lawrence, who seems to be a somewhat exploded myth in these parts.

30 January *King David Hotel, Jerusalem*

Up early, icy cold – we motored for nearly two hours, accompanied by Mr Fixit [Samer Bey] and escorted by the Sheik of Ma'an. At last we arrived at a Foreign Legion-looking out-post of a place, a high white fortress and were given coffee; coffee, always coffee in the East, and then mounted me on a horse. No-one hates horses as much as I. I prayed that I should not fall off or be terrified, and I wasn't. We left at nine, a strange caravan. The country was lovely, but the road winding and stony. We descended the whole way, and came at length to a sort of gorge where it was colder still. The over-hanging rocks were pink-ish: I was prepared to be disappointed. After some minutes in the gorge we emerged into the sun-light, and before our eyes was a

21. One of Chips's idiosyncrasies was a pathological horror of chickens.

pink baroque basilica of the greatest beauty. We dismounted – I gasped, I panted. It was breathtaking: 16th century baroque in manner and reminiscent of The Salute or any grand Venetian Church. We scrambled about like goats, went into raptures: at last we left and continued our journey, passing more ruins, until we were en plein Petra. To the right was a hill of carved-out houses, like Pueblo ones, and there were more palaces, more temples. All was pink. The sun was out, the façades glowed like tourmalines. There was a vastness, a stillness, something frightening about them and yet they breathed a gay aristocratic air of disdain and plenty and perfection. . . . I felt that we had reached the end of the earth: the summit of earthly peace and paradise . . . again we dismounted, and explored more temples, doorways, caves and arches. We came upon a few natives who handed us coins and fragments and we, ourselves, found more – meanwhile luncheon was being prepared for us, as we were the guests of the local Sheik by the orders of the Emir, who had himself telephoned last evening to Ma'an to enquire after our comfort. As we sat on a carpet surveying the classic scene and ate our luncheon of sheep stew, dreading being offered the eyes, we suddenly heard strange and plaintive shouts from on high. They came, as it was explained to us, from a fugitive from justice, a murderer who was pleading for mercy. He shouted from a high, inaccessible rock, and I was sorry for him. At last he went away and we went back to devouring our sheep – a very nasty dish I thought, though we plunged our fingers into it, and made the best of the feast prepared in our honour. Later, reluctantly, we left Petra with its pinkness, its queer atmosphere of elegance and light-hearted disdain, its remoteness. At the head of the gorge we left our horses, drove to Ma'an to the Sheik's slightly sinister house (all the door-knobs were shaped like hands), and we found the trolley awaiting us and started off in the gloaming for Amman, the Allenby Bridge and Jerusalem. One of the most fantastic and successful expeditions of my life was over.

2 February *King David Hotel*

We drove to Tel-Aviv which I thought horrible, overlooking a lovely blue sea, which reminded me somehow of Berlin in 1928 with its squalor and rude, unattractive people.

Back in Jerusalem, we paid yet another visit to the Church of the Holy Sepulchre and I prayed on the tomb of the Saviour for my little far-away boy, and prayed that my friends would come safe and unscathed through the war – this horrible war which I have almost forgotten for a few days.

5 February *The Embassy, Cairo*

This evening the Lampsons and I drove in some state to a cocktail party given on a Nile barge by the Australian General (Blamey) and Lady Blamey; and I was warmly greeted by Lady Wavell whom I now like enormously. She is a vague, motherly, lazy, humorous creature. The General calls her 'Queenie' because her name is Eugenie and she is said to be a God-daughter of the old Empress. . . . He, of course, is altogether more charming, more cultured, more silent – a very rare bird indeed.

There was an impressive dinner party at the Embassy to meet Mr [Robert] Menzies, the Australian Prime Minister. He is jolly, rubicund, witty, only 46 with a rapier-like intelligence and gifts as a raconteur . . .

Sun, oranges, ease, bad taste, heat, dazzling shops – how I love Cairo. It is the occidental-ised East, without the dirt of the usual Eastern town. I shall live here after the war, if we win it, which I think extremely doubtful in spite of the thousands of Italian prisoners, including Generals, captured every day.

7 February *The Embassy, Cairo*

I feel and fear that I ought to get back to England. Meanwhile the victories continue (Benghazi was captured yesterday) and we become correspondingly more popular with the Egyptians. . . . Today Cairo is en fete.

9 February *The Embassy, Cairo*

To Air House to dine with Longmore who had a banquet which had begun by being a small dinner for me. I was between Tedder[22] and Wavell, who was silent and bored at first. He only

22. Deputy Air Officer Commanding-in-Chief, Middle East, 1940–41; AOC-in-C, Middle East, 1941–3; Commander-in-Chief, Mediterranean Air Command, 1943; Deputy Supreme Commander, 1943–5. Created 1st Baron Tedder, 1946.

thaws gradually. I noticed that he focuses badly with his one eye and that he sometimes upsets things. ... After dinner we listened to the Prime Minister's broadcast which was none too well received, particularly his references to the Middle East. Then Wavell, who knew what was coming, hid behind a doorway. As the Churchillian compliments to him were handed out that magnificent language seemed rather forced, almost comic. I was embarrassed as the only English politician present. When the broadcast ended Wavell came and sat down next to me and we had a long conversation and he was charming, almost affectionate to me. After an hour Menzies rose and the party broke up; General Wavell offering to drive me back to the Embassy but I refused politely as I was already going with the Prime Minister of Australia ...

I cannot get over Wavell's modesty, his lack of surface brilliance, his intellectual detachment and seeming boredom with military matters. He is on a high scale and as great as he is charming.

10 February *The Embassy, Cairo*

Only a few more days. ... It is decided; I am to fly home with Menzies and Donovan.[23] I ought to be thrilled; instead I am bored by the prospect of such close proximity with the great. We leave on Thursday, probably. My entire Egyptian episode has been enthralling and successful beyond every expectation.

13 February *The Embassy, Cairo*

Accompanied by Madame Sirry, the gay alert wife of the Prime Minister, and Bob Menzies, I went shopping in the Mousky. We had two amusing hours together and I piloted them to the best shops. Menzies wanted to buy a present for his wife and at last decided upon an emerald brooch in the shape of a peacock. There was much Eastern haggling and at last I got it for him for £45. He was enchanted. I was called Excellency everywhere.

14 February, St Valentine's Day *The Palace, Khartoum*

About 12.30 we arrived at Khartoum. ... We were whisked off to

23. Colonel Donovan, President Roosevelt's personal observer in Europe.

the Palace and rested for two hours and then had tea on the lawn of the Palace which was Kitchener's house and is huge, but there is no real splendour. It is built on the actual site of Gordon's original house.

Thus ends my fabulous Egyptian visit.

16 February *Guest House, El Fasher*

We took off at 1.30, all the Sudanese Government being lined up to see us off. Menzies is a sympathetic travelling companion, highly intelligent, but he looks much more than his 46 years. . . . He says he does not intend to be blitzed by Winston, but he will be.

19 February *Palace Hotel, Estoril, Lisbon*

A dreadful day, really, overcrowded and exhausting. . . . We arrived in Lisbon Bay before nine o'clock a.m., having dozed most of the way from Lagos. . . . Everywhere else there had been officials and red carpets, but here the Embassy had done nothing, and the Prime Minister of Australia was allowed to land like any ordinary traveller. Luckily I had my laissez passer given me by the Portuguese Ambassador in London: thanks to that our luggage was not examined. Menzies, hungry, unshaved and affronted, was in a rage. I tried to calm him by ringing up the Embassy but there was no reply. At last we got into a car, Menzies and I, and drove to Estoril where no rooms had been reserved. I made a row and procured one which we shared for a few hours . . . whilst he bathed I slipped below and rang up Noel Charles[24] and told him of the situation. Later Menzies and I had breakfast together, and Charles, sleek and apologetic, arrived. The Embassy obviously had been caught napping. The Hotel is full of spies, impoverished grandees and nondescript people, including Rothschilds down to their last two millions . . .

In the afternoon I went to Queluz. The Palace is a dream of pink paradisical beauty, like a seraphim asleep. . . . The sophisticated garden, the tired statues, the tiled canals, all too rococo and beautiful: it makes the Trianon seem tawdry, even Bruchsal look

24. Sir Noel Charles, Minister at Lisbon, 1940–41; Ambassador to Brazil, 1941–4.

rough. Aged Infantas still inhabit the wings. I was in a daze from the heat, the pinkness, the faded splendour . . .

Back to Estoril to bathe and drink cocktails with the Australian Prime Minister, and drive him to the Embassy . . .

I fear I am reluctant to return to beleaguered Britain.

20 February *Belgrave Square*

I was called at five in Estoril, not by the waiter as arranged but by the loud complaint of the Duchess of Santona, next door, who was called by mistake instead of me, and drove alone to the airport, as Menzies was not yet up. A long wait for him, the luggage and the light. There was some doubt about the weather, and whether we should get off. However we did, before eight – and all the way back to England as I dozed over 'War and Peace' I wondered what disappointments, what problems, what difficulties will I find awaiting me? No matter what happens – and it may be much – I shall have had one of the happiest, most successful and glamorous trips of my life. And I owe most of it to Peter, who was the animateur, and to both Rab and Harold who made it possible . . .

The excitement of Menzies' Australian entourage was touching to see as they approached England for the first time. We came down at Poole and were met by the same officials who saw me off on 17 December. The Kangaroo party disappeared and I chartered a car for £8 to drive me to London. England was cold and dark – blackout again – and my gaunt woman driver drove recklessly. I was wretched to get back, and I heard the sirens as we approached London. But I found Rab and Harold dining at my house, and the warmth and affection of their welcome cheered me. Rab is now Acting Foreign Secretary but he exhaled an atmosphere of gloom and disappointment with the recent attitude and activities of the Prince Regent.

3 March

My dinner for the Prime Minister of Australia. Mr Menzies arrived on time and my dinner party was a huge success from the very start, one of the gayest and most riotous festivals I have ever arranged. There was a round table; too little to eat but much to drink, the three supreme ingedients of gaiety. Menzies told lengthy stories with great gusto and imitated me in the Mousky of Cairo, etc. He is immense, a raconteur . . . full of sense and charm. 'Shakes' Morrison came in for a drink afterwards and added his curious flavour to the banquet.

4 March

All day in my twin haunts, the FO and the H. of C. The Foreign Office, having longed for Anthony Eden's return, is now both bored and disappointed with him; apparently he is nervous, exigeant, fretful and the FO boys are pining for the Halifax days again.

7 March *Kelvedon Hall*

Never had I had so depressing a centenary! Only a short note from my mother-in-law to cheer me.

I came here with Christopher Hussey, editor of 'Country Life' and he took notes for articles. We talked of Edward Marjoribanks with whom he once shared digs, and of Michael Davies (Barrie's ward) who was his other great Oxford friend. I lunched once in the early summer of 1920 or 1921, with Michael Davies, a friend of his, Edward Marjoribanks and my beloved Ivo Grenfell. Michael Davies and a friend whose name I forget, went off on a bathing expedition whilst Edward, always hard-working, retired to his classics. Michael and his companion were drowned near Nuneham: Ivo and I heard the news when we came back late in the afternoon. Ivo was killed in 1926 in a motoring accident, Edward shot himself in 1932. Of the five, only I survive in this horrid world.

9 March *Kelvedon*

Last night's raid was really serious. Buckingham Palace was badly hit, and at the Café de Paris, over eighty people, including the Manager, were killed.

London presents a melancholy appearance this morning – un vrai visage du lendemain.

I came to Kelvedon in the afternoon and now regret doing so as it is so noisy; planes everywhere, and bombs falling – 10.05 It is maddening and nerve-racking. Tonight has decided me to let this house to the Red Cross.[25] I can no longer cope with it – an awful bang! Are we the target? Is the beam bent over Kelvedon? The dogs are fretful.

10 March *Belgrave Square*

All day in Southend where I received many people and attended an important luncheon of prominent businessmen. . . . Back to London in time for a bad raid. I care now very little whether I am killed or not, and I shall not go down to the cellar. . . . Declension, declension, all is going.

12 March *Farnham Park*

Winston, looking truculent and cross, made a statement in reference to the Lend and Lease Bill; he sat up late last night redrafting it. He spends much time drafting. Words are his delight.

14 March

Rab lunched at the 'Mirabelle', and ran into Winston and Max Beaverbrook who were in high spirits and à deux. He sat with them for some time, noticed that the PM had two whiskies and sodas and two kümmels – now a very rare commodity. They decided that it would be an excellent idea if Anthony were to remain in the Middle East and orders are being sent off immediately for him to stay . . . that is if he has not already left. The PM was vituperative about everyone, but he kept his gems for Wavell who he likened to a man one might propose as President for the local Country Golf Club. He abused him roundly, and probably from motives based on jealousy. . . . I am angry with the PM for nicknaming my Regent 'Palsy' and for being abusive about Wavell.

19 March *London*

It appears that Anthony Eden is restive in Cairo and wants to come home.

22 March *Kelvedon*

The Yugoslavian crisis worsens daily: I feel that the Regent is

25. As a convalescent home; the offer was made and accepted.

playing for time while his army is being prepared. He has now turned out old Stoyadenovitch. I knew the old ruffian well; a dark, huge man, not devoid of charm, but pro-Axis in his leanings and shaky financially. He was personally pleasant, but later his head was turned by Italian flatteries, and he saw himself as a second Mussolini. Paul told me that after discovering his treachery one morning – the man was Prime Minister at the time – he waited until the evening, when all was quiet in Belgrade, and Stoya had gone to bed, to dismiss him from his post and have him arrested. This was some time ago. Poor Paul was considerable shaken by the man's treachery: but no Balkan can ever be relied upon.

24 March *London*

Atmosphere at the Foreign Office tense about the Yugoslavian situation. I cannot believe that the Regent, whom I love more than anyone on earth, could do anything either dishonourable or against the interests of England which he loves as I do. Beyond all else England has been the passion of his life . . . but even now I have not abandoned hope.

Rab came in from the Cabinet looking pale and tired, and when I said that the news looked bad, he answered 'Let's not talk about it'. Later, in my car, driving home through the wet and the black-out, he explained that he knew how much grief and disappointment the denouement would bring to me, but he had to tell me that tonight the Yugoslav Prime Minister Tsinovitch, and his Foreign Minister, Markovitch (ever the *Bonnet* of Belgrade) were leaving for Vienna to sign a pact with the Axis. That there were reported risings and disturbances in Yugoslavia. . . . My heart aches for my poor Regent: I know his minor weaknesses, his occasional Slav unreliability, but his character is loyal.

25 March *5 Belgrave Square*

A dreadful day. We heard confirmation of the news that the Yugoslav delegates left last night . . . and when they arrived at the station, the engine driver and others had vanished – the inevitable comic note in any Balkan drama. But eventually they left on their sinister errand. I went to the House of Commons, and was immediately surrounded. Jay Llewellin[26] remarked that my 'Garter' had gone West. I felt an unfriendly atmosphere. Harold Nicolson gave me a drink in the smoking room – a very depressing sign, for he always makes a point of being kind to his friends when they are 'down'. But I did not care, and my heart bled only for my poor distracted Regent.... It was only in the evening that we knew that Yugoslavia had definitely signed the pact; has the Regent gone back on his sentiments and declarations, or, has he had a complete nervous breakdown? I am distracted.

26 March *London*

The news is official: in spite of risings, protests and serious demonstrations in Belgrade and elsewhere, the Regent's emissaries have signed the pact, and have returned today to Belgrade...

Much talk of Yugoslavia's defection. The Regent's name is mud in this London which he so loves; he is stamped as a Leopold... as a traitor.

27 March

News reached the Foreign Office of more extraordinary events in Belgrade. There was a coup d'état in the small hours of this morning. Little Peter was proclaimed King, the Ministers who signed the pact have been arrested and the three Regents have resigned: Paul is reported to have fled; some say he has been arrested too. No-one knows what to think but there is much jubilation here. I can see the dramatic happenings in that Palace which I know so well; the boy King awakened; the generals taking control; the Regent at bay; it is pure Ruritania; and certainly a blow to German prestige. I rang up the Duchess of Kent to break the news gently to her... I telephoned Queen Marie of Yugoslavia and told her that her son has assumed power, sacked the Government, and entrusted the formation of a new one to General Simovitch. Rumours all day... I was relieved, and yet anxious for my poor Regent.

Tommy Dugdale, the dawning power, Rab and the usual group of laughing cavaliers and important politicians dined; it

26. Conservative MP for Uxbridge; Parliamentary Secretary, Ministry of War Transport.

was Tommy Dugdale's first incursion into the Belgravian Citadel of Chamberlain Conservatism, and he seemed curious about it. I think he expected serious stuffy conversation, instead he found us gay, and jocular and affectionate to one another and I think he went away impressed . . .

What a fall; I dread every wireless bulletin lest it tell us that Paul has been butchered in the traditional Balkan manner: as for myself all my Yugoslav fun is over; no more Bled, Brdo and Belgrade, no more palaces and pomp, no more Regent; I may never see him again.

28 March *London*

I woke early and eagerly turned on the wireless. No bloodshed in Belgrade . . . and the Regent left last night by train for Athens. . . . May tomorrow bring safety to my beloved Paul.

29 March *Coppins*

At the Foreign Office the feeling against the Regent is growing. He has done worse, they say, than Boris, Carol or Leopold: he sold out England. I cannot yet believe it and am distraught about him. He arrived in Athens today, and the King of Greece went to meet him. It must have been a frigid and dramatic meeting: the last time they saw each other was in my house.

30 March *Coppins*

The Kents left for Chequers – a little apprehensive, I thought. They have not seen Winston to talk to since before the war. They returned about six, worn out. Lunch at Chequers had been fairly successful – the Duchess sat between Winston and Winant, the dark American Ambassador to whom she quite lost her heart. She handled W. C., she told me, as an ally, not as an enemy, and he reacted and was pleasant. But he repeated that of course Prince Paul could not possibly come here. It was being arranged to send him either to India or to South America. (It will kill him, I fear.) But he went on to say that efforts would be made to make him comfortable anywhere he was sent as a sort of semi-prisoner-of-State, and added, 'He has very loyal friends'.

All Fools' Day *London*

I was nervous about my reception at the House of Commons, and was relieved and surprised to be received as a sort of hero: several Members congratulated me on the recent coup in Yugoslavia: it seems that someone had started the hare – and there is nowhere on God's wicked earth anywhere where hares start and run so quickly as in the Lobbies of the Mother of Parliaments – that the Belgrade Revolution is a result of my trip to the Balkans! . . . Lady Astor rushed up to me, screaming 'I don't believe that Prince Paul did anything wicked'. So did others . . . but the Prime Minister, whom I happened to run into several times, did not smile at me . . .

The Bath Club has been burnt almost to the ground, and not by enemy action: no-one knows the cause. They employed four fire-watchers who observed nothing until too late. One more of my haunts is now no more: how transitory everything is. I am in despair: no Honor; my baby in America; now the Regent dethroned and cut-off from all communication with me. Gone, too, are the Chamberlain-Halifax days when I basked in the favour of the great.

I drank before dinner with Bob Menzies at the Dorchester. His Yugoslavian mot about 'robbing Paul to pay Peter'[27] has gone around London; it always irritates me.

3 April

I am convinced in my heart that Paul behaved as he thought best for the welfare of his country, and a long perusal of the telegrams confirms this theory . . .

At the House of Commons I had several conversations with Members inducing them to remove Questions about Yugoslavia – I have never had a failure yet all these years.

5 April

Virginia Woolf is dead, a grey, highly-strung woman of dignity and charm; but she was unstable and often had periods of madness. She led the Bloomsbury movement, did much indirectly to make England so Left – yet she always remained a lady, and

27. King Peter.

was never violent. She could not stand human contacts, and people fatigued her.

6 April *London*

I turned on the early wireless and heard that Germany has declared war on both Yugoslavia and Greece. I foresee terrible complications, and the immediate spreading of the war. Belgrade has been bombed already, and I thought sadly of beautiful Beli Dvor with its exquisite contents, and the Sèvres dinner service made for Madame du Barri: it was last used when the Regent entertained Teleki, the Hungarian statesman who has recently committed suicide. Life becomes increasingly drab and horrible.

7 April *London*

I walked to the Foreign Office where there is an atmosphere of great depression partly attributable to the invasion of Greece and Yugoslavia, but also to the imminent return of Anthony Eden, who is due back on Wednesday, when the Prime Minister wishes to exhibit him in triumph . . .

A cable has just come from Princess Nicholas in Athens saying that 'all well – Love'; this, of course, is an inspired message from the Regent. I am infinitely relieved.

9 April *London*

A gloomy, dejected day . . . I hurried to the House in order to hear Winston make a statement on the course of the war. The moment was ill-chosen, indeed: he had tabled a resolution thanking the Armed Services for what they had done in Africa – just as news of defeats[28] is pouring in. I arrived late, just in time to hear him refer to Paul as 'a weak and unfortunate Prince'.

Rab, still acting Foreign Secretary, went to a late Cabinet. The situation is very grave, and there is a tendency to blame Wavell who, after all, only obeyed – and reluctantly, I have reason to believe – orders in withdrawing his forces from Libya and sending them to Greece. Meanwhile the Italo-German combined forces rush on in Africa, though Rab says we shall hold Tobruk, and that Egypt will be safe. I wonder?

28. In North Africa.

10 April *London*

The Foreign Office was in a state of excitement as Anthony Eden, Dill and Co all arrived back. Their great trip has certainly been a failure. Why not leave the prosecution of the war to Generals? The Prime Minister sent a special train, which cost the tax-payer £250, to Plymouth to bring him to London. An ordinary train was leaving within an hour!

11 April *Good Friday*

Rab accompanied Anthony Eden to the Cabinet to hear his apologies: certainly he has brought back nothing but disaster. The military were much criticised, particularly by Menzies, it seems, who was present. Wavell is down and is, so A. E. reports, dejected.

12 April *Esplanade Hotel, Dover*

I came down to Dover to see Alan [Lennox-Boyd]. The town is full of military and many houses have been hit by shells. The Lord Warden Hotel is now the Headquarters of HMS 'Wasp',[29] the torpedo-boat in which Alan is serving. Alan leads a dangerous life: last night he was sent to the French coast, shelled Boulogne and got back safely. I cannot imagine a more horrible existence; and he does not look well, or enjoy it.

This ghastly little pub has been shelled and there are no windows in my room. Every few minutes there is an 'alerte': the atmosphere is much the most war-like I have come across.

The Regent has been sent to Egypt.

13 April, Easter Sunday

As I was dressing Alan burst in; he is on half hour's notice, and must stay near his boat. We breakfasted, and went to the Lord Warden Hotel where we gossiped. About 11 o'clock we walked down to the jetty where his torpedo-boat is moored, and at that very moment planes appeared, guns roared, everyone ducked, a balloon came down, and in the midst of the excitement – my baptême du feu – I saw thirteen parachutes descend; they were mine-laying ones. Alan jumped aboard and called out 'good-bye'.

29. 'Wasp' was the HQ base of a flotilla of MT boats.

It was one of the most exciting five minutes of my life. But active service, most decidedly, is not my line.

15 April *London*

I dined with Bob Menzies, and went with Jay Llewellin and Harold, not expecting so brilliant a gathering, as we found fifty men, all the Government, Simon and Portal, etc. I had half-an-hour with Bobberty Cranborne about Paul; he still believes in him and has done everything possible to plead his cause (not very successfully so far) with Winston. ... He ... promised to meet me in six months' time when we could review the situation. I then had a long talk with General Dill, the CIGS, about Wavell. He was delightful; but isn't he a bit too mild for the job? He told me that Wavell has been both to Tobruk and to Athens during the past ten days – he was fairly optimistc: but on the whole there was an atmosphere of intense gloom re the Libyan and Balkan situations. Jay Llewellin told me that he had said to Beaverbrook as he went to the fatal War Cabinet Meeting when it was decided to send troops to Greece – 'Remember three words: Gallipoli – Narvik – Dunkirk'. Beaverbrook had been impressed but later repeated that it was hopeless to stand up to the Prime Minister and that no one ever did except Portal and Wavell. What a terrible error in strategy. I also talked to Winant, who apparently knew of me well and proposed himself to dine one night. He is dark and magnificent looking; but shy and difficult.

22 April *London*

Wavell is in Greece where the situation is, I fear, hopeless. ... Paul and Olga leave on Thursday afternoon for Kenya ...

I went to the House of Commons, or rather to Church House where we now meet as the Palace of Westminster has been damaged again. Winston announced that the Navy had bombarded Tripoli and he did it deftly, thus disarming a somewhat hostile House.

23 April *London*

I met Anthony Eden in the House and he was charming, said 'Bless you' three times, gave me messages from the Lampsons, etc. I asked him to get a Privy Councillorship for Miles Lampson, and he agreed to do so: he had not thought of it. Thus the meeting, which I somehow dreaded, passed off extraordinarily well.

24 April *London*

The political atmosphere grows more tense . . . there are rumours that Anthony will leave the Foreign Office, etc. As Eden is down I thought this an opportune moment to be friendly and so – meeting him in the passage – I asked him to dine next Wednesday, and he has accepted . . .

The House of Commons is restive and the Government's popularity is declining, but the Prime Minister's position seems secure. There was a leader in today's 'Daily Mail' attacking Anthony: it must have been inspired by Winston – perhaps as a ballon d'essai, as I discovered that Esmond Harmsworth dined with him at Ditchley on Sunday night. Is Winston preparing to throw Eden over if the going gets too hot?

29 April *London*

Anthony Eden, Jay Llewellin, Harold, Rab and I dined. The feast was by way of a reconciliation between Anthony and me, and I was determined to be decent to Daniel as he entered the lion's den. He walked here from the Foreign Office with Rab, and was immediately charming, with his fluency, and his glib descriptions of his expeditions to Greece, and conversations with Wavell. He rarely drew breath and drank much. We had claret and Krug 1920. It was a perpetual flow of conversation for which he apologised; but he did the trick: we were reconciled and I agreed, without saying so, to support him next week, when he will need it most. He said 'Bless you' – a mannerism of his, I should think, a dozen times. I found him fluent and facile and the evening was a huge success. But more than ever am I convinced that it was an unforgiveable fault on the part of the Government – or rather of Churchill's, since he IS the Government – to send him abroad on so important a mission though no doubt he did his best. Foreigners find him frivolous and light-metal. It is only in England that he has a following.

The Regent and his family have arrived safely at Nairobi. . . . They are being treated as 'privileged prisoners'; later they will be sent farther south. No-one hits a man so hard when he is down as do the English – but no-one does it for so short a time. In a few months' time Paul may be a hero, or, forgotten.

30 April *London*

I walked a bit in London and was horrified ... the capital looks like a battered old war horse. St James's Palace is the worst and the most poignant. ... All the big houses overlooking the park ... Spencer House, Bridgewater House, Mrs Macquire's, Stornoway House, Esmond Rothermere's – all badly battered. The Press Lords seem almost to have been singled out for attack.

Winston made a statement to the House about the evacuation from Greece: it has been less of a disaster than we feared, for over 45,000 men have got away. The House, whilst restive, was relieved. Anthony also made a statement reading out a message from the Greek Government agreeing to, indeed suggesting, the withdrawal of our troops.

1 May

I went to the House to do some lobbying for Anthony Eden, to smooth his path for the big Debate when he will be under fire on Tuesday. My dinner-party, if it did not heal certainly went a long way to patch up a wound in the Conservative Party.

Harold [Balfour] came in before dinner and whispered to me that the Government changes are to be announced tomorrow: Max leaves Aircraft Production, and becomes Minister of State, a sort of roving commission which is scarcely promotion. Brabazon succeeds him. An unknown Mr Leathers[30] is created a Peer – made Privy Councillor and becomes Minister of Communications. Poor Ronnie Cross is to go to Australia as High Commissioner! Dégommé. I told Rab that he would soon be sent to the Falkland Islands, and he was annoyed.

6 May *London*

The first day of the great Debate: and I wonder will Anthony

30. F. J. Leathers, adviser to Ministry of Shipping on matters relating to coal, 1940–41; Minister of War Transport, 1941–5; Minister for Co-ordination of Transport, Fuel and Power, 1951–3. Created Baron, 1941, and Viscount, 1954.

survive it, or rather would he have survived had it not been for 'our' sudden and unexpected decision last week to support him? He opened the Debate with an appallingly bad speech; no cheers greeted him and he gave a dim account of his travels and failures. He sat down amidst complete silence. I have never heard an important speech so badly delivered: and Duff Cooper said afterwards that the most damaging speech against the Government was Anthony's. He was followed by a series of speakers all of whom attacked him and the Government. Maurice Petherick said that he wanted a Panzer Government, not a Pansy Government: the whole debate was acriminious and rude, rather than particularly damaging. . . . I rushed about doing yeoman service to Anthony who said I was 'Angelic'. I wanted to be friends with him but could not help taking some secret delight in his discomfiture. Winston looked uncomfortable and aware of Anthony's shortcomings.

I despaired of England and of democracy all day, and yet I seldom enjoyed a day more, thanks to the intrigues.

7 May *London*

In attendance on Anthony, and he was markedly cordial, even grateful. He took his Questions and at twelve o'clock the big Debate was resumed. Lloyd George fulminated for a full hour: he was weak at times, at others sly and shrewd, and often vindicative as he attacked the Government. I sat immediately behind these three gentlemen of Westminster, and watched Anthony chew his nails as he whispered to Winston who was obviously shaken, for he shook, twitched, and his hands were never still. He kept up a running flow of commentaries and, indeed, he was right, for L. G.'s attack could help nobody except the enemy, as he was even rude about Turkey and America. Several times the Prime Minister rose and contradicted him; and several times, too, Anthony and Winston turned to me for confirmation of statements mentioned by L. George. I was very conspicuous. I enjoyed my role, for it is a year ago today that we had the great Norway Debate which brought about the fall of Mr Chamberlain. Today was different; again the Government was attacked but the personal position of the Prime Minister was not in question: Anthony was the victim and he was rattled, even pathetic. Yet I could not but experience a rather subtle pleasure in the proceedings: he was my Chief, so I was loyal; he has been my friend so I was indignant; he has also been my enemy, so I was enchanted and I half agreed with his attackers. Soon after 4 o'clock Winston rose, and never have I heard him in such brilliant (although sometimes irrelevant) form; he was pungent, amusing, cruel, hard-hitting and he lashed out at Lloyd George and Winterton with all his inimitable wit and venom. He was completely at his ease and enjoyed himself: a magnificent effort, and he tore his opponents to shreds and captivated the House. When the Division came the figures were 447 to 3. A triumph on paper, but in reality the Government has been shaken and both Anthony and Winston know it. These two days are the thunder before the real storm which I predict will break in July. Everyone went away exhilarated . . .

I had Winant, the American Ambassador, to dine with Geoffrey Lloyd; Jay Llewellin – now a Right Honourable; Harold and Rab. Winant, with his ebony locks, his farouche charm, his Abraham Lincoln ways and inarticulate sincerity, completely seduced us all . . . he stayed until 11.30 and was fascinating but he did not seem as pleased to see Alan as I had supposed he would: during dinner it came out that they had differed over Franco. Nothing so divides people, not even Munich. Never have passions run so high on an issue.

12 May *London*

I left the lovely May countryside with regret and drove up to London; where I found burnt bits of paper fluttering about in the street, and broken glass everywhere. The rubble and debris are heaped high in the streets. I tried to get to the House of Commons but the crowd was so large I could not fight my way through; but I could see the huge hole in the Westminster Hall roof. I met Jim Thomas who tells me that the Chamber is gutted: no more shall we hear fiery and futile speeches there . . . gone is that place, as I always foresaw. Itself the cradle, the protector of democracy, in the end it went a long way to kill what it created . . .

I met Leslie Belisha and he walked with me for some time; he was vitriolic about the Government. The country would soon wake up and realise that speeches were not victories he said, and that we were drugged with Winston's oratory. He is gloomy about the future; and sees little hope if we continue as we are now doing. He is very anti-Russian. Rab, curiously enough is not, and still flogs his red horse.

There is an extraordinary rumour at the Foreign Office that a German peace envoy has arrived, and that he has some connection with the Duke of Hamilton.

13 May

The wireless announces that Rudolph Hess, the third and most important personality in the German Reich, arrived alone and by plane in Scotland on Saturday night. . . . A most hazardous and remarkable performance. All day people talked of a crack in the Nazi Government but I do not believe it. Hess once invited Honor and me to lunch in Berlin when we were there for the Olympic Games; we refused – but I remember that 'Duglo' Clydesdale, as he then was,[31] did go, as did Pat Jersey. The world does not know that the Duke IS thus concerned in the story. He came to the Foreign Office yesterday and spent an hour with Anthony.

14 May

A stupendous letter came from Peter from Cairo describing in vivid melodramatic language his trip to Greece with Wavell, the day before Greece cracked and collapsed. It is one of the finest letters I have ever had from him and he gives rivetting details of the visit of the 'Robinsons'[32] to Cairo. As I was devouring it, a telephone call came from Anthony Eden asking whether he might dine? And though I felt socially bankrupt and longed to be alone, I agreed, and collected Rab. He and Anthony walked home to Belgrave Square and we all drank too much – champagne, burgundy and Kümmel, and got heated and so argumentative that Rab tried to stop us. Anthony Eden seemed against all Kings, but I retorted that they were bulwarks against both dictatorships

31. The Duke of Hamilton.
32. A 'code' name for Prince Paul and Princess Olga.

and socialism. At last at 11.30 he left – to join Winston. The PM certainly keeps his henchmen up until all hours!

15 May

I woke early with the dead, doomed feeling that I had been foolish last night, and it was with some trepidation that I waylaid Anthony at the House; but he was affectionate and said that he had 'never enjoyed himself more'. So that passed off. ... Anthony made a brief statement about our relations with France which have become acute during the past 48 hours, as the Vichy Government have agreed to allow the Germans to use the Syrian air-bases. Is this the prelude to war with France?

18 May

In my loneliness I have been brooding over Peter's letter: the Regent, he tells me, seems to have little idea, little realization of what he did: is he then mad? He sent me a hundred messages and, as his plane took off, leaving Europe and the past, for Africa and obscurity, he was still talking of me ... Peter's letter almost broke my heart.

19 May

A letter which the Duchess of Kent has had from Princess Olga from Athens goes a long way to vindicate the Regent. It appears that the whole Greek Royal Family went to the station to meet the Regent's party on their arrival from Belgrade. There had been no real difficulty about their departure from Yugoslavia; they travelled in their own train in dignity and safety. Princess Olga's long letter, which is an historical document of importance, goes on to describe how young King Peter had been with her throughout the day of the coup d'état, and knew nothing of the proclamation which he was supposed to have signed. Nor did he broadcast: the new Government had arranged for someone with a voice slightly like his to speak. It is a fantastic story. I had the letter copied by my secretary, and the Duchess is sending a copy to the King tonight: I kept one, which is in the Bank.

20 May *London*

The long-expected attack on Crete has begun with parachutists and air-borne troops arriving in large numbers. No-one knows what the outcome will be ... General Freyberg is in command ... the King is still there; the Crown Prince has arrived in Alexandria. ... It has been decided to send them to South Africa, rather than to bring them here. The invasion of Crete is regarded in some quarters as a dress-rehearsal for the invasion of England.

I walked to devastated Ebury Street, past George Moore's house where I often used to go and see that old pink petulant walrus: it still stands; and curiously enough, as I passed it I heard – there are no windows and the door was half-broken – the tinkle of a telephone – a telephone was the one thing he would never tolerate: messages had to be sent in from a neighbouring chemist's. He used to say that a telephone distracted him, but others were convinced that his ban on them was to prevent Lady Cunard from ringing him up ... I see what he meant.

David Margesson dined with me alone and I built up Wavell tremendously and said that he was *adored* in the Middle East, and that to change him would almost cause a revolution amongst our troops. He listened, admitting all I said, but added that Winston and Wavell did not hit it off, and that Wavell came off very badly in Committee. But he inferred that no immediate change was contemplated.

24 May *Kelvedon*

I came here alone having refused five week-end invitations, to the Kents, the Kemsleys, Loelia Westminster, Mrs Greville's and Jay Llewellin. There is a Chips boom on ... but I have been through so many.

27 May *London*

Winston made an announcement at the end of Questions, a guarded statement to the effect that 'A great German battleship' had been disabled, was a wounded mallard, etc. A few minutes later Brendan Bracken hurried into the Chamber (Church House still) with a bit of paper which, after he had climbed over the PPS's, including myself, he handed to the Prime Minister. The PM fidgeted and at last, after a brief delay, owing to procedure, got up for the second time and told us of the sinking of the crack German battleship *Bismarck*. The House cheered – and for a moment forgot Crete.

29 May

The Cabinet have decided to clear out of Crete; but the news is not yet out.

1 June *Kelvedon*

The big news this morning is clothes rationing. Oliver Lyttelton is only going to allow us 66 coupons per annum. A suit takes 26. Luckily I have 40 or more. Socks will be the shortage. Apart from these, if I am not bombed, I have enough clothes to last me for years . . .

The evacuation of Crete is announced and we are told that over 15,000 men got away in our ships. I doubt whether the defence of the island was even worthwhile. It may have delayed the attacking forces in their downward march but it means also a further decline in our prestige. British Expeditionary Forces are now known as 'Back Every Friday'!

6 June *Kelvedon*

On all sides one hears increasing criticism of Churchill. He is undergoing a noticeable slump in popularity and many of his enemies, long silenced by his personal popularity, are once more vocal. Crete has been a great blow to him.

13 June

Harold went to Shoeburyness in a special train with the Prime Minister, Beaverbrook, Archie Sinclair and others, to inspect tanks and the new anti-aircraft guns and devices. How luxuriously the PM lives, a most lavish lunch and grand train. 'Baron Berlin', as Lindemann[33] is called was, of course, there too . . .

There are rumours of an imminent German-Russian war and huge German concentrations of troops are reported all along the Russian and Roumanian frontiers.

15 June *London*

A lovely English day but my miseries are many. I am haunted by the unhappiness of poor Paul and Olga languishing 70 miles from Nairobi. Their pathetic letter took over a month to arrive. People

33. Professor Lindemann's elevation to the House of Lords, as Lord Cherwell, had been announced on the previous day.

in Kenya and Government House have been beastly as only the English middle-class can be! What can I do to ease their position?

20 June *Pyrford*

Russia will be invaded on Sunday by Germany – if he is successful Hitler will be Master of Europe.[34]

1 July

At the Foreign Office I heard that General Wavell has been removed. I could not get the rumour confirmed, but came home miserable.

2 July

The dreaded blow has fallen: I awoke and saw 'Wavell Removed' in large letters in every newspaper. I feel indignant and revengeful.

I feel this blow acutely. First the Regent shorn of his pomp and power – and now Wavell, who has been sent to India,[35] a sacrifice to Winston's personal dislike. No General in all history has had so difficult a role, fighting on five fronts and harassed daily by contradictory cables.

15 July *London*

Our days at the Foreign Office are ending and I am wretched, yet relieved. I came there on 7 March 1938, full of hope and promise of happiness. I have learned much and been considerably disillusioned. Owing chiefly to neglect of my work since October, due to various personal reasons, I have not been an outstanding success recently – I fear not enough to qualify me for the office which normally I should have had. Life is a disappointment.

I called on the Amerys and sat with them for an hour. Leo listened as I praised Wavell, and told me that after dear fat Lampson had broken the sad news to him, adding banally: 'You could have knocked me down with a feather'. General Wavell's only comment was 'Some feather!' Terse and true.

34. Chips's information was exact. Germany invaded Russia on Sunday 22 June.

35. As Commander-in-Chief.

16 July

If Rab goes to the Colonial or Dominions Office I remain with him. If however, he gets to the Ministry of Health, Labour, or Board of Education I leave him, as the boredom would be too terrible. I really could not cope with school-mistresses and children in provincial towns.

17 July

I walked to the Office – for the last time. Soon it will not be mine to go to. However the break will come at a psychological moment. . . . Rab and I worked late tonight. . . . He was loyal and affectionate tonight, but we both knew that we shall soon separate.

18 July *Pyford*

This evening a telephone message from the Obese Almighty came asking Rab to come to No. 10 (the Annexe really) at 5.40, and Winston offered him the Board of Education which he accepted willingly. A mistake, I think, as he is now in a backwater. . . . Brendan Bracken goes to the Ministry of Information to replace Duff who is being sent – so I am told – to Singapore.[36] What will happen to me?

21 July *London*

I spent the day at the Foreign Office packing up. . . . I was wretched, and could not bring myself to say goodbye to anyone. I have loved the office, though in my ironic moods I have called it 'Bourbon House' . . . for they can never either forget or remember anything. Back to Belgrave Square, depressed and down.

22 July *London*

I went to the House, feeling dépaysé, but I was embarrassed by the many questions: 'Are you staying at the Foreign Office?' or 'Are you going to look after little boys and girls?' etc. . . . As, evidently I am to do neither, I hedged, pretended to be gay – but soon I could bear it no longer and came away. I am no longer a

36. Duff Cooper, after an unhappy spell as Minister of Information, was appointed Chancellor of the Duchy of Lancaster and sent by Churchill to Singapore to report on the situation there. (See *Old Men Forget*, 289–313.)

PPS. I am no longer anything; I am a genius at finding other people jobs and advancing them but I push myself clumsily or insufficiently. I am out of the racket, which is always a bore. . . . Shall I go away and write, and bury my shame?

CHAPTER SEVEN

Dégommé: July 1941–April 1943

Chips was now, to use a favourite word of his, dégommé. He was no longer able to pick up the latest information at the Foreign Office, although his political and official contacts were still close, and he was still well-informed. He felt his official exclusion intensely. He kept his diary carefully throughout this period but the narrative is of less interest. I have accordingly made some selections to form, as it were, a number of disconnected snapshots of himself and his life at this time.

1941

26 July *The Bothy, Culham Court, Henley*

I drove here to this dwarf Thames-side Trianon to pass a simple Sunday with Raymond Mortimer. The house is pink and pretty, and costs £10 a year in rent. I bathed in the Thames; it looked very Corot.

The Bloomsbury boys stimulate me with their eager quick alert intelligence and their new books and utter detachment from life. Roger Senhouse is also here. He is one of the most charming people alive, a very old and gentle friend.

29 July *London*

A dreary lonely day. I went to the House of Commons, which I now dislike: it has an opaque glow and I seem to see it through a different lens; everything is out of focus. The PM, sober and determined, made an important speech. The theme was production, and it was meant to be a reply to his critics. He held the House which was interested certainly, but not enthusiastic, though there were few of his usual oratorical tricks. Someone has told him that we are weary of his eloquence.

22 August *Kelvedon*

All day alone. It has been wet, and the rain always lures me out-of-doors. I went for a walk in the woods, overgrown and alive with pheasants and partridges and stinging with nettles. The views are surprisingly rural still, and much as they were centuries ago. I got soaked, picked roses and plums and gazed at my fields which, with their pretty cattle, looked like a picture by Paul Potter. I thought much. Is my life really over? Have I reached the end of my development? I do not think so really: after a blow, one must have a pause. One must mark time, and that I am doing. Perhaps I shall marry again, for I should like children about me, more and many children.

14 September *Pyrford Court*

A pleasant day. The Halifaxes arrived at Pyrford and I spent much of the day with him: he is so long, so lean, so distinguished and so bored. He looks more clerical than ever. I pleaded Paul of Yugoslavia's case, and he advised me to write and tell him not to worry: that all would in time be forgotten and forgiven. Halifax was friendly, even affectionate and he was smooth, simple and gracious; but it is always difficult to make any impression upon her. He was rivetted by 'Dorian Gray' and kept looking at an old copy and quoting from it, discussing the famous ritualistic passage with his youngest son, Richard, an immense auburn young subaltern. What a strange book for Lord Halifax to read, now, after all these years. After a picnic lunch he retired to work (or to sleep as I suspected) but kept saying: 'Chips, don't let me miss anything. Come and call me if there is any fun!' By fun he meant a long walk to the farm and back . . .

17 September *London*

Harold [Balfour] came to my room early this morning. He had been up until nearly 3 a.m., and had sat in Beaverbrook's long room at No. 12 Downing Street with him, David Margesson and Brendan Bracken. About midnight there was a tap at the door and a muffled throaty voice was heard: 'May I come in?' It was the Prime Minister dressed in his famous purple siren-suit over which he wore his heavy coat, and smoking the inevitable cigar. He was in an angry mood. . . . He began to abuse everybody and everything, and said that we were at war with almost every country 'including Australia'. Then he attacked the Army, said that it always refused to fight, and thus roused David Margesson to a spirited defence of his Department! Winston went on, 'The Army won't fight': 'The Army always wants more divisions, more equipment.' Said that he had 'sacked Wavell', and now he would 'Sack Dill and go himself'. Dill was no use, little better than Wavell, etc., etc. He ranted, roared, and walked about the room. Brendan and Beaverbrook were not in the least surprised, David was annoyed but Harold, new to this technique, was amazed. . . . Beaverbrook tried to apologize to Harold for the Prime Minister's strange conduct and the PM had said to him 'I hope I did not go too far in front of Balfour?' and Beaverbrook had reassured him that all is well.

18 September

As I was sitting with my always delightful in-laws the telephone buzzed and I was flattered and enchanted to hear General Wavell's voice. I hurried around later to the Service Club to see him. He looked rested and well and his face lit up with his charming shy smile. I sat with him and his son, Archie, for an hour, we drank whisky and chatted, and I found Wavell, the great soldier, the War's hero, as quiet, modest and as unassuming as ever. He told a tale or two, and said how busy he had been, and asked whether anybody knew that he was in England. I laughed, told him that half London was aware of his visit since he lunched out and walked in the streets. He is quite unaware that he is a popular hero. I understand why it is that the Prime Minister dislikes him: he is too silent for Winston's more flamboyant taste.

4 November

Jay [Llewellin] told me of his week-end at Cherkley with Beaverbrook, who was asthmatic, but all smiles. Dinner at nine, a long film and conversation until 2 a.m. or after. . . . I could not stand it.

11 November *London*

In the Commons the Prime Minister was in a bellicose mood: he answered Questions ungraciously especially one about the 'Prof',

Lord Cherwell. Alan and I went to the smoking-room and ordered brandy and ginger ale. Nearby sat Sir Waldron Smithers,[1] an ass of a man, alone. Suddenly the Prime Minister, attended by Harvie-Watt,[2] entered and they, too, sat down. Suddenly the Prime Minister saw Smithers, and rose, and bellowing at him like an infuriated bull, roared: 'Why in Hell did you ask that Question? Don't you know that he (Lord Cherwell) is one of my oldest and greatest friends?' The unfortunate Member for Chislehurst tried to defend himself – but the Prime Minister, still shaking, refused to listen or be pacified, and went on 'You make protestations of loyalty – I won't have it. President Roosevelt was most impressed by him.' And so forth – It was an extraordinary scene. The 'Prof' otherwise 'Baron Berlin', or, correctly, The Lord Cherwell, has long been a subject of speculation to the House, and from time to time there have been questions and veiled innuendos reflecting on his Teutonic origin. But Winston's almost blind loyalty to his friends is one of his most endearing qualities.

14 November

A long, cold day at Southend, too boring to chronicle. But one gets nearer to the war in one's Division: the cold, the black-out, the unhappiness, dislocation and misery of people . . . the sacrifices and separations. I fear I live in a gilded world.

'The 'Ark Royal' has been sunk off Gibraltar, happily with almost no casualties.

4 December

Today I had one of my usual 'dust-ups' with Lady Astor. How I loathe the interfering termagant. She came up, without the slightest provocation, and attacked Geoffrey Lloyd for not being in uniform. 'You ought to be ashamed of yourself.' Geoffrey was mute and cowed but I sang out at her, 'Well, you are nearly seventy so they can't get you!' She flushed with rage, and walked away. Later she accosted me, and asked why I always attacked her.

1. Conservative MP for Chislehurt.

2. Mr George Harvie-Watt, Conservative MP for Richmond; Churchill's Parliamentary Private Secretary, 1941–5.

I retorted that I was flattering her as she did not look a day over sixty.

8 December *Leeds Castle*

As I lay awake in bed last night something prompted me to turn on my little miniature wireless, a present from Alan from New York. I was flabbergasted to hear that Japan had declared war on the United States and Great Britain, and that bombing of Honolulu had already begun. So this vast war spreads. America's participation of course ensures final victory for the Allies. ... I rushed to Geoffrey Lloyd's room, and awakened him with the startling news, then I told Adrian and Olive Baillie who were still up ... much talk, and finally to bed again about 2 a.m. this morning. An historic hour ...

The House of Commons, so quickly summoned, was crowded. There was an immense queue and I rescued Pam Churchill[3] and led her into the inner lobby. Coming back I actually collided with her father-in-law, Winston, who, closely followed by Clemmie and Harvie-Watt, was pushing his way through the crowd. And after Prayers the Prime Minister rose and made a brief and well-balanced announcement that the Cabinet had declared a state of war to exist at 1 o'clock with Japan. Nobody seems to know whether this recent and dramatic development is helpful to the Allied cause or not. It means immense complications, but will probably bring about America's immediate entry into the war ... Geoffrey Lloyd whispered to me how lucky Winston was. Now. Libya will be forgotten. Russia saved the Government in July; now Japan will do likewise ...

The war has taken a tremendous leap forward, and deepens in intensity. As I write I am listening to President Roosevelt's address to Congress – it is remarkably clear and audible.

9 December

I dined in with Harold and the auburn alluring Pam Churchill. ... Kathleen Harriman and her dark, distinguished father, Averell, also came and we drank one of my last magnums of Krug 1920. Averell is sallow, distinguished and pleasant. Much talk

3. Wife of Randolph Churchill.

of a possible Japanese invasion of California. Averell hopes that the American cities will be blitzed, so as to wake the people up. He attacked the American isolationists bitterly.

10 December *London*

A dreadful day of despair and despondency. The Prime Minister stalked into the House and seemed anxious to speak. After a preliminary parley and getting up and sitting down twice, he announced the sinking of both the 'Prince of Wales' and the 'Repulse' at Malaya. A most shattering blow for our Pacific fleet and Naval prestige. . . . A wave of gloom spread everywhere. The House was restive, the Government suddenly unpopular . . . Dejected I came home and gave luncheon to the Iveaghs who had been at the Lords. They, too, were depressed. I could have cried.

At dinner Mrs Greville said, 'If only the Prime Minister could have permanent laryngitis we might win the war.' An allusion to his unfortunate reference on Monday to the menacing presence in the Pacific of our battleships at this convenient moment. A heart-breaking remark viewed in the light of subsequent events. Thousands of lives lost – it is terrible.

11 December *London*

Just before twelve o'clock the Prime Minister, looking worn, entered the Chamber and announced that Members of Parliament would be allowed a free choice between entering the Armed Services or attending to their Parliamentary duties. I was relieved, for I know how utterly hopeless I should be in uniform, although at times I hanker for it. I am too old, too flat-footed, too unfit and too temporarily hopeless – besides, I am gun-shy. Then he made a perhaps over-long statement, a spirited yet slightly defensive explanation, of the recent Cairene communiqués which were, everyone now realises, over-enthusiastic and misleading. By putting too much emphasis on this feature of this extraordinary week the Prime Minister increased the very suspicions which he wished to allay, and I watched Members shift uneasily as they do when they are irritated, and think that they are being imposed upon. Then he turned to the larger theatre of war and he had his usual exhilarating effect on the House. . . . Later I read on the tape that the City had reacted quickly. Yesterday shares fell dramatically and Guinness dropped to 90 from 96. Today they are recovering.

As I sweated in a Turkish Bath this afternoon the evening newspapers were brought in, and I read that both Italy and Germany had declared war on the United States. It must be galling for that great Republic to be treated like Poland or Czechoslovakia.

15 December *London*

After three days of 'do's' in Southend, I was on my way back to London in the train and discussed myself with an unknown man who was unaware of my identity. He said that I was well-known as being 'democratic' and 'not a snob' in my constituency. I was tempted to get him to put this rather unorthodox view on paper, but refrained.

18 December *London*

The war outlook is bewildering, certainly . . .

To the House, where we sat in Secret Session. There was continued criticism of the Government, a barrage of questions, bickering and obvious dislike. It was another Narvik night. The Government, as it is, is doomed: I give it a few months. No Government could survive such unpopularity for long. Of course, the Members behaved rather like schoolboys with the Headmaster away and no doubt Winston, on his return,[4] will, as usual, harangue us, and possibly pacify the House once more – for a short time. I want Winston to remain Prime Minister certainly, but he should reconstruct his Government.

30 December *London*

Anthony Eden's great visit to Moscow is now announced, and he is now back. I gather that there was disagreement between him and Stalin on the future of the Baltic States, which Russia has annexed. His statement has caused some amusement. He described his talks with Stalin to the Press as being 'full, frank and sincere.' Good God!

The Coopers are being bombed at Singapore.

4. From Washington.

31 December
A desperate, incoherent scrawl has come from the Regent, forwarded to me by the Duke of Kent.

1942

5 January *Belgrave Square*
I gave one of the most réussi dinner parties I have ever given, the clou being Stewart Menzies who is 'C', that is, head of the entire Secret Service. . . . As we were finishing dinner Bill Mabane arrived, accompanied by Mr Attlee, who is always pleasant in society. . . . The Acting PM left about one a.m. saying that he was going back to sleep in his dug-out, and to read the latest telegrams which ought by now to be arriving from the USA. 'Winston will just be getting up from his Washington nap,' he laughed. He was extraordinarily amiable.

8 January
The Government had another bad day. Without Winston it would not last a week; and I wonder whether even he will be able to save it?

9 January
Seventeen MPs dined last night at the Dorchester, collected by Erskine Hill,[5] who sees himself as a sort of Lord Younger[6]. Anthony Eden was present, and seemed upset when every MP present told him that the Government was doomed. It was no use, they said, the PM coming back and making one of his magical speeches. This time, it would serve no purpose. The Government must be reformed, and that soon.

13 January
A tiresome letter has come saying that the Kelvedon gates are to be requisitioned; they were expensive, and I shall regret them. All

5. Alexander Erskine Hill, Unionist MP for North Edinburgh since 1935 (died 1947).

6. Lord Younger of Leckie had been Chairman of the Conservative Party in the early 1920s.

iron is being collected and the first drive is to be made in Essex. The gates are very fine. Black, with gilded wreaths and fasces and my monogram on shields; damn.

16 January *Leeds Castle*

... The old Duke of Connaught is at last dead, aged 91. He was handsome, amiable, courtly, stupid, inclined to attach too much importance to etiquette and military detail, such as buttons and decorations. I used to meet him at luncheon parties long ago at Lady Essex's house – in the early '20s. Of recent years he has been ailing, but I wish that my child had seen him – I could easily have arranged such a meeting, and it would have been an interesting link with time since the old Duke was Wellington's godson and sat on his knee. Indeed he was named Arthur after him.

18 January *5 Belgrave Square*

The newspapers splash the Prime Minister's return and his welcome, and all my agents report that he will defy, or at least forestall his critics, by playing for time; he will ask the indulgence of the House and plead pressure of work, etc., before making any important statement. A wise course. Probably he is unaware how great the prevailing anxiety in political circles is.

20 January

At the House the Prime Minister arrived and was given a cheer, though hardly could his welcome be called enthusiastic – civil, perhaps. He looked fat and cross, and when he rose to answer his questions it was obvious that he was disappointed with his reception, and that he had a cold, since his voice was husky. Such was the reappearance of the great hero, and I was almost sorry for him. ... He has announced that he will make a broadcast speech next Tuesday, and the House took his suggestion ungraciously; indeed, Members were querulous but I remembered Rab's words last night at dinner when he warned us that Churchill is the greatest asset the Conservative Party has, and we had best exploit him. Rab said many wise things; how difficult it was for him to cooperate with Winston, etc.

21 January

Winston bowed to the will of the Members by withdrawing his motion for his speech to be broadcast direct. The feeling of the House was strongly against it; and in deciding not to challenge it, he has acted wisely. It is better to placate Parliament on a small matter than to have a row on a minor issue. The boys – the naughty boys – have won a round.

One hopeful incident occurred today; the Archbishop of Canterbury has resigned. This aged prelate has done irreparable damage to the Church of England; narrow, snobbish to a fantastic degree, cold, political, vengeful, he has emptied the Churches and alienated thousands of people. He has never been right on any issue, and is hated by Laymen and Ecclesiastics alike. His evil face, thin lips, hard, small, terrible eyes, are enough to frighten even an adult. Only his voice redeemed him, and his dignity – though it was the dignity of a Grand Inquisitor. Winston loathed him.

22 January

I picked up all the gossip. No. 10, now known as 'The Dixième Bureau', is in a flap. The 1922 Committee has sent an ultimatum, or at least a strongly-worded request, to the Prime Minister asking him not to insist upon a Vote of Confidence in the coming full-dress debate, as many Conservative Members would be obliged by their consciences to accept the challenge, and many more might abstain. At first the PM was adamant, but is now alarmed, though he still refuses to re-construct his Government. He may climb down, but he is in angry mood; the ineffectual Whips are in a frenzy and a first class crisis, no doubt chuckled over by the Germans, is upon us.

27 January

One of the great days in Parliamentary history is over, and it was a splendid spectacle. I went early. As I arrived, I met the whole Churchill family. Mrs Churchill, her hair grey now, was with Diana Sandys; both were hatless. Clarissa was with her father, Jack Churchill; Pam was not far behind, and she pressed my hand in her affectionate, conspiratorial way: immediately behind them, followed by his secretaries, came the Prime Minister.

He had his angry bull manner and seemed to charge into a rope barrier which he did not see; indeed, he very nearly toppled over it; he was greeted with perfunctory cheers, but when he rose, he quickly revealed that he was in high fettle, with his voice clear, and his manner confident. I watched the House; there was not an empty place, and I had to sit on the steps[7] between Anthony Eden and Brendan Bracken. The PM's carefully prepared speech rolled on like a vivid film, and it completely captivated the House for 90 minutes or more. I was won over, as were many others. Opposition was dead, or so it seemed. But perhaps he was just too long, for some Members left before he sat down, and when he did, the atmosphere had chilled. But another great Parliamentary moment had passed into history. ... The House emptied. The lobbies buzzed; one's first impressions were entirely favourable, but I soon detected an undercurrent of hostility, and of criticism, for he had mollified nobody. Soon the debate began to lose reality. ... Pethick-Lawrence was dull; Erskine-Hill (of the 1922 Committee) recanted and tried to insinuate himself in the Government's good graces; Herbert Williams openly attacked Winston, who by that time was sitting in the smoking-room, with his bull neck bulging over his collar, surrounded by Members. ... It is always a bad sign when the PM comes to the smoking-room; he is either angling, or anxious. I will not vote against the Government on Thursday, if vote there be. I do not think it would be in the interests of the country to do so. But why is the PM so unpopular in the House, he, a life-long House of Commons man? Perhaps his intolerance, his arrogance and his bad judgement are the reasons, and yet his many magnificent qualities are obvious to all.

28 January

The most colourful moment in today's debate was an excursion by Randolph Churchill[8], who was quick, witty and amusing and made the House laugh, although he added fuel to the fires of bitterness. ... And afterwards Winston remarked to Harold,

7. Of the Royal Throne; the Throne itself had been removed when the Commons took over the Chamber of the House of Lords in 1941.
8. He was MP for Preston 1940–45.

whom he met in the smoking-room, that Randolph had had a rough passage, which was true. I saw him again later – he was alone reading the 'Manchester Guardian', and he looked up and smiled at me, so I had a few words with him and conveyed that I would support him tomorrow; he at once became amiable and gracious, and we talked of Diana Cooper's homecoming, and I suggested giving a party for her; he half intimated that he would come, if he could. Several people watched me maliciously and then twitted me later about being 'in' with Winston. Yes, I have decided to go over to HMG, but only because I see no alternative.

29 January *London*

I went to the House; the Lords' Chamber, which we continue to occupy, was packed. Half a hundred Members had to stand; the Prime Minister was already speaking and again he held the vast audience enthralled. He was conciliatory, tactful – and, finally, successful. He spoke for 42 minutes and after glancing at the clock, sat down. The Speaker, in his tired voice, put the question twice and called a division. The Aye Lobby, or more accurately, the 'content Lobby', since it is the Lords, was at once so crowded that many of the Members were forced to wait in the Chamber. The six-minute rule was suspended and it was a quarter of an hour at least before we filed through; one good bomb would have destroyed the whole democratic apparatus of this country – or does Hitler think that the House of Commons is doing that on its own? When at last the figures were announced – 464 to 1 – there was a faint cheer. The victory is a triumph for Winston, though there was no alternative and he knows it. Nevertheless, he is the most inspiring leader we have, and the masses and the Americans both adore him.

1 February *London*

It is only lately, as the world plays Götterdämmerung, that I have been lonely; it is a new and distressing emotion and I realise that it will perhaps be my future fate. Only a few years ago I was handsome, lustful, a favourite at Court, a protégé of Mr Chamberlain's, a millionaire, happy at the Foreign Office; now I am none of these things. So I will now go to bed and finish

'Doctor Thorne', which I am enjoying for the second time. I am still a tremendous Trollopian, whatever else I no longer am.

2 February

Vsevelode,[9] who is a wine merchant, has had an SOS from Badminton for more hock; Queen Mary, it seems, drinks a half-bottle every night with her dinner, and has done so all her life; sometimes at luncheon too. And the stock of hock is running low in this country. I hear she still keeps up some state at Badminton where her tireless energy quite exhausts her long-suffering but devoted entourage . . .

4 February

I walked to the House where I quickly picked up the Government changes which have been rung tonight, and I congratulated Jay Llewellin. Surprised, he turned to me and said 'How did you know? I have only just left the Prime Minister'. So Jay is now President of the Board of Trade. Later the 1922 Committee was addressed by Beaverbrook who, with his curious Canadian accent, his small physique and dominating personality, soon captivated us all. He was confiding, charming and out to please – with the Ministry of Production in his pocket, I know. There are other changes but the consensus of opinion is that the reshuffle is inadequate and reminiscent of Mr Chamberlain's last, and fatal, attempt to re-organise his Government. The early edition of tomorrow's 'Daily Sketch' was sent to Lord Kemsley (where I was dining) and it contained a short, sharp leader story offensive to Mr Churchill. We persuaded him to eliminate it.

8 February *Queen's Hotel, Portsmouth*

We[10] drove to Hayling Island and called on Princess Yourievsky, whom I have not seen for 7 years. She greeted us cordially, pleased, I think, by our surprise visit. This daughter of an Emperor, descendant of all the Romanovs, lives in squalor and poverty which my £300 per annum makes possible. Otherwise she would starve. Her little house is horrible; and she has no

9. Prince Vsevelode of Russia.
10. Chips and his brother-in-law, Alan Lennox-Boyd.

servant of any kind; and has to look after herself in this cold. She is lonely, and over 60. But somehow she still exudes a certain atmosphere of grandeur, and still has her pearl ear-rings, the only tangible touch of the past. She chatted of her royal relatives, her various nephews and nieces, reigning still or in exile. She is an historic link, since she is actually the daughter of the Czar Alexander II, and great-great-granddaughter of the Empress Catherine whose name she bears. It was a depressing visit, but she was so cheerful that she has obviously achieved a certain philosophy of life. As we left her to her loneliness and drove away, I remarked that she is one of those people to whom every misfortune falls. She even found her last servant dead in bed a few weeks ago; and her three beloved Pekinese all have died recently.

12 February
The King of Greece and Crown Prince and others dined, and in spite of Royal unpunctuality, lack of servants and the depressing news, dinner was a success. The blue room shimmered in the candle-light, and looked more lovely than ever, since it is a touch tawdry now. I provided oysters, eggs and bacon and champagne – all rarities. Everyone was gay. . . . Then Harold rushed in at 10 o'clock, and whispered to me that the 'Scharnhorst' and 'Gneisenau' and other German ships had escaped from Brest, and that there had been a big naval-cum-air attack on them which had failed. Can we never do anything right, or even have a stroke of luck? I told nobody . . .

Singapore has practically fallen; only a few more hours are left to it of British rule. Already there are celebrations in Tokio. It is the most grievous single defeat since the fall of France. . . . What will happen now to Wavell and the Far Eastern Command?

13 February (Friday the 13th)
Woke ill and very sleepy, indeed, and my first thoughts were of last night's party, and then sleepily I stretched for the newspapers which were emblazoned with 'Scharnhorst' and 'Prinz Eugen' and 'Gneisenau' – and the whole story. Everything seems to be going against us. Then Harold rushed into my bedroom,

'Read this!' he said. He referred to a violently anti-Churchill, anti-Government leader in the 'Daily Mail'. It is the first that has ever appeared. Everyone is in a rage against the Prime Minister. Rage; frustration. This is not the post-Dunkirk feeling, but ANGER. The country is more upset about the escape of the German battleships than over Singapore. . . . The capital seethes with indignation and were Londoners Latins there would be rioting. I have never known so violent an outburst. At the House I heard that there is a flap on at 10 Downing Street and that Winston, angered by the 'Daily Mail' leader, is in a defiant, truculent mood. Attlee hinted to someone this afternoon that 'outside men' would be brought into the Government, that is non-parliamentary. And there is some talk about the formation of a so-called 'Centre Party' composed of Liberals, disgruntled Conservatives, etc., with Beaverbrook at its head.

15 February *London*

The hero of the battle of the Channel is Colin Coats, Peter's brother, who commanded the 'Worcester'.

17 February

The House of Commons was restless, crowded and angry, yet it does not seem to know its own mind. . . . The PM came into the Chamber and I saw him scowl. No cheer greeted him as he arrived. Nor as he answered Questions. He seemed to have 'Lost the House'. Then at twelve o'clock he rose and in a curiously nonchalant, indeed uninterested, manner, read a prepared statement about the passing through the Channel Straits of the German ships. He convinced nobody, and particularly his attempt to turn an inglorious defeat into a victory displeased the House. There was soon a barrage of questions. Several times the PM intervened and each time his reception was increasingly hostile; never have I known the House growl at a Prime Minister. Can he ever recover his waning prestige? He is such a Schwärmer that he basks only in approval; smiles and praise encourage him; criticism irritates and restricts him. Today the august assembly nearly blew up; he was only saved by several dull speakers who so bored the House (Hugh O'Neill and Gallacher, the Communist) that members began to file out in dozens. It was a disgraceful scene which lasted an hour and there was no dignity or force; all sense of reality seemed to have left the elected representatives of the people. We have the first dictator since Cromwell, and much as I distrust Winston (and I fear that he has the evil-eye, or ill-luck – certainly nothing that he has ever touched – Dardanelles, Abdication, India Bill, has come off well), I have even less faith in the Commons – a more moribund collection of old fogies and nit-wits I have never met. Eventually the House resumed its ordinary business after having extracted a promise for a two days debate next week from the Prime Minister. But he was obviously disgruntled and shaken by his reception. I felt sorry for him . . .

I called on the Coopers who came back last night from Cairo via Malta. Poor Diana, who loathes flying, and is always terrified, has flown right around the world, in itself almost a record. She was looking lovely, slim and glamorous and embraced me affectionately. Duff was amiable.

20 February

It appears that Max Beaverbrook, who seems disgusted at being dropped from the Government, will soon turn against it. He is going to America on some trumped-up mission, but really to heal his asthma and sooth his pride in Florida. During the recent crisis which is far from being over, he and Lord Camrose have supported Churchill, whilst the Kemsley, Rothermere and Astor press have been hostile and as critical as they dared. The Government is doomed.

23 February

The changes have been announced, and a wave of indignation has swept over London at the dropping of David.[11]

25 February *London*

I drank at the Dorchester with Mrs Greville who seemed ageing and silent, and the King of Greece, who told me that he could hardly look at food since it made him think of his starving compatriots. Dickie and Edward Mountbatten were also there, both

11. Margesson had been replaced at the War Office by Sir James Grigg, formerly Permanent Under-Secretary of State.

cool, chic and completely charming; Edwina M is now a complete Socialist, which for anybody in the position of a millionairess, a semi-royalty, and a famous fashionable figure, is too ridiculous. But she works very hard at the WVS and Red Cross. She looked a dream of beauty and seemed fond of Dickie. I went to their wedding, years and years ago.

2 March *London*

Rex Whistler has arrived to stay for a few days; elegant, vague, gentle and strange, like an exquisite goat, he is a delightful satyr, and full of charm. His newly-grown moustache lends him a French air. He is in the Welsh Guards, and is in charge of a tank. Anyone more unsuitable, I cannot imagine.

What should arrive this evening but a long typewritten letter from General Wavell; it was written at Batavia; and a most friendly, chatty missive, beginning 'My dear Channon' and ending 'Yours ever, Archie Wavell'. It is like having a letter from Napoleon, and I was touched, exhilarated and enchanted all at once.

7 March

My 45th birthday. From now on I shall live a grimmer life, spend less, be kinder, devote more time to my diary, my health and the House of Commons – my youth is over, faded, and I am kept alive now only by a desire to see Paul and bring him up well. I am ambitious to put my affairs, financial and otherwise, in order.

My mother's silence is strange; I am a little anxious about her.

11 March

Winston rose and without a preliminary cheer announced that important decisions had been made about India and that Cripps was going there at once (which I knew). The House appreciated the solemnity of the moment, and that our great Empire of India was perhaps to be bartered away.

19 March

At the H. of C. P. J. Grigg addressed the all-Party Committee, and his début was a dramatic disaster; he rose rudely and said grudgingly that he would attempt to answer any questions. No opening speech; no remarks – and he thus offended the largely-attended Committee; most of the audience got up and left as a protest. No Minister can live down a performance like that. Why he was not warned or advised, I don't know. Perhaps I am prejudiced, but I am prepared to think him a farouche and dreadful person. I walked away with Ernest Brown, who said he thought that Grigg could never recover . . .

I hear that Dickie Mountbatten is to have a new and most important appointment.

22 March

Walked in the Kelvedon gardens early this very sunny morning before leaving. The many trees and shrubs I have had planted are growing and the yews are doing splendidly. Even the copper roof to the swimming-bath pavilion is at last turning green – One day this place will be a paradise, I trust, for Paul. Today I thought much about my son and his future.

24 March

I lunched at the Spanish Embassy, where Mr [J. L.] Garvin, a colossal man in age, physique and mentality, was fascinating. He was anecdotal; and repeated to me many of the more out-worn Curzon stories, but was nevertheless diverting. He has only recently resigned the editorship of the 'Observer' owing to differences with Lord Astor. He maintained that 1942 is *the* year in the history of the world, the year that will decide the future for generations, perhaps centuries, to come. He thinks that Germany has had a blow in Russia from which she may never recover; with the flower of her youth sacrificed, killed and frozen. He compared the German-Russian campaign, to the Russian defeat in 1915 at Tannenberg. He was interesting, optimistic, and intensely critical of Lord Baldwin, whom he dismissed as a dangerous mediocrity with a fatal touch of talent. Had he been a greater man, either he would have been all right, or so unpopular that he could have been soon defeated; had he been completely incompetent, he could never have kept his high position; it was that fatal touch of talent . . . and England and the Empire and the world are suffering now in consequence . . . so he went on.

25 March

The PM arrived at the 1922 Committee today, looking shrunken and almost apologetic; yet I was surprised by the warmth of his reception, and he seemed much touched by it. I noticed that he saw I was not applauding – his eyes are often on me – and I hurriedly beat the table with my fist. The PM spoke for over half an hour and apart from attacking the 'Daily Mirror' (and I am with him there) told us very little. He wound up well; and made a dramatic bid for more loyal support. Indeed I was almost moved.

30 March *London*

We are living in a Gibbonian age – Decline and Fall, though the Prime Minister still repeats to his immediate circle that when he signed the Atlantic Charter, the War was on. That it is only a matter of time. This, he believes.

4 April *West Coker Manor, Yeovil*

Where I am staying with Violet Trefusis. Today Violet, Leslie Belisha and I drove to East Coker Manor, picked up Mrs Keppel, very Edwardian with her veil and gloves, and then drove to Wells, passing Glastonbury Abbey on the way . . . at Wells we went over the Cathedral, and then went to the Palace where we lunched with the Bishop. . . . Much talk of Barchester. 'There is nothing I like better than to lie on my bed for an hour with my favourite Trollope', the Bishop said, to everybody's consternation. . . . Mrs Keppel full of charm and vim. She sees much of Winston, but considers him 'bust' . . .

13 April *5 Belgrave Square*

At the re-opening of Parliament, the PM uneasy, halting, almost inarticulate, made a short, and far from comprehensive, or eloquent, statement about Singapore, Cripps and the recent loss of ships. He has lost his self-confidence and the House listened rudely.

17 April

Désœuvré and depressed, with nothing pleasant from any quarter. Life is all shadow. I envy Harold his active life. He is flying off today. I must expand and develop. I feel, however, that I am slipping, and have never quite recovered from the various emotional troubles which have convulsed my life these past three years.

19 April *London*

In the evening I walked in the gloaming through the Green Park, passing what was once my lovely and historic house, 21 St James's Place. I saw the vacant aching void of what had once been my home, the home too of Lord Harvey and Molly Lepel. It was where my little son, Paul, was born. Now all that remains is rubble, some remnants of the basement, and a few daffodils which I myself planted in the once so charming garden.

21 April *London*

Rab told me today that Edward Ruggles-Brise is dying. Old men who marry young wives always do. I must remember that.

22 April

I walked to the House half hoping to find Gerald Palmer, who has just returned from India with Cripps. I thought that possibly he might be my Mercury, and would bring letters from Delhi. As I entered the Chamber I saw him sitting on the PPS's Bench (where I lorded it so long) and looking up, he caught my eye, and his face lit up and he made frantic signals for me to go to him. I climbed over snoring Members, and finally reached him. He handed me an immense packet. I rushed with it to Rab's room, but he came in just as I was undoing it, so I fled to the library and wallowed in the luxury and fun of opening it. There was another historic account from Peter of his latest trip with Wavell to Maymyo and Mandalay . . . potted history, and then more about the beginning of the Cripps visit with what he described as 'dusky Metternichs prowling about, avid for power' (he clearly foresaw failure too). A wave of loyalty and affection for him came over me, especially as there were six packets of razor blades enclosed which are almost unobtainable at the moment.

In the afternoon I attended two enthralling committees. The first, the weekly Wednesday meeting of the 1922 Committee which was addressed by Vansittart. He was persuasive and less violent than usual, though he preached for nearly an hour about the iniquities of the German race, and how they can never be trusted, nor treated with, a doctrine of despair I thought. The large audience was interested, since he has charm and speaks enjoyably, but they were not especially enthusiastic. There was an interval during which I re-read my letters, and then I went back to the Committee Room just in time to hear Oliver Lyttelton speak to the All Party panel. He was gay, cynical, cheerful and rather over the heads of his many hearers. He painted a vivid picture of the Middle East, the complications, the Cairo Court and so on, and his rows and recriminations with de Gaulle. He was followed by Casey, his successor in Cairo. The Australian spoke well too, and with no trace of an accent but he is less brilliant than Oliver who, I think, has sized up the weakness of the institution of political life and the paucity of ability in the House of Commons. He has decided to capitalise all this, and perhaps make himself Prime Minister one day. But it is a pity that he must always turn a facile cynical phrase at the expense of our friends and allies, and indeed of everyone. It was, altogether, an enthralling afternoon.

23 April *Bognor*

The House went into Secret Session at noon, and Winston at once rose majestically and began his long review of recent events. He painted a magnificent and vast canvas. I went up to the gallery and . . . looked down on the crowded House. Every seat was taken. Black coated dullards, they looked, with only a light sprinkling of khaki among them. For nearly two hours the PM spoke with almost no interruption; it was a tour de force. No humour or tact, little oratory, no mea culpa stuff, but straightforward, brilliant and colourful, a factual résumé of the situation. Only at 1.50 when MPs began to think of their stomachs, was there any restlessness. His account of the situation was definitely encouraging and heartening, and we left the Chamber confident that the War would, after all, be won, thanks chiefly to the stupendous American production.

In the afternoon, I picked up a bag and came to Bognor on the 5.30 reading 'The Claverings'. It was cold but the countryside looked green and lovely with that curious English vernal haze. Diana Cooper, wearing amber slacks, met me in her little car, and drove me here. She looks a dream of golden beauty, and like Honor, she is now obsessed by farming. Still in my London clothes, I helped her to drive pigs, and feed rabbits. Then we walked to the water's edge which is framed in barbed wire, spikes, railings and what-not against a possible invasion. It looked formidable. 'If only poor Singapore had been like that' Diana sighed. She showed me her poultry and the swill for the pigs, of which she was very proud. The world's most beautiful woman showing off her swill. Then we dined quietly à deux, with a glass of vodka instead of a cocktail, and dined off onions and eggs cooked by her maid, and sat over the fire and gossiped. Diana was, as always, beautiful, delicious, simple and affectionate. As we talked we heard aeroplanes roaring overhead.

28 April *London*

To the House, where I heard Cripps make his statement on his abortive trip to India. He was clear, concise and convincing, but the House was bored in spite of his eloquence, as it always is with the fait accompli, or rather *pas* accompli. Ava Anderson was in the gallery; she has become, at the age of 47 or 48 a real beauty – pretty and provocative. Success does much to improve a woman's looks.

30 April *London*

Lunch with Mrs Greville in her suite at the Dorchester. The old lady received me, covered with jewels, sitting in her bath chair at the door, and she looked well though apparently she is always in pain and greeted me with the words 'Chips is my only vice'. It was a pleasant party. The Kents, she, lovely and amber-coloured, he in an Air Force uniform. . . . Both Mountbattens. What a dazzling couple they are. I sat between them and found Dicky much grown in stature since he took up his highly important, indeed vital, command.[12] But he remains simple and unaffected, and only when I talked of his nephew, Prince Philip of Greece, did his sleepy strange eyes light up with an affectionate, almost paternal light. Molly Buccleuch, in spite of just recovering from a tonsil operation, looked radiant but pretended to have caught a cold from walking for an hour in the Downing Street gardens yesterday, with Winston. Also, Brendan Bracken, bombastic, imaginative, and kindly, with his teeth blacker than ever, and his red hair greying. And the Duke of Alba. We stayed until 3. I felt sleepy after the rich food and Moselle wine.

I dined with Bill Mabane, to meet Lord and Lady Woolton. They are an amazing couple, bustling, dynamic, the New Order indeed, and immensely and comically impressed by their Peerage and position. Apparently before they made their great wealth, he was a Socialist and he even canvassed and spoke for Victor Grayson, the first Socialist MP. But nobody could be more Conservative or realistic than the ménage Woolton now. He wanted to keep his family name but the King demurred at creating a Lord Marquis. I much enjoyed them and their prattle . . . we talked coronets and ration cards the whole evening. We also discussed the new vitamin bread, the National Loaf and I asked whether it was really an aphrodisiac? His Lordship looked startled.

1 May *Coppins*

Geoffrey Lloyd dropped in, as he so often does, before I had finished my letters, and I walked with him through St James's Park. He seems to love trees, beauty and books, and longs for a cultured, leisurely existence. He is a rare creature. He told me that he had dined last night with Harold Mitchell, at the Savoy, a party of 14, including the PM, who happened to remark in the course of the evening that he had never read a single novel of Trollope in his life, which surprised me. Later I left with Alice Harding for Coppins, where the Duchess was awaiting us. Dinner was excellent and we had a delicious evening. Backgammon and gossip. The Duke kept me up (in a very cold room) until 2 a.m.

12. Chief of Combined Operations.

How gemütlich Coppins is, and how full of rich treasures, and gold boxes, étuis and pretty expensive objects always being exchanged or moved about. The Duke adores his possessions . . .

Her, I am completely devoted to. Her loyalty, her gentle sweetness and charm, which equals her beauty and her saintly character, make her an outstanding woman.

4 May *London*

All day in Southend, interviewing constituents. Amazing Balzac dramas unfolded themselves to my ears, and no doubt eventually to my pocket book.

5 May

To the House early as I had heard privately that there would be fun and frolic; and so there was. In fact a deplorable scene occurred. Brograve Beauchamp asked that the House go into Secret Session to hear charges of a serious nature against a Member. Geoffrey Shakespeare also made a statement naming McGovern. Most Members assumed that both charges applied to the same Member, but such was not the case. I was sitting next to Geoffrey Lloyd, joking about an announcement which appeared in this morning's press, about the arrival of an infant to Mrs Tommy Dugdale. On the front page of 'The Times' it is described as a son, and on another page as a daughter. Then the storm broke. Brograve Beauchamp rose and intimated that he wished to bring a charge against a Member for having revealed what happened at the last Secret Session. There was a momentary sensation and he was followed by Geoffrey Shakespeare who made a similar charge naming the Honourable Member for Shettleston [McGovern]. The House was soon in an uproar, and we at once went into Secret Session. Then followed an interminable foolish, farcical wrangle over procedure. I despaired of democracy or Parliamentary government and longed to remind the demented, as it seemed, assembly, that there was a war on, and that Madagascar had, that morning, been attacked by British forces. However, the scene dragged on. Tempers rose, and even the imperturbable Speaker seemed confused, since there was no possible precedent to help him, and we were, indeed, though clumsily, making history.

Cripps intervened several times and was, at least once, contradicted, by the irritated Speaker, who as usual tried to lower the atmosphere. The charge was finally made by Bro Beauchamp who related how he had been telephoned by a Doctor who reported that Edgar Granville, the Member for Eye, a National Liberal, had on last Thursday attended a cocktail party where he had quoted remarks alleged to have been made by the Prime Minister. The Doctor, who met him on that occasion for the first time, denounced him. The House was silent with stupefaction, for a second, since most people supposed that McGovern would be brought in, and no-one realised that there were two separate charges. Granville, looked very red and uncomfortable, then rose to make his statement, and he did it clumsily, convincing nobody of his innocence, which he did not even proclaim. He harped too long on the Gestapo methods employed in spying on Members of Parliament, etc., and soon lost whatever sympathy he may have had. He then withdrew, as is the custom, and once more there was a wrangle too tedious to chronicle, that he should be brought back. To this the Speaker consented, and I saw Bobbie Cunninghame-Reid dart from the Chamber to find him. (A few minutes later I met them together in the lobby, hurrying back.) More argument, and then I left, meeting Duff in the corridor. I told him the story and he was amused. He's very charming now and we have tacitly agreed to bury our ancient political hatchet.

7 May *London*

A big House of Commons day. First another long wrangle and investigations into an alleged indiscretion supposed to have been made by McGovern. He made a manly and spirited defence and when the division finally came, the voting was only 148 to 115 against him. A very thin majority. I voted with the noes as I have always had a sneaking sympathy for the ILPs who are usually sensible, always eloquent, and often charming. Then Winston suddenly appeared in the House, and rose at the end of the division and made a colourful statement about the British seizure of the Island of Madagascar, which capitulated today. He was cheered. I think he only comes to the House now when searching for kudos.

Eden's shares are very down just now, and Leo Amery is reported to have said that Anthony Eden, along with Walter Elliot, Shakes Morrison and Oliver Stanley, have joined the ever-growing group of ex-future Prime Ministers.

16 May

The beauty of Kelvedon this late afternoon almost broke my heart, but I felt so lonely. The fruit trees, the tulips and the lilac cast a spell on me. May is a miracle here . . .

I feel again the stirrings, the urge, once more to write. Shall I? And I fear that I have been corroded by wealth. I am Midas, I am a horrible Harpagon, and think only of money. But now having achieved my own financial goals, I only want money for Paul.

I slept fitfully. Simple food always gives one indigestion.

21 May *London*

Molotov arrived last night secretly in Scotland where he was met by the Royal Train, and brought to London. He is now hidden. Nobody knows of this, or hardly anyone. I had much pleasure in telling Rab this evening, who was astonished.

I went early to the House determining to speak . . . it was crowded, but uninterested and uninteresting. It is sad to see democracy slowly committing suicide, and every debate, I think, lowers parliamentary prestige. And there is so much political plotting at the moment, and of course the chief instigator is Max Beaverbrook. He cannot bring himself to forgive the Conservative party . . .

When the adjournment about retail shops came I went to my place and waited to be called; Member after Member spoke, but the Speaker ignored me. Suddenly I became shy and only wanted to bolt and after someone opposite got up I thought that the debate had ended and fled, relieved, from the Chamber. But I was wrong, as it was reopened and, feeling cowardly and disgusted with myself I came away and walked home. Later I dined with Helen Fitzgerald and David Margesson at the Dorchester. Gossip and politics, hock and seagulls' eggs.

Afterwards we were joined by the Butlers, who had dined with Sybil Colefax upstairs. She had had a gala, at 10/6d a head. She calls them her 'Ordinaries' and it is a wartime measure. Her dinner tonight was for the Mountbattens. We discussed the mysterious arrival of Molotov. I am sure that Anthony Eden has done this, and that a new Anglo-Russian Treaty will be sprung on the House, and the country during the Whitsuntide recess. It would be a dreadful mistake, a calamity, for the future of sinking England. Immorality in politics never pays, and to wink at the annexation of the Baltic States by Soviet Russia is too Jesuitical and shocking. . . . Victor Cazalet however, threatens to vote against the Government if need be.

22 May *London*

Diana Cooper rang up and asked whether she and Duff could stay the night and I was enchanted, and made arrangements accordingly. She duly arrived, lovely and radiant. She, Duff and I dined and talked. They are 'Anthony Adverse' and Duff says that he is an old donkey. He wrote him recently to protest against the proposed Russian Treaty, and he was indeed startled when I told him about Molotov being hidden somewhere in the suburbs. Duff was charming tonight . . . he didn't know about Molotov, nor that Gwilym Lloyd George is being heavily tipped for India, nor about the Beaverbrook plots, but I liked him quite enormously and we were suddenly at ease together.

2 June *London*

In the evening I dined with Esmond Rothermere at the Dorchester, and after dinner Duff Cooper appeared, who had been dining à deux with Winston Churchill, who told him the details, or rather the spirit, of the recent Anglo-Russian Treaty, still so deep a secret. The PM whispered that not even the Cabinet knew of it, whereupon Duff retorted, or so he said, 'Chips told me about it days ago'.

21 June

Tobruk has fallen, and Jay [Llewellin] thinks that this appalling defeat may endanger or even bring down the spineless Government. I doubt if silly Attlee will be able to hold the House tomorrow. The war outlook is bleak. Libya gone, Egypt and Suez threatened, Malta isolated and starving, the whole of the Middle

East in grave danger and the shipping problem desperate. But the public seems unaware of all this, and rants on about a Second Front.

23 June

I walked, in the heat, to the House and I found an atmosphere of disappointment, bewildered rage and uneasiness. There were all the signs of a crisis. Anthony Eden, who more than the Prime Minister, is reponsible for the present position for it is to him we owe the folly of the Greek campaign, remained at the House all day testing opinion. First there was an unreal hour during Question Time, while everyone waited for what really mattered – Attlee's statement. This he duly made, in his usual colourless style, and he really handled the House well, which was unexpected. Questions at first were restrained, given the dramatic circumstances and he almost got away with it. But towards the end of a wild barrage, John Wardlaw-Milne rose and demanded that the debate should take place immediately, suggesting Thursday as an appropriate day. Attlee refused, and intimated that it would be better to await the arrival of facts before trying to find out who was guilty, and that next week would be time enough. Obviously playing for time until the Prime Minister could get back. Wardlaw-Milne then threatened a Vote of Censure, and the House was electrified and cheered. The Lobbies soon hummed, and everyone I saw was suddenly as excited as an aged virgin being led to her seducer's bed. . . . Everybody agreed that Winston should cease to be Minister of Defence, and Belisha said to me 'When your doctor is killing you, the first thing to do is get rid of him'. Ernest Brown admitted that it was extremely difficult for 'those in the family' as he described the Government to be loyal to Winston. The House was in a ferment . . .

In the street I met Virginia Cowles, who was exceedingly cordial. We chatted, and she said that when we sent that mad expedition to Greece, it was the turning point of the war. I heartily agreed. She thinks the Middle East as good as gone, and added that Churchill and Government ought to go, but echoed the eternal cry 'but there is nobody else'. Always that – there *is* nobody else – if only Mr Chamberlain was alive. Many a Member who voted against him would willingly now withdraw his vote.

24 June

The House is still in a turmoil, and people intrigue in corners. Wardlaw-Milne will put down his motion, and the Government will survive, but scared and shaken ... I am still hesitating. I want to vote against the Government ... yet caution (or is it cowardice wedded to self-interest?) warns me not to. Perhaps I too will abstain. Meanwhile there is a pause in the battle in the Middle East, while Rommel masses his troops against the Egyptian frontier, which he will no doubt soon attack. Meantime the PM is flying back,[13] today I believe, to take charge of the crisis. It will be a battle, certainly, but one always gets back to the old problem, there is no alternative to Winston.

25 June

I got up (one must always get up) ... and walked to the House. It was still excited but the movement against Winston is subsiding and I have now almost decided not to vote against the Government. Both Rab and Hore-Belisha have urged me not to.

30 June

I attended the 1922 Committee, and Member after Member expressed the view that the big debate should be cancelled, as never had we been in more peril. The House was in a hubbub. But I now see that nothing will happen ... the PM will come down on Thursday, do his stuff, that is, make a magical speech, and will get a huge vote of confidence. He always does, and I personally would never vote against Winston to make Anthony King. ... Public anxiety is growing.

1 July

John Wardlaw-Milne moved his much publicised Vote of Censure in strong and convincing language today, and I watched the front bench squirm with annoyance. Winston looked harassed and everyone was emotional and uneasy. I thought it all rather horrible. Wardlaw-Milne held the House well, he was fair, calm and dignified, and he was listened to with respect, until he made an unfortunate suggestion, that the Duke of Gloucester should be made Commander-in-Chief of the forces. The House

13. From America.

roared with disrespectful laughter, and I at once saw Winston's face light up, as if a lamp had been lit within him and he smiled genially. He knew now that he was saved, and poor Wardlaw-Milne never quite regained the hearing of the House.

In the p.m. Oliver Lyttelton spoke for the Government and he made, as he afterwards remarked to Somerset de Chair, 'a proper balls of it'. His canvas was too large, he was too diffuse and altogether too unconvincing. He suffered a parliamentary setback and I did not wait to hear him finish, thus missed Clem Davies' novel suggestion that he should be impeached. I went to the Lords, which was also crowded, and there I was soon surrounded by all my friends, Camrose, Kemsley, Gage, David Margesson and my father-in-law all rushing up to ask how Oliver was doing, and for news of the Windsor by-election. I had the figures; a majority of 2,740 for Mott-Radclyffe. I saw Max Beaverbrook rise, and the Lords shivered a little, for he very rarely puts in an appearance. He looked puckish in his dark clothes, but seemed aged, though he spoke with punch in his usual exaggerated Canadian accent, he disregarded the usual polite forms of address to their Lordships, but he was effective, and spoke at great length to an enraptured audience . . .

2 July

Today Belisha made what proved to be a brilliant, eloquent and damning attack on the Government. He was skilful and deadly, and I admired his courage and accurate marshalling of the facts. Surely Churchill, I thought, could not answer him, but answer him he did, and for over an hour we had all the usual Churchillian gusto. . . . But his magic had no magic for me, we might as well have Macaulay or even Caruso as Prime Minister. He skated around dangerous corners, and by clever evasion managed to ignore the question as to whether he had ordered Tobruk to be held. Nevertheless he had his usual effect of intoxicating his listeners. I left before he sat down and went to the library, put my head into my hands, took a deep breath and prayed for advice. . . . The argument against voting against the Government is strong and, on balance, I decided I hadn't 'the guts', so slowly walked into the very crowded Aye Lobby to the derision of the few abstainers, perhaps 20 in all. I saw Winterton and Archie

Southby muttering to one another. They had abstained, as had Lady Astor, Megan Lloyd George and others who sat silent on the benches. I waited until the final figures were announced. 475 to 25, a Government majority of 450. The PM rose, looked up at the Speaker's Gallery, smiled at Mrs Churchill, and then walked out of the Chamber to go to the Smoking Room. As he left he received a polite but lukewarm ovation.

9 July

Before dinner Julian Amery,[14] who is the cleverest young man I have ever met, dropped in. He was scathing about the Egyptians and gave me much Cairene gossip. He thinks that Auchinleck is a greater personality than Wavell, but has nothing like Wavell's prestige or popularity with the troops. He reported a plot to bring Wavell back to Cairo. Meanwhile the position in Egypt remains much the same, we hold the enemy at El Alamein, and the battle wages furiously.

16 July

Mrs Neville Chamberlain and her step-mother [in-law], the aged white haired but exceedingly spry Mrs Carnegie[15] and Lord Halifax, bland and insinuating, the hard old hypocrite, lunched with me as did Alan and Patsy and Portia Stanley. Mrs Chamberlain talked of Neville, saying I was always his favourite amongst the young MPs and that he used to chuckle in the evenings, and repeat to her the silly things I had said. He was well aware of the affection I bore him. Mrs Carnegie must be nearly 80 since she was married in 1888 to Joe Chamberlain. . . . She is very Boston, is Mrs Carnegie, sheer Henry James – How many people can remember Gladstone?

4 August

I went to the House of Commons, which was in Secret Session, and Cripps clumsily announced to the astonished Chamber that Winston and Co are in the Middle East en route for Russia. Everybody gasped. The House of Commons is once more several

14. Younger son of Leo Amery.
15. Formerly Mrs Joseph Chamberlain.

laps behind London society, which is already well aware of the trip.

9 August

Leeds Castle, chez Olive Baillie. Only the flapping of the swans on the moat disturbed me, and I slept eleven hours and woke like a pygmy refreshed. We sunbathed, overate, drank champagne, gossiped all day. I was gay and amusing and for once forgot the war and our anxieties.

During the following weeks, unrecorded, Chips lost two great friends – the Duke of Kent, killed on active service, and the famous London hostess, Mrs Ronnie Greville.

19 September

I have found my diary, temporarily mislaid, and will resume writing in it.

20 September *Kelvedon*

Slept late. Diana Cooper rang up, inviting me to Bognor, today, and Alan begged me to join him at Ramsgate. I hesitated between these two marine invitations, finally decided to accept neither and came here for a let down. I must occasionally be alone, but Kelvedon is melancholy. . . . 'Bleak House', and for once, I do not love it.

21 September *London*

A wet morning at Kelvedon. Diana Cooper and Alan both sought me out by telephone in my retreat, and a gay, rather amused cable came from India, from Peter, about my Buckfast visit.[16] He also writes asking me who is to be the next Viceroy? The waiting list, apparently, is Lord Green, Rab, Bobbety Cranborne, Miles Lampson, Oliver Lyttelton, Sam Hoare. We'll see.

23 September *Back in London*

I attended a memorial service for poor Mrs Greville, which was

16. Chips had recently spent a few days' retreat in the monastery at Buckfast.

crowded with Ambassadors and all the usual funeral faces. I afterwards invited the Sitwells, Sachie and Georgie, and the Carisbrookes, to luncheon at Claridges. Irene Carisbrooke, a great lady, was gentle and charming. Her husband Drino talked of Mrs Greville and of her famous 'mots'. A few are worth recording. When Lady Chamberlain returned from Rome in early 1940 Mrs Greville remarked: 'It is not the first time that Rome has been saved by a goose'. Apropos of another woman well known for her loose morals, she said: 'I don't follow people to their bedrooms. It's what they do outside them that is important.' And her final polishing off of poor Emerald. 'You mustn't think that I dislike little Lady Cunard, I'm always telling Queen Mary that she isn't half as bad as she is painted.' Yet another of her remarks was about Mrs Keppel, who was making heavy weather about her escape from France. Of her, Maggie said: 'To hear Alice talk, you would think that she had swum the Channel, with her maid between her teeth.' No one yet knows what will happen to the world-famous Greville jewels. Luncheon cost me £10 including tips and three bottles of Moselle.

At 6 o'clock people poured in, among them Sydney and Rab Butler. Rab very gay. He fairly danced into the room hotfoot from a visit to Maisky, but he described the Soviet Ambassador as a crafty old fox and no friend of this country. Bobbety Cranborne has been offered, it appears, the Viceroyalty of India, but hesitates to accept because of his own and his wife's delicate health . . .

I am well, though bored, but everyone says that I look handsome, which is something.

27 September

The old Archbishop, heaven knows, was foolish and wicked enough, but the new obese one[17] is positively dangerous. He now openly preaches Socialism from the platform which he shares with Cripps – Is England mad, and doomed? But perhaps it is as well that the Revolution should come from the top, rather than the bottom. But almost everything that I loved has disappeared in under three years. I've only my adorable dauphin, a few friends, my money and, like Cyrano, 'mon panache'.

17. Dr William Temple.

30 September *London*

At luncheon, at Lady Willingdon's, I was next to James Grigg, the sournois new Secretary of State for War, who only unbent after I had turned all my artillery on him. He said that he thought Lloyd George the greatest man who he'd ever met, and he named 11 others, including Stresemann, Snowden, Bruning and Philip Chetwode. 'You have omitted the Prime Minister' I said, and he looked startled. Perhaps, he, too, is for the high jump. It seems that there is a cabal against him, and that pressure is being brought upon the Prime Minister to dismiss him. Already their honeymoon appears to be over. I smell a reshuffle when Parliament is dissolved. With both Cripps and Grigg out of the Government, drastic changes will be necessary.

10 October *Princes Hotel, Brighton*

I took a morning train to Newhaven where Alan [Lennox-Boyd] met me. He showed me a vast armada of small ships, tank carriers, landing boats, mine-sweepers, MTBs, etc., surely over 100, which had been assembled in Newhaven harbour as another raid, such as the Dieppe one, is about due to take place.

The afternoon was not, I fear, a success, as it was too cold, wet and disagreeable. At first we sat on the deck of Alan's MTB in the sun, but it was too cold and we moved to a neighbouring boat, a mine-sweeper, where we had drinks with Peter Scott, the artist who does sketches of animals, and particularly birds. His father was the famous Scott of the South Pole, and his mother is Lady Kennet. We then came on to Brighton, to this famous hotel, which is closing soon as it has been requisitioned. The war is slowly closing its clutches on us, on everybody, on civilisation. Every day something goes . . .

After a quick, hot, bath, we went to see Lord Alfred Douglas, whom neither of us had ever met before. He now lives in a tiny semi-basement flat at 1 St Anne's Court, Hove, and opened the door to us himself, and was generally gracious and friendly. He ushered us into his small sitting room where there were books and a few rather pathetic bibelots, relics of his youth. He is 72, looks much younger, and is lithe, lean and smiling, and has pleasant eyes. But he no longer listens to what one says, and scarcely took in our conversation at all. He just rattled on himself. We had resolved not to mention Oscar Wilde, prison, Winston, Robbie Ross or Frank Harris, but we were soon well embarked on all five subjects, though not at once. He told us much of Wilde, and after some sherry, said that although the Wilde story had ruined his life, he did not regret him. That throughout his imprisonment he had only waited for his release, and had received him in his villa at Sorrento where they lived together until his family ordered them to separate, threatening to cut off his allowance if they did not do so. Refusing to leave Wilde utterly penniless, Bosie wrote to his mother, Lady Queensberry asking for £200 to give him, and the old lady sent the money. Then the two famous lovers parted for all time. He made no secret of his being Wilde's catamite, and he showed us the photograph of a drawing of himself taken about that time. It was Dorian Gray himself . . . a young man of almost unbelievable good looks, staggeringly handsome. He went on to tell us that both Ross and Harris had behaved like scoundrels, and that he himself had served six months in Wormwood Scrubs in the second division, for having libelled Winston Churchill, to whom he had recently (and with the Prime Minister's permission) written and dedicated an ode. He was very pathetic . . . alone, poor, almost friendless, and married to a woman whom he rarely sees – but who does live in another flat in Brighton. Alan and I melted towards him, especially when he told us that he can no longer afford to keep his flat, for which Francis Queensberry pays the rent. I do not know what will become of him. I think I shall give him a small allowance, and then perhaps someone will be kind to me in my advanced age.

We left him reluctantly as we were pledged to dine with Sir Roderick and Lady Jones, at Rottingdean in a house where Kipling long lived. Although it was pitch black we finally found it and were warmly welcomed. Lady Jones is a buxom, vital blonde, who writes plays and books under her maiden name of Enid Bagnold. She is highly social, and full of fire and energy. She remarked that she had heard of me for upwards of twenty years, and had often wondered what I was like. Sir Roderick seemed ineffective compared to his wife, and I should have thought scarcely up to his former important job of being Chairman and Managing Director of Reuters, a position he relinquished a few years ago. He told us the whole story of Reuters, and we reminisced about old days when I knew Mrs Gordon Bennett so well. In the last war I used to go out to her villa at Versailles with Cecile d'Hautpoul, where we would meet Papa Joffre. Mrs Gordon Bennett had been Baroness de Reuter and she has long since been dead . . . but I am getting old and anecdotal myself. We ate rabbit and washed it down with a vintage burgundy, and we talked first, naturally, of Alfred Douglas, and then of young Julian Amery, and I related tales of his brilliance, which surprised the Jones' as they had only known him as a precocious child.

Back at the Hotel, we found Gilbert Frankau, the author, waiting up for us. He took us to his suite, and we drank whiskies and sodas with him and his third wife. . . . He advised me to write for 3½ hours a day, as he does, and never to depart from that rule. He insisted I would be famous if I did. Others have said the same, and I wish I had the application, but I am too weary and unstrung for that.

Bed about 12.30 after a fascinating day full of new personalities.

11 October *Kelvedon*

Kelvedon is blue but icy, and all day I have been unhappy. . . . Certainly I am lonely and sometimes foresee a dreary Alfred Douglasish old age. In fact, I am haunted by that sad, solitary leftover, eking out his existence surrounded by his few remaining possessions. How clumsily he must have arranged his life. He is a lesson to one.

15 October *West House, Bognor*

I travelled down here by a fast comfortable empty train to stay with Diana [Cooper]. She is more lovely, fair, and splendid than ever, and her great talents are now closely harnessed to farming. She milks her cows, feeds her rabbits, and sells swill. We had a happy evening together dining on Chianti and cheese, and gossiping.

16 October *Great Swifts, Cranbrook, Kent*

Diana drove me in her dirty, disreputable-looking car, with a trailer full of swill behind, into Bognor where we bought some large lobsters.

20 October

Walking in St James's Street after lunch, with Geordie Sutherland, I met de Gaulle ... strutting along insolently, and we crossed over to avoid them. Nobody can stomach de Gaulle. His intolerable swagger and conceit infuriate everyone.

21 October *Trafalgar Day*

I drove to Southend and inspected the damage done on Monday by the German raiders. Clarence Street is a shambles and my offices almost totally destroyed. The Conservative Club likewise. There were four fatal casualties and more than 39 injured, of whom 17 were seriously hurt. The little town I found rather excited, even stimulated, and seemed like a woman who has just been ravished. ... I walked about, and showed myself generally, and then attended a Trafalgar Day luncheon at which I both spoke and presided.

Directly after, I drove back to Westminster where the Smuts meeting had just opened. The Royal Gallery was crowded. At the end, seated at a table, were the Speaker, Lloyd George, Smuts, Winston and the Lord Chancellor. Lloyd George, in clear but a touch affected Welsh tones, introduced the Field Marshal, who was warmly received. He looked trim and fit, bronzed and wiry. He spoke, or rather read out his text, for 44 minutes and it seemed far too long. His stuff was no doubt excellent (it was a résumé of the whole war and so bromidic that I guessed that Anthony Eden must have written most of it, and later I discovered that such was the truth). But there was nothing new in it, and his accent was really too Afrikaans. The truth is that the speech was a disappointing flop as far as the gallery, packed with Peers and MPs and the press, were concerned. But to the outside world, it will be a tremendous triumph, for the scene and circumstances were inspiring. I understood little that he said as he rarely looked up. A long drone which might have been in Chinese, occasionally broken by a familiar word. People nearer to the table, although they heard better, later confirmed my impressions. At the end of the applause, there was a polite silence, since everybody appreciated the historic importance of the occasion, which was broken by Winston who made a few adequate and well chosen remarks – his clear voice was a relief after the Field Marshal's mumbo jumbo. The PM then called on the assembly to cheer Smuts, which we did, and sang with some constraint, 'For He's a Jolly Good Fellow'. There was then a little procession. The big Five trooped out – I was in the aisle and compared Smuts' ruddy, bronzed complexion and his taut little figure, with Lloyd George, Winston, the Speaker, all of whom seemed grayer, pale and years older than our distinguished guest. Winston's face, often impish, looked intensely bored during the speech as no doubt he had read it. He and Simon exchanged little notes, and each time Winston went through all his pockets, as he he does when he is irritated, searching for his spectacles. It was very cold, and I fled from the Royal Gallery directly I could and rushed to the Smoking Room to order a drink. It was nearly deserted, but I found, sitting at one table, the three grand old men together, who had just been speaking, Winston, Lloyd George and Smuts. Winston and Smuts, who had once fought each other in the Boer War, were having a drink together, and there were glasses before them. Of the three only the bronzed South African looked fit. As I ordered my drink Leslie Belisha looked in, and I was rather surprised to see Winston leap up and take him by the arm and lead him up to Smuts and introduce him. Smuts rose politely, and I left them all in conversation.

10 November

I want to be a Peer. There are many ways of becoming one. The quickest would be for Leslie Hore-Belisha to become Prime Minister, and to do that he would first have to be a Conservative. So I had a confidential chat with him, and later walked from Westminster to Stafford Place with him, trying to persuade him by every weapon in my armoury, to go over to the Tory party. He was surprised. He had never considered it, but promised that he would do so seriously. I suggested January as a psychological moment. Such an event would embarrass and annoy Winston, but why not? For Leslie's talents are too great to be thrown away as a free lance in Opposition.

11 November

Today, the anniversary of the Armistice, Hitler has announced that he is to occupy all France . . . All of lovely France gone.

There was a great fog today. The most impenetrable in human memory. There were accidents, delays, late trains and general dislocation. Of course it quite threw my day out of joint. I tried to walk to the House of Commons since taxis were unobtainable, but I couldn't see, and so turned back. Thus I missed the formal opening of the new session by their Majesties. In the afternoon when I finally got there, I was in time to see Peter Thorneycroft, looking a mere boy, rise and with very little shyness, though just enough, hold the House as he seconded the Gracious Speech. It was an admirable performance. Winston followed and for 76 minutes we had a dramatic treat, as he described the African landings, the victory in Egypt,[18] etc. But whilst vivid and boisterous, he said nothing, or little, that one had not heard on the wireless. Indeed, events just now seem to happen with such dramatic celerity and frequency, that we are breathless. The Germans have occupied Tunisia, the Italians have taken the Riviera. Darlan is rumoured to be treating with us. We listened enthralled. At last I crept away, and slept solidly in the library for 20 minutes, and when I returned, Winston was winding up. It was a creditable, indeed amazing, performance, for an overworked man of 68. He was cheered when he sat down, and the House emptied, or almost. The announcement that the Church bells are to be rung on Sunday in celebration of the Egyptian victory, was enthusiastically received, and I was reminded of the Greek bells which I heard announcing victory of Klissura, when I was in that ghastly train between Athens and Belgrade in January 1941.

12 November

Rab asked if he could live at Belgrave Square for a few months and I said that I would be delighted, as indeed I am.

14 November *Southend*

I attended and addressed three large meetings – the first at the hospital, the second a gathering of the Conservative Association

18. At El Alamein.

at Garon's, and thirdly a smaller one held here. Today is the seventh anniversary of my election for this Borough. Someone at the meeting handed me this quotation from Genesis: 'And Jacob served seven years for Rachel and they seemed unto him but a few days, for the love that he had to her'. . . . I was touched.

16 November *Belgrave Square*

I dined with Lady Cunard and Harcourt (Crinks) Johnstone at the Ritz. Emerald was gay, exquisite, full of life and fun and we sat enthralled for three hours. She is an amazing dazzling creature. She calls Crinks, 'le Misanthrope'. . . . At last he left, and I had an hour alone with my favourite woman. Her spritely gaiety is infectious. She kissed me affectionately goodnight and I admired her courage for I know her heart is broken over Thomas Beecham's desertion. She loved him for 34 years.

17 November

Harold, Rab and I dined rather hurriedly, and at nine o'clock sharp I went to the front door and a moment later a huge military car drew up, and out stepped Captain Smuts, who is acting as ADC to his father. He was followed by the Field Marshal, bronzed, with a boyish complexion, fine clear sky-blue eyes and gentle manners. He simply radiates charm. He refused a drink, but chatted most amiably of the Lampsons and of the Crown Prince and Princess of Greece for a few minutes, whilst several MPs, all junior Ministers, arrived. . . . When they were all more or less assembled and had taken drinks and sandwiches, the Field Marshal sat on a sofa and began a sort of monologue, and answered some rather amateurish questions. I was immensely and immediately impressed by his simplicity, his sweet smile and his incisive way of speaking; his language is a masterpiece of clarity, though he has a pronounced accent. He has an old man's charm, and an affectionate manner which is most endearing. He gave us his views of the past few years and of the future. He thinks that Baldwin deserves a high place in history for his management of England in a difficult period, but regrets that he was so uninterested in Europe. Hence his mistakes. Said that Hitler, indeed the whole German race, is pathological. Was grateful to Mr Chamberlain, etc. Admitted to being frightened of Europe and its entanglements. Thought that Germany has always been a destructive power (it broke the Russian Empire and nearly, but not quite, broke the British). Then he described in dramatic phrases the famous division in his parliament in Cape Town, the decision to support the war, which he won by only thirteen votes, and after a long struggle and a tremendous debate. The Opposition was largely isolationist, though not necessarily anti-British. If the voting had gone the other way South Africa would have remained outside the war, neutral like Eire, and the war might have already been lost. England could never have hoped to have won without her ports. Harold Macmillan who is so intelligent, asked searching questions. Someone mentioned the dreaded subject of Munich, and Harold Macmillan at once lost control; for he is obsessed by it, and was always violently hostile to it. But it was Bill Mabane, as everybody stirred uneasily, who asked the tremendous question: 'Did the Field Marshal think that this famous all-important division which he had described so vividly, would have been won had we gone to war at the time of Munich?' 'There would not have been a chance of it,' he replied, and he explained once more how far away Czechoslovakia, Danzig, and Poland seemed to the average South African. At that moment Germany had done little to estrange or frighten South Africa, and if anything opinion was Pro-Sudeten. It was only the later betrayal of Mr Chamberlain, the occupation of Prague, etc., and the actual invasion of Poland which swung the doubtful votes. This is the best vindication of Munich that I have ever heard, and Harold Macmillan was silenced. Gloomy Smuts Junior sat in complete silence, drinking whisky and soda. At 11.30 the Field Marshal rose, shook everybody genially by the hand and left, Harold and I seeing him to the door. As he got up he mentioned Runciman, and how sorry he had been for him at the time of his mission, and wondered if he had been sorry for himself? Rab chipped in. He had been present at No. 10 with Mr Chamberlain when the offer was made to Runciman, who had said pathetically 'I feel like a lone man whom you are putting to sea in a small boat in a big storm and I shall certainly drown.' Everybody laughed. At the door the Field Marshal whispered to me that he is leaving tomorrow for Cairo in his private plane. I hope that the beautiful good old gentleman will arrive safely.

When I came back the MPs were gathered about the drink table and were drinking and eating. Harry Crookshank was affable and I wonder whether it was good manners or a change of heart? The evening all in all, was a huge success. Here endeth one more great day in Belgrave Square.

18 November *London*

I walked back to 16 Stafford Place with Leslie [Hore-Belisha] to lunch and we spent three hours together. I begged him to join the Conservative party. Would I, he asked me, make him Prime Minister if he did? Only I could have that power, he said (in all seriousness) and I recalled Max Beaverbrook's famous message to Honor when he wrote asking her to see Sam Hoare with the idea of making Sam Prime Minister in succession to Mr Chamberlain. Honor was immensely amused and flattered at the time, and it is true that our house was then the centre of political, or at least Conservative, London.[19] Leslie Hore-Belisha told me much, described once again how he had been ousted from the Government, how he had sent for Brendan Bracken, who had been indignant, and how they had put a call through to Winston, who was then staying at the Embassy in Paris, and how Winston had promised to reinstate him, etc. (he was First Lord of the Admiralty at the time). Later Winston wrote him a charming letter in which he 'looked forward to the not distant day when once more they should be colleagues in the Cabinet'.[20] A few months later Winston was Prime Minister, but did not offer him a portfolio.

23 November *Coppins*

The Duchess has rearranged her sitting room, kept the Duke's just as it was, and has shut up the music room. . . .

We went up to bed about midnight, and I was haunted by the spirit of the Duke. Every room and object is so inspired by him, the house, in fact, is him. I met him on the staircase, saw him sitting at the end of my bed, as he so often used to do, and was constantly aware of him. The house still vibrates with his vivacious personality.

19. See p. 197.
20. See R. J. Minney: *The Private Papers of Hore-Belisha.*

24 November *London*

Early this morning Princess Alexandra rushed into my room – she is a whirlwind of a girl – and told me that she had 'prayed' to be taken up to London today and was to have a 'perm'. She is most vivacious and attractive.

Once in London I hurriedly changed and went to the House of Commons. Anthony Eden was cheered as he answered his first question as Leader of the House. He handled [Richard] Stokes[21] clumsily who asked an embarrassing question about de Gaulle's banned broadcast. However, Anthony had the House with him. Much discussion of Africa, where the political position is complicated. The Americans back Darlan, who apparently has gone over to them completely. As he is alleged to be bitterly anti-British (I don't know the truth) there is naturally political feeling about it.

26 November *London*

The Duke of Alba told me about his luncheon party yesterday for the Prime Minister, to which he had invited 'mes amis des mauvais jours' meaning Rab and Croft, who had been helpful over Franco. The PM, talking of India, had said, chuckling, 'Since the English occupation of India the native population has increased by a hundred million. Since the American War of Independence, the Red Indian population has practically died out.' What a wonderful riposte to the American critics of our Colonial policy. Alba is an ardent Anglophil.

1 December

The Beveridge Report has been made public. It will revolutionise life in England – but at first glance I am in favour of it.

2 December *London*

I attended a meeting of the 1922 Committee, which was addressed by Sir William Beveridge. He is a pleasant, earnest, professional little man, obviously capable of immense work. He explained the report, which surprisingly enough irritates the Socialists more than it does us. I think it should be adopted ...

21. Labour MP for Grimsby.

At dinner Peter Loxley, somewhat slyly, suggested that I should keep a diary, as it would be an important document. I brushed aside his remarks and laughingly said that I did in fact do so, but only 'sometimes'.

6 December

Later I went to see Pam Churchill in her flat at 49 Grosvenor Square. While I was there Averell Harriman and Max Beaverbrook both rang up. As she talked on the telephone I played with the infant Winston aged two and half. He is the most bumptious little boy I have ever seen; he rushes about, talks and makes a noise, a real Churchill. Pam pointed to a photograph of President Roosevelt and asked Winston who it was. 'Grandpa' the child replied.

I hear that the Linlithgows will stay on for another year in Delhi since Winston will not invite Rab to be Viceroy, and the Cranbornes, Sinclairs and Devonshires have all, after reflection, turned it down.

I listened to Smuts' broadcast, lying on the sofa where he had sat for nearly three hours a fortnight ago. It was an odd sensation.

7 December

Dined in with Lady Willingdon, who arrived with Vice-regal punctuality at eight o'clock. Emerald on the other hand was forty-five minutes late, as she so often and irritatingly is. At one point Emerald with mischief in her old, over-made-up eyes, declared that no man was ever faithful to his wife for more than three years. 'That', she added, 'is a biological fact.' 'You can never have known my Freeman' Lady Willingdon retorted. 'Perhaps better than you think,' was Emerald's reply. She is lunching with Winston on Wednesday.

10 December

Secret Session, and as we waited for the 'Strangers' to be cleared, I counted thirty-seven Peers in the gallery. Winston proceeded to hold the House enthralled for an hour as he described in dramatic detail the whole story of the African expedition and General Eisenhower's sudden decision to accept Admiral Darlan's cooperation. Winston, au fond a Conservative, was enjoying himself and seemed to be relishing the unexpected turn of events. He told much which surprised the House but which was no news to me. How the French hated de Gaulle and how the Americans refused to have anything to do with the Free French movement, etc. And how Darlan's sudden help had saved time, lives and perhaps even the succcss of the whole expedition. He was in the highest fettle, and I have never admired him so much. Pétain he pronounced Petaigne and described him as an antique defeatist. When he finished the House cheered him lustily; only a few left-wingers were irritated.

12 December

I am having domestic difficulties with my staff, as the Ministry of Labour wish to call up both my butler and the cook. I mustn't grumble as I have had three years and three months of comfort, even of luxury, whilst everybody else has pigged it . . .

At dinner at Emerald's, Duff was in a violent, vehement, tipsy mood, and attacked everybody and everything, particularly Mr Chamberlain. He still harps on that, and finally I gently asked him how long he had served under him. Duff, rather nettled, went red in the face. He can be so difficult and opinionated.

14 December

I dined with Barbie Wallace. She is intelligent, but has been bitten by that insidious bug, Edenitis. It is an instinct for self-destruction which one finds in the more intelligent social element of high society; it is fin-de-race, a desire for suicide, the last volupté, after they have had everything else. Otherwise she is an extremely sensible woman.

17 December

An extraordinary assembly today in the august Mother of Parliaments. It was sublime. Anthony read out a statement regarding the extermination of Jews in East Europe, whereupon Jimmy de Rothschild rose, and with immense dignity, and his voice vibrating with emotion, spoke for five minutes in moving tones on the plight of these peoples. There were tears in his eyes, and I feared that he might break down; the House caught his spirit and was deeply moved. Somebody suggested that we stand in silence to pay our respects to those suffering peoples, and the House as a whole rose and stood for a few frozen seconds. It was a fine moment, and my back tingled.

At Mrs Keppel's completely pre-war cocktail party, Duff arrived late, and came up to Bettine Abingdon and me and remarked: 'May I join beauty and fashion?' The world is being socially kind to me now. I bask in its smiles. But how long will it, can it last? I now don't really care.

18 December

At luncheon today Emerald remarked that she had long since ceased to be unduly depressed by the Crucifixion, in fact she had got used to it. She then went on, coyly, to read us a short note from George Moore in which he compared her to Socrates. Such was the conversation at Lady Cunard's in the third year of the Second World War . . .

My windows are being replaced, and they are very welcome after two years of blackness.

20 December *Pyrford*

I drove here in balmy warm weather and spent the day with my in-laws. Lady Iveagh, reminiscing about old country-house customs, thinks that those days are over for ever. She said that the last time the King and Queen stayed with them at Elveden they brought a suite of twenty-two, including a page, a postman, dressers, etc., and they stayed a week.

24 December

Raymond Mortimer lunched, whose brilliant little book 'Channel Packet' is having such a deserved success, though I find it slightly spoilt by his splenetic political theories and constant gibes at the class which secretly he admires and cultivates. However with his warm and generous charm, his piercing intelligence, he is a perfect companion, and I see him all too seldom.

Later I went to a cosy Christmas party which Laura Corrigan had taken endless trouble to organise. There were presents, holly, champagne, sherry, Christmas pudding and every other kind of rarity. What would have been a charming evening was somewhat spoilt by Emerald's absurdly plaintive announcement that she never had enough to eat in England, and 'What are the Merchant Navy doing?' Alan, fresh from the dangers of the sea, took offence, and snapped at her.

Later he and I went to Westminster Cathedral for midnight mass, which was most impressive. It was dark and crowded with soldiers, many of them American and Canadian, praying in the flickering candlelight.

Christmas Day *The Gardener's Cottage, Elveden*

My tiny faithful grey car, a present from Peter when he left for the wars in 1939, crowded with parcels, was ready at ten and Alan and I started off to spend Christmas with our in-laws at Elveden, where the children, rosy and beautiful as Hoppners, made me nostalgic for my own lad so far away in America. I am profoundly unhappy and lonely, really. My life is a mess, though the Iveaghs are consolingly gentle and affectionate.

1943

1 January *London, 5 Belgrave Square*

The New Year has dawned, and I have decided not to make any foolish resolutions. I only know that I am older and less attractive, though people go about saying that I am the Horace Walpole of the age. But is that a compliment?

4 January

At dinner at the Carlton (food most unappetizing) old Howard Whitbread,[22] who is well over 80 and a bucolic grand seigneur, talked of the House of Commons, and how he had once gone up from Eton to hear Disraeli speak on some great occasion. He described how the ageing Prime Minister had, from time to time, paused, taken out a coloured bandana from his pocket, and blown his nose. This was the signal for his supporters to cheer, which they did with considerable gusto; he then replaced the handkerchief and continued his speech.

22. Samuel Howard Whitbread (b. 1858). Liberal MP for Luton, 1892–5; Huntingdon, 1906–10.

25 January

Rab and I sat up late discussing old days, the political set-up, the possible re-birth of the Conservative Party and his own chances of both the Premiership and the Vice-regal throne . . .

I am devoted to him, and I think he is fond of me. But I do not think that he is advancing: in fact he is contracting. I have seen many do this, notably 'Shakes' Morrison, once the hope of enlightened Tory England, now an amiable white-headed boy taken seriously by nobody and fobbed off with the new Ministry of Town and Country Planning. And Rab has such obvious defects . . . is lacking in imagination . . ., and so simple in his way of life as to be almost irritating. Yet he has great gifts too – shrewdness, calm judgment, and ambition. But he is au fond a civil servant. I hinted much of this to him tonight, and he was depressed thereby, and has now gone to bed.

28 January *Belgrave Square*

Emerald tells me that Duff Cooper, who is in the gentlest of moods these days, remarked to her that all his life he has tried to make people like him, and always failed. He cited me as an example: praised me and added that he knew I only tolerated him because of Diana. This is, of course, true, though I do like him better of late.

1 February

On this date I spent my first night in this house, and remember it well: only my room was ready: the servants were still unpacking: there were crates and unhung curtains and general confusion. What a seven years! 5 Belgrave Square has played a considerable role in politics and society, and since the war has been, if it was not already so before, the centre of London . . . no true chronicler of the time could fail to record its glories and its influence. Today begins my eighth year of residence in Schloss Chips.

3 February

The 1922 Committee was addressed by Brendan Bracken, that kind-hearted, garrulous, red-headed gargoyle, whom I have always considered a fraud, au fond: he is an indifferent Minister, promising all and doing little – inoperative in fact, and prejudiced. He made a bid for popularity with the old-fashioned Tories today.

11 February

Dined with Mrs Carnegie in her really hideous house at 41 Lennox Gardens. She is 80, and still fine-looking in an old fashioned way. Her first husband, whom she always calls 'Mr Chamberlain' was 27 years older than she, and he was born in 1836. Much talk of early Endicott – she was née Endicott – days in Boston: and she showed me a few ugly treasures with some pride. Heirlooms she called them. Fresh from my reading of 'The Ambassadors' I guided the conversation on to Henry James, whom I thought she might have known. She had, and described him as a cold, unintimate man, though she had liked him, and seen much of him for many years. She again described Sir Austen Chamberlain's maiden speech, and told me how, at a ball in Washington, she had been dazzled by the chic, glamour and loveliness of Miss Adele Grant, who, as a débutante, had recently broken off her engagement to Lord Cairns. This was my beloved Lady Essex of later years. Mrs Carnegie had always admired her. . . . The food was atrocious – rabbit – but the claret superb, and the two old male servitors looked after us in the grand manner. Upstairs the drawing-room was lit and enlivened by one of the most magnificent Sargents I have ever seen – her portrait: a billowy girl in white, with blue sleeves. This correct Edith Wharton woman must have been extraordinarily attractive. She is so to talk to still.

16 February

Arthur Greenwood opened the much-heralded debate on the Beveridge report. The House was crowded and I saw little Beveridge himself, an alert, excitable, determined little sexagenarian. John Anderson replied for the Government, in what I thought the best, most balanced speech of his career. One listened without boredom: indeed he seems to have thrown off his usual tedious manner. Later I took Sydney and Rab (they were reluctant, even shy, about accepting) to dine with Emerald at the

Dorchester, whom we found gay, provocative, appetising, and altogether at her very best . . . the others were Diana Cooper, Eddie and 'Moucher' Devonshire and funny old Chester Beatty. A brilliant party and highly successful evening: but I was soon aware that there was an under-current of tragedy as Diana whispered to me that Emerald had just heard from Courtland Palmer in New York that Thomas Beecham had just married. Apparently she reeled on receiving it, but was being brave now, and was what Diana called 'doing a Marie Antoinette'.

I was desperately sorry for her tonight and loved her deeply. The others were unaware of the drama – and we sat in the candle-light listening to Emerald's and Eddie Devonshire's remarkable conversation, first about literature – Henry James again – and then cock-fighting! The Butlers were impressed and capitulated completely to Emerald's charm and high conversational powers.

I hear that Winston is really quite ill: he attended a Cabinet swathed in a shawl: apparently he caught cold on his return,[23] and the dramatic daily changes of climate and temperature were too much for him. He is an impatient patient, strong but not fit, and a life-time spent drinking brandy is not conducive to a speedy recovery from the pneumonia which they now say it is.

18 February

Beveridge Day. I spent most of it in the House and watched the revolt grow. The Whips are ill-informed, insensitive to opinion and rumour: and the much-abused Margesson is now missed. . . . Herbert Morrison wound up for the Government in a balanced, clever, eloquent speech which revealed his increasing Conservatism – was it a bid for the future leadership of a Coalition Government? The crowded House listened with interest and even the more truculent Socialists, whilst later prepared to vote against their leaders, were too cowardly to attack Morrison. 119 votes were recorded against the Government in a Three-Line Whip! Practically the whole rank and file of the Labour movement threw over their leaders, and there were ironical cheers when the result was announced. Coming into the Lobby I saw old Beveridge and his recent bride; they were surrounded by sympathetic Socialists.

23. From North Africa.

25 February

In Belgrave Square I found chaos. Champagne was being unpacked, furniture being moved, waiters changing, and I was soon joined by the bride and bridegroom themselves, Lord and Lady Dudley. They had been married at a Registry Office, then had some form of religious service, a luncheon, and come on to me. Laura was simply dressed in brown velvet and Eric was in a lounge suiting. They then left me, and I had an hour in which to tidy the house, dress and rest. About 5.30 they came back, and by that time the house was looking a dream of candle-lit beauty and the blue dining-room shimmered. Within a few minutes, on the dot of 5.30, Herbert Morrison walked in, escorted by three Home Office henchmen: Socialists never really know how to behave, but before too long he was surrounded by fashionable ladies, and seemed to enjoy their company. I led up 'Kakoo' Rutland and Mollie Buccleuch to him, and his one eye roved at them with approval. Within an hour, all London was there (the butler, Trehern, afterwards told me that 325 people had come). Half the Government: Ernest and Mrs Bevin: 'Shakes' Morrison: John and Ava Anderson: Malcolm McCorquodale, Harold and Rab, etc. Others – Averell Harriman and Dickie Mountbatten – came late. And there was a sprinkling of Ambassadors. Champagne and cocktails flowed and I was in a benign mood, and charming to everybody, and have not heard so much chatter since the war. Everybody was enchanted to see everyone else, and the party had really immense stimmung. There was atmosphere of gaiety, youth and distinguished grandeur about the reception which invigorated everybody. Finally the bride and bridegroom, after thanking me profusely, left for Claridge's about 8.30. The Mountbattens (Edwina is always particularly charming to me), Sutherlands and the Carcanos left together later, and I was sorry when it was over.

8 March

I met Mrs Keppel in St James's Street and walked with her to Partridge's shop: as we passed an urchin pointed at her, and I heard him say 'Look at her blue hair'. She told me much, and seems very intimate with the Prime Minister, though she pretends to be more so. She says that she had rebuked him for two major mistakes – moving Wavell, and appointing Temple as Archbishop. She is right. She also added that I was much the most popular man in London Society now that I was a bachelor again: I hope she is right about that too.

9 March

Clifton-Brown has won the Speaker stakes, and I went to the House to watch his election as the new Speaker. . . . Clifton-Brown is well-liked: has good manners, is simple and straightforward: is audible (perhaps a disadvantage as a Speaker) and a good House of Commons man. He is only 63, and now goes practically into purdah for the remainder of his days. No more intimacies: no more smoking-room colloquies. After luncheon, I brought Emerald back to see his Installation, and as we arrived the sirens sounded. We bombed Berlin heavily last night: this was probably the reprisal. I went into the Chamber, and saw Clifton-Brown in Court dress and wearing a short clerk's wig. At that moment Black Rod knocked, entered, bowed several times and summoned us to the Lords. We marched in solemn procession through the Princes' Gallery, but the little Robing-Room, the present abode of the Lords, was too small to admit many of us. I stayed outside with Emerald and, joined by Max Beaverbrook, we listened to the very short proceedings, and Emerald was soon surrounded by Peers of the Realm. . . . The procession returned, and somewhere en route Clifton-Brown must have changed his wig, for when I reached the Chamber he was already be-gowned and be-wigged in full Speaker's paraphernalia. There were a few perfunctory remarks from Anthony Eden, the new Speaker then rose, and declared the House adjourned. As he walked out with dignity, with his train-bearer and secretary, I heard him turn to the attendants and Serjeant and say – as if he had done it all his life – 'Usual time tomorrow'. All this quaint, rather Alice-in-Wonderland ceremony went on whilst a severe air-raid was in progress.

23 March

At the Requiem in honour of His Eminence,[24] General de Gaulle

24. Cardinal Hinsley.

made an idiotic entrance – a real entrée de souverain: he sat immediately in front of me. Sikorski, who had a grander place, was far simpler in his manner. There must have been a 1,000 or more priests, monks, prelates and bishops, all wearing their grandest surplices and most glittering vestments. In the procession I saw my friend, the Abbot of Buckfast. Soon the endless ceremony began: the intoning, the candles, the singing, were all impressive – and I watched for a long time, transfixed. Soon I was aware of a different smell from the heavy incense and, looking up, I saw it was the very seductive Argentine Ambassadress, Madame Carcano, arriving late and exuding through her sables an aroma of Chanel. . . . The interminable Service continued: but my bladder began to disturb me and, after an hour, began to be painful. Soon I could think of nothing else, and the scene became blurred: I wondered, would I hold out? It was impossible to escape except by tripping over General de Gaulle, and almost entering the conclave of officiating purple-robed priests. . . . Why must all Roman Catholic functions be so interminable? By midday I was in pain, by one o'clock I was almost fainting. Meanwhile two men had collapsed. At last it was over. I held my breath, and staggered to the Army & Navy Stores where at last I found relief.

26 March

The guest-of-honour at the Lobby lunch at the Savoy was Herbert Morrison, and to my surprise I was next to John Anderson, at the top table. Attlee was one off me, to my right, and Alexander to the left. I was the only MP at the top table who was not in the Cabinet, and I am sure there will be comment, as busybodies are already asking why I should have had so grand a place at the Cardinal's Requiem.

After lunch Herbert Morrison beguiled us amusingly, but in doubtful taste, for 45 minutes. He has rich humour, a caustic wit, and much conceit, all indispensable ingredients for a good speech. And so perhaps it was. He only said one important thing: that he would live and commit suicide with the Socialist Party, if once again it was determined to commit suicide: perhaps he wanted to quash a growing report that he was prepared to follow Churchill and head a Coalition Government: and it is true that he has much of the Tory in him. . . . My mind wandered, and I thought of other Lobby luncheons: last year it was Winston and in 1940 it was also Winston who, as First Lord, was the Guest of Honour, and Neville Chamberlain sat silent, a little sad and a touch neglected;[25] these Lobby lunches are always great occasions, Parliamentary institutions of importance.

13 April

Big news. I heard that Wavell may come here next week: also permission has been granted to Paul and Olga by the Government and Smuts, to go and live in South Africa.

17 April *Leeds Castle*

Today I behaved badly for I awoke weary, and could neither face Southend nor the intense tedium of having to write a speech, so I chucked a meeting, and, instead, I drove to Leeds Castle for the week-end, picnicking in the intense heat on the way. It was a lyrical day – the heat, the gauze-like mist rising from the fruit blossoms, the spinach green fields, all were intoxicating, as was the grey castle rising from the moat as I approached it. Black swans followed by cygnets were swimming around.

18 April

The hottest day I can ever remember in England. I lay almost naked until 7.30 p.m. wearing only slacks for luncheon, when I revelled in plovers' eggs and champagne.

25. See p. 287.

CHAPTER EIGHT

Wavell: April–October 1943

Chips's friendship with Field-Marshal Wavell seemed to many people to be an oddity. In fact, it emphasised the gayer part of Wavell's personality and the more serious one of Chips's. It was a genuine and sincere friendship on both sides, and Chips's comments on Wavell at this stage of his career are of such interest that they justify a chapter to themselves, although, to maintain chronology, I have included other extracts as well.

1943

21 April

The guns opened heavy fire last night, and people are beginning to complain that our planes keep them awake, which is not unfunny.

22 April

Wavell, accompanied by Peter [Coats], has finally arrived in London.

23 April *Good Friday*

Peter went to the War Office, and rang me later to say that the Field-Marshal much wanted to see me, and would look in about 6. Frantically, in spite of it being Good Friday and everyone away, I tried to arrange a cocktail party, and finally collected some twenty people, rather a mixed bag. On the dot of six, Wavell arrived, greyer, deafer, gentler and shyer than ever.

The greatest general of our day walked in simply and sat down, and I led up various people, including the Belgian Ambassador, the Carcanos (our fashionable Argentines), etc. He drank several cocktails, stayed for nearly three hours, and was charming . . .

25 April

In the morning Peter and I went for a long walk. And we talked of Winston and his uncontrollable and unfortunate disapproval – indeed jealous dislike – of Wavell.

28 April

A Wavell day. I had the Field-Marshal here for several hours, six in all, and my axis and friendship with him have already caused considerable comment. The day began when he proposed himself to luncheon, and I hurriedly collected not only food, but some guests as well, and we had a distinguished and successful little party. Lady Wilson, wife of General Sir Jumbo[1], self, Lady Willingdon, the Field-Marshal, Diana Cooper, Rab, Virginia Cowles and Peter. Lady Willingdon was abrupt and direct but almost comically pleased to meet Wavell, whom she had never met, while Diana made him talk, and Virginia Cowles fascinated him. As he left, he rather shyly and affectionately asked me if he could have a cocktail party here in the afternoon as he had so many people to see, and in due course nearly 30 people came. My additions were the Kemsleys, Oscar Solbert and Lady Colefax, who were all enchanted, and the party went on till 8.30, when Wavell left to dine with Winston at Number Ten.

30 April *London*

I lunched with the Amerys in Eaton Square. She was away, but Leo and I had a confidential chat, but I found out nothing about the Delhi appointment.[2] At 4 o'clock the Field-Marshal, accompanied by Sir Arthur Wauchope, came here to see me, and they were soon joined by General Andrews and his Chief of Staff, General Bath. Andrews is the Commander-in-Chief of the European operations, and a grey, shrewd, kindly old man. The typical American soldier, but lacking charm. He has been here several times; I left them in the Morning Room, and disappeared upstairs while they had a confidential conversation about high military strategy in the Far East, but the interview was brief, and I soon heard the door slam. I then found myself alone with the

1. General Sir Maitland Wilson.
2. To the Viceroyalty.

Field-Marshal and we gossiped for half an hour: he was playful about Winston, but I knew at once that he doesn't really like him. Our talk was interrupted by the arrival of an antique couple, old friends of the Wavells, who had travelled up from Gloucestershire especially to see him, whom he soon seemed rather bored by. He's easier, I have noticed, with my friends than with his own, for his mind is still young, and antiquated crocks depress him, though he remains loyal. I was polite and ADC-ish.

Diana Cooper, rapturously lovely and gently affectionate and altogether perfect, has left No. 5 for Bognor, but the Field-Marshal has proposed himself, and now wants to move in.

1 May *London*

Wavell is devoted to Peter, and is both possessive and utterly dependent. He trusts him completely, and relies on his judgment. From time to time I notice him looking at him affectionately as if to seek his approval, and there is much human understanding in this curiously sensitive relationship.

3 May

What I had half hoped for, yet rather dreaded, has come to pass. The Field-Marshal has arrived to stay. He wanted to come last week but I quite honestly did not encourage the idea. However, his luggage arrived this morning, and here he is. Not only that, but the two Miss Wavells, the maiden sisters who lived at Ringwood, have come up for the night to stay too, and my household is in confusion; the depleted and inadequate staff are demented.

I took my distinguished guest to luncheon at the Belgian Embassy where we found a large party including Winant, whose fascinating appearance is most impressive, the Polish Ambassador, D'Arcy Osborne,[3] half the Belgian Government and others. Later, I drove him to the Dorchester to call on the Kemsleys as Gomer wanted a quiet talk with him, and I played ADC and left them together for half an hour, waiting in the corridor. The meeting was a success (Wavell had never heard of the Kemsleys until I introduced them to him a few days ago). We then drove grandly

3. Resident Minister at the Vatican.

in his impressive War Office car to call on Virginia Cowles, who received us rapturously. I again left him to her charms for twenty minutes, and she was entranced, as are all those who are able to thaw him. He is easy, amiable, even affable and affectionate to people he likes, but he has lapses, or rather, long periods of brooding silence – luckily, he's always easy with me. This evening I heard him swearing in his room because he had mislaid something. I think his eye troubles him sometimes: he seems to have difficulty in focusing, and bumps into things. He finally came down to dinner in a shabby tweed suit, and said it was a relief to be out of uniform. ... He described his long interview with Queen Wilhelmina this afternoon and showed us the impressive Grand Cordon of Orange, or whatever the decoration is called, which she gave him. The ribbon is yellow, the stars are of steel and it makes a good show. I gather conversation with Her Majesty was sticky. 'She has little S. A.', he remarked dryly. I gather he is going to America on Wednesday, and I hinted to him that he might bring my Paul back to me in his plane (or would it be a battleship?).

4 May

The Field-Marshal insisted on being called at 7, and I heard him moving about in the next room, coughing and muttering. ... About 6 o'clock my own cocktail party (farewell for Wavell) began. It was crowded and distinguished ... about 45 came. The FM said he'd never met so many interesting people, and he seemed to enjoy himself, and he was easy and affable to all. A few cocktails loosen his tongue, and he made an immense impression as he invariably does.

When everyone had finally left (about 9 o'clock), he showed me his Field-Marshal's baton – a gold and red and plush affair, made by Spinks, which the King had given to him this afternoon during a long audience at Buckingham Palace. When he left the FM half hugged me, and murmured affectionate words of gratitude for my hospitality and kindness. I almost cried. He is now on his way to America, and the house is silent and deserted after his extraordinary, historic visit. I feel worn out and exhausted. Sad, too. For I have just heard that General Andrews and General Bath were killed on Monday in Iceland; on Friday afternoon they were both here in this house for a secret conference. The war seems endlessly tragic.

9 May *Leeds Castle*

A cold tempest rages and I shiver and am bored. Old Lord Hardinge came to lunch, on sticks, and Lord Queenborough (aged 80) who is about six months his junior, remarked to me 'Poor Charlie Hardinge. He looks an old crock, doesn't he?' Queenborough is an octogenarian of immense vigour, having produced three daughters by his second wife, when he was over sixty. Much banter here, and Lady Willingdon, who had been rather cruelly chaffed by Emerald, reasserted herself with the announcement that Flaubert had been in love with her when she was seventeen. We gasped, and wondered if she was the original of Salambo?

18 May

From all accounts, Winston and Wavell are not getting on together [in Washington]. I foresaw as much.

19 May

At 6 o'clock the great Te Deum to celebrate our victory in Africa was held in St Paul's Cathedral. Owing to a ridiculous tale the time had to be altered from noon. It seems that Charlie Londonderry's butler opened his 'whip' at Mount Stuart, and telegraphed it to him in London. The censorship stopped the telegram, and informed the authorities, who at once decided that the great church, crowded with all the notabilities of England, might prove too tempting a target for the Luftwaffe; so it was decided to alter the time. Even so, there was some uneasiness all day that the Germans might get to know and bomb us. But nothing of the sort happened. Instead, though it had been hurriedly organised, we had an impressively effortless English service. I took Laura Corrigan as my guest, and she was enchanted. We arrived at 5.30 and already the church was half full with Peers, MPs and Socialist Ministers looking self conscious and awkward in their tail coats. Attlee appeared with Mrs Churchill. Soon the choir, including the Archbishop of Canterbury, magnificent in full regalia, white satin and gold, went to the Grand Entrance to receive the

Royalties. After a pause, the procession returned, solemn, stately and dignified, the King and Queen looking small, though she was gracious and smiled, leaning back, a new walk she has recently acquired; immediately behind them came the two Princesses dressed alike in blue, which made them seem like little girls. . . . Then followed the Kings of Norway and Yugoslavia an oddly matched brace of monarchs, one so immense and the other so small. Then Princess Marina, in black and pearl, looking rich and resplendent, and as ever, the cynosure of all admiring eyes. . . . The Service was short and impressive with an anthem superbly sung. I looked up at the painted cupola and thought of the grandeur of England, and was moved. The proceedings lasted for about forty-five minutes, then the procession filed out. They were followed out by the ambassadors and by the tall, striking De Gaulle, etc. A big rectangular doorway had been opened, and sunlight flooded the church, and the bells began pealing. The bells of victory.

20 May

The newspapers give a vivid account of Winston's speech to Congress, and report that the Windsors were cheered on their arrival and departure: never before have they had an ovation in the USA. This is Winston's doing, and his attentions to them have obviously affected American opinion: people here are a touch annoyed

27 May

At 12.30 I was given a message from the Air Ministry that the Field-Marshal was back in England, and would arrive in Belgrave Square in the hope of staying with me, sometime this afternoon. I was at once in a fever, and frenziedly rushed home to make arrangements. What a mercy that I didn't go to Kelvedon as I had planned. I hurriedly tidied up the house, telephoned frantically, and by four p.m. when he was due, I was waiting for him, flanked by Diana Cooper. Soon he walked in, smiled in his gentle humorous way and said 'Hello Chips', greeted Diana and bewailed Peter's illness[4] and absence: then George Gage dropped

4. Peter Coats was seriously ill in the Doctors Hospital, New York.

in, and was considerably impressed. As the FM changed into blue mufti, I sat with him, and at 8 o'clock we sailed forth to dine at Pratt's Club, where I had invited Lord Rosebery to dine with us, and we found him already waiting. They are very old friends, and Harry is one year older, though he seems much younger. . . . They were enraptured to see each other and talked of the last war, of Allenby and T. E. Lawrence, etc. Gradually, the other members sitting at the round table joined in and the subject turned, not unnaturally, on India, and the much-debated question of the future Viceroy. The Field-Marshal expressed no opinion but listened. At the end of the table sat a KC . . . who suddenly intervened with 'Why not send old Wavell?' An amused shudder went round the table, and I tried to save the situation by pointing to the Field-Marshal, and suggesting . . . that he ask him direct. The poor man blushed deeply, swallowed his port, and bolted; we sat on for a bit, then Harry Rosebery left for Scotland, and the Field-Marshal and I walked home via St James's Park. He is gentle, affectionate, vague, yet shrewd, and when he is attending to the subject, darts rapier-like to the point.

28 May

The FM went off at 9.30 to the War Office and I was left to cope with his correspondence, messages, and to make engagements, of which he has none. Luckily I caught Duff Cooper, who said that he would be enchanted to see him and give him lunch. Then I hinted discreetly on the telephone to the Amerys that they invite him to dine, which they did. The Secretary of State for India was unaware that he'd arrived. After a blessed morning to myself, I walked to 11 Downing Street, where the FM was closeted with Attlee, and we drove to Buck's Club where Duff Cooper had engaged a private room and arranged matters en prince. However, as we went through the public room I introduced Esmond Rothermere, Freddy Birkenhead and Christopher Chancellor and others, and we made quite an entrée. Duff had collected Shakes Morrison, and an American called John Cowles who is Wilkie's right-hand man. The food was delicious, and whenever the conversation flagged I gave Wavell a prod or lead and all was well. A trick Peter taught me. I told Duff how much he had enjoyed 'David',[5] which pleased him, and the conversation continued for twenty minutes on that theme, while the FM quoted the Bible, Kipling and Shakespeare; he has a prodigious memory. Morrison capped him once or twice, and the Americans were impressed and breathless. I have now just walked with him to the Amerys in Eaton Square, having refused to dine with them, have returned and fallen into my bed. The second successful Wavell day is over, but I'm worn out.

29 May

The FM and I left London for the weekend at 9.50. The roads were deserted, and we drove furiously. Occasionally the FM would tap the window and order the driver to stop, to give lifts to soldiers. It was amusing to watch their manner change when they twigged who he was. We talked the whole way, and I gather he is annoyed (indeed he said so) with Winston, who wrote him rude, pontifical notes on the ship and in Washington. They didn't get on well this time at all, and he saw little of him intimately in Washington; but one day lunching with him and the President and one other (the CIGS I think) at the White House, Winston openly attacked him in front of the President, who gently took Wavell's part. The FM was very annoyed, and I wonder whether the rift between him and the PM is not seriously widening.

We rushed through Oxford ... and I was immensely struck by the Field-Marshal's quickness in reading a map, and knowing his whereabouts: the old campaigner coming out. We arrived here[6] at 1.10 and were greeted by Captain George Churchill, our host. He is the FM's oldest and perhaps closest friend, and has been for nearly 40 years. He is an old maid of a man aged 66 or 67 – pleasant, houseproud who must have been handsome at the time of Queen Victoria's Jubilee. The house, built of yellow Cotswold stone, however, is fascinating. It was the seat of the Lords Northwick, a Dutch merchant family who settled in England at the time of Charles II. The second Lord was immensely rich and spent most of his 94 years of life collecting pictures and other

5. Duff Cooper's biography of King David.
6. Northwick Park, near Moreton-in-Marsh.

treasures. He had luck, flair and great taste. It was he who added the vast picture gallery, which spoils the symmetry of the house, though its contents are magnificent. Almost every painter except the moderns, are represented. Leonardos, Saverys, Holbeins, Kuyps, Sir Joshuas, etc. The Madonna of the Cherries (perhaps by Leonardo da Vinci) is the Field-Marshal's favourite. George Churchill's whole life is his house and his collection, and one could say that it has either ruined or made him. But the house, while rich in atmosphere and overladen with priceless and rare possessions, is stark and uncomfortable. After an only moderate luncheon I hoped to go to sleep, but the FM came to my room and suggested a walk, and I couldn't well refuse. The walk developed into a hike, and we must have tramped six miles, passing a brick kiln where we were stopped by the Home Guard sentry, and the FM modestly refrained from saying who he was.

30 May

We skilfully avoided going to Church, and went for another hike. Various unexciting people came for luncheon, and I am afraid the great soldier was very bored. I know now when he is, because his face goes grey, and he doesn't speak, and there are long silences. He whispered to me: 'Let's get off soon', so I ordered the car quickly, and after he had signed half a dozen autographs we departed, though I was almost sorry to leave our gentle host and his hospitable house, so crowded with loveliness. At Oxford we stopped to call on an old General, Sir Something Swinton, who is about 76 and the old man was delighted and his wife and Sir Harold Perceval, the Steward of Christ Church, joined us and gave us tea in their very North Oxford front parlour of the little house. Swinton is a dear and a gay old bird; unaware of my Guinness connections, he told us tales of old Lord Iveagh and of the Elveden picture collection, which of course quite eclipses even the Northwick one. We then drove back to London. On the way the FM disparaged Mr Chamberlain, and said slightly damning things about him, remarking that we had made a mistake in giving up Czechoslovakia without a fight. It is the old Munich schism, which so divides people. ... I was piqued; though he is the gentlest and goodest of men, and almost (but luckily not quite) a Saint. He's kindly, affectionate, yet shy and detached, and is often dreamy and vague, but withal the soldier of all time.

Back at Belgrave Square I tried to remember all the things he had told me during the past two days – of his disagreements with Winston (he fundamentally both hates and admires him). He and the PM had two tiffs on the trip [to America], and he said, 'Winston is always expecting rabbits to come out of empty hats'. Lately the PM has been very angry and disappointed by the Burmese campaign, which though it has not exactly been a triumph, has kept the Japs occupied and anxious for many months, at small expense to us. 'An unreasonable genius is this Winston.' I feel in my bones that he [Winston] will either move or dégommer Wavell when he dares.

As soon as we got back to London the FM changed from his blue flannel suiting back into uniform and we drove to the Dorchester to dine with Lady Cunard. I had proposed ourselves, and was rather apprehensive lest her party would be more than usually ill-chosen, and it was a scrap Sunday collection of boys and girls. Bridget Parsons, Enid Paget, Jim Lees-Milne, James Pope-Hennessy. However, Wavell was in high spirits, and as he was treated like royalty, soon dominated the dinner and made it hilarious. Afterwards we were joined by Francis Queensberry and before long Wavell was quoting from Keats and Kipling, and it became a duel between him and Queensberry. Then we were interrupted by General Nye, the Vice-CIGS telephoning, and I had to escort him to Kings Cross, where he was to board the special train to take him to an exercise in the North. I piloted him to the train where we were received by General Paget, C-in-C Home Forces, and taken aboard, and given drinks in the luxurious saloon. They begged me to come along, but I had no luggage. I put Maurice Collis's book 'The Land of The Great Image' in the FM's wagon-lit, and then finally left, driving home in his grand car.

31 May

My great new friend Field-Marshal Sir Archibald Wavell gay, debonair and affectionate returned about 5 o'clock. The man is both an inspiration and a saint.

1 June

Lunched at the 'Senior' with the FM and Rupert Hart-Davis, a publisher nephew of Duff's.[7] General Montgomery was at the next table, and he joined us for a little. He was in battle dress – a tiresome pose since, inconsistently, he is staying in the grandest suite at Claridges.

2 June

Today the FM went to Aldershot, but returned early. He's so gay and garrulous these days, though I think lonely. This evening I collected Alan Moorehead and Mrs George Bambridge for drinks. She is an old acquaintance whom I haven't seen for many years, but as she is Kipling's daughter I knew that Wavell would like to meet her.

3 June

Before lunch I walked to the War Office to fetch the FM, and as I waited in the vestibule I chatted with Lady Grigg, General Paget, Dickie Mountbatten and others. We then drove to Kemsley House to lunch with His Lordship of that name. A brilliant party, I must admit, though I arranged it myself. G. M. Young, the writer and thinker, Arthur Bryant,[8] and Deneys Reitz.[9] Good conversation. Reitz told me an amusing tale how at Dunkirk time the King had consulted the Chief Rabbi, and they had chatted. The Rabbi, whilst assuring the monarch that all would finally be well, added that 'All the same, Sir, I should put some of the Colonies in your wife's name!'

5 June *Kelvedon*

I came here alone to rest, quite worn out, and thought much of Wavell. 'In war was never lion raged more fierce. In peace was never gentle lamb more mild.'

7. He subsequently published Lord Wavell's anthology *Other Men's Flowers*.

8. Historian and author; b. 1899.

9. South African High Commissioner; author of the Boer War classic *Commando*.

6 June *5 Belgrave Square*

I returned after lunch, and about six received the FM for whom I had collected a small dinner party of Lord and Lady Londonderry, Lady Willingdon, and Harold Balfour, and it was a great success. Wavell likes Society, with a capital S and has had little of it. Yet I fear that this good, gentle, affectionate warrior is unhappy, and fears that he may be for the high jump, and that Winston will sack him. I don't think that he will dare to do it: more likely he'll make him Viceroy.

8 June

Today Winston addressed the Commons and I took the precaution of obtaining a seat for the FM. The Prime Minister was less discursive and amusing than usual, and looked bored and so, I fear, did we: he paid no tribute to the Field-Marshal although he mentioned several other Generals. I hear that he cannot make up his mind about Wavell, and oscillates between possessive admiration of him, and ridiculing and belittling him. None the less, in the Lobby afterwards, Wavell had an ovation, and we were soon surrounded by Lady Astor, Ned Grigg, Archie Southby and even Ellen Wilkinson. I saw Lloyd George approach, his white mane falling over his bright blue suit, and I introduced them. A great moment.

Afterwards I took him to dine with Emerald to meet Professor Joad, not a very successful evening, as one guest (female I regret to record) was so much the worse for drink that she behaved in a Hogarthian manner, and raved, ranted and was coquettish in turn and finally threw all the spoons at David Margesson and told incoherent tales about elephants and earwigs. We were all most embarrassed, except the Field-Marshal who seemed oblivious, though later he remarked that he was sorry for her as she must be desperately unhappy to have made such an exhibition of herself.

9 June

Lady Astor came up to me in the lobby today, and confided in me that Wavell is for the high jump. A Cabinet Minister, so she told me, had remarked after seeing her talking with him yesterday: 'So you are burying your dead?' She thinks that Winston is determined to get rid of him. I only told Peter, who was much depressed.

10 June

Peter has been making a little quiet investigation, and learns that it is on the tapis to make Wavell Governor-General of Australia. Dégommage indeed! I doubt whether this will happen, and think that it will be Delhi, as Winston would not dare to shelve him completely. The public would not stand it . . .

Later we had drinks with Amerys – sherry – in their gloomy but highly friendly house in Eaton Square.

The Field-Marshal is an angel, but he is an exhausting one; he seems to fill the house. He is called at 7.15, though he does not come down till 9 o'clock: but all the time I am aware of his presence. He sleeps in the big Empire bedroom next to mine, and through the communicating bathroom door I hear him muttering to himself, quoting poetry, etc. It is all a bit of a strain, and he seems quite oblivious of the attention lavished upon him, although he is occasionally affectionate and always gentle and good-natured. There is no news yet as to when they are returning to India. Peter is depressed and fears that all is over. Possibly retirement, or at best, Australia. The Merry Major thinks that he may be a Lieutenant next week. I personally still think that it will be Delhi, and indeed this is what my agents all inform me.

12 June

We packed the FM off to Bailiff's Court after we lunched here. He had absolutely no plans, so I secretly rang up the Amerys and persuaded them to invite him for the weekend. And so off he has gone.

15 June

A big day. I did not see the FM when he returned to London as he went direct to the War Office, but he rang up that he wanted to see me, and would soon return. He did, and in high spirits, as I soon saw. He paced the Morning Room, almost distractedly, and then confided in me the following tale which nobody (he added) as yet knows:

The night before, in the country, he had received a summons to come up to London last night to dine at No. 10. His first impulse had been to refuse, as he thought it inconsiderate of Winston to ignore him all this time, and then so suddenly want to see him on a Bank Holiday: however, up he came, and at No. 10 he found himself alone with the PM who was in rollicking mood: almost at once he offered him the Viceroyalty, and Wavell admits that he was dumbfounded, as he had never taken my hints and jokes on the subject seriously. He accepted, provided that Lady Wavell agreed, and an urgent cable was written out and despatched to her. I congratulated him, and begged him to tell Peter, which he did, and the loyal devoted Major was stunned, surprised and overjoyed. Afterwards (P. had a date) Wavell and I drove to the Athenaeum, where we lunched and discussed the appointment at length . . .

I had a long talk with the FM and begged him not only to accept the Vice-regal offer, but to rejoice in it. Delhi and Vice-regal trappings, rather than Cheltenham and the simple life: it is not given to every soldier to have so brilliant a retirement.

16 June

The secret is still inviolate: though rumours are flying about: nothing can be announced until Lady Wavell replies, and the King returns from his successful but too long-delayed African tour. We lunched in. Eileen Sutherland, Bettine Abingdon, Norah Lindsay, P., the FM, Mrs Samuel Whitbread, and Desmond McCarthy. Most successful, and the FM seemed enchanted with me and with life. No wonder, for he has eclipsed his model and hero, Lord Allenby: his victories have been greater, and he is to be a Viceroy, while Allenby was only High Commissioner in Egypt. P. says that I am the FM's best, and perhaps only, friend. I must say that his own are a mummified lot who have failed to keep pace with life, and 'Archie' likes life, and youth.

18 June *London*

A cable was on my breakfast tray announcing that my mother died yesterday in St Luke's Hospital, Chicago, where in the days of long ago (1927 I think) I had my tonsils out. I find I have no regrets, little remorse, still less sadness, yet. Her death is a release to her, to me, and to everybody. For years and years she has been a problem, and she was always eccentric, always unattractive, and selfish. I think she was, as doctors and psychiatrists as long ago as '23 declared, a paranoiac. She was always untidy, careless, suspicious, strange and depressed. Lately, she led a ghastly life. . . . But still, her sudden death is a shock . . .

I chucked Emerald's dinner party, preferring to be alone on the first evening of my mourning. However, I escorted the FM there, and deposited him with her in her suite at the Dorchester. And then I walked home alone, motherless and an orphan.

19 June *Himley Hall, Dudley*

I decided to come here to stay with Eric and Laura Dudley in spite of my poor mother's death. Since there is nothing I can do at this distance. So the FM, P., and I lunched and left at 2 o'clock in his fast car. We chatted all the way, he very gay, Peter as ever somewhat subdued in his presence. We stopped at Northwick to have tea with George Churchill, and to see the Madonna of the Cherries, the pseudo-Leonardo about which the FM has written so lovely a poem; he has given me a copy of it.[10] It expresses much of his personality, as a writer and a soldier. What an unexpected man he is . . .

The Vice-regal appointment is public. It was announced this morning, and every newspaper is full of it. Eric Dudley is enchanted to be entertaining the great man.

20 June

The new Viceroy is having the time of his life, and this gay bachelor existence suits him. This morning he went out riding (neither Peter nor I can abide a horse) and curiously enough he had a fall, quite a nasty one, at exactly twelve o'clock noon, the very moment when he ceased to be the Commander-in-Chief in India. He joked about it later, and was not hurt at all. What he minds more, he says, was that his pay stops from noon today, except for his Field-Marshal's emolument, until he assumes the Vice-royalty on 19 October. During the afternoon, we looked at

10. Subsequently printed in Wavell's *Other Men's Flowers*.

the monument of Rosie Ednam, and suddenly conscience-stricken I thought of my old mother being buried today at four o'clock, in the little La Belle Cemetery, at Oconomowoc, where she was born.

21 June *London*

We drove back to London in glorious summer weather: the roads were deserted. I am finding it a slight strain having the Field-Marshal in the house, as he is un peu sur le dos, and has a habit of always being there. As he sleeps next door, I am always hearing him coughing and muttering and blowing his nose. He is noisy and heavy in his movements.

22 June

The Field-Marshal now wears my clothes, since he is out of uniform, and today he wore my blue suit, and looked well in it, almost skittish. I lent him everything, shirt, socks and studs . . .

Tonight was the Kemsley's banquet in honour of the new Viceroy, and though it was hurriedly arranged, it was a huge success. Beforehand I had to break it to the Field-Marshal, both that it would be a large and important affair, and that he must dress. As he had no clothes, I lent him an old dinner jacket, and helped to dress him, putting in his links (mine) and tying his tie. He then had to be primed that he must make a speech, which he has hardly ever done before. The Kemsleys had collected half the Government and in fact most of London. The Amerys, the Spanish and Belgian Ambassadors, the fat, foolish Archbishop, and Mrs Temple, Brendan Bracken, the Greenwoods and many, many more. Wavell sat on Lady Kemsley's right, facing Lord Kemsley. The table was a vast empty square. After dinner, Kemsley spoke, proposing the health of the great guest, and then my poor Field-Marshal rose shyly to his feet, and began his speech by saying that two very unexpected things had recently happened to him. One, that he had become Viceroy of India, and two, that his entire wardrobe had been supplied by me. Everybody laughed, but I felt a touch foolish since everyone stared at me, and I also felt a pang of anxiety, since I know he hates speaking. At first he seemed shy and ill at ease, though after a moment or two he acquitted himself better than I should ever have thought, and it was obvious that he made an excellent impression. I felt somehow that perhaps tonight was the high watermark of the Wavell visit, at least as far as it concerned me. The banquet was a stupendous send-off for the Viceroy designate. He was both charmed and charming, and Peter was blissful; the dinner will perhaps rank with the farewell one for Lord Curzon, attended by all the 'Souls'.[11]

The World's Press is favourable to the Wavell appointment. London Society blames it on me, or gives me the credit for it, I do not know which, but I have certainly had several letters of congratulation.

23 June

After a too-long dinner with Emerald, Peter and I had a long talk at home, and we were both a touch tipsy, tired and irritable: he broke it to me that there was mischief afoot: a woman friend of his who works in the War Office had rung him up, and warned him that she had heard from a high War Cabinet source that Wavell was being much criticised for going so much dans le grand monde, now that he was Viceroy; and Peter hinted that I, too, was being abused for my kindness and hospitality. Such is the jealousy of this world. I have surrounded this poor lonely man with affection, have literally made his London life, and now people gossip.

24 June

I didn't sleep, suffering from too much tobacco, wine, society and surfeit, and this morning I felt cross with everybody; indeed I did not get up; but the FM came up to my room, and was affectionate, and asked anxiously if he could do anything for me? . . .

Bill Astor attacked me in the House of Commons about Wavell. I think he is jealous, and I told him that he was a scold like his old mother; but we parted friends.

25 June

This morning Cecil Beaton photographed the Field-Marshal in

11. In 1898, when Curzon was about to leave for India to take up the Viceroyalty. It was in fact an Etonian dinner.

every room of the house, and in every position, though I was rather against the whole performance.

Rab came to see me later. I pumped him; he inferred that I was generally believed to have 'rigged' the Vice-royalty. He hadn't heard a word of criticism, and even Ismay has been pleasant about the whole episode.

29 June

This evening I escorted my illustrious guest to the Dorchester, where we dined with the Camroses, Alba, Doreen Brabourne, Abingdons, and others. I fear he was bored, yet it was important for him to go, and he owes the Camrose link, like so many others, to me. But he cheered up after a glass of champagne, and finally became almost hilarious. Much later, I heard doors banging in the wee hours, and I think he must have fallen asleep in the morning room, and awakened hours later: he is inclined to do that, sometimes.

30 June

After some discussion this morning, the FM and I decided that the Dorchester is the most suitable hotel for him to stay in, and I have selected a suite and reserved it. Lady Wavell is expected soon. It will be a relief, because I am rather worn out by so big a dose of society and constant companionship. All my life, I have had occasionally to be alone for an odd day or evening, or more. Now I scarcely ever have an hour to myself, and my batteries are fast running down. I look like a skeleton.

1 July

I lunched at the Spanish Embassy, where Brendan Bracken announced, before everybody, that I had been the first to say that Wavell should be Viceroy. 'We have done everything you wanted, Chips,' he added, 'made him a Field-Marshal, a Viceroy and now a Viscount, in spite of Alec Hardinge.' He then went on to explain that Alec Hardinge had tried very hard to fob off Wavell with a barony, and had even written a memo to the King on the subject, which infuriated Winston. Brendan Bracken hinted that this small act might prove his undoing, as small acts often do, in the end. I have high hopes that he will soon be dégommé. It's high time.[12]

Brendan also told a fantastic tale, which I believe to be true, of how Woodrow Wilson for nine months refused to receive Lord Grey of Fallodon when he was Ambassador in Washington, because of an alleged indiscretion of one of his subordinates, a man who has recently been killed in an air raid at Folkestone; apparently he made indiscreet remarks about the President and Mrs Wilson's early relations, which were repeated at the White House. Wilson never got over it, and for nine months, England's Ambassador, and a man of such integrity and high reputation as Lord Grey, was not received, and was unable to present his credentials.[13]

5 July

In the lobby of the Ritz I read the horrifying news that a plane had crashed at Gibraltar and that General Sikorski, the leader and hero of Poland, had been killed. I thought at once of Victor Cazalet, and wondered whether he had been with him, and then of Lady Wavell who is also supposed to be somewhere en route. A moment or two later the tape ticked out the words that Colonel Cazalet, MP for Chippenham, was among the victims, and everything blurred. I felt sick, and cold and numb, for Victor was one of my oldest friends, and a loyal and loving lad.

What an appalling year; the death roll grows, and soon all my contemporaries will be gone. Victor is a great loss. He had the hardness of a Christian Scientist, combined with the kindest heart imaginable. No service was too trivial or too great for him to perform for a friend, and he made friendship a cult, and though he much preferred friends to be high-born, rich and famous (he was a colossal snob, and admitted it), he was nevertheless equally painstaking with the poor and unimportant. His hobbies were Poles

12. Lord Hardinge resigned as Private Secretary to the King 'for reasons of health' a fortnight later.

13. The story is in substance true. The episode that caused so much coolness was the repetition of the famous Washington story that Mrs Wilson had declared 'When Woodrow proposed to me I was so surprised that I nearly fell out of bed'.

and Jews, and his phobia was Russia, and he did not live altogether in vain, for he recently frustrated Anthony Eden in his attempt to cede the Baltic States to the Soviet Union. Eden, who was an old friend, is now near to admitting that Teenie, as everybody called Victor, was perhaps right. Victor had not changed in appearance since the Versailles days of 1918 when he was ADC to the Allied Council there, and ever since then he has been a character in London Society, and known the world over. Too many people accepted his hospitality and abused him afterwards, indeed people were malicious about him who were never unkind about anyone else, for in some, usually men, he roused something akin to fury. Women were ever his allies, especially old ones. Since the war, it was as if he had prescience that he would not live, for he spent his life being kind to his old friends, and doing them services. He was intimate with Baldwin, and had been with Lloyd George. But in later years, his passion, which was reciprocated, was Edward Halifax, and they were inseparable.

6 July

The PM paid a suitable tribute to both Sikorski and to Victor Cazalet in the House. Incidentally, there was another MP in the plane, a good-looking but unexciting man, Lt. Col. Whiteley, who sits for Buckingham. Nobody mentioned him, and although married with children, who doubtless loved him, it is the social, répandu Victor who gets all the publicity . . .

The Field-Marshal's social career, and his new bachelor life, is a long astonishment to him. He has never known anything of the sort before, and although probably the finest soldier since Wellington, he is a child in society. Only his greatness and charm save him.

9 July

A muddled morning. Messages by the dozen, and a terrific telephone bombardment. I lunched with Colebox, with Duff Cooper, Oliver Lyttelton, Loelia Westminster, Esmond Rothermere and Barrington Ward, the Editor of 'The Times'. The conversation was brilliant, led by Emerald and consisted of a volley of wit and indecency which continued until 3.30. In the course of it,

Emerald announced 'The trouble about Wavell is that he is riddled with idealism.'

12 July

The FM has finally moved to the Dorchester, but this evening he appeared at Belgrave Square unannounced and stayed for two hours. Peter says that he is obsessed with me, and that I am 'better with him than anyone he has ever known'. There seem to be further delays over Lady Wavell's arrival, who was due tonight.[14]

13 July

A vast dinner party (which I had half arranged) at the Egyptian Embassy, where the host was Amir Bey, the Ambassador whose chief claim to fame is the fact that he was once squash champion of the world. About forty people. Lady Willingdon picked me up, and we arrived together. Wavell arrived alone, and did le cercle like reigning royalty, speaking to everybody, and he did it well. I was next to the Indian High Commissioner, Sir Somebody Something, who had Emerald on his side, and I heard her opening remarks to him – 'Are you an Untouchable?' Her indiscreet remarks and inspired triviality may well have caused much of the Wavell mischief. This evening the FM obviously avoided her. The party consisted of the Cromers, Kemsleys, etc., and had great style; uneatable food, magnificently served.

18 July *Brighton*

I gave Bosie, Lord Alfred Douglas, lunch at Sweetings, and found him ageing, but still gay and young in manner. He now boasts of his relations with Wilde, and was fascinating about him and them. He's still rather litigious, and wants to fight everybody. I don't know quite how he lives, though I, and several others, help him financially.

21 July

The Field-Marshal and Lady Wavell, he wearing my black striped suit, and Lady Wavell in a hat I think she had made herself, lunched at Buckingham Palace, while I lunched with Sibyl

14. She arrived on 14 July.

Colefax and Diana Cooper at the Ivy. Sibyl had collected Maurice Collis for me whom I so wanted to meet. He is my new literary hero, and author of those absorbing books, 'The Great Within', 'Siamese White', and others. In appearance he is a typical retired civil servant, which for many years he was. Luckily he resigned, so literature is the richer.

22 July

Returning home this evening, I found the Field-Marshal awaiting me . . . and he was gay, and garrulous and told me many tales of his youth and his relations: he asked me to dine, but I refused, as I had arranged to go to Emerald's, and she now complains that I neglect her. . . . I left early, and meeting Sir Lancelot Oliphant in the corridor, heard the astonishing news that Mussolini had resigned, and that Fascism in Italy had been overthrown. Could it be true? I rushed back to Emerald's party, but nobody would believe me. I said I had secret agents, and Gladwyn Jebb, who after all is an important FO official, rang up the Foreign Office, and the resident clerk confirmed the news. Everyone was stunned and excited. Dazed and jubilant, I walked home.

27 July

An historic day in the House of Commons, where Winston made his pronouncement on Italy. . . . The House was packed and the excitement intense, and I thought the PM's speech the most statesman-like of his utterances, for he avoided cheap jibes or wit at the expense of the fallen Duce, and he deplored too much jubilation. It was restrained and subtle, and prepared the Commons for greater things to come. The consensus of opinion was that Churchill had been masterly.

When he finished I went to lunch with the Parliamentary Empire Association at the Savoy, a small lunch arranged for Wavell, whose face literally lit up when he saw me; I fetched him his cocktail, introduced MPs to him, and generally ADC'd him. He is apt to be a lonely and isolated figure, in public. (Peter was not there.) Leo Amery, in a completely inaudible speech, introduced him, and then the Viceroy Designate rose, and rather shyly, made a charming simple speech in reply. We then adjourned to the House of Commons, where he gave another excellent address to a very crowded mixed all-party meeting, and he made a most favourable impression. I organized a deafening clap. He actually seemed a bit dull to me, as I have heard all of it so often before; in fact it was a re-hash, but to newcomers, enthralling, and he looked somehow, so lovable, and lonely and almost pathetic. I am devoted to him.

28 July
All up early, as another Wavell day dawned. I breakfasted with Peter before 8, as he wanted to see about the Field-Marshal's robes for taking his seat in the House of Lords, to say nothing of Lady Wavell's clothes. I followed him to Westminster, where I gave Lady Willingdon lunch at the Commons, while the Wavells lunched in the Lords. Afterwards we joined up. Lady Wavell was lunching alone with Lord Denman (who has lent her a tiara for India), and the FM was with his supporters, Lord Lee of Fareham and Lord Trenchard, both Viscounts. I introduced Lady Willingdon to Lady Wavell, and B[15] took Q in, and they chatted for a few minutes while they sized each other up. Then we passed into the robing rooms, where already Wavell was donning his ermine and velvet, and Lady Oxford rushed up to me in her dominating manner. 'Will you introduce me to Wavell. He is the Empire's hero.' And so I led her up to the Field-Marshal, who was trying to get into his robes. He smiled and chatted with her for a minute, rather taken aback by her onslaught, and she was enchanted: she looks like a scarecrow, or a mad raven, yet there is still fire in that antique skeleton, and she has ever been my friend and my ally. I then escorted Lady Wavell to the entrance of the Lords. The peers were still at Prayers, but eventually the doors were flung open and we went in. Places had been reserved for the family, and I stood at the bar, as the procession entered with Wavell immensely dignified and somewhat diffident. He bowed correctly, answered audibly, and removed his hat the endless times required. He has taken the name of Viscount Wavell of Cyrenaica and Winchester. There were other more imaginative suggestions, but it appears that the Garter King at Arms has been unhelpful and pompous.

15. Lady Willingdon's nickname was Bee; Lady Wavell's was Q.

29 July

Rab introduced his famous Education Bill, or rather presented it in its preliminary stages. He did it well, and unostentatiously. He is unassuming by nature.

2 August *Kelvedon*

I am here alone, and I have been thinking much about Wavell. I have seen him almost every day for the last two months, and when he is not there I now miss his gruff gentleness . . . he has a grandeur of character and genius which is transcendent. It is his detachment and long sudden silences which disturb and worry people.

5 September

Wavell asked me about the Pilgrim's Banquet; was it important, and what ought he to say? I had accepted the invitation for him weeks ago and I had impressed upon him how important it was to make a good speech; I told him in fact, that he should go 'all out'; it would be a magnificent opportunity; a fine platform; I advised him to tell about his Texas connexions, and to quote Walt Whitman. He caught fire from my enthusiasm and sat down this evening in the upstairs gallery, and made notes for two hours. For all his tremendous erudition, he is curiously childish and even ignorant in some ways. He had hardly heard of the Pilgrims.

11 September *Bailiff's Court, Nr Climping, Sussex*

I came here to stay with the Amerys via the Coopers at Bognor whose house, once so charming, is now untidy and down at heel; and there are geese, hens and rabbits in coops disfiguring the lawns, for Diana, rapturously lovely, is now an advanced agriculturalist. Staying . . . John Julius, who declaimed to us in Russian (he is to answer questions before the Brains Trust on Monday); Lady Hardwicke, Conrad Russell and his aged sister, Miss Flora. A pleasant al fresco meal was followed by a sleep, sun-bath and long walk along the beach though it was sad to see the barbed wire and the huge concrete pillboxes everywhere. At length I arrived at the Amerys. Bailiff's Court is indeed a rich man's folly. A Norman feudal monster entirely created overnight by Honor's cousins the Moynes; it has a certain attraction: peace, gorgeous sea air and new trees, planted in many thousands, and it is comfortable . . .

The Amerys are a kindly, cosy, gentle family. Angels all. Julian is shrewd and remarkably alert and intelligent.

12 September *Bailiff's Court*

The house is comfortable, but the gadgets, the bible boxes, the wrought iron and other feudalities are faintly ridiculous. Leo Amery and Julian and I went for a 'five-miler' around the estate, taking what is called 'Lady Moyne's Walk'; Walter Moyne must have spent tens of thousands of pounds on his trees which he imported fully grown from Burgundy. On our walk Leo Amery, whose tremendously well-stocked mind is not always revealed to full advantage, because of his deafness, let drop an inconsequent remark à propos the governorship of Madras. I did not quite understand: did he mean that I had been considered and turned-down? Or was he sounding me?

16 September

Ava Anderson gave rather an old fashioned Proustian tea-party in her enchanting little house in Lord North Street. What an excellent maitresse-de-maison she is, and how clever at creating a distinguished atmosphere. She told me that old Margot Oxford had lunched with her and complained that all she had to live on now was macaroni and memorial services . . .

21 September

Two deaths: Kingsley Wood and Lord Kenmare. Kingsley Wood collapsed this morning at the age of 62. He was a small shrewd solicitor, Amery-size, with a twinkle in his eye; he was ambitious and sensible and always a secret Chamberlain sympathiser. I got on well with him; and the nation owes him a debt of gratitude for the admirable manner in which he has conducted the complicated finances of the country. . . . He was liked, but not loved, and I fear, there is no real grief today. Indeed, all the Upper Ministers, whilst expressing perfunctory regret, seemed secretly excited at the prospect of promotion. They looked like kittens awaiting a bowl of cream, and the lobbies buzzed with expectancy and speculation; who will be Chancellor? Will it entail a major re-shuffle?

Valentine Kenmare was a very different character ... An immense, kindly, jovial witty creature, Falstaffian, funny and boisterous and always grossly overdressed; yet with a kindly heart and was not quite the fraud he pretended to be. He has survived his father only by a short time. His present consort, Enid, has now buried three husbands. Valentine made a precedent in writing gossip, and by becoming a journalist in the days when it was still thought extraordinary and in bad taste to be either. He had a Jewish wit, and was the supreme raconteur.

23 September

More deaths: now the Reaper has bagged Elinor Glyn; she was an extraordinary woman; feline, theatrical, a 'poseuse' and a vulgarian, but a personality. She was a little in love with me in 1918 though I always, perhaps unkindly, called her 'Grandma'. I once saw her every day for months in Paris: her long red hair was famous, as were her tiny green eyes that used, all too often, to light up amorously. But she was a brave old girl, tough, upright, and unexpectedly religious. She tried hard to marry Lord Curzon; and, indeed, redecorated Montacute in her own appalling taste, with tiger skins and mauve carpets. But it was Lord Alistair Innes-Ker who was (as she often told me) the love of her life, and he is the hero of that period-piece, the once fashionable and so daring book 'Three Weeks' which made her famous.

24 September

I had Ava Anderson, always gay and engaging, to lunch alone, and told her that her husband, not Sam Hoare, would be Chancellor of the Exchequer. She did not believe me. But I heard this morning ... that Winston just hasn't the courage to offer Sam the Exchequer; he is too afraid of the Eden-ite clique, who would never agree to having so senior a rival to Anthony in the Cabinet. ... Later in the day, we were proved right and it was confirmed that Anderson had been offered the coveted post ... Ava was fetched from Belgrave Square by her Chancellor-to-be.

28 September *London*

There is indignant consternation in London over the recent Government changes; it is felt (and he has been told) that Winston let a great opportunity slip; for recently he had begun to woo the Conservative Party, with some success: and now, suddenly he snubs it, and takes back his old crony Beaverbrook, making him Lord Privy Seal, and so affronts a large and powerful section of his supporters. The minor promotions are all too Eden-ite in character. One expected favouritism, which is legitimate in politics, but the Prime Minister was ill-advised to ignore the party as a whole. It is a scandal that Alan Lennox-Boyd was not sent to the Admiralty.

7 October

This evening I had my big party for the Wavells ... [it was] quiet, elegant and certainly distinguished. At 5.30 punctually my first guest, Lady Halifax, arrived, and was charming: she was followed by the Duke of Alba and his delightful dreamy daughter Tana; then came Portia Stanley, the Chetwode ménage; Mr Philips, the American Ambassador at large, and after that I lost count – for three hours people poured in; young and old; gay and great; tight and sober; and soon the blue dining-room, with its flickering candles, was crowded. Over 105 people turned up. Who do I remember? ... Freya Stark, dressed like an Eskimo in a white fur coat; Eva Curie, chic and military, in French uniform; Violet Trefusis, grandly got-up in an 1860 affair; Loelia Westminster in green; Mrs Amery wandering sad-eyed, like a ghost; the Belgian Ambassador bow-wowing; Harold Nicolson in a corner with Lady Wavell; Audrey Bouverie wearing a curious bird hat; Daisy Fellowes, elegant but ageing; and ever so many more. Hore-Belisha said it was the most glamorous party he had been to since the war. And certainly so it seemed. The black-out fell at 7 o'clock, and there were taxi difficulties, old Princess de Polignac sitting in the porter's chair in the front hall for an hour awaiting a conveyance, while people chattered and made dates; the candles guttered, and the cocktails were passed and it was after 8.30 before the room emptied. Wavell and Amery arrived late together and I gave them the last drinks. It was all a huge glamorous success, and I hope the Wavells were pleased. They are off soon.

11 October

A grey, gloomy day dawned and I half-hoped, half-dreaded, that the Wavell departure would be postponed, but it was not to be. Just before two, I drove in my little car to Airways House where the departure was to take place, and found the Vice-regal train drawn-up; there were police, and soon friends, relations and the Government began to arrive; it was a distinguished galaxy, but emotional.

12 October

There was excitement at the House and I knew at once that there was something afoot. After Questions Amery read out a long statement about the famine in Bengal, and then Winston rose and announced our recent occupation of the Azores. He did it with relish and skill and the House was enchanted.

There are many references in the Diaries to later meetings with Wavell, but it may be most convenient to insert at this point what Chips wrote about his friend on 26 May 1950, two days after Wavell's death:

What a curious man Lord Wavell was ... great in his way, full of humour, a touch deaf, with the power of shutting his mind, or almost all of it, to the assembled company or what was happening to him. He often gave the impression of being dull and even 'ramolli' and he could, at times, ask the same question of the same woman several times at dinner. But if he liked somebody or was amused – and especially after a few cocktails – the problem was not how to make him talk, but how to stop him. He was not a politician or a statesman, and his judgment was frequently bad, even childish: but as a writer, a friend and a general he was supreme.

His one eye had an uncanny way of seeing through one's weaknesses ... he remained in some ways a simple soldier, and would talk of 'billets', but his humour overflowed, though it was of the acrostic kind. He could do 'The Times' crossword in 20 minutes.

He was untidy, he cordially disliked Winston, he was fond of his family, particularly of Archie John, and of his formidable old sisters who live at Ringwood . . . but he was bored, really, by them all. Lady Wavell worshipped him, and he was increasingly touching and tender with her, but rarely listened to what she said . . . sometimes I wonder how sincere he was: he should have protested against the folly of the Greek campaign . . . he should have resigned in India: he was anti-Munich and really quite silly when he discussed Neville Chamberlain . . . but I shall always remember him with much affection, and am proud and pleased that so great a man gave me his loving trust.

CHAPTER NINE

The End of the War
October 1943–June 1945

13 October, 1943
I turned on the wireless and heard the official announcement of Italy's declaration of war on Germany. So now the wheel has turned full circle.

16 October *Kelvedon*
People are agreed that the Prime Minister's handling of the Coal Debate was masterly, and his speech has done much to please and placate the aggrieved Conservative Party. Whenever he is in trouble he veers towards us, and leans on us.

23 October *Palace Hotel, Suite 38, Southend-on-Sea*
It is a year since the vital battle of El Alamein began. What a year of disillusion for Germany, and of triumph for the Allies.

28 October *London*
Rab dropped in and remained for two hours; and he told me much that I was able to piece together with what I already knew; on the day of my giant cocktail party for the Wavells, he [Wavell] had put in an ill-fated memo on the future policy for India, which was debated in the War Cabinet for hours: in it he advocated releasing Gandhi, and other extreme left-wing measures. The Cabinet was stunned, and Churchill exploded; in fact nearly cancelled the appointment altogether. How could Wavell have been so ill-advised? Never has there been such a political faux-pas. . . . A man who can be so politically inexperienced may easily make another similar mistake, and Wavell's Vice-royalty may end sooner than one expects.

5 November *London*
I gather from Diana Cooper, Geoffrey Lloyd and Rab, all of

whom came to see me during the day, that the grand re-shuffle has been postponed until the end of the month. Alan [Lennox-Boyd], though he is as yet unaware of it, will be taken back into the Government, but Winston won't finally make up his mind, and in any case enjoys the spectacle of his Ministers – fearful and hopeful – dancing like cats on hot bricks awaiting his decisions.

Geoffrey furthermore, told me that the Government is seriously concerned about the prospect of aerial bombardment of London, on a mammoth scale, by rockets: they know that the Germans are straining everything to produce a rocket which will destroy London. A pleasant outlook.

10 November

The Government appointments are to be made public tomorrow; Duff becomes a Minister of State in the occupied regions of Africa at £5,000 per year, and will be Ambassador in Paris, thus splitting Harold Macmillan's job. Diana is enchanted, and yet saddened by the prospect . . . and doesn't want to be away for five or six years. But more exciting than the Coopers' plans, is that the Prime Minister rang up Alan at Edinburgh today, was charming and considerate and offered him the Parliamentary Secretaryship of the Ministry of Aircraft Production, under Cripps. Alan jumped at it.

14 November *London*

Much talk of imminent aerial bombardment, and rockets that will half demolish London. It will be unpleasant, and there is no doubt that the Germans are 'up' to something.

16 November *London*

There is serious unrest amongst the Conservatives at the growing influence and power of Beaverbrook; it is said that the new triumvirate of Bracken, Cherwell, and Beaverbrook rule the country when the PM is abroad, and dominate and fascinate him when he is at home.

19 November *London*

I gave a dinner-party at which Mrs Keppel was the 'show' piece;

she looked magnificent in black sequins and jewels, and her fine white hair and gracious manners are impressive: she is so affectionate and grande dame that it is a pity she tipples, and then becomes garrulous and inaccurate in her statements. . . . Fine food and adequate wine, candlelight and conversation. . . . Cecil [Beaton] told us that he had been to see the Queen, who told him that the Buckingham Palace balcony has become unsafe; they want to use it for their victory appearance, and are ordering cement.

23 November *London*

The last day of the dying session was largely given up to argument's about Mosley's inopportune release, which has caused considerable excitement in the country, largely whipped up by the Communists and Jewish elements. I walked to the House with Geoffrey Lloyd and saw nothing unusual, though I was told later that an angry crowd had surrounded the St Stephen's entrance, and policemen had had to use batons: then the public lobby was crowded with young factory workers indignantly protesting at his release. I rather enjoyed the ironical scene of the Labour Party so enraged by the release of one of their ex-Ministers by a Labour Home Secretary! Their indignation seemed great. Morrison made an excellent case for his order; he is an able Parliamentarian, and he put it over with skill and persuasion, explaining that Mosley had been examined by five eminent physicians, who reported unanimously that his health demanded his release from Holloway. I know Mosley intimately or rather did: he is an unscrupulous but not unattractive fellow, dominated by an urge for power and publicity. . . . His first wife, Cynthia, Lord Curzon's daughter, was one of God's gentlest and loveliest creatures.

We then went into Secret Session and heard Attlee's announcement of Winston's meeting with Roosevelt and Stalin. It fell flat, as most of us were already aware of it; and the others were too angry about Mosley to be interested. Yet their meeting is the most sensational since Tilsit. The Prime Minister went to the Azores in the 'Renown', and on to Cairo, and is now at Teheran with Roosevelt and Stalin. A fantastic page in history.

4 December

At lunch with the Londonderrys, Charlie held forth about his cousin Winston, who, he maintains, has few Churchillian qualities: the Churchills, he said, were a dreadful family: Winston's genius, according to him, comes from the Vane-Tempests, and his vitality from his American mother. Perhaps. The Prime Minister's grandmother was a Vane-Tempest, she was the daughter of the Vienna Lord Castlereagh, and became Duchess of Marlborough. Charlie Londonderry went on to tell us how his political prospects were blighted by an unfortunate dinner party at Emerald's before the war, when he argued with Winston, and said that France was unreliable and rotten and could not be depended upon. Winston lost his temper, being a fanatical Francophil; and could not forgive Londonderry then, and certainly not later, for being proved right. Charlie thinks that Smuts' surprising reference to France, predicting that she would be a second rate power after the war, is inspired, and probably by Winston himself. Certainly the remark has caused universal astonishment, and may act as a warning to de Gaulle. I don't know; but certainly Smuts is the only statesman who could have said it. I heard the speech on the 25th at Westminster, and am surprised that it has been published.

13 December

A Proustian incident. In a Bond Street jewellers, I saw an extraordinary marionette of a woman – or was it a man? It wore grey flannel trousers, a wide leather belt, masculine overcoat, and a man's brown felt hat, and had a really frightening appearance; but the hair was golden dyed and long: what is wrongly known as platinum; the mouth was a scarlet scar. Bundi began to growl, and as I secretly examined this terrifying apparition, I recognized Gladys Marlborough, once the world's most beautiful woman . . . the toast of Paris, the love of Proust, the belle amie of Anatole France. I hadn't seen her since my wedding, but there seemed no reason to cut her, and I went up to her, and smiled, and put out my hand which she took shrinkingly and then, breaking into French (as she always did) said, 'Est ce que je vous connais, Monsieur?' 'Yes,' I said, 'I am Chips.' She looked at me, stared vacantly with those famous turquoise eyes that once drove men insane with desire, and muttered: 'Je n'ai jamais entendu ce nom là,' she flung down a ruby clip she was examining, and bolted from the shop ... and I remembered how we had been allies for twenty years or more; how she used to telephone to me every morning; how I used to give her sugar in the last war when she was still dazzlingly beautiful; and how we used to lunch with Proust; and of the story that D'Annunzio fainted when he saw her, such was her beauty; then of the Blenheim days.... Le temps qui coule.... What an adventure.

14 December *5 Belgrave Square*

Up betimes and went shopping, and on to the House where Anthony Eden, smartly dressed, delivered a pretty travelogue which interested nobody particularly. He has not got the gift of holding the House, and there was little wit, humour or eloquence in his tedious description of the momentous meetings in Teheran and Cairo. After twenty minutes Members got up, and began to trickle out.

16 December

At the House of Commons, I was quickly aware that there was something up – what I didn't know, but at the end of Questions, Attlee rose and in his usual monotonous voice announced that the Prime Minister was ill, and that pneumonia had set in in his left lung. The House, taken completely by surprise, gasped, for the immediate and important eventualities which this may mean occurred to everybody. A few moments later I saw Anthony Eden and John Anderson, the two rival claimants to the succession, deep in grave conversation in a lobby, and when I went into the lavatory, there were Attlee and fat funny old Bevin, blustering with importance; they were amiable to me, and we agreed that the illness is serious: a man in poor condition physically, and nearly 70, cannot have pneumonia twice within a year without running grave risks. Attlee rather hinted that the Prime Minister was in the Middle East, and later I learnt from Emerald that he was in Algiers. Mrs Churchill left today by air to join him. Somehow everything went flat, and I came away.

17 December

An official announcement from Downing Street last night said that there was some improvement in the Prime Minister's condition: even if he lives, he will be ill for many weeks, and his powers will be delegated to others.

24 December *Christmas Eve, London*

Two deaths: Lady Wilson, Lord Ribblesdale's eldest daughter, who married Sir Matthew ('Scatters') Wilson. . . . She was a grey, bony, clever, boring, bas-bleu of a woman, who wrote dim sketches about France, dressed badly, and looked like a witch. He, on the other hand, with his boisterous spirits and zest for cards, horses, and pleasure, is a full-blooded Regency character . . . and the other is old Victor Bowring-Hanbury who was 76.

31 December *5 Belgrave Square*

What will this year unfold? The return of my son, I hope; my divorce, I dread. The Second Front? The aerial bombardment of London? Exhorbitant expenditure? What? My senses are deadened and I really don't much care. I feel my real life is over; I am 46, and I hate it.

1944

1 January

I enter the New Year lethargic in spirit, waking so out of sorts that I could not bear to lunch with Diana Cooper, Emerald and George Gage – my three dear friends: if only I knew of a comfortable monastery I would hie myself to it; the world, or what is left of it, means little to me now, and never have I started a new year in so dejected a state of mind. Indifference is warping my susceptibilities.

2 January

I went round to see Emerald, who was in tears, to say goodbye to the Coopers, who are leaving for Algiers: in fact we all cried, though little John Julius did more than I did to hide his tears. Duff, too was unusually attentive and affectionate and gentle.

7 January

Peter writes from Delhi, that the Viceroy has a new trick to get him through the tedium of Indian dinner-parties. He turns to his female neighbour, when conversation flags, and asks 'If you were not a woman – what animal would you like to be?'

I dined again with Emerald – her rooms at the Dorchester are like a 'garde meuble' so stuffed are they with fine French furniture. The set piece this evening was Lady Oxford, looking like a witch in the flickering candlelight. How she and Emerald dislike each other: and Margot began by accusing Emerald of 'bunking' to America to escape the bombing: for a moment there was atmosphere, but it passed. I sat next to Margot at dinner, and she held forth to the effect that though our hostess thought she was a clever woman, she was not: in fact she, Lady Oxford, had never met a clever woman: doubtless she had been unlucky – but she sometimes wondered if a clever woman existed. 'Women are barren', she added, 'they can do nothing without the stimulus of a man's love.' I suggested that they were the world's greatest letter-writers. She agreed, and cited Norah Lindsay, Lady Desborough – Mme de Sévigné and herself. . . . As she had twice said I was the kindest man in London I tried to stick up for her – but Emerald delivered a tirade, and dismissed her as being 'black and wicked and with only a nodding acquaintance with truth'.

10 January

There is a me-wave on and I am feeling better. My depression of last week is passing. At Peggy Crewe's cocktail party I was soon surrounded by everyone. I went with Madame Carcano and indeed had spent the day with her. Ava Anderson whispered to me to drive home with her, and when I said that I was pledged to the Ambassadress, she replied that she did not wish to upset my sense of hierarchy. Mrs Keppel was a touch tiddly, and the Spanish Ambassador, I thought, was dressed a little too saucily for a man of his age. There were about fifty more, including Mademoiselle Françoise Rosay, who was the star piece.

11 January

Ciano has been shot. He was forty-one, and nobody has ever

risen so high, and fallen so low. I knew him, and always found him cordial, gay, fashionable and painstaking: he was pro-Fascist certainly, but not anti-English. He three times invited me to luncheon and once I went, a grand affair at the Palazzo Barberini. He was shot on Mussolini's orders, and I find it rather shocking to shoot one's son-in-law.

13 January

I collected two volumes of diaries dating from October 1940 until now, and took them to the British Museum where I was received with deference and respect by the Director, John Forsdyke, the Custodian of Manuscripts, and he led me through caverns measureless to man, where after unlocking many doors we came upon the tin boxes containing my older diaries, all the ones in fact that I did not destroy,[1] though gone are all the Proust letters which in my youth and folly I burnt. I deposited the recently written dozen and added them to the other store of frivolous chronicles . . .

15 January

I went early to the House hearing that the PM was due back. The secret had been well kept, but I soon twigged that they wanted to stage a demonstration of enthusiasm and the surprise would add to it. It did. He came in just before 11.30 and smiled. The House cheered and rose, a courteous, spontaneous welcome which under the dramatic circumstances was legitimate, but curiously cold. Churchill is not loved in the House. He has never had any ovation to equal several of Mr Chamberlain's, and this morning's performance proved it. I thought he looked disappointed, but his health and colour have returned. Later I overheard him chatting with Mr Speaker, and telling him that he felt 'wobbly' in his legs. Mrs Churchill, radiantly proud, and Mary Churchill were in the Gallery, smiling. The girl is pretty . . .

Gossip says that Grigg will be made a peer or perhaps go to the India Office, thus relieving poor Amery, who is to be dégommé, also that Max Beaverbrook will go to the War Office.

1. This is one of the few references to the probable existence of diaries before 1918 and for the years 1919-22.

Winston considers that he can do anything, that he is omnipotent, and he was taking the temperature of the House today. Later Ernest Brown and I had a conference, and he is convinced that Beaverbrook is the âme damnée of both the Prime Minister and the country: he must indeed be wicked to be so hated by an honest man like Ernest Brown. Max is now known as the 'Minister of Midnight' and is said to be plotting thickly.

2 February
I went to the House of Commons, and listened to Rab make a shrewd speech to the 1922 Committee. He was clear, cunning and convincing about his Education Bill. It has made him known to the country as a whole, and well may make him Prime Minister one day.

3 February
It was a balmy day, and in the Green Park I ran into poor Sir Horace Wilson who often wanders about there, aimlessly and idly. He looked sad and déœuvré . . . he who was once the eminence grise of England! He seemed too distracted to speak to me.

14 February
I dined with friends, a Trollopian little couple with political and perhaps social ambitions . . . the Hinchingbrookes (I find him quite absurd and ingénu but well meaning) and Agatha Christie the novelist. She is a comely, ample woman with no outward traces of brilliance. I scintillated for ten minutes, and then subsided into morose silence.

16 February
My parents-in-law, the Iveaghs, called to see me, after having had tea with the King and Queen at Buckingham Palace. . . . I do believe that a marriage may well be arranged one day between Princess Elizabeth and Prince Philip of Greece.

19 February
This evening at Pratt's, Bill Astor and I were discussing the 'New

Statesman's' recent offer of a prize for four lines about world problems. One of the unpublished ones, apparently, ran:

> The solution
> Is revolution
> But that would be hard
> On Lady Cunard! . . .

In spite of his ducal backing and background Billy Hartington has not been elected at West Derbyshire and . . . a Liberal, Alderman White has got in with a majority of five thousand. A shattering blow for the Government. As Loelia Westminster remarked on the telephone, 'Duchess's kisses are not what they used to be.'

22 February

I awoke after a peaceful night, and feeling alive and vibrating, walked with Master Geoffrey Lloyd, who I like almost more than anybody, to the House of Commons. It was crowded, with every seat taken, and many ambassadors. . . . Winant, fine featured and magnificent, sat alone brooding like Rodin's Penseur. The Prince of Luxemburg waved to me, from the Distinguished Strangers' Gallery. I sat at the Bar, and watched the tense House. The PM came in, answered questions with gay nonchalance, and then left the Chamber. Members were bored with the unimportant questions, and seemed restive as they invariably do before a big speech or a momentous occasion. Meanwhile Mrs Churchill, white haired and elegant had arrived with Mary Churchill; they went to the Speaker's Gallery, and I saw her kiss Edwina Mountbatten. Soon the PM returned, and was again cheered. Locker-Lampson, who sometimes seems demented, rose and waved his Order Paper, as he always does when Winston appears.

There was then the ignominious presentation of Alderman White, who just won the disastrous by-election in West Derbyshire: when he marched up, flanked by two Independents there was a stony silence, interrupted by a few catcalls and an occasional cheer. Winston glared at him. The PM rose for his big speech about 12.12 and spoke without interruption until 1.30. He was fluent, informative, friendly and discreet, and the House listened attentively, until almost the end when people became restless. Many peers leant over to catch every Churchillian word. Camrose was with Freddy Birkenhead, Kemsley with the Duke of Marlborough and so on. The PM was at his best, and most interesting when he described the precarious and delicate political conditions existing in Yugoslavia and Greece and Poland. He became lyrical (and misinformed?) about Marshal Tito's guerilla campaign in Yugoslavia, and so enthusiastic was he that I suspect that his views had been coloured by Master Randolph, who, as we know is at Marshal Tito's secret headquarters. About one o'clock he glanced up, and began to race for time, but he slowed down for his peroration, and ended eloquently: many members had left to eat, telephone or relieve nature.

23 February

In the afternoon I went to the House of Commons. There are parts of St James's Park roped off, as there are live bombs there and Whitehall, bits of it at least, are really frightful to look at.

I attended a crowded Conservative meeting which seemed in a state of panic over the recent by-election: Member after Member aired his views. I think they exaggerate the danger, as the Government has lost only seven seats since the war, out of fifteen. Later I heard Anthony Eden winding up for the Government. Well dressed, hot and with a very hoarse voice, he was gesticulating and managed for once to please the House, or at least not to annoy it. . . . His manner of uttering platitudes as if they were world shattering pronouncements is too irritating. I find him a man of tinsel, and yet today he was not without charm as he waved, smiled and placated. Not a brilliant parliamentary performance, but at least he talked sense.

26 February

Spent half the morning trying to get hold of Augustus John on the telephone as I want to be drawn by him before either of us die or are bombed. I have always regretted that I arranged too late to be sketched by Sargent; he was taken ill just before we had arranged a sitting.

Later, unable to reach Augustus John by telephone, I walked with Bundi, my delectable white dog, to 33 Tite Street where he lives and works, and as I arrived, I saw a very grand Rolls-

Royce drive up, from which emerged General Montgomery. He went in and I waited for a few minutes, and then rang the bell, and wrote John a note, not wishing to disturb so distinguished a sitting. As I was scribbling against the wall, there was a feeble knock at the door which I opened, and there stood Bernard Shaw. I don't think he recognised me, but we chatted for a second and he remarked that I had a nice dog, and he patted my famous Bundi, who I thought rather resembled him. G. B. S. looked aged and feeble and was dressed in very dark tweeds and a black overcoat. His white whiskers and pink face looked like an enamelled portrait and had that pink lifeless quality of the very old.

7 March

I opened my presents which included Wavell's Anthology[2] which came from him. It has only just been published and contains, at my persistent request, his sonnet 'The Madonna of the Cherries' which he actually wrote in this house. We had thought of it at Northwick Park, when he took me there in May or June, not April, as he has dated it in the book. The manuscript he gave to me, and it is in my Commonplace book.

Then I changed, and came down to put the finishing touches on the house. . . . Huge vases of boughs from Kelvedon, candles and beautiful bibelots produced an atmosphere of splendour. By 8.15 my thirty guests or more began to arrive. . . . There was gaiety, stimmung, even some drunkenness; the food was good, oysters, salmon, dressed crab, minced chicken, etc. Conversation flowed. After the brandy had been passed, the King of Greece gracefully proposed my health! I was happy and gay and exultant that my forty-seventh birthday should pass off so glamorously: I am on the top of the world still. . . . I counted nineteen cars parked outside my house.

No raid disturbed our revels, and we all wished that Hitler could have seen so luxurious a festival in London at the height of the war.

8 March

There were ministerial headaches all over London this morning,

2. *Other Men's Flowers.*

and I myself felt shaky but exalted. In the p.m. I went to 33 Tite Street to the very studio where I once saw Sargent, and sat to Augustus John. The drunken old Druid was gracious; he is like some great force of nature, so powerful, immense and energetic. We made friends at once, and he drew me, or rather my head. He last saw Wavell, he told me, at Lawrence's funeral. When I asked him how old he thought me, he answered 'approaching forty'.

Later, I dined in, with a curious collection of guests, including Sir Stafford Cripps, who has charming manners, and is honest, if demented, but agreeable to meet and to talk to. He ate three scraped carrots, some salad and an orange, nothing cooked. . . . The conversation was dull, and everybody left at 11.30. Cripps had only drunk orange juice; a very different set-up from last night.

21 March

I am in a nostalgic mood, occasioned by too many late nights, too much gin and by the receipt of a late birthday present of food sent by my poor mother. She must have arranged for it nearly a year ago, since she died in June. I was touched and saddened and as I ate her chocolate, I thought of her frustrated life.

23 March

I walked with Brendan Bracken to the Lords to hear Beaverbrook make one of his dynamic diatribes which amused, bewildered and galvanised their Lordships. Herbert Morrison told me today that while he disagrees with the Beaver on every possible subject, he likes and admires him immensely. As I had been thinking much about my American project, I had a sudden inspiration to go and see Morrison (as Home Secretary) and I rang him up. He immediately received me, and I told him that I wished to go to the States, and he promised that he would give sympathetic consideration to my request for an exit visa. I was most impressed by his cordial efficiency, and found him businesslike, punctual and simple in manner. I told him about the urgent necessity of bringing Paul back to England. If he is Prime Minister one day, we might fare much worse. Coming away, I was reminded of Edward VIII's remark to me when he last dined here. Discussing politics, he prophesied that England for a long time would be governed by Morrisons, 'Shakes' and Herbert, perhaps alternately. 'Shakes' is now but a ghost of his former self, and has lost all but the vaguest vestiges of power. He suddenly aged, and disappointed us; only his impressive appearance and his charm remain. Herbert, on the other hand, is high in the ascendant.

This evening, as I dined in and alone and perfectly happy, I thought of a tiny episode that occurred this afternoon, when I followed Lady Astor into the Lords. She had barged in, with the usual jangle of bracelets, and I happened to see Lord Astor's tired lined face light up, as he smiled at her with infinite tenderness: and I realised that that mad witch is still loved by her husband, after nearly forty years of marriage.

24 March

A Secret Session discussing tanks and their production. Stokes attacked the Government, and a little later Bill Anstruther-Gray[3] made a damaging onslaught, accusing the Government of slackness and dilatory methods of production, of antique models, etc., etc. He shook the Government to its very foundations, and had there been a Division HMG would certainly have fallen. Later the atmosphere cooled a little. Grigg, the Secretary of War, ever insensitive, behaved tactlessly, and actually left the Chamber, against the advice of the Speaker, while Bill Gray was speaking, but was quickly summoned back. Duncan Sandys wound up for the Government, redder in the face than usual. I was sorry for him, and he had an uneasy passage.

28 March

An historic and altogether unexpected day. I walked to the House where the Education Bill was being discussed in the committee stage, and soon realised that the House was in an odd, restless, and insubordinate mood. At about 4.45 Thelma Keir, nice but tactless, like all Cazalets, moved the amendment to the famous clause

3. Unionist MP for North Lanark, 1931-45; Assistant Postmaster-General, 1945; MP for Berwick and East Lothian, 1951–66.

82 in the Education Bill for equal pay for men and women teachers. The House was crowded, and it was obvious that a storm was brewing. Rab for the first time held firm, and was resolute. The principle of equal pay had nothing to do with him, and he ought not to be placed in that position . . . after further parley and rising heat the House divided, and the result was announced of 117 against the Government and only 116 for it. The first defeat Mr Churchill has sustained. The House gasped, as it began to realise the implications, and I was appalled at the Government's defeat on the very eve of the Second Front. This will cause jubilation in Germany. The young Tory reformers, led by Quintin Hogg, Hinchingbrooke, and Lady Astor are to blame. The Socialists, too, as a whole, with the exception of their Ministers, voted against us. The situation is serious, and might herald the break-up of the Coalition. I am so sorry for poor Rab.

29 March

Newspapers (and the German wireless) talk of little else except the Government's defeat, and I found the House was excited, ashamed and packed. Both the PM and Rab were wildly cheered as they entered. It was soon common knowledge that Rab's offered resignation had not been accepted by the PM with whom he was closeted until 2 a.m. The Cabinet had met and taken a stern decision which the PM announced at the end of Questions in a grave, solemn voice. He looked tired, wounded, and was barely audible. The offending amendment is to be withdrawn, the clause passed without it, and the vote treated as a vote of confidence. The House gasped at the hard (but just) terms and the rebels looked foolish, dreading the prospect of having to eat their words. The House suspended until 2.30. Later the PM had come up to Rab and said, patting him (I was next to him) 'Well I don't think you will have to go now.' The PM's blue eyes were watery, and he remarked to somebody else, 'If only the Chancellor of the Exchequer could have been induced to break into a gentle trot, the Government would have been saved.'

31 March

Herbert Morrison writes that I may go to the USA. I found his note at the Commons, and was immediately operative, and arranged my passage, etc. The horizon clears. I am both bored and enchanted by the project.

5 April

To the House. My American plans have not crystallised yet, but I hope to get off about the 17th or so, and shall close my diary for the period of the trip. The censorship would be too close . . .

22 August *Brighton, 4 months later*

In a frightful furnished flat facing the forbidden sea at Brighton I turn once more to my old confessor, my diary, neglected for over four months. Since that time I have done much, enjoyed much, and reflected more.

On 19 April, I left Belgrave Square, the devoted Alan Lennox-Boyd driving me to Euston, where I left by train for Glasgow. Jimmy Maxton was in an adjoining compartment, and we chatted late. . . . Next morning I embarked on the 'Queen Mary' and the huge ship was almost empty. I slept and ate much, and we wore lifebelts the whole of the six days crossing, but saw nothing. The last day out, we passed an immense convoy. Docked at New York on the afternoon of 26 April, and I rushed at once to the Volney Hotel, where I was soon reunited with my altogether adorable son. He knew me, but I shouldn't have easily recognised him, though he is me 'en petit' and not so petit either. I found that he is doing well at his school on East 74th Street, where he tops his class, and is a general favourite . . .

For weeks afterwards I philandered in New York, dining, wining, lunching, dancing and revelling in the luxuries of a city untouched by war. The shops were a delight and not expensive. Luxury abounded. Everyone gave grand galas in my honour . . . I was fêté ad absurdum, and almost ad nauseam. Never have I felt so well, never so triumphant.

I saw much of Somerset Maugham, who never before was a friend. He has put me into a book, 'The Razor's Edge' and when I dined with him I asked him why he had done it, and he explained, with some embarrassment, that he had split me into three characters, and then written a book about all three. So I am Elliott Templeton, Larry, himself the hero of the book, and another: however I am flattered, and the book is a masterpiece . . .

Washington I hated, but was pleased to go. It was hot and humid and horrible. . . . The Halifaxes asked me to stay, and were kindness and hospitality itself, and I was very happy with them, going for long walks with the Ambassador, and drives with her. She took me to Mount Vernon where the magnolias were out. There were parties every day both at the Embassy and elsewhere . . .

Eventually, reluctantly, yet relieved, I came home, but only after many complications. . . . I packed Paul and Nannie off in a convoy ship in under twelve hours notice, leaving most of their luggage behind. . . . Then on 21 June, a Wednesday, I left myself by Clipper . . .

I found London upset, bewildered, but in no way demoralised by the constant attacks of the so-called secret weapon. They are manless planes, nicknamed doodlebugs, which cause havoc and consternation, and shatter glass: really rather eerie and sinister.

The news on all fronts is encouraging. We are winning everywhere, yet doodlebugs poured into London today, killing many people.

23 August

The wireless has just announced the liberation of Paris after four years and three months of German occupation. . . . One is dizzy, and too excited to write coherently.

25 August

The news is increasingly wonderful; and it is important now not to be killed during the next few weeks. There is still fighting in Paris, but everywhere in France our troops are making sensational advances. Rumania is on our side, Bulgaria is asking for peace, Russia marches on, yet the bombardment on London by doodles continues.

The Marne, Chateau Thierry, the Allied Victories. It is so like 1918, the same names and places and forward triumphant march towards victory.

29 August *Brighton*

By this time next year my divorce will be through, and I shall be free. 'Going where I list, my own master, total and absolute' as

Walt Whitman wrote: it will be a testing time indeed. Shall I pull myself together, and be great, or just remain successful, or deteriorate, and go to the dogs? I know that I have been slipping recently: but is fame worth the effort, position the constant dancing attendance on the powerful? . . . I don't foresee the future clearly. It is so ghastly growing old, and my heart and body are still far from antique, but I dread failure and the shelf. Yet what have I, apart from my son, to live for except myself, and perhaps, as Cyrano said, mon panache?

31 August

The Allies march on to victory, more triumphs everywhere. What a fortnight it has been. 'Key towns', of which one has never heard, fall daily, and Paris has been liberated twice in three days. Coats are turning inside out in the Balkans, and old Hindenburg must be turning, too, in his grotesque tomb at Tannenburg.

5 September

I lunched at the Ritz with Diana Cooper who was looking lovelier than ever and Master John Julius: she is not looking forward to the Faubourg St Honoré, and the Parisian splendours of an established Embassy, though she will certainly do it well. Duff's career really resembles Talleyrand's more closely every year. We then went to a film 'The Liberation of Paris': it was de Gaulle's great moment, and yet somehow I thought he looked and acted absurdly. Diana whispered 'If Winston sees this he will have a stroke': nevertheless, one must admit, he is brave.

6 September

I had a long talk with Robin Barrington-Ward, Editor of 'The Times'. He thinks that politically there is no serious swing to the Left; and says the country is 'centre of centre': so much for the foolish prophecy of that very nice ass Harold Macmillan who goes about saying that the Conservatives will be lucky to retain a hundred seats at the election.[4]

4. The 'nice ass' was rather more accurate than the Editor of *The Times*. At the 1945 Election the Conservatives and their allies won 213 seats, with Labour winning 393.

12 September

The mysterious rocket bombs still arrive occasionally, and do damage, but they are supposed not to be mentioned, and officially they are a secret. Like that it is hoped to bluff the Germans.

13 September

The Coopers, escorted by thirty-six Spitfires, have left with a fanfare of trumpets to take over their diplomatic duties in Paris.

18 September

Billy Hartington has been killed in France. He was an extremely good looking boy and combined Cecilian sensitivity with Cavendish charm. I am so sorry for the distraught Devonshires, and cannot help wondering whether the flibberty-gibbet little Lady Hartington, née Kennedy, is pregnant of the future Duke of Devonshire? She recently went to America, to everyone's annoyance.

19 September

Dined with 'Coalbox' where I met Edwina Mountbatten, very sweet and lovely and fresh from Paris. However, politically, she talked tripe, and pretended to be against all monarchy, she who is cousin to every monarch on earth. According to her, they must all be abolished. How easy it seems for a semi-royal millionairess, who has exhausted all the pleasures of money and position, to turn almost Communist!

29 September

I was wakened by the French Ambassador telephoning to me to ask me if I would lease him my house to use as the French Embassy – and offering me a liberal rent: it is tempting, but I cannot face moving out.

I dined with Juliet Duff in her little flat stuffed with French furniture and bibelots – also there, Sibyl Colefax and Master Terence Rattigan, and we sparkled over the burgundy. I like Rattigan enormously, and feel a new friendship has begun. He has a flat in Albany.

2 October

Thought much about the French offer – the saving would be little, though I suppose that it would help, and it would be distinguished to have the French Flag flying over No. 5. But I would miss my own house deeply, and I feel I would lose my cachet – my point. Eric Crankshaw, whom I met in the Park today, said that I was a national asset, and that my entertaining did a world of good. He ought to know, as he is the head of Government Hospitality, and I have often helped him out.

3 October

The 54th birthday of my oldest friend Serge Obolensky . . . Still young-looking, still fascinating, still liked and respected by everybody. To lead a paratroop division at 54, and to jump repeatedly in France and Sardinia, is a remarkable feat. To celebrate the auspicious day, I organised a gala dinner for him at Belgrave Square, which was a huge success, although he would not let me invite any Kings. . . . The house, as always, 'dressed up' well . . . Came, among others – two Ministers, Geoffrey Lloyd and J. Llewellyn (Petroleum and Food), two under-secretaries, Harold Balfour and Alan Lennox-Boyd (Air and Aircraft Production), Bill Astor, Angier Duke, Junkie Fleischmann, Olive Baillie, Mrs Corrigan, Loelia Westminister, Portia Stanley and Juliet [Duff].

There were high spirits and fun and speeches. Vsevelode of Russia made the best one, when he said that Serge successfully bridged the gap between the old dead world and the new.

11 October

I suddenly decided to speak on the War Time Liabilities Bill and did; but I was bored and nervous, and stammered, I fear: yet I delivered a short pointful speech, and was congratulated on it afterwards: it ought to do me good in the Division . . .

Sydney Butler, always a staunch ally, came to see me, and told me that Rab is never in the least interested in people – only in facts.

23 October

Lunched at the Saintsbury Club, and was next to Compton

Mackenzie whom I had never met before. He looked like a Velasquez with his pointed beard, and wore a green velvet tie and diamond links: he began the conversation by saying 'So you are the famous Chips Channon, Wavell's great friend', and we talked for two hours over the wines. Distinguished company: Lord Woolton, Dalton, Osbert Sitwell, the Spanish Ambassador, and of course, Vyvyan Holland, the animateur of the Club, and son of Oscar Wilde.

25 October

The PM buzzed about all day at the House, and I saw him deep in conversation with Ralph Assheton, whom I assume has now been offered the Chairmanship of the Party. He is sound, safe and honest though Alan would have made a better showman. When they went into the smoking room, several Ministers collected in little groups ostensibly to chat and to drink, but in reality to waylay the PM, to have a private word, to catch his eye and perhaps obtain a decision. Leo Amery, in particular I thought hung about; he is terrified of Winston, and fears that his job (India) may be in jeopardy.

26 October

Death, who has been on holiday, bagged both old Princess Beatrice, the Queen of Spain's mother and the Archbishop of Canterbury, today. . . . The Archbishop was . . . a fat fool of 63 with a fuddled, muddled brain, who really looked more like Queen Victoria than her daughter did. He was a Socialist, and Winston was much criticised for appointing him: now after 2½ years he can put that right. Temple often consulted Rab in the Foreign Office days, and we were frequently obliged to alter his broadcasts, as they were so injudicious. He was then York. Winston is quoted as being jubilant about his death, and remarked 'Look, only 63, a teetotaller, and look at me, not a teetotaller, and 70'.

27 October

Winston was in high spirits today, and gave a résumé of his recent travels and of the developments in the international situation: he seemed a touch more pro-King in both Greece and

Yugoslavia. But he always backs both sides, and whilst helping Communists like Tito, he expects the King to be accepted, and reinstated on his shaky throne.

This afternoon I drove Nicholas Lawford to Coppins, where the Duchess warmly received us . . .

As I signed the visitors' book I noticed 'Philip' written constantly. It is at Coppins that he sees Princess Elizabeth. I think she will marry him.

31 October

Today the PM was gay, enjoying himself, and seemed in such high spirits that no-one doubts but that he will lead the Conservative Party triumphantly to victory at the Polls: though he wisely dispelled any hopes of an early dissolution, and it now looks as if we shall have another year of this wondrous Parliament which has already lasted nine years.

7 November

My uncle murdered![5] I went to sleep last night with strange emotions. Walter Moyne was an extraordinary man, colossally rich, well-meaning, intelligent, scrupulous, yet a viveur, and the only modern Guinness to play a social or political role, being far less detached than most of his family. He collected yachts, fish, monkeys and women. He had a passion for the sea, and for long expeditions to remote places. He had a curious frenzy for the very early Gothic, and all his many houses were in that style, and hideous. . . . Walter with his steely-grey hair, turquoise eyes, had a distinguished appearance, and also the curious Guinness money traits. He was careful of his huge fortune, though he had probably about three millions.

Lord Strathmore has died aged 89. I am surprised he was not more, for I stayed a week or more with him at Glamis in 1922 once, and he seemed to me to be a very old man then. The then Duke of York, afterwards King, used to come into my bedroom in the evening, and we would talk of the Glamis monster and the admittedly sinister atmosphere in the castle and of the other ghosts. . . . One rainy afternoon, we were sitting about and I pretended that I could read cards, and I told Elizabeth Lyon's

5. In Cairo, by members of the Stern Group.

fortune and predicted a great and glamorous royal future. She laughed, for it was obvious that the Duke of York was much in love with her. As Queen she has several times reminded me of it. I remember the pipers playing in the candlelit dining-room, and the whole castle heavy with atmosphere, sinister, lugubrious, in spite of the gay young party. Lord Strathmore's death recalled all this to me.

8 November

I went to inspect the model of the proposed new Chamber of the House of Commons, and it seemed to me adequate and a definite improvement, but it seems short-sighted not to build a massive modern Assembly Room that would do for all time. Occasion manquée.

11 November

At luncheon, I made a gaffe. In talking to Lord Cavan about Dill's recent death, I said 'Old men who marry young women always die soon after'. 'I did not' he retorted drily.

6 December

Dined with Lord Beaverbrook, at the Savoy – a party of 21 – a farewell to Harold Balfour, who goes to West Africa on Friday. Max was jovial, presided genially, and mixed the cocktails. Speeches. I over-ate and drank, and came home by Underground, where I was shocked to see the stations still full of people sleeping in bunks, miserable heaps of dirty humanity.

11 December

Fritzi of Prussia came to see me, and told me of his engagement to my sister-in-law Brigid [Guinness]: I am entranced, and was so moved that in a sad flash I remembered the days when we were all so happy, and did not know it.

1945

22 January

I drove to Lancing to the house of Mr & Mrs Coleman who are harbouring 'Bosie' Douglas in his illness: he is dying, and seemed enchanted to see me; but I was shocked at his appearance, he looked like an aged French Duchess. I sat with him for two hours, and he chatted feebly of Oscar Wilde and old days. I fear I shall not see him again.

6 February

Later. I have just heard the terrible news that one of the 24 planes taking the PM's party to Yalta for the great meeting of the Big Three has crashed, killing 15 people, including my beloved Peter Loxley, always so gentle, wise, indolent and devoted. I shall miss him for the rest of my life.

13 February

A dreadful day: the Iveaghs have had a message to say that their son Arthur Elveden has been killed by a bomb, I think in Holland. ... No two men were less alike than my brother-in-law and I – yet for 15 years we were very fond of each other. ... I am beginning to realise what an ally I have lost ...

28 February

All afternoon at the Commons, it was magnificent, the supreme debate, the conscience of the gentlemen of England and of the Conservative Party has been stricken by our failure to support our pledged word to Poland. The Prime Minister and Anthony Eden's abortive attempts to explain away, to justify our ignominious surrender to Stalin,[6] whilst they pleased some sections of the Left, have deeply shocked public opinion. People, gentlemen, not easily excited, like Alec Dunglass and James Willoughby D'Eresby made eloquent pleas for Poland, and the unfortunate and pathetic and charming Polish Ambassador, Count Raczinski, was in the Gallery. I was moved by the debate, and when the division was called at 5.58, particularly after listening to Eden's extremely weak winding up, I was tempted to join the insurgents. But there seemed little use in trying to fight the inevitable, and eventually I voted for the Government. 25, however, supported the Socialist amendment in the lobby, a serious thing to do, as it was a three-line whip. I am horrified by the inconsistency of some

6. At Yalta.

Members of Parliament, members of society, who went about abusing Mr Chamberlain about appeasement in 1938 and 1939, and now meekly accept this surrender to Soviet Russia. Victor Raikes and Maurice Petherick were really quite magnificent.

1 March

I went to the House of Commons for the winding up of the Big Three Day debate. Winston, who looked and seemed in cracking good spirits, decided that the crisis was over and left Anthony Eden to speak, for the second time, which he did with little effect. ... The division was interesting, 413 to 0, but I watched about 40 Conservatives and some Labour members deliberately abstain. I voted for the Government.

2 March *London*

Crinks Johnstone died suddenly last night from a stroke. He was only 49, and can really be described as having dug his grave with his teeth, for all his life he over-ate and drank. ... I rather liked him, though I long ago recognised that he was a Liberal hypocrite. He was a Regency figure ... immense, noisy, and an intelligent bore.

8 March

Lord Scarbrough is dead at Sandbeck. He was nearly 90. The greatest gentleman of England, he had the appearance and character of a chivalrous crusader. He was calm, gentle, good-mannered and completely charming and for many years I adored him. He was overwhelmingly in love with his warm-hearted, brilliant, loyal, rather vulgar wife and we all feared that her death in 1931 would kill him. But as often happens, with particularly devoted husbands, he seemed to take on a new lease of life. Lady Scarbrough's malapropisms were famous, but I loved her and she me; she was a sort of Lady Bracknell. Lord Scarbrough was uncle to all England and his four sisters, the 'Roses of Lumley', all married well, one was Lady Bradford, another Lady Grosvenor, mother of Bendor Westminster; the loveliest was Lady Zetland. I knew the three of these great Yorkshire ladies well; the fourth, Lady Bolton, I never saw.

15 March

At the Conservative Conference, I was impressed by the large attendance and great enthusiasm of the audience. Rab presided with skill and patience. At noon precisely, the PM accompanied by Mrs Churchill arrived, and were given a tumultuous reception. Winston spoke for 50 minutes – a good fighting speech which ought to win the next election.

16 March

The country's reaction to the PM's speech is favourable. Even the Labour people half admit that he has won the next election already by his address yesterday. I sat a few rows behind him, and watched his every gesture.

18 March *Weston near Towcester*

On my way here, I lunched with Mary Marlborough at Blenheim, who only lives in the left wing of the Palace, as the rest is occupied, or rather, taken over, by the War Office. A large party – mostly children. Caroline Churchill and the youngest child, Lord Charles, aged about 5 . . . a very pretty, petulant, sophisticated Hoppner of a child.

I came on here to stay with Sacheverell and Georgia Sitwell, at this small but atmospheric place. A Commando, Paddy Leigh-Fermor, is staying too . . . over-loquacious and pedantic but goodlooking. A warm welcome; then a cosy tea, and a long walk followed by many cocktails. The Sitwells are staunch allies and good hosts. Delicious dinner with old Burgundy and delectable sweet Sauterne.

20 March

At the House of Commons, I found a telegram from Coleman, the kind man at Lancing who has been looking after Lord Alfred Douglas for some months, to say that Bosie died this morning. Poor Bosie. He was a man of charm, even genius. It is indisputable that he was a great poet whose genius was overclouded (and perhaps unappreciated) because of his ardent association with Wilde. Even now, after 50 years exactly, his name is always linked with Oscar's. Bosie was litigious, difficult, quarrelsome, petulant and difficult about money. I have sent him many sums during the years that I have known him . . . He had a grudge against the world, and seemed to bear it a grievance. His whole life was unhappy, a frustrated one, and he never lived down the Wilde scandal. He retained his charm, even some looks until the end, and I am glad to have been of some service to him. I now wish I had done more . . .

In the afternoon I drove to see the bomb damage in Park Lane, where windows are out, etc., though only eight people who were out walking their dogs on Sunday morning at 9.30 were killed. The lie-abeds were all safe, and all the Dorchester inmates unscathed. I rang Emerald to ask her if she had been all right, and she answered insouciantly 'Quite, I was under the table with the telephone and Shakespeare'. She is quite undaunted by the bombing.

21 March

It is announced that the Wavells are arriving, but I have decided not to run them or run after them this time.

22 March

I spent much time with Rab today who was particularly charming. He said that he would do something about an Honour for me soon, perhaps in the dissolution Honours List. I doubt if he will succeed . . .

More V2s today, but we are almost used to them by now.

23 March

I went to the House of Commons where the Debate on Housing continued . . .

Later, I had a message through the India Office to go to the BOAC Station to meet the Wavells 6.40 this evening. But I did not go. The Viceroy can telephone to me when he feels so inclined.

Political gossip has it that the Conservatives will be re-elected with a reduced majority, and that Leslie Belisha will come back into the Government soon.

The war cannot last much longer now. Our armies are deep in Germany.

27 March

Old Lloyd George died yesterday, and has been a long time doing it. He was an unscrupulous rogue of charm, but a tremendous personality. The House of Commons rose, after Questions, as a mark of respect to him.

4 April

Paul and I joined the Wavells at 'Midsummer Night's Dream'. Lady Wavell was very friendly and gay, and took immediately to Paul, as did the Viceroy. During the interval H. E. remarked that the first time he had appeared on the stage, was when he had acted Cobweb in 'Midsummer Night's Dream'. We repeated this to John Gielgud whom we visited in the next interval, who capped it by telling us that Queen Mary, the only time he had ever met her, had confessed that her only Shakespearean role had been 'Wall'.

10 April

At the House of Commons the PM was in a fighting mood, but already one smells the odour of dissolution about, though the country is against an unnecessary election at this time. Meanwhile, our troops go triumphantly on.

13 April

At 8 o'clock I heard on the wireless that President Roosevelt died yesterday. I never saw him, but he was frequently very kind to my son, Paul, who often went to tea at Hyde Park, and adored him. Paul's first remark when I told him was 'Poor Falla', which is the name of the President's dog, a Scottie. This death bears out all the rumours that one has heard of the President's poor health at Yalta. It is a tremendous tragedy.

17 April

I took my son with me to the House of Commons where I picked up two tickets for the Service at St Paul's in memory of President Roosevelt. Then we drove through the crowded traffic and parked our car in Amen Court. The great church was not full, though there were many people in the nave where we sat, surrounded by peers, MPs, soldiers and notabilities. The Lord

Mayor stood at the steps of the Cathedral to meet the sovereigns and he held the Sword of State high and erect. We saw the Royal Procession form, and then slowly advance up the aisle. We were very near. The King was in Naval uniform, the Queen in black. Immediately behind them was Princess Elizabeth in ATS uniform. Following them were the King of Norway, escorting the Queen of Holland. . . . The Norwegian King was tall and slender and stately. Next came George of Greece and Peter of Yugoslavia, both in uniform, Olaf of Norway, the Princess Royal looking as cross as ever; the Duchess of Kent, a dream, was with Lord Harewood. Four Kings and Queens made an impressive array, and the service then began. Winant read from Revelation. The Star Spangled Banner was sung like a negro spiritual, and the words of the Anthem were magnificent. The service lasted three-quarters of an hour, and then the Royal Procession defiled past us again, and left the Cathedral as the bells slowly tolled. The Last Post and Reveille were sounded, and then Winant, dark and romantically handsome, escorted Winston, who was in tears, to the door. After that, everyone in England walked to the exits. Paul and I slipped out, and turning back towards St Paul's we saw Winston standing bare-headed, framed between two columns of the portico and he was sobbing as the shaft of sunlight fell on his face and the cameras clicked. We hurried sadly home to lunch in the nursery.

Later the House of Commons was crowded. At the end of questions, the PM announced that the Big Debate on Thursday had been postponed (which means, I fear, that the war is not yet over, and that greater opposition is expected). Then the Speaker called to Members desirous of taking their seats to come forward, and there was a surprise, for the recently elected Scottish representative for Motherwell advanced alone. The Speaker asked him if he had any sponsors, and he replied 'No', thus staging a historic demonstration. An unexpected debate followed for it is against procedure for a member to be introduced without sponsors. For an hour, whilst Winston waited impatiently to pay his tribute to Roosevelt, the house debated, raged and stormed, and finally a division was called. There was a majority of 74 – 199 to 273 – that McIntyre should not take his seat, and an hour later than schedule, we finally got down to ordinary business. The

PM made a glorious and moving speech in honour of 'England's greatest friend'.

It has been Churchill day. I ran into him twice in the lobby, heard him exchange banter in Westminster Hall, saw him weeping at St Paul's, admired and listened to him as he paid his tribute to Roosevelt. His command of English lies in apt phraseology, and never ceases to impress me. How long, one wonders, will he live?

The Pundits are now predicting that the election will be deferred as victory has receded. Indeed pessimists think the Germans may make a last stand which will last for weeks.

19 April

The black-out is to end officially on Monday and on Tuesday Big Ben will be lit up after a five years' eclipse. Slowly life reverts to normal.

25 April

I am reading an advance copy of Evelyn Waugh's new novel 'Brideshead Revisited'. It is obvious that the mis-en-scène is Madresfield, and the hero Hugh Lygon. In fact, all the Beauchamp family figure in it . . .

27 April

The Government has had a smashing defeat at Chelmsford where the Common Wealth candidate has got in with nearly a 7,000 majority. I'm in despair about England.

In the evening I dined alone with the Viceroy and Lady Wavell in their suite at the Dorchester. He was gentle, loving and lovable and gave me a book, and listened, almost rapturously it seemed, to my foolish conversation. He saw me to the door of the hotel, when I finally left. Lady Wavell, too, was enchanting and affectionate. . . . Both the Wavells seemed very pro-me.

Goering has resigned. Germany is practically prostrate; events move beyond one's power of comprehension, and there are more rumours of peace.

29 April

Mussolini has been shot ignominiously by Italian patriots. The

Duce, for whom no bootlicking was once bad enough. I must say, I do not admire the Italians for their disloyalty to their misguided leader, who at one time had genius and even greatness.

1 May

To the House, where Winston was in gay form. I dined at home with Paul. I don't feel well. I don't know why. I think it's because I smoke too much, and don't rest enough.

It is said that Hitler is dead, but nobody now cares.

2 May

I gather from Rab that the end of the war will not be until next week, and that Wavell will not return to India as soon as he expects. He was not wanted here at all, but insisted on coming now, though he had been advised that if he must come, June would be the best month or the Autumn. I fear he has made an unfavourable impression in high political circles, who consider him a great man, an angel and a gentleman, but a very unastute politician.

In the Lords, I had an hour's chat with Sam Hoare, now Lord Templewood, and known as Lord Tempelhof. He begged me to use any influence I have to force an early Election, preferably in June. Later, in the Chamber, there were rumours that the PM would be making an important statement, and he came in flushed and pleased and announced the complete capitulation of German resistance in Italy. This was a tribute indeed to General Alexander, but most members were disappointed as they expected that his rather dramatic appearance meant the end of the war. Everybody is bored by the proposed celebrations. We have undergone too much to be interested, and the prospect of even one evening's frivolity is depressing.

Will peace be declared tomorrow, or will VE Day be on Friday, as most people expect?

4 May

I had dinner with Mrs Keppel who, in spite of her years, looked magnificent. We discussed the war, and I really wondered, as we talked, which war we were on to, the last war, the Boer War or the Crimean War, so eternally charming is she. After dinner,

I went along the corridor of the Ritz, being, like everyone else, in a restless mood (all London has been on edge these last few days, waiting for the final announcement) and went to read the latest news on the tape machine. There I read that at 9.13 a communiqué had been issued at SHAEF that the Germans had capitulated in Holland, Western Germany and Denmark, and that the cease fire will begin tomorrow at 6.0 a.m. We were all immensely moved, and celebrated in Kümmel, the Linlithgows especially as it means that their prisoner-of-war son, Charles Hopetoun, whom they had not seen since Dunkirk, will soon be home.

6 May

The Wavells have now been here over six weeks. Will they never return? Their visit was ill-timed, even tactless. HMG was against it but Wavell whilst a scholar, a good man, and a great soldier, is no politician. He has been blundering and a bore to both Winston and the Cabinet. I am sorry for him, as he is in real jeopardy. To be dégommé after only a year and a half of Vice-royalty would be a tragedy, but Rab Butler thinks that he may survive.

8 May *VE Day, at last*

The night before war was declared, I was in the Cabinet Room of 10 Downing Street, watching Neville Chamberlain, who looked broken-hearted, and running errands back and forth from the FO and telephoning to Nevile Henderson, and coping with Red Boxes, when a thunderstorm broke – a storm such as I have never seen.[7] It did not stop and Peter Loxley and I had to sally forth, and arrived home drenched. There was rain as if the very gods were weeping (only once had I known a storm like it in England – the night Mme Fahmy murdered her husband at the Savoy, while I, the Prince of Wales and Prince Paul were dancing at Mrs Rupert Beckett's ball).

Early this morning, too, I was awakened by the rain – intense, Wagnerian rain, which lasted for a long time; the noise brought back, as nothing else could, that September night of 1939 . . .

7. See pp. 260–65

Before lunch I walked through the Ritz, which was beflagged and decorated: everyone kissed me, Mrs Keppel, the Duchess of Rutland and Violet Trefusis all seized me alternately. ... The streets were almost empty, as there is a bus-strike, and taxis refused to go out – there were a few singing people, that's all.

At the House, Questions lasted interminably, and there was an atmosphere of expectancy in the crowded Chamber. Every seat was occupied; the Ambassadors were all present, peers queued up. At three o'clock, in the Whips' Room, I heard the PM make the official announcement over the wireless that the war in Europe was at an end. I then returned to the Chamber, but owing to the ovation Winston was having in the streets he was delayed, and for a few embarrassed minutes we had nothing to do. Members, amused, asked desultory questions, keeping their eyes on the door behind the Speaker's chair. The Serjeant-at-Arms was in Court Dress, the Speaker wore his robes with gold braid, etc. (I have never seen this done before – though I suppose it was done at the Coronation.) At last Winston, smiling and bent, appeared, and had a tremendous reception. Everyone (except the recently elected cad for Chelmsford) rose and cheered and waved handkerchiefs and Order Papers ... Winston smiled and half bowed – as he often does, and turning towards the Speaker, read out the same short announcement of the surrender of Germany which he had already given over the wireless. The House was profoundly moved, and gave him another great cheer; but his reception, even at a supreme moment like today, did not equal Mr Chamberlain's great ovation after Munich. Then Winston, in a lower voice, added his personal thanks and praise for the House of Commons and the Democratic System: some Members wept, and the PM moved that we repair to St Margaret's to offer thanks to Almighty God using the identical phraseology employed by Lloyd George in 1918. The Speaker headed the procession, followed by Winston, who walked with Arthur Greenwood. We walked through St Stephen's Hall and outside, where there was a terrific crowd, the sun was shining. There were bells, police carved a way for us, and we must have looked like a picture by Giovanni Bellini as we filed, 500 strong, into St Margaret's for a short and impressive service.

10 May

It is my private opinion that the PM is universally admired but little liked, which is sad. But for the last few days he has certainly enjoyed his moment of triumph, and his car has been frequently mobbed: people climbed all over it on the way to the House on Tuesday and thus delayed him, and I am told that last night he stood on top of it outside the Ministry of Health. Today in the House, he was buoyant and gay, and later in the Smoking Room, when he was sitting with Jay Llewellin he smiled at me, and I murmured a few conventional words of congratulation. He thanked me, but, as always, made me feel shy. As I walked away I thought of Coronation evening, and how he had telephoned and proposed bringing Mrs Churchill and two of his daughters to Belgrave Square, which he duly did, and stayed half the night[8] . . . how much has happened to us all since then.

13 May

I went to St Paul's for the great Thanksgiving Service, very hot in my morning clothes: the great cathedral was crowded, and I watched all the notabilities of the earth come in, and listened to the cheers of the crowds outside. At length the procession of clergy moved to the door to receive the Sovereigns who then proceeded up the aisle. Their Majesties looked young and smiling – though the King looked drawn; but he has the Windsor gift of looking half his age. Behind him walked Queen Mary whom I had not seen since before the war. She looked magnificent – even beautiful, and was gloriously arrayed and bejewelled in a pink-heliotrope confection. She was upright and splendid despite her 78 years, and seemed as tall as the lean, lanky King of Norway – her brother-in-law, who walked with her. Then came the young Princesses, shy and uninteresting, and the Kings of Greece and Yugoslavia, the Duchess of Kent in uniform with her two elder children, making their first State appearance, and behaving beautifully. . . . The service was impressive, but long – Winston was all smiles and Mrs Churchill, safely back from Russia, bowing and gracious. At last it was over – and after tripping over several Field-Marshals, I walked to the Savoy. As always in England

8. See p. 158.

my top-hat was a Sesame, and got me quickly through the crowds.

15 May

I had one whole hour at the House with Quintin Hogg. His brain is like a rapier, and he is fascinating company, though his appearance is Dickensian.

16 May

Lunched at the 'Senior' with the Wavells. Lady Wavell was enchanting – amusing and provocative, but he – the Viceroy – is down and a bit disillusioned: he thinks that the PM has treated him shabbily: the Cabinet have completely ignored his proposals, and neglected him. He realises, of course, that everyone is preoccupied by the Victory, but feels that soon they must come to some conclusion. Already he has lost face, both here and in India by the long delay: I wondered if he would ever go back? Though he is in a strong position. Were he to resign now, on the eve of an election, Winston would be embarrassed. I advised him to go to Scotland – to forget all his problems and to play golf – till after the Whitsuntide holiday, as for the next few days all the politicians will be out of London enjoying their last holiday before the Election – now definitely, I am told – fixed for July.

20 May

From Sturford Mead – where we are staying – I took Terence Rattigan over to Longleat, which is now being used as a Girls' School. Henry Weymouth took us all over the house and showed us the famous Shakespeare folios of which they have the 1st, 2nd, 3rd and 4th. Terry was fascinated and impressed, and I saw his face light up as he took one down from the shelf, and fingered it. There are about 15 Caxtons at Longleat, and dozens of historical letters from Queen Elizabeth and others. In the evening we drove over to Ashcombe to dine with Cecil Beaton, a long melancholy beautiful drive through isolated country. The house is romantic and amusingly arranged, and Cecil received us in

Austrian clothes. Also there, an uninteresting couple, the Graham Sutherlands. He is a painter.

23 May
Winston has resigned, and the Coalition Government which has lasted five years and thirteen days, has ceased . . . at 5 o' clock he agreed to form another government: all this after two audiences with the King, The country is startled, but the PM has shown skill and political technique and acumen worthy of Talleyrand; he has all through, been encouraged and inspired by Beaverbrook.

24 May
The Viceroy telephoned, and I asked him to dine at Pratt's. He accepted gleefully, and we were joined there by Sir Philip Chetwode and the Duke of Devonshire. I doubt whether two ex-C-in-C's of India have ever dined together at Pratt's – and both Field-Marshals. Everyone stood up when we left. Eddie Devonshire thinks that we will lose the Election.

1 June
Went to the BOAC station to say goodbye to the dear, sweet disappointed Wavells. Only Lady Simon was there to see them off, and a few relations. It was very different to their triumphant departure in 1943.

5 June
The PM delivered a Broadside against the Socialists over the wireless last night: it was heavy pounding, certainly; and today the Labour boys seem very depressed and dejected by Winston's trouncing. I met Attlee in the lavatory, and he seemed shrunken and terrified, and scarcely smiled, though Bevin seemed gay and robust enough. I personally feel that the prevalent Conservative optimism in the Commons is overdone: everyone today was chattering of 'another '31 or at least another '24'. Everyone is cock-a-hoop.

6 June
A spirited debate in the House during which Herbert Morrison called Beaverbrook and Brendan Bracken 'Companions of the

Bath', a sly allusion to Winston's bathing habits, which have long amused the inner coterie.

8 June

Next week I leave for Southend to electioneer, and will close my diary for a while.

CHAPTER TEN

Post-War: July 1945–December 1950

1945

28 July

On 10 July I was operated on at the London Clinic for hernia and for ten days was prostrate, too ill and angry to reflect seriously on the disastrous Election results. I am stunned and shocked by the country's treachery, and extremely surprised by my own survival. I must nevertheless take up my diary again.

... I predict the Socialist régime will soon come to grief: I give it three years, and then we shall be returned to power; but do we deserve to be? I wrote Winston a note on Thursday night, posted it on Friday. Today, Saturday, a telephone message came through, with a kind message of thanks.

This morning Puffin Asquith rang up to announce the death of his valiant old mother, Lady Oxford. She was 81, and had long been ill. She was one of the most remarkable, though irritating, women I ever met. ... However, she was divine to me for twenty years, and a tremendous personality.

1 August

I went to Westminster to see the new Parliament assemble, and never have I seen such a dreary lot of people. I took my place on the Opposition side, the Chamber was packed and uncomfortable, and there was an atmosphere of tenseness and even bitterness. Winston staged his entry well, and was given the most rousing cheer of his career, and the Conservatives sang 'For He's a Jolly Good Fellow'. Perhaps this was an error in taste, though the Socialists went one further, and burst into the 'Red Flag' singing it lustily; I thought that Herbert Morrison and one or two others looked uncomfortable. We then proceeded to elect Mr Speaker, and Clifton-Brown made an excellent impression. It is a good sign that the Labour Party have decided to elect a Conservative Speaker unanimously.

3 August

Terry Rattigan rang early and we gossiped. He is getting on with his play about the Archer-Shee case.[1] I went to the Commons and took my seat, wrote many letters and put my affairs in order. My shares have declined by £5,000 in value since the Labour Party came in. Their Appointments are out tonight, and I find them harmless. Will they prove the Girondins of our age? I hear that Bevin is already doing well at the already pinkish Foreign Office.

5 August *Kelvedon*

The world has been electrified, thrilled and horrified by the atomic bomb; one has been dropped in Japan today. It devastated a whole town and killed a quarter of a million people. It could mean the end of civilisation.

10 August *Belgrave Square*

The Stock Market has recovered and is actually soaring. Evidently it does not fear the Socialist Government, now that the first shock has worn off.

Terry came to lunch about 12.55. He said (he is a wireless addict) – 'Turn on the news'; and we did, as we sipped our pre-prandial cocktails. The wireless announced that Japan had asked for peace, but insists on the rights of the Emperor. They want to save the Mikado. At long last the war is over, or ending. The streets were crowded with celebrating people singing, and littered with torn paper. People tear telephone books to bits and throw them into the streets, which by now look like a Victorian paperweight.

14 August *London*

One should always spend August in London. It is enchanting . . .

I went to St Margaret's, Westminster, for poor old Margot Oxford's Memorial Service. Somewhere in her biography she prophesied that she would have a crowded Memorial Service, but she was wrong. The cold church was half empty and forlorn, and there was an incredibly inaudible and boring address.

1. *The Winslow Boy.*

15 August

Up betimes, wearing morning clothes and top hat. I drove through immense crowds to the House of Commons, which met in St Stephen's Hall. I went at once to the Lords, where I had an excellent place. It was crowded with peers and peeresses. The Ambassadresses, all wearing extraordinary hats, sat on the right with the Duchesses. Mme Massigli, the French, wore a white tea tray. They all appeared so absurd that Mrs Wellington Koo, the Chinese, really seemed the most distinguished. There was a wait; the many new Socialists looked dazed and dazzled, and I was sorry for their sake that the peers were not in robes. At last the royal procession entered, led by the Heralds, the King in an Admiral's uniform and with his cap on. The Queen, in aquamarine blue, though dignified and gracious, was dwarfed by her Mistress of the Robes, the Duchess of Northumberland, who looked far the more regal of the two. The Crown was carried on a cushion. HM read out his speech, which announced the end of the war, and mentioned the nationalisation of the mines and of the Bank of England. His voice was clear, and he spoke better than usual and was more impressive. But they say that the word Berlin had been substituted for Potsdam, which he could not have articulated. The Labour people were subdued and impressed and everybody behaved in an exemplary manner. There was some good-humoured chaff between them and us, and coming out, Mrs Shakes Morrison stopped me and said that she had stood in the Lobby with Mrs Churchill, as neither could get into the Chamber. How are the mighty fallen!

... We walked in ceremonial procession to St Margaret's, and the Speaker, in full robes, led us through a good-natured crowd of cheering citizens. He was followed by Winston, who had a tremendous reception, and who walked with Eden, Attlee and Herbert Morrison. I sat with Alan during the service, which was impressive, and I was moved. On coming out, the crowd roared a welcome, and about a dozen spectators shouted 'Good old Channon', they must have been Southend constituents. Then I came home and slept, and about ten-thirty the Regent of Iraq, who I like more and more, arrived. We are very intimate. ... I never can resist a Regent. He brought a suite of six and we drank and gossiped for two hours; they had been in the crowds outside

Buckingham Palace, and were most impressed by the enthusiasm.

19 August

Terry read me out the first act of his new play about the Archer-Shee case. I suggested the title of 'Ronny versus Rex', and he has temporarily adopted it. So far it is brilliant, dramatic and full of a sense of period.

20 August

I went to the House of Commons and heard Bevin make his first big speech as Foreign Secretary. He was cheered and applauded by our side. It was almost a Tory speech, full of sense, and much the wisest exposition of foreign policy that I have heard for years. Anthony Eden squirmed, but replied politely.

21 August

Winston, accompanied by Anthony Eden, addressed the 1922 Committee. He seemed totally unprepared, indifferent and deaf, and failed to stir the crowded audience. I came away fearing that the Tory party was definitely dead.

An announcement in the evening newspapers staggered me. Wavell is expected back at any moment.

28 August *5 Belgrave Square*

The Viceroy of India, fatter and browner, and wearing a tweed suit, called on me and stayed an hour. He invited me to Delhi in the Autumn though he regretted that he could not take me back in his plane as there is no room (he is taking all his relations).

5 September *London*

I went to the Air Ministry and to the India Office, to try to get myself out to India, but I have failed so far, although the Viceroy himself approached Arthur Henderson and old Pethick-Lawrence, whom he described to me as a sort of saint. Saint or not, he turned my application down, as there are literally thousands of people waiting to go. All my summer plans have thus gone awry.

7 September

My telephone rang at 8 o'clock and I recognised Diana's voice ... just arrived from Paris: and I was thrilled, then dashed, later, by a letter from Arthur Henderson which finally puts an end to my hopes of going to India.

8 September *Kelvedon*

Walked to Buck's Club, where I ate a tin of potted shrimps for lunch, and came home. At 6 o'clock punctually Wavell arrived on foot, followed by a detective. I had collected Diana Cooper, Juliet Duff and Nicholas Lawford. We sat about talking, and had tea and cocktails. Suddenly, in walked Noel Coward unexpectedly, and very red in the face. He has an old looking neck. John Julius Cooper, who has grown, also came, he is a charming boy. The party went on till eight, and I was already late, as I wanted to leave for Kelvedon. However Noel ... settled down and remained till 9.30. I was famished. He was flattering (he is an arch-flatterer), insinuating, pathetic and nice. I have never liked him so much, though he talked mostly about himself.... At length, after many compliments and vows of eternal friendship, he left, and I leaped into the car and came here.

9 September

In the evening I dined alone with Wavell at Claridge's. At first he seemed detached and silent, though he gave me an expensive, handsome book. Then we went down to the restaurant, and had a good dinner ordered by an ADC. The Aly Khans were nearby. I talked with Princess Meg de Bourbon Parme, and a woman, whom I did not immediately recognise, came up to me. It was Princess Andrew of Greece. I hadn't seen her for years. She was very sweet, and said what a mistake it was for her daughters all to have married Germans.

12 September

I met an American who promised to help me get to India, so I rushed to see Wavell at the India Office. He was affectionate, but will he do the 'necessary'? He flies back tomorrow, and how I wish I were going.

13 September

Lord Wavell telephoned me early to say that he would try to help me to get to India later, but that he feared that at present the difficulties were insuperable. He added that he hoped I would see him off today at 11 o'clock. So I took Paul to the BOAC station, and we had an affectionate conversation. The Viceroy is really an old sweetie, but very cautious in his dealings with Government officials. I was sad to say goodbye; Paul and I watched the luxurious Vice-regal train pull out. There seemed to be lots of room for me.

17 September

Terry returned to London, and we discussed his play, which he has now all but finished. It is being typed, and there are only a few touches still to do. I advised against the title 'The Hamilton Boy' and we decided on 'The Winslow Boy', which I suggested. Terry thinks only of his play, dreams and lives it, and it really is magnificent. What a genius he is. He has completed it in six and a half weeks.

19 September

Terry came to lunch, and afterwards we took off our coats and settled down comfortably while he read me the script of his play which took till six. I adored it, and made many comments, suggestions and criticisms.

22 September

Honor telephoned in the friendliest vein, and I sent Paul off to have tea with her. Later I fetched him, and we went to 'Arsenic and Old Lace', and the little fellow laughed uproariously at this absurd, melodramatic affair. Later we dined à deux.

14 November

I lunched with the pleasant but black avized Rita Elliott, and found myself next to Mrs Attlee, the pretty, well-dressed wife of the Prime Minister. I instantly liked her, and made up to her, and turned on the full battery of my charm, and she told me how surprised they had been at the result of the Election, having quite expected Winston to win. She is very self-possessed, very much the lady, though without much elegance. We made friends, but I rather spoiled the effect by foolishly quoting – while discussing the flowers on the table – Osbert Sitwell's remark about chrysanthemums smelling like drowned sailors. Mrs Attlee looked startled.

15 December

Maurice Baring is dead at last. He was so ill and shaky when I last saw him that it must be a relief. He was mad, inconsequent and charming, and I loved him. He was about 70. Full of pranks and fun and foolishness.

1946–47

10 January 1946

At the fashionable, carefree Carcano-Ednam wedding reception I remarked to Emerald how quickly London had recovered from the war and how quickly normal life had been resumed. 'After all', I said, pointing to the crowded room, 'this is what we have been fighting for.' 'What', said Emerald, 'are they all Poles?'

Later, Grace Curzon and I talked of old days at Hackwood and Montacute and how jealous Lord Curzon had been. Once, she told me, he had removed her latch key, and King George V had had to intervene to have it restored.

1 August 1946 – 20 October 1947

Much has happened in the year and a bit during which I have idly let my diary go – a long, and needless gap ... Much happened during that time. Eight weeks of sunlight and splendour in India where I was the guest of the Viceroy. Tedious Delhi days in that cheerless Lutyens Palace – gay visits to dark Princes – to the white Alhambra of Jaipur three times, to Jodhpur for nearly a week with His Fat Highness, in his recently built and hideous Windsor (he has since died), beautiful romantic Bundi; Alwar, for the incredible splendour and colour of an Indian Wedding when the daughter of the late Maharajah, the wicked one, married. Bharatpur – heat – luxury – kaleidoscopic colour, and then back to the coolest English winter for centuries.

Now after a lapse of nearly 15 crowded full months, I reopen my diary.

22 October 1947

At the cold, wet, unveiling of George V's statue, trumpeters greeted the arrival of the Royal Family, and the King read a speech more effectively than I have ever heard him: the matter, a sincere tribute to his father's virtues, was a masterpiece. The ceremony itself was over in 20 minutes, but then followed that interminable pause whilst the Royalties greeted each other, inter-kissed and chatted. It is only in England that a crowd of several thousands can stand happily in the rain and watch one family gossip. It was a free close-up of the Windsor clan, and I suppose everyone enjoyed it. When the King, Queen and the Princesses had driven away, there was a pause of nearly two minutes, as the Queen Mary, tall, magnificent and sad, stood at the foot of the Memorial as she waited for her car to come up. The crowd sensed the pathos of the moment, and I wondered what were her thoughts as she looked up at the effigy of her husband. Then she was much cheered, as was Winston. No-one cheered Attlee, or even recognised Baldwin.

26 October

Is there anything more pleasant than an autumnal weekend in London? I lazed in bed – revelled in the almost royal splendour of my bedroom, and rose late to arrange my dinner party for the Regent of Iraq and his Minister of Defence. It was a great success. The Regent brought me a coffee set of silver as a present – six cups and a huge salver with palm trees engraved on it. The coffee pot has a spout like a pelican – hideous.

29 October

Big day at the H. of C. Winston opened the debate – it was on an amendment to the Gracious Speech, and he was magnificent, but there were touches of sadness in his patriotic eloquence, and at times I found him almost inaudible. He is ageing. But he impressed and moved the House, and Morrison's reply was, in comparison, weak and cheap. Later the atmosphere grew stormy over the Government's decision to abolish the basic petrol ration; the Socialists themselves sounded full of misgivings and several of them pleaded with their Front Bench to relent; but never has an administration been so blind, so bewildered and so unrelenting. When the closure was moved, their majority had dropped to 20; and on the actual issue – basic petrol or not – they won by only 27 votes . . .

Tonight 'The Winslow Boy' by Terence Rattigan opens in New York; the play was dedicated to my son Paul, and I shall always be interested in how it fares.

30 October

Another big Parliamentary day – one of those occasions when one is glad to have a permanent (and free – indeed one is paid to go) seat at the world's greatest play house, 'La Comédie Anglaise'. Two Labour MPs were tried at the House for disgraceful conduct, and for bribery. The proceedings opened with a harmless Editor of a newspaper being summoned to the Bar; the Speaker put on his black tricorne as the man made his apology, and was led away by the Serjeant-at-Arms – and the House was only slightly interested, and amused by the quaint ceremony. But when Mr Garry Allighan, MP for Gravesend rose, there was at once tension and human drama. Raymond Blackburn, my Socialist friend, had advised him to be simple, straightforward – a combination which always pleases the House – but he was neither, instead he was fumbling and ungracious and made a poor impression. Later we voted for his expulsion. He was severely rebuked by Mr Speaker in his Longhi chapeau, and the Motion was carried. He ceased immediately to be a Member of Parliament, and was escorted from the Palace of Westminster, somewhat roughly, by officials, and was never seen again; he was, of course, absent while he was being discussed. The opinion of the House was fairly united about him, but I don't suppose the Labour Party will relish a by-election at Gravesend after this scandal.

The next 'trial' was more complicated: many of us knew and liked Mr Walkden,[2] and we thought he was being hardly used:

2. Labour MP for Doncaster since 1941; subsequently sat as Independent MP until 1950.

there were shades of difference in the degree of his offence and I, for one, voted for the lesser punishment; at least I think I did, but the wording of the Motion was ambiguous. It was finally decided by the House not to expel him; but that he should be severely rebuked by Mr Speaker. He had been waiting about to know his fate, and was now sent for, entering with dignity. He was told to stand up: Mr Speaker once again put on his three-cornered hat and admonished him seriously. Then the House rose: as I came out into the Central Lobby, I saw Walkden hurry up to a homely dumpy woman and embrace her; it was his wife who was in tears.

4 November

John Winant has committed suicide in America, and there is much remorse; although I knew him, and he dined at Belgrave Square several times, I always found him unsatisfactory – and a quite inadequate ambassador. He knew few people, and judged England by the Cranbornes: but he had charm and his fine, sad eyes bewitched people. He had a curious elegance of his own; his likeness to Abraham Lincoln has often been noted – he was silent – only a lot of whisky could loosen his tongue and conquer his shyness. His views were leftish, and he was a Liberal Idealist; the sort of man who causes revolutions, and then regrets them.

5 November

My mornings are what Lady Brownlow calls 'quelque chose'. I am called early, pummelled by a sergeant; then a breakfast tray appears – eggs, coffee and prunes, and I lie back – revel in the beauty of my room; three telephones tinkle simultaneously, messages are brought in; letters opened, newspapers glanced at. . . . Soon it is mid-day and I rise, regretfully. Today was typical of this routine.

13 November *Another Socialist Scandal*

Dalton, as he walked into the Chamber yesterday to deliver his Budget speech was accosted, apparently, by the Lobby Correspondent of the 'Evening Star' to whom he revealed, verbatim, chapter and verse, the contents of his budget. 'The Star' consequently published an early edition at 3.45 which gave full details of the speech before it had been delivered. Dalton frankly admits his indiscretion, and it seemed as if the incident were closed. Winston was at first inclined to soft-pedal it. But – now – just past midnight, Leslie Belisha has just telephoned me to say that Dalton has sent in his resignation, and that Attlee has accepted it. How unlucky the Labour people are.

14 November

The newspapers splash the news – Dalton Down. Of course there is some Tory satisfaction, but most people are genuinely shocked. Winston was at the House early – chuckling. He has asked for an enquiry, and it was this demand which led to Dalton's resignation. His insufferable arrogance has had a fall, and the Government look crestfallen.

15 November *Bulbridge, Wilton*

I came here by train . . . Willy Maugham, in high spirits and agreeably anecdotal. He twitted me about my sex life, or apparent lack of it, and quoted Emerald as saying that I had once been a great voluptuary, but that now I was 'too occupied and too cerebral'; he then told Juliet Duff, who passed it on, that he thought I was one of the most colourful characters of the day. That from Willy!

At dinner we discussed Diaries, and Willy volunteered that mine would be illuminating. Other diarists he said, would be too cautious; that Eddie Marsh was too kind, and that Harold Nicolson was not in society. He thought that perhaps Nicholas Lawford's would live, but they would be too precious – too distinguished and that his style was too elegant.

17 November

The stage is now set for the Royal Wedding – which many people think has been mishandled. First, all the ridiculous fuss of Prince Philip changing his name and nationality – then the original intention of keeping the Wedding private . . . and someone in the Government apparently advised simplicity, misjudging the English people's love of pageantry and a show. Now it is too late and a great opportunity has been missed – when else in history has the heiress to the throne been married? Never.

Philip (still a secret) is to be given the Garter and made Duke of Edinburgh. I have been asked if I would lend or let my house to them for some months, but I have refused. Too much of an upheaval.

18 November

At the reception at St James's Palace to see the Royal presents I was struck by how ghastly some of the presents were, though the crowd made it difficult to see. Queen Mary's was magnificent, as was the wreath of diamond roses given by the Nizam of Hyderabad. My silver box (faux Fabergé) was in a conspicuous position. The King and Queen – and the young couple – were too surrounded to be approachable.

20 November

Royal Wedding Day. I was not 'commanded', but I had passes for the Parliamentary enclosure, and I drove there through the crowded streets – many people had waited all night to see the show. I thought Princess Elizabeth looked well, shy and attractive, and Prince Philip as if he was thoroughly enjoying himself. There were cheers of love and loyalty for Queen Mary and shouts for Princess Juliana of the Netherlands who is popular and whom the crowds take for a comic, which she is. But the warmest reception was reserved for Winston; and I hear that in the Abbey when he arrived, a little late, everyone stood up, all the Kings and Queens.

Rab, wandering about in the crowd outside, was affronted at not being asked – a foolish oversight of the Court, as Rab may well be Prime Minister one day and is, in any case, a leader of the opposition party.

25 November

My own big dinner, and as usual the house 'played up' and looked very grand and glittering, lit up and full of yellow chrysanthemums from Kelvedon. I 'laced' the cocktails with Benzedrine, which I find always makes a party go. Noel Coward arrived first, wearing what he called the 'Coward emeralds', and everyone was in gala dress – white ties and the women dripping with jewels. I never saw a lovelier sight. The Queen of Spain arrived punctually and I was on the doorstep to meet her. Five minutes later the Queen of Rumania drove up with her sister in a taxi – so there was just time to make the presentations to Spain before Rumania arrived...

After dinner we grouped ourselves about upstairs and the two Queens held rival Courts, and I led up the men to talk to them in turn. It was after midnight that Queen Helen – quietly elegant in black with an ermine jacket – rose and we went downstairs to the morning room which looked splendid with Prince Paul's tapestry[3] and the fine Nattier given to me by Laura, and we looked at the bibelots and the Mantegna panel which belonged to Isabella d'Este and is mentioned in one of her letters. I then ordered Her Majesty's car, and she left with the Duchess of Aosta – her sister and devoted shadow. I have always loved this pair of Greek swans who have been so buffeted about dynastically and matrimonially ...

Meanwhile, the Queen of Spain had settled down to enjoy herself and I found her ensconced on a sofa between Peter Coats and Sacheverell Sitwell (who had come in after dinner). The party went on.... It was 4 o'clock before they all left. A great, great success – as he left, Willy Maugham whispered to me 'This is the apogee of your career'. In a way it was, and I am sorry that Queen Freddie and the Duchess of Kent could not come too (they are on a secret visit to the affronted German relations, to tell them about the Wedding). Three Queens – it would have been like a hand at poker. But a pair is not bad.

26 November

London rings with tales of my party.... But I am haunted by Queen Helen's remark to me 'When I am back behind the Iron Curtain, I shall wonder whether this is all a dream.' HM of Spain, plump and bejewelled, is more terre-à-terre. She is a jolly, strapping Coburg all right.

15 December

The death of Lord Baldwin is announced. He died in his sleep at

3. A magnificent Gobelin tapestry which Chips was housing for Prince Paul.

his Worcestershire home. He was a grand old man, humane, and remarkably tolerant of human weakness. . . . He looked like a stalwart old oak, seemed unapproachable and seldom talked to anybody in the House of Commons. He had an odd habit of tearing up his Order Papers, and of grunting. Lazy and ill informed about anything outside England, he was in a way typical of his age, and accurately reflected the English people. Smuts once told me – one night he was dining at Belgrave Square – that probably the world had rated Baldwin too high when he was at the zenith of his power, and certainly in more recent years had rated him too low. History, he said, would surely restore the balance.

Later, in the House, many tributes were paid to Lord Baldwin – the most impressive, because it was so unexpected, came from the comic Communist Gallacher; an emotional hush fell on the Chamber as he sat down, and the House adjourned as a mark of respect to the dead Prime Minister . . .

As I walked away from the House I looked up at the red bones – the steel girders, of the new House of Commons; and I wondered when my small son's voice would vibrate in it.[4]

I forgot to record – how could I – that my beloved white dog Bundi, had to be 'put away' last week. Thank God I was not at Kelvedon when it was done. My companion for fourteen years. . . . But grown so senile and ill that it was a kindness. He was the only dog I ever loved. Shall I miss him? I have so selfish a character that no-one means much to me unless I happen to be in love with them at the time.

17 December

In the afternoon there was a rumpus in the House of Commons and the Royal Family had, I think, a deserved jolt. . . . The annuity to be paid to the Edinburghs was discussed, and the Socialists were in favour of reducing the proposed sum of £40,000. We then had the unpleasant spectacle of the Royal Family's finances being discussed in the House of Commons for 4½ hours. Had they all been invited to the wedding this would never have happened, and the larger sum voted instantly.

4. Paul Channon succeeded his father as MP for Southend after Chip's death in 1958.

1948

2 February

I had a long, exhausting, moving day which began with a Memorial Service which I organised at St Mark's Church, North Audley Street in memory of poor Laura Corrigan, who died suddenly and unexpectedly in New York on 22 January. Her kind old heart just gave out. ... I was stunned: all next day people kept ringing up: London was grief-stricken. Laura was an amazing woman – sexless, devoid of any outward physical attractions and never consciously amusing yet she made an international position for herself in the very highest society, which she wooed and cajoled. Her wealth and extreme kindness as well as her pretty snobberies and eccentricities were proverbial. ... Her death ends an epoch. Walter Buccleuch and Alan Lennox-Boyd helped me arrange the service, and we are sharing the expenses, and acted as ushers. I rang up all the Ambassadors and persuaded the Duchess of Kent to come in person – she had never before attended a non-royal Memorial Service, so it was a compliment.[5] The hymns were particularly well chosen, and everyone seemed moved. I had many compliments ... and was solaced for all my trouble. Incidentally, I telephoned her sister, Mabelle Armstrong-Taylor, at the Plaza in New York. She sobbed over the tranatlantic telephone, but she did mention, or I thought she did, that the Duchess of Kent and I are to inherit. Will it be one hundred pounds, or just a nice, cool million?[6] Whatever it is, good kind Laura will long live in my memory.

17 February

This evening, wearing my ruby and diamond buttons and very elegantly dressed, I went to pick up Miss Mae West, the famous comedienne. We were nearly mobbed – a crowd jumped at the car shouting for autographs, and I feared that the Rolls would be damaged. In the car she asked if she should 'make a knee' to the Duchess of Kent, and I said yes. We duly arrived at Georgia Sitwell's party, where we made a spectacular entrée, Miss West

5. She was to attend Chips's ten years later.
6. It was, in fact, £500, and the picture by Nattier.

looking like little Lord Faunleroy with her long blonde curls. I quickly presented the star to the amused Duchess of Kent, whom she shook warmly by the hand – no 'knee' – and I then led up Emerald, Mollie Buccleuch and others to her. Danny Kaye also arrived – a theatrical-cum-haute monde evening which lasted, alas, until nearly 5 a.m. Emerald suggested that Mae West should sing but she would not – I think because Danny Kaye was there.

1 March *Belgrave Square*

I had an immense supper party here at Belgrave Square, with 50 people, and all organised yesterday and today. The miraculous Danny Kaye was the attraction. First I went to the Palladium to hear him, he is mesmeric . . . like Hitler . . . and seems to pulverise his audience. Then we returned to Belgrave Square, where there was heaps of luscious food . . . champagne, candle-light: the Duchess of Kent was in a subtle shade of pink satin with two ropes of immense diamonds. Emerald, in a maddening mood, held court: Raymond Blackburn, Peter Thorneycroft, Hugh Fraser, were the MPs. Eventually Danny Kaye was persuaded to sing, and once on his feet nothing could induce him to stop, though Emerald irritated him by talking throughout his performance. At 2.40 the highly entertaining, successful rout came to a slow end . . .

12, 13, 14 March *Kelvedon*

The news of the Croydon by-election has sent a thrill through the country: it is an almost unbelievable Conservative victory. Our majority has increased by about 11,000 or more. Of course that nice silly Harold Nicolson was the worst candidate within human memory. How humiliating for him, though his ridiculous behaviour as the Labour Candidate cannot altogether explain the big swing-over. What can he think? He must hide his bald pink head in shame. Is it the turn of the tide?

17 March

Winston is in a jubilant mood ever since Croydon, which he accepts as a tribute to himself . . . his spectacular visit did much to help Frederick Harris.

Princess Helena Victoria – of what? – died a few days ago and has been buried at Windsor. When I last saw her, a few weeks ago, it was difficult to remember that she had once been a bouncing, fat, jolly Princess ... known to her intimates as 'the Snipe'. She was an old maid who may, however, have once known love. Certainly her first cousin, the Grand Duke of Hesse, wanted to marry her. When Honor and I stayed at Wolfsgarten with the Hesses years ago, the old Grand-Duke, still a fascinating Grand Seigneur, talked to me much of Princess Helena Victoria, and often used to see her. Her father, old Prince Christian, at the age of eleven, once took the Empress Marie Louise (Napoleon's wife) in to dinner. A story he repeated all his life.... She is survived by her even duller sister, Princess Marie Louise (named after the dinner companion of long ago). This female was married in her long-ago youth to a Prince of Anhalt, from whom she afterwards got an annulment. When she returned to England, King Edward VII's comment about his niece was: 'Poor Marie Louise. She came back just as she VENT.'

23 March *5 Belgrave Square*

Dined with Emerald Cunard who, as she was suffering acutely from bronchitis, looked about 100. She was charming, but for the first time looked what she is, an extremely old lady.... Dull evening, because of Emerald's indisposition.... And too much French furniture. It was like dining at Partridge's shop. I got up at midnight and broke up the tepid party.

5 April *London*

The garden at Kelvedon was lovely this weekend, with the orchard yellow with daffodils, lacy fruit blossom lending a nostalgic magic, and tulips in bud.

Dined in at Belgrave Square, lit-up and en fête.... At ten we drove to the American Embassy to a small reception for Mrs Roosevelt: it was not crowded – not more than 200 people. The American Ambassador and Mrs Douglas and their important guest, grinning and as massive as a caryatid, received us. Mrs Roosevelt gave me her famous 'tooth-y' smile, and asked how Paul was.... Then I bumped into the Prime Minister who wore a white tie and orders, and looked flushed. He was very friendly, as she was too. Bevin looked fat and tired, and later felt ill and had to be taken to a private sitting-room. That dreadful Aneurin Bevan wore a blue lounge suit which infuriated the Americans. In fact, the Socialist Government had turned up in force, and were enjoying the lavish atmosphere.

6 April

Cripps' penal budget. He spoke to a crowded house for about 2½ hours: the modern Savonarola was never offensive and always clear and logical, even when he announced his Capital Levy. It means that I must pay out more than I received last year. It is monstrous and a quite unnecessary piece of class legislation.

8 April

My chartered accountants seem to think that I shall not be completely ruined by the wicked Capital Levy. I walked to the House of Commons, where I heard John Anderson pontificate on the iniquities of this blundering budget. He is sound, but no spellbinder.

13 April

Much chat about the two last Windsor week-ends: Mrs Roosevelt was the guest-of-honour ten days ago and was a distinct success with everyone. It seems that after Queen Mary had gone to bed, the house party played 'The Game' and became quite childish with the Queen wearing a beard, etc. A wonderful scene it must have been. Mrs Roosevelt was exhausted.

6 May *Belgrave Square*

Augustus John, who is having an exhibition, came to the House of Commons to see me, and we sat for nearly two hours in the downstairs bar together, and drank two bottles of champagne. . . . Augustus still looks like a major prophet and his eyes sparkle with amusement and intelligence until he becomes be-fuddled, as he eventually always does, by drink.

8 May *Kelvedon*

A day of tremendous beauty: the lilac-scented air shimmered in the warm breeze: the sun blazed: the sky was clear: I bathed in the blue pool. . . . Never had Kelvedon been so lovely: is the place bewitched?

14 May *London*

The newspapers blazen more sad news: Kik Hartington has been killed in an air-smash; also Peter Fitzwilliam. They were a glamorous couple – gay, dashing, attractive, carefree, colossally rich – very much in love. Or at least he was. He has been wanting to marry her for some time but she objected, as a lapsed Roman Catholic, to his getting a divorce from Olive who is his official widow . . . Kik Hartington had an ill-starred life. She began by being a vivacious, simple, American girl when Joe Kennedy, her father, was made Ambassador here. She was gay enough, susceptible enough, to become be-glamoured by English life (and it was very grand then), and when Billy fell in love with her, and wanted to marry her, she couldn't resist and courageously defied the Roman Catholic Kennedys and married him: her gay, debonair brother Joseph was best man at their war-time wedding. Both he and Hartington were killed shortly afterwards. She seemed heartbroken and then, in time, recovered her spirits. . . . Then the fabulous Lord Fitzwilliam appeared. . . . Now they have died together.

20 May *London*

I am worried about Emerald and feel or fear that she will not live the year through. She is a-dying at the Dorchester.

26 May

Dined alone at Londonderry House with Circe Londonderry who was fascinating, and looked incredibly young. We dined in a small dining room overlooking Hertford Street, hung with some famous Lawrences. She gave me much ancient gossip, including the true story of the letters which convulsed London society in the late '90s, I think. I had often heard inaccurate versions before. It goes like this: Lady de Grey (afterwards Ripon) and Lady Londonderry (Circe's bell-mère) were great London hostesses: Lady de Grey owed her position largely to her somewhat romantic friendship with Queen Alexandra, and had had a long liaison with Luke, Lord Annaly. One August she went abroad for a cure, and foolishly entrusted her cavalier to her great friend, Lady Londonderry. Lady Londonderry was notoriously amorous, like all the Talbot family, and when Lady de Grey returned she strongly suspected them of having had an affair. In her indignation, she wrote Lord Londonderry a terrible letter in which she spilled the beans about Lady Londonderry's life-long 'collage' with Lord Helmsley. All London society, except Lord Londonderry, knew of this liaison. He was appalled and swore never to speak to his wife except in public. It was a terrible drama, and London was divided into two camps . . . though most people condemned Lady de Grey's caddish action. The non-speaking Londonderrys were the model for the Roehamptons in Vita Nicolson's famous book 'The Edwardians'.

30 May

I stayed with the Herberts, for the dance at Coppins, in their cosy, comfortable villa in Iver. . . . The dance was really for the Edinburghs, who were enchanting. She was in black lace, with a large comb and mantilla, as an Infanta, and danced every dance until nearly 5 a.m. I am beginning to doubt the supposed pregnancy . . . but Philip of Edinburgh, although as always extremely handsome and pleasing, looked worn out. But he was the success of the ball, and was wildly gay with his policeman's hat and hand-cuffs. He leapt about and jumped into the air as he greeted everybody. He went out of the way to be friendly to me, I thought, and we gossiped a bit. His charm is colossal, like all Mountbattens, and he and Princess Elizabeth seemed supremely happy and often danced together. . . . Towards 3 a.m. we danced the Hokey Cokey hilariously. . . . Then we went out of doors, and the Duchess in her shimmering white dress looked as lovely as the blue dawn itself. Meanwhile the tireless band played on. A glorious evening which made me re-live for a little my almost vanished and vanquished youth.

31 May

I had a note from my beloved Emerald in which she says that I am 'much too poignant and fantastic' for her to see in her weakened condition, but would I call next week? Perhaps she is rallying?

1 June *London*

I drove, with Felix Topolski, the Polish artist, to the Tower of London and there, on Tower Green, we saw Lord Wavell inducted as Constable. It was a brilliant ceremonial. The sun peered out from the grey sky at exactly the right moment: the uniforms shone, the Beefeaters looked splendid. Later we went to see the Crown Jewels, and had tea with the Wavells who were at their best and simplest – affectionate, muddled and charming.

2 June *London*

Went with Alan to the Savoy, where we attended the Conservative lunch for Winston Churchill. 'The boss' was in the gentlest of moods and made a wild, almost apologetic speech, which was yet not devoid of point and wit. I was very near to him and watched his easy smile and wet blue eyes that always look as if he had been crying. During his speech he made it clear that he expects to win the Election 'next year', or early in 1950, with a 'three-figure' majority. His reception was tepid, but not in the least unfriendly – though gone is the rapture of yester year. I think that the Party resents both his unimpaired criticism of Munich, recently published, and his alleged pro-Zionist leanings.

8 June

Emerald Cunard is desperately ill but is making an heroic struggle to survive.

9 June

Diana crossed from Paris by the Ferry last night, at my suggestion, to see Emerald. She was funny about her old friend whom she expected to find weak and aged, in fact, dying. Instead, she found a beautiful old lady in lace and pearls holding a black silk fan and wearing black lace gloves: she was propped up in bed, and evinced an intense interest in everything and everyone.

20 June *Kelvedon*

Norah Lindsay has died. She was one of the most brilliant, fanciful and altogether amazing of women. Her wit was extravagant, her conversation was ecstasy, her garden the finest in England, her appearance exotic to a degree. She had Renaissance hair, tight lips, treacherous eyes, but she was a fine friend, a lover of poetry and a worshipper and begetter of beauty. Everything that she touched sprang to life, and Sutton Courtenay, where she lived for so long, and where I spent the happiest days of my youth, was a terrestrial paradise. Long ago she influenced me more than anyone. Her funeral is to be at Sutton Courtenay in the little churchyard that she so loved. I suppose that she will lie near Mr Asquith.

27 June *Kelvedon*

Gore Vidal, the American novelist, and Tennessee Williams, the playwright, and I drove to Kelvedon. Vidal wears his hair like a Nazi, en brosse: he is dark. He has written four novels, and the most startling is 'The City and the Pillar', a book which has practically knocked America out. However, he is pleasant to talk to and not at all spoilt. Tennessee is 34 . . . a terrific Rodinesque character, of force and vitality and a great writer of poetic prose. Both were immensely impressed by Kelvedon, as they have never seen an English country house before. We were joined at luncheon by Field-Marshal Sir Claude Auchinleck and Violet Wyndham.[7] . . . An odd mixture but it went well. Tennessee retired to his room and began another play. This evening, in the House, when I told Beverly Baxter about my weekend guests – Tennessee in particular – he said that it was like entertaining Shakespeare.

8 July

Diana Cooper arrived from Paris to see Emerald this afternoon only to be told that she was dying. She had another heart attack, and it was agreed that she must be given a piqure which would put her to sleep for ever. All evening I was on the telephone . . . our beloved, dazzling, bright, fantastic Emerald dying. I cannot believe it.

9 July *London*

Diana Cooper told me that she sat with Emerald until 5.30 a.m. She was unconscious most of the time. Then Diana left her to

7. Authoress of 'Madame de Genlis'.

rest a little and now, this morning, Emerald has taken yet another turn for the better and is reading 'The Times'. So the crisis has not yet come.

11 July *Kelvedon*

I switched on the wireless this morning and heard that 'Lady Cunard, the famous London hostess', had died: and the newspapers confirm the horrible cold fact. She died at 6 p.m. last evening: and now I am more than ever alone. Laura and Emerald. Contemporaries, rivals, enemies but intimates. London society has had a horrible blow. There is only me left. Although I had not seen her so much during the past year I have nevertheless loved her since the first moment I saw her, in 1919. And with the exception of a brief estrangement caused by the old Queen of Rumania in Venice in 1925, we have been firm and fast friends ever since. Now she is no more: the elegance of the eighteenth century which she embodied and perfected are indeed gone. She was like a twittering, bejewelled bird. Her unexpected wit which was fanciful in the extreme, never failed to amuse and startle: and her kindness was proverbial. She always took it as a compliment to be asked to do a favour. She loved arranging people's lives: nothing was too much trouble for her. But her heart was lonely. Thomas Beecham had broken it.

Laura Corrigan, Norah Lindsay and now Emerald. 'Le monde' is now peopled only by mediocrities. I really haven't the time, money, cook or ambition to lead London society – but I perhaps will, well, just for a little.

14 July

I was married – and how debonair and confident I was – 15 years ago today. I rose early, dressed slowly, went to Delhez, the fashionable Figaro, to be shaved and coifféd, and there my best man, Freddie Birkenhead, met me: I then entertained 15 ushers to luncheon at Buck's Club – I remember every detail. Today was different.

17 July *Boughton, near Kettering*

Drove here to stay with the Buccleuchs. I had heard so much of the splendour of this place (palace is more apt), that I was afraid of being disappointed. However, I was soon reassured. It is a dream house with a strange, sleepy quality, but its richness, its beauty and possessions are stupefying. Everything belonged to Charles I, or Marie de Medici, or was given by Louis XIV to the Duke of Monmouth. Every 'enfilade' is elegantly arranged with Buhl chests, important pictures, Caffieri clocks, and the whole house is crammed with tapestries and marvellous objects. Gesso; white lacquer: signed pieces. There are 72 miles of drives in the park. But the place, for all its flowers and smiling furniture and lovely ladies, still has an asleep quality. It has hardly been lived in for 200 years. There is a writing-table which belonged to Cardinal Mazarin and 14 small Van Dycks in Walter Buccleuch's 'loo'. Over all this splendour Mollie reigns delightfully and effortlessly . . .

The long view from the terrace here is like a Claude Lorrain: and one hears the bees in the limes, a nostalgic soothing noise. But it is the stillness, the curious quiet of Boughton that impresses the most.

18 July *Boughton*

Coming down early for dinner I glanced onto the terrace and the long view and was overcome once more by the beauty of Boughton: and then I saw the Duchess of Kent in her blue Greek dress slowly advancing, and looking more lovely than ever. It was Shakespearian. A masque.

Brilliant games tonight, played in French, and excelled in by the Duchess of Kent. We sat in the drawing rooms overlooking the terrace . . . the beautiful, well-bred ladies so elegantly dressed: the many flowers; Boughton produces an atmosphere that is almost overwhelming.

20 July

I dined with the Palmellas at Claridge's in a private room. People stood up and clapped as Winston and Mrs Churchill passed through. We were about 22, and an agreeable party, but not the one that I should myself have given for Winston. Not sufficiently distinguished. I was between my sister-in-law, Patsy Lennox-Boyd, who was sweet, and Mrs Churchill, who looked most distinguished: beside her Lady Kemsley seemed almost naked. Winston entered like royalty, and bowed a little and made himself charming ... at the end of dinner the men remained behind and Gomer Kemsley appointed himself spokesman and tried to draw out Winston (I have long known of their hostility). But the great man needed no prompting: he was gay, he was grave, he was witty, he was provocative, and in the highest spirits, but he admitted, indeed insisted, that never before in our history had the position of England been so precarious. ... When asked by Gomer if he did not admire Attlee he replied, 'Anyone can respect him, certainly, but admire – no!'

Poor Massigli[8] showed every sign of the French weakening over Berlin (he is without a government, as Schumann's cabinet fell yesterday) and made a slightly defeatist remark to the effect that it would be better to clear out of Berlin and leave it to the Germans – in other words to the Russians, who would, of course, take over. Winston rose in his wrath and snubbed him. At length the Churchills left and everyone rose to say 'Good-night'. I left at 1.30 a.m., just too late to join Bob Menzies for supper at the Orchid Room.

22 July

At the Royal Garden Party Queen Mary was in a cloth-of-gold coat and looked magnificent, but ageing. A bit bowed, I thought, as she advanced slowly. Seeing me, she put out her hand but I could think of nothing to say – I am never particularly good at these impromptu meetings, and she smilingly passed on. Drino Carisbrooke who saw our meeting, whispered to me: 'My cousin May is rather over-dressed.' A curious way to describe Queen Mary.

Winston was in a grey morning coat, grey top hat and carrying a cigar. I saw him go up to the Queen and the Duchess of Kent, and bow to them. They appeared none too gracious, but Queen Mary rose slightly when he spoke to her. The Churchills were evidently bored for they soon left the Royal Pavilion, unfortunately, perhaps, for the thousands of guests suddenly began to cheer them. There was a stampede, and they were soon sur-

8. The French Ambassador.

rounded while the Royal Pavilion was deserted – except for the Royals. The excited, enthusiastic throng, still cheering, clapping and waving their hats, escorted the Churchills to the Palace. He was obviously enchanted by this reception, which almost amounted to a demonstration, and was quite extraordinary for Buckingham Palace.

30 July

At the House of Commons today, the Chamber was surprisingly crowded for an adjournment motion. Winston, in a short black jacket and light trousers, was in one of his righteous rages, and fairly trounced Attlee and his inept government over Hyderabad. The PM replied weakly, avoiding the issue, Winston interjected, and there was an angry scene. Meanwhile the Chamber glowed with an unusual reddish light resulting from the sun pouring through the mullioned windows and semi-drawn blinds: the temperature in the Chamber went up, so acrimonious was the debate. It is sad that it should part on a note of hostility, as lately the debates have been calm: there is an old belief that when the Catalpa trees in the Members' Yard begin to blossom it is time for Parliament to rise: I noticed them flowering a week ago today.

26 October

The State Opening of Parliament was magnificent; one had forgotten such splendour existed. . . . The long Royal Gallery was gay and red with peers in their robes moving about, and bejewelled peeresses . . . Circe Londonderry as always, was the most splendid: she was literally dressed in diamonds. That ghastly Nancy Astor looked magnificent, but haggard. . . . Looking at the incredibly romantic and moving scene she announced 'I hate the Peerage – it ought to be abolished', and then looking at me, added rudely, 'And the Beerage, too'. 'You are lucky, Margaret', I said, sweetly, to Margaret Case[9]: 'You are seeing the Opening of Parliament, and I have introduced you to the most unpopular woman in England'. The horrid old girl winced and I saw her withered bosom redden with rage. Our acrimonious exchange continued . . . and she said 'I can fill a Hall anyway'. 'So can

9. Miss Margaret Case, of New York.

George Robey', I replied. I knew that I had the upper hand, as I always do with her; nobody else has ever dared to be rude or to answer back, and she is always uneasy and disconcerted by me.

'In America I was the toast of everybody', she boasted.

'Is that why they tried to extradite you?' I asked, and she walked away, quivering with rage . . .

After the King read out his speech – a Socialist document which must have stuck on his lips, there was a charming moment when he turned and smiled at the Queen as if to say, 'Are we ready?' They rose, bowed to the assembled company and filed out followed by the Officers of State. It was like a Grand Slam in Hearts. I went quickly to an office window; the sun was shining, the streets were lined, the breastplates of the Blues glistened . . . and fat Mrs Leah Manning, MP for Epping, remained at her desk, and continued to dictate, not stirring when the Anthem was played and the Royal Cavalcade passed under her nose.

16 November

The Steel Nationalisation Bill. I returned to the H. of C. about 9.15, when Cripps in a particularly nauseous glib speech wound up for the Government, and made some startling statements; all through he was barracked, heckled, and interrupted by the rightly-indignant Opposition, led by Winston . . . Cripps lost his temper for a second, and made a damaging admission – 'If we cannot get Nationalisation of steel by legal means we must resort to violent methods.' This ill-timed threat of revolution threw the House into an uproar; there was a violent scene; we cat-called, and redoubled our interjections when he mentioned the Communists and the Communist peril.

24 November *Hotel des Bergues, Geneva*

I flew to Geneva, where I found my ancient ally, my beloved Prince Paul awaiting me. I had not see him since that day in January 1941 when I left Belgrade, and saw him and Princess Olga on the lawn of the Palace waving her handkerchiefs. . . . What years they have been. He, dethroned, disgraced . . . and now at length, almost absolved. I was at once struck by his altered, indeed, improved appearance, for he is fatter and better-looking.

We fell into each other's arms at the Swiss Airport. Princess Olga was waiting for me at the Hotel; she was almost overcome by the emotions and memories the meeting evoked. ... We had tea, and then he and I went for an endless walk. Two hours in the cold, arm-in-arm, we wandered about the Calvinistic city, which for the first time I found attractive. I suppose it is the shops which to my English half-starved eyes, seem paradisical. We gossiped and joked and so strong is the link between us, that it was as if those eight years of separation had never been. Paul and Princess Olga have money difficulties due mainly to the currency restrictions, and live in three smallish rooms. I thought of all their vanished, now Tito-occupied, palaces. We talked till two.

27 November *Geneva*

We decided that we had not enough money to take a car, a fantastic position for the ex-Regent of Yugoslavia and me to be in, and so we went, he, Princess Olga and I, to Lausanne by train ...

Then we walked to lunch with the Queen of Spain who was awaiting us at the door. She bubbled and said 'Do you understand?' every second second, but we had a splendid luncheon, which she had ordered especially in my honour, and I fear I wolfed the fine food. After luncheon we went to see Queen Helen, always divine, at the Beau Rivage Hotel, where we were soon joined by the young Rumanian couple. Queen Anne, as she is now called, is a good-looking girl, golden haired and wearing saintly medallions around her neck. Her nose is shiny, but I must say her accent is enchanting; it is a curious mixture of French and Danish, and makes her rare remarks a delight to listen to ... King Michael drove us to the station in his fast American car of which he is very proud. His face lights up when he talks of it.

30 November *Geneva*

After dinner, Paul sat with me until 2 o'clock, and he told me the whole long, sad tale of his interviews with Hitler which led to the Belgrade revolution and his overthrow ... I am absolutely convinced that he was innocent of all attempt to injure the Allied cause. Probably history will prove him right. He was in a terrible position with Germans surrounding his country, and Hitler pressing a pact upon him. For a long time he held out ... uneasy weeks of waiting and playing for time. Both he and his Government were against accepting the German pact of friendship. In Germany, he spent four hours with Hitler and Ribbentrop, who were affable . . . and said that the Axis powers would certainly win the war, and if he refused a Pact of neutrality and friendship – they asked for nothing more – Italy would be sure to demand most of Yugoslavia after the Peace. Paul knew, from other sources, that such were Mussolini's intentions. He returned to Belgrade and found that Dr Matchek, the two other Regents and most of his Cabinet were weakening, and now wanted to accept Hitler's offer, as was finally done – but all the conditions which have been so criticised about 'Sealed trains' for troops, etc. – Paul swears are untrue. We, the British (whom he has always loved and loves still) had let him down again and again, and never sent him the armaments we promised him. They were promised to him by Lord Chatfield at a secret interview in my house, in 1938, I think: I remember the incident well, as I had requested Mr Chamberlain to have the interview arranged.

1949

11 January

Loelia Westminster, Peter, Paul, and I went to Brighton for the great First Night of Terry Rattigan's 'Adventure Story'. Before the play, we went to the Grand Hotel to see him, and found him half dressed, rather tight and maudlin, but lovable, as he always is before a First Night. I gave him, for luck, a coin minted in the reign of Alexander. The play is an ambitious drama, or rather a series of episodes strung together on the theme of the gradual decay in Alexander's character. Though it was magnificently produced, Paul Scofield as Alexander did not particularly impress any of us. As the rich drama unfolded there were some of the usual mishaps which can occur in the provinces. The Brighton audience was puzzled by the play . . . they seemed to expect light comedy. We refused Terry's invitation to supper, and drove back to London, Loelia talking all the way.

20 January

Will I never learn the rudimentary secret of health and well being for a man over 50 (though I look 34 and have never had more physical success)? No red wine, no duck, no brandy, and I had all three at the French Embassy last night, and so feel like death today: are the sands beginning to run out? How much longer will I be strong enough – rich enough and youthful-looking enough to go on racketing about as I do . . .?

Winston has written me a personal note asking me to luncheon next Thursday. Why?

27 January

Woke with a violent headache and found that my temperature was 103°. This would happen on the day I was to lunch with Winston. But I was determined to go, and set off for Hyde Park Gate, where I found the street enlivened by the presence of a policeman, and three MPs – all too early, like me. We went in, and I was at once struck by the air of elegance and tidiness that the house has. Mrs. Churchill greeted me with 'Hello Chips' as did daughter Mary. . . . Winston soon joined us and was in a rippling mood. He looked small, even diminutive, and his face was as pink as a baby's. Clemmie referred to him as 'Winston darling'. She is obviously devoted to him. He greeted me affectionately and put me next to him at luncheon. The dining-room looks onto the garden. Food excellent – and four bottles of champagne. Winston talked of Southend, and suddenly, to my surprise, burst into an old Southend music hall song of the '80s, singing two verses of it lustily. Finally the conversation got onto politics and last night's debate.[10] He is immensely pleased with the figures and thinks that we may have deflated Bevin a bit. He then said that he was infinitely bored by the Lynskey Tribunal and its findings; and that the whole thing was a disgrace to our way of life. About 3.30 I rose and the party broke up. Very successful – but I still wonder why I was asked?

11 February

Charlie Londonderry died in the night at Mount Stewart, and I am very sorry; he was a good friend and a grand seigneur of the old school; even his appearance was almost theatrically 18th

10. The Palestine Debate. The Socialist Government's majority was only 90.

century. Slim, with an elegant figure and pointed features he was red in the face and dressed with distinction. He was always gay and amiable and completely sure of himself. In the long run he will be proved right politically; he always maintained that there were only two possible courses for us: either to make friends with Germany, or, if this was impossible, to re-arm. We did neither, and war was the result. But he was unpopular and much criticised at the time for his views.

I have come to the conclusion that I have no morals, no ideals, no principles whatsoever – except of that of good manners – and that I have had a most enjoyable life. I do not see that morals or religion are at all necessary to our happiness: but one has a richer, more varied life, if one keeps up appearances and a code of distinguished manners.

14 February

Diana Cooper tells me that poor Emerald Cunard's jewels have turned out to be false, and indeed all evidence points to the fact that she was really financially embarrassed during the last years of her life.

17 February

After Charlie Londonderry's Memorial Service, Arthur Henderson remarked to me 'possibly Londonderry was right all the time'. Of course he was.

20 February *Brussels*

I flew here two days ago for a gastronomic weekend and today went 'en tourist' to Waterloo, and tried to find the forgotten tomb – which has always fascinated me, of Lord Uxbridge's leg. Finally I discovered it, near the church and quite overgrown. I fear that this humorous memorial will be demolished in time. It bears an inscription commemorating visits to it paid by George IV and the King of Prussia in 1821. Then I went on to the 'triste et morne plaine' where the battle had taken place. I came here years and years ago, as a child, with my father, in 1913, and once again in 1926. I climbed 'the lion' puffing like an old engine. Occasionally I feel old, or, at least, middle-aged. I then drove to Belœil to the de Lignes' magnificent chateau (they were away) and walked in the magnificent garden, with its canals and allées of great trees.

6 April

Budget Day. We had all hoped for some cuts, some concessions, though fearing penal confiscatory legislation too. But nothing of the kind happened. Cripps, smiling articulate, between sips of orangeade, unfolded his review of our financial position. Then, to the rage of the Socialists and the amazement of the House in general he announced his changes: a penny off beer, higher telephone charges, higher cost of living, moderately increased Death Duties, but no reliefs or concessions. The Labour people snarled with anger. One remarked that the budget had 'malice for all – goodwill towards none'. In any case it was highly unpopular, and the Government has taken a knock. There is talk of a back bench revolt. Is Cripps making a bid for a coalition with the Tories?

7 April

The Conservative Press praises the budget, and it is true that it has brought me, personally, some relief; no additional taxation, while Brewery shares should now go up.

29 April *Villa Mauresque, Cap Ferrat*

Alan Searle[11] met me at Beaulieu, where I found blazing sun, and we drove to the Villa. Willie, looking like a mandarin and flanked by footmen, met me at the door. I was struck by his calm oriental manner – his youthful bearing and his stammer; he seems interested in everything, and we soon had an excellent luncheon in this almost too-tidy house. After a nap, we had a walk round the Cap – Willie, I and the bright-eyed, devoted Alan Searle. Alan is now Willie's housekeeper, companion and amanuensis. The Villa is white, Moorish in appearance and stands in an elaborate sweet-smelling garden. All is regulated, precise and spotless. Many good pictures – Zoffanys, Reynolds, etc., and several dozen theatrical pictures which Willie has left to the National Theatre. At dinner we had much chat and gossip, of a rather licentious nature. Willie and Alan appeared in elaborate dressing-gowns. I felt drab and ordinary in my dinner jacket.

11. Somerset Maugham's secretary and close friend.

30 April

I bathed, to Willie's astonishment, in the very cold pool, and then we walked down to the sea and saw many deserted villas; there is an Edwardian atmosphere, almost Ouida, about those abandoned, once luxurious houses, where lived the Duke of Connaught, Lady Essex, etc. The vegetation, after East Anglia, seems very rich and tropical.

Many reminiscences of every kind from Willie, who has had a long amorous career, and now at 75 is still lusty. He has been everywhere, met everybody, tasted everything. His interest in the world and in Society and food and drink, is acute, though he occasionally has flashes of amnesia.

3 May

Twice this evening Willie called Alan Searle 'Gerald', the name of his companion Gerald Haxton who died in New York in 1944 after having lived with Willie for over 25 years.

4 May

In the evening we dined in Monte Carlo where I do not remember ever having been before; many old trouts about, decaying old dames who have lived here for years. The Casino seemed tawdry, even municipal . . .

I do not really like the Midi – never have.

8 May *Paris*

A long, long day. I asked the concierge at the Ritz to find me a train to Chantilly and he told me of one that did not exist; so having walked to the Gare du Nord and found no train, I hired a car; almost immediately we got involved in a procession marching to celebrate Joan of Arc's birthday. I was already very late, but hesitated to tell the driver to blow his horn, as I felt it was scarcely the moment for an Englishman to make himself conspicuous. Finally, I arrived at the Chateau de St Firmin, and found Diana looking exquisite and Duff quite amiable, and very well dressed. Outside the waterfall tumbled and the grass and shrubs looked smiling. The little pavilion, which was lived in during the war by Seyss-Inquart, was enchanting in the May sunlight. There followed a large luncheon party – Bertha Michelham, Fulco Verdura, Cabrols, etc., and afterwards I slept in the sun, and was only wakened when a fox ran past and everyone shouted Tally-ho.

16 May *London*

Last night on my return home from the House I was surprised to hear what I thought was quacking coming from my Amalienburg dining room. On investigating I found twelve ducks in a basket in the blue and silver banquetting room, left 'to rest' there by Diana Cooper, who this morning fetched them and took them with her to Paris.

3 June

La vie joyeuse keeps one young. Today I drove to Syon in my little Ford and its romantic grandeur and beauty come as quite a shock after the down-at-heel suburbs of Brentford. Suddenly one enters a halcyon park with cattle and great green trees and, I am told, many rare birds; the facade of the house – Walpole Gothick – is disappointing but the interior rivals the Vatican. I was taken through room after room, until I reached the Long Gallery with its view over the Park towards Kew. There I found Hughie Northumberland waiting for me. It was a wonderful evening and we walked in the Park, saw the great glass house [designed by Charles Fowler, in 1830] and went to the river: what a sublime domain. But I fear it is doomed – some Government will surely requisition it. Elizabeth, sweet and unspoiled, who is still suckling her last baby, waved to us from a window. Then followed a grand tour of the house room after room – some tiny, some immense. One had only a mechanical bird hanging from the ceiling – others had Holbeins and Sir Joshua's by the dozen. Has any house – even Boughton, such treasures? One blue room, done by Adam, has life size gold statues on a colonnade to greet one. Hughie showed me dozens of huge crates that he had just opened, containing the cornices, doors, fireplaces from the old Northumberland House. Ever since 1875, when Northumberland House was pulled down to make way for Northumberland Avenue off Trafalgar Square, they have lain boxed up and forgotten in the Riding School.

4 June

My first 4 June with Paul at Eton. I drove down early and found him waiting for me, tidy and sleek and excited. We picnicked in Windsor Park and then went back and watched the cricket and greeted people . . .

The long day wore on, and ended with dinner at the Café de Paris with the Sitwells and the fireworks, which I thought very mediocre after the ones I remember at Goering's party in Berlin.

16 June *Ascot*

When we got back this evening there was a message, asking us all to Windsor Castle for a ball tomorrow night.

18 June

Paul rang up early this morning to give me racing tips – and I must say that they all won. What a quaint little fellow he is – he seems momentarily to have forsaken Hansard for the form book.

After a day's racing, we dined early – 2 Herberts, Diana Daly and I, with Sidney and me in white ties, and left in my car arriving at the Castle about 10; we went in by a small entrance and followed other guests (after our names had been taken) to the Green Drawing Room: there must have been 50 or 60 people, mostly young friends of Princess Margaret.

The rooms were banked with flowers and the lit vitrines full of china, though I saw none as fine as mine. Windows were open on to the terrace and the cool air was a relief. After we waited for about twenty minutes the doors were flung open, and we saw the King and Queen waiting to receive us, side by side: he seemed brown and she, though unfortunately very, very plump, looked magnificent in a white satin semi-crinoline number with the Garter and splendid rubies. . . Mrs Greville's[12] I suppose. They both called me Chips, and she said how pleased she was I had come. Just beyond was the dancing. . . . Soon, in a small antechamber leading to the long gallery full of family portraits, I came on the Queen, and we talked for a time, and she showed me the pictures, commenting on them, and then asked about Prince Paul and his sons. Friendly in the extreme she was, and

12. Mrs Greville had left many of the jewels to the Queen.

gay and gracious, and asked me to look at the Waterloo Chamber, which had been specially lit up for the evening. We walked along a long passage with magnificent Canalettos and Zoffanys, by the dozen, many of which have been rehung and cleaned since the war. The curving corridor was a rich sight. The Chapel, Throne-room and Waterloo Chamber were all brightly lit, and we had them to ourselves. Then we returned to the ballroom, and I danced with several people, and sat with Diana Daly in a long drawing room, of which the only other occupants were the King and Mrs Cecil Boyd-Rochfort, wife of his trainer. The King had his foot up on a foot stool to rest, though he seemed quite well and often danced. The Queen danced every dance vigorously, but not as violently as Lady Astor who, despite her 70 years, seemed positively frivolous. I gave Alice Winn supper and the Queen joined us with Reggie.[13] The Edinburghs made a somewhat late appearance (he had been to the Channel Islands or somewhere) and they looked divine. She wore a very high tiara and the Garter – he was in the dark blue Windsor uniform, also with the Garter. They looked characters out of a fairy tale, and quite eclipsed Princess Margaret, who was simply dressed. But already she is a public character, and I wonder what will happen to her? There is already a Marie Antoinette aroma about her. . . . I danced with the Duchess of Gloucester, who was mild and sweet, and we spoke of the old days. . . . The King smiled and showed his prominent teeth and I chatted again to the Queen. At a quarter to five, she told the band to stop; everyone bowed and curtseyed to the remaining Royalties and we left, and drove back in the dawn – looking back, the Castle rose romantic in the pink morning light. I was enchanted with the evening.

27 September

Six weeks later. Back from a sunlit holiday in my beloved Venice . . . Today Parliament, recalled because of the devaluation of the pound, met once more, and it was a crowded and cross House. The rule of the rabble. Outside, Winston was cheered lustily. Cripps brushed past me and looked irritable. He spoke with dialectical skill for an hour and a half. Said nothing. A plea for more production, and at the same time raising the tax on distributed

13. Winn.

profits – a fine way to encourage incentive. There seems no sequence or psychology in the man – why was he ever born? Even the Labour people did not like his speech, and his reception was tepid. While he spoke, his gloomy consort, voluminous and grey, sat in the gallery.

28 September

Winston's childish side is ever engaging. Today I saw him come into the Member's Lobby which was crowded with representatives of the people who prefer chatter to Prayers, and as we waited for the doors to open and the attendant to shout 'Prayers are over' Winston smilingly made his way towards one of the Porter's chairs and asked for snuff, which the attendant handed him from a silver box. Then, surprisingly, Winston looked at the Chair (which he must have known for 40 years) as if he had never seen it before in his life, got into it, and sat there for fully five minutes, bowing and beaming at other Members who looked at him through the little window. A boyish prank. How endearing he is, sometimes. A few minutes later, however, he was making what was to be one of his very greatest speeches ... to a crowded and anxious house ... a stupendous performance, highly audible, polished, unanswerable, and damning. He held the House entranced for over an hour. The Government supporters, while they interrupted, were more than usually puerile, and seemed uncomfortable. They even finally seemed to realise the solemnity of the occasion. For the speech was no ordinary one, but surely a clarion call to rouse the nation – an Election rally.

As Winston spoke, I looked about me. Attlee appeared wizened – Cripps oblivious of his weakened position – Bevan like an angry bull frog about to croak. In the Speaker's Gallery were Mrs Attlee in grey (she is always well dressed) and Mrs Churchill, who beamed at her husband below. Randolph was in the Journalists' Gallery over the clock, and at one moment the rays of the sun caught his face, and it seemed transfixed with filial pride; for all his faults, he adores his father.

8 November

Tomorrow is my father's birthday. He would have been seventy-seven. I never think of him.

1950

29 January *Kelvedon*

How I dread the electoral plunge . . . only twenty-five days from now till 'VE Day'. Though the Conservatives will surely gain many, many seats, the issue will probably be a deadlock, perhaps with a small Tory majority. I fear this would be disastrous, for us, politically.

30 January *Palace Hotel, Southend*

I have moved here, and here I shall remain until 24 February. I have laid the plans for a cunning campaign, and shall try to win over both the Catholics and the Jews. I know that I am popular, and my majority last time of only 3,077 should be greatly increased. It is lonely in Southend by myself. I wish I had a black poodle puppy as a companion; in fact I wish I had many things, but first and foremost a safe majority.

I have decided not to keep a diary during the election, for I have not either the time or privacy, and it would be of little interest since all election stories and comments are ephemeral. So this volume gets locked up for several weeks.

24 February

Three weeks later . . . the election is over, and I was re-elected by a colossal majority.

H.C.	34,100
E. C. Hutchison (Lab.)	15,354
MacCallum Scott (Lib.)	9,907
Majority	18,746

Last evening, after the polls closed at 9 p.m., I went back to the Palace Hotel, had a bath and a bottle of champagne and drove to the Kursaal, arriving at 10.30, for the 'count'. When I went down among the tellers I found I was already ahead, and had 10,000 votes already. It was exciting watching the little packets of votes mounting up. The Liberal, Scott, looked depressed. After the triumphant result was announced I spoke to the crowd, and went on to a celebration party. Returns of Labour victories kept coming in but I was too exhausted to care, for I had barely been to bed for two nights. This afternoon the two chief parties are neck and neck[14].

2 March

I took my oath in the House of Commons for the fifth time today. The first was to King George V in November 1935, and he died six weeks later; then to his successor Edward VIII in January 1936, then to George VI in December of that year. The fourth time was in the new Parliament in 1945. Now today again I pledged my loyalty to George VI.

6 March

The atmosphere in the new House is subdued, and even friendly; Attlee is all smiles, and his speeches and those of his followers are unprovocative ... altogether a very different set up from 1945, when the Labour people were cock-a-hoop and horrible. Tonight Geoffrey Lloyd, back after 5 years, was alone on the opposition Front Bench. I sat with him for a time, and several Labour MPs came up, and said that they were glad I was back. It looks as if nothing will happen for a bit, perhaps not for a long time. 'Rien ne dure comme le provisoire.' Meanwhile the Labour boys are most polite. The nicest of them all is Geoffrey de Freitas.[15] He asked me to pair with him, but I had reluctantly to refuse as it is now contrary to our regulations to pair at all. We want to keep them all here and wear them all out.

7 March

I am 53 today, and although I know I have aged during the past year. ... How I hate getting old, or rather time running out.

9 March

Odette Massigli told me that after her recent big dinner at the French Embassy for the King and Queen, a message arrived from Queen Mary, asking for one of the menus, and saying that if there were any sweets or flowers left over that had come from Paris, she would like to have them. This caused consternation

14. Labour had an overall majority of six – 315 to 309.
15. Labour MP for Lincoln 1945–1961; for Kettering, 1964.

at the Embassy and people tried frantically to collect the left-over friandises. Is Her Majesty's brain weakening?

14 March

I had a few people in for drinks, rather a motley crew, when suddenly the door opened, and the butler announced Lord Wavell. He really is an odd fellow, which is an understatement; full of loyalty and warmth for the few people he trusts, but impossibly shy with people he doesn't know, and thus sometimes making an unfortunate impression.

This evening in the House, Aneurin Bevan again wound up, but in a half-hearted manner, and our new technique of ignoring him (since he thrives on interjections) is having its effect, though sometimes it is almost more than Winston can bear; he often looks on the verge of bobbing up and contradicting some of 'Nye's' grosser lies. . . . He hopes to rule this country one day.

16 March

Winston spoke today in the Defence Debate for over an hour and seemed in the highest spirits. No extinct volcano he.

21 March

Tonight I am alone desœuvré, and depressed; even lonely; I am dissatisfied with my mode of life and ask myself why I go on being an MP. In fact, why do I do so much that both bores me, and for which I am unsuited? I really only like frivolity, and society; or else solitude, writing and love.

29 March

The Government was defeated by 26 votes today, 283–257. There was wild enthusiasm and cheers for Churchill as we shouted 'Resign' to the chagrined Socialists, who looked extremely glum. This must be the beginning of the end, but not quite yet as I doubt whether they will resign on this vote, and Winston does not want to force an election yet.

24 April

There is considerable political gossip and speculation about Wednesday's crucial vote, and I discovered that Winston and Attlee had a secret meeting at six tonight in a private room here at the House, as neither wishes to be seen visiting the other.

I think that Winston would form a Government, if the present one is defeated, but I fear that it will just scrape home on Wednesday.

1 May

We were eleven at my dinner party of Essex MPs and the evening was a great success, although we were obliged to rush back to the House because of a secretly agreed upon vote. I was sorry as all was going merrily at Belgrave Square, and it was a valuable and pleasant evening.

But back at the House there was a drama. As the Minister, when the House is not suspended, sits down at 10 o'clock, we had arranged to leave Belgrave Square at 9.50, which would have given us just time: 11 minutes. However, Alfred Barnes, Minister of Transport, whether by accident or design – I know not – sat down at 9.54. And when we luckily arrived a minute or so ahead of our schedule, a policeman shouted 'Division on, sir!' and added 'Run for it.' We did, and for the first time in my Parliamentary career I ran in the actual Chamber. All eleven of us got through, but with scarcely a second to spare. There was tremendous excitement in the House when the Whips announced a tie 278 to 278. Then Major Milner in the chair rose and declared that in accordance with custom and tradition he would cast his vote with the Government. Thus the Minister of Transport saved a £1,000 per annum reduction in his salary by one vote: but, more important, the Government was saved as, on such an issue, a defeat would certainly have meant an Election – or, as some people think, Mr Churchill would have been sent for to form a Government, which might have lasted some weeks or months. Who knows? Rumour has it that the Government did not expect a division until late in the evening, but by then had got wind of my party and hoped to rush the Division before we got back. If this was really a plot, it very nearly came off.

2 May

Great excitement and headlines in the newspapers proclaim the narrowness of the Government's majority – and by a casting vote.

A grand luncheon party at the Spanish Embassy, for Winston and Mrs Churchill, both very smiling . . . he came up to me and joked about my party and said 'I am creditably informed that owing to the abundance of your viands and the excellence of your wines, that you almost failed to support me in the Division lobby last night.' He was in the very highest of spirits, and joked with everyone and announced that he, too, had almost been late. 'I was told to be there at 10 – a merciful providence got me there at 10 to the hour.' As we walked towards the dining-room George of Denmark hung politely back and Winston, in a rollicking mood, tried to push him in front of him – to make him pass before him. 'I wouldn't dream of it' George said. 'Don't dream of it: just do it' Winston retorted, and went on prodding. . . . It was one of Winston's hilarious days (he has silent, truculent ones too) and he had obviously relished last night's frolic in the House. As he left he came up to the Duchess of Kent and apologized for leaving, adding '*The Prime Minister* wants to see me: I suppose he will suggest a coalition!!' There was scorn in his voice as he stressed the words 'Prime Minister'.

5 May

Just as I was leaving London for Southend, Archie John Keren telephoned to say that his father Lord Wavell had this afternoon a very serious abdominal operation. It is his 67th birthday. He is sleeping peacefully, but his condition is critical, and I am worried about him.

7 May *Kelvedon*

Peter is anxious about Archie Wavell, and a cloud of gloom has descended on us which not even a somewhat reassuring message from Lady Wavell could quite dispel.

21 May *Kelvedon*

Alone all day in this paradise. Kelvedon is almost too beautiful in May and the garden, deliriously lovely. I sunbathed and the quivering air was scented with carnations. About six o'clock I wrote a letter to Lord Wavell, and later I was told that the wireless had announced his serious relapse. I know now that he will die.

24 May

At the Commons I found a message to ring Peter who sadly told me that Lord Wavell had died peacefully this morning after a second haemorrhage – I was stunned, as much as one can be by a blow one has expected. I then happened on Arthur Moyle, the bland, smiling, kindly, efficient PPS to Mr Attlee and I sadly suggested that the Nation offer my old friend a State Funeral and burial in St Paul's. He said he would immediately tell Mr Attlee.

There is so much to be said about poor, great, granite Archie Wavell, but I am temporarily silent.[16]

25 May

Wavell has a wonderful Press and some of the newspapers describe him as one of the two greatest contemporary Englishmen.

2 June *Paris*

Suddenly I found myself face to face with the Windsors whom I now saw for the second time in 13 years – since, in fact, my famous dinner party in November 1936 on the very eve of the Abdication. She was elegant and gay and gracious, and we had a long talk standing up. She had, I thought improved, though she told a long incoherent tale of Civil Servants in Nassau. The Duke, rather desséché, astonished me by his opening remark which was 'Do you remember the night we dined together at the Saddle and Cycle Club in Chicago?' (This was in 1924 or 1925!) He watched me talking to Wallis; evidently he is still passionately in love. He came up three times and interrupted us by bringing her Scotch and water as he called it; each time she smilingly accepted the glass, and put it down undrunk. There was certainly understanding and affection in her glance. He turned to me and said 'Chips, do you know what tomorrow is? We shall have been married thirteen years.' 'It is already tomorrow: it is 1.15' I said. This evoked his only smile, and he nudged Wallis's elbow and said 'Chips says it is 1.15!' Again she smiled, and rather dismissed him, and we continued our conversation.

16. See pp. 460–61.

7 June *Lord Wavell's Memorial Service*

Peter and I drove to the Abbey early as Peter was ushering: the streets were lined with troops and traffic diverted. Lady Wavell sent me a ticket for the family pews in the South Transept. The Abbey quickly filled, and soon one could hear the distant piping of the Black Watch as they accompanied the coffin from Westminster Pier to the Abbey – it had come by barge from the Tower, as only Nelson's had ever done before, I believe. A long procession of antique prelates led the way: guardsmen carried the coffin, and pallbearers and the great military leaders of the war accompanied it: four officers carried Wavell's many decorations and orders. As I listened to the hymns and music I thought of our unexpected, strange friendship and suddenly, looking up, I caught Lady Wavell's eyes, and I looked away. She was immensely dignified. Everything she did was perfect, though she was not in heavy mourning, and wore white gloves and no veil. I sat with the Cholmondeleys and the Leicesters, and the coffin almost touched us as it passed: the family were weeping. Afterwards I joined my car waiting in the House of Commons courtyard and there found Peter, Charles Rankin and Hugh Euston, Wavell's three ADC's, and rushed them to Belgrave Square where they had a hurried snack and drank champagne to cheer them. Then I saw them off to Winchester where they attended the impressive funeral in the cloisters of the school Wavell loved so much. Nobody's burial arrangements have been so elaborate and magnificent, but then who else has been a war hero, who captured the imagination of the whole world, and who was, moreover, Lord Lieutenant of London and Constable of the Tower as well as once Viceroy of India?

14 June

It is now 11.30 and we are settling down to an all night sitting. Winston is in a dinner jacket and in a naughty boyish mood. He sits in the Division lobbies and twits us as we go by. He is incurably, irresistibly boyish.

In the lobby I passed Cripps and the air chilled. I felt as if I had breathed the dark, fetid atmosphere of beyond the tomb. He always gives me that impression. Later he went to the dining-room with Strachey, and death and the devil supped together.

15 June *After Ascot*

I went to Coppins for cocktails, which were served on the lawn. She was amazingly magnificent, the lovely Duchess, and carried an old-fashioned parasol with a long handle, almost entirely of jewels, mostly sapphires, which sparkled in the sunlight. As I was chatting with Mrs Douglas, the dark, divine American Ambassadress, the King and Queen appeared, accompanied by the Duke and Duchess of Gloucester. The Queen was still in her Ascot frock of white with pearls and rubies, but the King had changed into a blue suit. They came at once up to me and I had a long conversation with her about Paul and then George Gage. She was round-faced and smiled her world-famous smile, and smelt, to use her favourite word 'delicious'. Then she left me to talk to the Swedes (Hägglöffs) and the King in a rollicking mood – after several glasses of champagne – put his finger to my cheek – and asked me how I managed to look so young at my age? If only I had had some sleep (there was an all night sitting last night) I might have answered wittily, but I didn't, and just grinned like a Cheshire cat, though I talked garrulously enough with everyone else, and finally left – after the Sovereigns had departed. I was full of admiration for their easy informality.

Ascot this year was highly enjoyable, and obviously the King, who now dotes on society and parties, adored it. He looks much younger than the Duke of Windsor.

21 June *Christ Church, Oxford*

I drove to Oxford to attend the Gaudy here, and the beauty of Christ Church filled me with its usual sad and strange nostalgia. As I wandered about the crowded quads, I thought of my old happy days, the happiest of my life, when I lived a life of leisure and loveliness and my boon companions were Prince Paul, Gage, and dear, dead Ivo Grenfell. Dinner in the great hall was impressive, with Halifax looking like a saint (which he is definitely not) presiding. Robes, roses, choirboys in red, Burgundy, the lit pictures and cloying monastic atmosphere were all inebriating. Oxford always tears my heart.

13 July

Another ball ... at Olive Baillie's, where the garden had been transformed by M. Boudin of Jansen of Paris (who designed my celebrated dining-room) into a ballroom edged with floodlit herbaceous borders. Very elaborate and réussi . . . Princess Margaret was at the next table, and stayed until 4.30, looking very small and a wee bit Mongolian. Sinatra crooned for half an hour – to everyone's intense boredom. He is supposed to be a spellbinder, and the most famous singer in the world, but I consider all Cabaret stunts bores: we fashionable fools prefer our own banal chatter – and we are right.

Home again at 5.30 a.m. I haven't slept for months and moons.

15 July *Kelvedon*

Spent the weekend resting and re-charging the batteries among the roses at Kelvedon, and thinking of poor Elsie Mendl who died at Versailles on Tuesday, aged God knows what . . . I should guess about 97 or 98. She was a kind, good friend to me since 1917, and she was older than the Himalayas then. Elegant, gentle, with a shrieking voice, and high enthusiasms, she was a completely 18th century character. She invented fashionable interior decorating, and exotic entertaining. . . . I took my Paul to dine there two years ago and explained en route how aged and famous she was. He was bewildered, and fuddled by an unaccustomed glass of champagne, asked her if she had known Louis XV! Cleanliness was Elsie Mendl's mania and she had colonic irrigation every day, and used to stand on her head until she was past eighty.

8 August *London*

Lunched at the American Embassy in Prince's Gate, a very pleasant party. The Ambassador with his slightly Southern drawl, a black patch over the eye he lost in a fishing accident last year, and his easy, friendly manner and immense charm, is a delightful host: I was on her, Peggy's right, and she is really divine. Dark, gay, simple and yet very much with the grand manner, she makes an ideal Ambassadress . . . Lou Douglas was confidential. He has a deep contempt for the Socialist Government. That I had always guessed, but I never heard him say so before: and he thinks that they have no sense of the international position. He doesn't think that there will be a major war now – perhaps never – but believes that we are entering on a new phase: we shall have alarms, encroachments, Koreas, for many years to come.

23 August *Kelvedon*

Lovely weather and the garden and pool enchantments. My European plans have been dished by horrid old Attlee's (though I don't dislike him at all really) obstinacy in refusing to recall Parliament before 12 September. It seems as if I shall have to rush back from Italy almost directly I have arrived.

30 August *Brignoles*

We had two pleasant surprises: the car, repaired and ready,[17] was back, and Willie Maugham had arrived, so we all dined gaily in the garden, on luscious fare. Willie looked well and vigorous despite his 76 years: his mandarin manner remains, but he was friendly and witty. I think that he was slightly, but only slightly, put out that I had a grand suite on the first floor with a huge four-poster, whilst he was relegated upstairs.

2 September *Chateau de la Garoupe*

A day of sun-bathing and water-skiing. We went out in the 'small' yacht, and bathed blissfully, then had cocktails at the famous Eden Roc. Lunched at 3.30 p.m. As we came home in the speed-boat we saw a dark female figure silently fishing from the shores of the adjacent villa, the Chateau de la Cröe (where the Windsors lived for some summers): it was the old Queen of Italy, a famous fisher-woman. As she casts her lonely line, does she think of her daughter, Princess Mafalda, dying in a prison-camp? of Mussolini? of all her lost Quirinalian splendour? Or just whether the fish will bite?

2 November

Bernard Shaw is dead, that old fraud with his mania for publicity and money. I do not think that his works will live, though he tried to be the modern Voltaire, and up to a point succeeded. I met him several times, lunching at the Lavery's with his wife Charlotte, or at tea with Emerald Cunard. The last time I met

17. Chips's car had caught fire on the way to stay with Mrs Randolph Churchill.

him was going into Augustus John's studio. Lady Astor is making an exhibition of herself, as usual, about him, and behaving as if she was the widow.

Yesterday for the second time I had a private word with Attlee about an honour being bestowed on Lou Douglas on his much regretted retirement, and it may well now happen. Why do people in authority – of whatever party – seldom think of anything? Later I also approached amiable Arthur Moyle, Attlee's smiling, pleasant PPS about it. 'If we pull this off it will be the third time I've done something for you' he laughed. True. Laura Corrigan's decoration; and Wavell's State Funeral.

6 November

Ernest Marples, MP for Wallasey, made a remarkably good speech in which he attacked Bevan. A fine performance, simple, without elegance or eloquence, but direct and damning.

Later, there was an all-important Division on Housing, and an acrimonious Debate. I thought, perhaps for the first time, that Winston seemed old and his peroration fell flat – or half-flat. However I watched people in the Galleries, and they seemed enraptured; some even applauded, before they could be stopped. Expressionless in the Ladies' Gallery sat Mrs Churchill, Mrs Neville Chamberlain and Mrs Attlee.

7 November

The second vote today was on a Conservative Amendment against the proposed controls, and our attack was led by Peter Thorneycroft from the Front Bench. He was splendid, hard-hitting, effective and supremely confident; he has the grand manner, and I watched him with affection, admiration and envy. Carly, his now pregnant wife (as he told me himself) was in the Gallery.[18] This time our majority was 10. 288 to 278. . . . I saw old Arthur Greenwood being wheeled in in an arm-chair; he looked dying. His son, Anthony, also a Member, who has a Surbiton accent but a pleasant, well-soaped appearance, was in attendance.

8 November

Early to the House, where there was a plot afoot. There was a

18. The Thorneycrofts had met at Chips's house.

short, spirited debate on a question of procedure. At 4.35 the Bell rang, and I woke from my deep siesta in the library and went to vote. As I came through the Chamber Winston seized me and asked: 'How are the numbers going?' I went back and asked, and heard we were 235 which I told him and, at that very second, Patrick Buchan-Hepburn interrupted saying 'We have won! by six!' Winston smiled and remarked 'That is some sugar for the birds' and the tellers announced the Government defeat but not – I fear – their downfall. Nevertheless they looked glum and murmured 'Snap division', etc. But there is no question of their resignation.

9 November *Queen's Hotel, Southend*

My father was born 82 years ago today. He was a dull, charmless, uneducated, unexciting, unhappy, untidy little man who was weak with women and unpopular with men. . . . A cypher really. But I always quite liked him, and he doted on me.

26 November *Kelvedon*

I was shocked to hear on the news that Eddie Devonshire died suddenly this afternoon: he was 55. Poor dear Eddie! He was a frustrated man, hated being a Duke and was really a bit bored by all his possessions and palaces. But he was gay at heart and loved life, ladies – and, above all, port. . . . He was kindly, old-fashioned, shrewd and loyal and intelligent though just not quite intelligent enough to rise high politically. I always thought that he was a throwback of his French Flahaut ancestors, as there was nothing beefy or British about him. He looked entirely French . . . as do his children.

How terribly unlucky and ill-fated have been the male decendants of the old Lord Lansdowne (Talleyrand's great-grandson) whom I remembered well. Charlie Lansdowne killed . . . Waterford killed himself; Billy Hartington killed; my adorable Charlie Cavendish. And now Eddie dead at 55. What dread score has Destiny to pay off against the Devonshires? . . . Is it the end of Chatsworth and of Hardwicke?

28 November

Rab goes from strength to strength: this afternoon he presided over a secret meeting of the Tory Foreign Affairs Committee. It was an alarmist gathering – Rab would not commit himself but let it be known that we may well bring down the Government over their clumsy handling of Foreign Affairs. The Government is frightened and its supporters are turning in increasing numbers against Bevan. The Korean war situation is indeed appalling. 80,000 troops, mostly Americans, are trapped by Chinese Communist forces. The City has slumped, everybody is desperately depressed.

3 December *Bulbridge House, Wilton*

Staying here in this loveliest of small houses with Juliet Duff and Willy Maugham, who, as he approaches 80, is growing gentler and more mellow and is, in fact, sweetness itself. Before every meal he boyishly and with fiendish efficiency, mixes the Martinis, 'Maugham Specials'.

This afternoon Sidney walked over from Wilton, and took me for a long hike in the park, and we ended up at the House and went all over it. There is dry rot in the Double-Cube ballroom and other damage. He has recently caused the great statue of Shakespeare, erected in the early eighteenth century, to be brought in from the park where it has sat peacefully for two centuries. It is now in one of the Wyatt halls.

Wilton shimmering in the golden light looked very lovely. Sidney owns the whole property already, and he aches and itches to move in. Unfortunately his father Reggie Pembroke selfishly refuses to die . . .

I also heard the full story of the dinner-party given by Fulco Verdura in Paris for the King of Italy. It appears he arrived 45 minutes late, and omitted to apologise to the Windsors who by that time were hungry and cross. The Duchess was stung into saying half-jokingly, 'At least we weren't kicked out – we went of our own accord!' King Beppo was not amused.

7 December

The Abbey was cold and half-empty, in spite of dozens of Masons, for Eddie Devonshire's Memorial Service, and the Service was oddly unmoving and colourlessly Protestant. . . . If the Duke of Devonshire could not fill the Abbey, I doubt whether I could fill St Margaret's.

11 December *London*

I dreamt vividly that Queen Mary had died in the night though actually the casualty was not her splendid hoary old Majesty but Oliver Stanley. He is no loss to me, but a great one to the Tory Party. I have always thought him rude, cutting, cynical and charmless, though he could be witty – He looked a hundred, and has been dying for some weeks of cancer of the lungs, aggravated by excessive smoking.

14 December

Winston was 'booed' in the House by hundreds of enraged, roaring Socialists who will live to be ashamed of themselves – if Stalin spares them; but he carried on undaunted, unflinching and rather relishing the scene. My impression was that he deliberately created it; in veiled but vigorous language he told the country that there could be no question of a Coalition unless the Government abandoned their mad steel Nationalisation project.

CHAPTER ELEVEN

Last Years: 1951–8

1951

8 January *5 Belgrave Square*

I went to the deserted House of Commons and cleaned out my locker and collected my diaries; then I went to the British Museum where I deposited many volumes. They now fill two tin boxes and are kept in a special strong-room: I feel that one day they may see the light of day, and perhaps shock or divert posterity a little.

23 January

Parliament reassembled, but it was a dull day, and my contribution to the dismal proceedings consisted of sleeping for two hours in the library. The Government looks wretched for they know that they have lost the confidence of the country, and realise that they are, as a policeman at Westminster told me, 'on the way out'. As is Ernie Bevin who is extremely ill, and will die this week, methinks.

5 February

At the House I chatted with Anthony Eden and he asked me to attend a meeting with him which I did, to meet and hear the Belgian Prime Minister, Monsieur Van Zeeland. Anthony has much aged, and later as I sat with him, there was a resurgence of my old affection for him, for I realise that he is really the most civilised Member of the present House, and probably the nicest, although he is, always has been, and ever will be, a lightweight.

Much Election chatter: I am inclined to think that Attlee will be forced to resign this week, which would make an Election almost but not quite inevitable because there is always the possibility that Winston might agree to head a provisional Government for a few months: this is what many of the Labour

Members would prefer. Prefer certainly to an Election which would result in their certain defeat and loss of many seats. Probably 80 to 100.

6 February

There is a smell of Autumn or of 'Fall' in the air instead of Spring: The Government is on its last legs, and may resign on Friday. The Lobbies are humming with hustings chatter. Reggie Winster,[1] an ex-Labour man, but now very Tory, says that he scents decay. All the Ministers look depressed, with their arrogance gone, and their self-confidence shaken. . . . The Government is doomed. It is dull, is deadly, is dangerous. Can anything beat those three things?

8 February

I found the Lobby of the House of Commons this afternoon in an uproar, with hundreds of housewives haranguing, and almost attacking Labour MPs about meat. It was like the French Revolution – only they were on our side.

11 February *Mentmore, Leighton Buzzard*

I drove here with Diana Abdy, where Eva Rosebery, plump, pretty pink and not unlike the Queen, received us as did her son Lord Primrose whose 22nd birthday it is. He is a dark youth at Oxford; mad about theatrical lighting and of a scientific turn of mind. I remember holding him as a baby at Sandwich.

It must be 20 years since I have stayed here and I had forgotten what glorious meubles and pictures they have. There are twelve Fragonards in my bedroom, small ones, but Fragonards, and all over the large cold, icy palace are French pieces of the very finest quality; more and better, too, than the ones at Boughton. A pair of cupboards, not yet removed, they have just sold for £15,000. There is a pathetic Sèvres model of 'Papillon', Marie Antoinette's favourite dog, ordered in 1790, and found in her dressing-room at the Tuileries after it was sacked; several Rembrandts, and two pictures of Madame de Pompadour. I have never seen such richesse, not even at Lançut; the lanterns of the Bucentoro stand in the great hall . . . I am, I fear, sick with envy.

1. Lord Winster had been Labour MP for Basingstoke, 1923–4.

15 February

The newspapers blaze with Election talk; how can Attlee govern when all his energies are devoted almost daily to survival? In a crowded tense Chamber Winston opened the Great Debate[2]; though he was far from at his best, there were flashes of truth, of argument and of humour. After he sat down he began to search for something; and fidgetted so much that Gaitskell, who was speaking for the Government, asked what was the matter. Winston rose very gravely and solemnly announced 'I was only looking for a ju-jube.'[3] The House roared with laughter. Nobody seems to know what will happen tonight; much depends on the malcontents, 'the Peking Pinks', and the ever unpredictable Liberals. Some people think that Attlee will resign and that today is the last day of this mad, unsatisfactory Parliament. I cannot contain my excitement until 10 this evening.

Later. The big Debate had a disappointing end: the Government managed to get a majority of 21; six Liberals, Socialist malcontents, 'Peking Pinks', pacifists, made a Disunited Front – all the people who wanted to keep their seats more than to vote in the National interest filed into the lobby. Aneurin Bevan wound up brilliantly and, for once, without malice or even fireworks. We were told not to barrack or interrupt him; those were the orders from on high, since 'Nye' thrives on interjections. He was quick to detect our tactics, and so modified his manner and tone, which made him more effective.

16 February *Kelvedon*

Lunched, sat and later actually spoke at the House of Commons. The Southend line and its appalling service was my theme.

20 February

As I was walking in the Smoking Room corridor, I saw Winston immaculately dressed, pleased with himself and puffing a cigar, approach: immediately in front of us walked Attlee and Arthur Moyle, his PPS. There was almost a collision; Winston did not

2. A Vote of Censure on the Government's Defence Programme.

3. An episode immortalized by a Lobby Correspondent who described it as 'The Fall of the Pastille'.

make way (Attlee did, slightly) but made them one of his little courtly half-bows which he reserves for people he does not like. I was fascinated; as he passed me a second later he smiled, winked and passed on.

Later. A majority of only eight for the Government; their prestige has been much lowered. Attlee looks like a wasp that has lost its sting.

22 February

So André Gide is dead at last. He once scandalised an earlier generation though he became foolish and venerable with time. I used to see him fairly often in 1918 when I was in the literary as well as social 'swim' in Paris. He was a friend of Madeline Le Chevrel's and of Proust's, though Proust never did like him, and never thought him 'smart'.

5 March

I lunched with dear Mrs Neville Chamberlain at 8 Chester Square; she was always charming to me when I was Neville's pet at the time of her power, and I have always been a faithful friend to her in her 'Sunset Boulevard' days; but it was a déjeuner, indeed, of 'dug-ups'. Luncheon could only be described as 'genteel'; parlour maids, hideous furniture apart from one Buhl table, dull food and the shabbier aristocracy. Still, all very sweet people . . .

In the House we were kept up very late. At about 2 a.m. a division resulted in the close figure of 84 to 82. A few minutes later at the next division the figures were 82 to 82; and the Deputy Chairman, Sir Charles MacAndrew, whilst a Tory, gave the casting vote to the Government – at about 2.35. Now I am too excited to sleep.

6 March

A full Proustian Day. The day began horribly with a shock. Sleeping lightly, I switched on the news and heard of the sudden death in the night of Ivor Novello. He had played as usual in 'King's Rhapsody'; had then had supper with Tom Arnold in his flat in Aldwych, complained of being tired, and went to bed at one a.m. Before two he called for help, a doctor was fetched, and he was dead. Thrombosis again. The whole country is saddened; people in the streets and shops, servants, everyone mourns him. . . . I first met him in May 1919 in New York; and I gave a dinner at the Ritz to which he, Norah Lindsay and Ned Lathom, and others came – Now all, except me, are 'gathered' as charladies would say. . . . Ivor was gentle, good, kindly affectionate, lovable and loyal, and he gave pleasure to millions. His dark good looks were famous, and he might have been Neapolitan; actually he was Welsh and his hair, long since white, was carefully dyed. His little court of adorers kept him wrapped in emotional cotton wool; his oldest friend was Eddie Marsh, who for 20 years has been talking about his will, and how he would leave Ivor his pictures, etc.

14 March

This evening, at the House, the Socialists organized some rough tactics; directly after Prayers,[4] which they so resent, began, they deserted the Chamber and took up a stand in the tea-room where they formed themselves into a sort of Glee Club, and led by extremists, most of whom seemed drunk, they shouted and sang at every Tory who came in sight. When I entered they shouted a chorus 'Why is he so beautiful, why was he born at all?' They were fairly good-tempered, though I saw Dalton seize Charles Taylor who happened to be wearing a white tie. A more undignified proceeding could scarcely be imagined. They seem to have forgotten that they used to 'pray' against us. The late nights are getting the Labour-ites – and the Speaker – down, and this evening the Deputy Speaker, Milner, was obliged to send the Serjeant-at-Arms to quell the disturbance.

15 March

Another scene. At half past ten, about a hundred Socialists appeared in the Smoking Room. They immediately began to sing, roar and to become generally offensive, hooting at the Tory Mem-

4. At that time it was possible to put down a 'Prayer' to annul a Statutory Instrument after 10 p.m., and there was no time limit to such debates; subsequently the procedure was modified, and debates on Prayers had to end at 11.30 p.m.

bers, and jeering at some of their own. The feeling was worse than last night; one wondered whether there might not be a brawl. Fascinated yet repelled I sadly watched the happenings, and sat for nearly two hours surrounded by these drunken hooligans, though I was neither insulted nor molested. The unfortunate woman at the Bar was in tears and said to me: 'I never thought that I should live to see Members of Parliament come to this.' It was really horrible, particularly when they sang 'When Red Revolution comes'. I returned eventually to the Chamber, deserted by the Government but crowded on our side. The Speaker three times put his foot into it, and finally Rab Butler, usually so calm and Jesuitical, accused him of partiality. I was sitting on the steps of the Speaker's Chair and I could see the poor man tremble and shake with fury. He must really resign, and if we do have a Labour Speaker we shall at least gain two votes, vital ones.

16 March

In the House the atmosphere has cooled; indeed in a final division Tories and Socialists voted in the same lobby, and the wretched week, which has so weakened Parliamentary prestige, ended peacefully.

18 March

I drove once more to Eton in the rain, indeed in a cloudburst, picked up Paul and we debated what to do. Then Oxford, where he had never been, occurred to us, and we jumped into the car and were away. A flooded drive. Even so Oxford looked lovely though deserted. I thought of the happy times – the happiest of my life when I was there . . .

Paul was fascinated and, as ever, my choice companion. In the Ashmolean Museum I showed him the Piero di Cosimo oblong panel of 'A Forest Fire' or Hunt which long hung in my rooms in Mount Street which I shared with Prince Paul and George Gage. It moved me to see it again just as bright and brilliant as ever; though the rich picture did not recognise me, how much it has heard me say, and seen me do, in the golden days of my youth. . . . I wish now that I had bought it, and never quite knew why Prince Paul saw fit to sell it.

19 March

It was announced that Mr Speaker, on medical advice, could not attend today. Later we heard that he is suffering from nervous exhaustion. Now each side blames the other, and the Speaker's breakdown has led to a curious Socialist démarche. Something was obviously afoot, as the Labour benches, deserted about 10 p.m. all last week, suddenly filled up. After a Prayer about steel had been moved by our side, Chuter Ede, the new Leader of the House, rose and astonished us all by offering to enter into negotiations with the Opposition about the intolerable Parliamentary position which we have got into. His tone was temperate, though his mild manners were somewhat contradicted by his veiled hint of coercion, of a threat to amend the Standing Rules of the House. The Opposition, caught unprepared, hesitated until Harry Crookshank rose, and was able to make the best of a very bad situation, for Ede's manoeuvre had completely outwitted us.

20 March

A row in the House. Winston could scarcely make himself heard, as he and Ede duelled about the so-called 'negotiations' which may lead to a truce, and thus bring to an end these dreadful continuous late-sittings which are really designed to exhaust the Socialists physically. ... All day the Government Front Bench was crowded, and old Bevin, sallow and shrunken, looked as if he had been kissed by death.

As I walked past the Houses of Commons Book of Remembrance – its pages are turned daily – I happened to look at it, and saw there inscribed in blue and gold letters the names of six MPs killed in the war. I was startled for one I had known well and long, though never intimately, both at Oxford and here; another was a Commons acquaintance; and all the others I had known well. How full my life has been, and how I wish that I were not on the last lap.

7 April *Kelvedon*

Spring is far behind ... only forsythia and daffodils out. All the other blossom is bashful.

I always remember that this is my grandmother Westover's birthday ... she loved colour, jewels, drink and display, and yet was a grande dame. She was also a dreadful liar. She died in 1911, I think, and we adored and understood each other; both sheer pagans, unencumbered by morals although we shared principles . . . which is not the same thing.

8 April

My plot to get Epping . . . for Leslie Hore-Belisha, or, failing him, Councillor Sidney Bates of Southend, has failed. Nobody will look at poor Leslie: he is quite a back number . . . a hundred pities.

10 April

Suspense and a brooding atmosphere at the House, when Gaitskell, rather nattily if unsuitably dressed and wearing a red carnation, began to address the crowded and attentive benches. Every seat was taken. The sun smiled in a desultory way, and for a bit there were brief shafts of light; six Tories wore top-hats and looked faintly ridiculous. Winston, who has seemed so boyish recently suddenly seemed sleepy and old. Perhaps he had had too rich a lunch. . . . Mrs Chamberlain and Mrs Attlee were in the Speaker's Gallery. Bevin, on the front bench looked thin, and had the parchment pallor one associates with death. . . . Doom has now struck. It is 4 o'clock, and we await the worst. If it is very bad the Government may decide to go to the country at once. Last night's defeat, although it was only on cheese, has further dampened their spirits. Many would welcome a face-saving dissolution . . .

Gaitskell has a Wykehamistical voice and manner and a 13th century face. He began in a moderate fashion, and at once put the House in a receptive mood by his clear enunciation and courteous manner; he was lucid, clear and coherent and there was a commendable absence of Daltonian sneers or bleak Crippsian platitudes. A breath of fresh air. Nevertheless there was anxiety as the House soon realised that he intended to raise taxation, to produce a balanced Budget rather than to issue loans . . . one listened sadly. Ambassadors peered over the Gallery: there were no interruptions. I stood by the Speaker's Chair, and Bevan, red in the face and breathing like an angry bull was next to me. He was standing as inconspicuously as possible, and it was soon evident why: he had recently declared that he would never serve in a Government which taxed the ridiculous health service: Gaitskell announced some charges. Everybody wondered whether that meant Bevan's resignation? Eventually Gaitskell announced a rise in petrol and 6d. on the income tax, and a heavy increase on distributed profits – that was all. Once again we have been let off revolutionary legislation, or confiscatory political contrivances.

14 April *Kelvedon*

On the wireless we heard of the death of Ernest Bevin; I am scarcely surprised as he has looked very ill for months and particularly lately. He is a great loss to the country, since he was a steadying, moderating influence in the Socialist Party.

18 April

There is something astir politically; is it Bevan's resignation or a General Election or both? The first, if it occurs, and I think that it will, as he is now in an impossible situation, might well lead to the second.

23 April

Bevan has resigned [over the Budget]. This means a serious split in the Socialist Party and possibly the fall of the Government.

He made the traditional explanation to the House after Questions: but it was not a success and pleased nobody, for he was savage, vindictive, dramatic and too long-winded. He in turn assailed Gaitskell, insulted the Tories and railed against the Government and Attlee. Twice during his harangue the Speaker half rose to silence him, but lacked the guts. At the end of 32 minutes he sat down exhausted and defeated – temporarily. It may be that his bubble has burst, but I think it is more likely that he has run away, to fight another day. Much whispering in groups and rumours of an Election, etc. On the whole the Labour people are furious at his 'betrayal'. Harold Wilson has also resigned as President of the Board of Trade . . . John Freeman also. In fact there is practically no Government since the Prime Minister is in hospital, and all his henchmen are deserting him. I watched Winston while Bevan was speaking. He sat grinning and dangling his watch chain. He looked like a plump naughty little boy dressed as a grown up.

22 May *Paris*

Today was a day of fantastic elegance. Arturo Lopez gave a luncheon party for me at 14 Rue du Centre in Neuilly, his small Versailles, with every object in it beyond price: it is, I suppose, the most elegant 'set-up' in the world, and he is now building a ballroom made entirely of shells in one of the wings. I was between the Duchesse de Fesanzac and Nancy Mitford. The food – superb, and I slept all afternoon to work it off. . . . Then, in the evening Alexis de Redé – the Eugène de Rastignac of modern Paris – offered me a banquet. Eighteen, semi-gratin, and very grand. Alexis lives in 18th century splendour in a huge apartment in the Hotel Lambert in the Cité. We dined in the Banqueting Hall with all the drawing rooms lit up, footmen with candelabra on the staircase; gold plate. . . . The Palazzo Colonna en petit. It is fantastic that this sort of thing can exist in this age. I was particularly glad to see the Etienne de Beaumonts again: They are so intelligent, so fin, so decadent, so old, so painted and so civilised.

Prince Paul, who has spent the day with me, and I, stayed very late. Never has there been a deeper link between two people than between him and I, and what an extraordinary friendship – a Yugoslav Prince and an Anglo-American. It has lasted and deepened unshadowed for just 31 years. . . . He is the most divine companion in the world, and so gay and funny. He is the 'Coq du village' now, and if no longer Regent of Yugoslavia he is certainly Le Roi de Paris: and, furthermore, he has become a great conversationalist. Because, of course, people don't talk in Paris; they just look lovely . . . and eat. I am sad to leave tomorrow after such a glorious week of recaptured youth. What a blissful idle life one leads in Paris, though the more I see of it, the more I like Rome.

4 June

How rivetting newspapers can be. It is terrible to contemplate that one day one will be dead, and never again be able to read 'The Times'.

10 June

I dined with Duncan and Diana Sandys at their pretty Vincent Square house, No. 86, with Johnny Churchill, looking like Napoleon III in his beard, and his pretty second wife: booming Bob Boothby and Miss Margaret Truman.[5] I have a penchant for Miss Truman; she has an easy sense-of-humour, and a fluency that attracts me. . . . We got on famously until midnight talking about the Pope, about England, about everything. Alas, she leaves tomorrow for the Continent.

11 June

All afternoon, all evening, I have been cooped up here at the House, with divisions to break the boredom of the Debates, which are also occasionally enlivened by wrangles about procedure, though the Government have been dictatorial and ridiculous. But Winston has been tactless too. Many scenes and now the corridors, the lobbies, the little rooms, the libraries are all filled with supine, ungainly, sleeping snoring men. Some look dead. Our minority is usually 9 or 10 . . . towards six a.m. as the dawn broke over the Thames the rumour that we were not to rise at all but to continue on until midnight, was confirmed. I am half-hysterical with exhaustion. Attlee is waspish . . . I talked with both Anthony Eden and Winston, both elegant and spruce; and later – such strange things happen during all-night sittings – I had a cup of coffee with Aneurin Bevan.

Later – Tuesday morning – 12.6.51 at 10.15 I realised the hopelessness of the Parliamentary position, and had to send a message to the Duchess of Kent that I would be unable to give her luncheon as arranged at Buck's Club at Ascot . . . it just cannot be helped – I am stuck. The world here is now divided into two camps: those who have shaved and are tidy; and those who look 'frosty'. I sent for fresh clothes, shirt and a carnation and now look extremely elegant, though I felt hungry and hysterical. What a farce it all is. These Hitler tactics on the part of the Prime Minister (whose personal decision, I am told it is) to keep us going for 36 hours or so will do him no good. Though, so far, nobody has collapsed, except Clifton-Brown.

5. Daughter of President Truman.

14 June

Today I got away and went to Ascot: it was lovely and green and I thought rather empty in the Enclosure. The Queen was in lilac and looked sublime. I watched all the real Princesses of the Blood Royal as they kissed and curtsied to her, and really marvelled at her self-possession. She had an ovation, as did Winston, whose horse Colonist II was second favourite for the Gold Cup. The excitement was immense, for the King's horse, too, had a good chance. Everybody bet frantically. The whole Course, half-a-million perhaps of people, prayed for Winston to win, and he nearly did. The King's horse led at first, then Colonist was in front, but was just passed by a French outsider Pan II. The crowd groaned their disappointment. I came back with John Hare (and what a Jehu he is) and John Hope. We took only just the hour, and arrived at the House in good time, having missed no divisions. Winston soon followed and was clapped (unusual and not allowed) when he entered the Chamber. Later at the 1922 Committee he spoke for some time, perhaps even too long. He seemed tired and boyishly disappointed. He meandered and really made very little sense. For the first time we were conscious of his age.

2 July

I watched Winston today, with his hand to his ear, listening to a fellow MP in the Division Lobby. He has this trick of pretending to be deafer than he is, when he wants to shed a bore, or protect himself from importunities.

28 October

Three months since I kept my diary. Three months during which much has happened, first and foremost the Election. I am at Kelvedon trying to recuperate. ... But I still feel as if I had been squeezed dry. Indeed an election is like a violent love affair; one must be charming all the time; one is keyed up and every ounce of vigour and vitality goes ... I have over 100 cables and letters of congratulations to cope with. My son Paul has nicknamed me 'Channon, the People's Choice'.

31 October *1 p.m. House of Commons*

The first day of a new Parliament is always pleasant and stimulating; particularly this one: policemen smile a warm welcome, MPs are humming. . . . There was a crowded meeting of the 1922 Committee – and it was announced that 'Shakes' Morrison has been selected Speaker. A good choice; a palace for Alison and security for him. I hope he doesn't sleep all day in the Chair, as he has done for years in the library. He is ageing, and when I congratulated him and said: 'This is the last time I shall ever call you Shakes' he seemed sad. He was a Ministerial flop, but may succeed as Speaker. The debate on his appointment was short but acrimonious and undignified. Alison watched sadly from the Gallery – her private Gallery now. Eden was well received, and all the appointments seem popular.

I am exhausted. Reaction after the Election, and now I cannot eat even my own delicious food!! What a three months the last have been, Venice . . . four sunlit weeks on the Zattere with cloudless skies and bliss and balls including Charlie Beistegui's incomparable fête – then my feverish journey back, just in time to be ready for the Election.

What will this new Parliament unfold? The deaths of Winston, Queen Mary and the Monarch? A Coronation and some sort of show down with Stalin? Shall I survive it? Shall I die, or be made a Peer, or just resign? I look astonishingly well, but feel antique inside and I now cough and have nervous indigestion.

1 November

I took the oath for the 6th time at 5.45. By then the queue was short, so I was able to chat with 'Shakes', looking very austere and dignified. At 6.14 Winston came in; the Chamber was almost empty, a few attendants, two Whips and a few desultory spectators in the Gallery. The old man, smiling, good-tempered slowly signed his name, beamed, and approached the Chair and I heard him apologise to 'Shakes' whom he correctly called 'Mr Speaker' for being late. He has a new habit of raising his voice. Then, still grinning, he passed through the door. Only four MPs witnessed Winston taking the oath, perhaps for the last time. The light and the atmosphere made it a touching little scene . . . now I go home.

1952

2 February *Kelvedon*

I watched the television, and saw the King, bare-headed, cross, almost mad-looking, waving farewell to the Edinburghs, who have flown to Kenya en route for Australia. He is reported to be going out duck shooting next week, suicidal.

6 February

An unbelievable day began normally. That is, all my telephones buzzed, and I arranged my luncheon party, read my letters, chatted to Princess Olga[6] on the house telephone – and then soon after ten she walked into my room, followed by her son Alexander. They looked gloomy, and she said simply: 'You might as well know at once, the King is dead', and then bursting into tears, added, 'Poor Bertie'. Philip Hay had rung her a few minutes before, to break the news; the world did not yet know. It seems the Monarch was called at 7.15 this morning as usual by his valet, who found him dead. Doubtless coronary thrombosis. The Royal demise was kept secret for a few frantic hours whilst messages were sent to Princess Elizabeth in Kenya, and to Queen Mary. Later brief announcements were made over the wireless, and I heard the mid-day one. . . . I rang the House of Commons to ask what was happening, to be told that 'Her Majesty's wishes are not yet known'. Le roi est mort, vive la reine.

9 February

The late King, whom I knew fairly well at different times, was uninteresting and unintellectual, but doubtless well-meaning . . . he improved with the years. His natural shyness and an inferiority complex towards his eldest brother made him on the defensive. He had no wit, no learning, no humour, except of a rather school-boy brand. He was nervous, ill-at-ease, though slightly better after some champagne. He had no vices and few interests other than shooting. He had few friends and was almost entirely dependent on the Queen whom he worshipped: she was his will-power, his all. He was an affectionate father and a loyal friend to

6. Princess Olga was staying with Chips at Belgrave Square.

the very few people he liked. ... Let us hope that there will now be a clean-out, a clean sweep.

But when broadcasting His Majesty never got one in the throat as his father did. George V somehow stirred one; after hearing him one wanted to shout, to sing patriotic songs; and those wonderful blue eyes, can one ever forget them? ... The late King looked a boy at his Coronation, but he aged quickly after his accession, and of late was lined and wrinkled. ... I do not think that he concealed very skilfully his dislike of the Socialists for all the ones who had been in waiting are vitriolic about him. But no one hated him – he was too neutral; hence he was a successful and even popular sovereign.

11 February

A marvellous day. Mirabile dictu ... The young Queen has invited Paul over for the funeral ... Princess Olga rang me from Coppins to tell me. I am overjoyed and dumbfounded. So that long sad chapter is over, and he is coming. I rejoice in the new reign and welcome it. We shall be the new Elizabethans. ... I am rapturously happy that my old friend is now shriven and respectable. My long, anguished loyalty is rewarded ... and how right I was. Never for a single second was I weaned away from my deep love for Prince Paul – and it was not always easy ...

At the House of Commons everyone was in black – Parliamentary crows; only the Speaker, 'Shakes' Morrison, wore his gold and black robes. Winston spoke, and I thought he was sublime, so simple and eloquent with his Macaulay phrases pouring out. The attentive House was electrified. He was followed by Attlee and he, too, was excellent; a simpler delivery, calmer, less spacious yet effective. At 3.40 we filed, two by two, to Westminster Hall. The Speaker led the sombre procession, and was followed by Winston who walked with Mr Attlee. The Great Hall, recently refurbished and re-lit, was spacious and comparatively empty. Choristers from the Abbey and prelates stood at the top of the stairs. ... I was near the great North door. Slowly, solemnly, silently, sedately, the gorgeously apparelled Heralds followed by the various heraldic Kings, all of them in red and blue and gold tabards, advanced to the door and went out; they were preceded by Bernard Norfolk as Earl Marshal who walked with Roc Cholmondeley, the new Lord Great Chamberlain of England. He was superb in a splendid uniform. I have never seen a man look so aristocratic. . . The cortège was five minutes late or more. I shivered (most of the MPs wore overcoats, I did not) as I recalled a similar scene in January 1936, just slightly more than sixteen sad years ago.[7] At length there was a loud knock at the big door which was quickly opened and the Heralds, followed by the heraldic Kings, returned. Behind them, bearing the King's coffin, were eight Grenadiers who almost stumbled under the weight . . . very slowly they made their way to the catafalque. The Great Hall was cold, splendid and impressive . . . a few paces behind, the Royal Family followed, walking in measured paces like figures in a Greek tragedy. First walked the young Queen, all in black but wearing flesh-coloured stockings; behind her, to the right, was the Queen Mother – unmistakable with her curious side-ways lilting walk. On her left, was Queen Mary frail and fragile, I thought, with her veil and her black umbrella and steel-coloured stockings. I was very sorry for her as she must have known and realised that she is next. Then the others. The Service was short, and conducted by the Archbishop of York, as Cantuar is indisposed. At the end of the Benediction there was a brief pause, and I watched the new Queen nod to Bernard Norfolk and then the Gentile Bellini-like procession re-formed and left slowly. . . . Everyone, including the Socialists, were deeply impressed.

15 February

After too little sleep I got up, and dressed in a morning-coat and top hat; drove with Diana Cooper and John Julius to the Horse Guards Parade, where I had tickets for the Parliamentary enclosure. It was cold and muddy underfoot and we tramped about for some time; the crowd was thin; at length the procession nearly a mile and a half long began to move under the Horse Guards Arch; the Household Cavalry on their shiny black horses looked superb. I could have touched the gun carriage. . . . I recognised many friends. Eddie of Kent, his mouth too open, and wearing his father's morning suit, walked with the other Royal

7. See p. 73.

Dukes. Windsor jaunty – what must have been his thoughts and regrets? – Gloucester and Edinburgh correct – then the coaches. The Queen Mother easily recognisable. Nylon veils make matters simpler. With the coachmen in their scarlet cloaks; it was a dazzling procession, as it crawled up the Mall and away.

Later. The King of Yugoslavia complained to me of the cold at St. George's Chapel where the guests were obliged to sit for over two hours awaiting the arrival of the Royal remains . . . the Yugoslavian position was tense, for Tito's President of the Praesidium officially represented Yugoslavia: quite near him sat Queen Marie with her two younger sons, with King Peter and Queen 'Xandra' opposite; Prince Paul was in his own Garter Stall. None of them exchanged any form of greeting with one another.

My son was among the Eton OTC which lined the streets of Windsor.

26 February

Royalties poured in all day, No. 5 was a living Gotha . . . I had to have a luncheon party, for no better reason than that the Queen and Prince Philip wanted to be alone with the Duke of Windsor.

In the evening I drove Prince Paul to Victoria. He seemed emotionné. The Station Master met us, and he was royally treated . . . I took him into his compartment, embraced him, and saw his tears at leaving the England he so loves after a fortnight of such fun and happiness. He was miserable. Thirty-two years of loyal friendship we have had. Thus ends the Royal Opera, with 'God Save the Queen'.

4 March *5 Belgrave Square*

I am the Lord of Hosts; the only person with a large London establishment who entertains on the grand scale and enjoys it. Today I had a luncheon party, which consisted of Madame Massigli, the gay affectionate French Ambassadress, always unaffected and friendly and beautifully dressed; Jock Colville, dark and erudite and now secretary to Mr Churchill; Lady Margaret Colville, his wife, an Egerton; Philip Hay, the handsome Comptroller to the Duchess of Kent, who looks like a policeman and is well-meaning, but, like all courtiers, slowly becoming pompous; Lady Margaret Hay, his wife – she had to hurry off to Clarence House as she is in-waiting on the Queen ...

Gay conversation, during which we got on to middle-classisms; phrases which begin by being impossible, in time become tolerated and finally good usage. We all now say 'bus' and admit 'week-end' – both formerly very common; I say 'sweet' but the Ladies Margaret insist on 'Pudding'; all agreed that 'note-paper', 'mantelpiece', 'mirror', 'radio', are now often heard in 'Good Society' whilst 'town' is now lower-class exclusively ... quite fun, but the poor French Ambassadress was bewildered.

6 March

In the House of Commons, early this morning I found myself alone in the lavatory with Nye Bevan, who was particularly agreeable. He remarked that the House of Commons had sunk to a 'new low' when we could discuss reformed-spelling for hours in the early morning. Is he mellowing? Is he maturing?

9 March

Courtauld Thompson remarked at luncheon 'Of course I did not know Mr Gladstone very well'. He is 87, remarkably young-looking, vigorous and in full possession of all his faculties.

11 March

To the House for the Budget; crowded and excited. Rab looking sleek, calm and well ... spoke for nearly two hours, and he was clear, concise, calm, good-tempered. His performance was magnificent. He played politely with the Opposition, who revealed themselves in a really despicable light. They only cheered bad news, as when Rab announced cuts in food subsidies. When tax cuts were revealed they were glum and grim. His is a brilliant bourgeois budget; instead of being stern there is something in it for everybody – even the rich. He was cool, calculating and clever. He is like a Howitzer and mows down the Opposition, in their awkward embarrassed attempts to make 'phoney' attacks.... Dalton was disgusting; he is the most — biped, all in all, that I have ever met.

Rab had a great triumph, and afterwards smiled broadly, blandly. It was a bold bid for the floating middle-class vote and possibly for the Premiership. A wave of enthusiastic relief has surged over the House and later over the City. There is a new festival spirit about. A young Queen; an old Prime Minister and a brave buoyant Butler budget. Has he put us in for a generation?

15 March *Kelvedon*

I am alone and revelling in my solitude. I spent my evening reading a life of Pepys; his diaries covered only nine years, from 1660 to 1669 – from when he was 27 to 36. Mine are far longer and more, at times, although such is not their intention, improper.

3 April

Paul and I walked to the House, chatting politics all the way. He mugs up his Hansard, and knows almost every Member by name, and can tell one his Constituency. Parliament is in his blood, from his Onslow side. He is largely Onslow in mind; Channon, or rather me, in manner and looks; Guinness in size.

9 April *House of Commons*

Could there be any more nauseating performance than that of half a hundred hale young Socialists howling at Mr Churchill, jeering at his pronouncements and even at his entrances and exits into the House, taunting him with his advanced age and growing deafness? The man who may be the wrecker of the Tory Party, but was certainly Saviour of the civilised world? It happened again today. However in the 1922 secret Committee he had a rapturous reception, and stood the strain of speaking and answering questions well for over an hour.

10 April

I have a 'hunch' that Iain Macleod, the Member for Enfield West, will go far; he is shrewd, has a rapier-like brain, is ambitious and clear-minded; he is bald and limps, and is unattractive, except for his old man's smile. He is quite young.

22 April *5 Belgrave Square*

Cripps died last night in Switzerland. He was a Savonarola who did more harm than any other individual to England, though the one night that he dined at Belgrave Square I must admit that he was polite, agreeable and almost charming. He ate only carrots, mashed at his request, and drank orange-juice. He could be well mannered and ill mannered too. But why these hypocritical sycophantic phrases only because he is dead? Everyone says that Winston's tribute was a masterpiece of oratory; so it was, but wasn't it also playing politics, to disarm the turbulent Opposition?

24 April

Lunched in: as I awaited the arrival of my guests I saw Herbert Morrison drive up in a shabby little car next door. I went out, and brought him in, and gave him two cocktails; he was breezy, perky, friendly and alert with all his 'cocky' cockney manner. . . . He told us that his father had been a Tory policeman, and had turned him out when he became a Socialist. I asked him whether his father had lived to see his son famous, and 'Herb's' face softened and he said sadly 'No, he died too soon'. I felt that I had touched a sore part of his heart. This was the man who had kept us up half the night discussing the Guillotine. He was very friendly and gay.

In the Lobby this afternoon I suddenly saw a painted old crone, wearing a red wig, being escorted in by a chauffeur in livery; in raucous tones she demanded to see the Home Secretary. And then was too deaf to hear the policeman's reply. It was the Duchess of Portland. She looks a million, and is indeed very old. Always stupid, but loved, she has survived into an alien age. Recently I believe she drove to the City, lost her car and asked a policeman where she was; he told her. 'The City?' she replied vaguely, 'I have only been here in processions.' She was once Mistress of the Robes to Queen Victoria.

1 May

I dined with Tony Lambton[8] at St. Stephen's Club; he is very elegant with his long hair, effeminate features and mild surprised manner, all of which cloaks a strong courageous character. He is full of wit, penetration and charm.

8. Conservative MP for Berwick-on-Tweed.

8 May

The England I wooed and won and love still, is dying; thus I am determined to enjoy what remains to me of it and of life here: the few declining years, the few rapidly diminishing thousands of pounds; if I survive the collapse of the country or of my personal fortune, I shall slip off to some remote part of sun-lit California to die – on my American income, so far untouched, or rather unimpaired. Perhaps I can look for another five years.

12 May

I passed a quiet solitary evening at the House where the turbulent Opposition were deflated by Rab's sudden concession of £17,000,000 per annum on Purchase Tax. He is the ablest Parliamentarian of our time, cold, courteous, suave and seemingly simple, he outwits everyone . . .

I have dropped a word about Michael Redgrave, and hope that he will be included in the Birthday Honour's List.

13 May

To hear cockney spoken one must go to the House of Lords where Labour Peers scatter their 'aitches' all over the red benches.

23 June *5 Belgrave Square*

I paid out 18,000 francs for back rent of a Safe Deposit box of my mother's (she died leaving about fifty scattered all over the world). Today the contents were delivered to me – bundles of newspaper cuttings, old hoarded rubbish and a mass of well-written but horrid snubbing letters from me which, when I read them, rather saddened me. I destroyed most of them, though I lapped up the reviews of my first novel 'Joan Kennedy'. What a writer I could have been.

26 June

Huge cocktail party at Mrs Chamberlain's; over 100 people attended, including Halifax and the fabulous Mrs Carnegie, now nearly ninety and Neville Chamberlain's stepmother. Last year there were only eight people there – is it the turn of the tide? A demonstration for Neville, who I have always said will live in time in the hearts of men as a great patriot, leader, and humanitarian?

1 July

Winston spoke on Korea and the recent bombings, and the divided Socialists tried to turn the Debate into a Censure Motion. But the old lion, coolly dressed in light grey trousers and a short coat, fairly pulverised his attackers; rarely has he been more devastating; perhaps he is aware of the growing Tory discontent.

The catalpa trees in the Yard of the House are in bloom. This means that the House should rise.

23 July

I watched Duff Cooper be inducted[9]; he was dignified and impressive and immensely pleased, as he strutted into their Lordship's Chamber. He was introduced by Rob Hudson and David Margesson, his old-time political colleagues. Diana in the Gallery looked lovely but was furious; she dislikes her change of status and name and intends to go on calling herself Lady Diana Cooper. I am told that Duff's 'mot' on his elevation was 'A little Norwich is a dangerous thing'.

5 November

Awake all night listening to American reports on the wireless, and finally at about 6.40 I heard the news that Adlai Stevenson had conceded the Election to Eisenhower. I am overjoyed. All sensible people must be. . . . Then I dozed till morning, got up, and later lunched at the Austrian Embassy and arriving late having waited for the news of the Wycombe result. We have increased our majority. I was able to announce the good news to the party, including Anthony Eden, who I thought in a highly nervous state. He was affectionate, but in a sudden burst of nerves and temper revealed to me that he is on bad terms with Winston. 'I get all the knocks; I don't think I can stand it much longer', he suddenly said. We talked for some time and I had the feeling that he was fed-up and almost hysterical.

19 November

At the House of Commons I had a long surprising tête-à-tête with Ernest Marples; . . . I like this alert, able, squirrel-like urchin; he

9. Into the House of Lords as Viscount Norwich.

lacks distinction and the usual charming qualities – but he has a broad smile, and is a tiger for work. He goes to bed at 11 o'clock and is called at seven by a new-fangled machine which makes his coffee. Then he works until it is time to go to his Ministry.[10]

24 November

People are prattling of the Coronation already, of whom will and will not be summoned, of their robes and places and arrangements. The Dowager Peeresses are nervous lest they are not invited. Members of Parliament, too, are in a ticklish position. In fact, conversation has taken on a Gilbert and Sullivan quality. Coaches and robes, tiaras and decorations. Winnie Portarlington announced at luncheon that she has harness but no coach; Circe Londonderry has a coach but no horses; Mollie Buccleuch has no postillions but five tiaras. People are obsessed by their Coronation prerogatives. There is something unreal about it.

25 November

Another heart attack. Dr Gottfried says, who called and examined me, that my condition is rather serious but neither grave nor fatal. Of course I cannot take it reasonably.

28 November

I drove Maxwell-Fyfe[11] in the Rolls to Southend where we drank cocktails with the Mayor, then dined at the Queen's, a party of fifteen, all terribly silent. A big Meeting at the Queen's followed; in an ill-arranged, half-empty Hall; inefficiency and disappointment. David Maxwell-Fyfe is a man of the highest integrity and good intellect, with some warmth, but devoid of imagination. He deplored the lack of social life between MPs, Ministers and their wives. Shall I begin entertaining again, politically? But they are all so damned dull, I cannot face it.

10. He was Parliamentary Secretary at the Ministry of Housing.
11. Home Secretary 1951–4; Lord Chancellor 1954–62.

1953

26 January

The fashionable complaint is now known as Coronation Thrombosis. People talk of nothing else, except who is and who is not 'Abbey Happy' and people prattle all day about places, tiaras, coaches, postillions, robes and coronets – and, more seriously, of ballots. . . . One peer, who had been divorced, suggested to the Earl Marshal that he feared he would be ineligible for a place in the Abbey: the reply is said to have been 'Of course you will; this is the Coronation, not Ascot.'

5 February

I lunched with Leslie Hore-Belisha. What a bore the old boy has become . . . the tragedy of a good mind unharnessed.

10 February

Mrs Ogden Armour has died in Chicago, aged about 83. She was a very beautiful old woman of great charm and was my very first 'grand' friend when I was about 14. I adored her and she used to take me to plays when I had my first dinner jacket, and I used to stay with the Armours, in 1914 or before, at their lovely place, Melody Farm, near Chicago. Mrs Armour had an elegance which dazzled me, and her lame, limping daughter was the first heiress I ever contemplated marrying. At first Mrs Armour, like Mrs W. K. Vanderbilt thirty years later, was terrified that I would marry her daughter, then ended by fearing I would not.

16 February

Dined with the Beddington-Behrens where I had a long talk with John Tweedsmuir who recalled old days, which I had half forgotten, at Elsfield Manor, and he told me how his dear father, John Buchan, had prophesied a great future for me: have I let him down? I fear so: he was always very fond of me, very, and I owe him a great debt of gratitude, for he made me write. His was a successful, happy life.

4 March

Queen Mary, who has been rather better for a few days, had a serious relapse this morning, and all day we have been waiting for the glorious old girl to die, and as Oliver Lyttelton was speaking the rumour flew round that she had at 4.02; there was an atmosphere of hushed excitement. Winston came into the Chamber, so did Ralph Verney and the dreaded official announcement was expected any moment. Christopher Soames darted in and out. Then there was a detente, as we gathered that the story was untrue. I waited for an hour, and saw Attlee go into the PMs room, as did Harry Crookshank and the Serjeant-at-Arms, dear old Sir Charles Howard. I was then informed that Queen Mary was unconscious, but alive still. Everyone, Socialists, policemen, everyone seemed deeply moved and sad. Certainly I was. . . . I drove past Marlborough House, saw the old Queen's Standard still flying, rather limply, and there was a silent crowd at the gates. Just as I left the House of Commons, where Winston had waited all afternoon for the bad news, I was told by Robert Cary, who always knows everything, that the PM had been summoned to Buckingham Palace by the Queen. Evidently, death was not expected then for several hours.

Later. It is now 10.19, and the latest news is that the Queen's 'Strength is ebbing, but that she is sleeping peacefully'. That means, I suppose, that she is unconscious, and will probably die within the next twelve hours. There is a softening in the general public, moved beyond words, by Queen Mary's illness. The Socialists, especially, seem touched, and are a little boring with their reminiscences of having once seen her somewhere.

At 10.35 we heard that the old Queen was dead, and presently Winston entered the Chamber, and looked solemn as he whispered to the Speaker. Henry Hopkinson was speaking to an inattentive audience as the Chamber soon buzzed in subdued tones, with the sad news. Winston decided not to interrupt the proceedings as we were so soon to rise. Henry Hopkinson wound up courageously, but whether he was aware of how few people were listening to him I do not know. We had a majority of 44 for the African Federation. At 11 o'clock, Winston rose, and moving the adjournment of the House, announced the death of Queen Mary. There were cries of dismay from the Gallery, and, indeed on all sides there seemed to be grief, again particularly from the Socialists. She had long captured their imagination, and they rightly thought her above politics, a kind of Olympian Goddess. I drove sadly home, passing Marlborough House once more. It was plunged in darkness, and there was a large crowd outside; women were weeping.

25 March

The Press have been unanimous in their eulogies of Her Late Majesty. A wave of emotion has swept over the land, and there has not been a word of criticism of the grand old lady; she was magnificent, humorous, worldly, in fact nearly sublime, though cold and hard. But what a grand Queen. Her appearance was formidable, her manner – well, it was like talking to St. Paul's Cathedral; yet she was easy and pleasant to meet. The world is poorer. This afternoon, Winston and Attlee paid tributes to her, as did Jo Grimond for the microscopic Liberal Party, and Walter Elliot for the Back Benchers. Winston was adequate, but definitely not at his best. Curiously enough, Attlee was the more moving, and Winston, realising this, looked restless and nettled. Possibly he did not like the old lady, or did they cross swords over the Abdication?

29 March

The scene in dimly lit Westminster Hall was so impressive that several vignettes will always remain in my memory – Winston, almost next to me, waving away a chair that someone had brought for him; the single wreath from the Queen on the coffin; the royal ladies wearing short veils, steel coloured stockings, ropes of pearls and jewels – an English fashion which always amazes foreigners. Some of them, I thought, in fact, a little too made up, for one can see everything through the Nylon veils which they now all wear. The Duke of Windsor looking nervous and fidgety, but was obviously very unhappy. . . . I was struck too by the appearance of that loyal old courtier, Lady Airlie, aged 83 walking in, with immense dignity: for her it means the end of a long, splendid association, for the old Court will be disbanded in a few days time. I will remember too, the whole family, except the Queen, curtseying and bowing, one by one, to the coffin, and then slowly filing out.

1 April

Fascinating reports of yesterday's funeral and dinner at

Windsor: they were 28 at dinner (the Duke of Windsor was not invited, which I think quite extraordinary) and they used the famous blue Sèvres china. The women were in black, of course, but with many jewels, and the men in dinner jackets. Paul sat between the Queen and the Queen Mum. Ernst August of Hanover, another great favourite of Queen Mary's, was on the other side of the Queen and next to his sister, Queen Frederica who, it seems, did not make herself as popular on this visit as she did last time. She is getting spoiled. The shy dishevelled King Baudouin refused to stay for luncheon, and flew back to Brussels directly after the Service. Why? His odd behaviour has made a very bad impression. But they seem to have had a good time ... how royalties love funerals.

14 April

Great excitement in the House, about Rab's budget, as he rose this afternoon, and humorously, good-naturedly unfolded his plans. He announced various tax cuts – 6d. off income tax in particular: this means nearly £1,000 more a year for me. He had a tremendous reception and the Socialists were breathless with ill-concealed annoyance tempered by admiration. It is another step forward on the road to recovery. Rab has recently quietly enhanced his political position and reputation both in the House and in the country. This just comes at a time unfortunate for Anthony Eden, who is in the London Clinic for a gall-bladder operation.

Next Day. Rab has had a splendid Press and the whole country is relieved and grateful. It thinks his budget is a masterpiece. Only the Socialists are silent and dismayed. Everywhere, in fact, the outlook is brighter. Rab and the changed attitude of the Russians have done much to help. Are we in a new and better phase: are we entering a new cycle? Out of the fertile womb of time, the unexpected always comes. I have been re-reading Proust, and thinking much of him, and the days when I knew him well. Could I have written like him, once?

23 April

I had just put Mollie Buccleuch in the Gallery to hear Winston and Bevan speak, when there was a storm of gibes and ribaldry and noise. One Socialist . . . shouted out 'Bloody lie'. The Speaker tried in vain to restore order: Bevan looked at poor, plain Florence Horsbrugh and hailed her with the words 'That's the face that sank a thousand scholarships'. Later, when Winston got up to leave the Chamber the squawking Socialists rudely shouted 'Good night' at the old man. The PM, surprised, turned and, with his little mocking bow, blew kisses to the Opposition, who were somewhat startled by this response.

25 April

Winston was yesterday given the Garter by the Queen at Windsor. What a romantic picture – the aged Prime Minister kneeling at the feet of the young Queen: like Melbourne and Queen Victoria. What a scene, one day, for a painted window, or fresco.

21 May

Dined with the Bruntisfields – an amusing mixture. . . . The very French Louise de Vilmorin, with her great conversational powers, her wit and racontage, and the very English Duke of Norfolk, red in the face, and amazingly calm about the arrangements for the Coronation, of which he has complete charge. He is doing a splendid job – and now that all the peers have been invited to the Abbey, there are fewer complaints. The decorations are transfiguring London. David Eccles – Minister of Works – affectionately known as the Abominable Showman, has taken tremendous trouble over them, and assures me that they will be beautiful.

31 May *Kelvedon*

This evening Fleur Cowles, President Eisenhower's personal representative at the Coronation arrived, and brought with her General Marshall and Mrs M. of Marshall Aid fame, an elderly distinguished grey couple. After admiring my now famous gardens, they asked for whisky but their faces puckered with disgust when they found we had given them Scotch and not Bourbon. The General anecdoted, long-winded but a dear, and was delighted to find Mary Burghley, an old friend, staying here. What an unexpected invasion – even for Kelvedon.

2 June *5 Belgrave Square*

The day of days. I woke, with a guilty conscience as I had two, excellent unallocated places in my wallet ... at 4.15. Peter, magnificent in his green Hussar uniform, and my Paul, still in pyjamas, came to my room and at 6 o'clock we had coffee, and filthy it was, in the Black Room, and soon left for the Abbey, after picking up Susan Ward resplendent in a tiara (Jackie Ward, as Silver Stick was to ride by the Queen's coach). Westminster Hall was already filling up with Peers in robes and glittering Peeresses and other Abbey-bound guests. ... We had breakfast in the Commons dining-room, and then Susan and I went to the Abbey. All was comfortably, smoothly arranged (even the traffic arrangements had been excellent and there was no delay getting there) as a covered bridge had been built from St. Stephen's entrance to the East Door. But there was a slight drizzle and an overcast sky. It was at 8.25 that I took my seat which was almost identically the same one as I had occupied at the last Coronation.

Below, empty in the golden light, stood the throne. Opposite the Peeresses' benches were gradually filling up; the front row of 13 Duchesses was a splendid sight. Mollie Buccleuch on the extreme left [and] her daughter Elizabeth. ... The Duchess of Portland, grey and dignified and magnificent was between Argyll and Sutherland who talked across her. The new Duchess of Westminster made a dark note; she looked well, and so did 'Debo' Devonshire, wearing, I was told afterwards, the 18th century robes of Duchess Georgiana. The long wait was enthralling as every few minutes a procession of distinguished guests, relations, minor royalties entered and were escorted to their seats. Finally the Royal Family ... The Duchess of Kent was fairy-like, and there was a well-bred gasp as she walked in with her children and attended by Rachel Davidson whose little boy, Duncan, page to Bernard Norfolk, was later to 'steal the show' for a time. Queen Mum was OK, but compared badly with Queen Mary's entry last time. Dignitaries and ecclesiastics flittered about; peeresses got restive and retired to the Ladies' Room in red groups. Finally came the magic moment of the Queen's arrival: she was calm and confident and even charming, and looked touching and quite perfect, while Prince Philip was like a medieval knight – the Service, Anointing, Crowning, Communion were endless, yet the scene was so splendid, so breath-taking in its solemn splendour that it passed in a flash. The Homage was impressive, it was then that Duncan Davidson, standing by the throne, held the Coronets of the obeisant lieges: his big moment, and he did it to perfection. The Great Officers of State swished their robes with dignity. Harry Crookshank without, of course, a coronet, amongst them. From time to time my eyes wandered, and I saw Aneurin Bevan in a blue lounge suit, as unsuitable as possible, whilst Jennie Lee, his wife, wore a little veil and was the better of the two. . . . Privy Councillors in their uniforms, men in levée dress, the little Queen at one moment simply dressed in a sort of shift, and then later resplendent: the pretty pages; the supreme movements, and entrance of Helen, Duchess of Northumberland, who, as Mistress of the Robes to the Queen Mother, was the finest, the grandest and most impressive of all – the nodding, chatting, gossiping Duchesses; the swan-like movements when they simultaneously placed their coronets on their heads . . . it was all finer, and better organised than last time, although the Archbishop's voice was not as sonorous as that of the wicked old Lang . . . once or twice I slipped out on to the parapet for a cigarette and a chat. The Four Garter Knights rather bungled the canopy and were clumsy. The Buccleuch-Northumberland clan were all carrying trains or orbs or sceptres. I could have watched for ever. The red, the gold, the sparkle, the solemnity . . . finally a fanfare, people began walking about, and Winston was very recognisable in his Garter Robes as he smiled and strutted . . .

People were let out in batches, and as our numbers were called out by a loud speaker, there was some indignation amongst MPs at the delay; but it proved providential for as we came out, under cover of course, it was pelting, but the royal cortege was just leaving the Abbey. I stood on the bridge with the Devons and Hardwickes. As the Gold Coach turned into Parliament Square the sun smiled for a second and I saw the Queen's white gloved hand and her great crown. Then the procession curled up Whitehall. At this moment I ran into Paul who had stolen over from St. Stephen's and he, too, had witnessed the departure.

There was a pause as we waited for our car and it was diverting to see some hundreds of ermine-d, be-coronetted friends standing in the covered way waiting. The Fairbanks were obviously enchanted to be present, and waved triumphantly and endearingly.

I thought of the poor people who had taken up positions on Sunday and sat drenched.

What a day for England, and the traditional forces of the world. Shall we ever see the like again? I have been present at two Coronations and now shall never see another. Will my Paul be an old man at that of King Charles III?

15 June *Spithead*

Fireworks, illuminated ships, excitements; late hours, miles of battleships and yachts. The old world persists, thank God. Yet I always feel claustrophobic at sea.

1 July

There are various and conflicting rumours circulating about Churchill; I have sifted them, and it seems that he had a stroke last week at the end of his dinner party for de Gasperi, though the few guests who happened to notice his strange manner thought him intoxicated. On Wednesday he was too ill to answer Questions; he is now a semi-invalid with swollen feet; he has long flashes of lucidity, humour and bad temper, but his heart is failing and he must rest for many hours a day, and he walks with difficulty. He has at long last decided not to continue in office but will not resign until after Eden's return. There may be important far-reaching results, cleavages and decisions then, perhaps not until September; certainly not until after the House rises at the end of July. When next we meet in the Autumn we shall have a new Government. No word of all this has appeared yet in the Press.

20 July

So Bendor the great Duke of Westminster is dead at last; magnificent, courteous, a mixture of Henry VIII and Lorenzo Il Magnifico, he lived for pleasure – and women – for 74 years. His wealth was incalculable; his charm overwhelming; but he was restless, spoilt, irritable, and rather splendid in a very English way. He was fair, handsome, lavish; yet his life was an empty failure; he did few kindnesses, leaves no monument.

21 July

There was a bad fire next door; lots of smoke, but it turned out *not* to be the four bereaved Duchesses of Westminster committing suttee.

26 July

Rab's big speech this week on Foreign Affairs was not up to his usual standard, and in fact was considered a 'flop'. But of what use are Foreign Affairs Debates? None; they are always dangerous and do harm.

He is deeply affected by his mother's death and all day today I thought much of Lady Butler who adored her Rab. A tall, stately, grande dame she brought Rab much; his charm and humour and softer side; from his tiny father he got his Civil Servant's brain and brilliance and coldness. Physically, he resembles his mother who overwhelmed him with gentleness.

30 July

Diana Cooper, looking like a Goddess with youth and briskness in her gait, has left me after a stay of three weeks, to motor to the South of France. Adorable, divine, inspired creature, the character of the age: glamorous, gay and good, she is supreme among mortals and towers above them.

I shall not come back to the House of Commons for many a moon, and so shall shut my diary now for months. Goodbye, wonderful Coronation Summer. I have revelled in you and drunk your pleasure to the dregs.

20 October

The long holidays are ended: and the House crowded, friendly and excited, met today. I have enjoyed my twelve weeks holiday. Weeks of Venetian bliss, Casanova adventures; of my Paul's triumphs; Winston's illness; Anthony's recovery.

I lunched with the Austrians[12]; where I found the Soames', Walter Lippman and others. Mary Soames, who has become a ravishing beauty, drove me on to the House, where we saw Winston's long-awaited (and some prophesied never-to-be) return

12. The Austrian Ambassador and Baroness Wimmer.

acclaimed. He seemed self-confident, though a touch deaf in spite of his hearing aid, but apparently more vigorous than before. But I doubt whether he can carry on for long. The added strain of the House of Commons will be too much.

21 October
A hush-hush meeting at the House of the Foreign Affairs Committee which was addressed in turn by Anthony Eden, Lord Alexander and Winston – all three. Canal Zone. Anthony Eden brief and boring; Alexander factual; the Prime Minister rambling and repetitious ... but vigorous still. Is it the last flickering of that great flame?

26 October
Anthony Eden, elegant, but looking extremely old and tired, answered a barrage of questions in his usual bland, pleasing, ineffectual way.

3 November
In the House, Winston, who had not been present at the Opening of Parliament this morning, rose amidst cheers, and it was immediately clear that he was making one of the speeches of his lifetime. Brilliant, full of cunning and charm, of wit and thrusts, he poured out his Macaulay-like phrases to a stilled and awed house. It was an Olympian spectacle. A supreme performance which we shall never see again from him or anyone else. In 18 years in this honourable House I have never heard anything like it ... then he sought refuge in the Smoking Room and, flushed with pride, pleasure, and triumph sat there for two hours sipping brandy and acknowledging compliments. He beamed like a schoolboy.

18 November
I gave a cocktail party for King Umberto who appeared punctually – though already some 40 people, women in the majority, had arrived; all the usual Duchesses, plus Walter Buccleuch and the Charles Clores, who were a last minute inspiration, and were a success; a nice couple, abundantly rich and highly ambitious socially. But I felt worn out when it was over. How long shall I

continue this hectic life? Will retirement, the Reaper, bankruptcy, ill-health one day soon afflict me? But every day is a day gained.

The Diaries end at this point and on this note. Chips's health had been deteriorating for some years, and he had already had several heart attacks. But there was little change in his way of life until his sudden death in London, on 7 October 1958. He was buried at Kelvedon, which was, in more senses than one, a very long way from Chicago. A Memorial Service in London was attended by Royalty, politicians, the corps diplomatique; R. A. Butler read the Lesson; Lady Diana Cooper wrote a moving tribute in 'The Times'.

On the headstone of Chips' grave at Kelvedon were inscribed the words of Du Bellay which had been his special favourite:

'Heureux qui comme Ulysse a fait un beau voyage.'

Index